EUROMONITOR INTERNATIONAL

European Marketing Data and Statistics

DUNDEE

European Marketing Data and Statistics

2013

48th edition

Euromonitor International Ltd,
60-61 Britton Street,
London EC1M 5UX

European Marketing Data and Statistics 2013

First published 1964
Forty-eighth edition
ISBN 978-1-84264-587-1
Published by:

Western and Southern Europe
Euromonitor International Ltd – Head Office
60-61 Britton Street, London, EC1M 5UX, United Kingdom
T: +44 (0) 20 7251 8024; F: +44 (0) 20 7608 3149; E: info@euromonitor.com

North America
Euromonitor International Inc
224 South Michigan Avenue, Suite 1500, Chicago, Illinois 60604, USA
T: + 1 (312) 922 1115; F: +1 (312) 922 1157; E: insight@euromonitorintl.com

Asia Pacific
Euromonitor International (Asia) Pte Ltd
3 Lim Teck Kim Road, #08-01 Singapore Technologies Building, Singapore 088934
T: +65 6429 0590; F: +65 6324 1855; E: info@euromonitor.com.sg

China
Euromonitor International (Shanghai) Co., Ltd
Tian An Center - 21/F, 338 Nanjing Xi Lu, Shanghai 200 003, China
T: (+86 21) 6372 6288; F: (+86 21) 6372 6289; E: info@euromonitor.com.cn

Central and Eastern Europe
Euromonitor International
Jogailos Street 4, Vilnius, LT-01116, Lithuania
T: +370 5 243 1577; F: +370 5 243 1599; E: info@euromonitor.lt

Middle East and North Africa
Euromonitor International
Dubai Silicon Oasis (HQ), F- Wing Office 606-607, PO Box 341155, Dubai, U.A.E.
T: +971 4 372 4363; F: +971 4 372 4370; E: info-mena@euromonitor.com

Central and South Africa
Euromonitor International
The Forum, Unit GS04, 6473 Northbank Lane, Century City, Cape Town, 7441, Republic of South Africa
T: +27 21 552 0037; F: +27 21 552 7071; E: info-africa@euromonitor.com

Latin America
Euromonitor International
Avenida Apoquindo 4501, 11th Floor, Oficina 1102, Las Condes, Santiago, 7580125, Chile
T: +56 2 9157200; F: +56 2 9157201

Australasia
Euromonitor International (Australia) Pty Ltd
Suite 26, Level 32, 1 Market Street, Sydney NSW 2000, Australia
T: +61(0)2 9275 8870; F: +61 2 9275 8793; E: info@euromonitor.com

Japan
Euromonitor International Ltd
Level 16, Shiroyama Trust Tower, 4-3-1, Toranomon, Minato-ku, Tokyo, Japan 105-6016
T: +81 3-5403-4790; F: +81 3-5403-4799

Website
http://www.euromonitor.com

data
publishers
association

Summary of contents

Table of contents

1

CHAPTER ONE
Foreword and Guide

Foreword

European Marketing Data and Statistics 2013 is a compendium of statistical information on the countries of Western and Eastern Europe. Published annually, it provides a wealth of detailed and up-to-date statistical information relevant to pan-European market planning. The information is regularly updated and held on an international database of market information comprising 23 subject areas.

Published annually since the late 1960s, **European Marketing Data and Statistics**, or EMDAS, is now in its 48th edition. All data sections have been thoroughly revised for this new edition.

The data are presented in table form and a number of extrapolated tables have been included. The data coverage includes a considerable number of long-term time-series (dating back to 1980 as available) which permit the analysis of socio-economic trends over a longer time span as a basis for forecasting. The inclusion of figures from the most recent complete year (in this edition 2011) for key parameters ensures that up-to-date information is available for analysis.

In addition to reporting on major European countries, the country coverage also includes smaller European countries and principalities. Although the availability of statistical information on these countries is limited and they are minor markets, it assists in building up a more comprehensive picture of the total European market and will be of interest to academic users.

Readers requiring detailed guidance on sources of information used in the compilation of the data are referred to the World Directory of Business Information Sources (Euromonitor International, 2010) for more comprehensive listings.

A companion volume of marketing data, International Marketing Data and Statistics (IMDAS) is also available. Country coverage in IMDAS 2013 provides a comprehensive worldwide context, and data are provided in the same format for ease of comparison with the European figures presented here. The data included in both volumes are also accessible as part of the Global Marketing Information Database (GMID) on the web.

User comments are welcomed concerning the databases in **European Marketing Data and Statistics**. Also, whilst the editors have made every effort to ensure accuracy, Euromonitor International cannot accept responsibility for any errors which may have occurred.

Guide to Using the Handbook

Scope of the Handbook

European Marketing Data and Statistics (EMDAS) is a statistical yearbook of business and marketing information, featuring over 500 pages of up-to-date and detailed marketing statistics on 23 principal subject areas. These statistics are stored on a database of international marketing information and are regularly updated by Euromonitor International's research team.

The sections of EMDAS cover a wide variety of marketing topics, ranging from socio-economic trends and background information through to key consumer marketing parameters. Data covering international trade, transport, industrial output and agricultural resources are included, as well as sections on service industries such as tourism and retailing.

In EMDAS 2013, each statistical tabulation presents pan-European comparative information, either in the form of time-series from 1980 to 2011 or with single-year data for the latest year available. All the countries are listed down the left-hand column, presented in two geographical entities (Western and Eastern Europe).

Where data is in value form, units have been generally left in national currencies. However, the spreadsheets on which the data are stored facilitate calculations in US dollars. These are calculated only for the latest year available (usually 2011) as fluctuations in exchange rates and contrasts in rates of inflation render year-on-year conversions meaningless.

In addition, calculations have been made where deemed appropriate to show growth rates over a defined period, and per capita data. These permit easy cross-comparisons between countries, regions and markets.

Using EMDAS 2013 is easy. Whatever topic is of interest, you simply look up the tables (using the contents) and the table will show the relevant data for all countries. The heading shows the relevant section, title summary and title of the table, and unit. A guide to the sources used in the compilation of the data appears at the foot of the table, along with any relevant notes.

The aim of EMDAS is to locate in one handbook the essential statistical information relevant to European market planning. The handbook will save the busy marketeer or researcher hours of time trawling through statistics from many sources and provides a wealth of hard-to-get information drawn from the many reports and studies compiled by Euromonitor International over the last 2-3 years - many based on trade interviews and original extrapolations. Business users and librarians will find the handbook especially useful.

Subject Coverage

EMDAS 2013 is presented in 23 separate sections or "databases" which have all been specially compiled by Euromonitor International. The subjects have been selected as those most appropriate for strategic planning and European market analysis, covering both background marketing parameters and detailed consumer market information. The 23 databases are outlined below.

1 Advertising
This section includes a range of data on advertising expenditure trends, organised into seven tables.

2 Agricultural Resources and Output

This section presents key data on land use and output of various agricultural and forestry products. There are 11 tables on the database, mostly including figures for 2011.

3 Automotives and Transport

This 25-table database covers the circulation, manufacture and sales of cars, commercial vehicles and two-wheelers, including tables on automotive fuel prices; it also covers major movements in terms of the road, rail, air and shipping transport sectors.

4 Banking and Finance

This section features tabulations mainly showing data from 1980-2011 and covering bank assets, liabilities, claims and interest rates, as well as information on credit card holders and accepting outlets.

5 Consumer Expenditure

The presentation of this section comprises total consumer spending, a consolidated breakdown by product sector, and a series of tables analysing each major consumer sector. New 2011 data have been included with growth rates since 1980 and 2011 dollar comparisons.

6 Consumer Market Sizes

Per capita consumption and retail market sizes are included in 17 tables for 2011. The information is drawn from Euromonitor International's market information database, which forms the basis for the publication Consumer Europe (28th edition, Euromonitor International, 2012).

7 Consumer Prices and Costs

Trends in consumer prices and selected European living costs are included in 14 tables of data.

8 Economic Indicators

This database features tables of key economic data, again with the emphasis on time-series data. All the main economic indicators are covered, including GDP, GNP, inflation, money supply, public and private consumption, government finance and exchange rates.

9 Education

A range of educational statistics are included in this seven-table section, from pre-primary through to higher and university education.

10 Energy Resources and Output

This section consists of 18 tables on energy supply and demand. Coverage extends to household energy consumption with several tables containing data for more than 20 years.

11 Environmental Data

This section includes tables covering various environmental factors. Coverage includes pollution, recycling, waste generation, protected areas and threatened species.

12 External Trade

This section includes 11 tables which give a cohesive and structured trade overview covering total imports and exports and external trade breakdowns by origin, destination and commodity.

13 Health

This database comprises seven tables covering major health indicators (including a table on obese population).

14 Home Ownership

This section includes comparative data on housing stock and new dwellings completed, as well as numbers of households by tenure and type of dwelling.

15 Household Profiles

This section comprises 12 tables of comparative statistics on households. Data on average number of occupants per household are included, as well as possession of household durables.

16 Income and Deductions

This section includes six tables covering gross and disposable income parameters, as well as savings.

17 Industry

This section provides key industrial indices for a 30-year period and includes output tables covering major industrial materials.

18 IT and Telecommunications

This section features information on a number of communications and information technology topics including Internet statistics and data on mobile telephony.

19 Labour

This database covers the key employment indicators including numbers employed, unemployed and hours of work. The structure of the economically active population by age group and sex is included for latest years available, along with a breakdown of the total workforce into industry sectors.

20 Media and Leisure

This section includes eight tables covering available data on cinema, newspapers, and TV households including cable TV, satellite TV, and digital satellite pay-TV.

21 Population

This database features statistical compilations covering population trends, vital statistics, urbanisation, demographic analysis by age and sex, and population forecasts. Much of the data included are from 1980 to the latest year, forming a basis for forecasting and projections.

22 Retailing

This section has drawn on Euromonitor International's extensive European retail research in recent years, with tables covering retail sales and channels and breakdowns for different retail sectors.

23 Travel and Tourism

This database consists of 12 tabulations covering tourism values and movements, tourist accommodation and its usage, reflecting holidaying habits across Europe.

Data Coverage

Each of the statistical compilations is presented in one of four data periods:

(1)   A 31-year trend table from 1980-2011, with data for each country drawn from the same consistent source. Some intermediary years have been excluded for reasons of space.

(2)   A different period trend, eg 1990-2011 (21-year trend) or a recent period.

(3)   Latest year available, with the years differing between countries. These are used where the information is drawn from occasional studies, eg a census, or where statistical offices vary in the speed of publishing statistics.

(4)   A single year, eg 2011, where space does not permit trends or where an interactive range of information is provided (eg imports by origin, usage of GDP, etc).

The statistics in this volume are as available during the compilation period (June-October 2012). Figures for 2011 (in some cases provisional or estimated) have been included where possible. Various one-off surveys cover earlier years only.

1

Foreword and Guide

Country Coverage

This edition of EMDAS includes a total of 44 countries in both Western and Eastern Europe. These are grouped into two geographic entities, as follows:

Western Europe

Austria	Belgium
Cyprus	Denmark
Finland	France
Germany	Gibraltar
Greece	Iceland
Ireland	Italy
Liechtenstein	Luxembourg
Malta	Monaco
Netherlands	Norway
Portugal	Spain
Sweden	Switzerland
Turkey	United Kingdom

Eastern Europe

Albania	Belarus
Bosnia-Herzegovina	Bulgaria
Croatia	Czech Republic
Estonia	Georgia
Hungary	Latvia
Lithuania	Macedonia
Moldova	Poland
Romania	Russia
Serbia and Montenegro	Slovakia
Slovenia	Ukraine

Country Note

Data for Germany prior to 1991 refer to the former East and West Germany, for the Czech Republic data prior to 1993 refer to the former Czechoslovakia, and for Serbia and Montenegro data prior to 1992 refer to the former Yugoslavia.

Sources

European Marketing Data and Statistics is based on an extensive and on-going programme of research into European markets and industries. A Europe-wide network of market analysts and researchers work to pull together available data on socio-economic patterns, market conditions and trends, living standards and background information relevant to business, export and market planning.

The principal sources used in the compilation of EMDAS are as follows:

— International and European organisations, such as the United Nations, OECD, and the International Monetary Fund.

— National statistical offices and central banks in each country.

— Pan-European and national trade and industry associations.

— Industry study groups and unofficial research publishers.

— Euromonitor International's own research publications, including one-off reports and statistical compilations.

— Original research specially commissioned for the handbook, including consumer research, trade interviews and retail surveys.

A guide to the main sources used in the compilation of each table is included at the foot of each table. For reasons of space the main sources are only briefly cited; in some cases, many different reports and publications are used in the preparation of just one table. For example, we may have extracted data from publications by the national statistical offices for all the countries covered in order to compile one table. In other cases, statistical compilations are from secondary sources, which have in turn used many different sources.

A brief guide to the main sources used in each of the databases follows.

1 Advertising
Drawn from data published by the World Association of Newspapers and various other media study groups, advertising associations and agents in various countries.

2 Agricultural Resources and Output
Mainly based on the publications and databases of the Food and Agricultural Organisation of the United Nations (FAO).

3 Automotives and Transport
Automotives data are drawn from national statistics, and the publications of various motor trades organisations. Transport statistics are based on national statistics and on various UN publications; the International Civil Aviation Organisation; the International Road Federation and Lloyd's Register of Shipping.

4 Banking and Finance
The major source of comparative financial data is the IMF's International Financial Statistics.

5 Consumer Expenditure
Drawn from the OECD and the national accounts of each country (generally published by the national statistical offices). Euromonitor International estimates have been used to reach levels of consolidation.

6 Consumer Market Sizes
Drawn from Euromonitor International's consumer market database; primary sources include trade associations and interviews with industry leaders in all countries.

7 Consumer Prices and Costs
Mainly from national statistics, the International Monetary Fund and the OECD; living costs from the International Labour Organisation.

8 Economic Indicators
The principal international sources are the OECD and the International Monetary Fund (IMF). National statistical offices (yearbooks, national accounts) and economic bulletins by leading banks are also used.

9 Education
The key international source is UNESCO with data from national statistical offices incorporated as available.

10 Energy Resources and Output
This compilation draws mainly on data from BP, the UN and the OECD/IEA, national statistics and various industry publications.

11 Environmental Data
Drawn largely from the OECD, United Nations, and the World Resources Institute, as well as national statistics.

12 External Trade
The IMF, UN and OECD track external trade flows in some detail. National statistical yearbooks are also utilised.

13 Health
Compiled from various publications from national statistical offices, OECD and UN publications and incorporating Euromonitor International estimates and calculations.

14 Home Ownership
Data are compiled from national statistical offices of each country.

15 Household Profiles

Compiled from various publications from national statistical offices, and from Eurostat and UN publications, and incorporating Euromonitor International estimates and calculations.

16 Income and Deductions

Data from national statistical offices of each country. Specific sources include Household Budget Surveys and National Accounts. Euromonitor International estimates have been used.

17 Industry

Mainly drawn from UN and OECD publications, and from national statistics. Various industry sectors are covered by associations as stated.

18 IT and Telecommunications

Mainly based on national statistics and UN data, particularly the publications of the International Telecommunications Union (ITU), and incorporating some data from the World Bank.

19 Labour

In addition to national statistics, the primary international source is the International Labour Organisation, which publishes both a statistical yearbook and quarterly bulletins.

20 Media and Leisure

Mainly drawn from the UN, UNESCO, the Council of Europe and national statistical offices.

21 Population

Drawn mainly from the statistical yearbooks of the national statistical offices supplemented with population data and forecasts from the UN, Eurostat and the Council of Europe.

22 Retailing

Drawn from a wide number of Euromonitor International's own surveys and market reports on European retailing, including Retail Trade International (Euromonitor International 2010), and also original research. Primary sources include retail trade censuses (various countries) by national statistical offices, retail trade associations, major retailers etc.

23 Travel and Tourism

A compilation sourced from the World Tourism Organisation and Euromonitor International's own research.

List of Abbreviations

BLEU	Belgo-Luxembourg Economic Union
EFMA	European Financial Management and Marketing Association
EFTA	European Free Trade Association
EU	European Union
FAO	Food and Agriculture Organisation of the United Nations
FT	Financial Times
IAA	International Advertising Association
IATA	International Air Transport Association
IBRD	International Bank for Reconstruction and Development (World Bank)
ICAO	International Civil Aviation Organisation
IEA	International Energy Authority
ILO	International Labour Organisation
IMF	International Monetary Fund
IMMA	International Motorcycle Manufacturers' Association
IRF	International Road Federation

ITU	International Telecommunication Union (a UN agency)
OECD	Organisation for Economic Co-operation and Development
SMMT	Society of Motor Manufacturers and Traders
UN	United Nations
UN ECE	United Nations Economic Commission for Europe
UNESCO	United Nations Educational, Scientific and Cultural Organisation
WHO	World Health Organisation
WTO	World Tourism Organisation
EAP	Economically active population
GDP	Gross domestic product
GNP	Gross national product
LPG	Liquefied petroleum gases
NGL	Natural gas liquids
SITC	Standard International Trade Classification
'000	thousand
gWh	gigawatt-hours
ha	hectare
hl	hectolitre
kg	kilogramme
km	kilometre
km2	square kilometre
kWh	kilowatt-hours
m2	square metre
m3	cubic metre
mn	million
MTOE	million tonnes of oil equivalent
MW	megawatts
R/P	reserves/production
TJ	terajoules
0	denotes less than 0.5 where no fraction given

Country Currencies

Albania	Lek (ALL = 100 quindarka)
Austria	Euro (€ = 100 cents)
Belarus	Rouble (BYR)
Belgium	Euro (€ = 100 cents)
Bosnia-Herzegovina	Marka (BAM = 100 pfenniga), pegged to the euro at €1 = BAM 1.95583
Bulgaria	Lev (BGN = 100 stotinki), pegged to the euro at €1 = BGN1.95583
Croatia	Kuna (introduced May 1994) HRK = 100 lipa
Cyprus	Euro (€ = 100 cents)
Czech Republic	Koruna (CZK = 100 heller)
Denmark	Danish krone (DKr = 100 ore)
Estonia	Euro (€ = 100 cents)
Finland	Euro (€ = 100 cents)
France	Euro (€ = 100 cents)
Georgia	Lari (GEL = 100 tetri)
Germany	Euro (€ = 100 cents)
Gibraltar	Gibraltar pound (G£ = 100 pence), at par with pound sterling
Greece	Euro (€ = 100 cents)
Hungary	Forint (HUF = 100 fillér)
Iceland	Icelandic krona (ISK = 100 aurar)
Ireland	Euro (€ = 100 cents)
Italy	Euro (€ = 100 cents)
Latvia	Lat (LVL = 100 santims)
Liechtenstein	Swiss franc (SFr = 100 centimes)
Lithuania	Litas (LTL = 100 centu)
Luxembourg	Euro (€ = 100 cents)
Macedonia	Denar (MKD = 100 deni)
Malta	Euro (€ = 100 cents)
Moldova	Leu (MDL = 100 bani)
Monaco	Euro (€ = 100 cents)

1

Foreword and Guide

Montenegro	Euro (€ = 100 cents)
Netherlands	Euro (€ = 100 cents)
Norway	Norwegian krone (NOK = 100 ore)
Poland	New zloty (PLN = 100 groszy)
Portugal	Euro (€ = 100 cents)
Romania	Leu (= 100 bani)
Russia	Rouble (RUB = 100 kopecks)
Serbia	Dinar (RSD)
Slovakia	Euro (€ = 100 cents)
Slovenia	Euro (€ = 100 cents)
Spain	Euro (€ = 100 cents)
Sweden	Swedish krona (SEK = 100 ore)
Switzerland	Swiss franc (CHF = 100 centimes/rappen)
Turkey	Turkish lira (TL=100 kurus)
Ukraine	Hryvnia (UAH = 100 kopiykas)
United Kingdom	Pound sterling (£ = 100 pence)

2

Advertising

Advertising Statistics   **Table 2.1**

Adspend by Medium 2011

US$ million

	Television	Radio	Print	Cinema	Outdoor	Online	Total
Western Europe							
Austria	982.8	259.4	2,427.3	20.6	285.8	626.1	4,602.1
Belgium	2,123.2	583.9	1,745.1	36.6	367.9	260.3	5,117.0
Cyprus							
Denmark	416.8	37.2	972.7	14.1	105.3	642.3	2,188.4
Finland	393.3	78.5	1,000.0	4.5	56.4	324.0	1,856.7
France	4,885.9	1,073.7	3,405.9	137.3	1,705.6	2,531.2	13,739.7
Germany	5,758.3	1,003.1	13,328.1	109.1	1,107.6	4,684.9	25,991.0
Gibraltar							
Greece	621.7	121.5	1,314.7	17.8	212.5		2,288.2
Iceland	15.2	10.3	23.4	1.2	3.4		50.0
Ireland	409.1	160.1	1,121.5	11.6	154.6	170.9	2,027.7
Italy	6,295.9	812.4	2,651.3	75.9	309.3	628.6	10,773.5
Liechtenstein							
Luxembourg	21.6	41.0	158.2	2.8	8.0	4.4	236.0
Malta							
Monaco							
Netherlands	1,230.4	317.9	2,303.6	7.2	209.1	1,203.7	5,272.0
Norway	577.5	106.2	1,165.4	26.3	95.0	786.7	2,757.1
Portugal	638.0	62.2	199.8	4.8	140.3	35.3	1,080.4
Spain	3,455.2	778.9	2,158.8	36.8	590.1	1,212.1	8,231.9
Sweden	895.6	115.6	1,607.4	20.9	185.1	1,019.7	3,844.4
Switzerland	1,601.5	201.4	2,574.1	34.9	520.3	577.8	5,510.0
Turkey	1,569.7	74.7	673.8	35.1	189.3	219.7	2,762.3
United Kingdom	5,329.9	713.1	5,505.2	256.5	1,200.5	5,825.6	18,830.9
Eastern Europe							
Albania							
Belarus							
Bosnia-Herzegovina	522.4	6.2	41.4		21.3	2.2	593.5
Bulgaria	488.6	73.4	119.8		45.1	31.9	758.8
Croatia	1,732.1	24.9	250.8		37.5	34.5	2,079.7
Czech Republic	836.1	74.0	636.0	8.4	69.6	341.4	1,965.5
Estonia	37.6	11.5	36.6		10.1	17.7	113.4
Georgia	123.3	17.7	19.1		9.8	1.1	170.9
Hungary	318.1	47.1	296.4	6.2	97.1	176.8	941.7
Latvia	52.7	16.5	25.6	1.0	13.3	15.9	125.0
Lithuania	71.4	12.2	35.6	0.4	9.9	12.7	142.3
Macedonia							
Moldova	16.7	2.3	3.4	0.6	12.6	0.5	36.1
Montenegro							
Poland	1,312.2	157.8	393.5	39.5	181.8	394.7	2,479.6
Romania	349.6	32.6	37.9	2.8	71.5	41.7	536.2
Russia	4,343.0	367.4	547.6	131.5	983.4	1,039.0	7,411.8
Serbia	164.1	13.5	66.3	0.9	34.5	12.7	291.8
Slovakia	1,916.6	112.1	196.9	1.2	164.9	55.4	2,447.2
Slovenia	730.0	34.8	217.0	0.4	48.0	39.7	1,069.9
Ukraine	514.2	41.8	217.0	5.1	106.3	42.3	926.8

Source: Euromonitor International from national statistics

Table 2.2

Radio Adspend 1985, 1990, 1995, 2000, 2006-2011

National currency million

	1985	1990	1995	2000	2006	2007	2008	2009	2010	2011	US$ million 2011
Western Europe											
Austria	94.0	126.0	136.0	158.0	170.0	170.0	178.0	172.0	181.3	186.6	259.41
Belgium	21.0	48.0	100.0	186.0	327.0	375.5	377.2	357.7	399.0	419.9	583.86
Cyprus											
Denmark	34.0	81.0	165.0	213.0	279.0	285.0	250.0	217.0	199.0	199.5	37.22
Finland	55.0	43.0	28.0	38.0	46.8	47.0	51.0	50.0	52.5	56.5	78.54
France	256.3	355.8	488.2	602.9	844.0	802.0	776.3	707.0	744.0	772.2	1,073.75
Germany	295.0	425.0	608.3	733.0	680.0	743.0	720.0	678.0	692.0	721.4	1,003.06
Gibraltar											
Greece	5.0	20.0	69.5	71.3	96.0	115.0	189.0	147.0	107.0	87.4	121.54
Iceland					1,046.0	1,260.0	1,393.0	1,274.0	1,105.8	1,190.7	10.27
Ireland	13.0	20.0	33.0	55.0	124.0	140.0	148.0	137.0	112.0	115.1	160.06
Italy	238.0	217.0	201.0	454.0	521.8	563.5	575.3	531.3	572.2	584.3	812.43
Liechtenstein											
Luxembourg	5.0	7.0	9.0	12.1	20.5	22.1	26.2	27.3	28.0	29.5	40.96
Malta											
Monaco											
Netherlands	16.0	45.0	111.0	235.0	244.0	257.0	261.0	219.2	230.2	228.6	317.89
Norway	84.0	84.0	191.2	286.6	533.4	547.0	585.0	504.0	563.0	595.2	106.18
Portugal	95.6	42.7	25.0	62.0	51.8	50.5	47.0	45.6	45.6	44.7	62.17
Spain	2,139.0	899.0	346.0	502.0	636.7	678.1	641.9	537.3	548.5	560.2	778.88
Sweden		3.0	234.0	592.0	643.4	701.5	728.3	628.4	688.0	750.9	115.61
Switzerland	38.0	59.0	100.0	139.0	136.0	137.0	154.0	168.0	168.0	178.8	201.38
Turkey	0.0	0.0	1.7	47.4	101.0	111.0	111.4	88.0	103.0	125.5	74.73
United Kingdom	26.0	78.0	230.0	455.0	494.4	508.6	476.3	429.8	444.7	445.0	713.08
Eastern Europe											
Albania											
Belarus											
Bosnia-Herzegovina					5.9	9.8	11.7	11.7	10.4	8.7	6.21
Bulgaria	1.0	1.0	3.0	6.0	57.3	61.9	69.9	89.3	83.8	103.2	73.35
Croatia					0.0	0.0	0.0	0.0	101.5	133.0	24.88
Czech Republic	231.2	364.4	560.3	926.5	2,329.4	2,483.5	2,651.2	1,716.0	1,416.6	1,308.9	73.97
Estonia		11.1	1.7	4.9	6.7	8.6	9.4	6.9	6.5	8.3	11.49
Georgia							10.1	14.1	21.9	29.8	17.66
Hungary	28.2	156.0	843.8	2,426.7	6,804.2	7,844.6	8,894.9	8,217.4	8,503.5	9,475.0	47.13
Latvia			0.8	4.9	8.5	9.8	10.6	6.7	7.0	8.3	16.46
Lithuania			4.7	11.7	28.0	34.0	39.0	28.0	26.0	30.2	12.17
Macedonia											
Moldova					23.0	24.3	27.0	24.8	25.2	26.6	2.27
Montenegro											
Poland	2.4	8.8	49.4	218.4	482.5	499.4	528.1	452.0	456.0	467.8	157.84
Romania			0.6	9.8	78.7	84.9	121.9	101.6	88.4	99.3	32.58
Russia			135.7	1,133.4	11,192.3	12,551.2	10,720.9	9,677.1	10,299.9	10,799.4	367.43
Serbia					425.0	600.0	729.0	611.0	824.0	988.1	13.47
Slovakia					71.1	64.3	68.3	68.4	73.3	80.6	112.13
Slovenia	9.0	10.1	12.6	21.4	19.0	20.0	20.0	21.0	22.5	25.0	34.83
Ukraine					136.4	212.1	210.7	126.6	232.2	333.3	41.81

Source: Euromonitor International from national statistics

2

Advertising

Advertising Statistics

Table 2.3

TV Adspend 1985, 1990, 1995, 2000, 2006-2011

National currency million

	1985	1990	1995	2000	2006	2007	2008	2009	2010	2011	US$ million 2011
Western Europe											
Austria	152.0	240.0	270.0	479.0	545.0	596.0	623.0	628.0	675.0	706.9	982.84
Belgium	150.0	234.0	393.0	782.0	1,071.2	1,161.3	1,204.8	1,246.8	1,414.3	1,527.0	2,123.20
Cyprus											
Denmark	240.0	612.0	1,510.0	1,823.0	2,471.0	2,516.0	2,431.0	2,059.0	2,165.0	2,233.8	416.78
Finland	75.0	127.0	161.0	213.0	242.9	262.1	268.0	237.0	265.3	282.9	393.33
France	1,446.1	1,597.0	1,721.8	2,484.4	3,433.0	3,557.0	3,392.5	3,020.0	3,358.2	3,513.9	4,885.90
Germany	814.0	1,642.0	3,420.1	4,709.0	4,114.0	4,156.0	4,036.0	3,640.0	3,954.0	4,141.4	5,758.27
Gibraltar											
Greece	53.0	200.0	836.6	676.4	705.0	855.0	784.0	648.0	521.0	447.1	621.67
Iceland					2,422.0	2,625.0	2,572.0	2,052.0	1,698.6	1,765.1	15.22
Ireland	33.0	51.0	112.0	200.0	326.0	374.0	363.0	312.0	284.0	294.2	409.09
Italy	2,360.0	2,864.0	2,595.0	4,134.0	4,704.5	4,760.9	4,701.9	4,224.7	4,478.1	4,528.0	6,295.94
Liechtenstein											
Luxembourg	3.0	4.0	6.0	7.9	10.6	11.4	13.8	14.9	14.8	15.5	21.61
Malta											
Monaco											
Netherlands	142.0	271.0	483.0	783.0	797.0	851.0	855.0	780.6	863.4	884.9	1,230.44
Norway	4.5	69.3	1,179.3	2,340.3	2,993.9	3,050.0	3,175.0	2,793.0	3,061.0	3,237.6	577.53
Portugal	44.5	99.5	216.0	519.0	512.4	532.6	529.2	465.7	475.7	458.8	637.98
Spain	1,833.0	1,696.0	1,323.0	2,311.0	3,188.0	3,468.6	3,082.4	2,377.8	2,471.9	2,485.0	3,455.20
Sweden	25.0	324.0	2,373.0	3,959.0	4,546.1	4,698.2	4,971.0	4,394.5	5,198.0	5,817.4	895.62
Switzerland	88.0	220.0	339.0	520.0	889.0	1,054.0	1,116.0	1,165.0	1,313.0	1,422.3	1,601.49
Turkey	0.1	1.0	11.5	284.5	1,442.0	1,760.0	1,686.9	1,442.0	2,017.9	2,636.7	1,569.71
United Kingdom	1,088.0	1,548.0	2,267.0	3,327.0	3,282.0	3,380.0	3,211.0	2,857.8	3,257.9	3,325.9	5,329.90
Eastern Europe											
Albania											
Belarus											
Bosnia-Herzegovina					266.7	293.4	414.6	520.3	599.5	734.9	522.45
Bulgaria	2.0	2.0	1.8	108.4	477.0	617.0	791.0	647.3	648.2	687.2	488.57
Croatia					3,218.0	3,612.0	3,706.0	5,760.8	7,908.0	9,256.2	1,732.11
Czech Republic	525.6	829.2	2,263.2	8,709.6	14,208.5	14,624.6	16,652.6	12,965.8	12,619.5	14,796.3	836.15
Estonia		122.0	5.0	9.9	23.2	30.6	30.0	20.8	21.1	27.0	37.56
Georgia					92.3	109.6	117.9	141.5	166.7	207.9	123.30
Hungary	104.5	697.4	3,530.4	24,304.9	65,088.0	70,163.0	71,509.0	59,954.0	60,039.7	63,960.5	318.13
Latvia	2.0	1.0	4.9	10.1	27.1	32.8	34.8	21.6	22.4	26.6	52.66
Lithuania		0.5	3.9	17.8	187.0	227.0	231.0	145.0	153.0	177.4	71.45
Macedonia											
Moldova					61.8	85.2	150.1	146.0	174.8	196.6	16.75
Montenegro											
Poland	11.5	54.0	290.6	1,601.3	3,010.0	3,527.8	4,015.2	3,561.0	3,678.0	3,888.7	1,312.22
Romania			8.3	165.0	745.8	950.8	1,297.4	1,084.4	947.2	1,065.8	349.61
Russia			840.0	6,800.3	76,913.3	95,355.4	96,324.5	100,823.4	110,798.5	127,648.5	4,342.96
Serbia					5,950.0	8,160.0	9,153.0	8,930.0	10,094.0	12,032.2	164.07
Slovakia					1,067.4	1,138.2	1,366.0	1,222.9	1,317.9	1,378.4	1,916.60
Slovenia	2.7	8.6	29.4	144.1	195.0	243.0	299.0	373.0	441.1	525.0	730.00
Ukraine					1,767.5	2,439.2	2,501.9	1,889.4	2,827.7	4,099.2	514.17

Source: Euromonitor International from national statistics

Table 2.4

Print Adspend 1985, 1990, 1995, 2000, 2006-2011

National currency million

	1985	1990	1995	2000	2006	2007	2008	2009	2010	2011	US$ million 2011
Western Europe											
Austria	180.0	403.0	671.0	1,134.0	1,320.0	1,444.0	1,525.0	1,468.0	1,663.7	1,745.7	2,427.31
Belgium	319.0	399.0	479.0	652.0	1,162.6	1,202.1	1,187.1	1,164.2	1,205.5	1,255.1	1,745.11
Cyprus											
Denmark	6,291.3	5,701.3	6,287.9	6,846.9	7,764.0	7,773.0	7,107.0	5,544.0	5,300.0	5,213.5	972.71
Finland	447.0	583.0	556.0	828.0	861.3	900.5	890.0	699.0	712.5	719.2	1,000.03
France	2,399.3	1,782.0	2,164.6	3,032.7	2,979.0	2,879.0	2,798.0	2,385.8	2,425.2	2,449.5	3,405.88
Germany	8,756.0	9,920.0	12,036.7	13,476.0	10,836.0	10,951.0	10,683.0	9,396.0	9,408.0	9,585.6	13,328.15
Gibraltar											
Greece	87.0	148.0	291.6	822.8	1,263.0	1,379.0	1,437.0	1,202.0	1,070.0	945.5	1,314.71
Iceland					6,121.0	6,318.0	5,725.0	3,673.0	2,815.7	2,710.8	23.38
Ireland	99.0	108.0	175.0	446.0	1,078.0	1,123.0	1,120.0	900.0	797.0	806.6	1,121.54
Italy	3,108.0	2,069.0	1,792.0	2,976.0	2,828.0	2,911.7	2,690.2	2,103.5	2,013.3	1,906.8	2,651.26
Liechtenstein											
Luxembourg	27.0	34.0	46.0	57.0	94.9	101.7	106.4	105.6	109.2	113.8	158.24
Malta											
Monaco											
Netherlands	1,313.0	1,475.0	1,793.0	2,721.0	2,273.0	2,303.0	2,205.0	1,754.7	1,724.1	1,656.8	2,303.62
Norway	1,885.1	1,885.1	3,229.1	4,822.9	8,092.8	7,839.0	7,520.0	6,152.0	6,388.0	6,533.0	1,165.38
Portugal	221.0	150.0	134.0	280.0	215.0	217.3	208.8	165.0	156.5	143.7	199.84
Spain	4,302.0	2,940.0	1,677.0	2,427.0	2,601.5	2,750.2	2,229.1	1,644.9	1,594.4	1,552.6	2,158.83
Sweden	9,040.0	8,788.0	9,751.0	11,952.0	11,315.2	11,598.5	11,311.6	8,933.1	9,799.0	10,440.5	1,607.38
Switzerland	2,653.0	2,600.0	2,569.0	3,033.0	2,136.0	2,287.0	2,297.0	2,063.0	2,217.0	2,286.0	2,574.07
Turkey	0.0	0.5	13.1	271.8	1,020.0	1,113.0	1,065.6	818.0	942.3	1,131.8	673.78
United Kingdom	2,595.0	3,163.0	4,103.0	5,987.0	5,545.4	5,472.3	4,856.1	3,727.3	3,657.1	3,435.3	5,505.22
Eastern Europe											
Albania											
Belarus											
Bosnia-Herzegovina					27.4	31.3	35.2	46.5	48.6	58.2	41.39
Bulgaria		1.0	1.2	54.4	154.0	176.0	189.0	175.6	157.5	168.4	119.76
Croatia					1,315.0	1,501.0	1,566.0	1,429.0	1,378.7	1,340.1	250.78
Czech Republic	117.1	572.4	2,175.3	6,652.3	11,265.3	11,373.1	11,787.8	8,715.0	9,374.7	11,254.2	635.98
Estonia		94.3	13.9	25.6	47.1	58.0	51.0	28.5	23.1	26.3	36.56
Georgia							15.0	16.0	24.8	32.1	19.05
Hungary	1,345.3	4,109.6	13,478.7	40,117.4	68,680.7	69,364.6	72,892.2	60,019.6	57,382.6	59,595.0	296.41
Latvia	1.0	1.0	7.5	13.2	30.1	37.0	32.0	13.0	12.0	12.9	25.58
Lithuania		1.6	17.1	67.8	173.0	187.5	205.0	108.0	94.0	88.5	35.62
Macedonia											
Moldova					27.0	33.8	37.0	36.0	37.3	40.3	3.43
Montenegro											
Poland	7.4	31.3	167.6	880.0	1,592.8	1,653.0	1,669.8	1,359.0	1,243.0	1,166.0	393.45
Romania			2.0	67.3	230.1	251.9	293.1	200.9	124.9	115.7	37.94
Russia			525.9	3,686.5	17,191.3	19,711.3	24,306.2	17,884.6	18,349.7	16,095.8	547.62
Serbia					2,082.5	3,200.0	4,374.0	3,384.0	4,223.0	4,858.4	66.25
Slovakia					178.2	193.2	187.8	162.3	150.7	141.6	196.87
Slovenia	16.1	23.4	35.7	70.0	124.0	144.0	159.0	142.0	148.9	156.1	217.02
Ukraine					843.4	1,252.4	2,099.5	1,359.6	1,516.0	1,730.3	217.04

Source: Euromonitor International from national statistics

Advertising Statistics

Table 2.5

Cinema Adspend 1985, 1990, 1995, 2000, 2006-2011

National currency million

	1985	1990	1995	2000	2006	2007	2008	2009	2010	2011	US$ million 2011
Western Europe											
Austria	3.0	4.0	6.0	11.0	15.0	15.0	13.7	11.5	14.3	14.8	20.60
Belgium	10.0	10.0	17.0	25.0	29.7	26.0	26.8	24.6	25.7	26.3	36.55
Cyprus											
Denmark	4.0	23.0	57.0	46.0	55.0	56.0	60.0	66.0	69.3	75.4	14.07
Finland	2.0	1.0	1.0	2.0	1.4	2.3	3.0	2.4	3.0	3.2	4.46
France	43.4	37.5	29.8	52.4	81.6	88.6	74.9	76.6	90.4	98.7	137.30
Germany	65.0	102.0	159.6	175.0	117.0	106.0	77.0	72.0	75.0	78.4	109.07
Gibraltar											
Greece	2.0	2.0	2.4	12.5	16.0	17.0	16.0	15.0	14.0	12.8	17.82
Iceland					130.0	154.0	157.0	147.0	126.4	136.4	1.18
Ireland	1.0	1.0	4.0	6.0	10.0	11.0	10.0	8.0	8.0	8.3	11.58
Italy	12.0	16.0	17.0	50.0	64.1	58.7	49.1	46.9	52.6	54.6	75.92
Liechtenstein											
Luxembourg			1.0	1.2	1.2	1.3	1.5	1.8	1.8	2.0	2.77
Malta											
Monaco											
Netherlands	9.0	9.0	11.0	13.0	5.0	5.0	5.0	5.0	5.0	5.1	7.15
Norway	42.1	42.1	51.2	87.0	121.4	127.0	143.0	115.0	139.0	147.3	26.28
Portugal				6.0	5.9	5.5	5.2	4.0	3.8	3.5	4.84
Spain	91.0	57.0	29.0	55.0	43.0	38.4	21.0	15.4	24.4	26.5	36.84
Sweden	68.0	70.0	81.0	78.0	73.7	90.6	103.5	103.0	119.0	136.0	20.93
Switzerland	47.0	30.0	34.0	45.0	50.0	47.0	45.0	30.0	33.0	31.0	34.91
Turkey	0.0	0.0	0.6	8.2	33.0	36.0	39.4	39.0	45.5	59.0	35.11
United Kingdom	20.0	32.0	59.0	109.0	131.0	144.0	145.0	152.0	155.0	160.1	256.55
Eastern Europe											
Albania											
Belarus											
Bosnia-Herzegovina											
Bulgaria											
Croatia											
Czech Republic					140.7	135.5	97.8	50.8	109.1	148.7	8.40
Estonia											
Georgia											
Hungary	0.9	9.9	109.8	968.3	1,151.9	850.0	800.0	810.0	1,031.5	1,243.5	6.18
Latvia					0.5	0.6	0.6	0.4	0.4	0.5	0.99
Lithuania					0.5	0.5	1.2	1.1	0.9	1.1	0.44
Macedonia											
Moldova					1.2	1.5	3.7	4.6	6.0	7.3	0.62
Montenegro											
Poland	0.3	0.7	1.0	9.3	60.0	71.9	95.0	94.0	103.0	117.2	39.54
Romania			0.4	0.4	8.1	8.3	9.9	8.0	7.5	8.6	2.80
Russia				75.6	1,611.7	2,021.7	2,209.7	2,300.9	3,100.0	3,864.5	131.48
Serbia						40.0	40.5	47.0	51.5	63.4	0.86
Slovakia					0.9	0.6	0.7	0.7	0.8	0.9	1.22
Slovenia					1.0	2.0	1.3	0.9	0.5	0.3	0.42
Ukraine					35.4	45.5	68.5	34.1	41.7	40.9	5.13

Source: Euromonitor International from national statistics

Table 2.6

Outdoor Adspend 1985, 1990, 1995, 2000, 2006-2011

National currency million

	1985	1990	1995	2000	2006	2007	2008	2009	2010	2011	US$ million 2011
Western Europe											
Austria	29.0	54.0	79.0	112.0	170.0	171.0	180.0	201.0	196.0	205.6	285.81
Belgium	183.0	138.0	129.0	162.0	226.6	238.8	249.5	248.1	254.0	264.6	367.94
Cyprus											
Denmark			153.0	338.0	405.0	473.0	516.0	491.0	530.0	564.3	105.29
Finland	14.0	21.0	24.0	35.0	37.0	42.0	44.0	36.0	39.1	40.6	56.40
France	894.9	871.5	915.3	1,194.2	1,221.0	1,237.0	1,265.0	1,127.0	1,188.0	1,226.7	1,705.58
Germany	288.0	377.0	540.4	746.0	787.0	820.0	805.0	738.0	766.0	796.6	1,107.56
Gibraltar											
Greece	4.0	13.0	66.6	240.2	306.0	330.0	184.0	202.0	166.0	152.8	212.50
Iceland				279.1	347.9	384.4	402.1	389.2	382.5	388.6	3.35
Ireland	4.0	13.0	20.0	70.0	134.0	183.0	196.0	142.0	116.0	111.2	154.60
Italy	596.0	296.0	171.0	318.0	312.3	318.2	309.2	230.8	234.0	222.5	309.32
Liechtenstein											
Luxembourg					3.6	4.1	4.2	4.9	5.3	5.8	8.02
Malta											
Monaco											
Netherlands	71.0	72.0	84.0	139.0	164.0	165.0	164.0	148.6	150.1	150.4	209.13
Norway	95.4	95.4	139.8	142.5	484.5	494.0	535.0	481.0	506.0	532.6	95.02
Portugal	37.8	35.0	48.0	99.0	114.3	120.0	118.8	104.5	105.1	100.9	140.34
Spain	876.0	400.0	160.0	308.0	529.0	568.0	518.3	401.4	420.8	424.4	590.05
Sweden	343.0	446.0	573.0	848.0	1,067.7	1,039.4	1,061.0	954.0	1,081.0	1,202.4	185.12
Switzerland	427.0	386.0	446.0	592.0	423.0	437.0	459.0	428.0	447.0	462.1	520.30
Turkey	0.0	0.1	2.3	56.9	160.0	235.0	242.4	198.0	252.0	317.9	189.27
United Kingdom	124.0	191.0	349.0	592.0	792.0	829.0	798.0	665.0	748.0	749.1	1,200.54
Eastern Europe											
Albania											
Belarus											
Bosnia-Herzegovina					17.6	15.6	17.6	23.5	24.8	30.0	21.31
Bulgaria				16.8	89.8	107.1	123.8	84.0	73.9	63.5	45.13
Croatia					311.0	275.0	267.0	218.2	213.5	200.3	37.48
Czech Republic				1,050.0	2,207.6	2,424.6	3,759.8	1,698.4	1,655.3	1,231.6	69.60
Estonia			1.1	2.0	5.4	7.9	8.8	5.7	5.8	7.3	10.09
Georgia					4.5	9.1	9.0	11.3	13.1	16.5	9.81
Hungary	0.5	42.0	1,632.7	8,235.1	19,000.0	19,093.0	20,460.0	14,340.0	18,006.9	19,515.8	97.07
Latvia			1.0	1.5	6.5	8.1	9.5	5.5	5.7	6.7	13.34
Lithuania	0.6	0.6	3.2	10.9	29.6	32.0	36.0	23.0	22.0	24.6	9.91
Macedonia											
Moldova					27.0	60.9	108.2	108.2	130.6	148.1	12.62
Montenegro											
Poland	2.0	9.8	66.1	448.1	523.2	669.7	707.2	587.0	555.0	538.8	181.82
Romania				3.9	34.7	101.0	131.5	209.3	180.6	185.7	218.1	71.54
Russia			400.1	4,155.7	29,637.1	34,031.4	34,617.9	26,356.3	29,699.6	28,903.2	983.37
Serbia					1,190.0	1,840.0	2,106.0	1,927.0	2,163.0	2,531.7	34.52
Slovakia					43.0	48.3	85.4	81.1	103.0	118.6	164.89
Slovenia	0.2	0.8	3.2	10.6	30.0	32.0	32.6	31.0	32.3	34.5	48.03
Ukraine					767.6	1,015.1	1,000.8	535.6	734.2	847.8	106.35

Source: Euromonitor International from national statistics

2

Advertising

Advertising Statistics

Table 2.7

Online Adspend 2000-2011

National currency million

	2000	2001	2002	2003	2004	2005	2006	2007	2008	2009	2010	2011	US$ million 2011
Western Europe													
Austria		10	22	10	22	28	37	81	108	143	362	450	626.14
Belgium	13	11	11	18	32	48	82	110	125	135	168	187	260.30
Cyprus													
Denmark		310	418	486	582	742	1,794	2,502	2,926	3,030	3,195	3,443	642.30
Finland	11	15	15	17	23	36	48	61	152	180	206	233	323.99
France	227	181	156	207	282	603	855	1,164	1,450	1,519	1,680	1,820	2,531.24
Germany	153	285	427	546	671	832	1,500	2,094	2,498	2,696	3,067	3,369	4,684.94
Gibraltar													
Greece		2	5										
Iceland		8											
Ireland	2	3	4	6	9	16	85	91	100	112	111	123	170.85
Italy	139	107	99	103	107	143	206	294	335	352	423	452	628.57
Liechtenstein													
Luxembourg				8	5	7	8	9	9	9	4	3	4.37
Malta													
Monaco													
Netherlands	154	137	129	162	267	392	554	720	782	795	835	866	1,203.75
Norway	247	193	205	267	374	1,726	2,563	2,906	3,500	3,518	4,013	4,410	786.68
Portugal	5	5	5	4	4	5	7	13	19	21	25	25	35.26
Spain	53	52	72	75	94	162	310	482	610	654	790	872	1,212.06
Sweden	1,037	895	1,139	1,325	1,325	1,974	3,005	4,054	4,850	4,999	5,759	6,624	1,019.73
Switzerland	37	36	44	64	78	107	156	223	300	390	452	513	577.84
Turkey		1	2	4	8	18	30	53	95	182	251	369	219.75
United Kingdom	132	141	162	295	700	1,162	1,713	2,391	2,848	3,005	3,435	3,635	5,825.60
Eastern Europe													
Albania													
Belarus													
Bosnia-Herzegovina							1	1	1	2	2	3	2.16
Bulgaria					3	5	12	19	32	34	37	45	31.94
Croatia						9	12	43	65	54	155	184	34.49
Czech Republic	82	165	198	287	547	684	1,670	2,806	3,680	3,740	4,358	6,041	341.39
Estonia	1	1	1	2	2	3	4	10	12	9	10	13	17.69
Georgia										1	1	2	1.08
Hungary					2,688	6,159	10,500	15,300	21,800	23,300	29,241	35,547	176.80
Latvia			1	1	1	2	3	6	8	6	7	8	15.94
Lithuania	1		2	6	6	6	12	16	30	20	25	32	12.69
Macedonia													
Moldova							1	1	2	3	4	5	0.46
Montenegro													
Poland		15	21	31	55	148	215	593	738	801	965	1,170	394.73
Romania				2	5	8	16	43	72	65	101	127	41.72
Russia	76	157	309	495	774	1,522	2,597	10,698	12,194	16,943	22,600	30,538	1,038.97
Serbia						34	77	136	203	235	670	928	12.66
Slovakia							12	18	23	27	33	40	55.43
Slovenia					3	4	7	11	18	20	24	29	39.65
Ukraine			5	5	11	10	30	56	111	148	203	338	42.35

Source: Euromonitor International from national statistics

CHAPTER THREE

Agricultural Resources and Output

Agricultural Statistics | **Table 3.1**

Agricultural Output Indices 1985, 1990, 1995, 2000, 2006-2011

2004-2006 = 100

	1985	1990	1995	2000	2006	2007	2008	2009	2010	2011
Western Europe										
Austria	89	93	97	102	98	102	104	102	98	98
Belgium				107	97	98	94	98	85	84
Cyprus	90	99	110	108	93	92	89	87	86	85
Denmark	89	95	97	99	98	101	104	104	100	101
Finland	105	108	95	99	100	101	100	100	94	94
France	99	99	99	103	96	95	96	98	96	95
Germany	107	108	94	103	97	100	103	107	103	103
Gibraltar										
Greece	95	86	105	107	96	90	90	88	81	78
Iceland	107	87	86	95	100	104	106	105	105	106
Ireland	93	98	98	104	100	101	97	95	100	100
Italy	96	90	95	100	96	95	97	97	94	93
Liechtenstein	95	99	96	97	100	99	101	98	99	99
Luxembourg				115	101	96	104	107	100	99
Malta	75	79	91	107	103	98	106	96	96	97
Monaco										
Netherlands	97	104	106	102	100	103	105	109	111	111
Norway	104	111	103	99	100	101	102	101	102	102
Portugal	81	99	96	100	98	96	99	99	101	101
Spain	73	83	71	100	102	100	100	104	104	104
Sweden	112	110	97	101	98	97	98	101	97	96
Switzerland	106	105	101	102	99	101	102	105	104	104
Turkey	68	80	83	95	104	100	104	106	107	108
United Kingdom	107	108	109	104	100	98	103	101	101	101
Eastern Europe										
Albania	66	72	86	87	102	104	108	112	119	122
Belarus			86	78	106	106	115	122	123	128
Bosnia-Herzegovina			66	62	105	99	107	112	105	109
Bulgaria	179	180	135	113	103	79	105	103	109	111
Croatia			99	96	105	108	109	115	103	105
Czech Republic			103	98	95	96	102	98	92	91
Estonia			109	84	103	104	109	112	112	114
Georgia			120	100	76	86	76	73	68	66
Hungary	118	119	85	89	94	79	104	95	83	83
Latvia			113	84	103	112	125	120	118	121
Lithuania			88	89	95	111	111	115	104	106
Macedonia			87	98	102	105	111	112	118	120
Moldova			128	91	100	79	99	86	87	87
Montenegro					100	93	96	98	103	104
Poland	104	111	91	92	101	100	102	106	100	101
Romania	114	95	96	83	96	80	97	96	95	97
Russia			95	88	103	109	106	112	101	103
Serbia					100	97	100	107	101	102
Slovakia			105	89	94	89	104	93	84	84
Slovenia			94	98	96	94	95	93	96	95
Ukraine			107	88	100	94	115	118	107	109

Source: Euromonitor International from national statistics

Table 3.2

Food Output Indices 1985, 1990, 1995, 2000, 2006-2011

2004-2006 = 100

	1985	1990	1995	2000	2006	2007	2008	2009	2010	2011
Western Europe										
Austria	89	93	97	102	98	102	104	102	98	98
Belgium				107	97	98	94	99	85	84
Cyprus	90	99	110	108	93	92	89	87	86	85
Denmark	89	95	97	99	98	101	104	104	100	101
Finland	105	108	95	99	100	101	100	100	94	94
France	00	00	99	103	97	96	96	97	96	95
Germany	107	108	94	103	97	100	103	107	103	103
Gibraltar										
Greece	98	86	103	106	98	92	93	92	84	82
Iceland	106	86	86	94	101	104	106	105	105	106
Ireland	93	98	98	104	100	101	97	95	100	99
Italy	96	90	95	100	96	95	97	97	94	93
Liechtenstein	95	99	96	97	100	99	101	98	99	99
Luxembourg				115	101	96	104	107	100	99
Malta	75	79	91	107	103	98	106	96	96	97
Monaco										
Netherlands	97	103	105	102	100	103	105	109	111	111
Norway	104	111	103	99	100	101	102	101	102	102
Portugal	81	99	96	99	98	96	99	99	101	101
Spain	73	83	71	100	102	100	100	104	104	105
Sweden	112	110	97	101	98	97	98	101	97	96
Switzerland	106	105	101	102	99	101	102	105	104	104
Turkey	68	80	82	95	104	100	106	109	110	112
United Kingdom	107	108	109	104	100	98	103	101	101	101
Eastern Europe										
Albania	62	69	85	86	102	104	108	113	119	122
Belarus			86	78	106	106	115	123	124	128
Bosnia-Herzegovina			66	62	105	99	107	112	105	110
Bulgaria	175	180	138	115	104	79	106	104	111	112
Croatia			99	96	105	107	109	115	104	105
Czech Republic			103	98	95	96	102	98	92	92
Estonia			109	84	103	104	109	112	111	114
Georgia			118	99	77	87	77	73	69	67
Hungary	118	119	85	89	94	79	104	95	83	83
Latvia			113	84	103	112	125	120	118	122
Lithuania			88	89	95	111	111	115	104	106
Macedonia			88	99	102	107	114	113	119	120
Moldova			126	89	100	79	99	86	86	87
Montenegro					100	93	97	98	103	104
Poland	103	110	91	92	101	100	102	106	100	101
Romania	113	95	96	83	96	80	97	96	95	97
Russia			95	88	103	109	106	112	101	103
Serbia					100	97	100	107	101	102
Slovakia			104	89	94	89	104	93	84	84
Slovenia			94	98	96	94	95	93	96	95
Ukraine			107	88	100	94	115	118	107	109

Source: Euromonitor International from national statistics

Agricultural Statistics

Table 3.3

Land Use and Irrigation 2011

'000 hectares

	Total Area	Land Area	Arable Land	Permanent Crops	Permanent Pasture	Irrigated Land	Irrigated as % of Land Area
Western Europe							
Austria	8,387.9	8,243.5	1,362.1	64.5	1,686.9	116.1	1.4
Belgium	3,053.0	3,028.0	839.1	21.3	493.9	23.0	0.8
Cyprus	925.0	924.0	72.8	30.9	5.2	46.0	5.0
Denmark	4,309.0	4,243.0	2,514.3	6.0	166.2	429.0	10.1
Finland	33,842.0	30,390.0	2,256.8	4.4	33.2	76.6	0.3
France	54,919.0	54,766.0	18,256.5	1,011.6	9,844.5	2,559.7	4.7
Germany	35,712.0	34,861.0	12,003.1	201.6	4,636.5	485.0	1.4
Gibraltar	1.0	1.0					
Greece	13,196.0	12,890.0	2,756.3	1,160.8	1,389.7	1,546.2	12.0
Iceland	10,300.0	10,025.0	7.0		2,274.0		
Ireland	7,028.0	6,889.0	1,073.4	3.0	3,058.4		
Italy	30,134.0	29,414.0	6,596.0	2,658.1	4,476.4	3,945.4	13.4
Liechtenstein	16.0	16.0	3.3		3.0		
Luxembourg	259.0	259.0	63.3	2.0	66.7		
Malta	32.0	32.0	8.0	1.3		3.3	10.3
Monaco	0.2	0.2					
Netherlands	4,154.0	3,373.0	1,046.4	37.4	833.9	474.3	14.1
Norway	32,378.0	30,547.0	819.3	4.3	176.1	95.7	0.3
Portugal	9,209.0	9,147.0	1,074.4	779.8	1,803.4	576.3	6.3
Spain	50,537.0	49,880.0	12,370.1	4,629.0	10,182.8	3,809.3	7.6
Sweden	45,030.0	41,034.0	2,624.9	9.0	393.9	158.3	0.4
Switzerland	4,128.0	4,000.0	405.3	23.7	1,096.6	25.0	0.6
Turkey	78,356.0	76,963.0	20,468.8	2,976.2	14,617.0	5,215.0	6.8
United Kingdom	24,361.0	24,193.0	6,017.7	41.3	10,945.1	239.3	1.0
Eastern Europe							
Albania	2,875.0	2,740.0	658.8	87.0	587.7	365.0	13.3
Belarus	20,760.0	20,282.0	5,554.2	119.2	3,243.7	131.0	0.6
Bosnia-Herzegovina	5,121.0	5,100.0	975.9	108.0	1,024.9	3.0	0.1
Bulgaria	11,100.0	10,851.2	3,175.2	152.4	1,627.2	98.6	0.9
Croatia	5,659.0	5,596.0	869.7	97.0	389.2	35.8	0.6
Czech Republic	7,887.0	7,725.0	3,165.3	76.0	987.8	17.0	0.2
Estonia	4,523.0	4,239.0	613.5	7.0	333.4	4.0	0.1
Georgia	6,970.0	6,949.0	437.4	124.0	1,940.0	433.0	6.2
Hungary	9,303.0	9,053.0	4,577.4	191.4	994.9	138.3	1.5
Latvia	6,456.0	6,218.0	1,145.5	5.0	675.2	0.8	0.0
Lithuania	6,530.0	6,267.5	2,223.4	24.3	508.7	1.3	0.0
Macedonia	2,571.0	2,522.0	408.3	33.4	478.4	128.0	5.1
Moldova	3,385.0	3,289.0	1,814.0	299.5	349.4	228.5	6.9
Montenegro	1,381.0	1,345.0	172.2	16.0	325.3	2.4	0.2
Poland	31,268.0	30,420.0	12,628.5	411.8	3,135.4	116.3	0.4
Romania	23,839.0	23,006.0	8,807.6	300.0	4,210.5	3,157.3	13.7
Russia	1,709,824.0	1,637,687.0	121,887.1	1,787.3	91,951.9	4,165.5	0.3
Serbia	8,836.0	8,836.0	3,288.8	296.8	1,465.3	82.7	0.9
Slovakia	4,904.0	4,809.0	1,385.5	23.3	517.5	112.7	2.3
Slovenia	2,027.0	2,014.0	173.8	25.2	250.7	10.9	0.5
Ukraine	60,355.0	57,932.0	32,506.9	897.2	7,871.8	2,170.3	3.7

Source: Euromonitor International from national statistics

Agricultural Statistics

Table 3.4

Livestock 2011

'000 head

	Asses	Cattle	Goats	Horses	Pigs	Sheep
Western Europe						
Austria		1,905.5	73.8	85.0	3,109.5	365.7
Belgium		2,439.2	20.6	37.7	6,414.5	111.0
Cyprus	5.2	55.1	178.4	0.7	437.5	208.9
Denmark		1,549.1		62.5	13,205.1	161.9
Finland		915.2	4.7	76.3	1,298.2	129.6
France	14.0	10,611.1	1,366.2	448.0	13,725.3	7,419.2
Germany		12,061.4	142.8	431.7	25,214.7	1,911.6
Gibraltar						
Greece	37.7	632.4	3,990.1	27.0	952.2	8,505.7
Iceland		74.9	0.8	78.0	37.8	481.9
Ireland	6.2	6,226.1	10.5	102.1	1,488.6	4,433.3
Italy	24.1	5,746.2	957.1	301.4	8,698.8	7,596.6
Liechtenstein		6.2	0.5		1.8	4.1
Luxembourg		200.2	5.5	4.8	83.7	9.0
Malta	0.5	15.2	5.8	1.1	64.1	13.0
Monaco						
Netherlands		4,002.4	437.1	134.6	12,406.7	1,066.4
Norway		820.2	63.5	37.9	858.9	2,283.6
Portugal	125.0	1,321.4	480.1	19.3	2,208.2	2,695.3
Spain	142.3	5,715.7	2,900.9	251.7	24,264.1	17,050.0
Sweden		1,450.7		94.9	1,398.7	581.6
Switzerland	6.2	1,608.3	89.6	53.5	1,591.1	401.8
Turkey	205.0	10,321.6	4,686.1	149.7	1.7	20,297.3
United Kingdom		9,326.3	79.2	391.7	4,124.8	28,846.9
Eastern Europe						
Albania	60.6	447.2	740.7	30.6	168.6	1,792.1
Belarus	9.1	4,171.8	76.5	111.5	3,846.1	47.6
Bosnia-Herzegovina		465.6	58.1	17.2	597.6	1,048.1
Bulgaria	126.6	520.0	309.0	106.7	665.1	1,292.2
Croatia	4.0	421.9	71.2	18.1	1,168.1	636.2
Czech Republic		1,244.1	23.8	32.0	1,677.0	218.8
Estonia		220.5	3.9	5.4	368.6	83.5
Georgia	10.0	940.3	66.4	39.6	90.8	572.3
Hungary	1.8	656.1	52.2	60.7	2,900.3	1,182.5
Latvia		358.2	13.2	11.4	348.4	76.3
Lithuania		719.3	13.3	45.2	909.2	58.1
Macedonia		259.9	98.6	23.6	186.3	712.6
Moldova	2.9	194.8	109.0	49.1	312.7	800.0
Montenegro		117.9		5.5	10.7	216.2
Poland		5,757.5	112.1	271.6	14,331.0	236.7
Romania	30.3	2,342.1	957.9	712.2	5,637.7	9,402.9
Russia	17.3	18,960.2	2,007.8	1,357.3	17,215.8	20,725.1
Serbia		864.0	113.9	11.9	3,305.7	1,398.5
Slovakia		432.6	32.9	7.8	583.1	385.7
Slovenia		472.8	31.0	20.4	371.0	136.2
Ukraine	12.0	4,191.0	578.5	395.9	7,344.2	1,232.3

Source: Euromonitor International from national statistics

Agricultural Resources and Output

3

Agricultural Statistics

Table 3.5

Selected Crop Production 2011

'000 tonnes

	Apples	Bananas	Grapes	Hops	Potatoes	Rapeseed	Sugar Beet	Tomatoes
Western Europe								
Austria	287.7		214.4	0.4	676.0	178.9	3,291.3	45.5
Belgium	247.1		0.1	0.4	3,671.5	43.6	4,164.3	268.6
Cyprus	5.9	5.7	23.8		70.6			25.9
Denmark	27.6				1,357.0	616.1	2,366.5	21.0
Finland	4.5				680.0	186.1	492.1	39.3
France	1,618.8		5,617.0	0.7	6,637.0	4,983.3	32,420.1	574.3
Germany	806.8		936.2	35.7	10,244.7	5,787.9	24,661.4	78.3
Gibraltar								
Greece	226.7	3.2	968.0		763.9	6.5	726.4	1,365.6
Iceland					12.1			1.6
Ireland	39.5			0.0	317.4	25.3	0.0	13.8
Italy	2,223.5	0.3	7,653.1		1,501.8	57.8	3,245.2	5,943.2
Liechtenstein			0.2					
Luxembourg	11.9		14.1		20.3	15.8		0.1
Malta	0.0		4.2		8.9			14.1
Monaco								
Netherlands	331.3		0.9		6,994.5	11.5	5,247.0	848.8
Norway	11.5				306.8	11.4		13.1
Portugal	141.3	35.0	924.0	0.1	327.2		137.0	1,511.8
Spain	582.4	383.8	5,985.2	0.6	2,218.6	40.0	2,975.7	4,440.7
Sweden	23.4				825.1	295.4	1,919.9	15.7
Switzerland	185.9		182.0	0.0	428.6	70.4	1,316.9	29.5
Turkey	2,749.5	218.2	4,318.7		4,585.8	120.7	18,814.6	10,101.3
United Kingdom	217.3		1.0	1.5	6,090.3	2,315.0	6,255.0	90.6
Eastern Europe								
Albania	61.4		199.2	1.3	219.4		37.5	207.9
Belarus	534.7				7,706.5	419.5	3,717.3	327.3
Bosnia-Herzegovina	75.0		23.6		370.8	1.2	0.0	35.6
Bulgaria	47.5		211.0	0.1	217.4	603.2	0.0	98.3
Croatia	115.2		214.8		154.6	36.3	1,171.5	35.0
Czech Republic	85.0		43.0	8.4	658.5	1,083.0	3,046.7	6.4
Estonia	1.8				166.1	142.6		4.8
Georgia	18.2		110.3	0.0	243.8		0.0	52.5
Hungary	486.8		258.5		408.8	578.8	941.8	116.7
Latvia	10.9				467.3	252.7	0.0	0.0
Lithuania	33.9				479.1	476.6	723.9	2.8
Macedonia	127.8		253.1		203.1	6.0	8.0	174.4
Moldova	198.5		808.8		219.6	115.5	304.8	89.2
Montenegro	6.1		40.6		153.4			22.4
Poland	1,747.5			2.5	8,712.0	2,184.2	9,409.9	684.2
Romania	543.5		697.1	0.2	3,100.9	1,029.7	759.3	751.9
Russia	884.0		344.4	0.0	18,911.1	707.1	20,151.7	1,896.3
Serbia	239.9		322.7	0.1	876.6	22.6	3,358.8	189.5
Slovakia	48.7		18.1	0.2	115.0	338.2	879.4	33.9
Slovenia	117.2		109.3	2.1	99.8	17.0	0.0	3.6
Ukraine	987.1		434.7	0.8	18,514.5	1,685.7	13,273.8	1,843.1

Source: Euromonitor International from national statistics

Agricultural Statistics | Table 3.6

Dairy Products and Egg Production 2011

'000 tonnes

	Butter and Ghee	Cheese	Fresh Cows' Milk	Hens' Eggs
Western Europe				
Austria	34.5	198.6	3,285.8	93.6
Belgium	83.6	90.2	3,124.1	192.9
Cyprus		5.3	151.5	10.1
Denmark	33.4	282.6	4,980.0	76.2
Finland	50.9	102.5	2,330.2	62.7
France	431.1	1,915.2	23,092.3	956.2
Germany	452.6	2,105.2	30,037.4	637.8
Gibraltar				
Greece	2.0	218.5	766.8	99.9
Iceland	1.8	9.3	122.2	2.7
Ireland	134.7	183.4	5,195.4	46.7
Italy	105.1	1,186.8	10,393.9	751.3
Liechtenstein			13.1	
Luxembourg	0.2		302.1	1.3
Malta		0.2	42.3	4.7
Monaco				
Netherlands	120.1	746.8	11,791.5	636.0
Norway	13.5	82.8	1,556.9	62.2
Portugal	21.2	75.5	1,964.8	134.0
Spain	36.1	212.9	6,398.5	843.3
Sweden	37.6	103.6	2,886.1	104.3
Switzerland	50.9	203.4	4,116.1	44.3
Turkey	162.9	161.2	12,883.3	741.7
United Kingdom	158.9	328.4	13,871.0	625.3
Eastern Europe				
Albania	3.4	16.3	936.5	32.4
Belarus	101.3	166.5	6,780.2	198.8
Bosnia-Herzegovina	0.5	4.6	723.8	20.6
Bulgaria	1.0	75.2	1,080.8	86.8
Croatia	4.0	31.2	739.7	40.4
Czech Republic	38.6	126.6	2,662.9	129.2
Estonia	4.6	16.2	671.3	11.4
Georgia	0.4	0.0	504.7	24.7
Hungary	4.2	93.1	1,647.7	148.7
Latvia	5.9	33.5	835.6	47.3
Lithuania	8.9	78.6	1,697.8	40.7
Macedonia	6.8	6.7	364.0	18.9
Moldova	4.4	7.6	533.1	40.5
Montenegro			171.6	4.1
Poland	167.9	685.3	12,352.8	638.8
Romania	8.3	88.7	4,210.4	285.7
Russia	194.4	607.5	32,072.3	2,300.8
Serbia	1.3	24.8	1,476.1	58.0
Slovakia	7.1	47.7	888.4	75.7
Slovenia	5.6	18.3	617.7	23.1
Ukraine	74.8	233.2	10,635.3	1,013.5

Source: Euromonitor International from national statistics

Agricultural Resources and Output

3

Agricultural Statistics   **Table 3.7**

Meat Production 2011

'000 tonnes

	Beef and Veal	Goat Meat	Horse Meat	Mutton and Lamb	Pig Meat	Poultry	Total (including others)
Western Europe							
Austria	226.9	0.5	0.2	7.3	546.5	122.4	906.5
Belgium	262.4	0.0	2.0	2.9	1,132.7	473.5	1,871.6
Cyprus	4.5	2.1		2.4	57.6	28.9	96.0
Denmark	133.2		0.5	1.8	1,674.0	189.5	1,999.1
Finland	83.1		0.4	0.8	206.6	108.5	401.6
France	1,553.2	12.6	4.3	121.7	2,088.5	1,756.7	5,780.1
Germany	1,202.4	0.5	2.6	33.7	5,668.0	1,438.6	8,449.6
Gibraltar							
Greece	71.1	53.2	2.7	89.4	99.0	118.3	440.4
Iceland	3.9		0.8	9.1	6.3	7.3	29.9
Ireland	556.8		1.5	45.4	213.7	117.1	934.1
Italy	1,068.1	2.0	16.5	51.1	1,692.5	1,194.8	4,307.2
Liechtenstein							
Luxembourg	16.1		0.8	0.0	9.8	0.0	27.1
Malta	1.4	0.0	0.1	0.1	7.4	4.5	15.3
Monaco							
Netherlands	382.8	0.7	0.4	12.8	1,259.0	838.5	2,490.5
Norway	82.8	0.3	0.4	24.6	131.4	89.0	335.0
Portugal	93.5	0.9	0.2	19.9	390.5	287.3	795.0
Spain	609.1	8.5	6.5	124.5	3,415.4	1,156.0	5,380.4
Sweden	148.5		0.9	5.5	262.3	117.6	550.1
Switzerland	144.5	0.5	0.7	5.5	252.1	71.3	477.4
Turkey	322.3	35.8	2.0	253.7	0.0	1,538.5	2,167.8
United Kingdom	946.6		3.1	274.3	764.3	1,564.9	3,552.1
Eastern Europe							
Albania	41.5	7.3		14.2	13.0	18.3	94.6
Belarus	318.5		2.3	1.5	409.9	295.1	1,009.6
Bosnia-Herzegovina	24.4			2.1	14.3	40.7	80.8
Bulgaria	18.5	3.5	0.0	12.4	67.5	108.6	210.0
Croatia	38.5	0.2	4.5	2.2	126.7	29.2	201.0
Czech Republic	71.6	0.1	0.1	2.3	281.6	193.2	586.5
Estonia	12.1	0.0		0.7	34.6	16.9	64.2
Georgia	33.2	0.0	0.1	4.7	12.0	11.5	48.7
Hungary	25.6	0.2	0.1	0.8	439.9	367.8	844.4
Latvia	18.2		0.1	0.6	37.8	25.0	82.2
Lithuania	42.1	0.4	0.0	0.7	73.3	82.8	198.6
Macedonia	7.2			5.1	7.9	3.1	23.2
Moldova	9.7		0.1	2.0	57.6	43.7	113.6
Montenegro	4.4			0.5	1.6	5.9	14.5
Poland	406.1		14.8	1.1	1,514.5	1,284.3	3,626.2
Romania	154.8	7.7	9.6	63.9	425.9	358.0	1,023.4
Russia	1,694.8	18.4	47.8	176.1	2,381.4	2,760.9	7,220.7
Serbia	91.0			22.9	266.4	83.7	469.9
Slovakia	12.1	0.2	0.1	1.0	63.3	78.4	156.6
Slovenia	35.3	0.4	0.4	1.7	43.0	61.6	142.1
Ukraine	405.3	11.0	12.7	10.6	631.4	1,029.4	2,107.6

Source: Euromonitor International from national statistics

Table 3.8

Cereal Production 2011

'000 tonnes

	Barley	Maize	Millet	Oats	Rice	Rye	Sorghum	Wheat	Total (including others)
Western Europe									
Austria	743.9	2,343.1	6.9	89.6		181.1		1,548.2	5,547.4
Belgium	374.9	788.4		24.4		1.8		1,896.5	3,131.4
Cyprus	37.3			0.5				16.7	54.5
Denmark	2,909.1			274.5		285.9		5,124.5	8,806.7
Finland	1,182.2			754.9		72.9		734.5	2,792.9
France	10,027.4	14,275.0	37.4	443.7	124.4	121.8	282.4	38,917.9	66,698.6
Germany	10,023.5	4,286.1		542.9		2,968.4		24,526.4	44,647.3
Gibraltar									
Greece	336.0	2,154.3		123.8	242.1	34.5	0.0	1,555.5	4,453.0
Iceland									
Ireland	1,244.5			148.7		0.4		636.0	2,037.2
Italy	917.9	8,617.0		250.3	1,693.2	13.9	283.8	6,829.6	18,693.5
Liechtenstein									
Luxembourg	41.2	3.4		4.3		4.9		85.4	167.4
Malta	1.4							13.8	15.2
Monaco									
Netherlands	188.4	200.8		7.6		11.3		1,415.8	1,836.5
Norway	525.6			302.9		33.5		277.0	1,139.0
Portugal	67.2	694.1		60.9	176.0	16.1		113.2	1,127.4
Spain	8,161.5	3,134.6	0.7	1,035.2	976.9	273.5	34.0	5,633.0	19,409.4
Sweden	1,257.5			548.2		125.4		2,238.7	4,384.0
Switzerland	160.1	141.3		8.2		15.0		518.5	901.2
Turkey	6,662.3	4,434.8	6.7	202.6	901.0	389.2	0.2	19,572.5	32,266.9
United Kingdom	5,255.3			674.3		19.6		14,910.8	20,953.7
Eastern Europe									
Albania	7.6	391.2		28.5		2.2		310.9	740.4
Belarus	2,000.4	631.9		414.6		651.2		1,906.8	6,990.7
Bosnia-Herzegovina	47.1	818.3		16.8		6.6		123.6	1,044.9
Bulgaria	905.1	2,158.2	6.1	42.4	60.6	18.7	9.7	4,168.2	7,400.5
Croatia	161.6	2,101.1	0.2	43.6		2.2	0.2	650.1	3,012.4
Czech Republic	1,506.2	714.2	1.6	134.0		129.0		4,325.4	7,005.6
Estonia	240.0			49.8		26.9		350.6	682.7
Georgia	21.5	122.0		2.2		0.0		43.1	195.2
Hungary	938.3	6,638.5	9.0	115.8	8.3	74.6	3.3	3,610.5	11,763.5
Latvia	208.8			102.9		65.8		1,066.7	1,481.2
Lithuania	498.9	54.0		93.6		85.9		1,932.8	2,995.1
Macedonia	124.1	124.4	0.0	5.9	28.6	8.9	0.0	230.6	522.7
Moldova	262.3	1,051.7	0.3	0.9		1.0	0.1	709.4	2,060.3
Montenegro	2.0	10.8		0.5		0.9		2.5	16.7
Poland	3,626.0	1,830.1	12.5	1,409.3		3,432.5		10,094.8	28,456.5
Romania	1,445.6	9,056.4	2.7	293.8	67.9	33.9	17.6	5,883.2	16,947.9
Russia	8,145.2	2,977.9	130.4	2,809.7	1,155.7	1,429.6	8.0	40,652.8	57,621.9
Serbia	236.4	7,504.8	0.1	63.4		9.2	6.7	1,569.2	9,509.6
Slovakia	319.7	980.8	1.5	21.9		39.4	0.4	1,199.1	2,562.9
Slovenia	84.7	319.9	0.3	4.9		2.8		158.2	590.1
Ukraine	7,770.8	13,334.9	115.5	400.6	160.1	435.2	60.8	17,577.3	39,979.4

Source: Euromonitor International from national statistics

Agricultural Resources and Output

3

Agricultural Statistics   **Table 3.9**

Forestry and Paper Product Production 2011

as stated

	Fuelwood and Charcoal ('000 cu m)	Household and Sanitary Paper ('000 tonnes)	Paper and Paperboard ('000 tonnes)	Printing and Writing Paper ('000 tonnes)	Roundwood ('000 cu m)	Sawnwood and Sleepers ('000 cu m)	Wood Pulp ('000 tonnes)
Western Europe							
Austria	5,065	132	4,901	2,284	18,696	9,636	2,005
Belgium	893	87	2,040	1,208	5,128	1,369	504
Cyprus	4				8	3	
Denmark	1,115		423	155	2,583	372	5
Finland	5,240	158	11,329	7,045	50,688	9,750	10,362
France	24,107	731	8,527	2,489	53,509	8,437	1,837
Germany	10,783	1,377	22,704	7,669	56,142	22,600	2,725
Gibraltar							
Greece	795	51	409		1,743	108	
Iceland							
Ireland	195		47		2,627	759	
Italy	4,643	1,502	9,130	2,858	6,306	1,250	401
Liechtenstein	16				25	4	
Luxembourg	18	21	21		261	78	
Malta							
Monaco							
Netherlands	290	121	2,748	693	1,229	313	80
Norway	2,121	9	1,492	655	10,679	2,271	1,912
Portugal	600	74	1,936	1,413	9,140	1,044	2,107
Spain	5,120	679	6,492	1,422	17,609	2,162	2,011
Sweden	5,900	352	11,298	3,347	72,103	16,800	11,858
Switzerland	1,539	77	1,376	503	4,861	1,457	142
Turkey	4,616	1,042	5,334	533	21,039	6,461	65
United Kingdom	1,234	765	4,353	454	10,021	3,279	234
Eastern Europe							
Albania	350				430	8	
Belarus	2,292	8	588	80	10,364	2,571	51
Bosnia-Herzegovina	1,316	36	128	8	3,851	1,135	75
Bulgaria	2,841	26	293	3	6,205	550	135
Croatia	1,422	8	540	230	5,258	754	99
Czech Republic	1,953	16	829	108	16,270	6,028	747
Estonia	2,016		73		7,470	1,800	220
Georgia	733		2		838	70	
Hungary	3,152	4	777	12	6,073	324	1
Latvia	1,184		64	2	13,017	3,432	
Lithuania	1,809	13	111		8,053	1,162	
Macedonia	583		22		667	2	
Moldova	309	2	98		352	34	
Montenegro	156	227	227		364	50	
Poland	4,960	350	3,800	745	36,878	4,605	1,087
Romania	4,014	30	297	20	14,359	4,442	
Russia	43,817	220	7,624	780	197,000	31,692	7,362
Serbia	6,345	47	382		7,706	512	
Slovakia	643	135	748	559	9,213	2,204	716
Slovenia	1,336	48	787	248	3,388	642	43
Ukraine	9,521	131	951	37	17,510	1,898	

Source: Euromonitor International from national statistics

Table 3.10

Organic Farming Land Use 1990, 1995, 2000, 2006-2011

'000 hectares

	1990	1995	2000	2006	2007	2008	2009	2010	2011
Western Europe									
Austria	21.5	335.9	272.0	477.8	482.3	492.6	518.8	543.6	560.1
Belgium	1.3	3.4	20.3	29.3	32.6	35.7	41.5	49.0	52.9
Cyprus			0.1	2.0	2.3	2.3	3.6	3.6	3.8
Denmark	11.6	40.9	165.3	138.1	142.9	150.1	156.4	162.9	169.1
Finland	6.7	44.7	147.4	144.7	148.8	150.4	166.2	169.2	175.3
France	72.0	118.4	371.0	552.8	557.1	583.8	677.5	845.4	918.6
Germany	90.0	309.5	546.0	825.5	865.3	907.8	947.1	990.7	1,032.0
Gibraltar									
Greece	0.2	2.4	24.8	302.3	279.9	317.8	326.3	309.8	314.0
Iceland		0.7	3.4	5.0	6.2	7.0	6.7	5.8	5.7
Ireland	3.8	12.6	32.4	39.9	41.1	44.8	47.9	47.9	49.8
Italy	13.2	204.5	1,040.4	1,148.2	1,150.3	1,002.4	1,106.7	1,113.7	1,105.1
Liechtenstein		0.4	0.7	1.0	1.0	1.1	1.0	1.0	1.0
Luxembourg	0.6	0.6	1.0	3.6	3.4	3.5	3.6	3.7	3.7
Malta				0.0	0.0	0.0	0.0	0.0	0.0
Monaco									
Netherlands	7.5	12.9	27.8	48.4	47.0	50.4	51.9	46.2	45.7
Norway	1.6	5.8	20.5	44.6	48.9	52.2	56.7	57.2	60.0
Portugal	1.0	10.7	50.0	214.2	229.7	211.1	151.5	201.1	197.8
Spain	3.7	24.1	380.8	736.9	804.9	1,129.8	1,330.8	1,456.7	1,564.6
Sweden	28.5	83.5	171.7	225.4	308.3	336.4	391.5	438.7	471.3
Switzerland	12.0	31.8	95.0	117.8	116.6	116.3	114.1	119.6	120.1
Turkey	1.0	10.0	21.0	100.3	124.3	109.4	325.8	383.8	419.2
United Kingdom	31.0	48.4	527.3	605.7	682.2	737.6	721.7	699.6	688.0
Eastern Europe									
Albania				1.1	0.3	0.6	0.3	0.3	0.3
Belarus									
Bosnia-Herzegovina				0.7	0.7	0.7	0.6	0.6	0.5
Bulgaria			0.5	4.7	13.6	16.7	12.3	25.6	28.0
Croatia		0.1	0.1	6.1	7.6	10.0	14.2	23.4	25.5
Czech Republic	3.5	14.1	165.7	281.5	312.9	341.6	398.4	448.2	481.5
Estonia			9.9	72.9	79.5	87.3	95.2	113.0	123.0
Georgia		0.1	0.1	0.2	0.3	0.3	1.2	1.4	1.5
Hungary			47.2	122.8	122.3	122.8	140.3	127.6	128.8
Latvia		1.1	20.0	150.0	150.5	161.6	160.2	166.3	170.4
Lithuania		0.6	4.7	96.7	120.4	122.2	129.1	143.6	151.4
Macedonia				0.5	1.3	3.4	1.4	35.2	38.6
Moldova				11.4	11.7	11.7	32.1	32.1	33.8
Montenegro				25.1	25.1	1.9	4.6	3.6	3.3
Poland	0.6	6.9	22.0	228.0	285.9	313.9	367.1	522.0	566.1
Romania			20.5	107.6	131.4	140.1	168.3	182.7	196.4
Russia		20.0	5.3	3.2	33.8	47.0	78.4	44.0	46.4
Serbia				0.7	0.8	4.5	8.7	8.6	9.2
Slovakia	15.1	18.8	48.1	120.4	117.9	140.8	145.5	174.5	188.0
Slovenia		0.2	5.2	26.8	29.3	29.8	29.4	30.7	31.7
Ukraine				242.0	249.9	270.0	270.2	270.2	274.5

Source: Euromonitor International from national statistics

Agricultural Resources and Output

3

Agricultural Statistics   **Table 3.11**

Organic Farms 1990, 1995, 2000, 2006-2011

Number

	1990	1995	2000	2006	2007	2008	2009	2010	2011
Western Europe									
Austria	1,539	18,542	19,031	20,162	19,922	20,089	21,000	22,132	22,625
Belgium	160	193	628	803	821	901	997	1,108	1,184
Cyprus			15	305	305	305	732	732	775
Denmark	523	1,050	3,466	2,794	2,841	2,753	2,694	2,677	2,648
Finland	671	2,793	5,225	3,966	3,971	3,991	4,087	4,022	4,036
France	2,700	3,538	9,283	11,640	11,978	13,298	16,446	20,604	22,285
Germany	3,438	6,642	12,732	17,557	18,703	19,813	21,047	21,942	23,038
Gibraltar									
Greece	25	568	5,270	23,900	23,769	24,057	23,665	21,274	20,618
Iceland		12	30	24	36	35	28	38	40
Ireland	150	378	1,014	1,068	1,140	1,170	1,328	1,366	1,441
Italy	1,500	10,630	51,120	45,115	45,221	44,371	42,925	41,807	40,980
Liechtenstein		22	33	41	39	37	32	31	29
Luxembourg	10	19	51	72	81	85	77	96	102
Malta				10	30	30	12	11	11
Monaco									
Netherlands	399	561	1,391	1,448	1,465	1,402	1,413	1,462	1,466
Norway	263	728	1,823	2,583	2,611	2,702	2,851	2,805	2,861
Portugal	50	349	763	1,550	1,949	1,902	1,651	2,434	2,655
Spain	350	1,042	13,424	17,214	18,226	21,291	25,291	27,877	29,876
Sweden	1,588	2,473	3,329	2,380	2,848	3,686	4,816	5,208	5,703
Switzerland	803	2,121	5,852	6,300	6,199	6,079	5,943	5,989	5,911
Turkey	313	2,000	10,000	14,256	16,276	15,406	35,565	43,096	46,539
United Kingdom	700	828	3,563	4,639	5,506	5,383	5,156	4,949	4,800
Eastern Europe									
Albania				100	140	104	61	110	113
Belarus									
Bosnia-Herzegovina				329	304	304	27	27	25
Bulgaria			50	218	240	254	446	709	783
Croatia		18	18	368	483	632	817	1,125	1,239
Czech Republic	30	176	563	963	1,318	1,834	2,689	3,517	3,836
Estonia			231	1,173	1,211	1,259	1,277	1,356	1,402
Georgia		5	5	47	49	49	23	64	68
Hungary			471	1,553	1,389	1,614	1,617	1,617	1,633
Latvia		90	225	4,105	4,108	4,203	4,016	3,593	3,465
Lithuania		29	230	2,348	2,348	2,797	2,652	2,652	2,728
Macedonia				102	150	226	327	542	591
Moldova				121	121	121	166	166	173
Montenegro				15	13	25	29	62	68
Poland	49	236	1,419	9,187	11,887	14,888	17,092	20,578	22,287
Romania			650	3,033	2,238	2,775	3,078	2,986	2,999
Russia		15	19	8	12	25	40	50	55
Serbia				35	35	224	2,969	3,887	4,224
Slovakia	36	34	100	279	280	350	363	363	379
Slovenia		40	620	1,953	2,000	2,067	2,096	2,218	2,284
Ukraine				80	92	118	121	142	154

Source: Euromonitor International from national statistics

4

Automotives and Transport

Table 4.1

Commercial Vehicles in Use 1980, 1985, 1990, 1995, 1999-2011

'000

	1980	1985	1990	1995	1999	2000	2001	2002	2003
Western Europe									
Austria	186.1	212.2	263.7	311.0	345.1	354.0	359.6	345.5	354.9
Belgium	343.1	329.3	410.0	471.7	553.3	574.2	595.1	607.6	623.9
Cyprus	25.2	45.0	76.6	103.9	114.0	117.6	120.9	120.8	122.9
Denmark	259.2	267.4	300.8	342.3	382.3	393.7	401.5	411.2	422.4
Finland	153.6	184.5	270.7	257.4	309.7	320.9	329.0	336.4	344.1
France	2,570.5	3,980.0	4,910.0	5,195.0	5,610.0	5,753.0	5,897.0	5,984.0	6,068.0
Germany			1,989.4	3,061.9	3,370.0	3,533.9	3,592.1	3,567.5	3,541.2
Gibraltar	0.7	1.0	2.5	1.1	2.0	2.3	2.5	1.4	2.0
Greece	418.7	565.0	776.7	847.5	974.0	1,055.0	1,112.9	1,136.4	1,158.2
Iceland	9.0	12.7	14.5	16.1	19.4	21.1	21.7	22.0	22.9
Ireland	63.3	91.0	137.1	139.8	188.0	204.0	219.3	233.1	251.1
Italy	1,428.8	1,910.1	2,494.5	2,863.4	3,413.8	3,581.5	3,755.6	3,976.0	4,166.0
Liechtenstein	1.2	1.5	2.0	2.3	2.9	2.5	2.6	2.7	2.6
Luxembourg	15.5	14.0	18.1	27.1	30.8	31.4	33.3	35.1	35.9
Malta	14.2	17.5	21.2	50.9	44.9	44.3	44.7	45.0	45.4
Monaco				2.7	2.7	2.9	2.9	3.0	3.1
Netherlands	376.0	428.0	560.0	658.0	807.0	883.0	950.0	996.0	1,039.0
Norway	164.5	249.7	329.5	382.0	440.1	451.0	462.2	464.8	470.3
Portugal	264.0	356.0	568.0	824.0	1,066.0	1,157.0	1,211.0	1,253.0	1,275.1
Spain	1,380.9	1,570.9	2,378.7	3,071.6	3,788.7	3,977.9	4,161.1	4,315.8	4,419.4
Sweden	194.4	231.4	324.1	322.3	369.2	388.6	409.9	423.0	435.3
Switzerland	170.7	202.0	285.6	298.0	311.3	316.3	324.1	330.4	334.2
Turkey	428.2	553.1	709.9	982.4	1,405.8	1,543.1	1,588.4	1,636.2	1,747.4
United Kingdom	1,912.8	1,650.0	2,861.0	3,208.7	3,395.3	3,463.5	3,418.0	3,501.3	3,569.1
Eastern Europe									
Albania				35.8	49.4	62.4	73.1	75.7	78.6
Belarus			70.8	96.5	116.0	118.9	119.9	151.7	190.8
Bosnia-Herzegovina					37.1	35.2	36.1	47.8	42.3
Bulgaria			155.3	166.2	180.3	182.9	186.8	189.4	209.0
Croatia			52.4	77.4	123.4	127.2	134.3	143.5	153.1
Czech Republic			162.7	239.1	308.4	316.5	339.6	370.8	386.4
Estonia			75.6	72.6	87.2	88.2	86.0	85.5	88.8
Georgia						68.9	66.8	69.7	69.6
Hungary	201.9	229.6	289.6	345.0	345.7	370.7	384.3	399.6	410.2
Latvia			71.7	85.2	101.8	108.6	111.0	113.9	115.6
Lithuania			98.2	118.5	112.2	113.7	115.6	120.9	126.1
Macedonia								23.1	23.9
Moldova			83.4	67.4	76.7	68.5	69.4	75.7	82.0
Montenegro									
Poland	637.8	799.7	1,081.6	1,368.0	1,675.6	1,865.4	1,958.4	2,518.5	2,518.5
Romania			287.0	385.1	458.4	467.9	478.8	487.9	505.0
Russia				3,065.0	4,196.2	4,510.0	4,618.0	4,726.0	4,762.0
Serbia							110.0	107.2	112.1
Slovakia			106.3	114.4	129.6	132.8	136.0	147.7	161.6
Slovenia			35.5	47.4	56.6	59.2	61.2	63.1	65.1
Ukraine					977.7	995.0	1,054.3	1,073.9	1,113.6

Source: Euromonitor International from national statistics
Note: There may be wide variations from year to year in SMMT estimates and in other figures due to interpretation of definitions

Commercial Vehicles in Use 1980, 1985, 1990, 1995, 1999-2011 *(continued)*
'000

	2004	2005	2006	2007	2008	2009	2010	2011	Number in use per '000 persons 2011
Western Europe									
Austria	362.5	367.4	373.6	381.9	388.4	397.6	405.3	412.0	49.02
Belgium	649.6	674.5	691.1	712.3	730.7	744.4	761.1	780.7	71.29
Cyprus	121.0	121.6	118.9	120.8	125.2	127.5	124.1	124.1	111.23
Denmark	445.9	479.4	518.7	546.4	541.3	545.9	543.6	547.2	98.40
Finland	372.9	394.2	395.1	414.6	444.9	464.9	476.4	489.8	91.11
France	6,139.0	6,198.0	6,261.0	6,333.0	6,362.0	6,385.0	6,428.0	6,483.8	102.71
Germany	3,539.7	3,133.2	3,172.0	2,837.0	2,859.3	2,895.3	2,959.6	3,036.0	37.14
Gibraltar	2.6	2.1	2.3	1.3	1.5	1.9	2.0	2.2	76.30
Greece	1,185.9	1,213.3	1,246.8	1,283.0	1,316.7	1,329.8	1,346.1	1,350.5	119.24
Iceland	24.8	27.4	30.0	33.0	33.8	32.8	32.5	32.3	99.77
Ireland	268.1	286.5	318.6	345.9	351.3	343.9	327.1	317.0	70.74
Italy	4,250.9	4,422.3	4,579.6	4,688.0	4,789.3	4,840.7	4,898.6	4,959.6	81.81
Liechtenstein	2.6	2.6	2.5	2.7	2.8	2.7	2.8	2.8	78.02
Luxembourg	37.2	36.1	32.1	34.0	36.0	36.4	37.3	38.1	74.12
Malta	45.7	45.5	46.7	47.0	47.5	46.8	47.0	47.2	112.79
Monaco	3.2	3.4	3.7	4.0	4.3	4.5	4.7	4.9	139.45
Netherlands	1,069.0	1,063.0	1,070.0	1,095.0	1,125.0	1,146.4	1,154.3	1,170.9	70.30
Norway	480.1	493.9	514.5	538.2	546.0	544.9	552.8	566.1	115.05
Portugal	1,305.7	1,323.3	1,335.0	1,348.1	1,349.4	1,350.3	1,351.3	1,352.1	127.12
Spain	4,660.4	4,907.9	5,174.7	5,414.3	5,467.8	5,405.6	5,390.1	5,364.6	116.23
Sweden	453.3	474.6	493.4	517.4	523.7	526.6	541.2	562.2	59.71
Switzerland	341.3	351.0	358.7	370.1	373.3	376.6	383.2	390.1	49.57
Turkey	2,379.0	2,653.9	2,938.6	3,181.4	3,393.7	3,517.3	3,720.9	4,000.9	54.57
United Kingdom	3,696.4	3,816.7	3,988.4	4,110.3	4,147.8	3,902.0	3,925.7	3,971.5	63.55
Eastern Europe									
Albania	73.8	76.8	77.3	91.1	87.7	88.5	93.3	93.9	29.21
Belarus	231.5	283.1	377.7	409.2	428.0	507.7	575.4	644.6	67.99
Bosnia-Herzegovina	42.0	44.9	48.7	49.8	57.8	62.2	79.9	102.5	26.68
Bulgaria	228.6	239.8	248.2	289.2	323.8	342.3	347.8	353.4	47.02
Croatia	159.7	157.5	164.1	170.8	175.8	169.8	162.6	160.0	36.26
Czech Republic	416.2	459.3	511.2	575.2	627.8	621.7	617.6	627.5	59.84
Estonia	91.0	91.4	98.2	84.5	87.6	85.2	85.4	86.4	64.46
Georgia	68.6	78.2	89.3	94.3	105.1	97.3	105.0	112.4	25.58
Hungary	413.6	430.5	463.0	477.3	488.7	464.6	467.7	478.5	47.92
Latvia	118.3	123.8	131.7	140.2	140.3	130.3	77.0	79.4	38.28
Lithuania	130.1	137.3	150.7	161.6	163.9	159.7	147.2	150.9	46.51
Macedonia	24.7	25.4	26.7	28.8	31.2	34.5	38.3	41.8	20.34
Moldova	93.5	101.6	105.1	115.9	137.5	141.5	152.6	167.5	47.10
Montenegro									
Poland	2,632.2	2,494.3	2,476.0	2,609.0	2,802.1	2,892.2	3,078.6	3,175.9	83.16
Romania	525.6	533.1	489.3	623.1	686.9	703.0	712.8	707.4	33.02
Russia	4,856.0	4,927.0	5,001.0	5,237.0	5,413.0	5,388.0	5,435.0	5,503.6	38.51
Serbia	120.0	128.0	137.2	140.3	149.5	158.5	171.9	181.3	24.92
Slovakia	161.0	183.6	198.4	226.5	259.1	297.7	306.4	314.8	58.34
Slovenia	68.7	72.1	75.9	83.8	90.5	90.5	91.4	94.6	46.14
Ukraine	1,093.4	1,056.4	1,090.2	1,107.6	1,164.2	1,115.7	1,116.7	1,126.1	24.70

Source: Euromonitor International from national statistics
Note: There may be wide variations from year to year in SMMT estimates and in other figures due to interpretation of definitions

Automotives and Transport Statistics

Table 4.2

Passenger Cars in Use 1980, 1985, 1990, 1995, 1999-2011
'000

	1980	1985	1990	1995	1999	2000	2001	2002	2003
Western Europe									
Austria	2,247.0	2,530.8	2,991.3	3,593.6	4,009.6	4,097.1	4,182.0	3,987.1	4,054.3
Belgium	3,158.7	3,278.8	3,833.3	4,273.5	4,583.6	4,678.4	4,739.9	4,787.0	4,821.0
Cyprus	92.0	120.0	178.6	219.7	257.0	267.6	280.1	287.6	302.5
Denmark	1,389.5	1,500.9	1,590.6	1,684.8	1,846.9	1,842.9	1,875.3	1,890.0	1,894.2
Finland	1,225.9	1,546.1	1,938.9	1,900.9	2,082.6	2,120.7	2,146.2	2,180.0	2,259.4
France	19,150.0	21,090.0	23,550.0	25,100.0	27,480.0	28,060.0	28,700.0	29,160.0	29,560.0
Germany			30,695.1	40,499.4	42,423.3	43,772.3	44,383.3	44,657.3	45,022.9
Gibraltar	6.5	10.6	19.8	18.4	22.5	25.8	27.4	12.9	12.8
Greece	879.8	1,188.0	1,735.5	2,204.8	2,910.0	3,150.0	3,423.7	3,477.1	3,696.9
Iceland	80.0	100.0	119.7	119.2	151.4	158.9	160.6	161.7	166.9
Ireland	734.4	709.5	796.4	990.4	1,269.2	1,319.3	1,384.7	1,447.9	1,507.1
Italy	17,686.2	22,494.6	27,416.0	30,301.4	32,038.3	32,583.8	33,239.0	33,706.2	34,310.4
Liechtenstein	12.6	14.8	16.9	18.8	21.2	21.8	22.6	23.3	23.5
Luxembourg	147.4	152.0	183.4	229.0	253.4	257.8	268.2	282.4	287.2
Malta	66.2	75.0	104.7	147.6	182.3	189.1	195.4	201.9	208.8
Monaco				20.7	22.6	22.9	23.0	22.6	22.7
Netherlands	4,515.0	4,901.0	5,196.0	5,633.0	6,120.0	6,343.0	6,539.0	6,710.0	6,855.0
Norway	1,233.6	1,514.0	1,613.0	1,684.7	1,813.6	1,851.9	1,872.9	1,899.7	1,933.6
Portugal	941.0	1,185.0	1,630.0	2,611.0	3,469.0	3,593.0	3,746.0	3,885.0	3,966.0
Spain	7,556.5	9,273.7	11,995.6	14,212.3	16,847.4	17,449.2	18,150.9	18,732.6	18,688.3
Sweden	2,883.0	3,151.2	3,601.0	3,630.8	3,890.2	3,998.6	4,018.5	4,042.8	4,075.4
Switzerland	2,246.8	2,617.2	2,985.4	3,229.2	3,467.3	3,545.2	3,629.7	3,701.0	3,753.9
Turkey	742.3	983.4	1,649.9	3,058.5	4,072.3	4,422.2	4,534.8	4,600.1	4,700.3
United Kingdom	15,437.7	19,458.2	21,989.0	24,428.6	27,010.4	27,959.7	28,640.3	28,484.0	29,007.8
Eastern Europe									
Albania			5.3	58.7	92.3	114.5	133.5	148.5	174.8
Belarus			604.5	939.6	1,351.0	1,385.9	1,432.2	1,515.9	1,620.1
Bosnia-Herzegovina				362.9	366.7	374.2	374.4	368.0
Bulgaria			1,083.9	1,398.7	1,490.9	1,536.0	1,624.8	1,656.2	1,689.3
Croatia			795.4	710.9	1,063.5	1,124.8	1,195.5	1,244.3	1,293.4
Czech Republic			2,520.4	3,043.3	3,439.7	3,438.9	3,529.8	3,647.1	3,706.0
Estonia			240.9	383.4	458.7	463.9	407.3	400.7	434.0
Georgia			485.0	360.6	247.9	247.9	244.8	247.8	252.0
Hungary	925.0	1,435.9	1,856.7	2,044.9	2,255.5	2,364.7	2,482.8	2,629.5	2,777.2
Latvia				331.8	525.6	556.8	586.2	619.1	648.9
Lithuania			493.0	718.5	1,089.3	1,172.4	1,133.5	1,180.9	1,256.9
Macedonia								308.0	293.3
Moldova			209.0	165.9	224.4	231.0	248.8	260.8	257.1
Montenegro									
Poland	2,269.9	3,450.0	5,261.0	7,517.0	9,282.8	9,991.3	10,503.1	11,243.8	11,243.8
Romania			1,292.3	2,197.5	2,703.1	2,777.6	2,881.2	2,973.4	3,087.6
Russia			8,986.3	14,195.0	19,496.9	20,247.0	21,152.0	22,342.0	23,271.0
Serbia							1,382.4	1,343.7	1,388.1
Slovakia			860.0	1,015.8	1,236.4	1,247.0	1,290.8	1,326.9	1,356.0
Slovenia			578.3	698.2	829.7	866.1	881.5	894.5	910.4
Ukraine			3,272.0	4,468.7	5,210.8	5,372.0	5,463.0	5,529.0	5,585.0

Source: Euromonitor International from national statistics
Note: There may be wide variations from year to year in SMMT estimates and in other figures due to interpretation of definitions

Passenger Cars in Use 1980, 1985, 1990, 1995, 1999-2011 *(continued)*
'000

	2004	2005	2006	2007	2008	2009	2010	2011	Number in use per '000 persons 2011
Western Europe									
Austria	4,109.1	4,156.7	4,205.0	4,245.6	4,284.9	4,359.9	4,441.0	4,558.1	542.35
Belgium	4,874.4	4,918.5	4,976.0	5,049.0	5,130.6	5,193.0	5,273.0	5,361.0	489.54
Cyprus	335.6	355.1	372.9	410.9	443.5	460.5	462.7	479.3	429.40
Denmark	1,914.4	1,961.2	2,013.9	2,058.9	2,105.0	2,099.1	2,142.1	2,197.3	395.15
Finland	2,331.2	2,414.5	2,489.3	2,570.4	2,700.0	2,777.0	2,859.8	2,945.1	547.89
France	29,900.0	30,100.0	30,400.0	30,700.0	30,850.0	31,050.0	31,244.6	31,455.8	498.29
Germany	45,375.5	46,090.3	46,569.7	41,183.6	41,231.2	41,737.6	42,301.6	42,751.6	522.95
Gibraltar	13.9	14.6	14.7	14.6	14.6	15.7	15.7	16.0	548.62
Greece	3,960.2	4,204.5	4,446.5	4,821.4	5,101.4	5,132.0	5,216.9	5,275.3	465.77
Iceland	175.4	187.4	197.3	207.5	209.7	207.2	206.3	206.4	636.86
Ireland	1,582.8	1,662.2	1,778.9	1,882.9	1,924.3	1,902.4	1,872.7	1,880.1	419.59
Italy	33,973.1	34,667.5	35,297.3	35,680.1	36,105.2	36,371.8	36,751.3	36,996.2	610.23
Liechtenstein	23.9	24.4	24.3	24.4	25.5	25.9	26.9	27.7	765.64
Luxembourg	293.4	299.8	304.5	314.3	329.0	331.5	337.2	345.2	671.42
Malta	211.4	212.6	218.2	224.9	229.4	234.9	233.6	237.1	567.03
Monaco	22.9	22.7	23.0	23.4	24.2	25.3	26.0	26.9	758.17
Netherlands	7,151.0	7,299.0	7,413.0	7,597.0	7,757.0	7,827.3	7,998.9	8,270.3	496.54
Norway	1,977.9	2,028.8	2,084.8	2,154.8	2,197.2	2,244.0	2,309.0	2,384.5	484.63
Portugal	4,100.0	4,200.0	4,290.0	4,379.0	4,408.0	4,441.7	4,560.8	4,604.6	432.88
Spain	19,541.9	20,250.4	21,052.6	21,760.2	22,145.4	21,983.0	21,979.4	21,918.8	474.92
Sweden	4,113.4	4,153.7	4,202.5	4,258.5	4,279.0	4,300.8	4,335.2	4,399.4	467.25
Switzerland	3,811.4	3,861.4	3,900.0	3,955.8	3,989.8	4,009.6	4,075.8	4,157.7	528.28
Turkey	5,400.4	5,772.7	6,141.0	6,472.2	6,796.6	7,094.0	7,544.9	8,172.0	111.47
United Kingdom	29,378.2	29,747.5	29,880.0	30,177.9	30,309.2	28,459.0	27,920.2	27,154.5	434.48
Eastern Europe									
Albania	190.0	209.6	228.6	247.6	264.8	281.2	294.7	310.2	96.49
Belarus	1,671.3	1,737.1	1,970.0	2,329.2	2,442.6	2,601.4	2,838.9	3,091.9	326.11
Bosnia Herzegovina	385.2	379.0	389.1	409.0	447.6	457.3	478.7	493.4	128.37
Bulgaria	1,720.6	1,751.8	1,767.7	1,971.5	2,366.2	2,502.0	2,613.2	2,725.4	362.58
Croatia	1,337.5	1,384.7	1,435.8	1,491.1	1,535.3	1,532.5	1,514.4	1,513.9	343.13
Czech Republic	3,815.5	3,958.7	4,108.6	4,280.1	4,423.4	4,435.1	4,496.2	4,606.2	439.28
Estonia	471.2	493.8	554.0	523.8	551.8	545.7	552.7	559.5	417.48
Georgia	255.2	312.1	375.4	416.3	466.9	500.9	536.1	595.7	135.59
Hungary	2,828.4	2,888.7	2,953.7	3,012.2	3,055.4	3,013.7	2,999.0	2,988.1	299.24
Latvia	686.1	742.4	822.0	904.9	932.8	904.3	636.7	665.0	320.56
Lithuania	1,315.9	1,455.3	1,592.2	1,587.9	1,671.1	1,695.3	1,721.4	1,754.0	540.60
Macedonia	279.2	253.2	242.3	248.8	263.1	282.2	283.1	284.6	138.34
Moldova	269.6	293.0	319.3	338.9	366.4	386.4	404.3	430.5	121.08
Montenegro									
Poland	11,975.2	12,339.4	13,384.2	14,588.7	16,079.5	16,494.7	17,239.8	18,004.6	471.46
Romania	3,225.4	3,363.8	3,220.7	3,554.4	4,027.4	4,244.9	4,348.6	4,444.5	207.45
Russia	24,091.0	25,461.0	26,656.0	29,405.0	32,021.0	33,084.0	34,736.9	37,074.4	259.42
Serbia	1,449.8	1,481.5	1,511.8	1,476.6	1,486.6	1,637.0	1,567.1	1,604.8	220.60
Slovakia	1,388.2	1,303.7	1,333.7	1,433.9	1,544.9	1,589.0	1,631.8	1,689.0	312.97
Slovenia	933.9	960.2	980.3	1,014.1	1,045.2	1,058.9	1,061.6	1,070.4	522.10
Ukraine	5,603.8	5,539.0	5,739.3	5,939.6	6,393.9	6,518.7	6,769.3	6,973.7	152.94

Source: Euromonitor International from national statistics
Note: There may be wide variations from year to year in SMMT estimates and in other figures due to interpretation of definitions

Automotives and Transport Statistics   **Table 4.3**

Two-Wheelers in Use 1980, 1985, 1990, 1995, 1999-2011
'000

	1980	1985	1990	1995	1999	2000	2001	2002	2003
Western Europe									
Austria	574.1	648.4	548.0	546.4	622.9	628.0	641.4	596.8	606.9
Belgium	113.0	130.0	139.0	200.0	261.0	278.0	294.0	306.0	319.0
Cyprus		40.0	51.0	50.4	44.8	43.3	42.0	40.3	41.5
Denmark				50.0	112.1	126.9	138.3	146.4	151.3
Finland			169.0	159.0	182.4	192.6	205.4	222.7	244.4
France				2,289.0	2,373.0	2,410.0	2,440.0	2,441.0	2,448.0
Germany			1,400.0	2,267.0	3,177.0	3,410.0	3,557.0	3,657.0	3,745.0
Gibraltar		1.6	2.8	6.6	6.9	8.5	9.6	5.7	5.6
Greece		162.3	256.6	475.7	710.8	781.4	853.4	910.6	969.9
Iceland		0.9	1.5	1.9	2.1	2.3	2.2	2.6	2.7
Ireland		26.0	22.7	23.5	26.7	30.6	32.9	33.1	35.1
Italy				7,905.8	9,367.9	9,773.1	9,979.9	10,149.5	10,295.4
Liechtenstein	0.6	1.3	1.3	1.7	2.4	2.6	2.8	2.9	3.0
Luxembourg		24.7	25.4	28.5	31.8	32.8	33.6	34.7	36.0
Malta				8.0	11.7	12.2	12.6	13.1	13.4
Monaco		4.0	4.7	5.3	6.3	6.6	6.8	6.9	7.0
Netherlands		728.0	612.0	848.0	964.0	970.8	964.8	1,002.5	1,015.6
Norway		186.6	203.5	197.8	239.6	249.9	261.9	277.0	292.3
Portugal	1,069.1	1,091.2	968.6	838.5	735.0	734.0	709.0	604.0	633.0
Spain		2,015.5	3,073.6	3,402.0	3,672.1	3,648.2	3,596.0	3,561.5	3,657.1
Sweden					96.8	114.7	137.7	163.0	188.3
Switzerland	808.8	862.1	763.9	721.6	744.4	732.6	751.4	745.1	762.9
Turkey	137.9	289.1	531.9	819.9	975.7	1,011.3	1,031.2	1,046.9	1,073.4
United Kingdom	1,457.0	1,148.0	879.8	900.2	1,041.1	1,157.7	1,212.0	1,256.4	1,314.0
Eastern Europe									
Albania			8.6	6.9	3.2	3.8	3.4	3.4	3.9
Belarus			404.1	504.2	533.7	523.6	536.0	525.0	506.4
Bosnia-Herzegovina					1.6	2.1	2.8	3.7	3.8
Bulgaria			54.4	58.6	58.6	59.0	59.4	59.9	60.5
Croatia					58.1	65.3	73.8	85.3	99.2
Czech Republic			1,442.9	1,425.6	1,254.1	1,178.6	1,193.5	1,204.0	1,190.0
Estonia			2.7	3.3	6.7	6.7	6.8	7.3	8.1
Georgia				28.6	7.6	4.0	4.6	4.0	2.8
Hungary			92.3	85.3	87.6	91.2	93.1	97.6	103.5
Latvia				15.7	20.1	20.7	21.4	22.2	22.9
Lithuania				19.4	22.1	21.7	25.2	27.5	28.8
Macedonia									
Moldova								13.4	14.4
Montenegro									
Poland		1,546.5	1,356.6	1,679.3	1,441.0	1,393.0	1,246.0	1,260.2	1,246.0
Romania		238.0	249.3	262.2	242.5	239.2	237.9	238.5	235.9
Russia									
Serbia							13.1	12.3	13.3
Slovakia			286.3	229.1	181.7	181.1	180.2	179.5	178.5
Slovenia			50.4	45.9	48.7	49.4	50.1	50.6	42.4
Ukraine			3,253.4	3,102.6	2,372.0	2,251.5	1,960.3	1,744.4	1,369.0

Source: Euromonitor International from national statistics
Note: Two-wheelers consist of motorcycles and mopeds

Two-Wheelers in Use 1980, 1985, 1990, 1995, 1999-2011 *(continued)*
'000

	2004	2005	2006	2007	2008	2009	2010	2011	Number in use per '000 persons 2011
Western Europe									
Austria	612.2	627.7	645.0	668.0	691.0	712.0	728.0	757.5	90.14
Belgium	332.7	346.0	360.0	374.0	388.0	403.9	419.3	434.1	39.64
Cyprus	41.4	40.4	40.4	41.2	43.2	42.7	40.7	39.3	35.21
Denmark	155.7	162.1	171.9	184.0	197.2	204.8	205.2	210.1	37.78
Finland	270.6	299.6	336.0	374.0	403.6	423.2	447.9	476.3	88.60
France	2,462.0	2,480.0	2,482.0	2,596.1	2,710.2	2,805.4	2,896.9	3,000.3	47.53
Germany	3,828.0	3,903.0	3,969.0	3,566.0	3,659.0	3,762.6	3,688.6	3,620.1	44.28
Gibraltar	6.2	6.6	7.1	7.7	7.3	8.6	8.9	9.3	316.72
Greece	1,042.6	1,124.2	1,205.8	1,298.7	1,388.6	1,448.9	1,489.0	1,515.4	133.80
Iceland	3.1	4.2	5.7	8.1	9.0	9.4	9.6	9.8	30.35
Ireland	34.9	34.3	34.9	37.2	39.4	39.6	38.1	38.5	8.59
Italy	10,224.6	10,263.4	9,649.4	9,585.8	9,211.0	9,314.2	9,216.5	9,062.4	149.48
Liechtenstein	3.0	3.1	3.2	3.3	3.4	3.6	3.7	3.9	107.08
Luxembourg	36.9	37.7	38.6	39.5	40.3	41.1	42.1	43.1	83.76
Malta	12.6	11.9	12.3	12.8	14.4	14.5	14.8	15.4	36.76
Monaco	7.2	7.5	7.8	8.1	8.4	8.8	9.1	9.5	267.01
Netherlands	1,038.9	1,112.9	1,220.0	1,310.5	1,371.3	1,371.6	1,383.8	1,390.7	83.50
Norway	302.9	313.3	328.5	343.6	360.0	373.2	387.8	403.0	81.90
Portugal	611.0	593.0	535.3	526.5	519.0	512.2	490.9	468.8	44.07
Spain	3,854.1	4,117.6	4,401.1	4,741.7	4,911.5	5,007.9	5,040.2	5,106.8	110.65
Sweden	222.7	258.2	297.8	328.5	357.3	370.4	356.7	379.5	40.31
Switzerland	770.6	770.3	783.5	788.7	804.1	806.6	815.7	822.0	104.45
Turkey	1,218.7	1,441.1	1,822.8	2,003.5	2,181.4	2,303.3	2,389.5	2,571.9	35.08
United Kingdom	1,338.3	1,367.1	1,315.1	1,263.0	1,290.7	1,292.2	1,234.4	1,200.6	19.21
Eastern Europe									
Albania	4.9	7.2	11.6	13.9	18.3	20.9	24.0	28.5	8.87
Belarus	454.6	444.5	427.9	377.7	358.0	349.2	319.6	288.4	30.41
Bosnia-Herzegovina	3.8	5.4	6.5	5.7	8.7	14.2	12.0	13.5	3.51
Bulgaria	69.5	73.9	76.3	78.9	106.9	117.6	133.0	150.2	19.98
Croatia	113.0	127.9	143.5	162.8	183.8	184.5	194.2	203.6	46.14
Czech Republic	1,196.0	1,254.0	1,292.0	1,336.0	1,371.0	1,376.0	1,403.1	1,435.9	136.93
Estonia	9.1	10.2	12.6	14.8	17.6	18.6	19.7	20.8	15.51
Georgia	3.3	4.1	4.9	5.5	5.0	4.9	5.3	5.9	1.34
Hungary	114.0	122.7	130.0	135.9	141.5	142.0	146.9	152.2	15.25
Latvia	29.9	32.5	36.9	44.4	51.3	52.0	54.3	57.1	27.51
Lithuania	29.0	30.5	32.5	35.3	45.6	51.4	56.3	62.8	19.36
Macedonia									
Moldova	15.7	16.9	18.0	19.1	21.9	24.7	27.1	30.2	8.48
Montenegro									
Poland	1,146.0	1,092.0	1,122.0	1,350.0	1,607.0	1,808.7	2,000.3	2,239.0	58.63
Romania	234.7	197.4	43.8	56.5	71.8	80.0	60.5	41.8	1.95
Russia									
Serbia	14.8	16.0	20.4	24.9	31.8	34.5	37.5	42.2	5.80
Slovakia	180.1	182.5	183.1	201.4	221.5	229.5	234.7	250.5	46.42
Slovenia	40.2	48.7	53.2	71.5	82.0	88.4	91.0	96.7	47.18
Ukraine	1,145.4	982.6	848.5	714.3	650.9	554.5	404.3	280.4	6.15

Source: Euromonitor International from national statistics
Note: Two-wheelers consist of motorcycles and mopeds

Automotives and Transport Statistics **Table 4.4**

Commercial Vehicle Production 1980, 1985, 1990, 1995, 1999-2011

'000

	1980	1985	1990	1995	1999	2000	2001	2002
Western Europe								
Austria	8.5	11.2	11.0	9.2	15.7	25.0	24.3	19.9
Belgium	47.0	48.7	90.0	103.6	99.5	121.1	128.6	120.3
Cyprus								
Denmark								
Finland	1.1	0.8	0.9	0.4	0.5	0.5	0.4	0.4
France	439.9	383.7	474.2	423.8	395.7	468.6	446.9	309.1
Germany	357.6	279.2	315.9	307.1	378.2	394.7	390.5	346.1
Gibraltar								
Greece								
Iceland								
Ireland								
Italy	165.1	183.8	246.2	244.9	290.8	316.0	307.9	301.3
Liechtenstein								
Luxembourg								
Malta								
Monaco								
Netherlands	32.1	14.3	17.3	17.6	45.0	52.2	49.7	48.9
Norway								
Portugal	58.4	26.5	77.5	85.7	65.3	68.2	62.4	68.3
Spain	152.8	187.5	374.0	375.0	570.8	666.5	638.7	588.3
Sweden	63.1	60.3	74.4	102.5	36.8	41.4	38.1	38.2
Switzerland								
Turkey	19.4	37.3	62.8	49.0	75.8	133.5	95.3	142.4
United Kingdom	389.2	266.0	270.3	233.0	186.9	172.4	192.9	193.1
Eastern Europe								
Albania								
Belarus								
Bosnia-Herzegovina								
Bulgaria								
Croatia								
Czech Republic					27.8	27.3	8.3	5.8
Estonia								
Georgia								
Hungary	15.2	14.0	8.1	1.2	2.3	3.4	3.9	3.3
Latvia								
Lithuania								
Macedonia								
Moldova								
Montenegro								
Poland	116.0	57.1	42.8	10.6	28.0	23.3	11.9	23.6
Romania	49.1	19.8	17.6	21.2	18.6	14.0	12.0	14.2
Russia			716.9	214.9	226.0	236.3	229.0	239.7
Serbia					1.5	1.6	1.5	1.7
Slovakia			0.9	0.2	0.3	0.5	0.4	0.3
Slovenia								
Ukraine		45.2	40.3	8.7	9.0	13.1	6.8	3.4

Source: Euromonitor International from national statistics

Commercial Vehicle Production 1980, 1985, 1990, 1995, 1999-2011 *(continued)*
'000

	2003	2004	2005	2006	2007	2008	2009	2010	2011
Western Europe									
Austria	21.0	21.5	22.7	26.9	28.1	25.4	15.7	18.8	22.2
Belgium	112.7	43.2	33.2	36.1	44.7	44.4	12.5	26.3	0.0
Cyprus									
Denmark									
Finland	0.4	0.5	0.4	0.4	0.3	0.4	0.1	0.3	0.0
France	399.7	438.6	436.0	446.0	465.0	423.0	228.2	305.3	363.9
Germany	361.2	377.9	407.5	421.1	504.3	513.7	245.3	353.6	439.4
Gibraltar									
Greece									
Iceland									
Ireland									
Italy	295.2	308.4	312.8	319.1	373.5	364.6	182.1	265.0	304.7
Liechtenstein									
Luxembourg									
Malta									
Monaco									
Netherlands	52.2	59.9	65.6	72.1	76.7	73.3	26.1	46.1	32.4
Norway									
Portugal	73.8	75.9	81.5	83.8	42.2	42.9	24.3	44.2	50.5
Spain	630.5	609.7	654.3	698.8	693.9	598.6	357.4	474.4	534.2
Sweden	42.6	49.9	49.9	44.6	49.2	56.1	27.7	40.0	48.2
Switzerland									
Turkey	239.2	376.3	425.4	442.1	464.5	525.5	358.7	491.2	549.4
United Kingdom	188.9	209.3	206.8	206.3	215.7	202.9	90.7	123.0	120.2
Eastern Europe									
Albania									
Belarus									
Bosnia-Herzegovina									
Bulgaria									
Croatia									
Czech Republic	5.4	5.3	5.5	6.0	13.6	12.5	6.8	6.9	7.9
Estonia									
Georgia									
Hungary	3.8	4.1	3.5	3.2	4.0	3.7	1.8	2.9	2.8
Latvia									
Lithuania									
Macedonia									
Moldova									
Montenegro									
Poland	15.2	78.0	85.4	82.3	89.6	104.5	60.2	84.4	97.1
Romania	19.5	23.2	20.6	11.9	7.6	14.3	17.2	27.3	25.0
Russia	268.4	276.0	283.1	330.4	371.5	320.9	125.7	194.9	249.9
Serbia	0.9	1.9	1.6	1.4	1.7	1.8	0.4	0.6	0.7
Slovakia	0.2	0.0	0.0	0.0	0.0	0.0	0.0	0.0	0.0
Slovenia	7.6	15.0	39.6	35.3	24.2	17.6	10.2	10.3	5.2
Ukraine	4.9	7.8	19.0	20.4	22.5	22.3	3.6	8.0	7.1

Source: Euromonitor International from national statistics

Automotives and Transport Statistics

Table 4.5

Passenger Car Production 1980, 1985, 1990, 1995, 1999-2011
'000

	1980	1985	1990	1995	1999	2000	2001	2002
Western Europe								
Austria	7.5	7.1	12.7	59.2	123.6	116.0	131.1	132.8
Belgium	281.7	248.5	311.8	385.9	917.5	912.2	1,058.7	936.9
Cyprus								
Denmark								
Finland	21.5	38.7	30.2	34.6	33.9	38.5	41.9	41.1
France	2,938.6	2,632.4	3,294.8	3,050.9	2,784.5	2,879.8	3,181.5	3,292.8
Germany	3,520.9	4,166.7	4,660.7	4,360.2	5,309.5	5,131.9	5,301.2	5,123.2
Gibraltar								
Greece								
Iceland								
Ireland								
Italy	1,445.2	1,389.2	1,874.7	1,422.4	1,410.5	1,422.3	1,271.8	1,125.8
Liechtenstein								
Luxembourg								
Malta								
Monaco								
Netherlands	80.8	108.1	121.3	100.4	262.2	215.1	189.3	182.4
Norway								
Portugal	45.5	61.0	60.2	73.2	187.0	178.5	177.4	182.6
Spain	1,028.8	1,230.1	1,679.3	1,958.8	2,281.6	2,366.4	2,211.2	2,266.9
Sweden	235.3	400.7	335.9	387.7	213.9	260.0	251.0	238.0
Switzerland								
Turkey	31.5	60.4	167.6	233.4	222.0	297.5	175.3	204.2
United Kingdom	923.7	1,048.0	1,295.6	1,532.1	1,786.6	1,641.5	1,492.4	1,629.9
Eastern Europe								
Albania								
Belarus								
Bosnia-Herzegovina								
Bulgaria								
Croatia								
Czech Republic				213.0	348.5	428.2	456.9	441.3
Estonia								
Georgia								
Hungary				36.5	125.9	134.0	140.4	138.2
Latvia								
Lithuania								
Macedonia								
Moldova								
Montenegro								
Poland	364.5	283.0	266.4	391.9	546.8	481.7	336.0	287.5
Romania	79.3	114.4	99.9	71.0	88.3	64.2	56.8	65.3
Russia	1,166.0	1,165.0	1,103.0	893.6	943.7	969.2	1,021.7	980.1
Serbia					3.8	11.1	7.5	10.3
Slovakia				22.3	126.5	181.3	181.6	225.4
Slovenia			74.7	63.5	118.1	122.9	116.1	126.7
Ukraine		167.5	103.4	58.7	10.1	18.1	25.0	50.4

Source: Euromonitor International from national statistics

Passenger Car Production 1980, 1985, 1990, 1995, 1999-2011 (continued)

'000

	2003	2004	2005	2006	2007	2008	2009	2010	2011
Western Europe									
Austria	118.7	227.2	230.5	248.1	200.0	125.8	56.6	86.2	130.3
Belgium	791.7	852.4	895.1	881.9	789.7	680.1	524.6	529.0	562.4
Cyprus									
Denmark									
Finland	19.2	10.1	21.2	32.4	24.0	18.0	10.9	6.4	2.5
France	3,220.3	3,227.4	3,113.0	2,723.2	2,550.9	2,145.0	1,819.5	1,924.2	1,931.0
Germany	5,145.4	5,192.1	5,350.2	5,398.5	5,709.1	5,532.0	4,964.5	5,552.4	5,871.9
Gibraltar									
Greece									
Iceland									
Ireland									
Italy	1,026.5	833.6	725.5	892.5	910.9	659.2	661.1	573.2	485.6
Liechtenstein									
Luxembourg									
Malta									
Monaco									
Netherlands	163.1	187.6	115.1	87.3	61.9	59.2	50.6	48.0	40.8
Norway									
Portugal	165.6	150.8	137.6	143.5	134.0	132.2	101.7	114.6	141.8
Spain	2,399.4	2,402.5	2,098.2	2,078.6	2,195.8	1,943.0	1,812.7	1,913.5	1,819.5
Sweden	280.4	290.4	288.7	288.6	316.9	252.3	128.7	177.1	189.0
Switzerland									
Turkey	294.1	447.2	453.7	545.7	634.9	621.6	510.9	603.4	639.7
United Kingdom	1,657.6	1,647.2	1,596.3	1,442.1	1,534.6	1,446.6	999.5	1,270.4	1,343.8
Eastern Europe									
Albania									
Belarus									
Bosnia-Herzegovina									
Bulgaria									
Croatia									
Czech Republic	436.3	443.1	596.8	848.8	925.1	934.0	976.4	1,069.5	1,192.0
Estonia									
Georgia									
Hungary	122.3	118.6	148.5	187.6	288.0	342.4	212.8	208.6	200.0
Latvia									
Lithuania									
Macedonia									
Moldova									
Montenegro									
Poland	306.8	523.0	540.0	632.3	695.0	842.0	819.0	785.0	740.0
Romania	75.7	99.0	174.5	201.7	234.1	231.1	279.3	323.6	310.2
Russia	1,010.4	1,110.1	1,068.1	1,177.9	1,288.7	1,469.4	599.3	1,208.4	1,738.2
Serbia	13.0	13.3	12.6	9.8	8.2	9.8	16.3	17.4	15.1
Slovakia	281.2	223.5	218.3	295.4	571.1	575.8	461.3	561.9	639.8
Slovenia	110.6	116.6	138.4	115.0	174.2	180.2	202.6	201.0	169.0
Ukraine	103.0	179.1	196.7	274.9	380.1	400.8	65.6	75.3	97.6

Source: Euromonitor International from national statistics

Automotives and Transport Statistics

Table 4.6

Two-Wheeler Production 1985, 1990, 1995, 2000, 2006-2011

'000

	1985	1990	1995	2000	2006	2007	2008	2009	2010	2011
Western Europe										
Austria	160.8	20.9	13.2	29.2	69.0	78.3	79.2	51.3	74.9	79.0
Belgium										
Cyprus										
Denmark										
Finland										
France			394.6	451.4	232.4	215.5	172.5	109.7	140.0	161.9
Germany	85.8	55.3	44.6	112.6	106.3	105.5	105.7	82.4	99.5	108.8
Gibraltar										
Greece										
Iceland										
Ireland										
Italy	808.3	894.9	1,101.1	1,048.2	708.6	692.5	641.0	477.0	596.8	601.6
Liechtenstein										
Luxembourg										
Malta										
Monaco										
Netherlands				9.3	8.0	7.1	6.3	6.8	7.0	6.9
Norway										
Portugal										
Spain	173.5	384.6	279.9	284.8	253.7	245.4	115.7	115.6	143.7	167.0
Sweden		1.3	0.1	0.1	0.5	0.6	0.5	0.4	0.4	0.5
Switzerland										
Turkey										
United Kingdom	2.0	1.9	11.2	25.6	42.1	32.4	33.9	22.7	29.6	30.8
Eastern Europe										
Albania										
Belarus										
Bosnia-Herzegovina										
Bulgaria										
Croatia										
Czech Republic				3.9	1.0	2.1	1.6	0.7	0.8	1.0
Estonia										
Georgia										
Hungary										
Latvia										
Lithuania										
Macedonia										
Moldova										
Montenegro										
Poland										
Romania										
Russia										
Serbia										
Slovakia										
Slovenia										
Ukraine										

Source: Euromonitor International from national statistics

Table 4.7

Automotive Diesel Price 1980, 1985, 1990, 1995, 1999-2011

National currency per ten litres (including tax)

	1980	1985	1990	1995	1999	2000	2001	2002	2003
Western Europe									
Austria	6.21	7.81	5.98	6.25	6.36	7.78	7.48	7.19	7.27
Belgium	3.46	4.51	5.28	6.07	6.40	8.10	7.81	7.26	7.56
Cyprus									
Denmark	20.00	28.14	22.79	43.82	56.15	70.91	69.49	67.93	67.85
Finland	3.29	4.70	5.19	5.91	6.82	8.50	8.19	7.84	8.08
France		5.82	4.94	5.87	6.88	8.45	7.99	7.71	7.93
Germany			4.89	5.73	6.38	8.01	8.22	8.40	8.87
Gibraltar									
Greece	0.43	1.04	1.94	4.10	5.03	6.65	6.34	6.22	6.37
Iceland									
Ireland	3.20	7.06	6.95	6.79	7.00	8.42	8.20	7.74	8.04
Italy	2.33	4.16	6.39	6.93	7.62	8.92	8.69	8.56	8.77
Liechtenstein									
Luxembourg	3.01	4.97	3.11	4.96	5.43	6.89	6.56	6.32	6.38
Malta									
Monaco									
Netherlands	4.38	5.70	4.74	7.02	6.97	8.45	8.20	7.90	7.95
Norway	18.42	23.50	27.46	67.58	83.17	98.98	86.45	81.98	83.88
Portugal	0.82	3.29	4.96	5.22	5.49	6.54	6.69	6.45	7.10
Spain	3.51	4.51	4.81	4.93	5.65	6.95	6.93	6.89	6.94
Sweden	14.65	30.73	49.22	63.46	66.52	84.46	86.48	83.38	81.14
Switzerland	12.72	14.18	11.23	11.94	12.35	14.36	14.00	13.35	13.58
Turkey				0.19	2.37	4.35	7.33	10.96	13.94
United Kingdom	2.78	3.65	3.98	5.43	7.25	8.13	7.79	7.55	7.79
Eastern Europe									
Albania									
Belarus									
Bosnia-Herzegovina									
Bulgaria									
Croatia									
Czech Republic		55.00	98.00	156.50	189.80	247.00	241.10	217.30	218.95
Estonia									
Georgia									
Hungary	65.50	93.00	300.00	834.10	1,663.00	2,150.80	2,086.31	2,013.35	2,098.85
Latvia									4.50
Lithuania									
Macedonia									
Moldova									
Montenegro									
Poland				10.01	18.35	25.55	25.52	25.80	28.36
Romania				0.42	5.32	8.48	13.22	15.90	18.87
Russia					34.98	57.83	74.11	90.62	107.13
Serbia									
Slovakia			4.29	4.54	6.12	7.47	7.07	6.59	7.21
Slovenia									
Ukraine									

Source: Euromonitor International from national statistics

Automotives and Transport Statistics

Automotive Diesel Price 1980, 1985, 1990, 1995, 1999-2011 *(continued)*

National currency per ten litres (including tax)

	2004	2005	2006	2007	2008	2009	2010	2011	US$ per litre 2011
Western Europe									
Austria	8.09	9.48	10.09	10.35	12.38	9.73	11.06	13.30	1.85
Belgium	8.81	10.40	10.79	10.94	12.52	10.21	12.02	14.40	2.00
Cyprus	7.22	8.24	8.84	9.00	10.85	8.34	10.06	12.53	1.74
Denmark	68.21	76.62	81.80	82.58	95.05	78.21	90.11	104.64	1.95
Finland	8.48	9.69	10.22	10.18	12.64	9.92	11.46	13.68	1.90
France	8.83	10.23	10.79	10.92	12.70	10.02	11.45	13.36	1.86
Germany	9.38	10.68	11.17	11.69	13.33	10.90	12.26	14.25	1.98
Gibraltar									
Greece	7.40	8.79	9.54	9.84	12.06	9.61	12.33	14.57	2.03
Iceland									
Ireland	8.82	10.36	10.95	10.80	12.72	10.19	12.05	14.13	1.96
Italy	9.38	11.08	11.65	11.63	13.42	10.81	12.14	14.47	2.01
Liechtenstein									
Luxembourg	6.90	8.43	9.17	9.35	11.09	8.45	9.97	11.67	1.62
Malta	7.17	8.78	9.83	9.48	11.19	9.61	10.46	12.96	1.80
Monaco									
Netherlands	8.89	10.23	10.87	10.87	12.87	9.96	11.70	13.48	1.87
Norway	86.80	98.30	106.48	103.50	122.75	107.20	117.59	126.92	2.26
Portugal	7.87	9.37	10.61	10.81	12.62	10.03	11.52	13.72	1.91
Spain	7.55	8.93	9.47	9.58	11.30	9.10	10.75	12.70	1.77
Sweden	85.47	103.53	111.33	110.08	133.58	115.12	124.63	140.10	2.16
Switzerland	14.46	16.38	17.40	17.68	20.25	15.96	17.21	18.63	2.10
Turkey	15.39	19.56	22.24	23.02	28.73	25.94	30.59	36.79	2.19
United Kingdom	8.19	9.09	9.52	9.69	11.75	10.39	11.93	13.87	2.22
Eastern Europe									
Albania									
Belarus									
Bosnia-Herzegovina									
Bulgaria	15.62	16.95	18.55	19.34	21.19	16.32	19.16	23.03	1.64
Croatia	59.90	70.20	71.83	72.70	85.00	67.93	78.65	90.94	1.70
Czech Republic	248.68	278.73	289.58	287.15	317.49	262.22	307.06	342.67	1.94
Estonia	6.90	8.37	8.69	8.67	11.46	9.06	11.05	12.68	1.76
Georgia									
Hungary	2,185.63	2,500.93	2,709.10	2,636.16	3,085.20	2,677.39	3,198.38	3,797.18	1.89
Latvia	5.60	6.03	6.08	6.30	7.68	6.48	7.55	8.99	1.78
Lithuania	24.60	28.44	30.65	30.30	37.70	30.68	35.13	42.69	1.72
Macedonia									
Moldova									
Montenegro									
Poland	31.69	36.82	38.18	37.66	42.19	36.43	42.47	50.37	1.70
Romania	24.67	30.32	32.85	31.50	40.30	35.88	44.10	53.01	1.74
Russia	123.64	140.16	167.83	172.54	226.60	187.68	194.93	247.77	0.84
Serbia									
Slovakia	8.44	9.76	10.68	12.54	13.82	11.07	11.30	13.46	1.87
Slovenia			9.62	9.73	11.29	10.10	11.49	12.43	1.73
Ukraine									

Source: Euromonitor International from national statistics

Table 4.8

Premium Unleaded Petrol Price 1980, 1985, 1990, 1995, 1999-2011

National currency per ten litres (including tax)

	1980	1985	1990	1995	1999	2000	2001	2002	2003
Western Europe									
Austria			6.84	8.21	8.14	9.42	9.04	8.74	8.80
Belgium			6.74	7.78	9.16	11.08	10.81	10.53	10.20
Cyprus				5.50	6.05	6.46	6.65	6.95	6.07
Denmark				60.58	72.10	83.59	82.06	83.82	82.15
Finland	6.60	6.68	6.48	8.38	10.16	11.58	11.31	11.00	10.90
France			7.53	8.62	9.63	11.12	10.58	10.37	10.20
Germany			5.77	7.93	8.74	10.15	10.24	10.48	10.92
Gibraltar									
Greece			3.18	5.59	6.22	7.69	7.54	7.35	7.40
Iceland									
Ireland			7.70	7.10	7.50	8.90	8.89	8.55	8.71
Italy			7.62	8.89	9.60	10.81	10.53	10.48	10.59
Liechtenstein									
Luxembourg			5.14	6.15	6.92	8.28	7.95	7.73	7.78
Malta									
Monaco									
Netherlands		8.49	7.43	8.85	10.30	12.08	12.02	12.10	11.59
Norway			59.44	81.08	92.37	105.66	95.85	92.70	93.73
Portugal			6.53	7.82	8.38	9.02	9.52	9.20	9.65
Spain				6.42	7.00	8.19	8.07	8.14	8.17
Sweden			64.70	75.04	83.35	95.12	94.50	96.83	94.03
Switzerland			10.20	11.83	12.29	14.48	14.14	13.55	13.12
Turkey			0.02	0.29	3.63	5.83	9.92	14.76	18.04
United Kingdom			4.20	5.86	8.29	8.73	8.28	7.98	7.60
Eastern Europe									
Albania									
Belarus									
Bosnia-Herzegovina									
Bulgaria									
Croatia									
Czech Republic			124.00	192.90	231.20	287.10	273.30	245.89	248.05
Estonia									
Georgia									
Hungary				971.30	1,855.40	2,324.10	2,252.50	2,228.60	2,327.90
Latvia									
Lithuania									
Macedonia									
Moldova									
Montenegro									
Poland				11.75	23.30	31.37	31.52	31.92	33.53
Romania				0.59	8.14	11.21	15.17	20.22	24.29
Russia					50.70	73.93	62.50	70.06	87.71
Serbia									
Slovakia			5.42	5.01	6.14	7.89	7.32	7.04	7.57
Slovenia									
Ukraine									

Source: Euromonitor International from national statistics

4

Automotives and Transport

Automotives and Transport Statistics

Premium Unleaded Petrol Price 1980, 1985, 1990, 1995, 1999-2011 *(continued)*

National currency per ten litres (including tax)

	2004	2005	2006	2007	2008	2009	2010	2011	US$ per litre 2011
Western Europe									
Austria	9.50	10.30	10.91	11.21	12.09	10.45	11.89	13.58	1.89
Belgium	11.40	12.80	13.53	13.84	14.56	13.16	14.56	16.05	2.23
Cyprus	7.86	8.47	9.19	9.46	10.26	8.80	10.40	12.16	1.69
Denmark	83.94	90.29	95.84	97.44	102.65	95.31	107.36	119.19	2.22
Finland	11.40	12.10	12.88	12.98	14.23	12.84	14.29	15.61	2.17
France	10.60	11.60	12.37	12.73	13.56	12.07	13.44	15.00	2.09
Germany	11.40	12.20	12.89	13.41	14.03	12.95	14.17	15.60	2.17
Gibraltar									
Greece	8.12	8.82	9.68	10.13	11.10	10.04	14.19	16.52	2.30
Iceland									
Ireland	9.50	10.50	11.17	11.16	12.25	11.00	13.01	14.82	2.06
Italy	11.30	12.20	12.86	12.98	13.79	12.32	13.63	15.54	2.16
Liechtenstein									
Luxembourg	9.00	10.20	10.82	11.22	11.78	10.35	11.63	12.88	1.79
Malta	8.71	9.46	11.05	10.40	11.32	11.22	11.96	13.82	1.92
Monaco									
Netherlands	12.53	13.52	14.15	14.59	15.37	13.43	15.03	16.40	2.28
Norway	99.85	108.16	114.57	116.83	125.28	118.80	126.89	136.73	2.44
Portugal	10.33	11.47	13.10	13.23	13.88	12.35	13.72	15.46	2.15
Spain	8.70	9.50	10.21	10.35	11.08	10.02	11.65	13.19	1.83
Sweden	99.64	109.55	114.55	116.48	126.01	121.38	130.31	139.78	2.15
Switzerland	14.01	15.27	16.43	16.84	17.85	15.07	16.37	17.32	1.95
Turkey	19.59	25.35	27.77	28.79	32.09	31.22	36.82	41.96	2.50
United Kingdom	8.02	8.67	9.12	9.44	10.71	9.93	11.69	13.33	2.14
Eastern Europe									
Albania									
Belarus									
Bosnia-Herzegovina									
Bulgaria	15.76	17.10	18.06	18.45	19.82	17.20	19.94	22.88	1.63
Croatia	68.98	75.44	76.90	77.20	84.80	73.28	83.88	97.16	1.82
Czech Republic	266.80	284.80	295.99	295.04	303.31	272.66	318.60	346.03	1.96
Estonia	7.24	7.97	8.66	8.79	10.42	9.21	11.11	12.40	1.72
Georgia									
Hungary	2,396.20	2,601.00	2,771.57	2,766.11	2,935.44	2,780.06	3,372.43	3,828.54	1.90
Latvia	4.74	5.70	6.11	6.38	7.19	6.75	7.71	9.05	1.79
Lithuania	26.90	28.60	31.12	31.06	35.51	35.22	40.59	45.67	1.84
Macedonia									
Moldova									
Montenegro									
Poland	37.36	39.91	39.81	42.10	42.98	41.22	45.42	51.22	1.73
Romania	27.20	32.40	33.48	32.90	37.23	36.55	45.13	53.50	1.75
Russia	121.03	152.84	177.22	189.57	223.30	203.50	223.68	252.66	0.86
Serbia									
Slovakia	8.78	9.66	10.61	12.62	12.86	11.18	12.51	14.52	2.02
Slovenia	8.91	9.52	9.95	10.30	10.68	10.50	12.02	12.91	1.79
Ukraine									

Source: Euromonitor International from national statistics

Table 4.9

Commercial Vehicle New Registrations 1980, 1985, 1990, 1995, 1999-2011

'000

	1980	1985	1990	1995	1999	2000	2001	2002
Western Europe								
Austria	21.8	22.3	30.9	29.2	34.2	36.5	32.5	29.9
Belgium	31.3	30.7	47.7	44.1	70.4	66.1	73.0	60.3
Cyprus		5.4	10.1	10.0	6.9	7.1	8.2	7.5
Denmark	18.9	37.6	22.8	30.0	38.7	38.1	36.3	36.7
Finland	17.3	18.1	28.9	10.7	19.9	18.1	18.2	18.3
France	323.3	342.2	447.0	357.8	433.5	477.2	496.3	460.9
Germany	194.8	149.4	225.7	259.1	323.7	314.8	296.6	270.6
Gibraltar		0.1	0.3	0.2	0.2	0.3	0.2	0.2
Greece		19.0	44.6	11.6	23.9	25.0	22.8	20.3
Iceland		0.8	2.0	0.8	1.7	2.0	1.2	0.9
Ireland	12.2	16.2	28.4	16.4	38.6	46.3	42.9	38.3
Italy	130.4	107.3	170.0	157.9	228.5	268.1	273.3	316.1
Liechtenstein					0.2	0.3	0.3	0.2
Luxembourg		2.8	5.1	2.4	4.4	4.6	5.2	5.0
Malta		0.6	1.4		2.3	2.0	1.8	0.4
Monaco								
Netherlands	48.0	63.1	69.0	65.1	116.4	114.3	101.4	95.5
Norway	13.9	39.0	21.1	34.9	33.0	35.6	37.5	28.5
Portugal	45.6	22.4	73.6	61.2	134.8	161.0	106.3	84.7
Spain	97.8	114.1	250.5	179.1	344.6	335.7	325.6	305.1
Sweden	19.7	22.9	33.1	14.8	35.3	38.5	35.3	34.6
Switzerland	22.4	20.5	28.9	20.1	25.9	29.3	31.6	26.8
Turkey			62.1	54.7	141.2	189.8	63.7	83.8
United Kingdom	272.0	286.7	293.5	249.9	292.0	301.5	316.1	324.7
Eastern Europe								
Albania								
Belarus								
Bosnia-Herzegovina								
Bulgaria			14.6	10.7	6.4	4.2	2.3	4.3
Croatia			3.0	17.0	6.4	7.2	10.4	13.3
Czech Republic					21.2	23.5	21.7	
Estonia			1.3	0.7	1.9	1.8	2.2	2.5
Georgia								
Hungary		25.3	21.9	14.0	28.5	27.9	29.7	35.1
Latvia				4.1	7.5	6.0	4.3	3.2
Lithuania					2.5	2.5	2.2	2.5
Macedonia					0.8	1.5	0.6	0.7
Moldova					4.2	4.7	5.0	4.3
Montenegro								
Poland		39.0	65.2	56.3	50.8	41.3	29.4	20.2
Romania			9.0	37.9	21.3	17.9	19.4	23.2
Russia					294.2	262.7	265.3	247.3
Serbia								
Slovakia				1.7	5.8	6.7	10.4	9.7
Slovenia			4.7	6.7	7.8	7.6	7.3	7.8
Ukraine								

Source: Euromonitor International from national statistics

Automotives and Transport Statistics

Commercial Vehicle New Registrations 1980, 1985, 1990, 1995, 1999-2011 *(continued)*
'000

	2003	2004	2005	2006	2007	2008	2009	2010	2011
Western Europe									
Austria	34.2	39.5	37.7	38.8	41.5	42.3	31.0	34.0	40.5
Belgium	62.4	70.1	75.1	72.1	81.7	81.3	63.4	61.2	72.0
Cyprus	5.1	4.9	4.8	5.8	7.3	8.9	7.1	7.0	5.8
Denmark	37.4	51.2	64.3	72.0	66.9	41.5	19.6	19.7	28.5
Finland	18.8	22.1	20.0	20.9	22.2	21.6	12.5	14.4	18.3
France	431.4	459.9	480.1	498.4	519.5	523.4	416.2	457.2	482.8
Germany	264.7	283.4	295.6	304.4	334.1	335.0	242.2	282.2	334.8
Gibraltar	0.3	1.2	0.6	0.3	0.3	0.3	0.2	0.2	0.3
Greece	20.7	26.3	25.5	26.4	27.1	25.6	17.4	12.3	7.0
Iceland	1.4	2.0	2.8	3.1	3.4	1.5	0.4	0.3	0.4
Ireland	34.6	34.4	42.0	47.2	50.0	34.0	10.6	11.5	12.5
Italy	242.6	255.3	249.9	272.0	282.9	261.9	198.2	204.2	197.3
Liechtenstein	0.2	0.2	0.2	0.2	0.2	0.3	0.2	0.2	0.2
Luxembourg	4.8	3.8	4.6	4.7	5.3	6.0	4.2	4.1	4.9
Malta	0.6	0.4	0.7	0.6	0.7	0.7	0.5	0.9	0.8
Monaco									
Netherlands	91.0	101.5	80.8	84.7	97.3	104.1	64.2	59.8	71.9
Norway	31.3	38.4	42.7	49.2	53.0	42.6	28.8	34.6	42.0
Portugal	73.4	76.5	72.0	70.5	74.8	61.7	42.7	49.3	37.9
Spain	334.4	374.1	430.6	318.5	324.5	201.4	121.5	132.1	123.4
Sweden	34.3	37.4	41.8	47.2	51.9	47.5	34.1	44.5	54.1
Switzerland	23.8	25.7	26.7	28.9	30.7	32.8	28.7	28.7	33.8
Turkey	170.9	290.1	319.9	292.3	276.7	220.5	206.1	283.4	317.3
United Kingdom	366.1	392.2	388.4	389.5	395.6	353.5	227.5	260.6	306.5
Eastern Europe									
Albania									
Belarus									
Bosnia-Herzegovina			9.8	9.5	9.3	6.8	4.9	5.4	5.6
Bulgaria	4.9	6.5	9.0	10.0	10.7	11.5	4.3	3.2	2.9
Croatia	15.1	13.3	13.6	14.6	14.9	13.9	7.3	7.1	6.9
Czech Republic	25.6	37.8	48.5	60.4	74.6	71.8	25.0	17.8	22.1
Estonia	3.1	3.1	3.9	5.4	6.6	4.4	1.5	1.6	2.8
Georgia									
Hungary	25.0	23.6	20.5	21.6	21.9	21.6	10.6	11.7	15.9
Latvia	2.0	2.5	3.0	4.9	6.9	4.3	0.9	1.2	3.1
Lithuania	3.1	4.1	5.7	7.5	9.5	6.7	1.4	2.4	4.7
Macedonia	0.6	0.5	0.7	0.5	0.8	1.1	1.1	1.1	1.3
Moldova	6.3	7.2	8.9	8.3	10.4	14.0	11.5	12.7	14.9
Montenegro									
Poland	34.3	48.9	47.1	56.0	79.0	81.2	51.9	50.7	61.3
Romania	28.5	35.8	40.9	40.8	51.2	53.1	17.8	9.6	13.3
Russia	273.0	281.0	286.3	331.1	383.1	177.2	79.8	111.0	156.1
Serbia									
Slovakia	12.1	13.3	18.2	24.4	29.4	32.3	18.0	9.8	9.7
Slovenia	8.0	8.6	8.5	8.3	9.7	10.1	5.3	6.4	8.0
Ukraine	70.0	60.7	75.2	133.8	93.2	95.7	32.1	54.8	86.2

Source: Euromonitor International from national statistics

Table 4.10

Diesel Car New Registrations 1985, 1990, 1995, 2000, 2006-2011

'000

	1985	1990	1995	2000	2006	2007	2008	2009	2010	2011	Diesel car registrations as % of all passenger car registrations 2011
Western Europe											
Austria	32.2	66.3	119.1	182.8	191.8	175.9	160.4	146.0	166.6	167.6	47.05
Belgium	95.0	155.4	168.0	290.3	392.3	404.1	423.4	358.6	415.4	430.8	75.29
Cyprus		1.7	1.9	2.6	1.4	4.1	6.3	6.3	6.2	7.0	20.93
Denmark	10.4	3.6	3.9	14.9	40.2	61.2	68.9	49.5	70.2	79.0	46.80
Finland	14.4	7.2	5.5	26.3	29.5	35.6	69.2	40.8	44.5	52.5	41.67
France	264.8	762.1	897.7	1,046.5	1,427.7	1,525.7	1,584.9	1,620.9	1,594.2	1,622.2	73.59
Germany	530.7	337.6	483.5	1,026.0	1,535.9	1,504.8	1,362.7	1,168.8	1,221.9	1,285.2	40.50
Gibraltar											
Greece				2.0	5.9	8.1	9.6	7.3	5.7	4.1	4.18
Iceland	0.4		0.5	2.3	4.2	4.8	3.0	0.7	0.7	1.1	21.76
Ireland	8.6	12.2	13.1	23.4	49.0	50.5	50.8	35.7	55.0	61.2	68.05
Italy	438.7	171.0	178.8	805.2	1,350.9	1,391.2	1,096.0	904.8	900.4	773.5	44.25
Liechtenstein					0.7	0.8	0.7	0.7	0.7	0.7	37.37
Luxembourg	3.5	6.4	8.0	21.1	39.3	39.6	40.3	34.5	37.4	37.4	74.91
Malta											
Monaco											
Netherlands	71.3	54.8	61.8	134.4	130.0	143.1	125.5	77.8	96.5	103.5	18.62
Norway	1.7	2.2	5.5	8.8	52.8	96.1	80.1	71.7	95.7	97.6	70.57
Portugal	2.3	10.3	21.3	62.4	126.4	139.9	146.0	107.2	149.9	102.4	66.72
Spain	125.2	136.2	274.2	733.4	1,114.8	1,144.9	804.7	667.9	693.3	570.1	70.55
Sweden	5.7	1.4	4.7	18.2	55.8	117.5	100.0	93.7	157.1	173.5	56.90
Switzerland	9.3	9.0	10.7	29.0	80.1	91.7	93.2	78.0	88.3	94.6	29.66
Turkey					184.0	174.1	168.3	147.0	194.6	216.1	36.41
United Kingdom	66.2	128.6	405.1	313.2	898.5	967.0	929.5	831.9	936.2	964.7	49.69
Eastern Europe											
Albania											
Belarus											
Bosnia-Herzegovina											
Bulgaria											
Croatia			18.2	19.6	49.9	46.5	34.5	20.4	19.6	21.1	36.31
Czech Republic											
Estonia				1.8	6.4	8.5	6.1	3.5	4.0	4.4	28.48
Georgia											
Hungary			6.1	7.7	36.1	59.6	56.4	24.7	21.2	45.3	100.40
Latvia			6.0	5.0	9.8	13.5	8.4	2.4	3.0	5.2	59.18
Lithuania					5.2	9.6	9.6	3.5	4.0	6.3	48.08
Macedonia											
Moldova											
Montenegro											
Poland			37.9	54.5	82.9	125.6	162.2	174.8	193.1	207.2	74.69
Romania											
Russia											
Serbia											
Slovakia											
Slovenia					24.8	29.2	27.5	19.9	20.6	21.0	35.93
Ukraine											

Source: Euromonitor International from national statistics

Automotives and Transport Statistics

Table 4.11

Passenger Car New Registrations 1985, 1990, 1995, 2000, 2006-2011

'000

	1985	1990	1995	2000	2006	2007	2008	2009	2010	2011
Western Europe										
Austria	242.7	288.6	279.6	309.4	308.5	298.2	293.7	319.4	328.6	356.1
Belgium	378.2	473.5	358.9	515.2	526.1	524.8	535.9	476.2	547.3	572.2
Cyprus	12.2	19.5	17.9	19.1	37.2	50.9	51.4	37.5	32.7	33.6
Denmark	157.5	80.7	135.8	112.7	154.4	159.3	150.1	112.2	153.9	168.7
Finland	139.0	139.1	79.9	134.6	145.7	125.3	139.6	88.3	112.0	126.1
France	1,766.3	2,309.1	1,930.5	2,133.9	2,000.5	2,064.5	2,050.3	2,302.4	2,251.7	2,204.2
Germany	2,379.3	3,040.8	3,314.1	3,378.3	3,468.0	3,148.2	3,090.0	3,807.2	2,916.3	3,173.6
Gibraltar	2.0	2.1	1.7	1.7	1.3	1.3	1.2	1.0	1.2	1.2
Greece	109.4	115.5	125.0	290.2	267.7	279.7	267.3	219.7	141.5	97.7
Iceland	5.7	6.8	6.4	13.6	17.2	15.9	9.0	2.1	3.1	5.0
Ireland	60.4	82.6	87.0	230.8	178.5	186.3	151.6	57.5	88.4	89.9
Italy	1,745.9	2,307.1	1,731.7	2,423.1	2,326.0	2,493.1	2,161.7	2,159.5	1,961.6	1,748.1
Liechtenstein			1.7	1.8	1.9	2.0	2.0	1.6	1.8	1.8
Luxembourg	26.9	38.4	28.0	41.9	50.8	51.3	52.4	47.3	49.7	49.9
Malta	4.1	8.9		11.3	6.7	6.5	4.6	5.5	4.1	5.8
Monaco										
Netherlands	495.7	502.6	447.9	597.6	484.0	505.5	499.9	387.2	482.5	556.1
Norway	159.1	61.9	90.5	97.4	109.2	129.2	110.6	98.7	127.8	138.3
Portugal	104.2	210.9	201.5	257.8	194.7	201.8	213.4	161.0	223.5	153.4
Spain	575.1	988.2	834.4	1,381.3	1,634.6	1,614.8	1,161.2	952.8	982.0	808.1
Sweden	263.0	229.9	169.8	290.5	282.8	306.8	254.0	213.4	289.7	305.0
Switzerland	265.5	329.9	268.0	316.5	269.5	284.7	288.6	266.0	294.2	319.0
Turkey	63.9	267.8	196.9	256.9	373.2	357.5	306.0	369.8	509.8	593.5
United Kingdom	1,832.0	2,008.9	1,945.4	2,221.6	2,344.9	2,404.0	2,131.8	1,995.0	2,030.8	1,941.3
Eastern Europe										
Albania										
Belarus										
Bosnia-Herzegovina					85.4	63.2	35.5	24.9	34.9	46.1
Bulgaria		33.4	74.4	63.5	32.5	41.0	43.8	25.0	15.6	19.1
Croatia		66.2	67.6	92.4	114.4	106.2	95.7	53.3	52.6	58.2
Czech Republic				148.7	124.0	132.5	143.7	161.7	169.2	173.3
Estonia			3.1	10.2	25.4	30.9	24.6	9.9	8.8	15.4
Georgia										
Hungary	101.3	83.9	127.8	133.2	187.7	171.7	153.3	60.2	43.5	45.1
Latvia			49.3	35.7	25.6	32.5	19.8	5.4	5.0	8.8
Lithuania				7.4	14.2	21.6	22.2	7.5	8.0	13.2
Macedonia					12.5	16.9	17.9	13.1	15.5	16.2
Moldova				12.1	16.2	19.1	26.1	19.8	23.0	25.7
Montenegro										
Poland	259.9	358.1	311.1	478.7	239.0	293.3	320.0	320.3	315.9	277.4
Romania		82.0	87.1	66.3	256.4	315.6	271.0	130.2	94.5	81.7
Russia				821.3	2,080.9	2,502.2	2,897.5	1,465.9	1,912.8	2,653.4
Serbia					67.0	77.3	150.0	126.9	56.3	68.6
Slovakia			0.0	54.4	59.1	59.7	70.0	74.7	64.0	68.2
Slovenia		69.3	61.7	64.8	59.6	68.7	71.6	58.0	59.2	58.4
Ukraine					378.0	514.1	610.2	175.2	172.8	211.5

Source: Euromonitor International from national statistics

Table 4.12

Two-Wheeler New Registrations 1985, 1990, 1995, 2000, 2006-2011
'000

	1985	1990	1995	2000	2006	2007	2008	2009	2010	2011
Western Europe										
Austria	49.2	20.1	29.4	45.1	47.0	53.0	53.0	50.0	47.0	53.6
Belgium	7.5	9.2	14.6	24.7	27.2	30.2	30.1	27.5	29.3	30.8
Cyprus	4.3	8.3	5.7	5.4	4.7	5.5	6.2	4.8	3.5	3.9
Denmark	2.6	1.7	2.3	13.1	12.3	14.3	10.4	6.5	5.3	8.1
Finland			95.4	11.6	36.8	39.0	34.3	29.9	26.2	30.4
France			302.4	371.8	414.2	448.4	427.9	357.0	343.1	388.0
Germany	214.7	171.2	342.7	361.3	275.7	261.1	245.8	213.7	190.3	190.7
Gibraltar	0.2	0.6	0.7	1.1	0.9	1.0	1.1	0.9	1.1	1.2
Greece	14.6	41.5	40.7	73.7	91.7	110.2	106.4	85.8	77.9	77.2
Iceland		0.1	0.1	0.2	1.5	2.4	1.4	0.5	0.5	0.5
Ireland	4.1	3.1	2.3	6.9	3.2	3.5	3.2	1.9	1.3	2.9
Italy			655.3	836.5	554.8	566.7	531.4	560.0	407.7	477.9
Liechtenstein			0.1	0.2	0.2	0.2	0.3	0.2	0.2	0.3
Luxembourg			1.3	1.7	2.0	2.0	2.0	1.9	1.9	2.0
Malta				0.5	0.5	0.5	0.7	0.6	0.5	0.6
Monaco										
Netherlands	47.7	74.4	77.0	86.6	63.6	73.7	86.6	112.1	107.6	112.5
Norway	23.6	8.8	10.1	17.3	26.2	32.3	34.2	25.7	28.5	31.1
Portugal	1.4	7.3	54.1	32.7	13.4	19.9	18.0	19.2	23.8	18.5
Spain			189.9	320.7	390.8	395.3	294.2	178.6	169.4	213.0
Sweden	11.3	7.6	10.1	28.4	42.0	62.6	51.6	33.3	24.2	30.4
Switzerland	34.2	31.1	27.1	50.8	45.7	47.9	48.8	44.9	43.0	44.7
Turkey				35.7	389.5	191.8	192.5	141.7	136.6	190.4
United Kingdom	123.6	94.4	68.9	170.1	133.1	144.4	139.4	111.7	96.2	110.6
Eastern Europe										
Albania										
Belarus										
Bosnia-Herzegovina					2.8	2.4	4.8	3.4	4.3	4.2
Bulgaria		6.1	1.4	1.1	5.8	7.7	9.4	6.8	8.9	9.6
Croatia			2.6	2.1	8.1	9.4	9.3	5.1	4.3	4.4
Czech Republic				3.9	19.6	25.0	27.2	19.7	18.5	16.7
Estonia		0.3	0.2	0.2	2.5	3.7	2.9	1.2	1.3	1.4
Georgia										
Hungary			0.2	2.2	7.6	6.3	12.3	3.8	6.0	6.5
Latvia				0.5	2.1	3.8	3.5	1.2	1.2	1.4
Lithuania				0.4	2.5	4.4	10.7	7.0	5.1	7.3
Macedonia				1.0	2.4	3.2	6.4	4.8	4.3	4.9
Moldova										
Montenegro										
Poland	50.0	31.4	5.3	7.2	24.4	36.8	54.5	46.2	42.8	49.0
Romania					5.1	4.8	7.0	8.6	7.8	8.7
Russia										
Serbia										
Slovakia				1.1	6.4	7.2	7.6	6.2	6.3	7.2
Slovenia		0.8	0.7	1.2	9.8	13.1	13.7	10.7	7.8	9.4
Ukraine										

Source: Euromonitor International from national statistics

Automotives and Transport Statistics

Table 4.13

Airline Freight 1980, 1985, 1990, 1995, 1999-2011

Million tonne-kilometres

	1980	1985	1990	1995	1999	2000	2001	2002
Western Europe								
Austria	21.7	35.3	62.2	147.7	340.8	422.4	373.8	424.1
Belgium	436.1	574.7	700.9	546.6	535.4	1,041.7	870.8	655.6
Cyprus	24.4	24.3	30.1	38.8	40.7	46.0	42.9	44.1
Denmark	159.7	154.5	147.7	144.7	196.1	215.8	201.2	199.4
Finland				224.9	303.5	300.5	190.0	215.6
France	2,287.2	3,258.5	4,300.5	4,567.9	4,726.6	5,428.0	5,029.6	5,229.8
Germany	1,974.5	2,920.3	4,781.9	6,006.0	6,598.8	7,281.4	7,205.7	7,391.9
Gibraltar								
Greece	58.1	67.5	88.0	115.3	103.4	149.8	116.7	91.8
Iceland		58.6	67.8	95.7	108.9	104.8	105.7	92.1
Ireland	93.9	98.7	111.1	95.7	138.0	174.5	165.7	122.3
Italy	484.0	692.6	1,091.1	1,334.6	1,614.6	1,773.2	1,555.7	1,440.2
Liechtenstein								
Luxembourg					2,506.1	3,523.3	3,768.4	4,157.7
Malta	3.5	2.5	3.5	8.5	10.5	15.7	15.1	13.2
Monaco								
Netherlands	1,109.7	1,769.7	2,434.6	3,852.4	3,967.6	4,521.2	4,303.4	4,388.4
Norway	168.8	160.5	152.7	148.1	200.6	224.6	207.2	205.1
Portugal	124.8	127.8	163.1	206.9	225.1	242.9	227.8	212.7
Spain	470.7	601.4	851.9	675.4	815.9	923.2	924.4	856.2
Sweden	252.7	245.5	232.4	209.3	291.0	308.9	283.1	283.9
Switzerland	427.9	670.1	875.5	1,562.1	1,877.3	2,033.8	1,698.9	1,088.9
Turkey			73.3	177.3	312.9	393.6	358.4	396.8
United Kingdom	2,664.3	3,519.4	4,711.9	7,214.1	4,925.2	5,340.1	4,650.4	4,997.1
Eastern Europe								
Albania						0.0	0.0	0.1
Belarus					1.8	1.9	1.7	1.4
Bosnia-Herzegovina								
Bulgaria				24.4	12.4	6.7	2.7	0.1
Croatia				1.8	2.0	3.4	3.6	3.4
Czech Republic				26.8	26.2	35.0	29.1	31.5
Estonia				0.7	4.1	2.1	3.1	1.8
Georgia					2.9	2.5	2.5	5.2
Hungary	8.5	9.3	6.3	19.2	39.9	55.1	35.8	28.7
Latvia				0.7	0.4	1.5	0.9	1.2
Lithuania				1.7	1.8	2.0	2.1	2.0
Macedonia					1.5	1.6	0.7	0.2
Moldova						0.9	0.3	0.4
Montenegro								
Poland	20.8	10.5	57.0	68.9	80.3	82.9	74.2	73.5
Romania	7.4	7.0	9.0	18.9	11.3	13.4	11.0	10.1
Russia				1,604.0	592.7	1,082.1	943.2	1,089.9
Serbia							4.2	4.8
Slovakia				0.1	0.2	0.5	0.7	0.9
Slovenia				4.1	3.7	3.9	4.1	4.5
Ukraine				24.7	13.2	13.0	12.9	12.8

Source: Euromonitor International from national statistics

Airline Freight 1980, 1985, 1990, 1995, 1999-2011 *(continued)*

Million tonne-kilometres

	2003	2004	2005	2006	2007	2008	2009	2010	2011
Western Europe									
Austria	467.2	539.8	580.3	621.6	483.9	420.8	341.5	357.6	379.6
Belgium	604.6	717.1	710.0	745.2	755.2	981.7	1,427.5	1,434.2	1,315.6
Cyprus	47.7	52.5	52.1	51.3	52.6	46.2	37.1	36.2	40.2
Denmark	184.6	189.0	174.2	177.5	190.9	286.9	237.5	218.5	245.5
Finland	255.7	325.2	353.6	408.8	489.7	542.6	484.4	728.9	804.3
France	5,262.2	5,776.7	5,995.9	6,296.0	6,555.9	5,838.3	4,632.4	4,722.4	5,531.5
Germany	7,503.8	8,288.2	7,949.5	8,520.3	8,798.6	8,176.1	6,669.0	7,424.2	7,716.2
Gibraltar									
Greece	70.4	67.3	74.3	82.2	81.4	69.7	61.1	55.5	49.0
Iceland	75.4	117.3	121.5	138.6	141.4	127.4	133.1	121.7	111.4
Ireland	127.5	130.2	113.5	130.5	125.3	122.3	120.9	120.2	127.6
Italy	1,413.6	1,438.1	1,411.1	1,458.1	1,588.9	1,279.0	1,133.9	1,176.2	1,090.7
Liechtenstein									
Luxembourg	4,347.9	4,670.3	5,149.8	5,270.4	5,512.4	5,357.9	4,877.8	5,110.4	5,853.1
Malta	13.3	12.5	11.9	12.4	12.7	12.5	7.1	11.9	11.6
Monaco									
Netherlands	4,526.8	4,978.6	5,089.1	5,122.7	5,169.6	4,645.5	3,959.5	3,698.2	3,708.2
Norway	195.1	197.9	198.0	202.0	205.4	191.6	199.8	214.4	220.5
Portugal	224.2	262.2	261.2	320.8	351.6	344.6	301.1	370.4	355.9
Spain	918.8	1,092.6	1,078.0	1,158.3	1,267.5	1,105.7	1,002.6	1,253.1	1,280.8
Sweden	271.1	276.8	274.7	240.5	221.8	180.4	85.7	82.8	84.1
Switzerland	1,305.2	1,152.2	1,161.5	1,085.8	1,172.6	1,142.0	997.5	1,276.0	1,313.2
Turkey	390.0	383.3	394.5	474.9	466.1	470.6	720.1	1,026.9	1,254.8
United Kingdom	5,214.0	5,779.2	6,088.7	6,314.6	6,266.0	6,283.8	5,063.9	6,071.5	6,293.5
Eastern Europe									
Albania	0.1	0.1	0.1	0.1	0.1	0.1	0.2	0.1	0.1
Belarus	1.3	1.3	1.3	1.4	1.4	1.4	1.2	1.4	1.4
Bosnia-Herzegovina									
Bulgaria	1.0	3.5	4.1	4.2	3.7	2.2	1.7	2.3	2.3
Croatia	3.2	2.9	2.9	2.7	2.9	2.3	1.9	1.5	1.7
Czech Republic	40.5	45.2	44.2	45.1	38.4	27.2	22.4	18.0	16.2
Estonia	2.0	1.8	1.8	1.5	1.4	1.3	0.8	1.0	1.0
Georgia	5.4	2.9	2.9	2.9	3.1	3.1	2.6	3.5	3.9
Hungary	33.1	28.1	25.5	28.1	30.8	13.3	11.1	18.5	20.0
Latvia	0.9	1.5	3.0	14.4	15.3	15.2	20.2	19.2	23.3
Lithuania	1.8	1.9	2.1	2.1	1.9	2.0	1.9	1.9	2.0
Macedonia	0.2	0.1	0.1	0.1	0.1	0.1	0.1	0.1	0.1
Moldova	0.8	0.9	0.9	1.2	1.2	0.8	0.7	1.0	1.1
Montenegro									
Poland	78.5	86.3	82.2	92.1	95.4	78.9	55.5	76.0	74.4
Romania	7.8	5.6	5.9	5.8	6.5	6.4	4.0	5.6	6.3
Russia	1,167.3	1,482.7	1,597.3	1,986.8	2,297.1	1,783.9	1,680.6	1,874.9	1,738.5
Serbia	4.7	6.5	4.9	4.2	4.0	3.4	2.0	2.1	2.3
Slovakia	0.9	0.7	0.5	11.5	34.1	34.4	19.8	25.9	35.2
Slovenia	3.6	3.2	2.6	2.3	3.7	1.9	1.7	1.5	1.6
Ukraine	20.4	27.2	42.6	47.7	55.5	63.4	52.3	69.3	73.1

Source: Euromonitor International from national statistics

Automotives and Transport Statistics

Table 4.14

Airline Passengers 1980, 1985, 1990, 1995, 1999-2011

Million passenger-kilometres

	1980	1985	1990	1995	1999	2000	2001	2002
Western Europe								
Austria	1,953.8	2,500.6	4,172.4	6,858.1	15,324.0	14,232.4	13,875.4	13,794.3
Belgium	4,966.2	5,818.6	6,960.3	7,716.9	17,953.1	19,378.7	15,319.8	2,606.1
Cyprus	660.5	1,089.3	1,606.9	2,713.6	2,941.7	2,785.1	3,011.9	3,436.3
Denmark	2,963.5	2,975.1	4,173.1	4,950.8	5,872.6	6,128.0	6,952.0	7,453.0
Finland	2,019.1	2,728.9	4,716.4	6,852.8	7,800.0	7,634.9	8,194.8	8,807.2
France	34,099.2	40,015.4	53,600.3	69,913.5	97,884.8	113,438.1	113,278.7	117,273.4
Germany	25,150.8	30,761.8	46,018.6	72,105.8	97,153.0	112,795.0	111,302.8	124,245.6
Gibraltar								
Greece	4,792.3	5,878.4	7,478.6	7,864.9	9,960.0	9,841.2	9,800.9	8,586.7
Iceland	2,292.1	2,761.5	1,876.7	2,643.0	3,944.6	3,937.2	3,713.7	3,187.6
Ireland	2,550.3	2,522.8	4,938.7	5,652.1	11,315.3	13,664.3	13,917.3	18,575.2
Italy	11,891.8	14,099.1	22,209.8	32,796.5	40,913.8	44,389.3	40,950.0	34,327.6
Liechtenstein								
Luxembourg		101.9	130.3	340.8	521.3	557.3	586.0	436.8
Malta	565.9	542.8	709.3	1,559.1	2,028.8	2,383.8	2,359.2	2,305.5
Monaco					1.0	2.5	2.3	6.9
Netherlands	23,490.6	28,498.5	43,401.4	57,333.8	70,236.0	74,425.9	69,317.1	69,492.9
Norway	4,261.8	4,078.7	6,440.6	8,348.1	9,945.5	10,366.7	10,460.9	10,546.3
Portugal	4,919.9	5,311.1	7,863.8	8,238.7	12,072.0	11,216.5	11,182.4	12,109.1
Spain	20,358.2	23,416.0	30,641.9	24,168.0	44,100.0	52,427.3	55,323.7	54,044.3
Sweden	4,368.5	5,137.0	7,006.3	8,580.0	10,140.0	11,192.2	11,277.4	11,662.5
Switzerland	10,390.8	13,157.5	17,420.6	20,813.8	31,920.0	36,624.8	33,469.6	26,712.0
Turkey			5,097.8	10,276.6	13,356.0	17,282.1	16,057.6	16,931.9
United Kingdom	83,589.4	80,111.0	133,847.8	161,337.0	192,420.0	170,686.7	159,020.8	156,594.4
Eastern Europe								
Albania					95.9	101.3	92.6	95.9
Belarus					282.8	316.5	339.2	308.1
Bosnia-Herzegovina								
Bulgaria			1,349.9	2,084.4	2,311.9	834.5	361.7	56.7
Croatia				486.0	643.0	643.8	735.9	783.3
Czech Republic				2,188.6	3,444.0	3,313.1	3,575.7	3,855.1
Estonia				138.0	297.6	235.0	246.8	282.6
Georgia				301.9	376.2	230.1	234.9	521.1
Hungary	1,027.3	1,284.1	1,475.6	1,768.8	2,662.0	3,572.6	2,951.9	3,076.1
Latvia				131.1	164.5	236.4	180.4	183.8
Lithuania				202.9	324.0	321.6	347.0	355.1
Macedonia						740.3	377.4	235.6
Moldova						125.0	146.1	161.1
Montenegro								
Poland	2,259.5	1,732.7	3,014.6	3,599.9	4,568.8	4,757.5	4,914.6	5,111.4
Romania	772.0	898.4	1,077.8	1,692.0	1,795.7	2,097.9	1,854.2	1,593.0
Russia				60,482.2	47,684.0	42,950.3	48,320.8	49,889.9
Serbia							831.8	1,080.9
Slovakia				68.6	72.0	107.8	84.8	93.8
Slovenia				325.6	516.0	562.5	656.7	675.1
Ukraine				2,029.8	1,560.0	1,387.4	1,418.2	1,578.1

Source: Euromonitor International from national statistics

Airline Passengers 1980, 1985, 1990, 1995, 1999-2011 *(continued)*

Million passenger-kilometres

	2003	2004	2005	2006	2007	2008	2009	2010	2011
Western Europe									
Austria	14,558.4	17,529.5	18,835.3	19,921.3	17,407.9	16,464.5	14,775.2	15,936.0	15,838.3
Belgium	3,958.3	4,737.9	4,918.3	5,311.8	6,212.3	9,826.6	7,815.5	8,646.4	8,893.1
Cyprus	3,934.5	4,229.6	4,183.9	4,293.1	4,478.3	4,522.0	4,163.0	4,374.7	4,406.5
Denmark	7,201.6	8,101.5	7,908.1	8,749.5	9,315.7	9,543.5	8,301.0	8,705.6	9,793.9
Finland	9,055.9	10,114.0	11,172.0	12,636.0	15,564.0	16,980.0	15,564.0	17,412.0	19,140.0
France	115,571.1	123,984.0	135,016.8	144,096.0	151,011.6	160,277.9	152,255.8	151,702.5	159,218.8
Germany	149,671.8	170,628.0	182,507.6	204,117.8	214,654.7	220,758.8	205,370.5	222,639.0	237,028.0
Gibraltar									
Greece	7,353.6	9,166.2	9,410.5	9,225.3	9,646.6	10,193.9	9,357.8	9,313.1	9,450.5
Iceland	2,997.5	3,634.9	4,307.7	4,253.4	4,280.1	3,756.7	3,632.3	4,036.0	4,254.8
Ireland	27,440.9	34,597.0	44,791.9	54,272.0	67,667.3	79,498.1	87,474.6	77,658.3	86,000.6
Italy	41,176.9	43,237.0	51,127.4	50,039.5	50,486.2	41,182.7	43,823.3	45,433.3	46,179.4
Liechtenstein									
Luxembourg	548.5	572.6	565.7	610.9	665.9	690.1	407.0	469.4	606.8
Malta	2,174.0	2,281.8	2,292.2	2,475.5	2,698.3	3,017.3	3,681.1	4,115.9	4,822.9
Monaco	6.0	3.8	4.9	4.9	5.1	4.2	2.8	2.5	2.7
Netherlands	69,236.4	76,310.7	82,268.9	86,833.4	90,914.5	95,189.5	90,184.5	92,989.2	98,733.5
Norway	10,506.4	10,321.1	10,309.7	10,437.5	10,401.0	10,923.3	8,878.5	10,217.1	10,610.6
Portugal	13,562.3	16,092.9	16,833.6	19,010.1	21,381.3	24,158.9	22,820.1	26,004.0	26,542.3
Spain	57,594.3	64,140.6	70,975.5	77,100.4	88,404.4	87,099.7	80,133.8	83,131.8	79,266.1
Sweden	11,411.1	11,976.2	12,330.2	11,939.8	13,273.7	13,794.2	11,939.8	11,842.2	13,145.7
Switzerland	23,294.8	20,602.2	20,476.5	22,139.8	25,150.1	30,268.1	29,560.2	30,865.9	34,843.3
Turkey	16,451.0	20,499.8	24,297.4	27,889.6	33,689.5	42,560.5	49,528.6	57,891.5	60,878.3
United Kingdom	164,208.4	182,736.1	200,332.8	213,335.5	227,501.7	232,591.6	230,595.8	225,672.0	226,596.0
Eastern Europe									
Albania	121.1	135.6	149.1	161.1	175.6	185.3	174.4	215.7	235.1
Belarus	337.8	398.8	383.3	414.0	451.2	459.7	442.2	480.8	513.1
Bosnia-Herzegovina									
Bulgaria	457.3	747.1	1,122.6	1,345.6	1,442.5	1,718.3	1,247.6	1,615.9	1,899.7
Croatia	869.2	940.5	973.5	1,004.5	1,084.0	1,216.6	1,151.1	1,056.0	1,263.0
Czech Republic	4,938.0	5,988.0	6,605.4	6,651.8	6,310.9	6,297.3	6,333.8	6,000.0	5,873.1
Estonia	415.3	547.3	660.1	682.1	754.2	801.4	407.1	459.0	660.2
Georgia	634.5	472.7	520.0	505.3	612.1	630.0	597.3	685.3	727.8
Hungary	3,316.3	3,509.7	3,806.4	4,139.9	4,435.3	4,061.9	3,842.6	4,043.3	4,263.6
Latvia	244.8	581.2	1,161.2	1,510.3	1,501.1	1,538.6	1,455.6	1,801.7	2,163.0
Lithuania	394.8	556.8	700.3	622.7	576.9	862.0	874.0	887.4	1,016.1
Macedonia	280.2	275.6	248.7	268.6	253.1	209.0	114.4	168.0	180.8
Moldova	222.8	257.3	325.0	363.2	434.3	528.9	493.5	641.9	779.6
Montenegro									
Poland	5,433.8	5,860.7	6,222.9	6,719.7	7,288.0	7,854.4	7,169.1	7,727.4	8,285.0
Romania	1,696.1	1,532.2	1,967.1	2,430.3	3,695.2	3,979.5	3,959.7	4,419.9	4,988.4
Russia	53,893.9	62,010.1	63,192.3	69,499.3	82,331.6	91,096.1	83,827.6	109,125.4	113,452.2
Serbia	1,041.5	1,095.0	958.6	1,088.0	1,136.7	1,145.7	946.6	1,105.1	1,208.9
Slovakia	220.4	847.9	949.4	2,289.9	2,202.4	2,614.2	3,263.6	2,410.6	2,980.6
Slovenia	700.3	711.0	706.8	772.9	863.3	1,002.0	920.1	945.5	924.8
Ukraine	2,580.3	3,826.1	4,086.9	4,928.8	5,730.6	6,532.3	5,958.5	6,948.0	7,185.6

Source: Euromonitor International from national statistics

Automotives and Transport Statistics

Table 4.15

Scheduled Flights: Distance Flown 1980, 1985, 1990, 1995, 1999-2011

Million kilometres

	1980	1985	1990	1995	1999	2000	2001	2002
Western Europe								
Austria	44.1	50.2	69.8	101.5	133.6	139.1	134.2	129.9
Belgium	71.8	65.6	91.4	141.9	209.7	215.7	186.2	114.6
Cyprus	6.6	8.2	9.6	16.8	21.2	20.9	22.0	25.0
Denmark	41.2	42.3	63.4	78.2	85.5	85.4	91.7	80.9
Finland	33.1	38.8	58.1	70.6	100.7	101.6	95.2	90.9
France	345.3	335.4	431.2	597.9	842.7	961.0	902.0	880.4
Germany	228.7	266.2	419.0	619.6	781.3	839.5	860.8	927.3
Gibraltar								
Greece	40.5	46.4	52.5	62.5	70.5	89.9	95.3	81.7
Iceland	17.9	20.2	19.0	25.3	34.0	34.0	31.7	26.5
Ireland	31.8	27.4	55.5	55.6	83.5	106.0	118.6	138.1
Italy	160.8	159.9	211.6	298.9	358.5	392.1	392.6	350.7
Liechtenstein								
Luxembourg						60.7	66.3	70.3
Malta	3.8	3.5	5.8	14.5	22.5	26.0	25.3	22.5
Monaco					0.4	0.6	0.5	0.7
Netherlands	139.2	158.3	210.9	351.1	420.5	463.9	434.2	433.3
Norway	64.2	64.3	89.3	115.3	139.8	148.9	148.8	129.4
Portugal	49.3	46.8	65.8	85.7	112.3	104.8	111.9	116.8
Spain	193.0	187.3	224.5	279.8	343.0	418.3	459.6	442.3
Sweden	63.0	72.9	105.4	115.3	153.1	166.8	166.9	129.6
Switzerland	113.1	124.8	161.7	210.1	275.8	317.0	303.6	256.1
Turkey	25.2	27.9	44.4	96.8	135.5	148.1	143.0	140.5
United Kingdom	575.4	535.9	672.1	917.7	1,013.2	1,016.2	1,052.7	1,048.0
Eastern Europe								
Albania					2.1	2.6	2.1	2.0
Belarus					5.4	7.1	7.3	6.5
Bosnia-Herzegovina								
Bulgaria	10.7	22.0	27.3	22.0	23.6	13.9	6.3	1.4
Croatia				6.5	10.2	10.3	10.9	11.4
Czech Republic				29.1	32.3	39.4	42.1	44.4
Estonia				3.9	6.7	6.2	6.1	5.9
Georgia				4.4	6.2	3.7	3.8	8.2
Hungary	16.9	18.7	21.6	27.4	37.1	42.1	38.1	38.7
Latvia				8.5	9.4	6.7	5.7	5.8
Lithuania				5.7	11.4	9.9	10.2	9.8
Macedonia						9.6	5.3	2.8
Moldova						4.1	4.6	4.6
Montenegro								
Poland	34.6	22.8	37.8	38.4	46.8	55.4	70.2	65.6
Romania	12.7	12.2	14.1	18.7	22.3	30.1	25.6	20.6
Russia				777.3	523.3	533.7	568.2	653.2
Serbia							11.5	16.5
Slovakia				2.4	3.5	2.0	1.6	2.7
Slovenia				6.5	9.1	9.8	11.1	12.1
Ukraine				53.8	24.0	31.5	30.3	31.7

Source: Euromonitor International from national statistics

Scheduled Flights: Distance Flown 1980, 1985, 1990, 1995, 1999-2011 *(continued)*

Million kilometres

	2003	2004	2005	2006	2007	2008	2009	2010	2011
Western Europe									
Austria	130.3	148.7	158.9	170.0	159.8	133.8	120.4	126.4	119.1
Belgium	103.0	125.3	124.1	131.6	162.6	168.0	167.5	166.6	175.6
Cyprus	29.5	32.4	31.7	32.0	34.2	34.3	32.8	32.3	32.7
Denmark	78.3	85.4	83.3	84.1	81.8	87.8	76.8	83.9	85.2
Finland	96.9	107.8	108.6	118.7	139.7	153.6	137.7	155.0	170.7
France	856.5	911.3	925.1	960.1	1,001.6	1,039.7	987.4	911.7	885.4
Germany	1,069.3	1,198.4	1,285.2	1,397.1	1,484.0	1,520.8	1,358.3	1,335.8	1,363.8
Gibraltar									
Greece	75.8	95.7	88.0	88.9	92.6	93.4	81.7	76.8	73.5
Iceland	25.1	29.2	32.2	33.8	37.2	32.4	34.1	35.5	36.2
Ireland	196.9	235.7	292.3	349.6	442.0	530.1	569.1	616.1	674.5
Italy	404.3	406.6	448.0	427.9	440.7	404.4	404.2	406.9	412.6
Liechtenstein									
Luxembourg	73.7	78.3	90.7	93.5	97.3	88.0	88.3	92.6	102.4
Malta	22.2	22.5	23.8	25.2	27.5	31.5	36.1	46.0	52.1
Monaco	0.7	0.6	0.6	0.7	0.8	0.7	0.6	0.6	0.6
Netherlands	438.1	469.8	481.3	502.6	520.8	516.3	552.1	572.8	591.1
Norway	127.4	128.0	127.7	125.7	123.5	124.9	125.9	125.6	125.5
Portugal	128.4	148.8	158.1	171.3	198.6	242.1	194.6	196.1	184.0
Spain	473.4	520.3	561.1	575.1	638.5	648.4	593.5	588.1	568.5
Sweden	125.3	133.1	133.3	137.3	141.3	144.3	138.7	138.2	144.4
Switzerland	217.7	171.9	165.7	164.5	180.5	190.0	191.5	195.8	202.9
Turkey	141.5	161.2	186.4	227.1	263.2	327.8	394.4	466.3	499.2
United Kingdom	1,086.7	1,204.7	1,324.2	1,399.8	1,472.0	1,436.3	1,364.9	1,247.8	1,236.7
Eastern Europe									
Albania	2.5	2.7	2.9	3.1	3.3	3.6	3.6	3.8	3.8
Belarus	6.7	7.1	6.3	6.7	7.3	6.9	6.7	6.7	6.7
Bosnia-Herzegovina									
Bulgaria	7.3	10.7	14.0	18.9	18.3	22.3	15.4	22.7	23.2
Croatia	11.7	12.2	13.5	13.3	13.4	14.5	14.3	14.8	15.3
Czech Republic	53.0	66.5	75.3	73.9	73.1	71.6	70.7	67.9	67.7
Estonia	6.9	8.1	9.2	9.1	9.5	13.8	7.7	8.3	9.4
Georgia	9.8	7.3	7.8	6.9	9.0	9.3	8.7	8.9	9.0
Hungary	44.5	52.3	53.7	56.8	58.4	51.8	47.6	47.1	48.6
Latvia	6.9	12.8	21.2	26.1	25.7	26.6	24.9	23.9	25.2
Lithuania	10.3	12.5	14.4	13.8	13.1	14.8	14.2	14.4	14.9
Macedonia	3.1	3.1	2.9	3.1	3.3	3.1	2.1	3.1	3.1
Moldova	5.1	5.5	5.6	5.3	5.9	5.9	5.7	5.4	5.8
Montenegro									
Poland	67.9	72.9	77.0	81.1	91.8	86.4	77.3	83.0	84.5
Romania	26.2	28.0	36.0	40.5	50.5	55.2	57.3	61.3	69.1
Russia	601.8	694.4	680.0	748.7	868.4	939.1	861.9	895.5	941.8
Serbia	15.5	16.8	14.7	16.6	16.9	16.6	15.2	15.2	15.4
Slovakia	5.0	11.8	13.0	22.3	18.4	14.5	18.4	22.5	25.8
Slovenia	12.9	13.7	14.6	15.4	18.4	19.1	21.2	22.6	23.5
Ukraine	43.8	54.4	56.5	61.6	68.2	72.9	75.1	85.2	93.2

Source: Euromonitor International from national statistics

Automotives and Transport Statistics

Table 4.16

Merchant Shipping Fleet 1980, 1985, 1990, 1995, 1999-2011

'000 gross tons

	1980	1985	1990	1995	1999	2000	2001	2002
Western Europe								
Austria	88.8	134.2	139.3	91.9	71.1	53.2	35.3	29.9
Belgium	1,809.8	2,400.3	1,954.5	72.0	132.1	141.5	151.0	186.7
Cyprus	2,091.1	8,196.1	18,335.9	24,652.5	23,641.0	23,206.4	22,761.8	22,997.0
Denmark	5,390.4	4,942.2	5,188.1	5,747.2	5,353.6	6,357.8	7,109.0	7,602.9
Finland	2,346.2	1,649.7	1,093.6	1,581.4	1,658.4	1,620.4	1,595.4	1,545.2
France	11,924.6	8,237.4	3,832.4	4,194.3	4,766.4	4,681.2	4,677.7	4,731.5
Germany	9,887.8	7,611.4	5,737.8	5,626.2	6,513.8	6,552.2	6,300.2	6,545.8
Gibraltar	2.3	583.3	2,008.5	307.1	628.0	722.0	816.3	960.9
Greece	39,471.7	31,031.5	20,521.6	29,434.7	24,833.3	26,401.7	28,678.2	28,782.8
Iceland	188.2	180.3	176.6	190.2	192.1	192.7	193.4	187.3
Ireland	209.0	194.0	180.8	213.4	218.9	259.6	300.3	279.6
Italy	11,095.7	8,843.2	7,991.4	6,905.0	8,048.5	9,048.7	9,655.0	9,595.9
Liechtenstein								
Luxembourg			3.3	880.8	1,343.0	1,406.1	1,469.2	1,493.8
Malta	132.9	1,855.8	4,518.7	17,678.3	28,205.5	28,170.0	27,052.6	26,331.4
Monaco								
Netherlands	5,723.8	4,301.3	3,784.8	2,903.0	4,813.8	5,167.7	5,605.0	5,664.3
Norway							22,590.8	22,194.5
Portugal							1,199.2	1,099.7
Spain	8,112.2	6,256.2	3,807.1	1,618.6	1,269.0	1,552.6	2,147.5	2,371.2
Sweden	4,234.0	2,620.0	2,782.0	2,880.0	2,946.9	2,887.0	2,957.9	3,177.5
Switzerland	310.8	342.0	287.5	381.0	439.1	470.6	502.0	559.1
Turkey	1,454.8	3,684.4	3,718.6	6,267.6	6,324.6	5,832.7	5,896.7	5,658.8
United Kingdom	27,135.2	14,343.5	9,836.0	8,935.0	9,061.5	9,702.5	12,143.1	13,773.0
Eastern Europe								
Albania	56.1	56.1	55.8	63.0	21.4	23.3	25.2	48.7
Belarus								
Bosnia-Herzegovina								
Bulgaria	1,233.3	1,322.2	1,360.5	1,166.1	1,035.8	989.6	955.3	889.3
Croatia					868.9	822.0	775.2	834.7
Czech Republic								
Estonia				597.7	452.6	399.6	346.6	357.4
Georgia				282.0	132.2	204.4	276.6	569.3
Hungary								
Latvia				798.1	118.1	93.2	68.3	88.7
Lithuania				610.2	424.3	408.8	393.3	435.3
Macedonia								
Moldova								
Montenegro								
Poland	3,639.1	3,315.3	3,369.2	2,358.0	1,319.1	1,119.2	618.3	585.6
Romania	1,856.3	3,023.8	4,004.6	2,536.4	1,220.6	766.9	637.7	622.0
Russia				10,818.0	10,649.0	10,485.9	10,247.8	10,380.0
Serbia								
Slovakia				19.3	15.2	15.2	15.2	7.4
Slovenia				2.1	1.8	1.8	1.9	2.3
Ukraine				4,613.0	1,775.2	1,546.3	1,407.7	1,349.9

Source: Euromonitor International from national statistics
Note: Ships of 100 gross tons or more. Gross tonnage (gt) is a measure of the total volume within the hull, and above deck, available for cargo, passengers, crew, fuel, stores etc. 1gt = 100 cu ft

Merchant Shipping Fleet 1980, 1985, 1990, 1995, 1999-2011 *(continued)*

'000 gross tons

	2003	2004	2005	2006	2007	2008	2009	2010	2011
Western Europe									
Austria	32.0	34.1	34.1	34.1	14.0	14.0	9.9	9.9	
Belgium	3,000.0	3,973.3	4,058.4	4,312.7	4,091.3	4,241.8	4,301.0	4,500.8	4,428.9
Cyprus	22,054.2	21,283.4	19,019.1	19,032.2	18,954.3	20,109.4	20,168.9	20,732.5	20,992.5
Denmark	7,726.7	7,763.1	8,290.4	8,799.6	9,476.3	10,570.0	11,336.5	12,126.4	11,601.6
Finland	1,452.1	1,428.9	1,475.2	1,422.6	1,570.1	1,564.9	1,459.3	1,450.2	1,581.3
France	4,859.2	4,974.9	5,611.1	6,164.8	6,350.2	6,323.5	6,842.3	6,667.9	7,051.9
Germany	6,111.8	8,246.4	11,497.2	11,364.3	12,934.2	15,282.8	15,157.1	15,282.5	15,319.5
Gibraltar	993.0	1,142.4	1,156.6	1,297.4	1,515.4	1,607.1	2,026.8	2,064.2	2,155.5
Greece	32,203.1	32,040.7	30,744.7	32,048.1	35,704.5	36,822.3	38,910.6	40,795.4	41,276.0
Iceland	187.4	194.1	188.5	184.2	180.0	168.7	161.6	155.5	168.9
Ireland	471.0	496.8	309.8	193.4	187.2	185.5	189.2	218.1	229.3
Italy	10,245.8	10,956.0	11,616.0	12,571.2	12,971.7	13,599.9	15,530.6	17,044.3	18,492.2
Liechtenstein									
Luxembourg	1,006.0	689.7	570.0	779.9	883.5	729.9	935.0	1,030.0	1,098.1
Malta	25,134.3	22,352.6	23,015.6	24,849.8	27,754.4	31,633.3	35,037.0	38,737.7	45,116.9
Monaco								0.1	0.1
Netherlands	5,702.6	5,622.9	5,669.4	5,818.8	6,139.8	6,684.2	6,966.2	6,738.0	7,570.4
Norway	20,509.3	18,936.2	17,531.9	18,222.3	18,156.0	18,311.3	16,614.3	16,528.7	16,511.9
Portugal	1,156.3	1,136.5	1,239.6	1,223.6	1,070.1	1,095.7	1,287.6	1,225.4	1,240.5
Spain	2,651.0	2,869.1	2,901.7	3,004.6	3,061.8	3,054.9	2,880.4	3,072.8	3,027.9
Sweden	3,579.3	3,666.9	3,765.7	3,876.5	4,044.9	4,389.3	4,044.9	3,560.5	3,369.3
Switzerland	588.7	487.5	479.6	510.0	588.6	640.4	640.6	704.8	742.3
Turkey	4,950.6	4,678.9	5,044.7	4,848.8	4,995.1	5,181.0	5,450.5	5,946.8	6,418.5
United Kingdom	17,314.2	18,344.3	19,652.0	20,835.7	21,947.2	24,262.0	27,201.7	28,147.8	30,992.7
Eastern Europe									
Albania	70.0	72.8	74.8	74.7	67.5	65.7	67.2	57.1	44.8
Belarus									
Bosnia-Herzegovina									
Bulgaria	747.9	789.5	894.2	875.5	911.1	876.1	522.8	422.2	317.6
Croatia	847.7	1,016.1	1,135.2	1,157.2	1,373.5	1,444.7	1,389.7	1,509.5	1,562.4
Czech Republic									
Estonia	358.2	334.9	292.5	416.7	389.8	363.5	374.9	375.1	319.1
Georgia	814.9	974.3	1,091.9	1,129.3	1,048.4	678.4	707.9	711.5	264.2
Hungary									
Latvia	90.9	294.3	304.0	333.3	261.8	289.7	263.9	263.6	187.1
Lithuania	442.1	453.4	476.7	448.6	425.8	423.7	433.7	417.5	406.8
Macedonia									
Moldova		3.7	11.4	15.7	50.1	178.7	351.2	362.8	483.7
Montenegro				10.5	13.1	14.3	7.7	5.3	26.6
Poland	282.4	162.7	190.1	193.4	193.3	212.9	203.8	162.2	109.5
Romania	563.1	426.7	336.5	272.1	269.5	261.8	246.0	91.7	84.1
Russia	10,430.8	8,638.9	8,334.5	8,046.0	7,587.3	7,527.0	7,650.0	7,710.7	7,590.8
Serbia									
Slovakia	29.2	126.4	211.2	232.7	233.3	189.9	146.8	56.3	19.0
Slovenia	1.7	1.5	1.1	1.6	1.6	2.1	2.1	2.1	2.6
Ukraine	1,378.8	1,144.8	1,154.0	1,136.5	1,144.6	1,087.1	905.0	787.1	710.1

Source: Euromonitor International from national statistics
Note: Ships of 100 gross tons or more. Gross tonnage (gt) is a measure of the total volume within the hull, and above deck, available for cargo, passengers, crew, fuel, stores etc. 1gt = 100 cu ft

4

Automotives and Transport

Automotives and Transport Statistics

Table 4.17

Public Railway Network 1980, 1985, 1990, 1995, 1999-2011

km at end-year

	1980	1985	1990	1995	1999	2000	2001	2002
Western Europe								
Austria	5,857	5,766	5,624	5,672	5,643	5,665	5,697	5,779
Belgium	3,971	3,667	3,479	3,368	3,472	3,471	3,454	3,518
Cyprus								
Denmark	2,461	2,471	2,344	2,349	2,760	2,758	2,770	2,770
Finland	6,075	5,900	5,867	5,880	5,836	5,854	5,850	5,850
France	34,362	34,676	34,070	31,939	29,113	29,272	29,445	29,352
Germany	28,517	27,634	40,980	41,718	37,525	36,588	35,986	35,804
Gibraltar								
Greece	2,461	2,461	2,484	2,474	2,299	2,385	2,377	2,383
Iceland								
Ireland	1,987	1,944	1,944	1,954	1,909	1,919	1,919	1,919
Italy	16,138	16,183	16,066	16,003	16,092	16,295	16,357	16,307
Liechtenstein								
Luxembourg	270	270	271	275	274	274	274	274
Malta								
Monaco								
Netherlands	2,880	2,824	2,798	2,739	2,808	2,802	2,809	2,806
Norway	4,242	4,242	4,044	4,023	4,179	4,179	4,178	4,077
Portugal	3,609	3,603	3,064	2,850	2,813	2,814	2,814	2,881
Spain	15,724	14,804	14,572	14,308	14,361	14,347	14,347	14,426
Sweden	11,377	11,266	10,801	10,925	11,044	11,037	11,021	11,095
Switzerland	2,943	2,986	2,978	2,987	5,108	5,062	5,053	5,049
Turkey	8,387	8,400	8,429	8,549	8,682	8,671	8,671	8,671
United Kingdom	18,028	17,122	16,924	16,999	16,984	17,008	16,986	17,020
Eastern Europe								
Albania	337	672	674	674	440	440	447	447
Belarus	5,461	5,459	5,488	5,543	5,523	5,512	5,509	5,512
Bosnia-Herzegovina		944	944	1,032	607	519	608	608
Bulgaria	4,341	4,297	4,299	4,294	4,290	4,320	4,320	4,318
Croatia	2,437	2,441	2,429	2,726	2,726	2,726	2,726	2,726
Czech Republic			9,451	9,430	9,444	9,444	9,523	9,600
Estonia	993	1,019	1,026	1,021	968	968	967	967
Georgia		1,465	1,583	1,575	1,545	1,562	1,565	1,565
Hungary	7,836	7,837	7,838	7,988	7,988	8,005	7,736	7,950
Latvia	2,384	2,384	2,397	2,413	2,413	2,331	2,305	2,270
Lithuania	2,008	2,014	2,007	2,002	1,905	1,905	1,696	1,775
Macedonia	696	696	696	699	699	699	699	699
Moldova	1,100	1,100	1,150	1,326	1,140	1,139	1,121	1,120
Montenegro						250	250	250
Poland	27,181	27,012	26,228	23,986	22,891	22,560	21,119	21,073
Romania	11,110	11,192	11,348	11,376	10,981	11,015	11,015	11,002
Russia			87,200	87,388	86,031	86,075	85,835	85,542
Serbia					3,809	3,809	3,809	3,809
Slovakia			3,660	3,668	3,662	3,662	3,662	3,657
Slovenia	1,058	1,058	1,196	1,201	1,201	1,201	1,229	1,229
Ukraine	22,553	22,698	22,799	22,756	22,472	22,301	22,219	22,079

Source: Euromonitor International from national statistics

Public Railway Network 1980, 1985, 1990, 1995, 1999-2011 *(continued)*

km at end-year

	2003	2004	2005	2006	2007	2008	2009	2010	2011
Western Europe									
Austria	5,787	5,675	5,691	5,818	5,818	5,664	5,356	5,066	4,934
Belgium	3,521	3,536	3,544	3,500	3,374	3,513	3,578	3,582	3,603
Cyprus									
Denmark	2,782	2,787	2,646	2,646	2,646	2,641	2,667	2,667	2,667
Finland	5,851	5,741	5,732	5,905	5,899	5,919	5,919	5,919	5,923
France	29,269	29,246	28,412	29,562	29,918	29,901	29,903	29,871	29,948
Germany	36,044	34,715	34,218	34,128	33,978	33,862	33,721	33,708	33,603
Gibraltar									
Greece	2,414	2,449	2,576	2,509	2,551	2,552	2,552	2,552	2,552
Iceland									
Ireland	1,919	1,919	1,919	1,919	1,919	1,919	1,919	1,919	1,919
Italy	16,288	16,236	16,543	16,627	16,667	16,861	17,004	18,011	18,149
Liechtenstein									
Luxembourg	275	275	275	275	275	275	275	275	275
Malta									
Monaco									
Netherlands	2,811	2,811	2,813	2,776	2,896	2,896	2,886	3,016	3,022
Norway	4,077	4,077	4,087	4,087	4,114	4,114	4,169	4,169	4,169
Portugal	2,818	2,849	2,839	2,839	2,838	2,842	2,842	2,843	2,843
Spain	14,909	14,785	15,015	15,212	15,554	15,550	15,553	15,835	15,853
Sweden	11,037	11,050	11,017	11,020	10,972	11,032	11,138	11,149	11,160
Switzerland	5,028	5,062	5,062	5,080	5,107	5,109	5,110	5,111	5,112
Turkey	8,697	8,697	8,697	8,697	8,697	8,699	9,080	9,594	9,616
United Kingdom	16,950	16,458	15,810	15,795	15,814	15,814	15,796	15,777	15,773
Eastern Europe									
Albania	447	447	423	423	423	423	423	423	423
Belarus	5,502	5,498	5,498	5,494	5,494	5,491	5,491	5,503	5,505
Bosnia-Herzegovina	609	608	608	608	601	601	601	600	600
Bulgaria	4,318	4,259	4,154	4,146	4,143	4,144	4,150	4,098	4,094
Croatia	2,726	2,726	2,726	2,722	2,722	2,722	2,722	2,722	2,722
Czech Republic	9,602	9,612	9,614	9,597	9,588	9,586	9,578	9,568	9,561
Estonia	967	959	959	968	816	919	919	919	919
Georgia	1,565	1,554	1,559	1,559	1,559	1,561	1,565	1,566	1,568
Hungary	7,950	7,950	7,950	7,960	7,942	7,892	7,892	7,893	7,894
Latvia	2,270	2,270	2,270	2,269	2,265	2,263	1,883	1,897	1,878
Lithuania	1,774	1,782	1,771	1,771	1,766	1,765	1,767	1,767	1,767
Macedonia	699	699	699	699	699	699	699	699	699
Moldova	1,111	1,110	1,139	1,154	1,154	1,157	1,157	1,157	1,157
Montenegro	250	250	250	250	250	250	250	250	250
Poland	20,665	20,250	20,253	20,176	20,107	20,196	20,360	20,228	20,200
Romania	11,077	11,053	10,948	10,789	10,777	10,785	10,746	10,777	10,777
Russia	85,394	85,286	85,542	85,253	84,158	85,194	85,281	85,292	85,293
Serbia	3,809	3,809	3,809	3,809	3,809	3,809	3,809	3,809	3,809
Slovakia	3,657	3,660	3,626	3,626	3,629	3,622	3,623	3,622	3,622
Slovenia	1,229	1,229	1,228	1,228	1,228	1,228	1,228	1,228	1,228
Ukraine	22,079	22,011	22,001	21,891	21,873	21,676	21,678	21,705	21,700

Source: Euromonitor International from national statistics

Automotives and Transport

4

Automotives and Transport Statistics

Table 4.18

Railway Statistics of Major National Carriers 2011

As stated

	Locomotives (number)	Rail motor vehicles (number)	Passengers carried (million)	Average journey length (km)	Total goods carried (million tonnes)
Western Europe					
Austria	1,436.0	2,084.0	218.5	49.0	119.0
Belgium	589.0	1,333.0	230.5	47.2	54.0
Cyprus					
Denmark	131.0	772.0	207.1	34.0	8.7
Finland	483.0	648.0	69.4	57.7	38.7
France	4,314.0	6,621.0	1,100.1	77.7	89.8
Germany	7,395.0	15,537.0	2,387.5	35.0	374.0
Gibraltar					
Greece	175.0	300.0	15.8	101.9	3.3
Iceland					
Ireland	143.0	580.0	41.7	43.9	0.6
Italy	3,053.0	4,608.0	621.5	72.5	99.0
Liechtenstein			0.1	10.3	1.2
Luxembourg	42.0	88.0	20.4	18.9	9.2
Malta					
Monaco					
Netherlands	281.0	2,027.0	337.9	45.9	41.7
Norway		200.0	59.8	54.6	30.3
Portugal	149.0	390.0	161.3	26.4	8.5
Spain	693.0	1,695.0	556.2	41.3	19.0
Sweden	680.0	1,800.0	179.6	62.9	72.1
Switzerland	1,878.0	2,270.0	382.9	48.8	48.6
Turkey	622.0	759.0	85.0	66.3	23.8
United Kingdom			1,311.0	41.6	98.7
Eastern Europe					
Albania	55.0		0.3	48.8	0.5
Belarus			84.7	91.2	151.2
Bosnia-Herzegovina	97.0	109.0	1.1	61.1	13.1
Bulgaria	511.0	715.0	30.5	69.3	14.9
Croatia	249.0	340.0	70.3	25.6	13.5
Czech Republic	2,134.0	3,080.0	165.6	40.4	85.2
Estonia	304.0	384.0	5.0	50.9	31.4
Georgia	322.0		3.3	203.8	18.0
Hungary	1,085.0	1,544.0	142.5	56.1	49.2
Latvia	197.0	300.0	21.4	35.4	55.2
Lithuania	273.0	329.0	4.4	83.8	54.7
Macedonia	55.0	65.0	1.6	101.8	3.9
Moldova	152.0		5.1	80.5	4.8
Montenegro					
Poland	4,253.0	5,451.0	278.9	67.0	224.4
Romania	1,797.0	2,140.0	56.3	87.2	53.7
Russia	9,448.0		981.8	148.2	1,337.9
Serbia	333.0		5.3	0.1	13.0
Slovakia	964.0	1,198.0	47.8	49.4	47.8
Slovenia	162.0	276.0	16.3	50.5	17.8
Ukraine	4,459.0		434.2	121.6	459.1

Source: Euromonitor International from national statistics

Table 4.19

Railway Freight 1980, 1985, 1990, 1995, 1999-2011

Million net tonne-kilometres

	1980	1985	1990	1995	1999	2000	2001	2002
Western Europe								
Austria	11,002	11,903	12,682	13,715	15,039	16,602	16,895	17,132
Belgium	8,037	8,277	8,370	7,304	7,392	7,674	7,081	7,297
Cyprus								
Denmark	1,620	1,756	1,787	1,985	1,938	2,025	1,961	1,906
Finland	8,335	8,067	8,357	9,293	9,753	10,107	9,857	9,664
France	67,862	54,225	49,677	58,153	52,112	55,352	50,396	50,295
Germany				70,500	71,900	77,500	76,165	76,283
Gibraltar								
Greece	801	724	600	306	347	426	379	327
Iceland								
Ireland	637	601	589	602	526	491	516	426
Italy	18,384	17,968	21,170	24,050	23,781	25,839	24,352	23,060
Liechtenstein								
Luxembourg	665	645	709	529	609	633	587	571
Malta								
Monaco								
Netherlands	3,396	3,274	3,070	3,097	3,988	4,522	4,293	4,323
Norway	3,001	2,867	2,600	2,700	2,900	3,000	2,900	2,700
Portugal	945	1,171	1,442	2,343	2,562	2,569	2,498	2,585
Spain	10,424	11,397	10,824	11,684	13,429	13,553	13,698	13,781
Sweden	15,914	17,331	19,100	19,391	19,090	19,468	18,954	19,197
Switzerland	7,799	7,434	8,958	8,686	9,825	9,937	10,091	9,639
Turkey	4,996	7,719	7,759	8,516	8,237	9,761	7,487	7,166
United Kingdom	17,600	16,000	16,000	13,300	18,200	18,100	19,400	18,700
Eastern Europe								
Albania	477	605	584	53	27	28	19	21
Belarus	66,264	73,243	75,373	25,510	30,529	31,425	29,727	34,169
Bosnia-Herzegovina				16	162	214	264	293
Bulgaria	17,681	18,172	14,132	8,595	5,297	5,538	4,904	4,627
Croatia	7,561	8,675	6,535	1,974	1,685	1,788	2,074	2,206
Czech Republic			41,150	25,459	16,713	17,496	16,882	15,810
Estonia	5,919	6,446	6,977	3,846	7,295	8,102	8,557	9,697
Georgia	13,748	13,487	12,354	1,246	3,160	3,912	4,481	5,065
Hungary	24,397	22,307	16,781	8,337	7,734	8,095	7,731	7,752
Latvia	17,586	19,933	18,538	9,757	12,210	13,310	14,179	15,020
Lithuania	18,237	20,927	19,258	7,220	7,849	8,918	7,741	9,767
Macedonia	712	993	769	169	380	527	462	334
Moldova	15,201	16,136	14,783	3,004	1,232	1,513	1,980	2,748
Montenegro								
Poland	134,737	120,642	83,530	68,206	55,076	54,015	47,656	47,747
Romania	75,535	74,215	57,253	27,179	15,927	17,982	17,960	17,494
Russia	2,316,000	2,506,000	2,522,915	1,213,711	1,204,547	1,373,178	1,433,617	1,510,203
Serbia	8	9	7	1	1	2	2	2
Slovakia			23,176	13,674	9,859	11,234	10,929	10,383
Slovenia	3,851	4,292	4,191	3,076	2,784	2,857	2,837	3,078
Ukraine	469,643	497,916	488,243	195,762	156,336	172,840	177,465	193,141

Source: Euromonitor International from national statistics

Automotives and Transport Statistics

Railway Freight 1980, 1985, 1990, 1995, 1999-2011 *(continued)*
Million net tonne-kilometres

	2003	2004	2005	2006	2007	2008	2009	2010	2011
Western Europe									
Austria	16,869	17,931	17,064	20,980	21,371	21,915	17,767	19,833	20,664
Belgium	7,293	7,691	8,130	8,572	9,258	8,572	6,374	6,268	7,268
Cyprus									
Denmark	1,985	2,147	1,967	1,885	1,776	1,863	1,696	2,240	2,359
Finland	10,047	10,105	9,706	11,060	10,434	10,777	8,872	9,750	10,139
France	46,835	45,121	40,701	41,190	42,623	40,548	32,130	29,965	30,841
Germany	79,841	86,409	95,421	107,008	114,615	115,652	95,834	107,317	116,452
Gibraltar									
Greece	456	588	611	662	835	786	545	435	440
Iceland									
Ireland	398	399	303	166	129	103	79	92	93
Italy	22,457	22,183	22,761	24,151	25,285	23,831	17,791	18,616	23,638
Liechtenstein		21	17	18	18	17	10	11	12
Luxembourg	523	559	392	441	287	280	200	248	305
Malta									
Monaco									
Netherlands	4,962	5,831	5,865	6,289	7,216	6,984	5,578	6,385	7,232
Norway	2,627	2,845	3,182	3,351	3,502	3,639	3,506	3,496	3,593
Portugal	2,442	2,675	2,826	2,763	2,586	2,549	2,174	2,141	2,226
Spain	14,156	14,117	11,587	11,524	11,065	10,224	7,349	7,844	7,984
Sweden	20,170	20,856	21,675	22,271	23,250	22,924	20,389	23,464	24,777
Switzerland	9,534	10,800	11,500	12,000	12,300	12,265	10,565	10,485	11,590
Turkey	8,612	9,332	9,077	9,544	9,755	10,552	9,681	11,030	11,137
United Kingdom	18,700	20,100	21,400	21,900	21,300	21,100	19,200	18,532	19,987
Eastern Europe									
Albania	31	32	26	36	53	52	46	66	69
Belarus	38,402	40,331	43,559	45,723	47,933	48,994	42,742	46,224	49,995
Bosnia-Herzegovina	312	612	1,176	1,089	1,148	1,237	1,026	1,227	1,266
Bulgaria	5,274	5,211	5,163	5,396	5,241	4,693	3,145	3,064	3,553
Croatia	2,487	2,493	2,835	3,305	3,574	3,312	2,641	2,618	2,992
Czech Republic	15,862	15,092	14,866	15,779	16,304	15,437	12,791	13,770	14,076
Estonia	9,670	10,488	10,639	10,418	8,430	5,943	5,947	6,638	7,184
Georgia	5,539	4,862	6,127	7,379	6,928	6,529	5,433	5,523	5,671
Hungary	8,109	8,749	9,090	10,167	10,137	9,874	7,735	8,809	9,353
Latvia	17,955	18,618	19,779	16,831	18,313	19,581	18,725	17,179	19,288
Lithuania	11,457	11,637	12,457	12,896	14,373	14,748	11,888	13,431	14,533
Macedonia	373	426	530	614	778	743	497	524	659
Moldova	3,019	3,006	3,053	3,673	3,120	2,873	1,058	958	1,086
Montenegro		94	132	133	185	184	101	121	133
Poland	49,573	52,316	49,972	53,623	54,253	52,043	43,446	48,705	49,667
Romania	16,942	18,426	16,582	15,791	15,757	15,236	11,088	12,375	12,459
Russia	1,668,921	1,801,601	1,858,093	1,950,830	2,090,337	2,116,240	1,865,305	2,011,308	2,059,486
Serbia	3	3	3	4	5	4	3	4	4
Slovakia	10,113	9,702	9,463	9,988	9,647	9,299	6,964	8,105	9,006
Slovenia	3,274	3,465	3,579	3,705	3,944	3,520	2,668	3,421	3,606
Ukraine	225,287	233,961	223,980	240,810	262,505	257,006	196,188	218,091	235,768

Source: Euromonitor International from national statistics

Table 4.20

Railway Passengers 1985, 1990, 1995, 2000, 2006-2011

Million passenger-kilometres

	1985	1990	1995	2000	2006	2007	2008	2009	2010	2011
Western Europe										
Austria	7,290	8,575	8,526	8,318	8,854	9,037	10,275	10,206	10,306	10,694
Belgium	6,572	6,539	6,757	7,732	9,607	9,932	10,403	10,493	10,609	10,887
Cyprus										
Denmark	4,716	4,851	4,684	5,327	5,903	5,992	6,096	5,980	6,586	7,046
Finland	3,224	3,331	3,184	3,405	3,540	3,778	4,052	3,876	3,959	4,006
France	61,828	63,761	55,319	69,571	79,483	83,179	88,284	87,667	84,883	85,516
Germany			60,514	74,015	78,764	79,098	82,428	81,206	83,033	83,606
Gibraltar										
Greece	1,732	1,977	1,568	1,886	1,811	1,930	1,657	1,414	1,594	1,604
Iceland										
Ireland	1,023	1,226	1,291	1,389	1,872	2,007	1,976	1,683	1,678	1,832
Italy	37,401	44,709	43,859	47,133	50,158	49,780	49,524	44,404	43,349	45,036
Liechtenstein					1	1	1	1	1	1
Luxembourg	229	208	286	332	298	316	345	333	347	387
Malta										
Monaco										
Netherlands	9,007	11,060	16,350	14,666	14,678	14,741	15,313	15,400	15,400	15,509
Norway	2,241	2,104	2,381	2,635	2,833	2,958	3,123	3,080	3,134	3,269
Portugal	5,725	5,664	4,869	3,834	3,876	3,987	4,213	4,152	4,147	4,256
Spain	17,231	16,733	16,594	20,144	22,105	21,857	23,969	23,093	23,136	22,954
Sweden	6,586	6,353	6,345	8,301	9,617	10,261	11,017	11,216	11,204	11,296
Switzerland	9,715	11,448	12,122	13,302	14,863	15,769	16,125	16,973	17,693	18,666
Turkey	6,489	6,410	5,797	5,832	5,277	5,553	5,097	5,374	5,491	5,632
United Kingdom	30,400	33,200	30,000	38,200	47,297	50,474	53,002	52,765	53,328	54,492
Eastern Europe										
Albania	564	779	197	125	80	51	41	32	19	15
Belarus	13,729	16,852	12,505	17,722	9,968	9,368	8,188	7,401	7,578	7,729
Bosnia-Herzegovina			63	47	66	68	78	61	59	69
Bulgaria	7,785	7,793	4,693	3,472	2,422	2,423	2,335	2,144	2,100	2,111
Croatia	4,063	3,429	943	1,252	1,362	1,611	1,810	1,835	1,742	1,798
Czech Republic		13,313	8,023	7,300	6,922	6,900	6,803	6,503	6,559	6,683
Estonia	1,649	1,510	421	261	260	273	274	250	248	257
Georgia		2,497	371	453	809	774	675	626	655	675
Hungary	11,209	11,403	8,336	9,693	9,584	8,752	8,293	8,073	7,692	7,990
Latvia	5,214	5,366	1,373	715	992	983	951	756	749	760
Lithuania	3,417	3,640	1,130	611	430	409	398	357	373	371
Macedonia	417	355	65	176	105	109	148	154	155	161
Moldova	1,648	1,464	1,019	315	471	468	486	422	399	412
Montenegro					123	124	125	99	115	124
Poland	51,978	50,373	20,960	19,706	18,240	19,524	20,195	18,637	17,921	18,679
Romania	31,082	30,582	18,879	11,632	8,092	7,476	6,958	6,128	5,437	4,908
Russia	246,300	274,440	192,217	167,054	177,832	174,085	175,872	151,466	139,000	145,543
Serbia	4	4	2	1	1	1	1	1	1	1
Slovakia		6,381	4,202	2,870	2,213	2,165	2,296	2,264	2,309	2,361
Slovenia	1,668	1,429	595	705	793	812	834	840	813	823
Ukraine	66,954	76,038	63,752	51,767	53,230	53,400	53,225	48,274	50,038	52,785

Source: Euromonitor International from national statistics

Automotives and Transport

4

Automotives and Transport Statistics **Table 4.21**

Car Traffic 1980, 1985, 1990, 1995, 1999-2011

Million car-kilometres

	1980	1985	1990	1995	1999	2000	2001	2002
Western Europe								
Austria	25,840	27,500	48,687	57,240	63,750	65,141	66,308	67,845
Belgium	34,888	35,947	43,090	72,745	78,713	75,750	76,980	77,990
Cyprus								
Denmark	19,928	22,608	26,885	29,423	32,026	31,759	31,363	31,540
Finland	22,180	25,970	33,430	35,760	39,190	39,815	40,680	41,675
France		222,503	310,931	343,018	375,552	375,974	391,690	395,448
Germany			431,488	514,414	541,900	555,800	569,700	583,600
Gibraltar								
Greece	9,392				47,457	48,573	50,909	54,465
Iceland	986				1,991	2,017	2,210	2,272
Ireland	14,798	20,540	19,271	24,826	25,212	23,532	24,664	25,142
Italy				329,000	348,000	353,507	359,989	364,647
Liechtenstein								
Luxembourg	1,382	2,191	2,971	2,954	3,339	3,408	3,478	3,548
Malta								
Monaco				1				
Netherlands	61,351	68,745	81,275	89,310	97,990	100,925	115,963	131,000
Norway	22,743	22,565			27,643	28,113	27,563	28,507
Portugal		22,500	30,300	44,250	49,463	52,339	54,517	56,518
Spain	93,293	99,515	143,782	137,904	169,000	180,908	189,167	197,597
Sweden	45,192	47,790	55,808	56,898	58,931	59,654	60,247	61,961
Switzerland	32,071	36,468	42,649	43,823	46,701	48,062	48,508	49,061
Turkey	7,444	9,415	14,755	21,061	30,771	36,224	34,047	33,204
United Kingdom	241,070	279,043	375,796	395,630	429,033	429,115	436,406	447,902
Eastern Europe								
Albania								
Belarus				935	1,114	966	889	760
Bosnia-Herzegovina								
Bulgaria			10,597	11,230	12,718	13,189	13,529	13,897
Croatia					11,454	11,158	12,337	13,432
Czech Republic				24,540	31,181	31,338	31,733	33,481
Estonia				3,957	5,095	5,140	5,238	5,430
Georgia								
Hungary			17,155		15,840	16,000	16,300	15,800
Latvia			5,853	1,834	4,161	4,789	5,359	6,160
Lithuania								
Macedonia								
Moldova				180	141	143	157	191
Montenegro								
Poland	20,494	20,193	34,194	75,150	92,800	94,600	94,600	102,941
Romania			19,681	24,019	28,895	27,545	29,029	30,593
Russia				14,711	16,317	17,099	17,778	18,961
Serbia								
Slovakia				8,251	9,754	9,754	10,268	12,134
Slovenia			7,847	9,673	11,933	12,094	12,397	12,732
Ukraine					3,362	3,347	3,636	3,786

Source: Euromonitor International from national statistics

Car Traffic 1980, 1985, 1990, 1995, 1999-2011 *(continued)*

Million car-kilometres

	2003	2004	2005	2006	2007	2008	2009	2010	2011
Western Europe									
Austria	69,167	70,148	71,511	72,512	74,417	75,669	76,362	77,004	77,435
Belgium	77,240	78,170	74,500	75,190	76,620	76,620	77,049	77,359	77,482
Cyprus		6,384	6,476	6,509	6,690	6,700	4,786	5,099	5,134
Denmark	31,971	32,811	32,751	33,062	33,921	33,912	33,741	33,464	33,388
Finland	42,565	43,530	44,220	44,610	45,560	45,285	45,950	46,173	46,276
France	398,946	398,779	393,956	392,964	396,180	392,355	394,855	398,065	398,065
Germany	577,800	590,400	578,200	583,900	587,500	584,600	584,245	585,066	584,660
Gibraltar									
Greece	59,241	65,236	67,939	71,787	75,094	78,400	81,569	84,569	86,148
Iceland	2,338	2,414	2,580	2,706	2,836	2,863	2,825	2,918	2,932
Ireland	26,037	26,913	27,972	29,015	30,349	31,173	30,920	32,598	32,972
Italy	370,934	372,681	374,427	381,124	385,177	389,709	395,194	400,155	402,651
Liechtenstein									
Luxembourg	3,532	3,623	3,729	3,841	3,981	4,185	4,084	4,125	4,158
Malta									
Monaco				77	79	80	80	81	81
Netherlands	133,000	134,900	133,600	133,700	135,000	129,500	128,817	128,003	126,837
Norway	29,162	28,935	28,708	29,880	32,247	32,714	32,631	32,737	32,819
Portugal	57,888	59,863	61,357	62,715	65,304	66,110	65,032	66,023	66,143
Spain	193,909	202,723	209,812	217,072	220,135	218,852	222,437	225,604	226,515
Sweden	62,549	62,971	63,188	62,980	64,391	63,658	63,731	63,856	63,967
Switzerland	49,526	50,018	50,464	50,811	51,207	51,948	52,851	53,191	53,522
Turkey	33,802	38,403	40,490	43,188	47,124	47,502	49,615	50,686	51,280
United Kingdom	450,911	458,861	477,660	486,036	491,348	487,134	465,782	469,407	477,583
Eastern Europe									
Albania									
Belarus	861	731	744	704	706	836	848	869	881
Bosnia-Herzegovina									
Bulgaria	14,698	15,237	14,619	15,797	16,101	16,623	16,723	17,243	17,433
Croatia	14,600	16,060	17,520	18,058	19,011	19,456	18,965	19,116	19,134
Czech Republic	34,718	35,561	37,175	43,289	47,629	51,327	51,821	53,763	54,786
Estonia	5,895	6,249	6,373	6,893	7,852	8,431	8,381	9,079	9,283
Georgia									
Hungary	17,200	19,400	22,100	24,556	25,917	27,174	26,702	27,060	27,250
Latvia	6,809	7,486	7,979	9,505	11,135	9,946	8,865	8,958	9,062
Lithuania	6,472	7,051	6,753	7,206	8,383	8,690	8,281	8,460	8,473
Macedonia									
Moldova	207	237	269	304	355	405	390	428	440
Montenegro									
Poland	111,282	119,623	127,964	133,602	139,239	144,877	153,509	156,827	159,758
Romania	31,356	32,268	33,413	30,464	32,029	34,887	38,077	39,346	40,565
Russia	19,795	20,517	21,731	22,773	25,140	27,394	27,946	29,160	29,830
Serbia									
Slovakia	11,451	10,736	11,468	10,987	11,374	11,791	10,750	11,202	11,188
Slovenia	13,007	13,441	13,725	14,036	14,851	15,170	15,717	15,997	16,188
Ukraine	4,241	4,697	4,788	4,995	5,303	5,363	4,687	4,736	4,925

Source: Euromonitor International from national statistics

Automotives and Transport Statistics

Table 4.22

Road-Transported Goods 1980, 1985, 1990, 1995, 1999-2011

Million car-kilometres

	1980	1985	1990	1995	1999	2000	2001	2002
Western Europe								
Austria	7,931	9,099	15,317	26,824	33,982	35,122	37,532	38,498
Belgium	18,311	22,106	32,049	47,136	46,878	51,047	53,182	52,889
Cyprus								1,322
Denmark	20,120	19,910	22,349	22,605	23,236	24,021	22,156	22,516
Finland	18,400	20,100	25,400	22,338	29,656	31,975	30,478	31,967
France		116,399	155,841	178,880	204,713	203,999	206,870	204,359
Germany	124,400	132,200	169,900	237,515	278,427	280,708	288,964	285,214
Gibraltar								
Greece	9,159	10,352	12,486	12,356	13,804	14,291	16,681	18,010
Iceland								
Ireland	5,011	4,521	5,130	5,493	10,206	12,275	12,325	14,275
Italy	119,600	144,129	177,945	195,327	177,291	184,677	186,513	192,681
Liechtenstein								
Luxembourg	278	206	383		6,313	7,609	8,700	9,179
Malta								
Monaco								
Netherlands	30,370	33,097	40,063	40,391	83,564	79,565	78,492	77,418
Norway	5,252	6,418	8,231	9,654	14,916	15,132	15,179	15,426
Portugal	11,800		16,193	18,826	26,087	26,836	29,967	29,724
Spain	89,500	110,500	90,530	101,874	134,262	148,717	161,045	184,549
Sweden	20,109	19,400	25,649	28,247	32,224	35,621	34,158	36,652
Switzerland	7,287	7,718	10,953	11,420	12,222	12,781	13,374	13,664
Turkey	37,507	45,634	65,710	112,515	150,974	161,552	151,421	150,912
United Kingdom	91,100	100,600	132,900	146,714	166,260	165,621	163,264	164,035
Eastern Europe								
Albania	1,302	1,221	1,195	2,077	2,011	2,164	2,231	2,352
Belarus	16,806	17,737	22,361	9,539	9,232	9,745	10,241	11,400
Bosnia-Herzegovina					252	228	221	221
Bulgaria							5,423	8,804
Croatia	2,630	2,723	2,852	1,251	2,424	2,816	6,783	7,413
Czech Republic				31,267	36,964	37,310	39,067	43,674
Estonia	4,218	4,407	4,510	1,549	3,975	3,932	4,677	4,387
Georgia	2,355	3,018	2,577	130	420	475	520	543
Hungary					15,770	16,046	18,486	17,913
Latvia	5,133	5,554	5,853	1,834	4,161	4,789	5,359	6,200
Lithuania	6,921	7,369	7,336	5,160	7,740	7,769	8,274	10,709
Macedonia	2,534	2,464	2,189	1,174	839	776	3,131	3,679
Moldova	5,573	6,159	6,305	1,159	1,073	1,088	1,060	1,257
Montenegro						60	64	71
Poland	44,546	36,592	40,293	51,200	70,452	75,023	77,228	80,318
Romania			28,993	19,748	13,456	14,288	18,544	25,350
Russia	241,371	265,047	299,362	156,483	140,013	152,735	159,852	167,238
Serbia					552	582	475	459
Slovakia				26,536	18,516	14,341	13,799	14,929
Slovenia					4,240	5,252	7,035	6,609
Ukraine			79,668	34,478	18,206	19,282	18,457	20,593

Source: Euromonitor International from national statistics

Road-Transported Goods 1980, 1985, 1990, 1995, 1999-2011 *(continued)*
Million car-kilometres

	2003	2004	2005	2006	2007	2008	2009	2010	2011
Western Europe									
Austria	39,557	39,186	37,044	39,187	37,402	34,313	29,075	28,659	29,990
Belgium	50,542	47,878	43,847	43,017	42,085	38,356	36,174	35,002	36,947
Cyprus	1,401	1,119	1,393	1,165	1,202	1,308	963	1,087	1,184
Denmark	23,009	23,114	23,299	21,254	20,960	19,480	16,876	15,018	14,767
Finland	30,926	32,290	31,857	29,715	29,819	31,036	27,805	29,532	30,127
France	203,608	212,201	205,284	211,445	219,212	206,304	173,621	182,193	203,360
Germany	290,745	303,752	310,103	330,016	343,447	341,532	307,547	313,104	335,345
Gibraltar									
Greece	19,340	36,773	23,761	34,002	27,791	28,850	28,585	28,704	27,572
Iceland									
Ireland	15,650	17,144	17,910	17,454	19,020	17,402	12,787	12,291	14,528
Italy	174,088	196,980	211,804	187,065	179,411	180,461	167,627	175,775	189,452
Liechtenstein			390	339	339	328	263	303	297
Luxembourg	9,645	9,575	8,803	8,807	9,562	9,382	8,400	8,694	9,272
Malta									
Monaco									
Netherlands	79,765	89,695	84,163	83,193	77,921	78,159	72,675	68,242	67,962
Norway	16,590	17,460	18,247	19,387	19,375	20,595	18,447	19,751	20,073
Portugal	27,425	40,819	42,607	44,835	46,203	39,091	35,808	35,368	36,658
Spain	192,596	220,822	233,230	241,788	258,875	242,983	211,895	210,068	215,825
Sweden	36,638	36,949	38,575	39,918	40,540	42,370	35,047	36,268	40,257
Switzerland	14,168	14,509	14,860	15,385	15,989	16,218	15,359	14,967	16,165
Turkey	152,163	156,853	166,831	177,399	181,330	181,935	176,455	193,561	196,155
United Kingdom	167,143	162,654	161,285	165,479	170,991	160,296	139,536	134,531	145,436
Eastern Europe									
Albania	2,530	2,798	3,210	3,306	3,584	4,098	4,445	4,727	5,050
Belarus	12,710	13,909	15,045	15,779	10,200	22,767	22,386	26,546	28,790
Bosnia-Herzegovina	221	483	671	854	1,241	1,230	1,081	1,250	1,289
Bulgaria	9,497	11,961	14,371	13,764	14,624	15,321	17,742	19,454	21,586
Croatia	8,241	8,819	9,328	10,175	10,502	11,042	9,429	8,780	9,496
Czech Republic	46,535	46,011	43,447	50,376	48,141	50,877	44,955	51,832	53,177
Estonia	6,428	6,837	7,641	8,857	10,660	8,279	6,296	5,986	7,241
Georgia	562	570	578	586	594	600	611	615	621
Hungary	18,208	20,608	25,152	30,479	35,805	35,759	35,373	33,721	34,320
Latvia	6,808	7,381	8,394	10,753	13,204	12,344	8,115	10,590	11,176
Lithuania	11,462	12,279	15,908	18,134	20,278	20,419	17,757	19,398	22,111
Macedonia	5,450	5,341	5,576	8,299	5,938	3,978	4,035	4,235	4,339
Moldova	1,577	2,161	2,405	2,567	2,743	2,966	2,714	3,232	3,772
Montenegro	71	65	61	73	91	139	179	167	196
Poland	85,989	102,807	111,826	128,315	150,879	164,930	180,742	210,846	232,336
Romania	30,854	37,220	51,531	57,288	59,524	56,386	34,269	25,889	40,431
Russia	173,146	182,141	193,597	198,766	205,849	216,276	180,136	199,000	212,775
Serbia	452	277	680	798	1,161	1,112	1,185	1,689	1,956
Slovakia	16,748	18,527	22,566	22,212	27,159	29,276	27,705	27,575	28,656
Slovenia	7,040	9,007	11,032	12,112	13,734	16,261	14,762	15,931	16,423
Ukraine	24,387	28,847	35,244	40,567	46,570	54,877	49,232	52,297	56,652

Source: Euromonitor International from national statistics

Passenger Cars: Average Annual Distance Travelled 1980, 1985, 1990, 1995, 1999-2011
Kilometres

	1980	1985	1990	1995	1999	2000	2001	2002
Western Europe								
Austria	11,500	10,866	16,276	15,928	15,899	15,899	15,856	17,016
Belgium	11,045	10,963	11,241	17,023	17,173	16,192	16,241	16,292
Cyprus								
Denmark	14,342	15,063	16,902	17,464	17,340	17,233	16,724	16,688
Finland	18,093	16,797	17,242	18,812	18,818	18,774	18,954	19,117
France		10,550	13,203	13,666	13,666	13,399	13,648	13,561
Germany			14,057	12,702	12,774	12,698	12,836	13,068
Gibraltar								
Greece	10,675				16,308	15,420	14,870	15,664
Iceland	12,325				13,150	12,691	13,760	14,049
Ireland	20,150	28,950	24,198	25,067	19,864	17,837	17,812	17,364
Italy				10,858	10,862	10,849	10,830	10,818
Liechtenstein								
Luxembourg	9,376	14,414	16,199	12,897	13,176	13,218	12,968	12,562
Malta								
Monaco				48				
Netherlands	13,588	14,027	15,642	15,855	16,011	15,911	17,734	19,523
Norway	18,436	14,904			15,242	15,180	14,717	15,006
Portugal		18,987	18,589	16,948	14,259	14,567	14,554	14,548
Spain	12,346	10,731	11,986	9,703	10,031	10,368	10,422	10,548
Sweden	15,675	15,166	15,498	15,671	15,149	14,919	14,992	15,326
Switzerland	14,274	13,934	14,286	13,571	13,469	13,557	13,364	13,256
Turkey	10,028	9,574	8,943	6,886	7,556	8,191	7,508	7,218
United Kingdom	15,616	14,341	17,090	16,195	15,884	15,348	15,237	15,725
Eastern Europe								
Albania								
Belarus				995	824	697	621	501
Bosnia-Herzegovina								
Bulgaria			9,777	8,029	8,531	8,586	8,326	8,391
Croatia					10,770	9,920	10,320	10,795
Czech Republic				8,064	9,065	9,113	8,990	9,180
Estonia				10,320	11,106	11,080	12,860	13,553
Georgia								
Hungary			9,239		7,023	6,766	6,565	6,009
Latvia				5,527	7,917	8,601	9,142	9,950
Lithuania								
Macedonia								
Moldova				1,085	628	619	631	732
Montenegro								
Poland	9,029	5,853	6,500	9,997	9,997	9,468	9,007	9,155
Romania			15,230	10,930	10,690	9,917	10,075	10,289
Russia				1,036	837	845	840	849
Serbia								
Slovakia				8,123	7,889	7,822	7,955	9,145
Slovenia			13,570	13,854	14,383	13,964	14,064	14,233
Ukraine					645	623	666	685

Source: Euromonitor International from national statistics

Passenger Cars: Average Annual Distance Travelled 1980, 1985, 1990, 1995, 1999-2011 *(continued)*

Kilometres

	2003	2004	2005	2006	2007	2008	2009	2010	2011
Western Europe									
Austria	17,060	17,071	17,204	17,244	17,528	17,659	17,514	17,339	16,988
Belgium	16,022	16,037	15,147	15,111	15,175	14,934	14,837	14,671	14,453
Cyprus		19,023	18,238	17,454	16,280	15,107	10,393	11,021	10,712
Denmark	16,878	17,139	16,699	16,417	16,475	16,110	16,074	15,622	15,195
Finland	18,839	18,673	18,314	17,921	17,725	16,772	16,547	16,146	15,713
France	13,496	13,337	13,088	12,926	12,905	12,718	12,717	12,740	12,655
Germany	12,833	13,011	12,545	12,538	14,265	14,179	13,998	13,831	13,676
Gibraltar									
Greece	16,025	16,473	16,159	16,145	15,575	15,368	15,894	16,211	16,330
Iceland	14,011	13,761	13,764	13,717	13,668	13,652	13,634	14,146	14,207
Ireland	17,276	17,003	16,828	16,311	16,118	16,200	16,253	17,407	17,537
Italy	10,811	10,970	10,801	10,798	10,795	10,794	10,865	10,888	10,884
Liechtenstein									
Luxembourg	12,296	12,348	12,441	12,614	12,666	12,719	12,319	12,230	12,047
Malta									
Monaco				3,363	3,379	3,300	3,169	3,098	3,013
Netherlands	19,402	18,864	18,304	18,036	17,770	16,695	16,457	16,003	15,336
Norway	15,082	14,630	14,150	14,332	14,965	14,889	14,541	14,178	13,763
Portugal	14,596	14,601	14,609	14,619	14,913	14,998	14,641	14,476	14,365
Spain	10,376	10,374	10,361	10,311	10,116	9,883	10,119	10,264	10,334
Sweden	15,348	15,309	15,212	14,986	15,121	14,877	14,819	14,730	14,540
Switzerland	13,193	13,123	13,069	13,028	12,945	13,020	13,181	13,050	12,873
Turkey	7,191	7,111	7,014	7,033	7,281	6,989	6,994	6,718	6,275
United Kingdom	15,544	15,619	16,057	16,266	16,282	16,072	16,367	16,812	17,588
Eastern Europe									
Albania									
Belarus	531	437	420	398	342	342	326	306	285
Bosnia-Herzegovina									
Bulgaria	8,700	8,856	8,345	8,936	8,167	7,025	6,684	6,598	6,396
Croatia	11,288	12,007	12,653	12,577	12,750	12,673	12,375	12,623	12,638
Czech Republic	9,368	9,320	9,391	10,536	11,128	11,604	11,684	11,957	11,894
Estonia	13,582	13,262	12,906	12,442	14,990	15,279	15,358	16,426	16,592
Georgia									
Hungary	6,193	6,859	7,650	8,314	8,604	8,894	8,860	9,023	9,120
Latvia	10,493	10,911	10,748	11,563	12,306	10,662	9,803	14,070	13,627
Lithuania	5,149	5,358	4,640	4,526	5,279	5,200	4,885	4,915	4,831
Macedonia									
Moldova	805	878	916	951	1,046	1,106	1,008	1,059	1,023
Montenegro									
Poland	9,897	9,989	10,370	9,982	9,544	9,010	9,307	9,097	8,873
Romania	10,155	10,004	9,933	9,459	9,011	8,663	8,970	9,048	9,127
Russia	851	852	854	854	855	855	845	839	805
Serbia									
Slovakia	8,445	7,734	8,796	8,238	7,932	7,632	6,765	6,865	6,624
Slovenia	14,287	14,392	14,294	14,319	14,644	14,514	14,843	15,068	15,123
Ukraine	759	838	864	870	893	839	719	700	706

Source: Euromonitor International from national statistics

Table 4.24

Road Network 2011

Kilometres

	Total	Motorway	National Highway	Secondary Regional	Other Local	% Paved	Density (km per sq km of land)	Motorway Intensity (% of total road network)
Western Europe								
Austria	112,980.0	1,700.0	9,988.0	23,677.0	77,615.0	100.0	1.4	1.5
Belgium	154,317.0	1,763.0	12,821.0	1,349.0	138,384.0	78.2	5.1	1.1
Cyprus	12,522.0	257.0	5,425.0	2,760.0	4,080.0	65.0	1.4	2.1
Denmark	74,334.0	1,133.0	601.0	9,948.0	62,652.0	100.0	1.8	1.5
Finland	78,162.0	789.0	12,659.0	13,453.0	51,261.0	65.7	0.3	1.0
France	1,054,344.0	11,464.0	9,736.0	378,239.0	654,905.0	100.0	1.9	1.1
Germany	643,716.0	12,857.0	39,592.0	178,267.0	413,000.0	100.0	1.8	2.0
Gibraltar	117.0						11.7	
Greece	117,037.0	1,270.0	9,288.0	31,628.0	74,851.0	95.1	0.9	1.1
Iceland	12,793.0		5,189.0	2,529.0	5,075.0	38.7	0.1	
Ireland	96,848.0	806.0	5,502.0	11,630.0	78,910.0	100.0	1.4	0.8
Italy	500,337.0	6,671.0	18,350.0	162,430.0	312,886.0	100.0	1.7	1.3
Liechtenstein	377.0		117.0	260.0		100.0	2.4	
Luxembourg	5,231.0	153.0	837.0	1,891.0	2,350.0	100.0	2.0	2.9
Malta	3,096.0		185.0		2,911.0	87.5	9.7	
Monaco	77.0					100.0	38.5	
Netherlands	137,660.0	2,657.0	2,469.0	7,855.0	124,680.0	90.0	4.1	1.9
Norway	93,896.0	376.0	27,544.0	27,355.0	38,621.0	80.8	0.3	0.4
Portugal	84,441.0	2,799.0	13,320.0	4,422.0	63,900.0	86.0	0.9	3.3
Spain	663,494.0	14,351.0	15,235.0	134,986.0	498,922.0	99.0	1.3	2.2
Sweden	627,139.0	1,921.0	15,353.0	83,161.0	507,985.0	23.4	1.5	0.3
Switzerland	71,495.0	1,419.0	381.0	18,019.0	51,676.0	100.0	1.8	2.0
Turkey	367,249.0	2,082.0	31,248.0	31,111.0	302,808.0	89.6	0.5	0.6
United Kingdom	419,677.0	3,676.0	9,779.0	39,265.0	366,957.0	100.0	1.7	0.9
Eastern Europe								
Albania	18,185.0		3,786.0	3,892.0	10,507.0	73.7	0.7	
Belarus	98,653.8		15,150.3	71,664.5	11,839.0	86.5	0.5	
Bosnia-Herzegovina	21,846.0	40.0	2,042.0	2,535.0	17,229.0	52.3	0.4	0.2
Bulgaria	40,374.0	440.0	2,969.0	4,032.0	32,933.0	98.6	0.4	1.1
Croatia	29,383.0	1,154.0	6,891.0	11,001.0	10,337.0	92.1	0.5	3.9
Czech Republic	130,700.0	747.0	6,266.0	48,768.0	74,919.0	100.0	1.7	0.6
Estonia	58,625.0	101.0	4,021.0	12,423.0	42,080.0	28.8	1.4	0.2
Georgia	20,389.0		1,499.0	3,355.0	15,535.0	94.1	0.3	
Hungary	198,701.0	1,437.0	29,734.0	76,757.0	90,773.0	38.0	2.2	0.7
Latvia	68,966.0		6,969.0	13,177.0	48,820.0	85.6	1.1	
Lithuania	82,367.0	309.0	6,364.0	14,585.0	61,109.0	88.0	1.3	0.4
Macedonia	14,213.0	263.0	911.0	3,771.0	9,268.0	58.2	0.6	1.9
Moldova	12,783.0		3,337.0	6,008.0	3,438.0	85.8	0.4	
Montenegro	7,823.0					69.3	0.6	
Poland	409,966.0	889.0	17,729.0	154,437.0	236,911.0	67.4	1.3	0.2
Romania	214,458.0	341.0	25,800.0	56,620.0	131,697.0	56.1	0.9	0.2
Russia	1,012,200.0	28,833.0	804,500.0	178,867.0		80.1	0.1	2.8
Serbia	45,023.0	539.0	5,079.0	10,390.0	29,015.0	67.8	0.5	1.2
Slovakia	43,912.0	408.0	3,545.0	3,608.0	36,351.0	87.1	0.9	0.9
Slovenia	39,036.0	825.0	770.0	5,199.0	32,242.0	100.0	1.9	2.1
Ukraine	169,509.0	15.0	21,181.0	78,852.0	69,461.0	97.9	0.3	0.0

Source: Euromonitor International from national statistics

5

Banking and Finance

Banking and Finance Statistics

Table 5.1

Private Sector Bank Claims 1980, 1985, 1990, 1995, 1999-2011

National currency billion / US$ billion

	1980	1985	1990	1995	1999	2000	2001	2002	2003
Western Europe									
Austria	54.8	83.7	122.3	162.0	197.1	213.0	224.1	229.5	234.9
Belgium	53.0	66.5	126.5	151.2	192.3	196.6	197.3	198.9	203.8
Cyprus	0.9	1.7	4.9	9.9	16.3	18.1	19.9	20.4	21.7
Denmark	94.0	190.4	429.2	312.9	420.6	1,749.3	1,902.2	1,996.8	2,123.2
Finland	15.2	34.2	75.7	58.9	65.0	70.1	77.8	83.8	93.4
France	321.2	555.8	969.3	1,028.3	1,115.3	1,225.2	1,314.3	1,325.9	1,407.6
Germany	649.8	889.9	1,250.7	1,856.4	2,326.4	2,445.7	2,497.1	2,505.8	2,497.4
Gibraltar									
Greece	2.6	7.0	14.2	26.8	52.0	63.9	83.1	94.5	110.4
Iceland	4.3	46.9	157.1	209.0	461.0	663.6	772.5	858.9	1,097.2
Ireland	5.5	10.4	17.3	37.0	91.8	110.7	129.1	142.4	160.2
Italy	111.2	212.5	385.2	530.8	788.2	896.8	966.6	1,030.8	1,110.8
Liechtenstein									
Luxembourg	4.0	5.6	11.1	13.0	19.8	22.5	29.1	24.9	26.5
Malta	0.3	0.6	1.3	2.6	3.9	4.3	4.6	4.7	4.4
Monaco									
Netherlands	102.0	122.9	193.8	284.4	484.0	560.8	605.7	656.6	705.8
Norway	96.8	241.3	461.7	527.5	849.7	969.6	1,075.5	1,144.6	1,232.5
Portugal	5.4	14.3	24.9	55.6	129.3	160.5	179.2	190.8	194.0
Spain	71.5	118.8	250.3	323.1	519.6	615.9	688.5	770.9	886.2
Sweden	219.2	340.6	791.2	596.7	848.4	958.7	2,298.0	2,421.7	2,540.3
Switzerland	195.8	335.2	532.8	611.7	676.5	668.9	660.9	662.9	687.0
Turkey	0.0	0.0	0.1	1.4	17.4	29.6	36.9	50.9	66.2
United Kingdom	63.7	167.4	645.3	829.1	1,094.4	1,254.3	1,367.8	1,479.4	1,624.6
Eastern Europe									
Albania				8.3	18.2	24.4	34.9	39.5	51.9
Belarus				7.4	279.7	802.5	1,400.8	2,364.1	4,283.5
Bosnia-Herzegovina					4.1	4.4	3.3	4.2	5.1
Bulgaria				0.4	2.9	3.4	4.4	6.3	9.4
Croatia				30.7	52.7	56.8	69.7	91.0	104.7
Czech Republic				1,036.6	1,098.5	1,029.9	916.4	720.6	782.5
Estonia				0.5	1.7	2.2	2.7	3.5	4.4
Georgia				0.1	0.3	0.4	0.5	0.6	0.7
Hungary		208.6	971.3	1,263.2	2,968.0	4,247.6	5,025.9	5,989.2	7,988.9
Latvia				0.2	0.7	0.9	1.4	1.9	2.6
Lithuania				3.9	6.3	6.0	6.6	8.4	13.0
Macedonia				39.2	43.6	42.2	41.2	43.1	47.2
Moldova				0.4	1.5	2.0	2.8	3.9	5.6
Montenegro								0.1	0.2
Poland	0.0	0.6	11.8	56.9	169.8	197.8	212.6	221.8	236.7
Romania	0.0	0.0	0.1		4.4	5.8	10.2	15.4	27.1
Russia				133.8	631.1	969.4	1,473.1	1,915.1	2,772.5
Serbia					59.2	188.7	257.6	167.9	216.7
Slovakia				5.5	10.4	11.3	8.8	10.2	9.1
Slovenia				4.1	7.0	7.8	8.7	9.5	10.7
Ukraine				0.8	11.0	18.8	26.6	39.8	65.6

Source: Euromonitor International from national statistics

Private Sector Bank Claims 1980, 1985, 1990, 1995, 1999-2011 *(continued)*

National currency billion / US$ billion

	2004	2005	2006	2007	2008	2009	2010	2011	US$ billion 2011
Western Europe									
Austria	247.7	282.5	298.8	313.9	337.7	345.5	347.7	357.6	497.16
Belgium	207.4	223.8	261.5	305.2	325.3	332.1	336.2	342.5	476.22
Cyprus	23.4	25.0	27.5	34.0	43.6	45.7	49.5	53.0	73.66
Denmark	2,318.4	2,654.0	3,029.2	3,432.5	3,791.9	3,703.3	3,897.2	4,114.2	767.60
Finland	102.9	118.1	130.6	146.6	159.6	161.5	170.4	182.6	253.91
France	1,499.8	1,591.8	1,769.2	1,991.3	2,102.0	2,102.9	2,211.3	2,318.8	3,224.19
Germany	2,479.7	2,504.6	2,536.1	2,556.0	2,686.9	2,692.9	2,669.2	2,709.4	3,767.25
Gibraltar									
Greece	129.7	153.4	177.5	209.3	226.8	217.5	263.2	253.8	352.83
Iceland	1,531.3	2,542.8	3,733.2	5,205.1	5,941.0	6,696.2	7,419.2	7,880.0	67.96
Ireland	200.3	260.7	321.8	377.7	396.5	376.7	335.5	324.8	451.56
Italy	1,178.9	1,271.5	1,403.1	1,555.9	1,646.2	1,682.1	1,903.4	1,930.3	2,683.98
Liechtenstein									
Luxembourg	29.1	39.1	52.5	69.3	72.4	70.0	74.6	72.7	101.07
Malta	4.7	5.1	5.8	6.3	7.3	7.8	8.2	8.5	11.88
Monaco									
Netherlands	775.2	847.3	903.2	1,075.3	1,148.3	1,227.6	1,172.7	1,192.1	1,657.58
Norway	1,354.1	1,583.5	1,879.2	2,027.1	2,176.6	2,308.4	2,442.1	2,512.4	448.17
Portugal	202.7	216.9	244.2	275.0	298.6	314.6	329.5	328.6	456.84
Spain	1,050.4	1,324.4	1,645.7	1,978.0	2,205.5	2,219.1	2,244.2	2,184.1	3,036.84
Sweden	2,696.3	2,986.9	3,321.5	3,797.3	4,090.1	4,220.5	4,433.8	4,572.9	704.02
Switzerland	716.8	762.3	831.6	904.8	896.2	935.4	961.4	993.7	1,118.87
Turkey	96.6	144.4	196.7	248.7	309.8	321.8	353.4	372.9	222.02
United Kingdom	1,807.6	1,994.9	2,256.2	2,625.9	3,030.3	2,973.2	2,965.6	2,831.2	4,537.12
Eastern Europe									
Albania	71.1	123.6	194.7	288.9	381.8	411.0	458.5	491.5	4.87
Belarus	6,928.0	10,063.7	15,437.8	22,988.5	35,331.2	46,097.6	52,364.7	56,980.6	11.45
Bosnia-Herzegovina	5.9	7.5	9.2	11.8	14.3	13.7	14.1	14.8	10.53
Bulgaria	14.0	18.6	23.2	37.7	49.6	50.2	55.3	59.3	42.16
Croatia	119.9	140.1	172.2	198.2	222.2	220.1	234.2	249.7	46.72
Czech Republic	886.8	1,076.9	1,312.9	1,686.4	1,937.9	1,957.5	2,107.4	2,306.0	130.31
Estonia	5.9	7.8	11.1	14.7	15.6	14.9	14.1	14.9	20.66
Georgia	1.0	1.7	2.7	4.8	6.3	5.5	6.2	6.4	3.79
Hungary	9,480.0	11,271.3	13,152.2	15,624.5	18,518.2	17,886.9	19,063.9	20,541.9	102.17
Latvia	3.8	6.2	9.8	13.1	14.7	14.0	15.4	16.1	31.90
Lithuania	18.0	29.5	41.4	59.2	69.9	65.3	71.9	75.7	30.49
Macedonia	58.6	70.9	92.7	129.0	173.1	175.5	191.8	204.2	4.62
Moldova	6.8	8.9	12.3	19.7	22.9	21.3	23.3	24.7	2.11
Montenegro	0.2	0.3	0.8	2.2	2.7	2.3	2.1	1.8	2.51
Poland	260.1	284.4	352.8	464.1	633.1	647.8	702.0	745.7	251.63
Romania	38.6	57.5	89.1	144.7	193.9	195.9	217.9	234.0	76.77
Russia	4,109.0	5,557.6	8,312.0	12,539.9	17,100.2	17,164.3	18,992.0	20,327.0	691.58
Serbia	316.8	487.4	571.5	801.1	1,069.7	1,166.2	1,285.1	1,374.3	18.74
Slovakia	10.1	13.5	17.2	23.2	27.4	30.5	33.3	37.4	51.95
Slovenia	13.1	16.2	20.5	27.2	31.8	32.8	33.4	32.6	45.27
Ukraine	86.7	142.0	241.2	419.0	700.0	685.1	768.8	834.8	104.71

Source: Euromonitor International from national statistics

Banking and Finance Statistics | **Table 5.2**

Deposit Money Bank Assets 1980, 1985, 1990, 1995, 1999-2011

US$ billion

	1980	1985	1990	1995	1999	2000	2001	2002
Western Europe								
Austria	21.71	36.75	65.99	92.04	62.99	69.68	74.78	91.22
Belgium	60.77	92.67	192.03	273.06	112.05	108.17	126.96	164.25
Cyprus	0.05	0.12	2.53	5.34	11.97	15.96	16.37	14.49
Denmark	4.83	14.16	45.55	56.59	68.43	70.56	60.06	71.59
Finland	2.76	7.67	27.00	24.17	15.72	19.91	35.26	41.88
France	160.21	184.38	455.78	705.08	430.98	435.49	447.01	538.48
Germany	85.17	112.93	395.49	578.20	513.97	579.53	641.34	774.43
Gibraltar								
Greece	1.19	1.98	3.46	8.96	13.85	12.63	16.39	21.77
Iceland	0.03	0.06	0.13	0.09	0.22	0.27	0.32	0.57
Ireland	8.78	3.21	13.45	46.68	78.11	135.34	173.20	236.53
Italy	35.09	50.44	102.73	145.84	90.84	85.89	75.04	94.26
Liechtenstein								
Luxembourg	104.83	130.95	355.12	504.84	178.65	174.95	207.51	237.00
Malta	0.16	0.21	0.96	2.24	6.81	8.60	6.89	9.42
Monaco								
Netherlands	62.63	72.88	185.92	234.14	155.62	163.90	211.40	256.24
Norway	0.63	3.64	7.82	7.47	12.42	15.28	15.09	17.64
Portugal	1.13	1.43	6.16	35.92	25.17	29.90	26.87	28.93
Spain	12.79	20.04	39.11	146.06	61.25	77.37	82.00	95.10
Sweden	8.04	8.94	34.92	36.16	53.09	67.36	62.01	72.53
Switzerland	66.45	85.24	153.25	212.37	463.67	465.83	446.49	557.85
Turkey	0.55	2.01	5.51	10.97	16.07	18.18	13.33	13.59
United Kingdom	356.32	590.07	1,068.96	1,350.86	1,802.43	2,059.96	2,168.52	2,477.29
Eastern Europe								
Albania							0.61	0.61
Belarus				0.29	0.34	0.33	0.30	0.26
Bosnia-Herzegovina					0.58	0.59	0.61	0.79
Bulgaria				1.06	1.49	1.94	2.10	2.02
Croatia				1.75	1.62	2.42	3.93	3.64
Czech Republic				3.78	13.30	13.26	15.61	14.64
Estonia				0.32	0.56	0.62	0.87	1.10
Georgia				0.03	0.05	0.05	0.08	0.10
Hungary		0.34	1.16	0.92	3.59	2.74	4.44	4.36
Latvia				0.60	1.49	2.11	2.27	3.02
Lithuania				0.12	0.42	0.69	0.75	0.72
Macedonia				0.25	0.40	0.43	0.64	0.56
Moldova							0.06	0.08
Montenegro						0.10	0.12	0.09
Poland	1.48	2.30	6.09	7.15	7.87	11.32	15.31	13.71
Romania	0.26	1.00	0.68	0.07	0.09	0.10	1.61	1.19
Russia				10.01	14.37	17.57	18.20	19.06
Serbia					0.77	0.82	0.98	0.74
Slovakia				1.82	1.62	2.35	2.39	2.05
Slovenia				2.40	1.81	2.01	3.27	2.26
Ukraine				1.04	0.85	0.92	0.77	0.85

Source: Euromonitor International from national statistics

Deposit Money Bank Assets 1980, 1985, 1990, 1995, 1999-2011 *(continued)*

US$ billion

	2003	2004	2005	2006	2007	2008	2009	2010	2011
Western Europe									
Austria	122.77	157.55	167.08	228.71	296.68	303.34	281.84	315.66	337.40
Belgium	194.31	236.40	274.52	314.10	399.43	331.54	287.77	354.98	365.20
Cyprus	17.72	23.85	33.10	49.06	69.22	48.96	56.54	42.81	42.90
Denmark	103.18	128.55	134.42	177.44	252.82	247.49	227.43	248.44	266.19
Finland	51.76	66.70	61.33	82.53	98.95	101.32	114.77	115.08	123.22
France	635.90	829.48	1,003.06	1,268.93	1,478.58	1,288.90	1,299.44	1,455.01	1,501.53
Germany	1,018.88	1,223.06	1,172.69	1,544.88	1,972.33	1,780.81	1,571.61	1,676.21	1,709.04
Gibraltar									
Greece	32.37	39.51	41.06	62.81	94.20	117.10	138.09	139.98	159.27
Iceland	1.59	2.86	8.55	18.58	19.13	21.74	23.31	25.40	27.11
Ireland	324.81	433.63	509.69	747.61	991.46	957.94	958.49	902.36	941.04
Italy	117.86	122.63	110.30	140.81	156.31	128.90	141.27	145.39	146.54
Liechtenstein									
Luxembourg	301.44	332.05	355.16	471.20	594.55	548.11	550.12	611.22	646.22
Malta	12.94	16.75	20.74	27.95	40.34	35.45	34.05	38.27	36.13
Monaco									
Netherlands	308.25	376.87	413.18	576.25	749.83	579.51	555.16	659.05	679.75
Norway	28.59	25.18	34.06	63.11	63.02	78.13	71.08	81.98	86.70
Portugal	34.88	37.67	36.83	46.10	49.35	44.23	49.36	45.08	44.82
Spain	101.13	153.24	167.65	226.89	293.58	276.02	276.57	271.81	283.05
Sweden	102.26	157.44	160.90	229.17	303.92	299.71	310.96	331.29	356.82
Switzerland	616.29	680.72	709.24	803.01	1,116.56	834.81	739.49	756.17	761.18
Turkey	14.55	21.01	23.47	37.47	43.99	52.27	45.92	35.19	38.78
United Kingdom	3,023.60	3,643.33	3,937.75	4,914.15	5,520.27	5,930.38	5,425.22	6,156.19	6,466.71
Eastern Europe									
Albania	0.73	0.91	0.86	1.17	1.27	0.98	0.90	1.19	1.67
Belarus	0.33	0.46	0.69	0.43	1.24	0.99	1.43	1.49	2.28
Bosnia-Herzegovina	1.01	1.33	1.26	1.57	2.67	2.20	2.19	1.92	2.01
Bulgaria	1.94	3.13	3.27	5.57	5.91	5.51	5.64	6.14	6.28
Croatia	5.78	7.78	5.77	7.19	9.41	9.80	9.82	8.55	6.90
Czech Republic	15.32	20.53	24.10	27.07	38.35	36.00	35.14	38.19	40.97
Estonia	1.38	2.49	3.47	3.66	5.93	5.51	6.27	6.33	7.00
Georgia	0.12	0.16	0.16	0.23	0.45	0.71	0.60	0.88	0.55
Hungary	5.94	7.20	6.97	12.43	17.04	19.86	21.66	21.79	24.13
Latvia	4.04	5.78	5.63	6.68	11.17	9.73	9.91	9.70	10.46
Lithuania	0.93	1.86	2.54	3.75	5.03	4.49	5.91	5.96	6.51
Macedonia	0.67	0.82	0.73	0.86	0.92	0.55	0.72	0.76	0.78
Moldova	0.11	0.10	0.15	0.25	0.21	0.25	0.44	0.38	0.30
Montenegro	0.07	0.08	0.20	0.37	0.50	0.35	0.47	0.53	0.59
Poland	14.92	24.96	25.51	29.54	29.93	20.39	15.27	17.03	13.91
Romania	1.08	1.81	1.45	1.81	2.47	2.43	4.94	4.83	5.58
Russia	20.68	25.52	38.02	62.55	93.53	159.35	160.37	169.33	210.50
Serbia	1.09	1.12	0.93	0.93	2.07	1.91	2.42	2.83	1.56
Slovakia	2.33	2.87	3.03	3.94	5.93	6.69	4.94	4.39	3.75
Slovenia	2.58	2.89	4.19	6.51	6.12	6.22	6.33	5.66	5.22
Ukraine	1.36	2.30	2.83	4.07	6.06	7.49	10.19	11.56	13.24

Source: Euromonitor International from national statistics

Banking and Finance

5

Banking and Finance Statistics   **Table 5.3**

Deposit Money Bank Liabilities 1980, 1985, 1990, 1995, 1999-2011

US$ billion

	1980	1985	1990	1995	1999	2000	2001	2002
Western Europe								
Austria	24.95	38.03	74.31	99.15	49.42	49.93	58.52	56.53
Belgium	72.95	112.93	239.79	302.86	181.82	163.88	176.33	199.01
Cyprus	0.18	0.41	3.24	6.00	13.33	17.14	17.84	16.76
Denmark	4.88	14.85	44.80	33.25	63.34	62.55	58.81	75.60
Finland	4.57	12.81	59.91	29.27	9.37	15.47	28.04	26.34
France	146.68	197.18	519.81	662.47	337.03	384.58	399.22	464.83
Germany	72.09	75.77	226.37	482.24	491.34	559.07	571.75	629.90
Gibraltar								
Greece	5.15	7.59	16.46	34.29	41.73	39.65	9.64	18.56
Iceland	0.18	0.42	0.71	0.42	1.99	2.65	2.50	2.81
Ireland	10.72	6.32	17.74	49.10	77.73	141.51	191.25	255.23
Italy	51.41	72.83	205.38	216.81	136.37	146.78	150.86	153.43
Liechtenstein								
Luxembourg	98.45	117.21	308.09	434.11	164.24	159.29	163.50	173.27
Malta	0.02	0.07	0.49	1.58	6.34	7.91	6.16	8.36
Monaco								
Netherlands	64.35	65.68	153.43	220.96	194.07	206.13	250.06	305.75
Norway	2.74	9.16	22.17	9.62	31.82	37.02	39.76	52.76
Portugal	0.81	1.64	5.78	32.43	31.35	47.62	50.01	62.15
Spain	24.50	20.94	63.99	109.25	125.66	147.33	157.56	176.27
Sweden	12.52	17.20	99.36	55.10	76.77	102.35	78.87	91.64
Switzerland	47.95	63.40	133.57	184.87	395.02	440.01	415.25	498.61
Turkey	0.70	3.06	4.46	6.11	20.10	25.17	11.74	11.17
United Kingdom	377.71	625.74	1,201.03	1,429.20	1,871.71	2,160.04	2,305.83	2,684.13
Eastern Europe								
Albania							0.09	0.11
Belarus				0.12	0.12	0.11	0.19	0.27
Bosnia-Herzegovina					1.69	1.59	0.69	0.96
Bulgaria				0.58	0.17	0.26	0.31	0.47
Croatia				2.85	2.25	2.18	2.62	4.90
Czech Republic				6.43	9.68	8.42	7.71	7.66
Estonia				0.14	0.88	0.98	0.99	1.58
Georgia				0.05	0.05	0.06	0.07	0.09
Hungary		1.20	1.69	2.88	5.58	5.51	5.97	7.43
Latvia				0.45	1.77	2.14	2.65	3.74
Lithuania				0.09	0.54	0.52	0.62	0.85
Macedonia				0.08	0.26	0.23	0.20	0.21
Moldova							0.05	0.05
Montenegro						0.20	0.21	0.02
Poland	25.32	26.68	1.92	2.07	6.75	6.61	7.77	9.07
Romania	8.38	6.05	1.72	0.82	0.61	0.51	0.66	1.00
Russia				6.90	10.05	11.09	12.94	14.77
Serbia					2.98	2.86	3.07	0.29
Slovakia				0.98	0.64	0.64	0.84	1.50
Slovenia				1.48	1.44	1.57	1.76	2.79
Ukraine				0.30	0.34	0.46	0.65	0.74

Source: Euromonitor International from national statistics

Deposit Money Bank Liabilities 1980, 1985, 1990, 1995, 1999-2011 *(continued)*
US$ billion

	2003	2004	2005	2006	2007	2008	2009	2010	2011
Western Europe									
Austria	70.38	81.78	85.74	103.95	114.25	106.65	110.75	114.93	117.67
Belgium	236.31	274.68	328.34	350.61	477.40	332.58	317.80	402.84	415.89
Cyprus	19.37	25.24	24.63	33.72	52.69	33.41	39.18	38.68	40.65
Denmark	110.79	129.87	128.69	165.11	239.00	213.75	210.99	226.20	241.48
Finland	25.27	34.95	39.52	48.61	69.02	82.53	98.79	99.50	112.22
France	547.13	701.86	899.66	1,237.77	1,611.18	1,380.99	1,400.73	1,590.88	1,679.16
Germany	719.20	787.91	740.01	842.36	974.61	928.19	860.76	889.44	901.21
Gibraltar									
Greece	27.72	44.53	53.22	76.86	115.46	103.53	102.65	116.12	125.93
Iceland	3.05	3.66	5.34	9.50	30.63	34.80	38.28	41.18	43.82
Ireland	338.47	428.83	487.80	696.75	918.17	871.00	884.31	832.54	866.49
Italy	201.52	214.47	212.37	253.35	310.24	270.40	271.96	282.28	289.51
Liechtenstein									
Luxembourg	198.97	221.67	235.53	284.00	332.35	292.49	227.67	302.72	307.40
Malta	10.92	14.27	18.40	24.70	35.82	24.57	25.29	28.19	26.86
Monaco									
Netherlands	328.22	392.49	427.83	564.21	717.98	624.57	559.71	651.57	673.41
Norway	69.46	76.04	93.24	140.23	141.55	168.59	155.49	173.93	178.15
Portugal	84.36	93.12	86.53	120.58	135.43	111.25	118.79	114.20	112.60
Spain	231.74	244.31	241.05	257.68	311.49	375.67	388.50	386.25	418.40
Sweden	109.49	157.60	139.93	184.51	196.71	228.79	217.40	228.28	239.22
Switzerland	546.82	608.31	634.71	717.63	1,044.11	810.24	752.44	769.05	841.47
Turkey	15.58	21.34	36.19	46.13	55.82	57.33	54.47	84.98	97.27
United Kingdom	3,276.43	4,033.35	4,251.40	5,254.85	5,929.43	6,346.03	5,815.75	6,586.58	6,753.04
Eastern Europe									
Albania	0.15	0.15	0.16	0.40	0.53	0.92	0.59	0.36	0.43
Belarus	0.40	0.62	0.85	1.38	2.48	2.36	3.55	5.73	5.99
Bosnia-Herzegovina	1.57	1.85	2.15	2.72	3.88	4.49	4.23	3.27	3.41
Bulgaria	0.96	3.38	3.22	4.25	8.87	13.27	12.61	12.72	14.84
Croatia	8.16	10.99	10.88	13.74	13.21	14.98	15.96	15.07	15.80
Czech Republic	10.09	10.27	9.79	12.05	19.69	22.70	19.65	21.92	24.39
Estonia	2.81	3.07	4.50	7.08	12.72	13.65	16.02	16.38	18.71
Georgia	0.10	0.14	0.32	0.56	1.31	1.86	1.49	1.59	2.02
Hungary	12.50	16.39	19.00	25.80	34.60	47.68	49.13	49.40	55.30
Latvia	5.30	8.06	10.00	15.68	25.66	25.79	22.85	23.06	24.90
Lithuania	1.88	2.81	5.07	8.14	13.83	17.15	16.24	17.41	19.73
Macedonia	0.20	0.24	0.28	0.37	0.57	0.55	0.68	0.78	0.74
Moldova	0.06	0.07	0.08	0.15	0.35	0.55	0.44	0.40	0.53
Montenegro	0.05	0.11	0.15	0.42	1.18	1.75	1.50	1.24	1.04
Poland	12.64	13.72	12.65	19.68	37.93	58.55	62.41	57.54	67.00
Romania	2.22	4.98	8.15	16.42	29.90	36.73	33.83	38.06	43.47
Russia	24.51	34.22	52.25	105.31	168.51	170.58	129.99	146.55	161.16
Serbia	0.43	1.44	2.65	5.13	5.58	5.56	7.49	7.69	6.77
Slovakia	3.15	5.83	10.01	7.09	13.23	17.02	2.38	2.66	2.91
Slovenia	4.59	6.26	9.75	14.02	4.54	3.62	3.23	3.14	2.65
Ukraine	1.63	2.25	5.24	12.83	28.61	36.86	28.86	24.83	23.81

Source: Euromonitor International from national statistics

Banking and Finance

5

Banking and Finance Statistics   **Table 5.4**

Annual Lending Rates 1980, 1985, 1990, 1995, 1999-2011

% per annum

	1980	1985	1990	1995	1999	2000	2001	2002
Western Europe								
Austria					5.64	6.33		
Belgium		12.54	13.00	8.42	6.71	7.98	8.46	7.71
Cyprus	9.00	9.00	9.00	8.50	8.00	8.00	7.52	7.15
Denmark								
Finland	9.77	10.41	11.62	7.75	4.71	5.61	5.79	4.82
France								
Germany								
Gibraltar								
Greece								
Iceland	45.00	32.60	16.18	11.58	13.30	16.80	17.95	15.37
Ireland	15.96	12.44	11.29	6.56	3.34	4.77	4.84	3.83
Italy	19.03	18.06	14.85	13.24	6.35	7.02	7.29	6.54
Liechtenstein								
Luxembourg								
Malta	8.00	8.00	8.50	7.38	7.70	7.28	6.90	6.04
Monaco								
Netherlands	13.50	9.25	11.75	7.21	3.46	4.79	5.00	3.96
Norway	13.00	13.41	14.15	7.60	7.61	8.93	8.69	8.71
Portugal								
Spain								
Sweden	15.18	16.89	16.69	11.11	5.53	5.83	5.55	5.64
Switzerland		5.49	7.42	5.48	3.90	4.29	4.30	3.93
Turkey	25.67	53.50		88.00	82.00	33.00		
United Kingdom	16.17	12.33	14.75	6.69	5.33	5.98	5.08	4.00
Eastern Europe								
Albania				19.65	21.62	22.10	19.65	15.30
Belarus				175.00	51.04	67.67	46.97	36.88
Bosnia-Herzegovina					24.29	30.50	30.99	12.70
Bulgaria				79.36	13.50	11.34	11.11	9.21
Croatia				20.24	14.94	12.07	9.55	12.84
Czech Republic				12.80	8.68	7.16	7.20	6.72
Estonia				19.01	11.09	7.43	7.78	6.70
Georgia				85.62	33.42	32.75	27.25	31.83
Hungary			28.78	32.61	16.34	12.60	12.12	10.17
Latvia				34.56	14.20	11.87	11.17	7.97
Lithuania				27.08	13.09	12.14	9.63	6.84
Macedonia				45.95	20.45	18.93	19.35	18.36
Moldova				39.60	35.54	33.78	28.69	23.52
Montenegro								
Poland	10.23	15.34	644.50	33.45	16.94	20.01	18.36	12.03
Romania				50.72	65.64	53.85	45.40	35.43
Russia				320.31	39.72	24.43	17.91	15.70
Serbia					46.06	6.30	34.50	19.71
Slovakia				16.85	21.07	14.89	11.24	10.25
Slovenia				23.36	12.38	15.77	15.05	13.17
Ukraine				122.70	54.95	41.53	32.28	25.35

Source: Euromonitor International from national statistics

Banking and Finance Statistics

Annual Lending Rates 1980, 1985, 1990, 1995, 1999-2011 *(continued)*

% per annum

	2003	2004	2005	2006	2007	2008	2009	2010	2011
Western Europe									
Austria	5.50	5.28	5.00	5.51	6.30	6.82	5.00	4.23	3.91
Belgium	6.89	6.70	6.72	7.49	8.57	9.21	9.50	6.42	6.15
Cyprus	6.95	7.57	7.09	6.69	6.74	6.22	6.05	5.84	5.63
Denmark									
Finland	4.13	3.69	3.70	4.52	6.13	6.43	3.27	3.13	2.79
France									
Germany									
Gibraltar									
Greece									
Iceland	11.95	12.02	14.78	17.91	19.29	20.14	18.99	10.26	7.70
Ireland	2.85	2.57	2.65	3.02	3.75	3.45	1.49	1.31	1.20
Italy	5.83	5.51	5.31	5.62	6.33	6.84	4.76	4.03	4.60
Liechtenstein									
Luxembourg									
Malta	5.85	5.32	5.51	5.65	6.24	5.89	4.47	4.60	4.75
Monaco									
Netherlands	3.00	2.75	2.77	3.54	4.60	4.60	1.98	1.75	2.00
Norway	4.73	4.04	4.04	4.70	6.65	7.28	4.28	4.42	4.35
Portugal									
Spain									
Sweden	4.79	4.00	3.31	4.05	5.49	5.75	2.93	2.81	2.50
Switzerland	3.27	3.20	3.12	3.03	3.15	3.34	2.75	2.73	2.72
Turkey									
United Kingdom	3.69	4.40	4.65	4.65	5.52	4.63	0.63	0.50	0.50
Eastern Europe									
Albania	14.27	11.76	13.08	12.94	14.10	13.02	12.66	12.82	12.43
Belarus	23.98	16.91	11.30	0.04	8.58	8.55	11.68	9.22	13.58
Bosnia-Herzegovina	10.87	10.28	9.61	8.01	7.17	6.98	7.93	7.89	7.43
Bulgaria	8.54	8.87	8.66	8.89	10.00	10.86	11.34	11.14	10.63
Croatia	11.58	11.75	11.19	9.93	9.33	10.07	11.55	10.38	9.68
Czech Republic	5.95	6.03	5.78	5.59	5.79	6.25	5.99	5.89	5.72
Estonia	5.51	5.66	4.93	5.03	6.46	8.55	9.39	7.76	6.12
Georgia	32.27	31.23	21.63	18.75	20.41	21.24	25.52	24.21	25.87
Hungary	9.60	12.82	8.54	8.08	9.09	10.18	11.04	7.59	8.32
Latvia	5.38	7.45	6.11	7.29	10.91	11.85	16.23	9.56	6.39
Lithuania	5.84	5.74	5.27	5.11	6.86	8.41	8.39	5.99	6.22
Macedonia	16.00	12.44	12.13	11.29	10.23	9.68	10.07	9.48	8.87
Moldova	19.29	20.94	19.26	18.13	18.83	21.06	20.54	16.36	14.44
Montenegro			12.11	11.15	9.20	9.24	9.36	9.53	9.69
Poland	7.30	7.56	6.83	5.48	5.68	6.13	5.87	5.74	5.81
Romania	25.44	25.61	19.60	13.98	13.35	14.99	17.28	14.07	12.13
Russia	12.98	11.44	10.68	10.43	10.03	12.23	15.31	10.82	8.46
Serbia	15.48	15.53	16.83	16.56	11.13	16.13	11.78	17.30	17.17
Slovakia	8.46	9.07	6.68	7.67	7.99	5.76	4.01	3.39	3.03
Slovenia	10.75	8.65	7.80	7.41	5.91	6.66	5.95	5.80	5.40
Ukraine	17.89	17.40	16.17	15.17	13.90	17.49	20.86	15.87	15.95

Source: Euromonitor International from national statistics

Banking and Finance Statistics

Table 5.5

Deposit Money Bank Reserves 1980, 1985, 1990, 1995, 1999-2011

National currency million

	1980	1985	1990	1995	1999	2000	2001	2002
Western Europe								
Austria	3,151.82	4,023.47	4,494.33	5,374.78	3,305.00	3,878.00	7,975.00	3,729.00
Belgium	520.58	545.37	629.65	939.52	3,509.00	7,130.00	5,945.00	4,482.00
Cyprus	61.06	146.32	306.97	344.10	425.00	472.88	582.63	898.49
Denmark	1,138.00	25,797.00	8,704.00	39,573.40	96,258.00	23,816.00	17,368.00	32,474.00
Finland	667.84	2,044.96	3,767.45	7,732.63	4,884.00	2,475.00	4,111.00	3,759.00
France	7,149.83	17,104.70	13,933.78	7,149.83	24,371.00	28,083.00	29,467.00	33,293.00
Germany	36,010.84	40,009.20	60,169.75	44,503.53	45,641.00	51,003.00	56,439.00	45,585.00
Gibraltar								
Greece	393.50	2,087.07	4,354.78	14,674.81	24,053.50	20,645.14	11,521.00	4,841.00
Iceland	1,045.00	7,365.00	15,042.00	10,325.00	29,026.00	25,731.00	20,701.40	25,293.80
Ireland	977.26	1,049.73	1,445.21	1,823.18	2,486.00		4,324.00	4,909.00
Italy	20,176.42	43,240.35	67,125.45	40,958.13	9,896.00	8,158.00	25,732.00	10,344.00
Liechtenstein								
Luxembourg	27.52	46.85	79.82	91.72	4,182.73	4,911.69	5,981.17	4,638.04
Malta								
Monaco								
Netherlands	467.40	953.40	1,304.17	1,401.73	7,138.00	9,242.00	9,676.00	8,365.00
Norway	2,652.00	4,314.00	3,000.00	5,153.00	38,362.00	27,815.00	29,747.00	65,871.80
Portugal	854.34	5,288.85	11,108.23	10,426.77	8,263.00	7,326.00	7,566.00	6,506.00
Spain	3,778.14	23,536.48	31,027.85	22,388.30	15,793.00	8,391.00	14,725.00	9,291.00
Sweden	5,646.00	7,708.00	24,908.00	9,415.00	30,668.00	9,803.00	16,010.00	12,085.00
Switzerland	16,500.00	15,775.00	8,274.00	8,270.00	17,169.00	12,511.00	12,741.00	13,619.00
Turkey	0.22	1.83	13.38	171.69	2,516.35	3,272.62	4,807.40	19,548.40
United Kingdom	2,385.00	2,884.00	5,972.00	7,558.00	11,536.00	9,752.00	8,556.00	8,919.00
Eastern Europe								
Albania				10,301.50	28,150.20	30,161.90	33,814.60	32,175.90
Belarus				2,841.79	92,002.20	158,118.00	312,321.00	438,923.00
Bosnia-Herzegovina					274.67	287.41	871.93	595.25
Bulgaria				67.64	745.27	598.06	864.44	1,071.15
Croatia				3,508.33	8,987.90	10,588.90	15,002.70	20,373.50
Czech Republic				160,933.00	296,541.00	310,927.00	333,319.00	60,197.00
Estonia				100.03	370.28	434.05	313.01	298.96
Georgia				38.00	56.37	76.65	82.45	126.13
Hungary		117,700.00	118,367.00	273,721.00	447,525.00	646,928.00	520,074.00	464,058.00
Latvia				64.15	144.46	135.11	153.25	213.73
Lithuania				522.70	1,342.30	1,282.40	1,343.10	1,391.80
Macedonia				1,836.00	3,861.00	6,192.00	6,195.00	6,364.00
Moldova				54.38	360.92	465.22	652.38	979.20
Montenegro								56.33
Poland	112.51	131.43	3,908.89	8,806.00	14,866.60	14,660.80	21,485.30	19,857.00
Romania	8.13	3.59	0.87	329.32	3,501.43	5,103.77	8,712.49	14,395.60
Russia				36,712.00	168,180.00	310,781.00	356,771.00	471,563.00
Serbia					10,711.00	44,534.00	60,301.00	60,927.00
Slovakia				195.73	277.32	1,204.46	1,039.70	1,139.63
Slovenia				76.66	170.19	178.66	269.25	375.72
Ukraine				960.25	2,613.25	4,749.59	3,687.92	4,516.01

Source: Euromonitor International from national statistics

Deposit Money Bank Reserves 1980, 1985, 1990, 1995, 1999-2011 *(continued)*

National currency million

	2003	2004	2005	2006	2007	2008	2009	2010	2011
Western Europe									
Austria	4,864.00	3,819.00	4,634.00	4,875.00	8,091.00	14,806.00	15,707.00	13,698.00	18,842.00
Belgium	8,325.00	5,416.00	6,786.00	7,928.00	17,789.00	10,804.00	14,777.00	12,996.00	22,570.00
Cyprus	684.54	714.88	862.69	1,203.03	1,453.51	1,304.00	3,050.00	2,336.00	3,165.00
Denmark	18,907.00	27,703.00	25,793.00	22,539.00	18,067.00	44,838.00	9,577.96	6,697.73	4,717.57
Finland	2,146.00	3,156.00	3,535.00	3,766.00	5,910.00	8,110.00	13,543.00	21,898.00	71,881.00
France	25,995.00	26,384.00	25,692.00	26,320.00	73,610.00	90,762.00	61,044.00	46,272.00	173,238.00
Germany	46,857.00	41,248.00	47,942.00	49,495.00	64,986.00	102,611.00	78,968.00	79,612.00	93,967.00
Gibraltar									
Greece	2,479.00	5,387.00	4,354.00	4,625.00	7,248.00	7,936.00	8,187.00	10,647.00	5,457.00
Iceland	13,293.50	29,412.50	36,906.50	47,358.80	80,214.15	101,423.19	120,614.89	136,894.02	144,355.28
Ireland	4,303.00	4,760.00	8,720.00	13,473.00	22,428.00	20,215.00	16,123.00	12,319.00	6,765.00
Italy	10,384.00	13,126.00	11,624.00	14,716.00	41,918.00	34,930.00	35,017.00	23,386.00	33,850.00
Liechtenstein									
Luxembourg	6,765.57	5,063.32	6,810.32	9,741.90	10,779.70	45,531.70	13,488.50	9,663.98	50,826.90
Malta						9.00	138.00	532.00	1,107.00
Monaco									
Netherlands	12,539.00	11,215.00	15,681.00	13,010.00	20,116.00	21,252.00	62,284.00	49,999.00	175,653.00
Norway	39,492.90	47,702.00	53,372.90	30,448.80	41,910.85	40,366.54	36,898.18	38,331.38	39,316.70
Portugal	12,670.00	6,252.00	4,665.00	5,049.00	9,266.00	5,402.00	8,771.00	4,921.00	5,691.00
Spain	14,409.00	13,091.00	16,531.00	20,559.00	52,321.00	54,315.00	35,089.00	26,964.00	50,934.00
Sweden	20,564.00	15,819.00	10,701.00	11,762.00	15,012.00	219,934.00	275,729.47	334,388.90	350,520.25
Switzerland	14,328.00	13,166.00	13,603.00	15,320.00	19,505.00	50,894.00	53,863.00	43,448.00	179,588.00
Turkey	21,772.50	23,104.90	35,188.40	38,653.70	43,938.20	64,879.10	46,283.12	47,978.55	49,144.15
United Kingdom	9,731.00	12,998.00	13,375.00	29,734.00	32,245.00	60,788.00	155,345.00	146,186.00	173,260.00
Eastern Europe									
Albania	35,245.20	40,626.60	49,967.80	60,303.10	72,660.00	76,560.60	71,070.87	73,463.71	75,108.78
Belarus	772,808.00	1,134,530.00	1,810,240.00	2,349,290.00	2,410,680.00	3,516,910.00	2,802,650.00	2,903,396.67	2,972,660.00
Bosnia-Herzegovina	1,004.55	1,566.58	2,233.86	3,061.92	4,022.28	3,394.50	3,631.86	3,680.54	3,289.87
Bulgaria	1,388.25	2,428.00	2,955.00	4,244.00	6,733.00	6,135.00	5,054.56	5,234.69	5,358.52
Croatia	26,783.70	33,743.40	41,789.30	48,402.70	50,201.50	40,721.50	44,412.19	43,525.41	42,915.75
Czech Republic	56,563.00	49,989.00	45,561.00	60,208.00	66,665.00	147,168.00	80,904.58	85,503.82	88,665.80
Estonia	399.10	567.36	852.20	1,201.01	1,240.38	1,766.41	1,814.21	1,158.73	1,153.44
Georgia	148.91	220.40	268.93	442.26	627.62	558.09	601.98	637.47	661.87
Hungary	406,811.00	677,319.00	599,145.00	595,805.00	723,774.00	467,332.00	659,322.75	673,437.81	683,141.91
Latvia	205.00	311.00	594.00	1,317.00	1,557.00	1,221.00	916.81	827.88	766.74
Lithuania	1,897.10	1,868.00	2,819.00	3,419.00	4,789.00	4,216.00	3,096.13	3,024.38	2,975.05
Macedonia	7,090.00	7,192.00	11,454.00	15,247.00	19,912.00	24,581.00	32,487.37	36,318.56	38,952.50
Moldova	1,155.98	2,842.09	3,526.31	2,411.82	4,673.69	7,020.37	4,945.99	5,509.14	5,896.31
Montenegro	37.82	41.57	101.30	233.78	342.44	262.17	238.30	276.16	206.07
Poland	16,902.70	18,398.00	13,579.00	18,302.00	25,765.00	36,297.00	38,820.06	43,379.63	46,514.34
Romania	16,912.80	26,853.50	34,068.30	55,519.20	68,545.60	77,650.00	39,289.93	35,683.43	33,203.96
Russia	768,914.00	837,433.00	873,086.00	1,236,500.00	1,717,000.00	2,580,600.00	3,035,937.07	3,435,811.97	3,710,725.97
Serbia	70,118.00	97,037.50	188,136.00	316,780.00	350,716.00	412,876.00	368,333.50	379,789.83	387,666.06
Slovakia	899.92	755.88	1,053.08	1,336.62	2,338.91	2,999.88	1,198.00	715.00	646.00
Slovenia	400.85	357.31	400.02	301.98	351.00	984.00	1,220.00	873.00	1,126.00
Ukraine	7,127.74	11,629.30	22,559.50	22,429.70	30,471.70	31,547.20	29,796.95	31,434.12	32,559.67

Source: Euromonitor International from national statistics

Banking and Finance Statistics

Table 5.6

Credit Cards in Circulation 2000-2011

'000

	2000	2001	2002	2003	2004	2005	2006	2007	2008	2009	2010	2011
Western Europe												
Austria	882.7	941.2	1,018.1	1,034.6	1,019.8	1,103.9	1,183.1	1,238.0	1,253.9	1,201.0	1,255.0	1,288.2
Belgium	144.2	170.1	224.5	312.9	381.2	488.8	581.9	753.8	925.8	1,093.5	1,178.6	1,257.0
Cyprus	102.5	119.8	138.2	160.9	188.4	218.2	252.3	289.1	334.9	368.2	366.8	367.4
Denmark	458.0	497.0	541.0	590.0	789.9	957.1	1,021.4	941.5	1,119.1	1,437.2	1,423.6	1,447.5
Finland	1,383.8	1,614.3	1,650.4	1,912.0	2,182.2	2,528.8	3,015.3	3,281.8	3,847.7	3,592.6	3,780.0	3,864.7
France	3,000.0	3,242.6	3,500.0	3,800.0	4,005.0	4,166.6	4,326.4	4,499.2	5,068.5	8,362.6	8,931.3	9,490.4
Germany	1,172.4	1,652.5	2,177.4	2,625.6	2,775.6	3,561.6	4,474.2	4,611.8	4,796.3	4,879.0	5,001.0	5,144.5
Gibraltar	11.1	11.9	13.6	15.4	16.3	16.3	16.2	16.0	15.6	14.6	13.9	13.4
Greece	3,030.2	4,144.1	5,157.1	5,579.9	5,642.0	6,045.5	6,284.8	6,707.3	7,039.6	6,005.8	5,126.6	4,369.8
Iceland	135.0	148.6	170.1	194.5	205.7	206.6	207.0	205.6	202.1	191.1	197.0	214.3
Ireland	1,360.3	1,752.3	1,888.6	2,025.5	2,035.8	2,060.9	2,248.7	2,399.4	2,488.0	2,665.9	2,793.6	2,684.0
Italy	1,696.9	2,699.6	3,965.0	7,270.0	8,500.0	10,159.1	12,199.7	13,900.4	14,612.4	14,579.5	13,555.7	13,416.6
Liechtenstein	0.1	0.1	0.1	0.2	0.3	0.4	0.7	0.8	0.9	0.9	0.9	0.9
Luxembourg	11.0	11.3	11.8	12.3	12.6	13.1	13.5	14.1	15.2	16.0	17.3	18.5
Malta	118.2	126.1	143.6	163.4	172.2	172.4	176.5	174.9	171.1	161.1	167.3	160.7
Monaco	0.9	1.0	1.0	1.2	1.4	1.5	1.7	1.8	1.9	1.9	2.1	2.3
Netherlands	4,630.1	4,636.8	4,626.7	5,331.9	5,416.8	5,653.8	5,839.2	5,635.9	5,334.9	5,409.0	5,430.6	5,451.8
Norway	955.2	1,008.3	1,244.0	1,624.6	1,967.2	2,345.2	3,005.0	3,647.0	3,713.0	4,877.0	4,877.0	4,683.4
Portugal	2,219.0	2,559.2	3,014.2	3,202.3	3,641.3	4,290.2	4,923.1	5,279.9	5,289.9	5,156.7	5,086.5	5,024.3
Spain	3,564.0	4,259.0	5,663.2	6,680.0	8,972.2	11,304.0	14,250.0	17,384.0	18,059.3	17,413.4	17,151.3	16,545.4
Sweden	2,462.0	2,319.0	2,584.0	2,827.0	3,336.0	3,610.0	3,968.0	4,349.0	4,962.0	5,158.0	6,157.0	6,420.0
Switzerland	2,945.7	3,109.2	3,158.2	3,179.4	3,202.8	3,249.9	3,661.8	4,102.7	4,303.6	4,441.0	4,677.6	4,932.3
Turkey	13,409.0	13,997.0	15,706.0	19,863.0	26,681.0	29,978.0	32,741.4	37,831.7	44,153.4	45,320.7	48,076.0	52,783.6
United Kingdom	47,862.3	52,541.6	59,840.3	67,941.1	70,795.2	70,802.5	70,813.4	69,049.1	67,190.5	59,227.9	56,882.2	55,878.5
Eastern Europe												
Albania	8.4	13.6	18.3	26.8	46.0	78.9	120.4	153.7	200.2	231.1	225.0	225.1
Belarus				27.6	69.7	118.0	273.2	410.4	813.6	838.6	798.0	851.6
Bosnia-Herzegovina	108.8	110.1	111.4	112.7	115.1	117.5	119.8	152.7	197.6	226.9	220.2	219.3
Bulgaria	1.8	5.5	8.9	19.3	57.9	126.9	382.6	543.6	609.1	552.0	530.7	529.8
Croatia	61.4	107.0	148.4	218.5	117.0	235.4	353.5	427.5	448.8	484.6	494.4	505.3
Czech Republic	56.1	74.3	139.5	282.9	1,149.5	1,739.9	2,187.5	2,638.4	2,890.7	2,760.3	2,780.0	2,854.5
Estonia	21.7	55.1	77.6	93.1	116.5	133.0	172.0	210.5	222.5	246.9	252.2	258.3
Georgia				6.8	14.9	28.6	65.9	98.5	194.3	199.1	190.0	203.6
Hungary	245.8	407.7	598.4	880.7	972.4	1,143.1	1,597.0	1,757.7	1,787.8	1,505.4	1,367.9	1,231.5
Latvia	3.5	5.5	4.3	4.6	30.6	58.8	106.5	242.4	258.5	267.3	268.5	273.5
Lithuania	4.6	6.5	18.1	26.1	43.0	73.5	122.5	168.5	255.0	254.9	259.9	259.7
Macedonia	49.8	79.5	134.9	208.3	301.5	451.6	593.2	794.9	1,113.8	1,221.0	1,259.1	1,293.3
Moldova	9.3	20.6	29.6	43.2	23.5	47.8	72.6	88.0	91.8	98.1	94.3	93.1
Montenegro				0.1	0.2	0.4	1.0	1.5	3.0	3.1	3.0	3.0
Poland	371.7	600.1	806.4	1,172.6	1,996.3	3,386.8	5,124.0	6,996.2	9,010.0	10,555.5	8,645.7	6,747.5
Romania	26.0	50.7	89.8	155.0	229.5	585.0	1,125.7	1,732.2	2,719.0	2,248.9	2,123.4	2,156.3
Russia				206.0	1,319.0	2,480.0	5,660.0	8,944.0	9,296.0	8,601.0	10,047.0	15,025.9
Serbia				1.2	2.8	5.3	12.4	18.7	37.3	38.4	37.1	36.8
Slovakia	1.3	8.7	126.1	234.6	343.0	367.0	497.4	580.1	643.6	505.9	518.1	531.0
Slovenia	16.7	21.1	26.5	33.2	36.4	44.6	52.5	58.3	60.3	60.9	63.0	60.6
Ukraine				461.2	2,341.7	3,717.0	6,078.0	10,045.0	9,032.0	5,188.0	5,619.0	8,180.0

Source: Euromonitor International from national statistics

Table 5.7

Charge Cards in Circulation 2000-2011

'000

	2000	2001	2002	2003	2004	2005	2006	2007	2008	2009	2010	2011
Western Europe												
Austria	910.1	995.1	1,027.5	1,045.5	1,041.4	1,068.0	1,121.0	1,172.4	1,267.3	1,333.2	1,400.4	1,410.2
Belgium	2,535.9	2,665.9	2,581.5	2,816.2	2,794.8	2,770.2	2,841.1	3,015.2	3,099.3	3,207.3	3,392.0	3,620.0
Cyprus	24.1	26.3	28.8	33.5	39.3	44.2	50.3	57.2	65.4	72.8	76.1	74.9
Denmark												
Finland	441.2	414.7	449.6	488.0	517.8	571.2	584.7	618.2	652.4	660.2	665.1	672.4
France	11,753.0	12,836.0	13,628.0	14,719.0	17,928.0	20,166.0	25,278.0	27,557.0	27,315.0	30,864.0	24,278.9	23,314.3
Germany	16,719.6	15,990.1	16,759.6	16,936.6	17,235.9	17,806.7	18,147.7	18,332.6	18,760.8	19,223.4	20,191.5	20,702.3
Gibraltar	0.9	1.0	1.0	1.0	1.0	1.1	1.1	1.2	1.2	1.2	1.1	1.2
Greece	373.7	334.9	334.4	325.3	83.8	76.0	72.3	74.2	73.4	72.8	75.7	63.2
Iceland	21.6	25.4	24.9	25.7	25.8	27.7	29.0	30.0	30.9	30.6	30.6	30.9
Ireland	243.1	287.3	283.9	295.5	298.8	324.6	345.9	363.1	378.0	377.6	366.1	373.6
Italy	15,272.1	17,296.4	17,792.0	18,375.0	18,520.0	18,732.9	19,074.4	20,604.6	21,371.6	20,449.8	20,309.1	20,264.3
Liechtenstein	6.8	7.5	8.3	8.7	8.9	9.4	9.9	10.0	10.4	10.6	10.8	11.2
Luxembourg	148.6	155.7	158.1	164.0	171.1	178.8	185.7	194.4	212.4	225.8	237.9	255.2
Malta	9.5	10.8	10.5	10.8	10.8	11.6	12.4	12.8	13.1	13.0	13.9	14.2
Monaco	4.5	4.8	5.2	5.7	6.2	6.7	7.2	7.8	11.8	12.4	12.5	13.1
Netherlands	370.4	367.2	363.3	378.1	377.2	394.3	401.6	391.2	387.5	399.2	376.2	362.2
Norway	415.7	445.4	438.0	451.1	469.7	450.6	478.0	522.0	535.0	534.0	528.0	593.0
Portugal	316.3	330.2	394.3	451.9	581.9	646.0	729.0	751.4	794.9	825.2	810.9	789.1
Spain	12,493.0	13,487.0	15,273.8	17,177.0	19,989.8	21,855.2	24,031.0	25,743.0	26,760.7	26,360.6	25,811.7	25,341.9
Sweden	1,009.0	1,025.0	807.0	839.0	807.0	620.0	648.0	686.0	709.0	706.0	665.0	636.8
Switzerland	185.3	172.0	174.8	179.6	188.2	204.1	210.6	207.7	197.1	224.0	226.6	230.6
Turkey												
United Kingdom	2,913.7	3,402.9	3,264.7	3,315.0	3,593.1	3,773.9	3,725.6	3,954.5	5,303.9	5,436.4	5,409.8	5,496.9
Eastern Europe												
Albania	15.4	14.1	12.8	7.5	8.0	8.6	7.5	7.3	8.0	8.5	7.7	7.9
Belarus												
Bosnia-Herzegovina	2.1	1.9	1.8	1.1	1.1	1.2	1.0	1.0	1.1	1.2	1.1	1.1
Bulgaria												
Croatia	1.6	1.5	1.2	2.5	4.0	4.2	4.6	5.2	5.4	4.2	4.3	4.2
Czech Republic	285.5	277.2	290.4	334.2	333.8	365.8	385.8	446.3	449.5	423.0	440.5	431.4
Estonia	9.2	12.2	15.2	18.2	21.4	23.7	27.5	40.0	35.5	32.2	33.1	34.3
Georgia												
Hungary	6.4	6.2	5.3	10.8	17.2	18.2	20.0	20.0	19.0	17.6	16.0	16.6
Latvia	0.2	0.3	0.2	0.4	1.8	3.3	5.9	13.1	19.9	26.3	32.1	33.0
Lithuania			9.0	59.5	66.4	56.2	58.5	85.0	75.3	68.1	70.0	70.7
Macedonia												
Moldova	0.2	0.2	0.2	0.4	0.6	0.7	0.8	0.9	1.0	0.7	0.6	0.6
Montenegro												
Poland	1,040.5	1,124.2	1,204.4	861.2	884.2	891.8	853.4	778.3	827.3	797.5	726.4	717.3
Romania		0.1	0.7	1.8	4.2	7.8	14.0	13.5	13.9	11.3	15.9	20.8
Russia												
Serbia												
Slovakia	4.3	5.0	6.4	9.0	7.9	8.0	8.4	7.0	7.6	8.3	8.6	8.7
Slovenia	75.6	76.4	79.0	82.4	85.4	87.2	90.9	93.6	96.1	98.5	102.4	104.3
Ukraine												

Source: Euromonitor International from national statistics

5

Banking and Finance

Banking and Finance Statistics

Table 5.8

Credit Card Expenditure 2000-2011

US$ million

	2000	2001	2002	2003	2004	2005	2006	2007	2008	2009	2010	2011
Western Europe												
Austria	1,575.0	1,815.8	2,068.3	2,540.8	3,291.4	3,663.4	4,027.1	4,735.6	5,400.2	5,197.1	5,588.7	5,998.5
Belgium	583.6	615.7	752.4	936.1	1,126.1	1,483.1	1,927.6	2,565.9	2,742.2	2,640.0	2,748.9	2,869.5
Cyprus	574.3	588.6	721.8	923.5	1,152.5	1,296.8	1,459.6	1,648.8	1,842.9	1,806.7	1,717.9	1,683.8
Denmark	1,358.2	1,434.3	1,651.7	1,980.0	4,500.1	5,066.1	5,545.5	6,776.3	8,393.2	7,141.0	6,990.6	6,188.5
Finland	837.6	959.8	1,035.8	1,108.1	1,228.5	1,202.8	1,437.8	1,488.0	2,039.1	1,772.8	1,779.4	1,873.8
France	4,331.1	4,609.4	5,274.9	6,909.0	8,085.7	8,513.4	9,032.7	10,381.7	12,234.6	14,451.8	16,119.9	19,366.6
Germany	1,553.1	1,773.1	2,201.8	2,992.4	3,542.6	3,865.6	4,054.1	4,712.2	5,246.7	5,046.5	5,136.6	5,655.6
Gibraltar	28.1	28.3	33.4	40.7	50.3	50.0	49.4	48.9	50.3	46.4	43.2	44.9
Greece	2,049.7	1,897.5	2,062.9	4,843.1	6,744.3	8,082.4	8,518.8	10,222.8	11,396.9	9,880.0	7,787.0	7,154.1
Iceland	683.3	708.3	834.6	1,023.6	1,266.9	1,267.1	1,132.8	1,037.4	1,019.6	1,015.3	1,021.7	1,042.9
Ireland	2,213.6	3,275.9	4,121.3	5,479.5	6,994.5	7,991.0	9,522.3	11,616.7	12,278.2	9,554.8	9,021.7	9,343.3
Italy	2,744.3	3,300.3	3,857.8	5,423.9	7,275.3	8,918.7	10,908.0	14,225.0	15,632.6	14,275.1	14,146.4	15,076.5
Liechtenstein	1.2	1.4	1.6	2.1	2.5	2.7	2.9	2.9	3.2	3.2	3.3	3.5
Luxembourg												
Malta	299.3	300.6	352.7	430.8	531.3	529.7	537.9	533.0	551.4	511.2	502.7	496.1
Monaco	2.7	3.1	3.6	4.6	5.5	6.0	6.6	6.8	7.3	6.4	7.4	8.0
Netherlands	4,716.9	4,768.0	5,088.9	6,070.1	7,119.4	7,677.8	8,768.0	10,509.4	12,584.6	10,841.4	10,442.2	11,060.0
Norway	1,035.2	1,145.7	1,566.5	2,286.6	3,080.3	4,148.6	5,585.4	6,897.3	8,499.5	9,131.2	10,510.0	13,503.7
Portugal	7,482.2	7,381.5	9,027.6	11,541.6	14,364.9	16,098.4	18,233.4	20,927.6	25,392.4	25,834.8	24,582.0	25,577.7
Spain	4,245.5	4,864.9	7,995.4	11,570.5	16,268.4	19,716.0	22,285.5	26,958.0	28,466.6	25,686.2	26,115.8	28,147.2
Sweden	1,808.5	2,217.5	1,927.4	2,853.2	3,074.6	3,614.6	4,202.9	4,881.0	5,462.8	4,965.1	8,324.5	11,659.6
Switzerland	14,256.0	15,309.0	15,633.0	15,390.0	16,038.0	17,091.0	18,732.1	21,821.6	22,023.0	21,327.0	21,707.9	21,977.0
Turkey	16,790.9	9,922.6	14,577.0	23,774.7	41,047.6	57,531.8	68,775.5	91,288.3	125,074.7	116,308.1	132,818.9	133,205.1
United Kingdom	114,958.1	118,292.6	141,158.5	171,485.3	208,370.2	206,789.1	213,798.3	240,785.5	220,038.1	180,478.7	182,912.4	191,133.5
Eastern Europe												
Albania	9.6	12.3	24.2	32.4	44.2	69.3	96.2	120.2	151.8	149.8	139.6	148.9
Belarus				8.4	13.5	21.9	30.6	57.0	94.9	127.3	120.7	147.6
Bosnia-Herzegovina	1.3	1.7	3.4	4.6	6.4	10.0	13.7	17.0	21.2	20.8	19.4	20.5
Bulgaria	7.4	10.0	18.2	33.1	113.5	141.3	86.9	256.6	415.5	356.6	368.9	389.4
Croatia	21.1	36.3	66.0	111.0	161.4	222.5	317.9	475.2	578.3	601.2	619.5	665.8
Czech Republic	9.0	10.7	26.4	71.1	426.2	756.7	1,045.7	1,424.0	1,764.1	1,535.4	1,519.7	1,830.3
Estonia				72.6	120.7	146.2	215.1	311.6	383.8	369.4	372.6	389.9
Georgia				2.6	4.9	9.9	19.0	32.6	62.4	76.9	72.8	89.3
Hungary	42.6	76.4	143.8	238.8	352.7	489.4	708.7	1,037.4	1,247.1	1,060.2	1,058.6	1,196.7
Latvia	6.1	9.4	9.7	24.6	43.4	90.5	133.7	284.1	489.8	477.8	457.9	476.8
Lithuania	12.1	18.7	19.5	48.2	73.5	145.8	306.6	496.8	551.0	512.0	531.5	542.2
Macedonia	7.5	14.0	30.3	57.4	92.0	150.1	223.4	257.5	348.0	406.4	441.7	472.4
Moldova	1.6	3.5	6.6	11.0	16.2	22.6	32.5	48.6	58.6	60.6	55.5	58.5
Montenegro				0.1	0.1	0.3	0.6	1.0	1.7	2.0	1.8	2.0
Poland	425.7	546.2	1,065.4	1,417.6	1,957.8	3,063.2	3,689.5	5,562.3	8,116.7	6,437.3	7,322.3	7,956.2
Romania	6.9	10.9	17.8	34.4	67.4	217.8	457.7	1,050.1	1,101.2	759.7	786.5	1,139.2
Russia				123.8	537.9	1,019.5	1,703.9	2,261.9	3,480.5	3,123.3	4,783.4	7,921.3
Serbia				0.8	1.6	3.5	7.0	11.9	21.6	24.5	22.6	23.9
Slovakia	0.1	13.5	33.7	62.5	120.8	198.5	333.3	482.7	709.4	614.7	642.5	672.4
Slovenia	27.2	43.7	55.8	88.6	103.2	116.5	131.2	143.4	193.2	165.5	163.5	161.3
Ukraine				19.1	112.1	201.1	346.9	660.6	1,325.5	480.1	614.7	888.8

Source: Euromonitor International from national statistics

Table 5.9

Charge Card Expenditure 2000-2011

US$ million

	2000	2001	2002	2003	2004	2005	2006	2007	2008	2009	2010	2011
Western Europe												
Austria	1,489.6	1,784.8	2,054.8	2,451.5	3,235.7	3,469.4	3,813.8	4,653.5	5,839.3	8,212.5	8,303.6	8,912.5
Belgium	5,888.4	6,461.6	6,481.9	6,552.4	6,749.0	7,089.3	7,957.8	8,838.2	9,554.8	9,639.1	10,332.5	11,196.1
Cyprus	68.2	73.1	79.1	99.2	119.7	130.8	139.2	146.9	155.5	148.1	159.1	153.3
Denmark												
Finland	2,572.5	2,621.2	2,824.9	3,632.3	4,113.1	4,387.3	5,588.5	6,309.5	6,672.8	6,610.5	6,644.6	6,719.4
France	30,746.5	40,276.4	47,097.6	65,477.2	73,280.9	93,212.6	122,945.6	164,240.9	200,496.0	220,296.2	140,203.0	138,058.3
Germany	20,269.6	21,176.6	24,421.8	31,835.5	38,833.6	40,858.6	42,892.3	48,638.3	51,829.2	49,111.0	50,901.6	56,425.1
Gibraltar	7.6	8.2	8.6	9.5	11.1	11.5	13.3	13.7	15.0	12.3	10.0	10.3
Greece	504.3	359.2	392.8	517.5	389.8	478.0	419.3	449.2	490.5	455.3	410.5	337.9
Iceland	183.7	206.1	215.9	238.1	280.7	291.3	338.0	349.5	387.9	320.5	320.4	318.1
Ireland	2,064.7	2,328.6	2,459.6	2,734.8	3,251.0	3,417.3	4,035.2	4,234.9	4,747.8	3,953.3	3,265.7	3,325.6
Italy	20,643.9	23,138.9	27,980.2	34,161.6	44,928.0	49,013.6	49,730.5	57,433.3	67,083.0	61,869.1	61,045.8	71,827.1
Liechtenstein	7.5	8.7	10.5	14.3	17.6	19.1	20.5	20.6	21.3	21.9	22.6	23.9
Luxembourg												
Malta	80.5	87.5	91.2	100.2	117.7	121.8	144.7	149.3	165.0	135.7	140.9	144.9
Monaco	18.5	21.0	26.2	36.6	45.7	51.2	57.0	62.5	67.3	65.4	67.7	72.1
Netherlands	2,014.9	2,003.5	2,173.6	2,632.5	2,992.3	2,973.5	2,829.0	2,855.7	3,316.0	2,676.6	2,795.9	3,057.1
Norway	1,949.9	2,013.1	2,194.7	2,390.1	2,633.5	3,054.1	2,962.5	3,907.2	4,451.1	3,640.8	3,391.9	3,870.9
Portugal	922.9	963.2	1,039.7	1,293.5	1,560.6	1,688.9	1,806.3	2,058.0	2,365.1	2,333.8	2,145.0	2,165.3
Spain	8,241.1	9,034.9	14,526.7	20,569.8	27,700.2	33,141.8	37,142.4	50,098.3	59,107.7	53,552.6	54,301.6	58,189.5
Sweden	5,584.2	5,040.5	5,109.0	6,552.7	7,292.0	5,221.1	4,067.3	4,881.0	5,462.8	4,573.1	4,578.5	4,840.3
Switzerland	3,344.0	3,591.0	3,667.0	3,610.0	3,762.0	4,009.0	4,167.9	4,078.4	3,942.8	3,888.4	3,803.8	3,802.9
Turkey												
United Kingdom	20,237.9	22,575.2	23,660.4	25,388.0	30,849.7	31,998.5	36,825.3	42,306.4	51,128.0	41,017.3	39,809.6	43,399.7
Eastern Europe												
Albania	10.2	8.7	12.2	11.6	6.7	7.7	8.1	7.8	8.8	9.1	11.0	12.7
Belarus												
Bosnia-Herzegovina	1.4	1.2	1.7	1.6	0.9	1.1	1.1	1.1	1.2	1.3	1.5	1.7
Bulgaria	4.0	3.8	3.0	7.0	16.6	21.5	35.4	54.1	67.7	50.6	59.9	68.9
Croatia	4.3	3.9	3.1	7.0	15.2	20.0	32.2	49.6	61.7	47.4	47.3	50.0
Czech Republic	281.7	292.8	365.3	515.0	533.3	642.8	745.7	1,012.3	1,326.0	984.9	1,043.6	1,223.7
Estonia				0.1	0.1	0.2	0.4	0.7	0.8	0.6	0.6	0.7
Georgia												
Hungary	8.6	12.0	17.0	24.9	32.7	45.2	71.6	106.3	130.3	86.2	84.9	129.1
Latvia	0.8	1.1	1.6	2.2	3.1	6.6	9.8	20.1	25.5	22.9	23.7	25.3
Lithuania			0.0	0.1	0.1	0.2	0.5	1.0	1.0	0.7	0.8	0.8
Macedonia												
Moldova	0.3	0.3	0.3	0.6	1.4	1.8	3.0	4.7	5.8	4.4	5.2	5.9
Montenegro												
Poland	855.7	1,264.7	2,350.8	2,685.9	2,816.2	3,456.9	4,756.6	5,921.7	7,705.0	5,622.3	5,541.4	5,787.1
Romania		0.2	0.9	1.7	3.7	7.2	14.3	23.5	25.5	31.0	25.3	30.2
Russia												
Serbia												
Slovakia	4.0	4.6	10.2	15.4	17.3	20.1	25.1	30.3	33.6	30.8	31.7	34.1
Slovenia	179.2	187.0	201.1	243.1	272.8	283.7	293.6	304.0	312.5	312.2	316.4	321.2
Ukraine												

Source: Euromonitor International from national statistics

5

Banking and Finance

Banking and Finance Statistics

Table 5.10

Credit Card Transactions 2000-2011

Million

	2000	2001	2002	2003	2004	2005	2006	2007	2008	2009	2010	2011
Western Europe												
Austria	14.2	17.4	19.2	19.2	26.5	28.2	30.2	31.8	33.1	34.0	36.2	37.2
Belgium	4.6	4.8	5.5	7.1	9.4	11.9	15.5	21.9	23.8	24.7	25.3	26.0
Cyprus	12.8	18.6	20.7	22.3	24.0	26.0	28.4	31.4	34.5	34.4	34.4	34.2
Denmark	13.0	13.0	14.0	15.0	36.8	44.6	49.4	57.2	68.5	65.1	69.7	59.6
Finland	18.5	22.2	23.6	25.0	26.5	28.5	34.5	36.2	44.5	43.0	44.3	46.7
France	66.0	73.0	80.0	88.0	93.9	98.9	104.0	109.6	122.0	153.8	179.7	202.7
Germany	25.7	28.2	32.2	35.8	39.1	42.5	46.6	49.8	52.3	53.4	57.5	59.6
Gibraltar	0.3	0.3	0.4	0.4	0.4	0.4	0.4	0.4	0.4	0.4	0.4	0.4
Greece	50.4	41.9	39.3	50.5	59.9	60.7	64.4	69.3	75.3	73.3	66.4	60.5
Iceland	4.9	5.2	5.7	6.2	6.8	6.7	6.6	6.5	6.7	6.5	7.7	9.0
Ireland	48.0	73.0	80.0	82.0	83.0	95.7	105.3	110.6	118.4	115.4	116.7	120.9
Italy	27.9	34.3	38.0	47.8	55.9	69.5	70.0	99.8	102.1	106.3	110.1	109.4
Liechtenstein	0.0	0.0	0.0	0.0	0.0	0.0	0.0	0.0	0.0	0.0	0.0	0.0
Luxembourg	0.0	0.0	0.1	0.1	0.1	0.1	0.1	0.1	0.1	0.1	0.1	0.1
Malta	3.5	3.7	4.0	4.4	4.7	4.6	4.7	4.6	4.7	4.5	4.5	4.6
Monaco	0.0	0.0	0.0	0.0	0.0	0.0	0.0	0.0	0.0	0.0	0.0	0.0
Netherlands	46.8	49.1	51.8	55.1	57.7	65.0	69.1	75.4	80.6	77.7	84.1	88.3
Norway	8.1	8.8	11.2	15.1	20.7	25.6	29.2	40.9	47.8	58.2	72.4	91.9
Portugal	116.6	164.9	183.1	197.0	212.1	228.7	249.2	269.8	280.3	281.1	279.2	282.9
Spain	41.5	48.7	75.8	88.4	115.0	135.0	178.6	259.3	320.0	327.0	359.0	371.1
Sweden	11.0	23.0	30.0	36.0	36.0	66.0	83.0	93.0	94.0	100.0	125.4	148.2
Switzerland	80.1	87.1	90.1	88.8	90.7	94.8	100.8	117.8	120.5	124.0	131.1	139.5
Turkey	465.0	511.9	594.1	787.2	1,079.2	1,247.5	1,283.4	1,382.4	1,623.4	1,780.0	1,987.4	2,215.7
United Kingdom	1,387.1	1,481.2	1,636.5	1,770.7	1,913.4	1,855.0	1,841.3	1,879.7	1,867.9	1,932.2	1,957.5	1,949.7
Eastern Europe												
Albania	0.2	0.3	0.6	0.8	1.0	1.2	1.3	1.8	2.1	2.1	2.0	2.1
Belarus				0.1	0.4	0.7	1.2	1.8	2.7	9.1	9.4	10.5
Bosnia-Herzegovina	0.6	0.7	0.8	0.8	3.0	3.2	3.3	3.8	4.1	4.2	3.6	4.1
Bulgaria	0.1	0.1	0.2	0.2	0.8	2.1	2.2	2.7	3.4	3.7	4.0	4.0
Croatia	0.6	1.0	1.5	2.2	3.2	4.3	6.9	9.1	11.7	13.2	13.9	14.2
Czech Republic	0.2	0.2	0.8	2.1	6.6	10.4	14.6	19.1	22.0	24.2	28.7	32.6
Estonia	0.4	0.5	0.8	1.0	1.8	2.0	2.6	3.3	4.0	3.9	4.0	4.5
Georgia				0.1	0.1	0.2	0.4	0.6	0.9	2.3	2.4	2.6
Hungary	1.2	2.0	3.2	4.7	6.9	9.4	15.2	19.8	23.1	25.5	24.8	26.7
Latvia	0.0	0.1	0.1	0.1	0.6	1.2	2.2	4.7	11.5	8.8	9.5	10.6
Lithuania	0.2	0.3	0.4	0.7	1.0	2.0	3.7	5.4	7.1	6.8	6.8	7.5
Macedonia	0.1	0.1	0.1	0.3	0.3	0.4	0.5	0.7	0.9	1.0	1.0	1.2
Moldova	0.0	0.1	0.1	0.2	0.3	0.4	0.7	0.9	1.2	1.3	1.2	1.3
Montenegro				0.0	0.0	0.0	0.0	0.0	0.0	0.1	0.1	0.1
Poland	9.6	12.9	27.3	34.1	45.1	67.5	81.5	107.9	138.1	160.0	174.0	187.5
Romania	0.1	0.2	0.4	0.8	1.3	3.4	6.8	10.6	17.4	16.4	16.3	22.4
Russia				1.4	3.0	5.5	9.4	18.0	28.1	36.0	52.7	85.4
Serbia				0.0	0.0	0.1	0.1	0.2	0.4	1.0	1.0	1.0
Slovakia	0.3	0.3	0.8	1.4	2.5	3.3	4.7	7.2	9.4	11.5	12.5	14.1
Slovenia	0.5	1.0	1.3	1.7	2.0	2.3	2.6	2.6	3.5	2.9	2.8	2.9
Ukraine				0.3	1.6	2.7	5.8	11.0	20.3	13.8	15.8	31.9

Source: Euromonitor International from national statistics

Table 5.11

Charge Card Transactions 2000-2011
Million

	2000	2001	2002	2003	2004	2005	2006	2007	2008	2009	2010	2011
Western Europe												
Austria	13.7	16.8	18.6	18.5	25.5	27.3	29.2	31.2	36.7	56.8	68.5	70.3
Belgium	62.3	65.7	66.2	64.7	66.2	69.5	80.0	93.9	101.6	107.3	111.9	119.2
Cyprus	3.7	4.2	4.2	4.7	5.3	5.8	6.2	6.7	7.3	7.4	8.1	7.8
Denmark												
Finland	43.5	42.8	44.4	45.0	46.5	47.6	53.5	53.8	55.5	55.0	56.0	61.6
France	309.0	426.0	497.0	584.0	632.0	813.0	1,077.0	1,328.0	1,529.0	1,791.0	1,595.1	1,550.9
Germany	239.9	255.0	263.9	304.7	322.4	325.1	331.7	382.4	373.5	390.3	413.4	419.0
Gibraltar	0.0	0.1	0.1	0.1	0.1	0.1	0.1	0.1	0.1	0.1	0.1	0.1
Greece	3.2	2.3	2.4	2.6	1.8	2.2	1.9	1.9	2.0	2.0	1.9	1.4
Iceland	1.2	1.4	1.4	1.4	1.4	1.6	1.7	1.8	1.8	1.6	1.6	1.6
Ireland	13.3	15.7	15.5	16.3	16.3	18.4	20.5	21.5	22.3	19.8	18.0	17.9
Italy	244.4	280.1	320.3	326.2	377.7	394.1	395.9	404.1	420.5	453.0	477.6	484.4
Liechtenstein	0.1	0.1	0.1	0.1	0.1	0.1	0.2	0.2	0.2	0.2	0.2	0.2
Luxembourg	2.7	2.8	2.9	2.9	3.2	3.4	4.0	4.3	4.6	5.0	5.3	5.7
Malta	0.5	0.6	0.6	0.6	0.6	0.7	0.7	0.8	0.8	0.7	0.7	0.7
Monaco	0.2	0.2	0.3	0.3	0.3	0.4	0.6	0.6	0.8	0.8	0.8	0.9
Netherlands	11.2	11.6	12.3	12.8	13.3	14.7	14.2	13.1	13.6	11.9	12.5	12.9
Norway	13.9	14.8	13.9	14.8	16.3	19.1	17.7	20.5	22.6	21.4	19.1	19.2
Portugal	37.4	41.5	41.8	47.2	53.1	57.7	62.0	66.9	73.9	79.5	77.2	74.4
Spain	180.5	210.3	325.2	376.7	463.0	540.0	641.9	777.8	824.0	842.0	909.5	931.8
Sweden	47.0	52.0	51.0	64.3	55.0	40.0	44.0	55.0	63.0	59.0	46.4	42.5
Switzerland	10.0	11.2	11.6	11.6	11.9	12.6	12.4	12.0	11.4	11.0	10.8	10.7
Turkey												
United Kingdom	150.5	179.0	176.1	186.5	191.5	198.6	211.8	216.0	278.2	277.7	268.7	280.8
Eastern Europe												
Albania	0.2	0.2	0.2	0.2	0.1	0.1	0.1	0.1	0.1	0.2	0.1	0.2
Belarus												
Bosnia-Herzegovina	0.1	0.2	0.2	0.2	0.2	0.3	0.3	0.3	0.3	0.3	0.3	0.3
Bulgaria	0.0	0.1	0.1	0.1	0.2	0.2	0.4	0.5	0.6	0.5	0.4	0.5
Croatia	0.0	0.0	0.0	0.0	0.1	0.1	0.2	0.2	0.3	0.2	0.2	0.2
Czech Republic	7.9	7.8	8.2	9.8	10.2	11.8	12.7	15.8	16.7	16.5	18.3	19.3
Estonia	0.0	0.0	0.0	0.0	0.0	0.0	0.0	0.0	0.0	0.0	0.0	0.0
Georgia												
Hungary	0.1	0.1	0.1	0.1	0.1	0.1	0.3	0.5	0.5	0.5	0.5	0.6
Latvia	0.0	0.0	0.0	0.0	0.2	0.5	1.0	2.0	2.0	3.1	3.2	3.4
Lithuania					0.0	0.0	0.0	0.0	0.0	0.0	0.0	0.0
Macedonia												
Moldova	0.0	0.0	0.0	0.0	0.0	0.0	0.0	0.0	0.0	0.0	0.0	0.0
Montenegro												
Poland	29.7	52.1	89.0	96.1	91.0	97.7	107.1	132.0	153.1	149.5	136.9	137.7
Romania		0.0	0.0	0.0	0.1	0.2	0.5	0.5	0.6	0.2	0.3	0.5
Russia												
Serbia												
Slovakia	0.0	0.1	0.3	0.3	0.3	0.2	0.2	0.2	0.2	0.2	0.2	0.2
Slovenia	8.8	9.2	9.2	9.4	9.4	9.6	9.5	8.9	8.5	8.3	8.3	8.6
Ukraine												

Source: Euromonitor International from national statistics

5

Banking and Finance

Banking and Finance Statistics

Table 5.12

Average Credit Card Expenditure 2000-2011

US$ per card

	2000	2001	2002	2003	2004	2005	2006	2007	2008	2009	2010	2011
Western Europe												
Austria	1,784.2	1,929.2	2,031.5	2,455.8	3,227.6	3,318.5	3,403.9	3,825.1	4,306.7	4,327.1	4,453.0	4,656.7
Belgium	4,047.2	3,619.6	3,351.4	2,991.7	2,954.1	3,034.2	3,312.6	3,404.0	2,962.0	2,414.3	2,332.3	2,282.8
Cyprus	5,600.3	4,915.2	5,223.7	5,739.0	6,116.0	5,943.6	5,785.4	5,704.0	5,502.3	4,907.2	4,683.9	4,582.4
Denmark	2,965.4	2,885.8	3,053.0	3,356.0	5,697.1	5,293.2	5,429.3	7,197.3	7,499.9	4,968.7	4,910.6	4,275.2
Finland	605.3	594.6	627.6	579.6	563.0	475.6	476.8	453.4	530.0	493.4	470.7	484.8
France	1,443.7	1,421.5	1,507.1	1,818.2	2,018.9	2,043.3	2,087.8	2,307.5	2,413.9	1,728.1	1,804.9	2,040.7
Germany	1,324.7	1,073.0	1,011.2	1,139.7	1,276.3	1,085.4	906.1	1,021.8	1,093.9	1,034.3	1,027.1	1,099.3
Gibraltar	2,531.7	2,384.2	2,455.8	2,636.4	3,085.0	3,072.6	3,047.6	3,048.4	3,223.4	3,173.1	3,103.2	3,345.0
Greece	676.4	457.9	400.0	867.9	1,195.4	1,336.9	1,355.5	1,524.1	1,619.0	1,645.1	1,519.0	1,637.2
Iceland	5,060.1	4,766.3	4,906.2	5,263.3	6,158.6	6,134.0	5,472.4	5,044.8	5,045.1	5,311.6	5,187.1	4,867.5
Ireland	1,627.3	1,869.5	2,182.1	2,705.3	3,435.7	3,877.3	4,234.6	4,841.5	4,935.0	3,584.1	3,229.4	3,481.1
Italy	1,617.2	1,222.5	973.0	746.1	855.9	877.9	894.1	1,023.4	1,069.8	979.1	1,043.6	1,123.7
Liechtenstein	19,353.4	17,092.2	17,781.9	11,186.3	9,992.0	6,147.4	3,990.8	3,641.8	3,723.3	3,724.6	3,708.2	3,730.2
Luxembourg												
Malta	2,531.7	2,384.2	2,455.8	2,636.4	3,085.0	3,072.6	3,047.6	3,048.4	3,223.4	3,173.1	3,005.5	3,086.4
Monaco	2,929.1	3,169.9	3,551.3	3,806.4	4,066.7	3,935.3	3,955.1	3,759.4	3,962.4	3,426.1	3,461.9	3,413.8
Netherlands	1,018.7	1,028.3	1,099.9	1,138.5	1,314.3	1,358.0	1,501.6	1,864.7	2,358.9	2,004.3	1,922.8	2,028.7
Norway	1,083.7	1,136.3	1,259.3	1,407.5	1,565.9	1,769.0	1,858.7	1,891.2	2,289.1	1,872.3	2,155.0	2,883.3
Portugal	3,371.8	2,884.2	2,995.1	3,604.1	3,945.0	3,752.3	3,703.6	3,963.6	4,800.2	5,010.0	4,832.8	5,090.8
Spain	1,191.2	1,142.3	1,411.8	1,732.1	1,813.2	1,744.2	1,563.9	1,550.7	1,576.3	1,475.1	1,522.7	1,701.2
Sweden	734.6	956.3	745.9	1,009.3	921.6	1,001.3	1,059.2	1,122.3	1,100.9	962.6	1,352.0	1,816.1
Switzerland	4,839.5	4,923.8	4,950.0	4,840.5	5,007.6	5,259.0	5,115.5	5,318.8	5,117.3	4,802.3	4,640.8	4,455.8
Turkey	1,252.2	708.9	928.1	1,196.9	1,538.5	1,919.1	2,100.6	2,413.0	2,832.7	2,566.3	2,762.7	2,523.6
United Kingdom	2,401.8	2,251.4	2,358.9	2,524.0	2,943.3	2,920.6	3,019.2	3,487.2	3,274.8	3,047.2	3,215.6	3,420.5
Eastern Europe												
Albania	1,145.2	910.1	1,321.2	1,208.9	959.0	879.0	798.6	781.5	758.4	648.0	620.5	661.6
Belarus				303.4	194.1	185.8	112.1	138.9	116.6	151.8	151.2	173.3
Bosnia-Herzegovina	11.9	15.5	30.4	40.5	55.2	85.1	114.5	111.5	107.4	91.8	87.9	93.6
Bulgaria	4,027.7	1,836.9	2,048.3	1,715.7	1,960.7	1,114.1	227.0	472.1	682.1	646.1	695.1	735.0
Croatia	344.0	339.1	445.0	508.0	1,380.0	944.9	899.2	1,111.8	1,288.3	1,240.8	1,252.9	1,317.5
Czech Republic	160.0	144.3	189.3	251.4	370.7	434.9	478.0	539.7	610.3	556.2	546.6	641.2
Estonia				779.8	1,036.4	1,099.2	1,250.5	1,480.1	1,724.8	1,496.3	1,477.4	1,509.2
Georgia				388.9	326.8	347.3	287.9	331.2	321.4	386.1	383.0	438.7
Hungary	173.2	187.4	240.3	271.1	362.8	428.1	443.7	590.2	697.6	704.2	773.9	971.8
Latvia	1,725.1	1,697.8	2,261.6	5,312.2	1,418.3	1,540.9	1,255.7	1,172.3	1,894.4	1,787.8	1,705.4	1,743.3
Lithuania	2,632.2	2,877.7	1,072.4	1,850.4	1,709.7	1,984.1	2,502.6	2,948.6	2,160.9	2,008.8	2,045.2	2,088.1
Macedonia	150.8	176.0	224.8	275.7	305.3	332.5	376.7	323.9	312.4	332.8	350.8	365.3
Moldova	171.8	169.4	222.3	253.7	690.3	472.1	447.6	552.0	639.2	617.8	588.4	628.1
Montenegro				683.9	596.1	662.1	561.1	635.9	578.8	637.2	609.1	649.9
Poland	1,145.2	910.1	1,321.2	1,208.9	980.7	904.4	720.0	795.1	900.9	609.8	846.9	1,179.1
Romania	266.5	215.2	198.3	221.9	293.7	372.4	406.6	606.2	405.0	337.8	370.4	528.3
Russia				601.0	407.8	411.1	301.0	252.9	374.4	363.1	476.1	527.2
Serbia				683.9	596.1	662.1	561.1	635.9	578.8	637.2	609.1	649.9
Slovakia	48.9	1,551.5	267.2	266.2	352.2	540.9	670.1	832.1	1,102.2	1,215.2	1,240.0	1,266.3
Slovenia	1,631.2	2,074.0	2,104.5	2,667.6	2,835.9	2,615.7	2,499.6	2,461.8	3,205.8	2,716.5	2,595.1	2,663.0
Ukraine				41.4	47.9	54.1	57.1	65.8	146.8	92.5	109.4	108.7

Source: Euromonitor International from national statistics

Banking and Finance Statistics | Table 5.13

Average Charge Card Expenditure 2000-2011
US$ per card

	2000	2001	2002	2003	2004	2005	2006	2007	2008	2009	2010	2011
Western Europe												
Austria	1,636.8	1,793.7	1,999.7	2,344.9	3,107.0	3,248.4	3,402.2	3,969.1	4,607.7	6,160.0	5,929.6	6,320.2
Belgium	2,322.0	2,423.8	2,510.9	2,326.7	2,414.8	2,559.1	2,801.0	2,931.2	3,082.9	3,005.4	3,046.1	3,092.8
Cyprus	2,828.9	2,784.0	2,744.8	2,962.6	3,043.1	2,961.3	2,768.6	2,565.9	2,378.2	2,033.3	2,089.9	2,048.0
Denmark												
Finland	5,830.9	6,320.6	6,283.5	7,443.0	7,942.9	7,680.5	9,557.7	10,206.1	10,228.7	10,012.4	9,990.7	9,993.9
France	2,616.1	3,137.8	3,455.9	4,448.5	4,087.5	4,622.3	4,863.7	5,960.0	7,340.1	7,137.6	5,774.7	5,921.6
Germany	1,212.3	1,324.4	1,457.2	1,879.7	2,253.1	2,294.6	2,363.5	2,653.1	2,762.6	2,554.8	2,520.9	2,725.5
Gibraltar	8,495.0	8,105.3	8,665.2	9,253.7	10,878.5	10,527.7	11,664.5	11,664.5	12,559.0	10,469.8	8,921.3	8,901.1
Greece	1,349.4	1,072.7	1,174.7	1,590.7	4,650.4	6,289.0	5,800.5	6,055.0	6,679.1	6,255.2	5,423.3	5,343.8
Iceland	8,495.0	8,105.3	8,665.2	9,253.7	10,878.5	10,527.7	11,664.5	11,664.5	12,559.0	10,469.8	10,479.2	10,300.9
Ireland	8,495.0	8,105.3	8,665.2	9,253.7	10,878.5	10,527.7	11,664.5	11,664.5	12,559.0	10,469.8	8,921.3	8,901.1
Italy	1,351.7	1,337.8	1,572.6	1,859.1	2,425.9	2,616.4	2,607.2	2,787.4	3,138.9	3,025.4	3,005.8	3,544.5
Liechtenstein	1,093.3	1,160.4	1,264.5	1,642.6	1,985.4	2,027.0	2,071.3	2,054.4	2,055.6	2,064.3	2,087.7	2,130.6
Luxembourg												
Malta	8,495.0	8,105.3	8,665.2	9,253.7	10,878.5	10,527.7	11,664.5	11,664.5	12,559.0	10,469.8	10,113.4	10,187.4
Monaco	4,088.3	4,380.7	4,995.6	6,418.2	7,420.8	7,671.5	7,950.8	8,021.8	5,715.6	5,286.6	5,399.3	5,511.3
Netherlands	5,439.9	5,456.3	5,983.2	6,961.8	7,933.4	7,541.7	7,044.8	7,300.4	8,557.3	6,704.3	7,432.8	8,439.7
Norway	4,690.9	4,519.6	5,010.8	5,298.6	5,607.0	6,777.6	6,197.7	7,485.1	8,319.9	6,818.0	6,424.0	6,527.7
Portugal	2,918.3	2,916.7	2,636.7	2,862.6	2,682.1	2,614.6	2,477.9	2,738.9	2,975.4	2,828.3	2,645.3	2,744.1
Spain	659.7	669.9	951.1	1,197.5	1,385.7	1,516.4	1,545.6	1,946.1	2,208.8	2,031.5	2,103.8	2,296.2
Sweden	5,534.3	4,917.5	6,330.9	7,810.1	9,035.9	8,421.2	6,276.7	7,115.2	7,704.9	6,477.5	6,884.9	7,601.5
Switzerland	18,051.3	20,877.9	20,978.3	20,105.8	19,985.1	19,639.4	19,794.4	19,636.2	20,004.0	17,359.1	16,787.8	16,490.6
Turkey												
United Kingdom	6,945.8	6,634.1	7,247.3	7,658.6	8,585.8	8,478.8	9,884.4	10,698.4	9,639.8	7,545.0	7,358.8	7,895.3
Eastern Europe												
Albania	659.2	620.4	953.7	1,550.1	839.2	888.6	1,075.1	1,065.1	1,101.7	1,070.3	1,416.3	1,616.0
Belarus												
Bosnia-Herzegovina	659.2	620.4	953.7	1,550.1	839.2	888.6	1,075.1	1,065.1	1,101.7	1,070.3	1,416.3	1,616.0
Bulgaria												
Croatia	2,657.5	2,638.7	2,511.9	2,772.7	3,817.6	4,805.9	7,072.0	9,549.8	11,396.4	11,224.3	11,119.4	11,895.6
Czech Republic	987.0	1,056.3	1,258.2	1,540.9	1,597.5	1,757.3	1,933.1	2,268.2	2,950.2	2,328.4	2,369.2	2,836.4
Estonia				3.3	4.5	9.9	15.4	16.9	23.8	19.5	19.4	20.2
Georgia												
Hungary	1,333.0	1,936.4	3,223.6	2,312.5	1,901.1	2,488.3	3,576.6	5,310.0	6,841.2	4,885.0	5,315.4	7,784.8
Latvia	4,378.4	3,827.6	7,166.7	6,051.6	1,747.4	2,003.9	1,661.7	1,532.3	1,281.1	870.8	740.5	768.2
Lithuania			0.0	1.0	1.8	3.8	7.8	11.3	13.9	10.9	10.9	11.3
Macedonia												
Moldova	1,381.7	1,368.4	1,304.1	1,483.7	2,209.3	2,697.7	3,920.9	5,097.5	6,062.3	6,062.3	8,022.0	9,153.6
Montenegro												
Poland	822.4	1,125.0	1,951.8	3,118.8	3,185.0	3,876.3	5,573.4	7,608.5	9,313.4	7,050.0	7,628.9	8,068.4
Romania		1,489.0	1,227.4	968.9	885.7	925.9	1,022.4	1,748.1	1,837.3	2,743.3	1,592.7	1,454.5
Russia												
Serbia												
Slovakia	922.1	918.5	1,591.5	1,704.2	2,186.6	2,497.0	2,976.2	4,319.4	4,433.4	3,724.1	3,702.1	3,908.4
Slovenia	2,370.3	2,446.3	2,545.4	2,951.6	3,193.9	3,254.1	3,229.5	3,248.1	3,253.4	3,168.6	3,091.5	3,081.1
Ukraine												

Source: Euromonitor International from national statistics

Banking and Finance Statistics

Table 5.14

Average Credit Card Transaction Expenditure 2000-2011

US$ per transaction

	2000	2001	2002	2003	2004	2005	2006	2007	2008	2009	2010	2011
Western Europe												
Austria	110.7	104.6	107.6	132.3	124.4	130.0	133.3	148.8	163.1	153.0	154.6	161.3
Belgium	126.9	128.3	136.8	131.8	119.8	124.6	124.4	117.2	115.2	106.9	108.9	110.4
Cyprus	45.0	31.6	34.9	41.5	48.0	49.9	51.3	52.5	53.4	52.5	49.9	49.2
Denmark	104.4	110.3	118.3	131.8	122.2	113.6	112.3	118.5	122.5	109.7	100.2	103.8
Finland	45.3	43.2	43.9	44.4	46.3	42.3	41.7	41.1	45.8	41.3	40.2	40.1
France	65.6	63.1	65.9	78.5	86.1	86.1	86.9	94.7	100.3	94.0	89.7	95.5
Germany	60.5	62.9	68.4	83.7	90.5	90.9	87.0	94.6	100.3	94.6	89.4	95.0
Gibraltar	84.4	82.0	87.7	98.9	111.9	114.5	115.0	115.0	117.3	112.7	108.8	108.7
Greece	40.7	45.3	52.5	95.9	112.6	133.2	132.3	147.5	151.3	134.8	117.3	118.3
Iceland	140.6	136.6	145.9	164.4	186.0	190.4	172.1	158.7	153.1	157.4	133.3	115.7
Ireland	46.1	44.9	51.5	66.8	84.3	83.5	90.4	105.0	103.7	82.8	77.3	77.3
Italy	98.4	96.2	101.5	113.5	130.1	128.3	155.8	142.5	153.1	134.3	128.5	137.8
Liechtenstein	112.2	116.5	116.0	134.5	143.1	139.7	133.1	126.2	127.7	126.4	125.5	126.2
Luxembourg												
Malta	84.4	82.0	87.7	98.9	111.9	114.5	115.0	115.0	117.3	112.7	112.3	108.2
Monaco	343.9	337.3	333.7	375.8	389.7	351.7	366.2	344.9	337.4	337.4	335.0	333.8
Netherlands	100.7	97.2	98.3	110.1	123.4	118.1	126.9	139.4	156.1	139.5	124.1	125.2
Norway	127.3	130.2	139.9	151.4	148.9	162.1	191.3	168.6	177.8	156.9	145.2	146.9
Portugal	64.2	44.8	49.3	58.6	67.7	70.4	73.2	77.6	90.6	91.9	88.1	90.4
Spain	102.3	99.9	105.5	131.0	141.4	146.0	124.8	104.0	89.0	78.6	72.7	75.9
Sweden	164.4	96.4	64.2	79.3	85.4	54.8	50.6	52.5	58.1	49.7	66.4	78.7
Switzerland	177.9	175.9	173.5	173.2	176.8	180.4	185.8	185.2	182.7	172.0	165.5	157.6
Turkey	36.1	19.4	24.5	30.2	38.0	46.1	53.6	66.0	77.0	65.3	66.8	60.1
United Kingdom	82.9	79.9	86.3	96.8	108.9	111.5	116.1	128.1	117.8	93.4	93.4	98.0
Eastern Europe												
Albania	44.3	42.3	39.0	41.6	45.7	60.1	72.2	67.2	71.4	71.2	69.0	72.0
Belarus				69.8	35.6	30.9	26.4	32.6	34.6	14.1	12.8	14.1
Bosnia-Herzegovina	2.2	2.6	4.5	5.4	2.1	3.2	4.1	4.5	5.2	5.0	5.3	5.0
Bulgaria	143.4	105.6	114.7	153.9	141.8	68.3	39.8	95.0	120.8	96.0	92.2	96.3
Croatia	35.8	37.7	44.1	50.7	50.8	51.4	46.1	52.2	49.3	45.6	44.7	46.9
Czech Republic	48.1	50.2	32.3	33.9	64.8	72.6	71.5	74.5	80.2	63.4	53.0	56.1
Estonia				70.2	69.0	74.0	82.7	94.3	97.0	95.1	93.2	86.7
Georgia				41.2	38.1	40.9	52.2	50.4	71.1	34.1	30.8	34.0
Hungary	36.1	38.0	44.5	51.1	51.2	51.8	46.8	52.4	54.1	41.6	42.7	44.9
Latvia	201.8	187.1	194.5	382.5	76.8	77.1	60.0	60.3	42.4	54.3	48.1	44.8
Lithuania	66.2	64.3	51.9	70.3	76.6	74.0	84.0	92.2	77.7	75.5	78.0	72.6
Macedonia	144.4	179.9	221.2	216.1	299.0	367.9	415.1	393.6	394.7	425.0	423.8	400.7
Moldova	35.8	37.7	44.1	50.7	50.8	51.4	46.1	52.2	49.3	45.6	44.4	46.3
Montenegro				35.9	38.0	42.9	48.3	54.4	60.0	24.1	23.6	24.6
Poland	44.3	42.3	39.0	41.6	43.4	45.4	45.3	51.6	58.8	40.2	42.1	42.4
Romania	69.2	49.1	41.7	42.5	53.4	63.4	67.5	99.3	63.4	46.3	48.3	50.8
Russia				88.4	179.3	185.4	181.3	125.6	123.9	86.8	90.7	92.8
Serbia				35.9	38.0	42.9	48.3	54.4	60.0	24.1	23.6	24.6
Slovakia	0.2	46.6	41.0	45.6	47.9	60.9	71.7	67.2	75.3	53.5	51.3	47.8
Slovenia	50.3	45.1	44.6	51.5	52.1	50.0	50.3	54.5	54.6	57.7	57.9	55.6
Ukraine				68.2	68.1	74.5	59.8	60.1	65.3	34.8	39.0	27.9

Source: Euromonitor International from national statistics

| **Table 5.15**

Average Charge Card Transaction Expenditure 2000-2011

US$ per transaction

	2000	2001	2002	2003	2004	2005	2006	2007	2008	2009	2010	2011
Western Europe												
Austria	108.6	106.4	110.7	132.5	126.9	127.3	130.7	149.4	159.2	144.5	121.2	126.9
Belgium	94.5	98.4	97.9	101.3	101.9	102.0	99.5	94.1	94.0	89.8	92.3	93.9
Cyprus	18.5	17.5	18.9	21.0	22.5	22.7	22.4	21.8	21.3	20.0	19.7	19.6
Denmark												
Finland	59.1	61.3	63.6	80.7	88.5	92.3	104.4	117.3	120.2	120.3	118.7	109.2
France	99.5	94.5	94.8	112.1	116.0	114.7	114.2	123.7	131.1	123.0	87.9	89.0
Germany	84.5	83.0	92.6	104.5	120.4	125.7	129.3	127.2	138.8	125.8	123.1	134.7
Gibraltar	155.7	148.2	158.3	168.0	199.7	185.6	197.0	197.0	213.1	199.3	181.3	185.8
Greece	158.7	154.9	163.9	197.7	213.0	213.0	217.9	240.1	240.6	229.6	218.4	239.8
Iceland	155.7	148.2	158.3	168.0	199.7	185.6	197.0	197.0	213.1	199.3	196.4	194.9
Ireland	155.7	148.2	158.3	168.0	199.7	185.6	197.0	197.0	213.1	199.3	181.3	185.8
Italy	84.5	82.6	87.3	104.7	118.9	124.4	125.6	142.1	159.5	136.6	127.8	148.3
Liechtenstein	76.8	81.2	92.2	105.5	121.6	128.1	130.5	122.3	123.9	125.0	126.6	130.6
Luxembourg												
Malta	155.7	148.2	158.3	168.0	199.7	185.6	197.0	197.0	213.1	199.3	199.7	199.1
Monaco	115.4	95.7	100.6	118.1	134.5	116.3	97.7	97.7	89.5	83.9	83.8	83.7
Netherlands	180.0	172.4	177.4	206.4	225.6	202.0	199.8	217.9	243.7	224.7	223.2	236.3
Norway	140.4	136.1	157.7	161.0	161.3	160.1	167.4	190.6	197.0	170.1	177.6	202.1
Portugal	24.7	23.2	24.9	27.4	29.4	29.3	29.2	30.8	32.0	29.4	27.8	29.1
Spain	45.7	43.0	44.7	54.6	59.8	61.4	57.9	64.4	71.7	63.6	59.7	62.4
Sweden	118.8	96.9	100.2	101.9	132.6	130.5	92.4	88.7	86.7	77.5	98.7	113.9
Switzerland	335.6	319.6	315.9	312.2	316.1	317.0	336.1	341.0	344.9	353.3	353.0	354.1
Turkey												
United Kingdom	134.4	126.1	134.4	136.1	161.1	161.1	173.9	195.9	183.8	147.7	148.2	154.6
Eastern Europe												
Albania	46.9	35.2	53.7	49.5	53.1	57.8	62.4	62.1	60.5	60.8	76.2	79.0
Belarus												
Bosnia-Herzegovina	9.5	7.2	9.0	7.8	4.1	4.2	4.1	4.0	3.9	4.0	5.0	5.1
Bulgaria	98.9	47.4	37.2	87.3	104.0	89.4	98.2	108.2	109.3	109.9	136.2	143.5
Croatia	103.2	99.5	77.9	174.7	193.3	174.8	194.6	223.0	223.5	223.7	215.1	220.4
Czech Republic	35.6	37.3	44.3	52.7	52.2	54.4	58.6	64.2	79.5	59.8	57.0	63.4
Estonia				64.6	55.4	77.2	75.8	75.1	103.7	84.6	84.5	84.8
Georgia												
Hungary	99.6	120.5	189.0	310.8	344.2	321.3	205.0	230.3	245.9	188.8	171.0	212.8
Latvia	67.5	50.5	70.1	79.7	13.1	13.0	10.2	10.0	9.0	7.5	7.4	7.4
Lithuania					142.0	53.1	63.8	79.3	47.8	21.1	24.1	27.7
Macedonia												
Moldova	169.9	99.6	73.4	186.5	197.9	177.9	195.4	220.3	220.5	219.1	274.3	284.7
Montenegro												
Poland	28.8	24.3	26.4	27.9	30.9	35.4	44.4	44.9	50.3	37.6	40.5	42.0
Romania		61.6	53.7	48.4	39.6	35.3	31.7	46.1	41.8	158.1	74.4	59.3
Russia												
Serbia												
Slovakia	103.2	44.2	40.0	56.5	69.2	83.7	104.5	159.3	160.2	142.2	143.8	147.0
Slovenia	20.3	20.4	21.8	25.9	29.0	29.6	30.8	34.0	36.8	37.8	38.0	37.4
Ukraine												

Source: Euromonitor International from national statistics

6

Consumer Expenditure

Consumer Expenditure Statistics

Table 6.1

Consumer Expenditure 1990, 1995, 1999-2011

National currency million

	1990	1995	1999	2000	2001	2002	2003	2004
Western Europe								
Austria	80,433	98,362	110,027	115,647	119,197	121,523	124,866	130,071
Belgium	90,516	109,067	122,956	130,619	134,935	137,147	139,998	145,438
Cyprus	3,618	5,729	7,163	8,022	8,571	8,608	8,872	9,369
Denmark	419,184	515,752	589,505	608,142	624,005	643,125	656,370	696,488
Finland	43,457	48,177	59,005	63,021	66,442	69,507	72,259	74,879
France	582,590	666,021	748,195	793,389	827,097	852,479	882,570	918,772
Germany	791,828	1,012,770	1,101,020	1,130,850	1,167,710	1,173,240	1,192,670	1,213,660
Gibraltar								
Greece	33,620	69,842	97,151	102,816	110,405	119,791	126,978	135,896
Iceland	202,927	242,254	349,626	380,083	403,252	419,255	446,675	488,654
Ireland	20,865	27,883	42,807	49,214	53,414	57,717	61,479	64,811
Italy	405,815	566,904	689,674	731,720	754,766	775,381	802,011	830,322
Liechtenstein	1,184	1,829	2,610	2,700	2,736	2,730	2,709	2,798
Luxembourg	5,294	7,195	9,326	10,249	10,527	11,360	11,456	12,170
Malta	1,581	2,311	2,931	3,060	3,133	3,196	3,354	3,457
Monaco	1,806	2,212	2,538	2,697	2,826	2,920	3,033	3,156
Netherlands	118,207	147,673	191,741	205,578	218,499	226,990	232,087	237,424
Norway	343,193	446,599	564,793	605,116	632,186	660,113	695,845	737,230
Portugal	37,156	57,730	76,204	82,021	86,109	89,552	91,770	96,705
Spain	195,616	281,192	365,484	397,805	424,620	446,281	473,188	508,538
Sweden	684,340	869,666	1,014,258	1,064,071	1,101,830	1,149,298	1,194,027	1,235,312
Switzerland	185,251	218,122	239,737	257,001	264,236	265,018	267,055	273,247
Turkey	366	7,499	74,994	124,768	179,987	259,441	345,723	423,620
United Kingdom	342,613	448,267	577,271	609,098	635,909	664,990	699,328	735,401
Eastern Europe								
Albania	12,226	203,334	418,345	418,532	438,267	482,939	525,889	595,262
Belarus	2	70,254	1,773,389	5,211,536	9,917,949	15,647,102	21,049,739	27,001,692
Bosnia-Herzegovina		3,264	9,336	12,097	13,477	15,032	15,627	15,701
Bulgaria	31	638	17,436	19,757	22,599	23,774	25,792	28,774
Croatia	209	81,021	111,808	126,185	140,872	152,042	169,921	177,933
Czech Republic	310,051	800,748	1,166,422	1,221,936	1,310,498	1,346,661	1,415,508	1,511,725
Estonia	1,586	1,668	3,331	3,694	4,171	4,656	5,095	5,747
Georgia		3,000	4,495	5,374	5,265	5,692	6,166	7,206
Hungary	1,017,363	3,292,181	6,632,759	7,634,264	8,737,335	9,635,218	10,713,493	11,426,818
Latvia		1,640	2,601	2,884	3,178	3,517	3,894	4,532
Lithuania	76	17,051	29,220	30,437	32,573	34,583	37,709	41,819
Macedonia	344	119,688	150,786	181,870	166,007	190,448	201,842	217,133
Moldova	8	3,616	8,945	13,641	15,901	18,020	24,072	27,582
Montenegro		649	586	739	962	1,090	1,110	1,210
Poland	27,674	205,751	419,854	474,790	502,459	536,052	549,894	592,705
Romania	56	4,907	39,969	54,639	80,460	102,826	129,102	168,407
Russia	289	688,038	2,459,553	3,167,498	4,182,382	5,215,968	6,332,020	8,137,258
Serbia		37,044	157,868	293,539	627,628	813,979	897,860	1,057,081
Slovakia	5,235	10,329	15,772	17,485	19,852	21,324	22,813	25,537
Slovenia	424	6,371	10,059	10,992	12,130	13,377	14,536	15,492
Ukraine	1	27,504	72,588	93,787	114,215	125,828	147,695	181,583

Source: Euromonitor International from national statistics

Consumer Expenditure 1990, 1995, 1999-2011 *(continued)*

National currency million

	2005	2006	2007	2008	2009	2010	2011	US$ million 2011	US$ per capita 2011
Western Europe									
Austria	136,556	141,789	146,696	151,883	152,899	158,346	164,638	228,917.57	27,238.30
Belgium	150,822	158,138	165,383	174,147	173,077	181,130	186,739	259,647.83	23,709.39
Cyprus	9,925	10,590	11,733	12,819	11,818	12,419	12,692	17,647.06	15,811.19
Denmark	735,377	777,066	806,552	826,129	799,004	834,444	848,130	158,239.79	28,457.18
Finland	77,838	82,371	86,930	91,681	89,651	94,368	99,746	138,690.50	25,801.56
France	955,919	997,568	1,042,154	1,073,996	1,065,655	1,090,284	1,114,519	1,549,662.38	24,548.03
Germany	1,238,170	1,272,270	1,287,380	1,317,261	1,319,330	1,358,920	1,414,562	1,966,851.93	24,058.88
Gibraltar									
Greece	140,491	151,061	161,247	174,880	172,622	173,217	165,809	230,546.23	20,355.67
Iceland	553,795	613,550	677,688	720,379	734,904	755,990	784,621	6,766.66	20,881.78
Ireland	70,305	76,807	83,502	83,550	72,450	71,250	71,366	99,229.84	22,145.28
Italy	857,017	892,032	921,092	941,351	925,040	949,853	977,241	1,358,787.40	22,412.46
Liechtenstein	2,952	3,166	3,404	3,370	3,287	3,370	3,484	3,922.51	108,509.42
Luxembourg	12,583	12,955	13,570	14,352	14,317	14,667	15,431	21,455.43	41,733.57
Malta	3,596	3,685	3,862	4,142	4,066	4,289	4,503	6,260.72	14,973.29
Monaco	3,297	3,555	4,162	4,318	3,925	4,030	4,200	5,839.12	164,821.21
Netherlands	245,144	249,657	259,096	264,994	257,816	263,194	266,292	370,261.49	22,230.18
Norway	774,472	825,348	883,512	926,871	948,031	1,003,436	1,036,382	184,874.46	37,573.78
Portugal	100,708	105,800	111,936	116,026	110,547	115,048	114,994	159,891.45	15,031.66
Spain	545,793	587,382	625,457	642,966	610,463	626,797	636,113	884,471.99	19,163.94
Sweden	1,287,641	1,347,172	1,418,909	1,462,990	1,497,581	1,571,168	1,624,973	250,173.96	26,570.24
Switzerland	278,904	287,833	299,844	312,929	316,529	324,552	329,254	370,737.09	47,106.83
Turkey	490,692	564,898	628,733	695,620	714,245	819,291	957,794	570,197.62	7,777.72
United Kingdom	773,118	806,575	849,551	862,644	850,835	896,022	928,455	1,487,908.23	23,807.06
Eastern Europe									
Albania	642,464	686,305	786,532	876,920	1,018,373	1,087,796	1,164,779	11,544.47	3,591.16
Belarus	34,170,019	41,158,150	50,862,554	68,224,331	76,903,494	90,808,799	144,123,313	28,971.66	3,055.70
Bosnia-Herzegovina	17,261	18,790	20,745	23,336	22,409	20,502	20,951	14,894.65	3,875.07
Bulgaria	33,074	36,561	43,961	48,476	45,827	45,869	48,332	34,364.32	4,571.70
Croatia	192,663	205,109	223,019	241,084	229,400	230,921	235,845	44,133.79	10,002.82
Czech Republic	1,589,399	1,699,628	1,815,972	1,944,902	1,937,982	1,960,319	1,976,173	111,674.47	10,650.10
Estonia	6,526	7,646	8,831	9,001	7,621	7,600	8,234	11,449.15	8,542.90
Georgia	7,850	11,064	12,300	14,945	15,069	15,951	18,466	10,949.40	2,492.31
Hungary	12,154,973	12,932,724	13,830,161	14,552,096	14,219,402	14,532,927	15,143,440	75,320.07	7,542.78
Latvia	5,440	7,045	8,902	9,736	7,886	7,986	8,775	17,362.82	8,369.22
Lithuania	47,578	54,329	63,153	72,285	62,604	61,101	67,813	27,308.12	8,416.48
Macedonia	232,824	256,138	285,559	337,361	320,727	328,425	352,500	7,969.56	3,874.41
Moldova	34,248	40,395	48,569	57,046	52,501	64,590	74,735	6,366.62	1,790.50
Montenegro	1,257	1,648	2,351	2,795	2,487	2,535	2,699	3,752.52	6,052.17
Poland	617,291	657,474	706,814	779,806	815,798	862,543	928,873	313,440.00	8,207.53
Romania	197,804	233,441	272,714	326,300	302,760	324,806	347,729	114,061.63	5,324.08
Russia	10,325,185	12,690,475	15,731,076	19,671,112	20,693,840	23,160,674	26,882,274	914,610.42	6,399.72
Serbia	1,286,735	1,498,987	1,723,241	2,036,305	2,162,202	2,300,465	2,585,413	35,255.60	4,846.19
Slovakia	27,819	30,945	33,884	37,531	37,527	37,747	39,013	54,245.46	10,051.56
Slovenia	16,394	17,234	19,037	20,694	20,728	21,270	21,810	30,325.46	14,791.54
Ukraine	254,761	322,969	428,562	591,379	592,257	699,733	874,790	109,728.52	2,406.42

Source: Euromonitor International from national statistics

Consumer Expenditure Statistics

Table 6.2

Consumer Expenditure by Object 2011

US$ million

	Food and Non-Alcoholic Beverages	Alcoholic Beverages and Tobacco	Clothing and Footwear	Housing	Household Goods and Services	Health Goods and Medical Services
Western Europe						
Austria	23,222.9	7,666.5	14,082.0	49,390.3	15,116.4	7,855.7
Belgium	37,010.2	9,687.4	12,897.1	62,246.1	15,162.8	13,928.6
Cyprus						
Denmark	17,712.0	6,010.1	6,687.0	47,910.9	8,296.7	4,396.8
Finland	16,676.6	6,509.8	7,296.8	38,272.0	7,438.0	6,425.3
France	205,737.5	50,121.3	66,317.6	395,371.0	89,965.7	59,751.8
Germany	218,392.1	60,204.6	98,925.4	476,391.2	121,350.9	100,488.6
Gibraltar						
Greece	38,765.2	9,521.9	10,564.7	51,600.3	10,373.2	15,972.9
Iceland						
Ireland	10,122.6	5,439.3	3,887.2	21,686.8	4,720.7	5,854.4
Italy	198,751.1	36,242.7	101,317.9	287,661.6	100,132.8	41,378.2
Liechtenstein						
Luxembourg						
Malta						
Monaco						
Netherlands	43,672.1	12,334.4	20,888.8	90,383.4	21,640.5	10,217.9
Norway	24,509.1	7,939.3	9,717.3	39,832.3	10,327.5	5,159.6
Portugal	26,048.0	5,249.8	8,862.9	26,582.6	9,918.1	9,752.6
Spain	125,593.6	26,617.2	44,970.7	180,787.9	41,777.5	30,752.8
Sweden	30,674.9	9,027.0	12,135.9	67,031.0	12,280.6	8,543.0
Switzerland	37,701.0	11,853.9	11,674.0	95,291.4	13,875.0	60,161.5
Turkey	124,213.1	23,871.4	27,985.0	120,605.2	43,245.3	21,781.9
United Kingdom	139,493.8	52,400.7	83,537.7	368,694.7	72,758.2	25,927.4
Eastern Europe						
Albania						
Belarus	11,984.8	1,644.1	2,313.2	3,917.6	1,538.0	766.0
Bosnia-Herzegovina	4,851.9	813.5	704.8	1,981.5	1,018.2	666.4
Bulgaria	7,535.1	1,347.5	889.7	6,617.0	1,051.0	1,521.5
Croatia	9,969.9	1,906.5	2,607.7	6,336.5	3,285.0	2,142.2
Czech Republic	14,780.6	10,500.0	3,206.7	30,461.2	6,062.9	2,776.4
Estonia	2,292.0	929.0	566.3	2,592.3	478.0	440.9
Georgia	4,471.6	543.9	465.0	1,492.8	355.7	1,129.5
Hungary	12,432.2	5,639.0	2,006.7	17,286.3	3,252.8	3,258.8
Latvia	3,059.5	1,256.9	947.3	4,525.0	665.7	688.5
Lithuania	7,251.4	2,245.0	1,936.6	4,140.8	1,157.0	1,507.0
Macedonia	2,605.5	301.3	477.8	1,282.0	432.5	172.2
Moldova						
Montenegro	1,276.7	120.9	234.4	744.9	177.3	96.8
Poland	62,927.7	20,464.5	13,495.6	77,236.3	13,675.6	12,829.3
Romania	33,511.4	4,326.8	4,139.5	24,859.6	5,765.7	3,962.1
Russia	285,800.8	65,257.2	81,024.7	80,390.4	42,804.6	35,094.1
Serbia	9,212.9	1,829.4	1,306.1	8,423.4	1,397.8	1,790.2
Slovakia	9,179.0	2,687.1	2,224.6	13,857.9	3,438.9	2,204.3
Slovenia	4,346.5	1,355.5	1,707.1	5,643.0	1,912.8	1,135.6
Ukraine	41,899.7	7,139.1	6,232.3	13,913.2	4,747.8	5,370.9

Source: Euromonitor International from national statistics

Consumer Expenditure by Object 2011 *(continued)*
US$ million

	Transport	Communications	Leisure and Recreation	Education	Hotels and Catering	Miscellaneous Goods and Services	Total
Western Europe							
Austria	30,067.3	4,561.4	23,589.8	1,680.3	27,113.9	24,571.1	228,917.6
Belgium	31,387.2	5,167.9	23,113.2	1,240.5	15,135.0	32,671.9	259,647.8
Cyprus							17,647.1
Denmark	18,960.2	2,814.8	17,123.2	1,210.4	7,526.0	19,591.6	158,239.8
Finland	15,897.3	3,206.1	15,400.9	632.0	8,707.8	12,227.9	138,690.5
France	216,120.5	43,115.4	131,864.7	13,897.5	109,844.6	167,554.9	1,549,662.4
Germany	278,110.1	52,662.8	177,140.5	19,372.2	114,349.1	249,464.3	1,966,851.9
Gibraltar							
Greece	26,229.7	8,108.9	13,249.7	6,185.5	22,146.8	17,827.4	230,546.2
Iceland							6,766.7
Ireland	12,049.9	3,076.7	6,667.9	2,314.9	13,650.2	9,759.2	99,229.8
Italy	177,517.6	34,306.6	93,046.2	12,723.2	139,902.7	135,806.9	1,358,787.4
Liechtenstein							3,922.5
Luxembourg							21,455.4
Malta							6,260.7
Monaco							5,839.1
Netherlands	47,179.0	14,304.4	35,844.5	2,406.0	17,588.3	53,802.0	370,261.5
Norway	27,635.7	4,858.8	23,364.4	831.1	11,097.0	19,602.4	184,874.5
Portugal	18,960.3	4,849.2	11,661.9	2,158.2	17,390.3	18,457.5	159,891.5
Spain	103,479.3	25,388.4	72,117.7	12,844.2	150,300.4	69,842.2	884,472.0
Sweden	33,426.6	8,398.7	27,657.2	737.2	14,071.8	26,190.1	250,174.0
Switzerland	28,761.3	10,629.2	28,460.5	2,051.9	28,261.2	42,016.0	370,737.1
Turkey	77,001.3	28,791.8	23,237.3	7,547.4	33,916.2	38,001.9	570,197.6
United Kingdom	214,234.8	30,830.4	163,798.0	22,770.5	147,769.9	165,692.2	1,487,908.2
Eastern Europe							
Albania							11,544.5
Belarus	2,219.9	1,205.6	1,052.1	431.2	690.9	1,208.1	28,971.7
Bosnia-Herzegovina	1,423.9	419.4	706.9	184.6	1,062.0	1,061.6	14,894.7
Bulgaria	6,136.0	1,815.4	1,659.3	207.0	4,118.0	1,466.8	34,364.3
Croatia	5,329.8	1,556.4	3,367.4	1,230.2	3,883.7	2,518.4	44,133.8
Czech Republic	10,071.1	3,556.5	11,462.2	857.3	8,501.4	9,438.1	111,674.5
Estonia	1,445.2	312.7	879.7	96.1	611.2	805.8	11,449.1
Georgia	854.2	189.9	623.2	116.7	237.2	469.8	10,949.4
Hungary	9,236.7	2,827.9	5,774.2	1,155.5	5,281.8	7,168.3	75,320.1
Latvia	2,155.6	606.4	1,404.0	332.9	800.2	920.8	17,362.8
Lithuania	4,342.1	610.9	1,444.0	244.0	681.4	1,747.8	27,308.1
Macedonia	979.5	693.6	241.0	147.7	232.6	403.6	7,969.6
Moldova							6,366.6
Montenegro	412.5	210.3	123.2	69.9	86.5	199.3	3,752.5
Poland	24,951.4	11,296.1	21,887.7	3,932.7	8,630.4	42,112.8	313,440.0
Romania	18,409.1	2,412.7	5,171.5	2,338.4	5,661.9	3,503.0	114,061.6
Russia	120,642.9	48,422.1	47,881.6	10,402.1	39,483.0	57,407.1	914,610.4
Serbia	4,994.1	1,583.5	1,854.2	429.9	807.5	1,626.5	35,255.6
Slovakia	3,928.6	2,062.7	5,315.5	857.9	3,007.4	5,481.7	54,245.5
Slovenia	4,508.9	1,010.0	3,113.0	413.2	2,276.2	2,903.6	30,325.5
Ukraine	12,767.3	3,754.5	4,503.9	2,250.2	3,023.0	4,126.6	109,728.5

Source: Euromonitor International from national statistics

6

Consumer Expenditure

Consumer Expenditure Statistics

Table 6.3

Food and Non-Alcoholic Beverage Consumer Expenditure 1990, 1995, 1999-2011

National currency million

	1990	1995	1999	2000	2001	2002	2003	2004
Western Europe								
Austria	9,995	11,244	11,766	12,101	12,572	12,800	13,043	13,617
Belgium	14,755	16,637	16,851	16,993	17,991	18,716	19,470	19,977
Cyprus								
Denmark	59,706	68,185	71,952	74,401	77,075	78,437	78,587	80,798
Finland	7,100	7,432	7,704	7,953	8,486	8,658	9,027	9,169
France	89,395	97,860	105,948	110,540	117,016	121,354	125,721	127,903
Germany	109,233	124,660	127,930	131,000	135,800	136,000	135,180	135,140
Gibraltar								
Greece	6,602	11,446	14,216	15,258	17,683	20,777	22,680	23,610
Iceland								
Ireland	3,817	4,243	4,843	5,515	5,931	6,144	6,184	6,287
Italy	76,667	94,667	105,533	110,229	112,947	116,484	120,889	123,977
Liechtenstein								
Luxembourg								
Malta								
Monaco								
Netherlands	16,442	19,221	22,363	22,992	24,488	25,547	26,009	26,211
Norway	57,643	71,135	84,709	88,763	90,541	92,695	97,001	99,702
Portugal	7,349	10,571	12,945	13,649	14,781	15,311	15,925	16,341
Spain	34,504	43,476	51,459	56,813	61,262	65,721	69,238	72,014
Sweden	104,761	122,994	125,076	128,239	135,983	144,621	148,480	150,797
Switzerland	22,254	24,384	25,500	27,148	28,482	28,671	29,141	29,211
Turkey	99	1,981	19,794	28,642	43,280	63,239	85,232	97,683
United Kingdom	42,285	49,700	57,750	59,403	60,584	61,850	64,411	66,158
Eastern Europe								
Albania								
Belarus	1	35,395	1,011,114	3,060,851	5,316,413	7,906,477	9,751,699	12,284,901
Bosnia-Herzegovina		1,134	3,110	3,992	4,398	4,868	5,024	5,009
Bulgaria	10	192	5,141	5,624	6,254	6,023	6,132	6,741
Croatia	53	19,471	26,163	27,268	33,333	36,915	38,483	39,979
Czech Republic	60,387	149,829	211,444	219,669	229,162	232,916	228,998	241,151
Estonia	624	482	692	749	825	907	962	1,094
Georgia		1,804	2,640	2,857	2,836	2,560	2,888	3,402
Hungary	266,220	769,800	1,303,070	1,455,244	1,653,013	1,762,194	1,897,365	1,972,098
Latvia		604	699	725	785	880	921	1,023
Lithuania	33	6,716	9,149	9,195	9,394	9,582	10,396	11,683
Macedonia	131	42,408	49,791	53,464	53,478	63,834	72,194	71,907
Moldova								
Montenegro		307	258	320	407	452	453	479
Poland	9,306	56,518	87,926	108,406	115,254	116,675	115,974	125,780
Romania	21	1,786	14,132	19,065	28,554	35,759	45,507	56,377
Russia	80	297,259	1,025,070	1,299,901	1,693,093	1,925,072	2,106,038	2,561,261
Serbia		13,803	57,210	104,571	218,166	275,609	285,047	309,801
Slovakia	1,247	2,861	3,883	4,085	4,401	4,674	4,810	4,936
Slovenia	75	1,146	1,719	1,858	2,052	2,219	2,380	2,433
Ukraine	1	15,040	37,884	47,720	56,163	58,392	63,118	68,488

Source: Euromonitor International from national statistics

Food and Non-Alcoholic Beverage Consumer Expenditure 1990, 1995, 1999-2011 *(continued)*

National currency million

	2005	2006	2007	2008	2009	2010	2011	US$ million 2011	US$ per capita 2011
Western Europe									
Austria	14,062	14,390	15,016	15,699	15,890	16,180	16,702	23,222.92	2,763.23
Belgium	20,217	20,355	21,241	23,198	24,026	24,929	26,618	37,010.20	3,379.54
Cyprus									
Denmark	82,133	84,519	89,310	94,128	91,060	93,049	94,932	17,712.00	3,185.25
Finland	9,407	9,814	10,460	11,431	11,636	11,691	11,994	16,676.60	3,102.46
France	130,000	133,109	136,984	143,408	143,116	145,753	147,967	205,737.45	3,259.06
Germany	135,960	138,900	141,500	149,432	147,087	149,606	157,068	218,392.09	2,671.41
Gibraltar									
Greece	22,765	21,918	23,434	27,869	28,447	28,006	27,880	38,765.21	3,422.71
Iceland									
Ireland	6,599	7,230	7,842	8,139	7,501	7,272	7,280	10,122.61	2,259.08
Italy	126,747	131,084	133,886	137,962	137,887	140,109	142,942	198,751.05	3,278.29
Liechtenstein									
Luxembourg									
Malta									
Monaco									
Netherlands	25,985	27,227	28,308	30,068	30,297	30,742	31,409	43,672.10	2,622.04
Norway	103,588	107,628	113,819	121,814	128,752	131,992	137,395	24,509.09	4,981.21
Portugal	16,530	17,339	18,140	19,227	18,728	18,560	18,734	26,048.02	2,448.82
Spain	75,396	79,926	83,761	88,061	84,941	88,230	90,327	125,593.64	2,721.25
Sweden	153,945	161,836	170,190	179,926	188,658	192,695	199,245	30,674.87	3,257.89
Switzerland	29,798	30,556	31,197	32,102	33,175	33,354	33,482	37,700.97	4,790.38
Turkey	112,018	125,083	135,615	153,810	162,111	187,332	208,648	124,213.06	1,694.31
United Kingdom	69,631	72,095	75,663	79,615	81,386	84,251	87,044	139,493.82	2,231.95
Eastern Europe									
Albania									
Belarus	15,546,259	18,725,634	22,687,513	30,037,828	33,227,939	38,227,947	59,619,784	11,984.77	1,264.06
Bosnia-Herzegovina	5,447	5,950	6,561	7,546	7,360	6,706	6,825	4,851.93	1,262.30
Bulgaria	7,210	7,820	9,508	10,426	9,886	10,083	10,598	7,535.10	1,002.44
Croatia	42,880	46,286	48,446	53,303	52,600	53,513	53,278	9,969.93	2,259.66
Czech Republic	238,439	249,182	265,964	290,162	270,359	270,774	261,556	14,780.64	1,409.59
Estonia	1,219	1,343	1,497	1,707	1,606	1,541	1,648	2,292.00	1,710.20
Georgia	3,472	4,924	5,230	5,956	5,786	6,591	7,541	4,471.59	1,017.83
Hungary	2,014,278	2,158,949	2,377,237	2,540,458	2,416,843	2,426,671	2,499,549	12,432.19	1,245.00
Latvia	1,214	1,390	1,606	1,760	1,490	1,493	1,546	3,059.48	1,474.73
Lithuania	12,469	13,963	15,806	18,066	16,393	15,746	18,007	7,251.44	2,234.93
Macedonia	79,159	84,198	93,762	111,285	105,985	108,127	115,244	2,605.52	1,266.68
Moldova									
Montenegro	484	637	820	979	855	874	918	1,276.65	2,059.02
Poland	129,952	137,310	145,555	159,278	165,844	174,237	186,485	62,927.68	1,647.78
Romania	58,877	67,948	76,200	91,508	88,668	96,446	102,163	33,511.35	1,564.22
Russia	3,010,574	3,649,608	4,380,332	5,618,863	6,144,048	7,293,677	8,400,270	285,800.76	1,999.81
Serbia	362,706	411,153	444,811	538,798	572,648	600,347	675,616	9,212.94	1,266.40
Slovakia	5,052	5,372	5,996	6,575	6,528	6,532	6,602	9,179.01	1,700.85
Slovenia	2,444	2,523	2,770	3,034	3,148	3,087	3,126	4,346.54	2,120.07
Ukraine	99,851	122,487	161,165	230,773	235,614	275,969	334,037	41,899.71	918.89

Source: Euromonitor International from national statistics

6

Consumer Expenditure

Consumer Expenditure Statistics | | | | | | | **Table 6.4**

Alcoholic Beverages and Tobacco Consumer Expenditure 1990, 1995, 1999-2011

National currency million

	1990	1995	1999	2000	2001	2002	2003	2004
Western Europe								
Austria	3,739	3,593	4,005	4,051	4,163	4,378	4,438	4,505
Belgium	2,861	3,645	4,529	4,685	4,733	4,991	5,458	5,654
Cyprus								
Denmark	24,616	24,725	25,917	26,514	27,214	27,586	27,964	27,269
Finland	2,852	2,917	3,265	3,479	3,914	4,055	4,152	3,915
France	17,442	23,049	27,017	28,175	29,500	30,652	30,525	31,052
Germany	35,006	38,260	40,000	39,550	40,500	42,510	42,310	42,070
Gibraltar								
Greece	1,132	2,700	3,856	4,018	4,542	5,455	5,843	6,097
Iceland								
Ireland	1,276	1,888	2,757	3,135	3,316	3,674	3,687	3,572
Italy	10,429	13,993	17,417	18,341	19,012	19,932	20,873	21,744
Liechtenstein								
Luxembourg								
Malta								
Monaco								
Netherlands	4,105	4,926	5,741	5,915	6,609	6,779	6,899	6,965
Norway	17,217	20,780	27,389	28,544	29,166	29,863	31,811	33,893
Portugal	1,511	2,221	2,911	2,904	3,113	3,203	3,371	3,483
Spain	5,822	8,868	11,041	12,065	12,812	13,606	14,463	15,331
Sweden	38,042	41,987	43,811	43,709	45,540	47,855	49,176	47,228
Switzerland	8,158	8,474	9,044	9,546	9,294	9,396	9,918	9,796
Turkey	7	178	1,801	4,413	5,575	9,625	12,849	15,991
United Kingdom	14,753	18,776	23,696	23,994	24,688	25,497	26,847	28,272
Eastern Europe								
Albania								
Belarus		6,756	119,613	350,424	590,215	805,763	1,341,039	1,624,636
Bosnia-Herzegovina		230	622	796	870	965	993	969
Bulgaria	1	17	494	662	774	733	919	1,083
Croatia	8	3,029	3,976	4,578	5,369	6,827	7,207	7,551
Czech Republic	32,000	78,313	104,186	105,498	106,674	112,182	117,059	119,392
Estonia	169	122	241	278	297	351	379	470
Georgia		92	138	174	202	225	275	347
Hungary	61,364	205,988	425,422	478,886	554,955	631,248	710,309	732,551
Latvia		126	200	238	240	268	292	325
Lithuania	8	1,605	2,366	2,464	2,509	2,809	3,014	3,092
Macedonia	16	6,682	7,043	9,207	8,765	7,804	7,912	7,337
Moldova								
Montenegro		37	30	37	46	50	49	51
Poland	2,632	17,062	30,415	32,994	33,827	35,362	36,038	38,763
Romania	3	281	2,020	2,978	4,413	5,194	5,973	6,865
Russia	51	72,441	264,757	344,196	440,921	489,445	592,267	707,156
Serbia		2,444	10,251	18,948	39,991	50,414	55,581	61,568
Slovakia	379	793	985	1,028	1,139	1,286	1,335	1,409
Slovenia	15	362	452	526	565	597	654	660
Ukraine		1,302	3,631	4,820	6,128	6,679	8,525	11,654

Source: Euromonitor International from national statistics

Consumer Expenditure Statistics

Alcoholic Beverages and Tobacco Consumer Expenditure 1990, 1995, 1999-2011 *(continued)*
National currency million

	2005	2006	2007	2008	2009	2010	2011	US$ million 2011	US$ per capita 2011
Western Europe									
Austria	4,752	4,669	4,945	5,128	5,213	5,306	5,514	7,666.47	912.21
Belgium	5,753	6,002	6,076	6,117	6,395	6,758	6,967	9,687.40	884.59
Cyprus									
Denmark	27,428	27,210	26,905	27,563	27,830	29,628	32,213	6,010.10	1,080.83
Finland	3,930	4,060	4,195	4,391	4,599	4,709	4,682	6,509.80	1,211.06
France	30,917	31,381	31,850	32,181	33,212	34,331	36,047	50,121.26	793.97
Germany	43,120	42,300	42,460	42,390	42,549	42,730	43,299	60,204.61	736.43
Gibraltar									
Greece	5,946	5,787	6,596	7,334	8,254	7,314	6,848	9,521.87	840.72
Iceland									
Ireland	3,874	4,076	4,359	4,292	4,136	4,035	3,912	5,439.33	1,213.90
Italy	22,434	23,591	24,024	24,553	24,281	25,195	26,066	36,242.74	597.80
Liechtenstein									
Luxembourg									
Malta									
Monaco									
Netherlands	6,992	7,212	7,530	7,865	8,276	8,425	8,871	12,334.36	740.54
Norway	34,597	35,703	37,568	40,695	42,394	43,331	44,507	7,939.30	1,613.58
Portugal	3,506	3,741	3,424	3,356	3,356	3,603	3,776	5,249.82	493.54
Spain	15,688	15,844	17,236	17,963	18,101	18,667	19,143	26,617.20	576.72
Sweden	46,995	47,145	49,439	51,581	56,040	57,059	58,634	9,027.01	958.73
Switzerland	9,811	9,910	10,122	10,279	10,850	10,617	10,528	11,853.93	1,506.19
Turkey	18,642	20,532	24,820	26,065	25,692	34,939	40,098	23,871.40	325.62
United Kingdom	28,545	28,615	29,242	29,820	29,980	31,471	32,698	52,400.68	838.43
Eastern Europe									
Albania									
Belarus	2,055,939	2,476,401	2,979,144	3,888,434	4,362,182	5,117,146	8,178,904	1,644.12	173.41
Bosnia-Herzegovina	1,085	1,163	1,186	1,234	1,224	1,120	1,144	813.47	211.64
Bulgaria	1,217	1,499	1,763	1,833	1,857	1,807	1,895	1,347.46	179.26
Croatia	8,610	9,174	10,469	10,171	10,299	10,215	10,188	1,906.54	432.11
Czech Republic	124,296	129,730	141,735	152,072	170,857	178,985	185,807	10,500.04	1,001.36
Estonia	532	566	617	638	633	616	668	929.01	693.19
Georgia	377	563	626	749	766	782	917	543.88	123.80
Hungary	746,999	849,696	970,277	1,065,862	1,079,633	1,072,314	1,133,737	5,638.95	564.70
Latvia	385	501	588	657	587	598	635	1,256.95	605.87
Lithuania	3,302	3,570	3,949	4,557	4,491	4,744	5,575	2,245.04	691.93
Macedonia	8,006	9,636	10,289	13,226	12,513	12,646	13,326	301.28	146.47
Moldova									
Montenegro	50	60	77	91	82	84	87	120.90	194.98
Poland	40,798	43,308	46,342	51,051	53,384	56,431	60,646	20,464.47	535.87
Romania	8,648	9,045	9,833	11,799	11,451	12,524	13,191	4,326.76	201.96
Russia	868,233	1,056,427	1,291,848	1,520,572	1,655,350	1,678,684	1,918,042	65,257.17	456.62
Serbia	65,310	77,138	86,984	97,687	117,656	124,104	134,158	1,829.43	251.47
Slovakia	1,475	1,577	1,742	1,819	1,836	1,898	1,933	2,687.08	497.91
Slovenia	733	777	837	916	962	961	975	1,355.52	661.17
Ukraine	15,772	19,909	25,108	32,354	38,628	44,497	56,915	7,139.14	156.57

Source: Euromonitor International from national statistics

Consumer Expenditure Statistics

Table 6.5

Clothing and Footwear Consumer Expenditure 1990, 1995, 1999-2011

National currency million

	1990	1995	1999	2000	2001	2002	2003	2004
Western Europe								
Austria	7,378	7,345	7,769	7,887	8,033	8,084	7,988	8,153
Belgium	5,980	7,017	6,897	6,706	6,734	6,885	6,973	7,232
Cyprus								
Denmark	22,197	26,312	29,679	30,350	30,957	31,559	32,581	33,735
Finland	2,440	2,224	2,898	2,905	3,058	3,224	3,409	3,586
France	39,492	38,737	40,778	42,324	42,536	44,170	45,445	46,156
Germany	65,314	67,300	67,510	68,360	68,140	66,470	64,150	62,840
Gibraltar								
Greece	2,145	3,923	5,276	5,670	5,535	6,433	6,802	7,530
Iceland								
Ireland	1,470	2,003	2,863	3,251	3,410	3,354	3,158	3,098
Italy	40,366	51,638	62,359	64,872	66,730	67,647	68,360	68,123
Liechtenstein								
Luxembourg								
Malta								
Monaco								
Netherlands	9,078	9,527	11,871	12,493	13,150	13,396	12,827	12,762
Norway	22,822	27,319	32,794	34,045	36,113	36,995	38,021	40,380
Portugal	2,619	3,716	4,482	5,176	5,365	5,818	5,812	6,043
Spain	14,744	17,626	22,799	24,643	26,093	26,675	27,300	28,630
Sweden	35,805	40,319	46,610	49,525	51,629	54,505	56,157	58,988
Switzerland	11,429	10,499	10,684	11,019	11,242	10,938	10,672	10,658
Turkey	56	997	6,909	10,852	15,860	23,512	32,647	38,475
United Kingdom	21,259	28,000	32,208	34,220	35,707	38,076	40,406	42,364
Eastern Europe								
Albania								
Belarus		5,374	179,333	440,577	930,484	1,460,374	1,737,666	2,133,872
Bosnia-Herzegovina		188	509	648	730	793	806	789
Bulgaria	2	40	832	719	866	854	888	938
Croatia	13	5,314	8,115	11,009	10,904	9,780	10,314	9,395
Czech Republic	16,508	41,236	60,303	61,662	65,956	66,005	65,739	68,881
Estonia	89	129	215	240	275	314	341	382
Georgia		178	320	381	347	306	360	413
Hungary	47,858	146,351	282,451	311,813	355,610	377,031	404,427	417,440
Latvia		104	204	241	238	266	278	328
Lithuania	3	896	1,823	1,822	1,944	2,027	2,165	2,678
Macedonia	31	7,474	8,945	9,621	9,210	11,877	12,874	13,036
Moldova								
Montenegro		48	41	51	65	73	73	78
Poland	1,812	11,802	21,334	24,308	24,847	25,851	26,231	28,226
Romania	3	220	1,415	2,020	2,993	3,749	4,688	5,638
Russia	65	95,562	377,139	453,274	531,511	658,874	744,138	872,504
Serbia		2,019	8,466	15,614	32,804	41,897	45,169	48,953
Slovakia	368	770	962	977	964	998	945	1,065
Slovenia	29	395	593	668	754	811	888	916
Ukraine		2,036	4,868	6,091	7,240	7,156	8,323	10,366

Source: Euromonitor International from national statistics

Clothing and Footwear Consumer Expenditure 1990, 1995, 1999-2011 *(continued)*

National currency million

	2005	2006	2007	2008	2009	2010	2011	US$ million 2011	US$ per capita 2011
Western Europe									
Austria	8,404	8,596	8,786	8,838	8,864	9,545	10,128	14,081.96	1,675.58
Belgium	7,537	7,721	8,263	8,630	8,745	9,045	9,276	12,897.15	1,177.69
Cyprus									
Denmark	34,847	36,785	38,808	38,336	36,238	36,910	35,841	6,687.04	1,202.57
Finland	3,781	4,028	4,298	4,499	4,481	4,778	5,248	7,296.77	1,357.47
France	46,639	47,440	48,892	48,407	46,830	47,271	47,696	66,317.56	1,050.53
Germany	63,610	64,180	66,430	67,205	65,369	68,829	71,147	98,925.38	1,210.07
Gibraltar									
Greece	7,674	7,957	9,062	9,567	8,846	8,172	7,598	10,564.73	932.79
Iceland									
Ireland	3,492	3,707	3,929	3,778	3,520	2,919	2,796	3,887.25	867.52
Italy	69,008	70,263	71,824	71,640	70,449	71,805	72,868	101,317.88	1,671.18
Liechtenstein									
Luxembourg									
Malta									
Monaco									
Netherlands	12,819	13,599	14,220	14,302	14,338	14,627	15,023	20,888.85	1,254.15
Norway	42,874	45,567	50,106	50,921	52,912	53,948	54,474	9,717.29	1,974.94
Portugal	6,116	6,330	6,501	6,581	6,482	6,615	6,374	8,862.93	833.22
Spain	30,994	33,924	35,776	35,203	32,291	32,697	32,343	44,970.70	974.38
Sweden	62,284	67,253	70,239	71,773	72,505	77,562	78,827	12,135.88	1,288.92
Switzerland	11,093	11,328	11,990	11,155	11,615	10,701	10,368	11,674.02	1,483.33
Turkey	35,975	37,498	38,986	39,988	36,996	43,746	47,008	27,984.96	381.73
United Kingdom	43,943	46,795	48,290	49,184	48,203	50,555	52,128	83,537.67	1,336.63
Eastern Europe									
Albania									
Belarus	2,700,365	3,252,619	4,128,188	5,537,174	6,165,141	7,303,348	11,507,086	2,313.15	243.97
Bosnia-Herzegovina	988	892	990	1,084	1,070	975	991	704.76	183.35
Bulgaria	1,062	1,137	1,405	1,486	1,252	1,128	1,251	889.70	118.36
Croatia	10,281	10,955	11,721	12,694	11,630	12,445	13,935	2,607.74	591.04
Czech Republic	73,358	73,753	75,107	77,410	64,231	59,326	56,746	3,206.73	305.82
Estonia	427	581	645	452	331	377	407	566.26	422.52
Georgia	428	565	576	669	625	681	784	464.96	105.84
Hungary	415,320	418,694	465,310	465,610	414,740	394,481	403,463	2,006.74	200.96
Latvia	386	548	756	738	429	438	479	947.28	456.61
Lithuania	3,812	4,348	5,198	5,071	4,810	4,578	4,809	1,936.64	596.88
Macedonia	14,228	16,409	17,666	20,202	19,261	19,720	21,136	477.85	232.31
Moldova									
Montenegro	81	119	164	179	156	159	169	234.45	378.12
Poland	28,446	30,157	31,954	34,831	36,001	37,531	39,994	13,495.60	353.39
Romania	6,894	9,057	10,120	12,290	11,020	11,723	12,620	4,139.48	193.22
Russia	1,066,570	1,329,849	1,530,051	1,851,749	1,931,885	2,092,305	2,381,482	81,024.69	566.95
Serbia	59,577	71,325	86,652	100,416	96,558	91,392	95,783	1,306.13	179.54
Slovakia	1,184	1,260	1,354	1,665	1,572	1,539	1,600	2,224.59	412.21
Slovenia	935	935	1,052	1,198	1,184	1,197	1,228	1,707.11	832.66
Ukraine	13,255	19,703	23,627	33,851	33,981	40,568	49,686	6,232.30	136.68

Source: Euromonitor International from national statistics

| Table 6.6

Housing Consumer Expenditure 1990, 1995, 1999-2011

National currency million

	1990	1995	1999	2000	2001	2002	2003	2004
Western Europe								
Austria	13,422	18,752	21,569	22,464	23,526	24,030	24,953	26,391
Belgium	19,872	24,809	28,734	30,579	32,014	32,392	33,445	34,505
Cyprus								
Denmark	109,405	135,540	155,217	162,043	170,925	176,348	179,881	188,073
Finland	7,921	11,923	15,001	15,625	16,491	17,438	18,365	19,033
France	116,777	154,732	177,274	183,369	190,739	196,994	207,052	217,130
Germany	145,346	228,240	252,050	258,860	271,490	275,580	285,270	289,470
Gibraltar								
Greece	6,387	14,233	18,714	19,549	20,300	21,980	23,630	25,565
Iceland								
Ireland	3,140	4,351	7,494	8,658	9,916	11,178	12,349	12,996
Italy	64,734	103,666	127,648	135,006	140,951	147,959	156,766	166,938
Liechtenstein								
Luxembourg								
Malta								
Monaco								
Netherlands	22,002	31,547	39,294	41,962	45,187	46,755	49,304	51,343
Norway	81,003	97,406	111,214	119,041	131,341	139,820	152,051	155,558
Portugal	4,902	7,787	9,861	10,646	11,331	12,116	12,961	13,796
Spain	31,019	46,372	56,802	61,000	65,610	71,003	76,886	82,821
Sweden	215,104	267,197	288,536	292,133	303,293	315,596	332,843	338,098
Switzerland	38,608	50,791	54,640	58,627	60,999	61,872	62,245	63,792
Turkey	28	758	10,799	19,655	30,291	42,114	54,681	67,064
United Kingdom	58,588	83,126	105,231	108,963	115,910	121,606	131,188	143,290
Eastern Europe								
Albania								
Belarus		6,373	89,003	290,529	713,836	1,372,582	2,466,318	3,321,916
Bosnia-Herzegovina		576	1,585	2,029	2,224	2,438	2,490	2,437
Bulgaria	9	172	4,695	4,664	5,240	5,356	5,729	6,002
Croatia	49	18,052	22,021	23,660	24,866	27,404	28,102	30,047
Czech Republic	66,246	166,053	241,204	256,690	283,797	310,883	333,304	354,842
Estonia	263	299	788	848	943	1,001	1,053	1,128
Georgia		214	339	475	487	843	756	832
Hungary	147,290	566,686	1,223,579	1,387,007	1,559,359	1,731,077	1,950,561	2,111,474
Latvia		336	578	619	709	758	836	970
Lithuania	19	3,606	4,907	5,111	5,066	5,483	5,617	6,019
Macedonia	62	21,895	27,616	31,632	29,662	35,059	41,994	45,712
Moldova								
Montenegro		121	112	143	187	214	220	244
Poland	4,935	42,500	94,535	97,182	110,440	123,580	127,634	135,405
Romania	8	856	8,259	12,450	16,814	23,500	29,151	36,499
Russia	12	35,718	110,685	155,681	245,288	375,348	548,173	718,090
Serbia		8,221	35,616	66,913	144,820	189,036	216,347	259,858
Slovakia	1,112	1,797	3,255	3,899	4,311	4,713	5,489	6,565
Slovenia	96	1,162	1,873	2,108	2,354	2,542	2,674	2,886
Ukraine		2,308	6,461	8,509	10,581	12,731	14,773	18,698

Source: Euromonitor International from national statistics

Housing Consumer Expenditure 1990, 1995, 1999-2011 *(continued)*

National currency million

	2005	2006	2007	2008	2009	2010	2011	US$ million 2011	US$ per capita 2011
Western Europe									
Austria	28,888	30,148	30,874	32,369	33,067	34,135	35,522	49,390.29	5,876.82
Belgium	35,822	37,474	38,002	41,542	41,248	43,408	44,767	62,246.10	5,683.92
Cyprus									
Denmark	198,739	209,448	218,010	228,649	234,027	248,683	256,792	47,910.90	8,616.09
Finland	19,694	20,615	21,488	22,869	24,261	25,467	27,525	38,271.97	7,120.00
France	229,991	242,862	252,684	264,463	268,059	277,530	284,351	395,371.04	6,263.03
Germany	298,530	307,840	309,080	324,992	325,820	334,346	342,621	476,391.22	5,827.30
Gibraltar									
Greece	26,482	29,642	31,621	34,732	35,893	38,674	37,111	51,600.33	4,555.96
Iceland									
Ireland	13,945	15,163	17,040	18,539	15,619	15,223	15,597	21,686.77	4,839.87
Italy	175,445	182,631	189,019	199,127	197,955	199,519	206,887	287,661.57	4,744.82
Liechtenstein									
Luxembourg									
Malta									
Monaco									
Netherlands	53,893	56,242	57,481	59,965	61,692	63,021	65,004	90,383.37	5,426.54
Norway	162,728	175,588	177,747	192,313	201,155	220,867	223,295	39,832.33	8,095.50
Portugal	14,532	15,084	15,991	16,867	17,230	18,406	19,118	26,582.64	2,499.08
Spain	90,393	99,704	108,824	116,948	122,127	126,895	130,023	180,787.93	3,917.15
Sweden	348,276	358,621	371,961	386,904	406,382	424,403	435,391	67,031.00	7,119.17
Switzerland	65,717	68,100	70,478	74,731	77,849	83,504	84,629	95,291.36	12,107.97
Turkey	81,982	100,252	119,517	141,245	157,022	167,933	202,588	120,605.23	1,645.10
United Kingdom	153,656	163,470	175,771	189,096	196,165	213,835	230,065	368,694.67	5,899.25
Eastern Europe									
Albania									
Belarus	4,203,809	5,063,532	6,348,151	8,697,990	9,937,058	12,151,500	19,488,582	3,917.59	413.20
Bosnia-Herzegovina	2,544	2,753	2,846	3,086	2,974	2,726	2,787	1,981.52	515.52
Bulgaria	6,627	7,244	7,705	8,888	8,974	8,862	9,307	6,617.04	880.31
Croatia	32,812	34,664	36,513	41,012	37,890	35,036	33,861	6,336.51	1,436.16
Czech Republic	382,048	407,423	438,018	481,279	526,668	524,513	539,036	30,461.21	2,905.00
Estonia	1,213	1,472	1,706	1,847	1,760	1,759	1,864	2,592.28	1,934.26
Georgia	969	1,344	1,531	2,119	2,229	2,149	2,518	1,492.80	339.79
Hungary	2,257,124	2,441,145	2,625,441	2,875,084	3,054,258	3,195,517	3,475,480	17,286.26	1,731.10
Latvia	1,149	1,449	1,944	2,280	2,041	2,021	2,287	4,525.01	2,181.14
Lithuania	6,813	7,728	8,557	10,081	9,206	9,058	10,283	4,140.76	1,276.20
Macedonia	46,196	45,507	50,033	57,054	53,068	53,492	56,704	1,282.01	623.25
Moldova									
Montenegro	252	337	486	559	493	502	536	744.86	1,201.33
Poland	146,777	155,815	169,479	188,145	198,077	211,499	228,888	77,236.27	2,022.46
Romania	41,262	46,760	61,460	72,162	66,056	70,295	75,787	24,859.60	1,160.38
Russia	1,076,706	1,286,180	1,518,264	1,847,162	2,001,219	2,064,239	2,362,837	80,390.36	562.51
Serbia	308,103	346,164	382,712	434,103	491,680	539,621	617,720	8,423.44	1,157.88
Slovakia	7,177	8,128	8,579	9,184	9,478	9,536	9,967	13,857.92	2,567.84
Slovenia	3,123	3,284	3,466	3,832	3,984	3,977	4,058	5,643.05	2,752.45
Ukraine	26,095	36,098	49,691	64,958	76,432	87,471	110,920	13,913.20	305.13

Source: Euromonitor International from national statistics

Consumer Expenditure Statistics Table 6.7

Household Goods and Services Consumer Expenditure 1990, 1995, 1999-2011

National currency million

	1990	1995	1999	2000	2001	2002	2003	2004
Western Europe								
Austria	5,748	7,185	7,699	8,081	8,235	8,243	8,394	8,808
Belgium	6,041	7,270	8,080	8,517	8,559	8,394	8,417	8,628
Cyprus								
Denmark	24,534	29,896	34,570	35,137	36,041	37,711	38,194	39,997
Finland	2,337	2,138	2,821	3,061	3,276	3,368	3,591	3,869
France	39,293	40,920	45,516	47,701	48,852	50,568	52,519	54,833
Germany	66,129	82,590	85,340	89,330	88,330	84,310	83,460	83,100
Gibraltar								
Greece	1,787	3,398	4,411	4,798	5,297	5,962	6,300	6,826
Iceland								
Ireland	1,528	1,943	3,156	3,520	3,871	4,007	4,238	4,369
Italy	37,597	49,308	59,022	60,376	61,063	61,794	62,506	64,408
Liechtenstein								
Luxembourg								
Malta								
Monaco								
Netherlands	9,071	10,427	14,012	15,152	16,163	16,135	15,793	15,521
Norway	21,257	27,455	34,159	37,965	39,550	41,353	42,071	43,826
Portugal	2,743	4,079	5,704	5,751	5,885	6,208	6,218	6,285
Spain	11,694	16,508	21,264	23,013	23,995	24,551	25,954	27,007
Sweden	30,881	35,658	42,635	46,611	49,058	52,119	55,042	58,808
Switzerland	11,595	11,155	11,443	12,136	12,307	12,276	12,238	12,432
Turkey	43	795	6,615	10,377	13,612	18,931	25,051	31,409
United Kingdom	19,936	26,287	33,809	36,428	38,779	41,392	43,585	43,423
Eastern Europe								
Albania								
Belarus		2,524	69,014	168,869	388,968	732,465	888,400	1,184,118
Bosnia-Herzegovina		253	699	897	989	1,097	1,124	1,128
Bulgaria	1	17	508	686	782	766	862	1,070
Croatia	23	8,634	10,344	10,527	11,473	12,427	14,758	15,133
Czech Republic	18,253	47,124	69,842	70,665	75,860	77,356	80,146	82,107
Estonia	63	103	160	181	200	229	252	282
Georgia		91	190	271	243	187	206	259
Hungary	72,741	218,731	416,081	476,916	535,416	587,735	667,726	774,835
Latvia		43	78	91	98	108	132	156
Lithuania	2	603	1,313	1,291	1,606	1,726	1,887	2,163
Macedonia	16	4,727	5,435	6,718	6,217	8,440	8,273	8,514
Moldova								
Montenegro		27	25	32	42	48	49	53
Poland	1,221	9,391	19,976	20,757	21,561	23,653	23,742	25,406
Romania	3	236	2,015	2,296	3,403	4,262	5,973	8,894
Russia	13	19,753	68,338	118,561	203,959	275,583	368,847	444,016
Serbia		1,675	7,151	13,211	28,231	37,329	38,643	47,034
Slovakia	288	518	783	817	1,014	1,092	1,151	1,286
Slovenia	27	376	583	659	735	805	864	908
Ukraine		778	2,132	2,808	3,576	3,709	4,736	6,620

Source: Euromonitor International from national statistics

Household Goods and Services Consumer Expenditure 1990, 1995, 1999-2011 *(continued)*

National currency million

	2005	2006	2007	2008	2009	2010	2011	US$ million 2011	US$ per capita 2011
Western Europe									
Austria	9,045	9,236	9,659	9,924	10,052	10,438	10,872	15,116.39	1,798.66
Belgium	8,828	9,107	9,623	10,092	10,231	10,615	10,905	15,162.75	1,384.57
Cyprus									
Denmark	41,652	44,380	46,803	47,044	44,768	45,203	44,468	8,296.66	1,492.04
Finland	4,158	4,426	4,747	4,935	4,672	5,093	5,349	7,438.05	1,383.75
France	56,919	59,032	62,145	62,779	61,906	63,296	64,703	89,965.66	1,425.14
Germany	81,860	83,950	83,170	83,128	81,297	83,848	87,276	121,350.90	1,484.39
Gibraltar									
Greece	7,032	7,268	7,767	8,105	7,954	7,845	7,460	10,373.21	915.88
Iceland									
Ireland	4,588	5,145	5,584	5,093	3,961	3,495	3,395	4,720.68	1,053.52
Italy	65,995	67,311	68,763	70,298	68,709	70,746	72,016	100,132.76	1,651.64
Liechtenstein									
Luxembourg									
Malta									
Monaco									
Netherlands	15,513	16,273	16,805	16,987	16,274	16,159	15,564	21,640.53	1,299.28
Norway	46,404	49,761	53,636	55,468	55,374	56,658	57,895	10,327.53	2,098.96
Portugal	6,499	6,780	7,124	7,224	6,738	7,149	7,133	9,918.07	932.41
Spain	29,144	31,331	32,668	31,866	30,007	30,284	30,046	41,777.55	905.20
Sweden	63,515	68,807	74,524	77,614	78,330	80,367	79,767	12,280.62	1,304.29
Switzerland	12,677	12,963	13,529	13,133	13,100	12,436	12,322	13,875.01	1,762.99
Turkey	40,237	45,720	48,989	49,848	49,183	59,221	77,642	43,245.29	589.88
United Kingdom	44,276	45,491	47,058	45,669	43,158	45,386	45,401	72,758.20	1,164.16
Eastern Europe									
Albania									
Belarus	1,498,474	1,804,928	2,308,192	3,176,542	3,708,983	4,629,334	7,651,179	1,538.04	162.22
Bosnia-Herzegovina	1,230	1,296	1,508	1,580	1,531	1,402	1,432	1,018.17	264.89
Bulgaria	1,308	1,599	1,922	1,985	1,882	1,724	1,478	1,050.98	139.82
Croatia	16,488	17,415	19,909	21,267	18,985	17,754	17,554	3,284.97	744.53
Czech Republic	87,293	90,584	96,994	103,910	98,241	104,653	107,289	6,062.93	578.21
Estonia	326	368	414	397	340	322	344	478.00	356.66
Georgia	279	386	463	521	522	519	600	355.73	80.97
Hungary	760,135	766,449	754,279	732,573	664,314	669,671	653,984	3,252.77	325.74
Latvia	199	285	396	409	294	297	336	665.69	320.87
Lithuania	2,695	2,963	3,497	3,862	3,014	2,799	2,873	1,157.05	356.61
Macedonia	10,001	13,881	15,945	18,156	17,078	17,575	19,131	432.53	210.28
Moldova									
Montenegro	56	74	102	133	118	120	128	177.33	286.01
Poland	26,892	28,618	30,815	33,911	35,512	37,634	40,527	13,675.56	358.10
Romania	9,724	12,388	15,008	17,252	15,115	16,274	17,577	5,765.70	269.13
Russia	550,458	657,952	821,190	1,025,657	998,707	1,076,344	1,258,114	42,804.58	299.51
Serbia	65,351	72,490	94,232	113,421	95,624	95,993	102,507	1,397.82	192.14
Slovakia	1,496	1,714	2,024	2,498	2,418	2,375	2,473	3,438.90	637.22
Slovenia	975	1,011	1,158	1,212	1,316	1,335	1,376	1,912.80	932.99
Ukraine	10,042	12,262	17,579	23,930	24,476	29,597	37,851	4,747.81	104.12

Source: Euromonitor International from national statistics

6

Consumer Expenditure

Table 6.8

Health Goods and Medical Services Consumer Expenditure 1990, 1995, 1999-2011

National currency million

	1990	1995	1999	2000	2001	2002	2003	2004
Western Europe								
Austria	2,317	3,281	3,892	4,039	4,298	4,455	4,656	4,747
Belgium	4,562	5,315	6,428	6,789	6,683	7,379	7,572	7,645
Cyprus								
Denmark	10,010	12,226	14,790	15,315	16,171	16,769	17,294	18,713
Finland	1,278	1,636	2,178	2,411	2,579	2,820	2,954	3,139
France	16,841	22,178	24,642	26,123	27,377	28,784	30,315	32,624
Germany	20,148	35,790	41,620	43,180	45,490	48,330	50,120	54,380
Gibraltar								
Greece	1,475	3,899	5,081	4,911	5,441	6,463	7,326	8,013
Iceland								
Ireland	591	902	1,296	1,463	1,705	1,959	2,239	2,484
Italy	9,576	19,029	23,873	24,524	23,764	25,289	26,097	26,730
Liechtenstein								
Luxembourg								
Malta								
Monaco								
Netherlands	5,618	6,095	8,371	8,736	9,761	10,962	11,580	12,189
Norway	8,189	11,309	15,063	16,441	17,650	18,850	20,305	21,570
Portugal	1,724	2,839	3,545	3,765	3,954	4,267	4,554	4,881
Spain	4,846	9,133	11,787	12,941	13,980	14,867	16,196	17,429
Sweden	14,218	21,228	26,750	30,275	33,507	35,713	36,885	38,645
Switzerland	19,596	27,512	32,390	35,145	36,782	37,537	38,750	40,607
Turkey	9	194	2,256	3,873	6,358	9,623	12,224	15,375
United Kingdom	4,432	7,000	9,018	9,610	10,373	11,043	11,618	12,040
Eastern Europe								
Albania								
Belarus		1,574	25,471	81,523	216,440	358,727	454,398	587,254
Bosnia-Herzegovina		89	307	415	481	558	603	627
Bulgaria	1	15	393	553	744	915	1,022	1,140
Croatia	4	1,835	2,902	3,304	4,220	4,439	5,884	7,078
Czech Republic	6,639	14,074	17,325	16,551	21,023	22,492	22,611	26,840
Estonia	18	37	85	106	124	140	161	178
Georgia		86	171	306	327	387	374	436
Hungary	27,675	98,188	234,178	282,437	346,815	381,339	423,294	445,270
Latvia		60	111	125	148	162	166	189
Lithuania	2	460	1,018	1,042	1,072	1,543	1,617	1,723
Macedonia	4	3,390	4,427	6,356	5,334	4,913	4,699	4,567
Moldova								
Montenegro		15	15	20	26	31	32	36
Poland	622	6,354	16,641	16,873	18,732	20,746	21,477	24,858
Romania	1	118	1,029	1,318	1,954	2,447	3,922	6,222
Russia	10	23,731	117,382	121,922	105,627	144,470	167,219	232,328
Serbia		705	3,265	6,320	14,232	19,950	23,834	31,079
Slovakia	74	254	349	390	483	500	586	799
Slovenia	6	152	290	354	400	454	499	525
Ukraine		877	2,533	3,401	4,267	5,003	6,295	7,710

Source: Euromonitor International from national statistics

Health Goods and Medical Services Consumer Expenditure 1990, 1995, 1999-2011 *(continued)*

National currency million

	2005	2006	2007	2008	2009	2010	2011	US$ million 2011	US$ per capita 2011
Western Europe									
Austria	4,929	4,985	5,247	5,331	5,499	5,582	5,650	7,855.66	934.72
Belgium	7,916	8,559	9,114	9,305	9,207	9,744	10,017	13,928.59	1,271.87
Cyprus									
Denmark	19,538	20,930	22,174	22,745	23,714	23,860	23,566	4,396.76	790.70
Finland	3,376	3,573	3,849	4,129	4,035	4,393	4,621	6,425.31	1,195.35
France	34,366	35,912	37,532	39,654	40,624	41,798	42,974	59,751.82	946.52
Germany	53,820	56,940	59,370	62,799	64,466	69,807	72,272	100,488.60	1,229.19
Gibraltar									
Greece	8,243	9,517	10,496	11,327	11,616	11,944	11,488	15,972.93	1,410.30
Iceland									
Ireland	2,816	3,169	3,312	3,672	4,026	4,148	4,211	5,854.43	1,306.54
Italy	27,406	27,968	28,538	28,983	27,340	28,711	29,759	41,378.21	682.51
Liechtenstein									
Luxembourg									
Malta									
Monaco									
Netherlands	12,733	5,742	6,178	7,297	7,210	7,372	7,349	10,217.94	613.48
Norway	23,041	23,517	24,565	26,258	26,929	27,878	28,924	5,159.56	1,048.63
Portugal	5,075	5,329	5,897	6,322	6,441	6,878	7,014	9,752.64	916.86
Spain	18,660	19,772	20,909	22,162	21,830	22,192	22,117	30,752.85	666.33
Sweden	41,093	43,005	45,126	47,491	49,704	52,589	55,490	8,542.96	907.32
Switzerland	41,533	42,136	44,173	48,343	48,738	51,809	53,430	60,161.55	7,644.29
Turkey	18,973	22,931	25,596	28,481	27,875	29,273	36,588	21,781.87	297.11
United Kingdom	12,454	13,486	14,577	14,203	15,126	15,311	16,179	25,927.36	414.85
Eastern Europe									
Albania									
Belarus	743,156	895,140	1,187,293	1,663,897	1,978,932	2,377,803	3,810,699	766.03	80.79
Bosnia-Herzegovina	712	811	923	1,067	985	909	937	666.43	173.38
Bulgaria	1,318	1,393	1,674	1,820	1,937	1,961	2,140	1,521.47	202.41
Croatia	7,900	8,344	9,479	10,854	11,186	10,881	11,448	2,142.21	485.53
Czech Republic	32,333	37,891	42,981	50,582	50,972	49,756	49,131	2,776.43	264.78
Estonia	201	206	230	278	290	298	317	440.86	328.96
Georgia	561	876	1,038	1,443	1,581	1,616	1,905	1,129.49	257.10
Hungary	488,362	509,132	527,981	559,686	567,781	611,091	655,190	3,258.77	326.34
Latvia	208	278	341	391	304	310	348	688.51	331.88
Lithuania	2,338	2,268	2,574	3,233	3,035	3,166	3,742	1,507.02	464.47
Macedonia	4,882	4,764	6,234	7,278	6,931	7,100	7,617	172.20	83.72
Moldova									
Montenegro	40	46	79	71	64	65	70	96.79	156.11
Poland	24,731	26,295	28,578	31,748	33,440	35,203	38,019	12,829.25	335.94
Romania	6,590	7,196	9,503	11,908	10,434	11,090	12,079	3,962.14	184.94
Russia	351,978	446,836	542,798	687,726	766,970	869,838	1,031,487	35,094.09	245.56
Serbia	45,471	60,525	81,704	96,933	108,525	116,718	131,282	1,790.21	246.08
Slovakia	910	1,037	1,232	1,347	1,457	1,520	1,585	2,204.27	408.45
Slovenia	570	593	666	721	782	778	817	1,135.61	553.90
Ukraine	11,191	13,133	17,175	22,573	29,990	34,360	42,818	5,370.87	117.79

Source: Euromonitor International from national statistics

Consumer Expenditure Statistics

Table 6.9

Transport Consumer Expenditure 1990, 1995, 1999-2011

National currency million

	1990	1995	1999	2000	2001	2002	2003	2004
Western Europe								
Austria	10,789	12,856	14,458	15,457	15,412	15,885	16,498	17,236
Belgium	9,813	12,184	14,877	16,154	16,176	16,589	16,544	17,499
Cyprus								
Denmark	48,453	68,181	78,062	73,916	71,524	76,537	72,296	85,663
Finland	6,299	5,912	7,640	8,146	7,965	8,494	9,279	9,430
France	86,644	94,178	109,437	116,130	119,232	121,097	122,289	129,109
Germany	120,533	137,560	156,050	156,960	161,350	163,860	165,280	171,670
Gibraltar								
Greece	4,515	7,789	10,114	11,501	12,487	13,648	14,616	15,861
Iceland								
Ireland	2,454	3,106	5,285	6,579	6,124	6,437	6,789	7,466
Italy	50,611	72,603	94,987	100,578	101,859	103,816	107,685	111,419
Liechtenstein								
Luxembourg								
Malta								
Monaco								
Netherlands	13,783	16,911	22,134	23,675	24,134	25,763	26,050	27,189
Norway	44,818	62,890	83,445	92,423	92,293	95,300	97,057	107,862
Portugal	4,871	8,181	12,058	13,490	13,399	13,222	12,809	13,817
Spain	22,486	30,996	47,296	49,471	51,558	51,351	53,876	59,379
Sweden	79,243	110,117	143,567	153,628	149,941	156,032	160,761	172,118
Switzerland	14,973	17,109	19,283	21,053	21,332	21,050	20,726	21,309
Turkey	31	732	9,001	17,286	21,240	31,923	46,315	57,526
United Kingdom	51,852	64,087	86,955	92,811	96,588	99,052	103,356	108,562
Eastern Europe								
Albania								
Belarus		4,351	101,886	318,085	619,768	1,031,869	1,609,288	1,978,146
Bosnia-Herzegovina		195	652	876	1,008	1,163	1,250	1,299
Bulgaria	4	74	1,933	2,643	3,250	3,622	4,094	4,638
Croatia	27	10,397	14,996	17,220	18,401	19,610	19,747	19,311
Czech Republic	27,118	77,679	116,115	124,836	132,191	125,060	136,735	153,289
Estonia	99	160	361	377	440	494	588	653
Georgia		230	255	341	293	523	494	548
Hungary	115,949	403,608	950,438	1,145,587	1,280,024	1,400,471	1,601,277	1,713,827
Latvia		129	244	265	294	323	374	486
Lithuania	5	1,351	3,647	4,271	4,623	4,674	5,550	6,262
Macedonia	31	14,598	17,553	25,832	19,462	21,778	18,327	22,920
Moldova								
Montenegro		18	25	35	50	63	70	85
Poland	1,588	15,673	42,064	43,477	45,835	48,696	50,079	53,527
Romania	8	646	4,860	5,942	9,233	11,771	15,001	21,057
Russia	16	56,521	203,378	273,180	384,354	579,721	693,965	979,888
Serbia		2,710	12,213	23,567	53,297	72,749	91,391	125,719
Slovakia	398	854	1,361	1,495	1,815	1,874	1,927	2,056
Slovenia	70	1,088	1,661	1,750	1,876	1,996	2,180	2,392
Ukraine		2,393	6,566	8,705	11,168	13,438	17,384	27,213

Source: Euromonitor International from national statistics

Transport Consumer Expenditure 1990, 1995, 1999-2011 *(continued)*

National currency million

	2005	2006	2007	2008	2009	2010	2011	US$ million 2011	US$ per capita 2011
Western Europe									
Austria	17,890	18,677	19,028	19,882	19,119	20,713	21,624	30,067.30	3,577.63
Belgium	18,121	19,370	19,947	21,023	20,126	21,873	22,574	31,387.15	2,866.08
Cyprus									
Denmark	96,510	106,244	108,645	102,381	88,189	99,738	101,623	18,960.24	3,409.73
Finland	9,921	10,222	10,171	10,732	9,149	10,392	11,433	15,897.26	2,957.48
France	136,837	141,073	148,129	152,976	146,632	152,336	155,434	216,120.47	3,423.54
Germany	174,890	184,610	179,970	183,130	188,593	182,736	200,017	278,110.13	3,401.89
Gibraltar									
Greece	17,781	21,328	21,550	23,205	20,254	20,420	18,864	26,229.68	2,315.90
Iceland									
Ireland	8,481	9,513	10,375	10,091	7,721	8,336	8,666	12,049.90	2,689.19
Italy	115,140	119,754	123,165	121,209	116,564	123,892	127,671	177,517.64	2,928.06
Liechtenstein									
Luxembourg									
Malta									
Monaco									
Netherlands	28,289	30,014	31,218	32,844	30,318	31,694	33,931	47,179.05	2,832.59
Norway	113,782	121,926	137,322	137,513	132,854	146,642	154,922	27,635.68	5,616.66
Portugal	14,788	15,235	16,071	16,206	13,993	14,165	13,636	18,960.32	1,782.49
Spain	65,608	71,150	75,583	76,696	69,428	72,480	74,422	103,479.28	2,242.10
Sweden	185,391	187,691	198,365	190,791	183,138	203,220	217,118	33,426.60	3,550.14
Switzerland	22,298	23,212	24,048	25,550	25,698	25,049	25,543	28,761.35	3,654.49
Turkey	69,419	82,085	87,235	98,218	91,831	111,653	129,344	77,001.33	1,050.33
United Kingdom	114,488	117,981	125,693	124,642	122,568	130,868	133,683	214,234.82	3,427.83
Eastern Europe									
Albania									
Belarus	2,503,298	3,015,249	3,733,677	5,018,617	5,758,763	6,878,127	11,043,332	2,219.93	234.14
Bosnia-Herzegovina	1,461	1,661	1,911	2,342	2,118	1,948	2,003	1,423.92	370.45
Bulgaria	5,939	6,862	9,163	10,104	8,232	8,318	8,630	6,136.03	816.31
Croatia	20,143	21,726	23,736	26,767	25,158	26,172	28,482	5,329.76	1,207.98
Czech Republic	166,760	176,664	191,283	201,238	174,896	180,870	178,216	10,071.07	960.45
Estonia	783	1,014	1,190	1,391	941	935	1,039	1,445.17	1,078.33
Georgia	632	815	914	1,205	1,215	1,245	1,441	854.20	194.43
Hungary	1,896,688	2,049,054	2,145,297	2,165,492	1,909,310	1,902,526	1,857,085	9,236.72	924.99
Latvia	614	890	1,082	1,065	961	988	1,089	2,155.63	1,039.05
Lithuania	6,995	8,763	10,525	12,775	9,920	9,874	10,783	4,342.09	1,338.25
Macedonia	23,181	27,874	32,522	40,192	38,783	40,100	43,326	979.54	476.21
Moldova									
Montenegro	98	130	220	292	268	272	297	412.54	665.36
Poland	53,709	56,307	59,798	65,101	67,019	69,619	73,943	24,951.43	653.36
Romania	34,568	42,051	43,825	54,011	47,877	52,023	56,122	18,409.09	859.28
Russia	1,257,452	1,598,943	2,217,135	2,818,543	2,542,126	3,000,599	3,545,941	120,642.87	844.16
Serbia	156,972	188,798	210,707	264,111	284,816	314,527	366,236	4,994.13	686.49
Slovakia	2,247	2,400	2,547	2,836	2,771	2,726	2,825	3,928.58	727.96
Slovenia	2,521	2,688	2,970	3,304	3,023	3,185	3,243	4,508.85	2,199.24
Ukraine	33,793	44,423	61,690	90,193	62,226	78,167	101,785	12,767.32	280.00

Source: Euromonitor International from national statistics

6

Consumer Expenditure

Consumer Expenditure Statistics

Table 6.10

Communications Consumer Expenditure 1990, 1995, 1999-2011

National currency million

	1990	1995	1999	2000	2001	2002	2003	2004
Western Europe								
Austria	1,520	1,907	2,785	3,249	3,320	3,353	3,521	3,681
Belgium	1,232	1,759	2,746	3,030	3,313	3,675	4,039	4,217
Cyprus								
Denmark	6,861	9,123	11,393	11,898	12,280	12,283	13,728	14,863
Finland	625	782	1,770	1,979	2,199	2,304	2,348	2,460
France	10,321	12,515	16,284	18,652	20,628	22,706	24,380	25,447
Germany	13,287	19,910	25,450	28,620	32,500	33,190	34,060	35,450
Gibraltar								
Greece	532	1,753	3,644	4,075	4,239	4,371	4,304	4,370
Iceland								
Ireland	328	538	866	1,111	1,297	1,509	1,795	2,162
Italy	6,330	10,481	17,322	19,401	20,721	21,590	22,416	23,584
Liechtenstein								
Luxembourg								
Malta								
Monaco								
Netherlands	2,188	3,280	6,787	7,997	9,096	10,228	10,890	11,009
Norway	7,063	8,176	14,332	15,910	17,208	18,208	19,673	23,827
Portugal	789	1,142	1,820	2,152	2,648	2,905	2,983	3,188
Spain	2,504	4,424	7,843	9,397	11,107	12,014	11,969	13,385
Sweden	9,889	18,837	32,062	32,804	37,866	41,471	44,646	45,946
Switzerland	3,554	4,707	5,141	5,590	6,231	6,444	6,746	7,220
Turkey	5	172	2,658	4,592	7,777	11,746	14,849	18,968
United Kingdom	6,510	9,067	12,237	12,979	14,019	14,605	15,734	15,733
Eastern Europe								
Albania								
Belarus		943	24,267	73,412	209,156	443,309	696,764	989,951
Bosnia-Herzegovina		67	220	292	340	386	408	447
Bulgaria		11	517	858	1,173	1,389	1,574	1,737
Croatia		426	1,330	1,928	2,482	4,542	5,305	6,456
Czech Republic	5,127	14,238	22,115	27,346	34,631	37,160	44,659	50,560
Estonia	15	30	89	110	130	138	163	182
Georgia		39	48	67	60	110	107	122
Hungary	7,605	60,421	248,407	298,372	369,149	437,550	452,113	460,347
Latvia		24	74	94	105	129	165	205
Lithuania		142	606	794	1,005	1,107	1,170	1,209
Macedonia	4	1,259	6,749	8,981	7,987	11,103	14,553	15,879
Moldova								
Montenegro		16	22	30	42	50	53	59
Poland	518	4,674	11,540	12,885	14,807	15,958	16,927	18,411
Romania	1	89	1,164	1,670	2,475	3,100	3,108	3,802
Russia	7	13,358	56,611	73,674	101,762	163,390	263,620	405,688
Serbia		1,401	5,970	11,051	23,618	30,819	32,706	39,389
Slovakia	58	215	473	562	756	791	851	925
Slovenia	6	116	218	250	302	406	443	506
Ukraine		821	2,349	3,212	4,127	4,564	6,598	8,463

Source: Euromonitor International from national statistics

European Marketing Data and Statistics 2013 – © Euromonitor International Ltd 2012

Communications Consumer Expenditure 1990, 1995, 1999-2011 *(continued)*

National currency million

	2005	2006	2007	2008	2009	2010	2011	US$ million 2011	US$ per capita 2011
Western Europe									
Austria	3,716	3,712	3,675	3,575	3,474	3,355	3,281	4,561.44	542.75
Belgium	4,330	4,142	4,174	4,071	4,073	4,036	3,717	5,167.95	471.90
Cyprus									
Denmark	14,844	15,299	14,949	15,556	15,353	15,792	15,087	2,814.80	506.20
Finland	2,191	2,200	2,237	2,227	2,009	2,071	2,306	3,206.10	596.45
France	26,880	27,370	28,569	29,633	29,671	30,030	31,009	43,115.39	682.99
Germany	36,230	36,230	36,200	35,881	36,060	36,878	37,875	52,662.82	644.18
Gibraltar									
Greece	4,359	5,152	5,446	5,190	5,490	5,885	5,832	8,108.87	715.96
Iceland									
Ireland	2,444	2,734	2,766	2,671	2,438	2,252	2,213	3,076.68	686.63
Italy	23,982	24,518	24,642	24,063	23,671	23,755	24,673	34,306.63	565.87
Liechtenstein									
Luxembourg									
Malta									
Monaco									
Netherlands	11,366	11,634	11,748	11,375	10,751	10,649	10,288	14,304.43	858.83
Norway	24,817	25,794	25,843	26,373	26,801	27,263	27,238	4,858.83	987.50
Portugal	3,265	3,373	3,427	3,516	3,352	3,498	3,488	4,849.16	455.88
Spain	14,320	15,287	16,545	17,458	17,252	17,790	18,259	25,388.38	550.09
Sweden	45,805	45,775	47,232	47,933	49,452	52,354	54,553	8,398.68	892.00
Switzerland	7,612	7,917	8,033	8,880	8,668	9,096	9,440	10,629.25	1,350.58
Turkey	21,190	23,616	28,440	30,370	32,647	40,754	48,363	28,791.78	392.73
United Kingdom	16,892	16,462	17,122	16,602	16,706	17,892	19,238	30,830.38	493.30
Eastern Europe									
Albania									
Belarus	1,252,760	1,508,963	1,943,481	2,691,946	3,129,962	3,722,838	5,997,612	1,205.64	127.16
Bosnia-Herzegovina	468	518	586	664	629	576	590	419.43	109.12
Bulgaria	2,019	2,139	2,423	2,473	2,345	2,432	2,553	1,815.43	241.52
Croatia	6,423	6,784	7,471	8,354	7,951	8,121	8,317	1,556.40	352.75
Czech Republic	51,947	60,001	62,014	63,765	62,591	62,415	62,935	3,556.46	339.17
Estonia	199	251	317	256	192	202	225	312.74	233.35
Georgia	144	189	215	288	295	275	320	189.86	43.22
Hungary	514,797	515,249	518,487	551,847	515,715	546,136	568,558	2,827.88	283.19
Latvia	229	301	358	370	276	273	306	606.36	292.28
Lithuania	1,233	1,343	1,542	1,560	1,472	1,404	1,517	610.94	188.30
Macedonia	16,963	18,186	18,977	25,867	25,743	27,490	30,681	693.65	337.22
Moldova									
Montenegro	65	85	122	132	135	138	151	210.25	339.10
Poland	20,780	21,780	23,844	26,830	28,573	30,791	33,476	11,296.14	295.79
Romania	4,008	4,604	5,727	6,768	6,492	6,905	7,355	2,412.68	112.62
Russia	546,509	656,505	858,888	1,037,357	1,111,500	1,195,298	1,423,224	48,422.08	338.82
Serbia	50,128	59,762	84,476	93,935	100,162	105,623	116,122	1,583.48	217.66
Slovakia	1,002	1,148	1,249	1,355	1,415	1,430	1,483	2,062.66	382.21
Slovenia	575	624	601	644	664	691	726	1,009.97	492.62
Ukraine	11,317	13,532	16,378	18,875	18,541	22,858	29,932	3,754.52	82.34

Source: Euromonitor International from national statistics

6

Consumer Expenditure

Consumer Expenditure Statistics

Table 6.11

Leisure and Recreation Consumer Expenditure 1990, 1995, 1999-2011

National currency million

	1990	1995	1999	2000	2001	2002	2003	2004
Western Europe								
Austria	7,921	9,999	11,639	12,411	12,905	13,038	13,126	13,533
Belgium	8,072	9,947	11,928	12,326	12,768	12,229	12,555	13,503
Cyprus								
Denmark	41,163	52,489	63,642	66,673	67,955	69,641	74,044	80,215
Finland	4,852	5,101	6,593	7,124	7,478	7,741	8,089	8,609
France	47,605	55,359	64,855	69,465	72,381	75,926	78,652	82,487
Germany	76,293	93,780	108,480	112,940	115,320	113,250	112,540	114,850
Gibraltar								
Greece	1,544	3,287	4,451	4,993	6,503	6,967	6,987	7,624
Iceland								
Ireland	1,749	2,143	2,892	3,563	3,991	4,113	4,275	4,779
Italy	30,769	40,246	50,551	53,729	54,706	55,696	56,475	59,491
Liechtenstein								
Luxembourg								
Malta								
Monaco								
Netherlands	13,650	15,921	21,738	22,826	24,139	24,817	24,367	24,427
Norway	33,441	50,764	71,846	76,761	81,389	84,803	90,082	95,489
Portugal	2,633	4,365	6,354	6,797	6,962	7,052	6,980	7,304
Spain	17,208	24,953	33,039	36,101	38,627	40,438	42,910	45,651
Sweden	71,081	91,088	116,574	125,531	130,397	134,595	140,207	144,371
Switzerland	17,639	20,322	21,349	22,512	22,843	22,989	23,053	23,274
Turkey	27	532	3,907	6,402	8,253	12,438	15,576	21,002
United Kingdom	35,494	49,274	67,041	71,393	73,668	78,118	82,052	87,713
Eastern Europe								
Albania								
Belarus		1,216	32,872	82,563	221,851	355,931	620,358	904,596
Bosnia-Herzegovina		73	292	405	477	571	623	652
Bulgaria	1	22	673	953	876	1,060	1,192	1,486
Croatia	11	4,091	5,789	6,446	6,980	7,996	10,284	14,749
Czech Republic	32,573	86,020	132,333	137,037	146,113	149,894	160,941	173,092
Estonia	41	98	264	298	342	394	426	492
Georgia		101	155	199	188	222	287	347
Hungary	87,129	275,458	543,296	627,648	731,077	801,855	906,224	970,074
Latvia		62	160	192	237	259	303	378
Lithuania	1	512	1,705	1,825	2,272	2,343	2,610	2,951
Macedonia	14	3,579	5,289	6,218	5,562	5,703	5,312	5,760
Moldova								
Montenegro		13	14	19	26	30	31	36
Poland	2,262	16,427	34,187	42,236	38,453	39,056	42,121	46,519
Romania	3	240	1,771	2,501	4,101	5,049	5,851	7,231
Russia	8	21,160	92,132	122,204	162,302	206,996	313,102	418,699
Serbia		911	4,179	7,999	18,087	25,162	28,573	40,207
Slovakia	504	732	1,274	1,476	1,768	1,837	1,940	2,169
Slovenia	36	578	1,047	1,136	1,268	1,422	1,565	1,695
Ukraine		651	2,014	2,771	3,600	4,656	5,838	7,704

Source: Euromonitor International from national statistics

Leisure and Recreation Consumer Expenditure 1990, 1995, 1999-2011 *(continued)*

National currency million

	2005	2006	2007	2008	2009	2010	2011	US$ million 2011	US$ per capita 2011
Western Europe									
Austria	14,022	14,805	15,140	15,845	16,122	16,429	16,966	23,589.83	2,806.89
Belgium	14,060	14,728	15,746	16,546	16,366	16,407	16,623	23,113.19	2,110.55
Cyprus									
Denmark	84,512	89,813	94,273	95,352	90,459	92,458	91,777	17,123.20	3,079.36
Finland	9,119	9,974	10,635	10,957	10,400	10,782	11,076	15,400.95	2,865.15
France	85,401	89,198	92,674	92,751	91,838	93,408	94,837	131,864.72	2,088.85
Germany	115,540	117,790	120,680	122,103	121,740	124,493	127,400	177,140.54	2,166.81
Gibraltar									
Greece	7,991	8,246	9,455	10,018	9,911	9,803	9,529	13,249.69	1,169.86
Iceland									
Ireland	5,164	5,500	6,040	5,631	5,074	4,886	4,796	6,667.88	1,488.08
Italy	58,896	61,541	63,786	64,368	63,239	65,263	66,919	93,046.17	1,534.75
Liechtenstein									
Luxembourg									
Malta									
Monaco									
Netherlands	24,795	25,974	27,533	27,951	26,289	26,437	25,779	35,844.55	2,152.08
Norway	99,840	106,681	114,519	117,551	119,178	126,200	130,978	23,364.39	4,748.57
Portugal	7,724	7,981	8,166	8,321	8,001	8,393	8,387	11,661.88	1,096.35
Spain	48,622	50,708	52,998	54,313	51,349	51,603	51,867	72,117.66	1,562.58
Sweden	146,536	154,655	165,554	169,417	170,616	176,313	179,644	27,657.20	2,937.39
Switzerland	23,479	23,497	24,191	24,693	25,508	25,221	25,276	28,460.50	3,616.27
Turkey	24,170	26,310	26,564	27,420	29,282	31,386	39,033	23,237.27	316.97
United Kingdom	90,832	95,127	100,191	100,682	97,477	100,495	102,210	163,797.99	2,620.83
Eastern Europe									
Albania									
Belarus	1,144,746	1,378,858	1,726,662	2,338,211	2,676,457	3,222,542	5,234,043	1,052.15	110.97
Bosnia-Herzegovina	784	862	974	1,121	1,050	966	994	706.93	183.92
Bulgaria	1,790	1,919	2,306	2,507	2,502	2,239	2,334	1,659.29	220.75
Croatia	15,914	16,791	18,176	17,221	15,090	16,679	17,995	3,367.40	763.21
Czech Republic	181,599	187,267	189,956	200,624	197,612	199,900	202,833	11,462.19	1,093.12
Estonia	590	642	837	681	544	580	633	879.71	656.41
Georgia	408	584	717	844	873	900	1,051	623.17	141.85
Hungary	1,056,880	1,119,270	1,152,045	1,143,824	1,107,043	1,139,664	1,160,920	5,774.16	578.24
Latvia	418	514	728	828	630	629	710	1,403.97	676.74
Lithuania	3,192	3,546	4,462	4,792	3,682	3,516	3,586	1,443.97	445.04
Macedonia	6,721	8,520	9,560	10,198	9,625	9,864	10,660	241.02	117.17
Moldova									
Montenegro	38	45	78	93	81	82	89	123.15	198.62
Poland	46,770	48,183	51,359	56,611	58,644	61,000	64,864	21,887.73	573.14
Romania	7,751	11,062	13,297	15,010	13,722	14,695	15,766	5,171.50	241.39
Russia	573,676	670,812	868,049	1,070,814	1,059,121	1,203,531	1,407,338	47,881.60	335.04
Serbia	55,659	73,094	94,122	117,887	118,685	122,078	135,971	1,854.15	254.87
Slovakia	2,429	2,678	3,084	3,599	3,604	3,651	3,823	5,315.50	984.95
Slovenia	1,787	1,864	1,990	2,042	1,921	2,162	2,239	3,112.99	1,518.39
Ukraine	13,916	16,783	22,341	27,298	24,689	27,999	35,907	4,503.93	98.77

Source: Euromonitor International from national statistics

6

Consumer Expenditure

Consumer Expenditure Statistics

Table 6.12

Education Consumer Expenditure 1990, 1995, 1999-2011

National currency million

	1990	1995	1999	2000	2001	2002	2003	2004
Western Europe								
Austria	454	689	773	807	877	960	999	1,033
Belgium	436	545	619	656	693	733	769	772
Cyprus								
Denmark	2,331	3,718	4,662	4,652	4,641	4,978	5,157	5,007
Finland	123	229	306	299	309	315	322	351
France	3,643	4,163	5,025	5,040	5,216	5,444	5,796	6,268
Germany	3,796	6,040	7,870	8,140	8,380	8,920	9,350	9,830
Gibraltar								
Greece	471	1,219	1,423	1,502	1,729	2,019	2,497	2,796
Iceland								
Ireland	180	402	415	547	540	683	820	750
Italy	4,032	5,723	6,640	6,846	7,036	7,095	7,475	7,686
Liechtenstein								
Luxembourg								
Malta								
Monaco								
Netherlands	896	946	1,108	1,161	1,216	1,299	1,409	1,491
Norway	2,005	1,926	2,746	2,881	3,588	3,784	2,717	2,737
Portugal	350	711	879	857	914	964	1,004	1,080
Spain	2,810	4,663	5,909	6,202	6,515	6,872	7,119	7,407
Sweden	42	40	39	33	26	24	2,756	3,117
Switzerland	701	900	1,047	1,117	1,227	1,279	1,338	1,438
Turkey	1	38	583	943	1,351	2,262	3,099	4,294
United Kingdom	3,222	6,197	9,367	10,015	10,105	10,558	10,756	10,910
Eastern Europe								
Albania								
Belarus		60	11,703	34,730	94,484	178,483	277,878	352,580
Bosnia-Herzegovina		29	92	122	140	158	170	177
Bulgaria		3	148	152	204	250	255	257
Croatia	7	2,422	3,063	3,152	3,462	3,243	4,068	3,747
Czech Republic	1,741	3,992	5,373	5,124	6,131	7,585	7,805	9,023
Estonia	11	13	32	40	46	53	61	66
Georgia		17	29	37	36	43	56	69
Hungary	19,881	58,238	93,796	104,724	126,381	144,733	187,833	186,916
Latvia		5	37	53	58	65	108	103
Lithuania		57	173	182	205	216	254	296
Macedonia	1	1,364	1,080	1,833	1,819	1,961	2,258	3,026
Moldova								
Montenegro		7	7	9	12	14	14	17
Poland	203	2,154	5,871	5,651	6,473	7,201	7,523	8,067
Romania		38	285	495	733	918	1,466	3,613
Russia	2	4,186	12,155	18,845	34,014	53,096	55,683	92,738
Serbia		431	1,892	3,563	7,784	10,374	11,693	14,687
Slovakia	35	59	82	108	157	164	239	360
Slovenia	5	57	82	96	107	122	135	157
Ukraine		271	971	1,421	1,900	2,774	3,774	4,594

Source: Euromonitor International from national statistics

Education Consumer Expenditure 1990, 1995, 1999-2011 *(continued)*

National currency million

	2005	2006	2007	2008	2009	2010	2011	US$ million 2011	US$ per capita 2011
Western Europe									
Austria	1,056	1,123	1,187	1,232	1,142	1,191	1,208	1,680.27	199.93
Belgium	784	800	830	852	878	908	892	1,240.46	113.27
Cyprus									
Denmark	5,184	5,514	5,542	5,788	6,064	6,295	6,488	1,210.44	217.68
Finland	334	361	385	403	410	414	455	631.98	117.57
France	6,722	7,502	8,038	8,744	9,198	9,301	9,995	13,897.51	220.15
Germany	10,550	10,930	11,870	12,528	13,000	13,448	13,933	19,372.22	236.96
Gibraltar									
Greece	3,070	3,249	3,502	3,805	4,076	4,456	4,449	6,185.52	546.14
Iceland									
Ireland	843	1,132	1,209	1,283	1,500	1,716	1,665	2,314.90	516.62
Italy	7,884	8,178	8,473	8,714	8,512	8,885	9,151	12,723.24	209.86
Liechtenstein									
Luxembourg									
Malta									
Monaco									
Netherlands	1,316	1,350	1,420	1,490	1,579	1,627	1,730	2,405.97	144.45
Norway	2,870	3,093	3,651	3,657	4,070	4,414	4,659	831.10	168.91
Portugal	1,150	1,218	1,277	1,394	1,434	1,543	1,552	2,158.24	202.90
Spain	7,927	8,244	8,522	8,505	8,789	9,032	9,238	12,844.21	278.30
Sweden	3,375	3,619	3,969	4,316	4,403	4,585	4,789	737.23	78.30
Switzerland	1,455	1,479	1,588	1,677	1,643	1,762	1,822	2,051.90	260.72
Turkey	5,771	7,098	8,199	8,888	9,341	9,993	12,678	7,547.36	102.95
United Kingdom	11,422	12,195	12,980	13,134	13,484	13,829	14,209	22,770.53	364.34
Eastern Europe									
Albania									
Belarus	446,181	537,430	688,946	932,910	1,094,622	1,317,515	2,144,959	431.18	45.48
Bosnia-Herzegovina	189	225	260	294	274	252	260	184.58	48.02
Bulgaria	279	270	271	293	256	286	291	207.04	27.54
Croatia	4,229	4,461	6,307	6,936	7,036	6,211	6,574	1,230.25	278.83
Czech Republic	10,522	11,027	13,256	14,688	13,332	14,891	15,170	857.28	81.76
Estonia	72	76	72	69	63	62	69	96.14	71.73
Georgia	82	119	147	175	183	168	197	116.66	26.55
Hungary	180,583	197,598	192,801	200,406	203,000	218,156	232,327	1,155.54	115.72
Latvia	137	151	178	229	137	138	168	332.86	160.45
Lithuania	361	513	689	602	590	579	606	244.03	75.21
Macedonia	3,797	4,098	4,861	5,938	5,680	5,930	6,535	147.74	71.82
Moldova									
Montenegro	19	18	46	51	46	47	50	69.86	112.67
Poland	7,727	8,510	9,148	10,022	10,366	10,821	11,654	3,932.68	102.98
Romania	4,104	4,171	4,644	6,054	7,655	7,069	7,129	2,338.41	109.15
Russia	129,837	164,795	204,255	243,532	238,192	256,783	305,739	10,402.08	72.79
Serbia	18,922	20,637	22,792	24,990	26,324	28,284	31,527	429.91	59.10
Slovakia	418	466	492	524	544	571	617	857.90	158.97
Slovenia	183	198	247	262	290	284	297	413.17	201.53
Ukraine	5,266	6,196	7,241	8,707	10,092	13,433	17,939	2,250.15	49.35

Source: Euromonitor International from national statistics

6

Consumer Expenditure

Consumer Expenditure Statistics

Table 6.13

Hotels and Catering Consumer Expenditure 1990, 1995, 1999-2011

National currency million

	1990	1995	1999	2000	2001	2002	2003	2004
Western Europe								
Austria	8,689	10,943	12,018	12,630	13,382	13,770	14,694	15,070
Belgium	4,939	6,029	6,841	7,335	7,568	8,036	8,320	8,608
Cyprus								
Denmark	22,077	25,798	29,728	31,118	31,575	31,767	31,860	33,803
Finland	3,323	3,393	3,833	4,036	4,283	4,360	4,626	4,955
France	38,622	44,732	52,083	56,376	58,720	61,294	63,766	65,862
Germany	45,131	56,710	60,690	64,350	65,300	64,210	64,300	65,460
Gibraltar								
Greece	4,058	9,791	14,657	15,166	16,688	16,278	16,533	17,418
Iceland								
Ireland	2,742	4,018	6,405	7,038	7,660	8,316	8,788	9,011
Italy	33,118	48,900	61,506	69,165	73,588	75,541	77,768	80,950
Liechtenstein								
Luxembourg								
Malta								
Monaco								
Netherlands	6,369	8,318	10,713	11,517	12,083	12,447	12,153	12,294
Norway	16,852	28,092	38,152	39,406	39,271	40,486	41,003	41,752
Portugal	3,858	6,109	7,753	8,844	9,473	9,918	9,965	10,607
Spain	33,128	51,800	65,692	71,984	75,887	80,962	87,242	94,286
Sweden	27,219	38,922	49,855	52,735	55,748	57,465	59,103	59,900
Switzerland	14,840	18,420	19,683	20,907	22,704	21,653	21,179	22,105
Turkey	25	502	4,404	7,820	11,517	16,031	19,760	25,549
United Kingdom	40,603	50,381	61,645	65,141	67,893	71,972	74,538	76,916
Eastern Europe								
Albania								
Belarus		3,388	55,934	149,944	250,571	381,710	440,835	688,212
Bosnia-Herzegovina		276	744	951	1,044	1,147	1,181	1,177
Bulgaria	3	57	1,633	1,702	1,905	2,010	2,232	2,569
Croatia	11	4,810	8,341	10,609	11,617	10,723	16,482	15,005
Czech Republic	23,632	64,558	94,297	100,656	102,529	99,506	102,928	114,854
Estonia	96	101	202	227	259	292	331	383
Georgia		46	67	86	80	94	119	142
Hungary	57,665	191,444	394,546	435,998	497,504	571,187	615,382	689,938
Latvia		90	132	143	161	166	160	188
Lithuania	2	514	1,014	1,003	1,100	1,158	1,220	1,299
Macedonia	10	6,051	6,755	9,405	7,503	7,241	5,657	7,116
Moldova								
Montenegro		16	13	16	20	22	21	22
Poland	912	6,634	12,641	14,736	15,076	15,515	15,994	17,169
Romania	4	306	2,028	2,704	4,007	4,462	5,074	6,658
Russia	13	21,052	32,693	56,860	106,902	128,366	192,613	276,960
Serbia		1,264	5,333	9,898	20,891	26,655	29,793	32,164
Slovakia	472	754	1,188	1,330	1,523	1,609	1,623	1,699
Slovenia	29	444	660	703	795	866	972	1,033
Ukraine		495	1,532	2,061	2,546	3,191	3,728	4,262

Source: Euromonitor International from national statistics

Hotels and Catering Consumer Expenditure 1990, 1995, 1999-2011 *(continued)*

National currency million

	2005	2006	2007	2008	2009	2010	2011	US$ million 2011	US$ per capita 2011
Western Europe									
Austria	15,323	16,223	16,982	17,787	18,211	18,630	19,500	27,113.94	3,226.22
Belgium	8,851	9,182	9,719	10,364	10,321	10,646	10,885	15,134.98	1,382.03
Cyprus									
Denmark	36,137	38,453	40,725	42,173	38,505	40,131	40,338	7,526.02	1,353.45
Finland	5,273	5,539	5,839	6,086	5,829	5,992	6,263	8,707.77	1,619.97
France	68,684	72,084	75,630	76,498	74,988	76,285	79,000	109,844.64	1,740.04
Germany	67,010	70,000	73,940	76,208	76,071	78,147	82,240	114,349.08	1,398.74
Gibraltar									
Greece	18,513	19,410	20,291	20,885	18,913	17,449	15,928	22,146.79	1,955.41
Iceland									
Ireland	9,548	10,058	10,957	11,168	10,236	10,032	9,817	13,650.17	3,046.33
Italy	83,584	88,302	92,592	94,393	91,547	96,811	100,618	139,902.66	2,307.62
Liechtenstein									
Luxembourg									
Malta									
Monaco									
Netherlands	12,540	13,124	13,838	13,881	13,251	13,172	12,650	17,588.32	1,055.99
Norway	43,497	48,342	52,378	57,015	56,834	58,428	62,208	11,096.98	2,255.34
Portugal	11,040	11,602	12,325	12,327	12,109	12,822	12,507	17,390.28	1,634.89
Spain	100,373	106,991	112,138	112,805	102,181	105,847	108,096	150,300.41	3,256.57
Sweden	64,561	69,357	74,182	80,163	82,206	86,886	91,401	14,071.78	1,494.52
Switzerland	22,219	23,138	24,152	24,899	24,074	24,577	25,099	28,261.23	3,590.95
Turkey	29,213	34,361	37,753	41,618	46,035	50,526	56,971	33,916.20	462.63
United Kingdom	80,018	81,938	84,926	86,164	82,296	88,279	92,208	147,769.90	2,364.37
Eastern Europe									
Albania									
Belarus	870,917	1,049,029	1,257,921	1,657,062	1,839,560	2,153,562	3,437,109	690.93	72.87
Bosnia-Herzegovina	1,254	1,388	1,540	1,636	1,606	1,466	1,494	1,061.96	276.28
Bulgaria	2,957	3,232	4,084	4,721	4,913	5,200	5,792	4,118.02	547.85
Croatia	16,691	17,623	18,373	19,779	19,833	20,954	20,754	3,883.70	880.23
Czech Republic	117,025	133,424	141,725	139,432	141,841	147,327	150,439	8,501.35	810.75
Estonia	452	508	594	543	401	398	440	611.23	456.07
Georgia	165	234	283	329	336	344	400	237.25	54.00
Hungary	750,406	796,607	888,291	947,104	954,287	999,002	1,061,928	5,281.79	528.93
Latvia	296	436	497	512	345	355	404	800.23	385.73
Lithuania	1,407	1,556	1,792	2,081	1,749	1,583	1,692	681.35	210.00
Macedonia	8,783	10,070	11,371	11,584	9,974	9,731	10,288	232.59	113.08
Moldova									
Montenegro	20	28	54	70	57	58	62	86.47	139.46
Poland	17,640	18,736	19,940	21,891	22,752	23,888	25,576	8,630.38	225.99
Romania	10,349	12,228	13,915	17,041	14,866	15,967	17,261	5,661.93	264.28
Russia	343,961	439,106	572,731	767,494	907,470	987,979	1,160,487	39,483.01	276.27
Serbia	37,643	42,925	48,647	51,483	50,357	54,402	59,214	807.47	110.99
Slovakia	1,893	2,272	2,351	2,472	2,172	2,154	2,163	3,007.39	557.26
Slovenia	1,071	1,146	1,410	1,501	1,523	1,592	1,637	2,276.20	1,110.24
Ukraine	7,643	9,025	11,603	15,402	16,621	18,795	24,100	3,023.00	66.30

Source: Euromonitor International from national statistics

6

Consumer Expenditure

Consumer Expenditure Statistics

Table 6.14

Miscellaneous Goods and Services Consumer Expenditure 1990, 1995, 1999-2011

National currency million

	1990	1995	1999	2000	2001	2002	2003	2004
Western Europe								
Austria	8,460	10,568	11,655	12,470	12,474	12,526	12,554	13,298
Belgium	11,954	13,911	14,426	16,850	17,703	17,127	16,437	17,197
Cyprus								
Denmark	47,832	59,560	69,894	76,125	77,646	79,509	84,786	88,352
Finland	4,307	4,490	4,996	6,003	6,403	6,730	6,096	6,361
France	76,514	77,600	79,336	89,495	94,900	93,490	96,109	99,901
Germany	91,612	121,930	128,030	129,560	135,110	136,610	146,650	149,400
Gibraltar								
Greece	2,972	6,403	11,308	11,376	9,960	9,437	9,461	10,187
Iceland								
Ireland	1,591	2,346	4,535	4,834	5,652	6,343	7,156	7,838
Italy	41,588	56,652	62,817	68,653	72,388	72,539	74,701	75,272
Liechtenstein								
Luxembourg								
Malta								
Monaco								
Netherlands	15,005	20,554	27,611	31,152	32,473	32,862	34,806	36,023
Norway	30,882	39,346	48,943	52,936	54,077	57,956	64,053	70,635
Portugal	3,809	6,010	7,891	7,991	8,285	8,567	9,188	9,881
Spain	14,849	22,375	30,552	34,175	37,174	38,221	40,035	45,198
Sweden	58,056	81,279	98,743	108,848	108,842	109,302	107,971	117,296
Switzerland	21,902	23,850	29,533	32,200	30,794	30,914	31,050	31,405
Turkey	34	621	6,268	9,913	14,872	17,996	23,440	30,284
United Kingdom	43,679	56,372	78,314	84,142	87,596	91,220	94,837	100,020
Eastern Europe								
Albania								
Belarus		2,299	53,180	160,030	365,763	619,411	765,095	951,510
Bosnia-Herzegovina		153	504	674	775	888	955	992
Bulgaria	1	19	470	542	530	795	894	1,112
Croatia	5	2,540	4,770	6,485	7,764	8,135	9,286	9,479
Czech Republic	19,827	57,632	91,885	96,202	106,431	105,622	114,583	117,694
Estonia	98	94	203	240	290	343	378	437
Georgia		101	143	180	166	193	244	289
Hungary	105,986	297,267	517,496	629,631	728,032	808,799	896,980	952,049
Latvia		57	86	99	105	133	159	182
Lithuania	3	588	1,500	1,436	1,777	1,916	2,211	2,444
Macedonia	24	6,262	10,104	12,600	11,008	10,734	7,789	11,360
Moldova								
Montenegro		23	22	28	38	44	45	50
Poland	1,662	16,561	42,724	55,284	57,153	63,758	66,151	70,573
Romania	1	92	989	1,201	1,780	2,615	3,388	5,554
Russia	11	27,296	99,213	129,199	172,650	215,607	286,355	427,930
Serbia		1,460	6,322	11,884	25,705	33,985	39,081	46,621
Slovakia	300	720	1,179	1,319	1,519	1,787	1,916	2,269
Slovenia	31	498	879	884	922	1,136	1,281	1,381
Ukraine		531	1,647	2,269	2,921	3,533	4,602	5,812

Source: Euromonitor International from national statistics

Miscellaneous Goods and Services Consumer Expenditure 1990, 1995, 1999-2011 *(continued)*

National currency million

	2005	2006	2007	2008	2009	2010	2011	US$ million 2011	US$ per capita 2011
Western Europe									
Austria	14,469	15,225	16,158	16,273	16,245	16,840	17,672	24,571.09	2,923.65
Belgium	18,603	20,699	22,647	22,407	21,461	22,759	23,498	32,671.91	2,983.39
Cyprus									
Denmark	93,852	98,472	100,407	106,413	102,796	102,698	105,007	19,591.63	3,523.28
Finland	6,653	7,558	8,626	9,022	8,169	8,586	8,794	12,227.94	2,274.85
France	102,562	110,604	119,026	122,502	119,581	118,945	120,506	167,554.86	2,654.22
Germany	157,050	158,600	162,710	157,464	157,278	174,053	179,415	249,464.34	3,051.49
Gibraltar									
Greece	10,634	11,587	12,025	12,843	12,967	13,248	12,821	17,827.42	1,574.04
Iceland									
Ireland	8,513	9,381	10,089	9,192	6,717	6,935	7,019	9,759.25	2,177.99
Italy	80,497	86,892	92,382	96,041	94,886	95,163	97,672	135,806.85	2,240.06
Liechtenstein									
Luxembourg									
Malta									
Monaco									
Netherlands	38,903	41,266	42,817	40,969	37,540	39,269	38,694	53,802.03	3,230.23
Norway	76,434	81,749	92,358	97,293	100,778	105,816	109,888	19,602.38	3,983.98
Portugal	10,483	11,789	13,594	14,686	12,684	13,415	13,275	18,457.46	1,735.22
Spain	48,668	54,501	60,497	60,986	52,168	51,082	50,231	69,842.17	1,513.28
Sweden	125,865	139,408	148,128	155,081	156,147	163,135	170,115	26,190.13	2,781.58
Switzerland	31,214	33,595	36,343	37,485	35,612	36,426	37,315	42,016.02	5,338.67
Turkey	33,103	39,403	47,011	49,670	46,230	52,534	63,834	38,001.88	518.36
United Kingdom	106,960	112,921	118,038	113,832	104,285	103,849	103,392	165,692.21	2,651.13
Eastern Europe									
Albania									
Belarus	1,204,115	1,450,369	1,873,386	2,583,720	3,023,896	3,707,138	6,010,024	1,208.13	127.42
Bosnia-Herzegovina	1,098	1,271	1,460	1,682	1,589	1,455	1,493	1,061.56	276.18
Bulgaria	1,349	1,445	1,737	1,939	1,790	1,828	2,063	1,466.76	195.13
Croatia	10,291	10,885	12,420	12,726	11,830	12,940	13,458	2,518.38	570.79
Czech Republic	123,779	142,682	156,939	169,740	166,382	166,909	167,016	9,438.14	900.09
Estonia	512	619	712	742	521	510	579	805.75	601.22
Georgia	333	467	561	647	656	682	792	469.81	106.94
Hungary	1,065,321	1,110,882	1,212,715	1,304,149	1,332,478	1,357,697	1,441,220	7,168.30	717.86
Latvia	208	301	430	497	390	446	465	920.85	443.87
Lithuania	2,960	3,770	4,563	5,605	4,242	4,053	4,340	1,747.79	538.68
Macedonia	10,906	12,996	14,339	16,380	16,086	16,650	17,853	403.62	196.22
Moldova									
Montenegro	55	68	102	147	132	134	143	199.26	321.38
Poland	73,069	82,456	90,002	100,386	106,185	113,888	124,800	42,112.81	1,102.74
Romania	5,029	6,931	9,182	10,497	9,405	9,796	10,679	3,502.99	163.51
Russia	549,232	733,464	925,535	1,181,643	1,337,252	1,441,398	1,687,313	57,407.13	401.69
Serbia	60,893	74,975	85,402	102,541	99,168	107,377	119,277	1,626.50	223.58
Slovakia	2,535	2,893	3,232	3,658	3,731	3,813	3,942	5,481.67	1,015.74
Slovenia	1,476	1,591	1,870	2,028	1,930	2,020	2,088	2,903.65	1,416.28
Ukraine	6,620	9,418	14,965	22,466	20,967	26,020	32,898	4,126.56	90.50

Source: Euromonitor International from national statistics

7

Consumer Market Sizes

Consumer Market Statistics

Table 7.1

Alcoholic Drinks: Per Capita Retail Sales 2011

Litres per capita

	Alcoholic Drinks	Beer	Wine	Spirits
Western Europe				
Austria	144.22	100.98	33.44	3.63
Belgium	119.92	87.26	28.14	3.43
Cyprus	78.31	61.30	16.38	0.59
Denmark	105.29	67.05	31.78	3.26
Finland	117.25	81.34	12.27	5.45
France	77.50	29.86	39.13	6.30
Germany	144.92	105.18	25.82	5.88
Gibraltar	40.15	26.76	8.86	1.68
Greece	62.84	31.87	27.81	2.91
Iceland	68.07	50.06	14.72	2.99
Ireland	149.72	110.31	17.96	4.42
Italy	71.48	27.05	41.04	2.44
Liechtenstein	87.54	49.18	33.88	2.06
Luxembourg	153.28	87.72	61.95	2.47
Malta	41.30	33.90	3.49	1.56
Monaco	80.48	35.70	34.98	7.42
Netherlands	98.18	68.35	25.02	3.42
Norway	73.80	52.87	15.50	2.89
Portugal	101.36	52.92	46.23	1.88
Spain	99.85	69.06	21.65	5.20
Sweden	79.22	50.35	22.35	2.33
Switzerland	99.56	56.24	38.16	2.78
Turkey	14.44	12.81	0.75	0.88
United Kingdom	113.24	68.79	22.37	5.07
Eastern Europe				
Albania	11.96	4.12	6.99	0.84
Belarus	95.35	53.52	25.16	15.24
Bosnia-Herzegovina	67.11	61.92	3.73	1.25
Bulgaria	81.03	67.23	6.51	7.24
Croatia	92.20	73.28	12.48	2.68
Czech Republic	173.32	144.83	18.72	8.57
Estonia	141.11	98.32	11.58	12.27
Georgia	38.09	29.06	6.59	2.44
Hungary	94.22	65.47	23.65	4.69
Latvia	100.56	76.34	8.95	8.48
Lithuania	112.76	92.25	6.68	7.59
Macedonia	44.17	31.83	11.30	1.01
Moldova	29.21	11.44	17.20	0.57
Montenegro	70.18	60.71	7.25	1.78
Poland	110.19	93.72	7.19	9.12
Romania	93.88	79.38	11.32	3.14
Russia	93.30	69.69	9.16	12.14
Serbia	75.54	66.68	5.94	2.75
Slovakia	97.77	72.89	15.64	9.02
Slovenia	145.54	94.99	36.46	2.93
Ukraine	77.97	57.22	7.77	10.96

Source: Euromonitor International from national statistics
Note: Alcoholic drinks data are off-trade

Table 7.2

Beauty and Personal Care: Per Capita Retail Sales 2011

US$ per capita

	Baby Care	Bath & Shower Products	Deodorants	Hair Care	Colour Cosmetics
Western Europe					
Austria	8.32	19.68	10.88	44.95	30.67
Belgium	7.87	21.05	14.34	31.64	27.79
Cyprus	5.24	7.59	6.08	17.99	11.63
Denmark	6.59	16.23	15.97	85.70	37.29
Finland	4.06	16.14	14.64	77.27	35.25
France	7.54	19.52	14.31	37.54	28.96
Germany	5.22	18.55	12.61	37.12	25.38
Gibraltar	3.66	7.63	7.03	14.54	13.54
Greece	8.07	11.82	6.72	28.62	12.28
Iceland	3.95	25.91	15.18	78.68	60.13
Ireland	12.66	22.52	12.18	44.41	29.42
Italy	7.58	25.33	10.94	29.05	22.34
Liechtenstein	3.49	19.40	7.60	29.43	25.02
Luxembourg	5.30	19.83	12.54	26.28	29.77
Malta	3.17	7.28	6.05	12.59	11.63
Monaco	5.93	17.80	12.22	33.65	29.27
Netherlands	7.00	23.37	14.73	44.88	33.43
Norway	8.86	35.51	19.95	94.67	68.86
Portugal	14.16	20.68	9.99	38.43	10.80
Spain	9.78	13.00	9.74	34.27	20.92
Sweden	6.24	16.99	10.44	55.62	44.11
Switzerland	10.36	36.10	13.50	52.31	46.94
Turkey	2.80	4.96	2.13	9.51	4.83
United Kingdom	10.35	21.06	15.64	36.82	42.11
Eastern Europe					
Albania	0.38	2.54	1.91	3.68	4.09
Belarus	2.05	9.43	2.88	12.54	11.06
Bosnia-Herzegovina	3.24	6.82	6.26	12.09	7.68
Bulgaria	1.14	7.11	3.89	11.01	5.88
Croatia	3.61	7.90	6.71	22.55	12.06
Czech Republic	4.28	12.91	8.61	27.20	19.00
Estonia	3.26	9.20	3.75	18.59	11.02
Georgia	0.91	3.75	2.60	8.07	4.54
Hungary	3.86	15.41	8.87	17.23	9.50
Latvia	1.72	5.72	3.83	14.53	8.23
Lithuania	2.30	8.23	2.87	13.38	9.06
Macedonia	2.51	5.73	2.08	7.41	7.27
Moldova	0.26	2.01	1.50	2.88	3.20
Montenegro	1.41	5.55	3.03	8.57	5.74
Poland	4.40	10.93	10.10	22.59	11.85
Romania	0.68	6.69	5.62	8.97	8.18
Russia	2.95	8.57	4.30	16.72	13.03
Serbia	4.16	5.21	4.55	13.05	5.93
Slovakia	2.22	12.50	9.36	23.58	17.31
Slovenia	3.46	10.13	7.62	24.10	14.20
Ukraine	1.66	4.46	2.56	10.84	6.15

Source: Euromonitor International from national statistics

7

Consumer Market Sizes

Consumer Market Statistics

Beauty and Personal Care: Per Capita Retail Sales 2011 *(continued)*

US$ per capita

	Men's Grooming	Oral Care	Fragrances	Skin Care	Sun Care
Western Europe					
Austria	23.51	38.30	26.28	49.41	6.97
Belgium	20.87	20.41	45.89	51.25	5.99
Cyprus	5.12	13.60	18.82	13.41	2.42
Denmark	24.90	23.11	40.28	45.06	13.13
Finland	13.47	19.87	10.93	55.53	6.50
France	23.00	20.83	42.48	66.42	7.01
Germany	25.89	24.24	32.97	59.12	2.94
Gibraltar	10.54	9.71	9.98	15.92	3.02
Greece	12.74	10.03	11.87	44.24	9.14
Iceland	21.13	28.04	20.57	51.05	8.47
Ireland	30.40	29.72	26.31	35.12	7.28
Italy	16.67	24.45	25.03	43.10	8.28
Liechtenstein	13.91	21.22	48.99	28.34	6.77
Luxembourg	18.38	12.49	46.97	39.80	4.46
Malta	9.06	8.34	8.58	14.00	2.59
Monaco	19.75	16.57	40.74	62.00	6.01
Netherlands	30.31	27.31	47.64	54.80	8.05
Norway	23.31	40.55	21.73	95.46	13.71
Portugal	17.73	21.16	32.43	40.67	6.85
Spain	16.43	19.95	36.41	51.22	12.35
Sweden	17.02	26.03	22.93	65.75	6.36
Switzerland	26.72	35.74	65.18	50.18	14.85
Turkey	3.81	5.54	6.63	6.95	0.49
United Kingdom	25.94	25.41	29.51	57.04	7.54
Eastern Europe					
Albania	1.58	2.85	5.11	3.00	0.43
Belarus	6.26	6.74	11.90	10.81	0.68
Bosnia-Herzegovina	7.58	4.91	6.80	9.81	1.22
Bulgaria	2.82	4.71	6.12	11.58	1.24
Croatia	11.32	5.41	7.27	17.37	3.56
Czech Republic	10.61	11.06	17.21	23.50	1.96
Estonia	6.29	5.19	10.41	28.71	1.81
Georgia	2.56	2.29	3.60	4.53	0.14
Hungary	13.98	9.43	11.71	22.21	1.30
Latvia	5.71	4.16	7.89	14.77	1.72
Lithuania	6.75	5.79	7.31	12.67	1.85
Macedonia	2.95	2.57	4.46	7.81	0.99
Moldova	1.24	2.24	4.01	2.35	0.34
Montenegro	4.03	3.87	5.02	7.60	2.01
Poland	12.88	9.25	16.52	20.80	1.25
Romania	4.31	3.58	13.37	13.45	0.70
Russia	8.52	8.21	16.02	18.58	1.00
Serbia	6.68	3.13	5.03	7.97	1.36
Slovakia	10.23	9.13	20.43	27.23	1.04
Slovenia	12.40	6.35	12.61	33.38	3.97
Ukraine	5.27	4.72	6.67	9.01	0.44

Source: Euromonitor International from national statistics

Table 7.3

Apparel: Per Capita Retail Sales 2011

US$ per capita

	Total Clothing	Men's Outerwear	Women's Outerwear	Footwear
Western Europe				
Austria	1,113.08	297.34	562.47	213.60
Belgium	645.44	166.52	290.09	176.99
Cyprus	154.54	44.01	63.25	29.70
Denmark	995.98	249.83	500.65	216.98
Finland	695.09	152.32	306.82	137.32
France	725.47	210.23	310.38	190.15
Germany	924.38	250.92	483.25	156.17
Gibraltar	129.68	29.84	63.07	24.28
Greece	556.98	141.38	256.87	138.92
Iceland	206.27	43.92	100.88	52.10
Ireland	774.98	197.62	358.25	139.25
Italy	965.64	243.05	337.95	209.00
Liechtenstein	914.06	269.53	440.17	184.99
Luxembourg	304.51	76.55	155.54	97.27
Malta	193.51	50.27	90.60	31.85
Monaco	269.98	74.63	98.92	101.33
Netherlands	881.60	269.23	370.73	215.64
Norway	1,569.47	436.40	690.26	337.40
Portugal	457.37	125.06	211.59	145.03
Spain	552.14	123.40	214.65	193.69
Sweden	1,154.38	284.88	542.51	209.72
Switzerland	866.10	258.92	423.76	160.99
Turkey	227.66	85.82	64.62	60.16
United Kingdom	1,011.99	258.89	467.16	169.82
Eastern Europe				
Albania	53.04	14.85	19.68	15.92
Belarus	146.09	39.00	64.15	91.49
Bosnia-Herzegovina	85.63	28.42	31.79	64.84
Bulgaria	67.13	22.79	26.72	43.36
Croatia	254.17	87.04	101.62	157.93
Czech Republic	284.37	85.52	137.35	68.19
Estonia	190.78	53.93	61.33	103.40
Georgia	53.66	14.33	23.55	33.56
Hungary	182.81	50.96	71.30	55.29
Latvia	255.94	72.65	82.05	139.29
Lithuania	241.06	68.53	77.03	130.95
Macedonia	110.77	37.90	44.34	69.90
Moldova	5.59	1.93	2.24	3.49
Montenegro	54.53	18.50	21.73	35.06
Poland	219.64	60.51	73.11	74.25
Romania	118.24	38.32	47.11	49.31
Russia	373.75	94.44	194.78	120.54
Serbia	89.53	30.38	35.68	57.48
Slovakia	217.97	65.12	96.50	110.53
Slovenia	261.37	49.11	125.84	246.08
Ukraine	164.06	45.22	66.64	80.69

Source: Euromonitor International from national statistics

7

Consumer Market Sizes

Consumer Market Statistics

Table 7.4

Consumer Electronics: Per Capita Retail Sales 2011

US$ per capita

	Digital Televisions	DVD Players	Audio & Cinema	Computers	Cameras	Camcorders	Media Players	Mobile Phones	MP3 Players
Western Europe									
Austria	84.27	2.59	17.90	94.75	35.65	5.32	10.15	72.46	1.49
Belgium	71.61	7.11	17.93	152.49	8.53	1.61	17.45	61.79	0.39
Cyprus	33.27	1.44	2.60	79.39	7.60	4.77	8.33	48.60	3.81
Denmark	81.35	1.25	30.74	134.87	18.70	4.08	23.88	149.80	2.25
Finland	83.98	5.42	15.38	186.36	24.54	8.29	28.64	122.43	11.88
France	81.15	1.70	30.68	108.35	24.82	4.22	20.36	72.12	0.05
Germany	105.00	0.83	19.31	96.25	30.46	3.54	9.57	90.74	1.48
Gibraltar		2.35	3.65	183.62	5.39		6.61	28.35	4.60
Greece	37.57	0.98	6.08	40.08	6.09	1.12	4.23	86.87	0.82
Iceland	47.10	2.57	8.68	204.29	13.75	4.64	16.07	67.94	6.67
Ireland	39.36	1.60	8.70	103.89	11.08	4.40	10.60	49.51	3.05
Italy	85.25	3.03	5.58	66.90	16.47	2.60	6.49	98.30	1.06
Liechtenstein	135.25	2.93	22.27	173.50	48.26	4.92	7.85	159.63	
Luxembourg	122.15	32.75	19.87	181.66	29.16	6.07	2.65	199.11	
Malta	40.11	1.66	9.58	52.74	14.29	2.59	9.10	44.72	
Monaco	87.54		31.36	17.12	12.76	8.48	21.15	97.33	
Netherlands	59.71	4.07	19.08	125.14	34.67	9.26	24.84	67.22	1.82
Norway	112.76	1.18	26.89	218.57	23.21	5.99	16.20	190.05	4.97
Portugal	35.28	2.34	3.23	59.82	13.41	1.47	6.24	50.86	1.55
Spain	117.24	3.60	5.20	95.09	15.15	5.82	5.52	81.26	0.12
Sweden	96.98	1.53	17.95	153.90	46.85	3.51	21.44	107.87	4.06
Switzerland	54.10	2.76	8.08	148.51	14.91	4.82	10.76	65.04	3.27
Turkey	16.12	0.70	2.14	32.29	4.76	0.27	0.86	46.17	0.22
United Kingdom	110.58	0.94	22.37	115.37	26.20	5.01	30.05	70.11	2.70
Eastern Europe									
Albania	2.31	0.44	0.29	7.68	2.86	0.06	0.90	19.21	0.55
Belarus	11.15	0.79	0.69	15.06	2.72	0.27	2.49	10.77	1.59
Bosnia-Herzegovina	1.97	0.37	0.25	7.46	0.73	0.05	0.76	16.46	0.47
Bulgaria	6.03	0.73	0.65	11.06	1.72	0.11	1.89	8.40	1.08
Croatia	10.54	0.96	0.94	19.48	2.36	0.16	2.65	16.70	1.50
Czech Republic	38.87	1.63	3.55	61.30	9.40	4.00	0.74	46.77	0.40
Estonia	24.64	2.32	3.39	65.15	7.83	0.52	7.55	41.70	3.79
Georgia	5.27	0.58	0.34	12.09	1.64	0.58	1.46	29.99	0.98
Hungary	20.01	1.69	2.60	28.35	5.68	3.26	1.54	50.76	0.29
Latvia	25.54	2.33	3.51	60.24	8.12	0.52	7.82	43.33	3.92
Lithuania	23.05	2.24	3.20	47.84	7.33	0.34	7.06	39.12	3.54
Macedonia	2.54	0.48	0.32	8.14	0.94	0.06	0.99	21.23	0.61
Moldova	4.13	0.45	0.26	9.72	1.29	0.07	1.14	23.72	0.77
Montenegro	7.00	0.54	0.52	12.90	1.65	0.11	1.82	11.61	1.04
Poland	39.24	0.53	4.18	51.13	10.22	1.49	2.03	30.94	0.41
Romania	14.57	0.45	1.43	13.42	2.01	2.31	0.44	14.59	0.18
Russia	31.82	1.08	1.92	39.83	8.84	2.13	1.75	43.82	0.41
Serbia	6.45	0.54	0.64	11.76	1.45	0.10	1.62	10.22	0.92
Slovakia	28.51	3.11	3.17	68.79	8.53	1.57	8.79	41.44	6.12
Slovenia	42.61	3.97	3.77	99.74	14.40	0.46	9.04	46.98	5.12
Ukraine	17.16	0.65	1.04	13.69	4.17	0.69	0.87	19.27	0.29

Source: Euromonitor International from national statistics

Table 7.5

Tissue and Hygiene Products: Per Capita Retail Sales 2011

US$ per capita

	Sanitary Protection	Nappies, Diapers & Pants	Toilet Paper	Tissues	Kitchen Towels
Western Europe					
Austria	10.10	15.07	24.81	9.08	8.54
Belgium	12.53	21.61	19.39	5.50	6.90
Cyprus	6.70	6.46	7.35	1.99	1.23
Denmark	19.40	22.20	20.72	1.87	11.14
Finland	12.81	17.04	27.17	2.28	10.25
France	10.84	17.66	19.36	5.56	7.88
Germany	10.92	11.82	23.42	5.36	7.80
Gibraltar	3.41	5.75	10.26	2.22	3.47
Greece	10.20	15.52	17.45	2.01	8.59
Iceland	15.81	21.25	27.67	0.99	13.31
Ireland	13.03	22.98	23.13	3.68	6.08
Italy	12.91	13.35	18.03	4.60	10.27
Liechtenstein	8.96	10.13	16.48	6.15	3.83
Luxembourg	7.51	15.95	15.35	2.90	5.35
Malta	2.84	4.96	8.78	1.90	2.97
Monaco	7.31	12.23	13.40	3.80	5.97
Netherlands	11.95	19.85	26.20	4.03	7.61
Norway	21.83	22.27	46.58	2.36	13.84
Portugal	8.66	13.46	18.12	2.14	5.02
Spain	13.21	14.85	18.46	2.83	6.09
Sweden	12.00	19.57	29.96	4.83	12.64
Switzerland	15.02	19.00	32.97	10.89	10.68
Turkey	4.77	8.45	4.68	0.37	1.94
United Kingdom	8.60	16.18	29.38	5.85	10.29
Eastern Europe					
Albania	6.13	3.51	3.99	0.32	0.31
Belarus	6.41	5.31	2.26	0.18	0.45
Bosnia-Herzegovina	5.60	7.86	9.99	0.79	1.04
Bulgaria	3.77	3.02	5.25	3.76	0.83
Croatia	10.60	10.84	11.87	2.06	4.62
Czech Republic	8.73	12.33	13.28	5.08	1.63
Estonia	4.85	12.10	6.72	2.25	1.25
Georgia	5.56	3.36	2.25	0.25	0.11
Hungary	7.13	8.04	12.64	5.70	3.32
Latvia	5.82	10.21	8.28	1.70	2.95
Lithuania	5.43	9.02	7.65	2.14	2.05
Macedonia	7.32	10.50	4.83	0.99	1.06
Moldova	1.63	0.93	1.06	0.09	0.08
Montenegro	3.18	2.37	5.40	0.85	0.74
Poland	8.19	10.11	10.92	2.96	3.43
Romania	3.39	7.88	5.68	0.70	1.19
Russia	7.53	11.95	3.70	0.39	0.40
Serbia	9.92	11.99	5.63	4.66	1.13
Slovakia	9.80	15.53	10.95	3.22	0.85
Slovenia	8.54	10.90	15.03	2.45	4.05
Ukraine	5.53	4.57	3.33	0.21	0.41

Source: Euromonitor International from national statistics

Consumer Market Sizes

7

Consumer Market Statistics

Table 7.6

Large Electrical Appliances: Per Capita Retail Sales 2011

Units per '000 inhabitants

	Refrigeration Appliances	Fridge Freezers	Freezers	Cooking Appliances	Microwaves	Laundry Appliances	Dishwashers
Western Europe							
Austria	46.01	21.41	12.88	42.14	20.68	46.25	24.63
Belgium	46.77	22.52	16.26	42.81	27.50	43.00	15.84
Cyprus	24.65	12.33	1.25	24.94	4.91	18.03	5.28
Denmark	51.70	19.94	11.44	55.77	39.42	52.86	28.30
Finland	47.49	16.82	14.31	54.11	22.02	32.27	17.19
France	54.39	26.33	11.78	65.61	36.66	49.59	23.86
Germany	50.51	19.43	13.03	61.55	17.75	56.26	25.53
Gibraltar	28.14	13.71	7.17	34.24	21.31	39.38	10.02
Greece	37.26	23.31	3.38	34.00	17.12	23.15	6.05
Iceland	50.06	24.01	12.38	65.87	43.74	81.50	13.96
Ireland	44.05	21.15	10.88	57.98	38.53	71.65	12.28
Italy	35.46	26.09	6.59	48.70	14.37	32.25	15.72
Liechtenstein	42.80	17.20	14.57	47.40	25.45	36.97	21.11
Luxembourg	41.99	16.37	16.34	47.71	27.33	41.83	19.94
Malta	23.71	11.26	5.90	31.80	20.57	38.29	6.68
Monaco	43.43	20.84	9.83	55.60	27.99	40.01	21.02
Netherlands	49.13	31.05	11.94	43.50	27.21	54.97	21.33
Norway	62.52	30.10	15.65	77.60	31.15	59.48	31.62
Portugal	35.69	14.76	8.45	61.16	23.62	46.72	15.14
Spain	27.28	20.26	4.54	52.65	23.73	34.03	14.02
Sweden	59.74	22.84	17.00	65.19	38.07	37.87	27.73
Switzerland	39.13	13.23	9.33	48.45	18.78	43.28	18.01
Turkey	31.33	26.63	3.46	24.35	3.08	24.09	17.31
United Kingdom	50.05	27.43	11.00	46.58	42.71	71.69	14.38
Eastern Europe							
Albania	5.11	3.26	0.13	8.17	2.32	9.01	
Belarus	6.01	3.84	0.15	9.58	3.10	10.31	
Bosnia-Herzegovina	2.25	1.90	0.11	3.42	1.15	5.46	0.65
Bulgaria	19.50	13.20	4.12	9.46	8.62	40.55	1.78
Croatia	28.02	18.97	5.92	8.79	12.18	58.27	2.19
Czech Republic	33.54	21.67	2.94	34.51	27.34	31.07	10.26
Estonia	10.81	6.90	0.27	17.03	5.50	18.54	
Georgia	17.17	16.67	0.14	4.61	8.26	42.48	0.54
Hungary	28.71	18.71	6.00	15.57	14.34	25.76	5.68
Latvia	12.74	8.13	0.32	20.03	5.99	21.84	
Lithuania	10.52	6.71	0.26	16.57	5.19	18.04	
Macedonia	2.82	1.91	0.60	1.37	0.83	5.87	
Moldova	3.24	2.19	0.68	1.57	1.42	6.73	0.54
Montenegro	7.67	6.53		5.70	5.98	20.59	0.23
Poland	25.83	21.84	1.31	33.29	11.43	26.58	10.57
Romania	16.41	12.98	1.86	12.84	6.57	14.28	1.68
Russia	27.70	22.76	1.27	17.39	20.12	33.36	1.50
Serbia	7.78	6.51	0.31	5.11	8.97	19.93	0.26
Slovakia	29.04	16.82	4.78	32.88	17.72	47.84	6.62
Slovenia	50.84	41.16	2.59	28.27	0.11	79.78	8.00
Ukraine	26.20	20.70	3.94	29.82	14.94	19.06	1.68

Source: Euromonitor International from national statistics

Table 7.7

Small Electrical Appliances: Per Capita Retail Sales 2011

Units per '000 inhabitants

	Food Preparation Appliances	Cooking Appliances	Personal Care Appliances	Irons	Body Shavers	Vacuum Cleaners
Western Europe						
Austria	66.75	144.55	146.87	33.55	45.05	92.68
Belgium	20.51	182.58	123.74	43.89	41.58	78.49
Cyprus	55.90	43.79	67.95	29.60	8.42	23.42
Denmark	100.81	156.18	214.31	23.00	11.73	76.28
Finland	63.59	117.29	119.92	26.09	30.49	41.43
France	111.53	219.94	197.30	57.00	42.87	75.16
Germany	82.21	182.01	222.08	46.51	51.16	64.23
Gibraltar	25.57	41.28	164.28	25.07	19.18	35.11
Greece	78.55	63.99	96.74	40.46	10.24	31.13
Iceland	54.84	133.00	239.43	50.01	34.31	71.60
Ireland	48.26	117.38	461.15	44.15	30.31	63.21
Italy	52.40	63.78	117.08	50.48	23.61	57.62
Liechtenstein	22.23	192.69	134.65	38.68	33.06	53.51
Luxembourg	20.25	187.35	128.75	50.07	10.56	64.47
Malta	24.94	62.00	144.73	23.72	16.33	33.88
Monaco	97.81	220.87	167.24	46.99	45.54	81.92
Netherlands	20.12	147.15	150.66	50.52	27.18	64.87
Norway	74.57	153.46	224.28	25.38	28.22	76.74
Portugal	115.83	150.97	100.78	51.43	23.30	46.72
Spain	95.16	90.52	109.83	39.97	25.51	25.50
Sweden	122.84	163.10	230.31	31.56	42.01	68.44
Switzerland	59.57	186.90	126.96	35.24	37.34	74.62
Turkey	45.05	82.71	77.87	42.55	13.57	41.53
United Kingdom	64.20	147.66	338.33	74.05	47.17	96.72
Eastern Europe						
Albania	17.59	7.64	29.74	18.14	9.74	15.95
Belarus	20.70	8.99	35.68	21.34	11.46	18.77
Bosnia-Herzegovina	4.81	1.95	9.52	2.41	3.51	3.07
Bulgaria	4.64	19.78	60.70	33.02	9.10	14.80
Croatia	6.67	28.42	89.44	47.44	13.08	21.27
Czech Republic	29.62	49.01	128.80	27.38	25.54	46.90
Estonia	30.07	16.08	62.97	38.40	20.62	33.77
Georgia	2.19	21.51	30.10	4.02	21.53	2.87
Hungary	12.95	34.93	96.33	44.41	12.80	18.84
Latvia	35.42	18.94	73.67	45.22	24.29	39.77
Lithuania	31.99	15.68	60.83	37.34	20.05	32.84
Macedonia	0.67	2.86	8.78	4.78	1.32	2.14
Moldova	0.77	3.28	10.08	5.48	1.51	2.46
Montenegro	8.29	4.79	19.40	10.06	7.99	8.28
Poland	50.44	22.28	117.33	27.81	34.98	31.58
Romania	3.12	15.03	25.54	17.97	5.54	9.02
Russia	20.50	17.47	59.63	32.99	20.36	28.07
Serbia	9.07	5.85	17.86	10.97	6.81	9.71
Slovakia	43.71	34.37	126.76	31.06	23.78	42.77
Slovenia	96.05	27.74	228.83	47.95	51.83	43.59
Ukraine	14.85	13.05	39.10	21.32	10.54	26.25

Source: Euromonitor International from national statistics

Consumer Market Sizes

Consumer Market Statistics

Table 7.8

Fresh Foods: Per Capita Retail Sales 2011
Kg per capita

	Meat	Fish and Seafood	Pulses	Vegetables	Starchy Roots	Fruits	Eggs	Sugar and Sweeteners
Western Europe								
Austria	105.06	15.15	0.32	72.64	66.08	75.77	9.89	7.57
Belgium	61.57	20.57	1.71	160.48	96.78	62.61	13.10	8.53
Cyprus	36.05	7.04	2.69	101.43	21.89	51.33	3.51	29.37
Denmark	74.14	9.17	0.71	82.29	71.96	102.44	14.14	6.67
Finland	37.27	22.29	1.24	61.68	51.03	55.45	7.51	4.07
France	53.75	5.27	1.95	43.56	27.49	36.52	12.63	7.34
Germany	61.65	9.40	0.11	63.21	23.11	65.83	6.90	5.30
Gibraltar	24.64	7.53	0.33	36.95	45.75	36.48	5.64	18.85
Greece	53.60	24.02	3.35	129.24	54.39	116.08	7.70	22.53
Iceland	43.98	40.12	0.92	58.05	58.37	109.00	9.50	54.51
Ireland	80.26	13.27	1.35	79.29	48.27	59.99	6.32	31.43
Italy	47.20	8.93	2.75	59.46	11.15	79.18	11.44	9.33
Liechtenstein	53.46	15.20	0.67	76.68	40.65	48.55	10.69	55.49
Luxembourg	66.24	24.85	2.09	159.38	93.65	64.02	15.79	58.33
Malta	18.88	5.77	0.25	28.31	35.04	27.84	4.32	14.44
Monaco	55.25	19.31	0.92	65.39	63.16	74.69	14.95	39.18
Netherlands	60.70	4.65	1.32	56.36	67.37	71.52	8.07	4.94
Norway	38.66	36.26	0.80	50.81	49.97	95.54	8.13	6.20
Portugal	107.77	46.26	2.32	107.10	97.01	68.53	11.86	24.08
Spain	47.29	28.71	4.74	70.55	30.62	108.98	11.32	6.59
Sweden	40.37	19.87	1.97	51.41	27.77	74.13	12.45	5.41
Switzerland	52.62	14.99	0.66	75.05	39.33	47.36	10.63	7.13
Turkey	20.84	8.91	11.46	153.56	69.55	90.87	6.67	19.79
United Kingdom	25.69	12.73	0.33	68.63	28.97	42.10	10.53	7.98
Eastern Europe								
Albania	47.60	2.42	1.25	170.85	87.92	44.37	12.94	24.55
Belarus	17.53	6.45	1.75	87.65	116.70	15.71	7.37	37.23
Bosnia-Herzegovina	23.96	0.88	1.64	76.11	14.67	18.08	7.43	15.83
Bulgaria	55.94	2.10	3.87	177.75	34.44	43.07	17.72	18.61
Croatia	25.29	1.54	1.81	46.88	45.36	30.20	6.92	26.51
Czech Republic	57.27	10.58	1.01	85.01	52.18	46.17	18.68	16.13
Estonia	37.82	2.30	2.71	70.11	67.84	45.22	10.35	39.66
Georgia	21.05	7.75	2.10	105.27	140.16	18.84	8.85	44.72
Hungary	59.55	3.48	5.31	126.07	58.44	44.69	15.99	35.09
Latvia	55.36	3.36	3.96	102.62	99.30	66.03	15.15	58.05
Lithuania	42.87	2.60	3.07	79.47	76.89	51.20	11.73	44.95
Macedonia	19.89	0.73	1.36	63.19	12.18	15.01	6.17	13.15
Moldova	12.38	0.63	0.32	44.43	22.86	11.51	3.36	6.38
Montenegro	50.63	1.86	3.46	160.82	30.99	38.15	15.70	33.46
Poland	74.30	7.71	1.80	109.15	116.68	43.56	12.16	20.43
Romania	54.76	2.81	1.42	193.09	98.43	49.82	15.06	13.87
Russia	42.27	16.04	2.14	69.19	107.87	45.53	9.62	22.58
Serbia	52.37	1.93	3.58	166.36	32.06	39.47	16.24	34.61
Slovakia	46.00	2.54	3.21	84.77	83.10	55.67	12.37	24.42
Slovenia	35.90	9.81	1.93	74.42	14.92	58.74	5.96	14.18
Ukraine	25.94	9.57	2.58	128.38	128.60	25.37	10.69	27.21

Source: Euromonitor International from national statistics

Table 7.9

Hot and Soft Drinks: Per Capita Retail Sales 2011

Grams per capita / Litres per capita

	Coffee (Grams)	Tea (Grams)	Bottled Water (Litres)	Carbonates (Litres)
Western Europe				
Austria	4,892.58	253.97	65.29	48.73
Belgium	4,142.78	122.84	97.03	83.77
Cyprus	731.51	278.42	34.14	19.31
Denmark	4,706.52	124.36	20.64	51.17
Finland	8,432.92	192.22	17.04	50.17
France	2,569.04	195.98	129.40	36.52
Germany	4,718.75	627.53	121.93	74.97
Gibraltar	389.81	736.96	48.98	27.94
Greece	1,711.28	21.69	39.17	34.09
Iceland	5,198.65	349.39	27.11	74.71
Ireland	702.38	2,197.03	36.57	87.85
Italy	2,676.95	123.66	146.13	29.91
Liechtenstein	3,349.94	388.29	33.71	54.48
Luxembourg	3,419.28	127.70	56.63	75.69
Malta	333.66	630.80	40.15	28.33
Monaco	2,923.15	200.69	76.99	30.82
Netherlands	5,063.17	583.88	20.05	57.66
Norway	5,753.43	218.33	17.45	90.47
Portugal	1,121.36	53.71	69.19	24.18
Spain	1,468.20	119.33	117.16	61.02
Sweden	6,253.18	382.91	18.89	57.72
Switzerland	3,266.76	403.40	75.77	51.55
Turkey	317.64	1,804.06	73.51	27.47
United Kingdom	1,002.26	1,801.56	34.92	64.45
Eastern Europe				
Albania	1,051.90	41.04	37.75	34.76
Belarus	491.26	493.66	29.33	37.72
Bosnia-Herzegovina	3,943.82	56.49	37.34	28.51
Bulgaria	1,579.46	93.91	64.29	43.38
Croatia	2,166.09	96.27	61.03	36.45
Czech Republic	2,319.34	411.66	112.11	39.96
Estonia	4,316.92	367.29	28.52	38.67
Georgia	957.36	180.69	16.23	18.91
Hungary	3,038.31	259.25	110.90	47.21
Latvia	2,283.18	436.14	26.58	26.01
Lithuania	2,699.60	520.67	33.35	22.77
Macedonia	2,542.56	473.40	68.51	35.69
Moldova	314.42	11.12	11.59	9.22
Montenegro	4,036.39	177.68	48.30	37.20
Poland	2,860.01	1,026.99	69.04	48.89
Romania	1,393.67	64.74	54.41	44.86
Russia	731.79	1,259.68	28.49	28.45
Serbia	4,385.70	396.10	72.41	65.00
Slovakia	2,337.33	335.05	85.05	56.50
Slovenia	4,846.12	72.97	44.63	25.67
Ukraine	783.79	545.75	32.46	26.63

Source: Euromonitor International from national statistics

7

Consumer Market Sizes

Consumer Market Statistics   **Table 7.10**

Home Care Products: Per Capita Retail Sales 2011

US$ per capita

	Laundry Care	Fabric Softeners	Hand Dishwashing	Automatic Dishwashing	Surface Care	Air Care
Western Europe						
Austria	41.40	5.67	3.85	10.54	12.10	8.71
Belgium	42.93	9.69	3.07	11.89	12.73	6.14
Cyprus	9.26	2.54	2.48	1.52	9.82	0.76
Denmark	34.22	6.00	5.84	7.82	11.84	1.13
Finland	26.55	6.63	4.97	7.82	9.49	1.40
France	43.57	4.31	5.20	9.52	11.46	8.74
Germany	31.86	5.29	3.53	8.35	12.89	3.81
Gibraltar	12.57	2.86	2.55		3.51	2.30
Greece	45.57	6.86	6.79	4.71	13.00	2.64
Iceland	26.13	5.71	6.41	5.97	13.07	1.76
Ireland	31.65	6.04	4.03	6.16	10.65	7.08
Italy	45.20	6.69	7.16	6.43	15.29	7.01
Liechtenstein	21.70	3.15	3.35	4.68	5.58	
Luxembourg	36.31	6.97	3.29	6.95	7.60	2.53
Malta	12.93	2.60	1.95	2.03	3.74	3.71
Monaco	23.84	2.97	4.71	6.76	7.99	3.80
Netherlands	36.94	5.96	3.35	7.62	10.82	5.61
Norway	35.38	7.39	8.42	9.39	17.59	2.06
Portugal	34.63	5.18	5.69	7.27	11.94	5.01
Spain	39.06	7.66	6.57	7.04	11.73	9.04
Sweden	25.54	5.91	4.84	6.54	8.32	2.02
Switzerland	74.47	7.31	4.42	19.24	20.27	10.15
Turkey	20.88	2.21	3.50	2.54	2.20	0.50
United Kingdom	46.01	9.23	5.17	6.38	15.35	9.80
Eastern Europe						
Albania	3.35	0.47	1.70	0.05	1.08	0.20
Belarus	23.98	0.56	5.64	0.61	4.74	1.39
Bosnia-Herzegovina	23.60	2.33	2.42	0.90	4.52	1.70
Bulgaria	19.07	2.77	2.42	0.80	3.78	2.22
Croatia	25.94	5.93	3.40	0.86	8.03	4.33
Czech Republic	26.44	3.17	3.89	5.78	5.64	2.48
Estonia	24.54	3.44	2.40	0.18	3.71	1.30
Georgia	12.44	0.03	1.80	0.25	2.14	0.15
Hungary	24.40	6.57	4.53	1.81	5.82	1.84
Latvia	24.27	3.20	5.67	0.32	6.80	2.20
Lithuania	21.89	2.07	2.84	0.19	1.77	1.50
Macedonia	13.71	2.31	3.45	0.97	3.28	0.76
Moldova	1.04	0.15	0.44		0.34	0.05
Montenegro	21.79	1.52	8.32	0.48	7.00	1.45
Poland	20.57	4.39	3.99	1.75	7.24	3.34
Romania	18.06	2.99	2.02	0.31	2.12	1.39
Russia	18.45	2.35	3.84	0.52	4.72	2.44
Serbia	13.07	0.91	4.99	0.29	4.20	0.84
Slovakia	20.29	6.46	3.16	3.91	5.59	1.50
Slovenia	34.72	6.27	4.21	1.05	6.12	3.41
Ukraine	19.50	1.17	1.70	0.24	4.76	0.57

Source: Euromonitor International from national statistics

Table 7.11

Consumer Health: Per Capita Retail Sales 2011

US$ per capita

	Analgesics	Cough, Cold and Allergy Remedies	Digestive Remedies	Medicated Skin Care	Vitamins and Dietary Supplements
Western Europe					
Austria	10.03	21.47	9.31	6.82	26.53
Belgium	20.59	22.43	12.62	6.37	34.46
Cyprus	2.21	1.65	1.41	1.58	5.58
Denmark	18.23	18.13	12.21	4.91	32.78
Finland	20.74	18.89	14.94	9.50	67.69
France	9.72	13.23	7.21	6.89	17.30
Germany	13.61	24.48	8.52	7.67	26.07
Gibraltar	3.19	4.64	1.49	1.97	4.09
Greece	9.93	5.43	1.62	3.26	18.25
Iceland	6.44	7.91	2.35	2.51	25.74
Ireland	22.37	22.91	11.42	8.77	19.74
Italy	13.18	18.18	9.15	7.54	41.61
Liechtenstein	6.49	16.91	5.57	6.16	8.83
Luxembourg	9.23	11.46	7.40	2.51	9.82
Malta	3.91	5.80	1.84	2.43	5.00
Monaco	4.72	5.29	2.82	2.73	6.38
Netherlands	8.38	18.83	2.86	4.86	21.90
Norway	20.57	35.51	12.43	9.33	87.29
Portugal	9.48	10.73	6.84	9.69	9.25
Spain	7.85	11.84	6.23	4.09	7.63
Sweden	21.08	23.63	10.92	9.95	40.87
Switzerland	29.99	47.51	19.05	24.13	34.41
Turkey	0.14	0.26	0.28	0.74	2.60
United Kingdom	13.41	16.09	7.55	7.37	19.62
Eastern Europe					
Albania	0.51	0.32	0.21	0.03	0.69
Belarus	3.58	7.91	2.74	1.38	5.11
Bosnia-Herzegovina	7.19	5.13	1.97	2.40	6.66
Bulgaria	10.33	5.96	1.52	1.56	8.82
Croatia	7.87	9.41	3.65	1.13	12.74
Czech Republic	12.81	15.07	6.76	4.19	11.96
Estonia	8.39	9.97	3.73	1.71	10.72
Georgia	3.73	6.75	3.30	2.76	5.61
Hungary	7.78	10.26	5.28	4.77	20.02
Latvia	17.19	12.70	5.18	1.05	12.18
Lithuania	3.35	6.33	2.55	1.80	16.45
Macedonia	6.95	2.79	1.08	0.85	5.78
Moldova	0.11	0.07	0.04	0.01	0.14
Montenegro	3.75	2.52	4.25	1.11	4.72
Poland	11.53	12.33	8.16	2.20	21.90
Romania	4.23	3.87	2.18	0.82	5.92
Russia	4.07	9.22	4.71	3.04	10.35
Serbia	7.37	6.46	4.94	2.14	4.30
Slovakia	7.46	12.08	5.28	3.47	9.53
Slovenia	8.13	11.76	3.04	3.30	8.39
Ukraine	1.88	5.24	2.14	1.25	3.84

Source: Euromonitor International from national statistics

7

Consumer Market Sizes

Consumer Market Statistics

Table 7.12

Dairy Products and Ice Cream: Per Capita Retail Sales 2011

US$ per capita

	Drinking Milk Products	Cheese	Yoghurt and Sour Milk Products	Other Dairy	Ice Cream
Western Europe					
Austria	72.55	87.56	44.32	53.79	41.33
Belgium	78.59	143.04	51.46	54.16	41.92
Cyprus	35.03	41.49	15.08	17.73	16.28
Denmark	115.15	196.77	65.18	54.01	78.36
Finland	147.25	232.42	112.50	94.27	117.21
France	54.27	179.16	55.24	70.77	36.99
Germany	47.31	103.10	44.61	58.29	39.53
Gibraltar	36.56	16.99	14.24	8.51	39.15
Greece	93.12	103.25	42.24	25.29	35.11
Iceland	124.01	266.38	22.30	174.48	87.26
Ireland	182.40	55.76	75.99	32.61	44.88
Italy	63.60	158.28	42.98	15.95	98.87
Liechtenstein	80.46	141.25	68.65	39.07	35.87
Luxembourg	68.21	97.63	38.54	79.72	45.36
Malta	31.26	14.52	11.79	7.28	13.56
Monaco	50.09	117.77	39.95	49.83	36.01
Netherlands	58.59	130.71	67.94	76.78	30.99
Norway	217.82	283.84	102.50	107.09	106.77
Portugal	69.78	99.15	69.67	18.51	43.96
Spain	102.92	67.31	58.64	25.85	40.74
Sweden	106.44	174.78	70.07	73.93	79.70
Switzerland	98.64	298.86	110.33	104.97	80.32
Turkey	12.59	14.12	26.79	2.04	18.75
United Kingdom	102.61	66.96	44.63	27.34	37.73
Eastern Europe					
Albania	80.60	7.02	2.99	4.98	3.49
Belarus	40.53	31.88	25.69	52.66	23.98
Bosnia-Herzegovina	38.03	25.16	19.94	16.96	8.24
Bulgaria	8.13	59.53	15.91	1.68	8.37
Croatia	97.44	82.04	46.81	23.55	37.26
Czech Republic	32.96	83.14	38.90	51.81	31.86
Estonia	43.43	49.97	32.73	36.12	28.10
Georgia	3.83	23.31	10.89	9.83	11.28
Hungary	64.66	45.43	28.39	39.92	23.11
Latvia	59.57	48.54	29.81	55.11	23.24
Lithuania	29.71	39.01	28.27	39.71	18.59
Macedonia	51.18	54.17	19.82	5.42	18.43
Moldova	13.80	2.16	0.90	1.53	1.28
Montenegro	7.37	57.10	15.26	1.61	8.13
Poland	31.20	37.70	27.74	29.78	11.04
Romania	14.84	15.69	16.52	15.36	11.92
Russia	33.45	48.59	28.29	22.07	13.99
Serbia	59.20	34.62	24.90	12.09	22.71
Slovakia	27.70	73.83	37.93	38.17	18.43
Slovenia	68.61	113.16	63.64	39.29	42.73
Ukraine	11.26	31.17	11.03	13.05	10.31

Source: Euromonitor International from national statistics

European Marketing Data and Statistics 2013 – © Euromonitor International Ltd 2012

Table 7.13

Bakery Products: Per Capita Retail Sales 2011

US$ per capita

	Bread	Pastries	Cakes	Biscuits	Breakfast Cereals
Western Europe					
Austria	315.09	39.24	58.05	44.96	10.25
Belgium	180.15	69.97	87.06	68.87	22.13
Cyprus	89.85	14.73	10.94	10.08	5.64
Denmark	236.79	16.95	35.79	34.25	28.87
Finland	224.93	31.46	49.88	59.85	28.82
France	165.17	59.52	76.89	47.99	15.14
Germany	159.52	19.87	47.55	24.71	11.40
Gibraltar	20.07	16.81	16.80	16.85	14.42
Greece	147.10	125.36	23.41	19.36	13.98
Iceland	327.58	1.34	26.15	22.36	47.59
Ireland	118.15	12.50	39.46	67.52	65.86
Italy	211.66	51.51	81.13	43.06	8.77
Liechtenstein	170.49	16.60	27.77	37.15	15.44
Luxembourg	202.66	23.27	64.69	56.80	10.93
Malta	17.16	14.37	14.36	10.03	12.32
Monaco	93.67	35.01	60.61	12.58	11.00
Netherlands	164.28	6.47	62.86	61.36	10.99
Norway	308.67	34.47	33.38	43.93	24.35
Portugal	72.88	16.93	11.79	26.46	17.24
Spain	110.80	32.11	9.19	25.78	10.83
Sweden	172.62	18.83	40.95	30.30	21.94
Switzerland	330.20	31.01	49.83	60.43	27.28
Turkey	238.85	2.65	13.47	13.42	1.61
United Kingdom	84.49	15.55	47.32	55.08	46.52
Eastern Europe					
Albania	64.13	0.49	4.03	7.00	0.67
Belarus	23.21	19.33	9.83	26.93	5.56
Bosnia-Herzegovina	52.87	10.41	3.46	27.98	3.78
Bulgaria	85.31	10.81	8.19	8.10	2.42
Croatia	140.47	14.46	12.18	29.41	6.10
Czech Republic	104.76	11.66	9.89	29.72	6.08
Estonia	59.97	20.55	19.13	9.52	7.75
Georgia	33.73	3.87	3.54	1.08	1.38
Hungary	81.36	4.87	11.37	19.61	6.04
Latvia	79.79	1.67	6.49	8.91	6.76
Lithuania	62.58	5.45	9.03	9.83	6.80
Macedonia	82.22	2.44	1.28	15.21	3.08
Moldova	19.71	0.15	3.67	2.18	0.21
Montenegro	91.20	10.90	3.57	6.65	2.44
Poland	66.07	3.81	11.90	15.80	7.06
Romania	114.57	4.00	22.43	12.46	4.67
Russia	58.37	5.72	10.19	20.04	3.04
Serbia	154.58	10.02	3.35	32.07	2.13
Slovakia	105.31	7.26	8.16	22.30	5.88
Slovenia	135.54	23.64	4.54	45.24	10.93
Ukraine	62.88	1.99	5.94	12.13	2.11

Source: Euromonitor International from national statistics

7

Consumer Market Sizes

Consumer Market Statistics

Table 7.14

Confectionery: Per Capita Retail Sales 2011

US$ per capita

	Total Confectionery	Chocolate Confectionery	Sugar Confectionery	Gum
Western Europe				
Austria	158.16	114.48	36.08	7.59
Belgium	141.20	94.02	35.02	12.16
Cyprus	27.00	13.49	6.70	6.80
Denmark	210.91	100.21	93.93	16.77
Finland	205.93	95.25	89.91	20.78
France	124.06	89.08	21.78	13.19
Germany	150.88	98.69	41.03	11.16
Gibraltar	49.11	36.17	11.48	1.46
Greece	60.92	39.40	5.36	16.16
Iceland	199.78	121.30	61.28	17.20
Ireland	249.71	175.37	55.27	19.06
Italy	99.48	57.79	24.37	17.32
Liechtenstein	187.40	136.60	37.38	13.42
Luxembourg	105.03	67.65	32.24	5.14
Malta	59.96	44.17	14.01	1.78
Monaco	84.43	59.48	15.75	9.20
Netherlands	131.71	61.46	52.01	18.24
Norway	338.38	203.39	100.73	34.27
Portugal	55.01	31.77	17.37	5.87
Spain	62.14	29.22	22.46	10.46
Sweden	193.98	101.36	72.76	19.86
Switzerland	282.49	212.35	52.94	17.20
Turkey	27.30	17.00	5.30	5.00
United Kingdom	201.04	148.18	45.36	7.50
Eastern Europe				
Albania	11.61	9.14	1.36	1.11
Belarus	63.07	34.28	26.09	2.70
Bosnia-Herzegovina	48.67	35.82	9.82	3.03
Bulgaria	36.59	26.78	6.08	3.73
Croatia	117.51	77.88	33.13	6.50
Czech Republic	70.66	47.95	15.07	7.64
Estonia	99.83	71.12	20.35	8.35
Georgia	41.45	27.36	10.17	3.91
Hungary	61.40	39.28	12.78	9.34
Latvia	74.85	43.36	22.11	9.38
Lithuania	60.03	41.13	12.43	6.47
Macedonia	42.83	32.96	6.32	3.56
Moldova	3.57	2.81	0.42	0.34
Montenegro	35.92	27.80	4.26	3.86
Poland	69.58	49.92	12.60	7.06
Romania	23.57	14.81	3.10	5.67
Russia	85.15	58.23	17.02	9.90
Serbia	53.86	36.11	13.85	3.90
Slovakia	87.71	66.18	15.43	6.10
Slovenia	99.91	72.09	14.93	12.89
Ukraine	49.43	36.91	9.91	2.61

Source: Euromonitor International from national statistics

Table 7.15

Other Selected Packaged Foods: Per Capita Retail Sales 2011

US$ per capita

	Canned/Preserved Food	Frozen Processed Food	Dried Processed Food	Chilled Processed Food	Oils and Fats	Sauces, Dressings and Condiments	Sweet and Savoury Snacks
Western Europe							
Austria	34.87	85.83	38.11	131.11	61.23	66.89	40.96
Belgium	77.58	102.20	35.04	238.90	61.05	54.21	33.95
Cyprus	13.31	19.38	11.82	16.29	19.78	10.81	17.14
Denmark	68.55	159.77	38.01	274.37	92.15	75.69	51.73
Finland	40.49	96.83	30.30	264.91	90.29	68.98	35.99
France	87.54	87.23	28.59	235.45	51.96	45.22	28.54
Germany	66.86	105.23	30.44	168.28	56.13	56.69	33.30
Gibraltar	27.26	46.75	9.68	110.67	16.32	22.66	40.03
Greece	22.34	38.45	27.67	43.54	47.64	36.82	34.46
Iceland	75.23	114.42	31.34	398.91	50.72	93.90	139.82
Ireland	43.61	136.53	43.14	144.29	54.53	59.21	130.72
Italy	55.69	64.49	57.60	250.88	48.27	43.42	24.14
Liechtenstein	61.46	89.36	28.92	161.92	47.50	30.96	23.94
Luxembourg	97.23	86.60	55.41	171.41	66.13	47.09	12.53
Malta	23.30	39.96	8.27	94.96	13.69	19.37	34.22
Monaco	68.54	46.42	17.54	177.27	40.68	30.80	15.25
Netherlands	40.25	63.14	31.71	181.08	51.23	55.31	56.84
Norway	98.04	208.57	65.83	308.95	89.04	116.15	155.02
Portugal	52.22	27.30	28.39	29.67	51.46	29.17	23.95
Spain	90.93	35.64	19.15	102.20	50.29	39.78	58.95
Sweden	75.08	157.22	38.94	226.87	74.22	88.44	66.75
Switzerland	102.13	116.77	55.17	281.36	90.50	59.17	58.55
Turkey	1.87	1.21	17.66	13.76	51.59	8.44	17.03
United Kingdom	69.86	119.05	33.96	252.34	39.29	68.83	113.49
Eastern Europe							
Albania	3.01	0.32	12.21	26.39	14.94	1.72	1.61
Belarus	29.28	11.54	16.12	107.69	35.39	22.69	6.70
Bosnia-Herzegovina	19.83	13.02	20.48	20.78	37.86	26.23	19.57
Bulgaria	11.94	18.83	15.99	55.43	28.25	12.47	5.66
Croatia	39.43	46.42	59.74	48.51	55.65	36.89	27.48
Czech Republic	46.26	38.38	30.30	69.10	50.92	33.01	18.79
Estonia	44.11	24.09	28.06	80.46	62.36	52.17	16.52
Georgia	10.76	6.98	10.89	32.44	45.66	14.77	4.77
Hungary	34.37	25.88	30.00	82.35	47.71	27.82	17.50
Latvia	36.43	25.67	42.47	87.47	58.11	33.85	12.13
Lithuania	26.21	27.00	20.60	98.51	53.02	59.91	10.93
Macedonia	24.52	8.87	23.87	42.84	74.96	18.83	10.57
Moldova	0.92	0.10	4.74	8.12	5.16	0.61	0.49
Montenegro	11.70	18.02	15.75	53.80	27.10	11.75	4.97
Poland	20.86	14.16	23.58	17.93	45.39	36.62	22.12
Romania	8.83	0.89	18.29	40.36	26.68	3.64	13.38
Russia	37.17	57.02	24.76	49.20	43.18	32.09	26.47
Serbia	35.98	33.44	22.83	85.07	35.77	21.79	33.87
Slovakia	38.35	30.07	34.31	68.97	48.10	34.74	24.75
Slovenia	48.08	44.37	40.80	119.60	45.07	20.95	22.23
Ukraine	16.31	11.51	11.39	33.61	40.01	19.61	16.14

Source: Euromonitor International from national statistics

Consumer Market Sizes

Consumer Market Statistics

Table 7.16

Tobacco: Per Capita Retail Sales 2011

US$ per capita

	Total Tobacco	Cigarettes	Cigars	Smoking Tobacco
Western Europe				
Austria	516.97	490.21	16.28	10.48
Belgium	465.44	325.46	46.70	93.28
Cyprus	225.11	221.42	1.81	1.88
Denmark	500.21	426.74	43.23	27.43
Finland	316.56	267.97	26.41	22.18
France	384.53	337.22	13.61	33.70
Germany	416.77	347.99	19.29	48.93
Gibraltar	181.74	168.19	8.02	5.52
Greece	610.88	562.30	12.26	36.32
Iceland	353.22	258.29	14.97	79.96
Ireland	603.23	561.12	9.06	33.05
Italy	443.12	425.83	7.93	9.35
Liechtenstein	342.09	281.46	52.57	8.06
Luxembourg	402.03	272.53	34.29	95.21
Malta	294.70	284.45	6.07	4.18
Monaco	327.01	310.14	5.11	11.76
Netherlands	405.08	269.58	24.08	111.42
Norway	588.55	305.37	14.04	139.23
Portugal	250.53	229.91	10.52	10.09
Spain	394.28	358.71	13.66	21.91
Sweden	382.21	217.94	7.79	28.28
Switzerland	725.24	635.55	70.90	18.79
Turkey	203.55	203.33	0.02	0.20
United Kingdom	428.01	376.06	14.19	37.76
Eastern Europe				
Albania	124.76	124.72	0.03	0.01
Belarus	142.88	142.45	0.31	0.12
Bosnia-Herzegovina	220.69	220.31	0.15	0.23
Bulgaria	191.19	189.48	1.46	0.26
Croatia	288.79	278.72	0.63	9.45
Czech Republic	449.31	409.17	15.72	24.42
Estonia	250.52	241.30	4.25	4.96
Georgia	95.10	94.98	0.10	0.03
Hungary	263.42	227.24	5.17	31.01
Latvia	171.85	151.65	17.15	3.05
Lithuania	145.20	139.96	3.79	1.45
Macedonia	140.43	140.28	0.13	0.02
Moldova	83.33	83.32	0.00	0.00
Montenegro	211.99	200.63	1.98	9.38
Poland	233.62	222.05	1.29	10.28
Romania	265.23	264.23	0.97	0.02
Russia	154.66	153.36	1.10	0.20
Serbia	282.04	263.86	0.25	17.93
Slovakia	266.02	256.93	8.84	0.25
Slovenia	477.21	469.44	2.42	5.36
Ukraine	99.60	99.26	0.32	0.02

Source: Euromonitor International from national statistics

Table 7.17

Toys and Games: Per Capita Retail Sales 2011

US$ per capita

	Toys and Games	Traditional Toys and Games	Video Games Hardware	Video Games Software
Western Europe				
Austria				
Belgium				
Cyprus				
Denmark				
Finland				
France	136.88	70.53	27.56	28.55
Germany	92.60	47.71	13.39	25.90
Gibraltar				
Greece				
Iceland				
Ireland				
Italy	67.61	30.12	15.80	15.32
Liechtenstein				
Luxembourg				
Malta				
Monaco				
Netherlands	109.29	64.39	16.15	21.84
Norway				
Portugal				
Spain	76.18	30.99	14.95	16.23
Sweden	142.77	65.50	22.37	44.73
Switzerland	121.73	65.39	16.19	29.21
Turkey	8.72	6.04	0.74	0.43
United Kingdom	151.73	72.63	28.38	36.96
Eastern Europe				
Albania				
Belarus				
Bosnia-Herzegovina				
Bulgaria				
Croatia				
Czech Republic				
Estonia				
Georgia				
Hungary				
Latvia				
Lithuania				
Macedonia				
Moldova				
Montenegro				
Poland	27.41	14.99	7.68	3.33
Romania	8.83	6.39	0.78	1.07
Russia	22.02	17.12	2.51	1.68
Serbia				
Slovakia				
Slovenia				
Ukraine	9.13	6.91	0.67	1.06

Source: Euromonitor International from national statistics

Consumer Market Sizes

7

8

Consumer Prices and Costs

Consumer Prices Statistics

Table 8.1

Consumer Price Indices 1990, 1995, 2000, 2006-2011

1995 = 100

	1990	1995	2000	2006	2007	2008	2009	2010	2011
Western Europe									
Austria	85.3	100.0	107.2	120.2	122.8	126.8	127.4	129.8	134.0
Belgium	88.6	100.0	108.6	122.7	125.0	130.6	130.5	133.4	138.1
Cyprus	79.3	100.0	115.4	135.5	138.7	145.2	145.7	149.2	154.1
Denmark	90.7	100.0	112.1	125.9	128.0	132.4	134.2	137.2	141.0
Finland	89.8	100.0	107.6	115.8	118.7	123.6	123.6	125.0	129.3
France	89.6	100.0	106.2	118.6	120.4	123.8	123.9	125.8	128.5
Germany	84.3	100.0	106.5	116.7	119.3	122.5	122.9	124.3	127.1
Gibraltar	82.0	100.0	107.0	121.8	125.1	129.7	133.3	137.5	142.6
Greece	52.3	100.0	126.7	154.5	159.0	165.6	167.6	175.5	181.4
Iceland	83.8	100.0	114.9	150.1	157.8	177.8	199.1	209.8	218.2
Ireland	88.3	100.0	113.4	140.1	147.0	152.9	146.1	144.8	148.5
Italy	78.3	100.0	112.8	129.8	132.1	136.6	137.6	139.7	143.6
Liechtenstein	85.3	100.0	103.8	109.4	110.1	112.8	112.2	113.0	113.3
Luxembourg	87.1	100.0	108.1	124.4	127.2	131.6	132.0	135.1	139.7
Malta	84.7	100.0	112.6	130.6	132.2	137.9	140.8	142.9	146.8
Monaco	83.7	100.0	109.4	124.7	127.8	131.1	131.7	133.8	137.2
Netherlands	87.4	100.0	111.2	127.2	129.3	132.5	134.1	135.8	139.0
Norway	88.9	100.0	112.0	125.1	126.0	130.7	133.6	136.8	138.6
Portugal	70.9	100.0	113.9	137.2	140.6	144.2	143.0	145.0	150.3
Spain	77.7	100.0	113.8	138.0	141.9	147.7	147.3	149.9	154.7
Sweden	81.5	100.0	102.2	111.4	113.9	117.8	117.2	118.6	122.1
Switzerland	85.6	100.0	103.8	109.4	110.2	112.9	112.4	113.1	113.4
Turkey	5.5	100.0	1,579.6	5,602.6	6,094.7	6,730.6	7,153.2	7,767.2	8,268.4
United Kingdom	83.1	100.0	108.2	119.0	121.8	126.2	128.9	133.2	139.1
Eastern Europe									
Albania	6.4	100.0	168.1	201.1	207.0	214.0	218.9	226.7	234.5
Belarus	0.0	100.0	4,576.7	18,825.8	20,411.2	23,439.8	26,474.3	28,522.3	43,704.3
Bosnia-Herzegovina		100.0	100.7	117.0	118.8	127.6	127.1	129.8	134.6
Bulgaria	3.6	100.0	3,200.0	4,454.5	4,828.7	5,428.8	5,581.0	5,717.3	5,959.1
Croatia		100.0	125.8	147.0	151.2	160.4	164.3	166.0	169.7
Czech Republic	39.6	100.0	138.7	158.9	163.5	173.9	175.7	178.3	181.7
Estonia	105.7	100.0	158.2	196.7	209.7	231.5	231.3	238.2	250.1
Georgia	0.0	100.0	129.5	187.1	204.4	224.9	228.8	245.0	265.9
Hungary	32.4	100.0	201.7	278.7	300.9	319.1	332.6	348.8	362.5
Latvia	1.0	100.0	140.2	182.1	200.5	231.5	239.9	237.3	247.7
Lithuania	0.3	100.0	145.1	157.1	166.1	184.3	192.6	195.1	203.2
Macedonia	0.2	100.0	109.8	124.7	127.5	138.1	137.0	139.2	144.7
Moldova	0.1	100.0	271.8	498.8	560.5	632.1	631.8	678.5	730.2
Montenegro	100.1	100.0	85.3	147.9	153.1	166.9	172.6	173.7	179.1
Poland	17.8	100.0	181.9	210.8	215.9	225.3	233.9	240.2	250.4
Romania	1.0	100.0	1,154.4	2,866.7	3,005.0	3,241.0	3,421.4	3,629.0	3,840.9
Russia	0.0	100.0	485.6	1,066.1	1,161.9	1,325.7	1,481.2	1,583.1	1,717.2
Serbia		100.0	765.3	2,822.1	3,002.5	3,375.2	3,649.1	3,873.3	4,304.7
Slovakia	40.2	100.0	148.5	206.0	211.7	221.4	225.0	227.2	236.1
Slovenia	8.1	100.0	148.5	198.7	205.9	217.6	219.4	223.5	227.5
Ukraine	0.0	100.0	363.6	582.9	657.3	823.4	955.3	1,045.1	1,128.7

Source: Euromonitor International from national statistics

Table 8.2

Food and Non-Alcoholic Beverage Price Indices 1990, 1995, 2000, 2006-2011

1995 = 100

	1990	1995	2000	2006	2007	2008	2009	2010	2011
Western Europe									
Austria	92.60	100.00	104.90	115.95	120.16	127.45	127.56	128.02	133.65
Belgium	87.04	100.00	100.98	116.38	121.20	128.42	128.80	130.31	133.42
Cyprus	78.20	100.00	122.19	154.77	163.36	175.77	183.73	182.69	190.14
Denmark	95.50	100.00	104.60	114.49	119.28	128.22	128.06	128.80	133.93
Finland	106.13	100.00	102.25	112.37	114.42	124.03	125.97	120.96	125.31
France	95.20	100.00	106.91	121.31	122.93	129.10	129.00	130.26	133.12
Germany	94.90	100.00	103.78	102.78	101.06	100.25	99.44	99.58	102.55
Gibraltar	87.90	100.00	110.24	132.78	137.15	145.63	158.08	164.84	173.41
Greece	55.25	93.15	113.80	134.09	141.21	148.80	149.55	150.27	154.97
Iceland	93.30	100.00	117.41	135.22	133.78	155.18	182.38	190.11	197.38
Ireland	94.08	100.00	106.95	115.80	120.53	130.88	129.20	125.85	130.73
Italy	80.73	100.00	107.59	123.22	126.80	133.81	135.99	138.40	142.46
Liechtenstein									
Luxembourg	92.60	100.00	108.06	127.05	131.32	138.36	140.34	141.56	145.18
Malta	87.30	100.00	109.90	125.52	130.98	141.49	150.51	152.03	157.89
Monaco									
Netherlands	84.95	100.00	102.45	111.60	113.17	120.12	121.93	122.20	124.91
Norway	93.97	100.00	114.63	119.79	122.97	127.95	133.00	133.48	133.53
Portugal	76.87	100.00	110.42	155.05	158.63	165.84	160.14	162.22	167.66
Spain	87.77	100.00	107.62	139.04	143.85	151.87	150.40	151.07	153.58
Sweden	88.99	100.00	96.43	102.85	104.99	112.33	115.39	117.02	118.45
Switzerland	94.80	100.00	101.94	106.73	107.34	110.65	110.44	111.21	112.09
Turkey	5.19	100.00	1,270.78	4,434.38	4,984.82	5,622.06	6,072.94	6,715.12	7,157.53
United Kingdom	88.73	100.00	103.71	114.25	119.42	130.19	137.29	141.73	149.48
Eastern Europe									
Albania	6.20	100.00	185.57	213.00	219.28	230.75	242.04	254.60	265.75
Belarus		100.00	5,441.97	16,535.48	17,924.38	19,284.74	21,746.97	23,308.58	32,613.94
Bosnia-Herzegovina		100.00	97.13	108.91	111.24	113.70	122.70	125.91	131.40
Bulgaria	3.64	100.00	2,430.71	2,635.37	2,990.60	3,475.87	3,443.24	3,427.79	3,649.75
Croatia		100.00	112.85	131.18	135.48	150.25	152.95	155.13	159.22
Czech Republic	45.84	100.00	115.73	118.60	124.04	134.14	126.54	127.27	133.81
Estonia	1.72	100.00	123.47	179.79	184.02	186.43	179.55	182.78	189.40
Georgia	0.00	100.00	194.17	307.95	348.21	392.67	399.91	455.26	502.90
Hungary	55.19	100.00	171.27	241.18	268.78	295.02	303.17	309.05	334.11
Latvia	5.67	100.00	118.79	166.96	187.97	228.26	226.30	219.84	229.32
Lithuania	0.25	100.00	85.63	94.09	104.34	122.81	131.13	131.78	141.56
Macedonia	0.20	100.00	105.20	109.30	113.50	120.90	120.60	122.87	128.17
Moldova	0.00	100.00	240.83	422.48	468.56	540.91	510.60	542.55	590.71
Montenegro		100.00	76.01	117.05	121.07	132.95	136.75	137.62	141.94
Poland	21.03	100.00	140.45	160.11	167.13	176.12	184.02	189.43	197.42
Romania	0.96	100.00	848.37	1,561.00	1,660.26	1,817.23	1,876.63	1,998.97	2,114.37
Russia	0.14	100.00	403.97	577.15	649.35	940.56	1,017.16	1,147.43	1,277.87
Serbia		51.17	384.47	1,229.20	1,319.27	1,585.34	1,695.11	1,780.13	2,054.65
Slovakia	42.93	100.00	131.32	147.41	153.04	165.62	158.36	161.54	171.14
Slovenia	10.06	100.00	141.64	177.34	191.22	210.06	210.91	218.20	223.13
Ukraine	0.00	100.00	361.20	639.22	742.79	1,057.69	1,135.71	1,262.47	1,388.69

Source: Euromonitor International from national statistics

Consumer Prices and Costs

8

Consumer Prices Statistics   **Table 8.3**

Food and Drink Costs: Selected Items 2011
US$

	Apples per Kg	Beer per 33cl	Butter per 250g	Flour per Kg	Fresh Chicken per Kg	Instant Coffee per 250g
Western Europe						
Austria	2.65	0.72	2.27	1.50	6.52	
Belgium	2.17	0.68	2.27	0.97	6.00	8.65
Cyprus	2.75	0.93	3.20	1.88	6.12	10.95
Denmark	3.15	1.14	2.90	1.60		13.67
Finland	2.81	1.11	2.18	0.86	2.57	11.06
France	3.16	0.70	2.32	1.50	13.02	9.13
Germany	2.90	0.70	1.80	1.04		17.28
Gibraltar	3.42	1.30	2.02	2.89	5.14	11.70
Greece	2.47	1.10	2.35	2.29	4.84	10.77
Iceland	2.63	1.43	1.27	0.64	5.09	8.98
Ireland	5.32	1.58	1.77	1.38	6.07	
Italy	3.25	0.78	3.10	0.98	6.61	
Liechtenstein						
Luxembourg	3.73	1.01	2.35	1.38	8.30	12.02
Malta	2.25	1.21	2.52	1.39	3.68	7.47
Monaco						
Netherlands	2.26	0.78	1.61	0.74	5.90	9.47
Norway	4.52	2.90	2.89	1.92	9.45	21.10
Portugal	1.81	0.63	2.30	1.43	3.31	10.83
Spain	2.62	0.70	2.95	1.15	4.33	8.76
Sweden	3.39	1.46	1.78	0.99	5.94	13.86
Switzerland	4.63	1.33	5.21	2.32	12.01	16.40
Turkey	1.06	0.99	2.74	1.19	3.10	10.35
United Kingdom	2.68	2.49	1.90	0.87	5.60	9.02
Eastern Europe						
Albania	1.95		2.25		4.28	
Belarus	0.93	0.29	0.96	0.62	2.53	6.42
Bosnia-Herzegovina						
Bulgaria	1.30	0.37	1.61	0.90	4.04	10.84
Croatia	1.59	0.67	2.75	1.08	4.61	13.16
Czech Republic	1.52	0.68	1.54	0.73	3.44	10.82
Estonia	2.18	0.60	2.17	0.90	4.07	8.04
Georgia	0.76	0.61	1.48	1.08	4.26	9.11
Hungary	1.01	0.53	2.81	0.76	4.07	14.13
Latvia	1.73	0.69	2.37	1.07	4.30	8.31
Lithuania	1.71	0.64	2.05	1.05	3.75	9.79
Macedonia	0.87	0.51	1.55	0.58	3.24	9.86
Moldova	1.01	0.77	1.76	0.87	4.08	10.73
Montenegro						
Poland	0.80	0.67	1.69	0.78	2.34	11.64
Romania	1.47	0.59	2.08	0.73	3.54	11.38
Russia	2.34	0.60	1.95	0.97	4.33	9.79
Serbia	0.92	0.33	1.94	0.79	4.02	
Slovakia	1.51	0.51	2.34	0.59	3.41	12.52
Slovenia	2.04	0.74	2.88	1.39	5.05	12.23
Ukraine	1.34	0.30	1.18	0.52	2.71	7.00

Source: Euromonitor International from national statistics
Note: 'Cost' refers to national average retail prices paid by consumers, including related costs, such as sales or value-added, taxes.

Food and Drink Costs: Selected Items 2011 *(continued)*
US$

	Milk per Litre	Potatoes per Kg	Red Table Wine per Litre	Soft Drinks (Cola or Orange) per 33cl	Sugar per Kg	Tea per 100g
Western Europe						
Austria	1.50	1.38	8.32	0.38	1.59	6.03
Belgium	1.30	1.32	10.46	0.44	1.47	
Cyprus	1.67	1.98	7.04	0.44	1.85	2.00
Denmark	1.72	2.05		1.12	1.95	3.05
Finland	1.30	1.11	12.72	0.59	1.48	4.30
France	1.79	1.99	2.66	0.37	2.01	
Germany	1.22	1.21	4.11	0.47	1.70	7.14
Gibraltar	1.62	0.86	13.64	0.77	1.16	1.01
Greece	2.13	1.19	6.62		1.29	2.29
Iceland	0.92	2.02	21.83	0.72	1.50	6.40
Ireland	1.54	1.94	16.63		1.41	2.40
Italy	2.47	1.73	3.44	0.46	1.36	5.17
Liechtenstein						
Luxembourg	1.82	1.89	2.26	0.44	2.13	4.30
Malta	1.08	0.78	3.47	0.82	1.24	1.42
Monaco						
Netherlands	1.43	1.08	6.52	0.38	1.30	1.89
Norway	2.59	1.84	23.44	2.23	2.70	7.63
Portugal	1.16	0.85	2.08	0.67	1.33	5.17
Spain	1.36	1.15	1.53	0.29	1.33	3.89
Sweden	1.35	1.92	11.10	0.89	1.64	3.79
Switzerland	2.04	2.58	13.97	1.01	2.24	5.64
Turkey	1.35	0.55	10.21	0.77	1.85	0.82
United Kingdom	1.41	2.17	9.56	0.70	1.48	1.27
Eastern Europe						
Albania	0.72	0.80			1.02	
Belarus	0.42	0.24	4.24	0.17	0.63	1.07
Bosnia-Herzegovina						
Bulgaria	1.23	0.74	5.93	0.28	1.45	2.31
Croatia	1.15	0.72	4.80	0.43	1.17	1.73
Czech Republic	1.47	0.50	3.94	0.12	1.13	2.37
Estonia	1.17	0.68	7.63	0.65	1.39	1.35
Georgia	1.66	0.47	4.92	0.32	0.93	1.46
Hungary	1.25	0.45	1.85	0.84	1.13	1.95
Latvia	1.24	0.65		0.35	1.54	1.27
Lithuania	1.16	0.55	9.50	0.60	1.36	3.41
Macedonia	1.09	0.60	1.93	0.37	1.04	1.96
Moldova	0.89	0.47	4.11	0.59	1.06	1.21
Montenegro						
Poland	0.42	0.38	7.71	0.54	1.01	1.06
Romania	0.96	0.48	2.57	0.47	1.21	
Russia	1.23	0.73	6.53	0.28	1.04	1.16
Serbia	1.24	0.40	1.95	0.39	1.00	1.91
Slovakia	0.94	0.50	3.40	0.26	1.34	2.32
Slovenia	1.14	0.76	2.66	0.37	1.25	6.20
Ukraine	0.73	0.46	1.26	0.18	0.70	0.48

Source: Euromonitor International from national statistics
Note: 'Cost' refers to national average retail prices paid by consumers, including related costs, such as sales or value-added, taxes.

8

Consumer Prices and Costs

Consumer Prices Statistics

Table 8.4

Alcoholic Beverage and Tobacco Price Indices 1990, 1995, 2000, 2006-2011

1995 = 100

	1990	1995	2000	2006	2007	2008	2009	2010	2011
Western Europe									
Austria	91.4	100.0	106.2	123.5	126.1	132.0	133.3	135.8	141.4
Belgium	84.5	100.0	108.0	133.4	141.6	147.1	151.3	154.6	155.5
Cyprus									
Denmark	95.8	100.0	108.5	114.0	115.7	120.1	123.0	132.1	137.5
Finland	82.9	100.0	109.9	102.5	103.5	110.2	118.8	123.4	129.3
France	75.4	100.0	118.7	155.2	158.9	164.7	168.3	174.3	180.2
Germany	105.6	100.0	96.2	79.5	77.2	75.5	73.7	72.6	73.6
Gibraltar									
Greece	39.1	89.9	126.2	151.3	159.5	162.3	169.8	188.2	197.4
Iceland									
Ireland	78.3	100.0	129.2	176.2	188.2	201.1	217.0	217.8	227.6
Italy	65.7	100.0	120.2	161.1	166.5	173.6	180.1	183.4	188.9
Liechtenstein									
Luxembourg									
Malta									
Monaco									
Netherlands	75.1	100.0	113.4	146.8	149.7	156.8	170.0	175.8	182.0
Norway	75.1	100.0	133.2	159.1	161.6	167.7	175.5	183.1	195.0
Portugal	71.1	100.0	120.6	157.5	166.0	179.9	185.9	189.9	198.4
Spain	64.0	100.0	135.7	172.4	184.6	191.7	207.8	232.0	255.7
Sweden	80.2	100.0	110.0	115.5	121.9	130.5	133.6	136.4	138.0
Switzerland	89.0	100.0	111.1	126.9	129.6	132.9	136.6	137.9	139.4
Turkey	5.1	100.0	1,746.7	10,253.5	11,271.6	12,068.1	13,601.7	18,331.4	19,854.8
United Kingdom	70.7	100.0	126.2	144.0	147.5	152.3	158.7	165.6	176.4
Eastern Europe									
Albania									
Belarus		100.0	3,575.4	15,255.3	16,973.1	18,575.9	21,011.0	22,592.5	31,690.8
Bosnia-Herzegovina		100.0	105.3	112.3	113.1	113.8	124.8	127.9	133.5
Bulgaria	3.4	100.0	3,362.5	7,625.5	7,688.1	8,454.7	9,967.2	12,351.8	12,998.6
Croatia		100.0	155.4	195.8	201.8	213.6	239.0	243.1	250.7
Czech Republic	47.0	100.0	124.1	138.3	150.9	165.9	171.9	178.8	184.3
Estonia	1.7	100.0	136.2	231.9	240.6	218.2	238.7	243.6	253.0
Georgia	0.0	100.0	196.9	401.5	377.1	379.1	380.6	417.7	453.8
Hungary	44.5	100.0	223.1	363.6	396.2	415.4	446.9	479.4	484.0
Latvia	5.5	100.0	158.2	195.9	218.3	276.1	311.1	306.5	325.1
Lithuania	0.2	100.0	142.6	145.4	153.0	174.9	194.8	205.7	206.2
Macedonia	0.2	100.0	108.4	150.4	153.7	155.8	161.5	164.2	171.1
Moldova									
Montenegro		100.0	95.2	182.8	182.2	187.4	194.7	194.6	199.5
Poland	17.4	100.0	176.7	204.6	211.8	227.2	252.0	260.6	273.7
Romania	0.9	100.0	1,397.7	5,196.8	5,507.0	6,043.0	7,324.6	7,878.0	8,465.1
Russia	0.3	100.0	169.4	343.2	355.1	480.2	546.6	591.3	655.5
Serbia		51.0	396.9	1,383.6	1,543.2	1,724.5	2,110.8	2,327.2	2,719.4
Slovakia	47.1	100.0	119.9	158.0	164.3	171.5	183.0	193.2	200.4
Slovenia	6.3	100.0	150.2	215.2	229.0	227.9	249.2	256.5	261.8
Ukraine	0.0	100.0	356.1	485.1	523.1	629.1	801.9	878.8	965.6

Source: Euromonitor International from national statistics

Table 8.5

Clothing and Footwear Price Indices 1990, 1995, 2000, 2006-2011
1995 = 100

	1990	1995	2000	2006	2007	2008	2009	2010	2011
Western Europe									
Austria	85.7	100.0	99.4	99.4	101.5	103.0	104.5	105.7	108.8
Belgium	89.7	100.0	99.2	103.8	104.3	105.3	106.6	107.3	108.9
Cyprus	81.1	100.0	113.8	100.3	100.6	99.3	95.3	94.6	93.1
Denmark	94.6	100.0	100.9	102.0	102.9	102.4	103.5	102.8	104.0
Finland	86.2	100.0	100.5	98.0	98.5	98.8	99.5	100.9	104.2
France	93.0	100.0	101.2	102.7	103.4	104.1	105.2	105.8	108.2
Germany	108.8	100.0	99.7	96.1	98.4	98.7	94.5	98.3	99.0
Gibraltar	90.8	100.0	102.1	101.9	101.7	100.2	101.2	102.4	104.4
Greece	49.7	89.6	119.5	147.5	151.8	155.6	159.7	162.7	167.4
Iceland	87.9	100.0	94.9	92.3	93.6	103.1	128.2	139.0	147.0
Ireland	95.3	100.0	75.3	60.4	58.1	55.2	48.3	43.6	42.6
Italy	80.9	100.0	114.5	130.9	132.7	135.0	135.6	137.4	140.7
Liechtenstein									
Luxembourg	87.6	100.0	103.3	110.1	110.6	111.1	111.6	111.8	111.8
Malta	89.7	100.0	95.2	79.6	79.9	83.5	83.3	79.7	79.6
Monaco									
Netherlands	87.0	100.0	102.1	103.6	104.3	103.6	103.5	104.0	105.1
Norway	93.2	100.0	91.5	66.5	63.2	60.7	58.7	56.3	54.6
Portugal	75.6	100.0	98.6	101.0	103.9	105.5	101.9	100.5	96.8
Spain	71.5	100.0	111.0	130.7	131.7	132.8	129.5	129.9	130.5
Sweden	94.2	100.0	105.7	106.3	108.8	108.3	111.1	113.9	116.4
Switzerland	90.3	100.0	102.6	96.1	96.4	100.2	102.6	103.6	104.8
Turkey	5.5	100.0	1,136.2	3,699.4	3,866.5	3,962.9	3,995.0	4,176.8	4,348.4
United Kingdom	97.3	100.0	84.3	60.3	58.1	54.2	50.1	49.8	50.3
Eastern Europe									
Albania	6.5	100.0	188.4	149.7	148.2	144.0	141.1	139.0	136.3
Belarus		100.0	5,523.0	24,758.9	27,174.8	29,481.8	33,294.9	35,742.0	50,072.4
Bosnia-Herzegovina		100.0	104.6	117.7	115.4	115.8	127.5	130.5	136.2
Bulgaria	3.6	100.0	2,501.4	2,696.9	2,886.4	3,190.7	3,331.5	3,293.0	3,358.3
Croatia		100.0	130.5	143.6	151.0	156.3	156.2	157.7	160.4
Czech Republic	43.3	100.0	124.6	96.9	97.6	96.8	87.8	87.3	85.4
Estonia	1.7	100.0	115.9	243.0	260.1	179.1	181.1	179.4	176.4
Georgia	0.0	100.0	187.4	230.1	220.9	212.9	200.9	191.1	201.3
Hungary	46.7	100.0	201.0	251.5	254.8	255.1	256.9	254.1	263.6
Latvia	5.3	100.0	175.0	182.8	197.7	203.2	197.1	208.2	214.7
Lithuania	0.2	100.0	180.9	153.4	145.7	139.6	127.8	120.4	118.1
Macedonia	0.3	100.0	105.2	121.2	123.6	133.4	132.6	135.0	141.0
Moldova									
Montenegro		100.0	83.6	145.2	146.6	148.8	153.8	153.7	157.2
Poland	21.9	100.0	166.4	144.1	133.9	129.0	119.9	120.4	122.2
Romania	1.0	100.0	1,090.8	3,891.0	3,929.2	4,047.1	4,145.6	4,378.4	4,593.8
Russia	0.4	100.0	349.1	742.2	723.2	836.7	952.6	1,005.0	1,096.3
Serbia		51.3	384.9	1,192.9	1,246.1	1,314.0	1,396.1	1,468.1	1,544.4
Slovakia	43.2	100.0	130.2	137.9	139.3	141.3	138.7	138.2	140.5
Slovenia	8.8	100.0	136.1	152.0	155.2	162.2	161.2	162.7	165.0
Ukraine	0.0	100.0	356.4	413.7	420.9	452.7	475.7	474.2	497.0

Source: Euromonitor International from national statistics

Consumer Prices Statistics Table 8.6

Housing Price Indices 1990, 1995, 2000, 2006-2011

1995 = 100

	1990	1995	2000	2006	2007	2008	2009	2010	2011
Western Europe									
Austria	79.8	100.0	114.3	138.3	143.2	145.6	149.4	153.3	158.8
Belgium	85.4	100.0	105.7	123.8	125.8	134.4	132.8	135.8	148.3
Cyprus									
Denmark	87.4	100.0	117.9	141.2	145.4	151.5	154.2	159.4	166.6
Finland	78.4	100.0	119.2	141.6	146.2	153.5	159.6	164.7	171.7
France	85.4	100.0	109.3	132.9	137.1	141.6	142.8	145.7	149.6
Germany	86.8	100.0	102.8	109.3	107.8	109.9	109.5	110.7	110.1
Gibraltar									
Greece	44.4	91.6	113.1	151.6	158.1	167.6	168.9	178.5	185.6
Iceland									
Ireland	81.0	100.0	164.0	219.8	236.9	247.2	208.5	200.4	200.8
Italy	66.9	100.0	124.5	162.1	168.0	175.3	175.3	178.2	182.9
Liechtenstein									
Luxembourg									
Malta									
Monaco									
Netherlands	74.1	100.0	115.7	144.2	147.7	151.4	154.6	154.3	159.1
Norway	86.3	100.0	115.6	149.5	147.3	155.4	158.1	168.3	170.0
Portugal	68.9	100.0	117.2	144.8	150.9	156.9	157.3	164.8	176.1
Spain	74.2	100.0	119.0	154.3	161.9	169.9	173.1	176.9	189.6
Sweden	69.6	100.0	107.6	126.8	129.2	133.5	138.0	141.3	144.5
Switzerland	81.1	100.0	104.8	113.4	115.7	122.2	119.1	120.1	121.1
Turkey	5.2	100.0	1,662.6	6,856.2	7,625.5	9,123.0	9,927.5	10,551.2	11,274.2
United Kingdom	70.7	100.0	121.9	164.5	174.9	186.3	195.7	208.9	224.3
Eastern Europe									
Albania									
Belarus		100.0	2,987.0	54,359.7	60,433.9	66,507.4	75,250.1	80,942.1	113,612.9
Bosnia-Herzegovina		100.0	99.8	109.1	104.2	108.4	116.0	118.6	123.8
Bulgaria	3.3	100.0	3,968.5	5,114.2	5,388.6	5,969.7	6,397.2	6,455.4	6,594.8
Croatia		100.0	131.4	174.8	179.3	193.0	202.5	205.3	210.7
Czech Republic	36.1	100.0	163.9	214.1	225.3	244.3	259.4	260.9	273.4
Estonia	1.6	100.0	148.8	171.3	169.3	177.9	168.7	171.5	178.1
Georgia	0.0	100.0	192.4	314.8	397.9	438.0	423.0	432.8	469.3
Hungary	39.9	100.0	227.9	341.3	377.2	409.3	444.2	469.2	498.2
Latvia	5.7	100.0	144.3	209.5	248.5	299.2	300.4	291.3	303.9
Lithuania	0.2	100.0	184.4	233.5	271.7	310.4	310.1	314.8	338.2
Macedonia	0.2	100.0	128.8	159.2	182.2	181.6	183.4	187.4	194.4
Moldova									
Montenegro		100.0	99.6	197.6	214.0	235.6	245.5	248.0	256.3
Poland	18.5	100.0	218.3	273.8	285.8	307.4	328.6	339.2	355.0
Romania	0.7	100.0	2,022.1	4,622.5	4,956.2	5,448.7	5,792.4	6,186.6	6,567.0
Russia	0.1	100.0	448.9	3,808.2	3,877.9	4,040.9	4,600.5	5,044.3	5,465.9
Serbia		51.0	403.3	1,692.5	1,836.4	2,040.1	2,336.4	2,555.2	2,884.5
Slovakia	41.5	100.0	144.5	259.7	273.4	292.9	308.3	308.6	330.0
Slovenia	8.2	100.0	164.2	227.8	235.1	252.5	246.8	250.3	254.2
Ukraine	0.0	100.0	375.7	830.9	1,191.3	1,448.6	1,802.5	2,072.3	2,284.4

Source: Euromonitor International from national statistics

Table 8.7

Household Goods and Services Price Indices 1990, 1995, 2000, 2006-2011

1995 = 100

	1990	1995	2000	2006	2007	2008	2009	2010	2011
Western Europe									
Austria	88.0	100.0	102.7	107.6	108.5	111.3	114.1	116.0	117.8
Belgium	90.0	100.0	99.5	107.6	109.7	112.5	115.5	117.1	118.7
Cyprus									
Denmark	90.4	100.0	109.3	119.0	120.9	123.2	126.5	126.8	128.5
Finland	88.8	100.0	102.8	108.9	110.1	112.1	114.3	116.5	120.8
France	92.1	100.0	105.2	111.6	112.7	114.5	116.3	116.6	119.4
Germany	90.9	100.0	104.5	95.6	93.6	92.0	88.2	90.0	92.8
Gibraltar									
Greece	50.3	93.3	116.3	132.3	135.6	140.2	142.8	144.8	148.7
Iceland									
Ireland	95.0	100.0	112.8	120.2	119.6	117.8	113.1	107.0	106.9
Italy	79.3	100.0	111.8	124.5	127.2	131.0	133.2	135.2	138.9
Liechtenstein									
Luxembourg									
Malta									
Monaco									
Netherlands	84.1	100.0	103.2	114.2	115.5	118.0	120.7	121.3	122.9
Norway	93.1	100.0	105.6	104.4	106.4	109.5	113.0	112.5	111.7
Portugal	70.8	100.0	113.7	127.3	130.1	132.2	132.0	134.5	136.4
Spain	69.5	100.0	111.6	127.6	130.6	134.1	135.6	137.1	138.6
Sweden	92.3	100.0	104.4	105.2	106.5	108.5	110.6	109.9	109.4
Switzerland	89.7	100.0	102.6	104.5	104.8	105.7	106.5	107.1	107.8
Turkey	5.5	100.0	1,258.1	4,096.7	4,407.9	4,711.2	4,752.3	4,856.5	5,068.1
United Kingdom	89.5	100.0	102.1	100.7	102.2	104.2	107.4	110.5	114.0
Eastern Europe									
Albania									
Belarus		100.0	3,011.7	19,582.4	21,946.7	24,058.8	27,229.1	29,297.6	41,108.9
Bosnia-Herzegovina		100.0	108.1	114.0	114.5	115.6	126.2	129.4	135.0
Bulgaria	3.6	100.0	2,288.5	2,396.7	2,498.0	2,627.1	2,728.0	2,725.4	2,718.8
Croatia		100.0	125.8	127.8	130.4	137.7	141.7	143.3	146.5
Czech Republic	49.3	100.0	115.7	104.0	103.4	104.4	103.2	103.0	101.4
Estonia	1.5	100.0	169.2	333.3	362.3	339.5	348.1	355.6	368.0
Georgia	0.0	100.0	185.6	219.9	230.8	261.2	264.9	269.8	294.8
Hungary	52.6	100.0	176.1	197.2	200.2	201.6	207.4	209.3	211.4
Latvia	5.7	100.0	137.8	152.5	159.6	167.8	168.2	171.8	177.7
Lithuania	0.2	100.0	134.7	120.2	122.2	127.4	131.7	128.8	127.6
Macedonia	0.4	100.0	130.1	129.5	129.7	142.0	140.7	143.2	149.7
Moldova									
Montenegro		100.0	75.0	110.7	111.1	113.0	115.9	115.7	118.3
Poland	16.3	100.0	177.9	199.1	201.4	207.8	212.1	217.2	225.2
Romania	0.9	100.0	797.3	2,057.1	2,085.0	2,127.5	2,178.1	2,299.3	2,409.6
Russia	0.3	100.0	466.4	1,400.2	1,383.6	1,525.5	1,736.8	1,779.1	1,925.4
Serbia		51.2	382.2	1,071.1	1,091.1	1,113.9	1,169.6	1,259.6	1,368.4
Slovakia	42.2	100.0	132.4	124.1	123.9	124.2	119.9	116.2	115.0
Slovenia	7.5	100.0	125.5	166.1	173.3	183.4	190.2	195.2	199.4
Ukraine	0.0	100.0	356.5	455.5	465.2	525.8	633.0	666.6	720.6

Source: Euromonitor International from national statistics

8

Consumer Prices and Costs

Consumer Prices Statistics

Table 8.8

Health Goods and Medical Services Price Indices 1990, 1995, 2000, 2006-2011

1995 = 100

	1990	1995	2000	2006	2007	2008	2009	2010	2011
Western Europe									
Austria	77.6	100.0	112.5	138.6	141.4	144.7	145.7	147.7	150.7
Belgium	94.8	100.0	104.4	114.2	118.1	119.8	115.6	120.7	120.9
Cyprus									
Denmark	95.6	100.0	104.6	113.1	113.6	114.4	116.0	116.6	119.9
Finland	77.5	100.0	114.4	130.9	131.0	133.6	138.2	138.9	143.9
France	92.7	100.0	102.7	105.7	106.3	106.8	106.9	106.7	108.8
Germany	67.1	100.0	112.9	133.8	138.1	144.5	146.3	157.0	158.4
Gibraltar									
Greece	57.7	103.7	86.7	107.0	108.9	109.5	112.0	118.0	121.3
Iceland									
Ireland	58.9	100.0	123.3	195.4	200.5	214.6	226.7	227.1	238.8
Italy	81.2	100.0	120.2	123.2	122.1	121.3	125.3	126.8	129.9
Liechtenstein									
Luxembourg									
Malta									
Monaco									
Netherlands	84.5	100.0	109.9	131.4	133.7	135.3	136.0	137.9	144.2
Norway	79.1	100.0	123.9	151.5	154.8	159.6	164.5	168.7	172.9
Portugal	69.0	100.0	120.9	138.5	149.6	151.6	146.8	145.3	152.1
Spain	69.6	100.0	114.2	133.3	133.7	135.5	135.2	134.6	132.9
Sweden	83.2	100.0	129.1	155.5	158.6	159.8	161.7	167.1	167.5
Switzerland	81.4	100.0	103.0	107.9	108.1	108.0	108.4	108.9	109.4
Turkey	5.0	100.0	2,006.8	6,393.1	6,698.5	6,725.5	6,923.5	6,973.8	7,227.6
United Kingdom	67.2	100.0	122.2	137.3	140.7	143.1	146.8	150.3	153.5
Eastern Europe									
Albania									
Belarus		100.0	4,457.9	39,675.9	44,043.1	48,385.5	54,733.9	58,860.2	82,599.1
Bosnia-Herzegovina		100.0	96.0	100.0	93.2	92.7	94.9	96.2	99.5
Bulgaria	3.1	100.0	4,125.2	6,598.8	6,898.6	7,360.4	7,685.7	7,895.1	8,365.0
Croatia		100.0	121.5	181.3	184.6	197.2	227.7	232.0	240.2
Czech Republic	45.4	100.0	132.7	128.4	134.1	147.4	143.0	138.8	143.1
Estonia	1.6	100.0	177.1	231.8	242.3	281.5	293.6	303.9	322.5
Georgia	0.0	100.0	184.2	238.9	271.8	314.0	352.2	367.4	407.0
Hungary	34.5	100.0	291.9	469.1	588.3	560.1	554.3	576.2	597.3
Latvia	5.9	100.0	120.5	183.2	205.1	242.5	284.5	281.8	298.4
Lithuania	0.2	100.0	95.9	122.5	129.9	143.7	170.1	172.2	172.3
Macedonia	0.2	100.0	108.2	135.8	140.6	150.0	149.5	152.3	158.9
Moldova									
Montenegro		100.0	70.2	102.5	102.7	104.0	106.4	106.2	108.5
Poland	20.4	100.0	248.1	298.5	304.7	318.1	328.8	337.6	351.0
Romania	0.8	100.0	1,185.4	2,852.2	2,798.8	2,773.9	2,914.0	3,067.7	3,212.7
Russia	0.2	100.0	383.5	1,593.5	1,675.9	1,971.0	2,243.9	2,276.4	2,477.6
Serbia		51.1	389.7	1,254.1	1,344.7	1,387.2	1,545.4	1,618.2	1,763.4
Slovakia	46.0	100.0	115.2	177.1	175.9	187.6	199.1	206.0	214.2
Slovenia	6.1	100.0	144.7	189.3	192.5	199.1	207.4	210.8	214.7
Ukraine	0.0	100.0	362.1	532.7	576.5	705.4	937.1	1,039.7	1,149.8

Source: Euromonitor International from national statistics

Table 8.9

Transport Price Indices 1990, 1995, 2000, 2006-2011

1995 = 100

	1990	1995	2000	2006	2007	2008	2009	2010	2011
Western Europe									
Austria	88.2	100.0	110.1	125.7	128.2	135.3	129.6	135.6	143.9
Belgium	85.7	100.0	108.7	127.3	127.9	133.4	128.3	135.1	144.0
Cyprus									
Denmark	90.5	100.0	110.2	124.3	126.0	130.2	129.0	133.2	137.3
Finland	82.7	100.0	112.4	121.5	122.1	124.8	121.6	126.9	131.2
France	88.6	100.0	109.3	125.4	128.4	135.3	131.1	136.0	138.8
Germany	104.2	100.0	103.3	106.4	100.1	98.4	102.8	96.3	100.3
Gibraltar									
Greece	61.9	96.4	113.4	131.9	133.6	142.4	136.8	153.8	159.6
Iceland									
Ireland	91.5	100.0	114.3	135.9	138.9	142.3	138.4	143.0	149.7
Italy	76.1	100.0	114.3	132.0	134.3	142.1	138.8	140.9	144.4
Liechtenstein									
Luxembourg									
Malta									
Monaco									
Netherlands	81.6	100.0	110.5	132.6	135.0	140.3	135.9	141.0	147.1
Norway	80.6	100.0	115.7	133.9	137.1	143.6	145.9	148.9	152.9
Portugal	68.9	100.0	121.9	160.4	163.8	166.5	157.1	164.5	179.8
Spain	70.5	100.0	114.6	143.0	146.0	154.5	147.7	158.1	170.8
Sweden	73.8	100.0	107.8	122.1	123.5	128.0	129.3	134.3	138.1
Switzerland	82.4	100.0	107.1	115.4	116.8	120.0	115.8	116.4	116.8
Turkey	5.1	100.0	1,582.4	6,517.6	6,883.3	7,431.7	7,449.4	8,166.8	8,593.9
United Kingdom	80.9	100.0	116.6	134.1	137.4	143.5	141.7	154.8	163.0
Eastern Europe									
Albania									
Belarus		100.0	3,933.2	27,005.0	30,119.1	32,971.0	37,299.9	40,115.2	56,274.0
Bosnia-Herzegovina		100.0	109.6	130.8	130.0	137.1	156.0	160.6	169.0
Bulgaria	3.3	100.0	3,920.4	4,988.9	5,314.2	6,109.6	5,819.4	6,166.2	6,535.8
Croatia		100.0	154.7	190.1	195.0	206.1	193.2	194.2	196.4
Czech Republic	49.4	100.0	115.1	108.8	107.8	108.7	97.3	93.4	95.8
Estonia	1.6	100.0	123.2	287.1	324.0	332.8	315.8	323.8	335.8
Georgia	0.0	100.0	185.5	246.6	263.5	305.7	293.3	327.4	359.9
Hungary	52.4	100.0	196.9	246.2	252.2	267.5	264.2	293.3	316.6
Latvia	6.0	100.0	195.0	258.3	294.3	337.3	333.4	326.6	338.8
Lithuania	0.2	100.0	158.7	182.4	194.2	215.7	213.6	225.7	242.0
Macedonia	0.2	100.0	131.5	157.6	159.3	171.2	171.2	174.2	181.9
Moldova									
Montenegro		100.0	80.5	175.1	180.1	206.5	214.6	216.6	224.6
Poland	19.2	100.0	204.5	257.3	259.9	269.9	266.7	272.6	281.9
Romania	0.9	100.0	1,204.2	3,139.2	3,194.6	3,530.8	3,639.1	3,866.8	4,092.2
Russia	0.1	100.0	268.6	712.3	865.9	620.9	706.9	740.9	758.8
Serbia		50.9	406.4	1,540.3	1,568.5	1,752.2	1,809.9	2,035.2	2,250.5
Slovakia	42.3	100.0	146.5	173.0	168.1	174.8	160.1	157.7	168.5
Slovenia	8.4	100.0	158.2	213.1	213.9	221.8	216.9	216.8	219.0
Ukraine	0.0	100.0	373.5	557.1	608.4	748.4	866.4	937.2	1,021.0

Source: Euromonitor International from national statistics

8

Consumer Prices and Costs

Consumer Prices Statistics

Table 8.10

Communication Price Indices 1990, 1995, 2000, 2006-2011

1995 = 100

	1990	1995	2000	2006	2007	2008	2009	2010	2011
Western Europe									
Austria	103.7	100.0	70.3	58.5	56.5	52.1	51.9	52.7	53.1
Belgium	83.9	100.0	96.8	91.5	88.7	86.1	85.6	83.7	84.1
Cyprus									
Denmark	98.7	100.0	92.3	74.6	66.9	67.9	66.9	66.4	68.0
Finland	98.9	100.0	87.3	60.4	64.0	61.7	60.6	57.3	58.3
France	103.3	100.0	72.4	59.5	58.4	58.2	58.0	57.4	58.4
Germany	72.5	100.0	187.4	264.4	268.0	275.5	282.9	294.3	286.2
Gibraltar									
Greece	36.3	88.8	86.2	81.1	81.6	84.2	85.0	88.6	91.0
Iceland									
Ireland	103.2	100.0	83.5	75.9	75.1	74.8	74.1	74.5	77.1
Italy	85.6	100.0	95.6	77.3	70.8	67.2	67.0	67.0	67.9
Liechtenstein									
Luxembourg									
Malta									
Monaco									
Netherlands	80.7	100.0	88.5	89.2	87.5	84.3	82.2	82.6	84.4
Norway	153.3	100.0	79.6	74.6	72.3	68.9	65.2	63.7	62.7
Portugal	77.3	100.0	90.9	85.9	84.9	83.1	80.8	79.5	82.0
Spain	73.2	100.0	99.4	90.8	91.0	90.3	89.5	89.5	88.8
Sweden	91.9	100.0	89.4	72.8	70.2	68.3	65.9	64.2	62.5
Switzerland	82.6	100.0	64.8	54.1	52.5	51.0	48.5	48.4	48.1
Turkey	4.7	100.0	1,764.8	5,953.2	5,903.3	6,010.0	6,217.1	6,202.0	6,435.0
United Kingdom	97.1	100.0	87.7	80.8	78.2	76.3	77.2	80.9	83.1
Eastern Europe									
Albania									
Belarus		100.0	6,917.2	76,906.8	86,115.5	93,747.5	106,044.3	114,035.2	159,871.7
Bosnia-Herzegovina		100.0	105.9	114.3	115.3	117.3	128.3	131.6	137.5
Bulgaria	3.4	100.0	3,100.6	3,637.9	3,635.4	3,572.8	3,392.1	3,359.9	3,312.4
Croatia		100.0	283.7	350.0	349.2	347.1	346.5	347.4	351.4
Czech Republic	38.3	100.0	154.0	200.5	202.1	198.6	190.7	187.0	185.2
Estonia	1.4	100.0	209.3	570.1	725.0	587.2	588.6	600.7	608.1
Georgia	0.0	100.0	186.1	193.8	196.3	205.0	212.0	211.3	228.8
Hungary	43.5	100.0	241.1	268.4	257.0	255.3	258.1	258.9	262.4
Latvia	6.0	100.0	213.6	165.5	155.7	151.6	148.9	148.4	151.2
Lithuania	0.2	100.0	305.1	299.9	283.7	250.4	217.2	206.3	198.5
Macedonia	0.3	100.0	274.7	596.5	535.7	643.9	622.7	632.0	664.7
Moldova									
Montenegro		100.0	128.5	266.7	275.9	339.0	354.4	359.5	375.5
Poland	30.7	100.0	110.6	114.7	114.7	116.2	115.8	118.1	121.9
Romania	0.4	100.0	4,926.1	10,655.2	10,955.6	11,877.1	13,318.4	14,222.5	15,153.1
Russia	0.2	100.0	234.1	1,196.0	1,205.5	1,353.9	1,541.4	1,536.3	1,661.1
Serbia		51.2	378.8	989.3	1,084.9	1,063.8	1,154.0	1,184.9	1,210.8
Slovakia	37.7	100.0	182.9	251.7	251.4	251.1	252.7	259.2	260.2
Slovenia	5.3	100.0	140.3	172.8	173.4	174.6	167.6	165.4	166.0
Ukraine	0.0	100.0	364.6	481.6	557.5	600.2	643.2	670.4	709.1

Source: Euromonitor International from national statistics

| **Table 8.11**

Leisure and Recreation Price Indices 1990, 1995, 2000, 2006-2011

1995 = 100

	1990	1995	2000	2006	2007	2008	2009	2010	2011
Western Europe									
Austria	86.9	100.0	98.7	99.2	98.9	98.7	97.8	98.7	100.7
Belgium	89.1	100.0	100.3	105.9	106.1	107.1	109.0	109.8	110.3
Cyprus									
Denmark	97.2	100.0	103.4	110.5	109.5	109.0	109.8	111.3	110.9
Finland	88.1	100.0	104.9	109.1	107.2	106.9	107.7	108.2	111.5
France	95.0	100.0	93.5	85.9	83.6	81.8	79.9	78.8	79.5
Germany	91.7	100.0	117.3	126.8	130.9	134.0	132.9	135.6	138.5
Gibraltar									
Greece	43.5	89.5	114.3	133.7	137.4	141.7	143.2	145.2	148.9
Iceland									
Ireland	88.9	100.0	104.0	113.9	112.9	113.4	109.3	103.0	103.7
Italy	79.5	100.0	106.7	116.1	117.2	118.1	119.0	120.6	123.4
Liechtenstein									
Luxembourg									
Malta									
Monaco									
Netherlands	86.4	100.0	102.2	106.0	105.3	105.1	105.1	105.4	105.7
Norway	90.9	100.0	102.6	103.8	104.7	105.4	107.5	109.4	109.2
Portugal	72.6	100.0	106.1	117.5	118.8	119.7	114.6	114.1	115.8
Spain	71.0	100.0	112.3	123.1	122.9	123.3	121.8	122.2	122.1
Sweden	90.1	100.0	94.7	87.6	86.2	84.7	85.1	84.4	82.8
Switzerland	92.5	100.0	98.1	97.2	97.0	98.3	97.5	98.0	98.6
Turkey	5.7	100.0	1,170.6	3,678.8	3,819.1	3,897.2	4,286.9	4,395.8	4,610.3
United Kingdom	87.9	100.0	93.4	81.6	79.6	77.0	76.5	77.0	76.2
Eastern Europe									
Albania									
Belarus		100.0	3,891.9	43,980.0	49,776.1	53,093.6	60,018.0	64,494.8	90,207.4
Bosnia-Herzegovina		100.0	97.2	103.8	102.0	104.2	110.4	112.9	117.5
Bulgaria	3.5	100.0	2,873.9	3,000.3	3,122.9	3,229.1	3,399.2	3,464.8	3,337.5
Croatia		100.0	125.6	150.2	153.4	156.6	159.7	161.0	163.8
Czech Republic	42.8	100.0	127.1	130.8	132.1	134.6	132.2	130.8	128.8
Estonia	1.5	100.0	176.3	350.7	428.8	344.9	350.6	356.9	361.6
Georgia	0.0	100.0	185.3	217.2	226.6	238.6	242.2	246.1	266.8
Hungary	52.7	100.0	183.4	235.6	240.6	248.3	255.0	262.4	265.6
Latvia	5.5	100.0	138.8	171.0	180.6	197.4	206.6	205.4	213.7
Lithuania	0.3	100.0	130.5	125.6	127.2	130.4	131.9	128.5	125.6
Macedonia	0.3	100.0	132.4	135.4	132.9	148.0	146.0	148.5	155.4
Moldova									
Montenegro		100.0	127.2	278.6	283.0	293.1	306.4	307.1	315.2
Poland	16.3	100.0	297.6	326.5	327.7	331.8	338.4	345.9	357.9
Romania	0.9	100.0	1,259.3	5,901.3	6,197.2	6,353.1	6,647.6	7,049.5	7,412.7
Russia	0.2	100.0	471.7	2,336.0	2,300.6	2,082.6	2,371.0	2,400.7	2,533.8
Serbia		51.4	384.2	1,247.3	1,324.1	1,367.2	1,464.3	1,578.3	1,672.0
Slovakia	44.6	100.0	131.8	149.3	151.2	152.6	150.0	152.3	153.0
Slovenia	9.5	100.0	144.5	181.5	186.1	191.6	195.8	198.4	201.5
Ukraine	0.0	100.0	358.2	475.7	488.0	539.6	621.7	644.1	689.6

Source: Euromonitor International from national statistics

8

Consumer: Prices and Costs

Consumer Prices Statistics **Table 8.12**

Education Price Indices 1990, 1995, 2000, 2006-2011

1995 = 100

	1990	1995	2000	2006	2007	2008	2009	2010	2011
Western Europe									
Austria	64.6	100.0	119.3	180.5	184.1	188.3	189.9	193.5	201.4
Belgium	88.7	100.0	103.6	117.0	119.7	122.0	124.9	128.9	129.4
Cyprus									
Denmark	89.0	100.0	113.4	138.0	141.3	149.6	157.0	164.4	172.0
Finland	87.4	100.0	113.6	143.5	149.0	154.4	159.9	167.6	174.7
France	83.9	100.0	105.2	130.3	135.7	144.2	157.1	162.0	169.7
Germany	103.6	100.0	112.1	134.8	137.5	145.7	160.2	167.5	167.6
Gibraltar									
Greece	37.1	98.6	123.8	157.6	163.7	171.4	178.0	181.3	187.8
Iceland									
Ireland	81.2	100.0	114.7	171.2	179.7	185.0	188.3	192.4	203.9
Italy	76.3	100.0	112.5	135.9	139.0	142.3	146.2	148.6	152.6
Liechtenstein									
Luxembourg									
Malta									
Monaco									
Netherlands	74.8	100.0	117.1	141.2	144.0	146.1	149.3	151.9	155.9
Norway	86.4	100.0	121.7	154.8	157.8	162.7	170.2	175.5	180.8
Portugal	67.4	100.0	123.4	178.5	186.2	194.0	197.1	203.2	207.8
Spain	66.6	100.0	121.2	154.0	160.2	166.8	171.4	175.7	179.9
Sweden	94.6	100.0	105.6	105.4	110.3	113.8	116.1	117.6	119.8
Switzerland	77.6	100.0	113.1	124.7	126.9	128.9	131.0	132.0	133.1
Turkey	5.0	100.0	1,997.4	9,037.1	9,687.8	10,341.9	10,942.3	11,532.6	12,140.2
United Kingdom	68.5	100.0	129.4	183.4	208.7	233.2	251.3	264.7	280.2
Eastern Europe									
Albania									
Belarus		100.0	9,588.5	114,082.1	124,485.3	133,390.0	150,448.4	161,283.4	225,581.5
Bosnia-Herzegovina		100.0	98.5	107.1	109.6	108.3	116.2	118.9	123.6
Bulgaria	3.4	100.0	4,296.2	5,644.3	6,058.3	6,879.8	7,921.8	8,390.5	8,617.8
Croatia		100.0	137.7	165.0	166.6	172.1	176.6	178.1	181.5
Czech Republic	45.6	100.0	136.3	184.4	190.5	198.5	202.4	205.8	210.3
Estonia	1.6	100.0	131.0	184.2	163.5	146.4	153.4	153.7	158.3
Georgia	0.0	100.0	184.3	206.2	214.5	217.8	256.8	338.2	379.4
Hungary	55.3	100.0	181.1	332.2	352.6	369.7	374.0	375.9	377.3
Latvia	5.6	100.0	148.4	212.6	246.1	300.1	356.0	333.5	352.7
Lithuania	0.2	100.0	190.4	198.8	212.5	236.8	255.7	274.4	273.7
Macedonia	0.5	100.0	129.1	166.1	189.8	186.4	190.2	194.3	201.4
Moldova									
Montenegro		100.0	87.2	133.1	132.0	132.7	136.8	136.4	139.2
Poland	22.7	100.0	183.7	225.3	229.1	238.3	245.5	251.8	261.7
Romania	0.7	100.0	3,901.0	15,631.5	18,409.0	19,444.5	21,210.3	22,763.4	24,141.1
Russia	0.2	100.0	396.6	1,149.5	1,299.8	1,359.4	1,588.1	1,676.7	1,815.2
Serbia		51.0	399.1	1,659.5	1,777.6	1,896.0	2,001.2	2,185.6	2,350.8
Slovakia	46.9	100.0	146.5	288.3	296.6	312.1	330.6	345.1	362.2
Slovenia	13.1	100.0	155.8	229.1	232.9	248.1	256.2	261.7	267.2
Ukraine	0.0	100.0	381.6	683.3	787.5	995.7	1,189.3	1,316.8	1,446.3

Source: Euromonitor International from national statistics

Table 8.13

Hotel and Catering Price Indices 1990, 1995, 2000, 2006-2011

1995 = 100

	1990	1995	2000	2006	2007	2008	2009	2010	2011
Western Europe									
Austria	82.9	100.0	109.3	127.2	130.1	134.9	137.7	139.1	144.2
Belgium	85.2	100.0	105.1	126.3	129.6	134.9	139.7	142.7	146.2
Cyprus									
Denmark	91.3	100.0	114.2	132.9	136.3	142.4	144.9	147.5	151.2
Finland	86.5	100.0	113.1	128.1	131.1	138.1	144.1	146.3	152.3
France	83.9	100.0	109.5	128.3	131.9	135.8	138.0	138.8	142.2
Germany	96.0	100.0	106.7	106.5	109.4	110.0	107.3	108.4	112.1
Gibraltar									
Greece	41.8	91.2	128.6	162.7	169.2	177.0	180.8	185.6	191.9
Iceland									
Ireland	81.0	100.0	119.1	155.0	159.5	163.2	162.3	156.4	161.3
Italy	73.9	100.0	117.2	142.9	146.7	150.4	152.0	154.4	158.3
Liechtenstein									
Luxembourg									
Malta									
Monaco									
Netherlands	79.0	100.0	108.5	133.5	138.1	143.8	148.3	152.0	156.0
Norway	86.7	100.0	117.5	140.3	146.7	154.3	160.2	165.2	170.0
Portugal	70.1	100.0	118.0	147.0	151.3	156.8	157.2	160.1	161.5
Spain	85.3	100.0	119.2	156.5	163.3	170.8	172.0	176.6	179.4
Sweden	84.1	100.0	109.8	129.2	133.2	139.9	144.1	148.5	152.8
Switzerland	75.8	100.0	106.0	116.6	118.1	121.0	122.8	123.9	125.0
Turkey	5.1	100.0	1,590.3	6,534.3	7,264.9	8,236.9	8,990.5	9,842.1	10,496.1
United Kingdom	77.0	100.0	120.2	147.4	152.9	158.9	162.8	166.7	172.6
Eastern Europe									
Albania									
Belarus		100.0	2,778.1	11,747.8	13,210.2	14,570.8	16,501.4	17,767.0	24,949.2
Bosnia-Herzegovina		100.0	99.4	110.6	112.2	112.9	122.1	125.1	130.4
Bulgaria	3.2	100.0	4,247.5	5,433.6	6,076.5	7,121.0	7,660.2	7,696.8	7,777.4
Croatia		100.0	136.7	168.8	172.5	184.3	192.8	195.3	200.2
Czech Republic	33.8	100.0	170.9	219.4	234.0	257.5	264.8	270.0	271.4
Estonia	1.7	100.0	141.6	251.0	271.8	227.9	225.2	227.2	230.3
Georgia	0.0	100.0	183.8	237.5	250.7	264.5	284.5	302.0	331.0
Hungary	47.4	100.0	212.6	368.4	396.5	423.2	447.0	461.4	473.3
Latvia	5.8	100.0	129.8	187.6	206.4	246.1	247.3	266.4	280.6
Lithuania	0.2	100.0	118.8	140.3	153.4	174.3	186.6	184.2	186.7
Macedonia	0.2	100.0	127.7	134.8	143.6	150.0	150.2	153.1	159.5
Moldova									
Montenegro		100.0	84.4	143.0	147.6	161.1	166.5	167.6	172.8
Poland	19.6	100.0	185.6	214.5	221.4	235.1	246.9	254.2	265.3
Romania	0.8	100.0	1,623.4	4,503.4	4,678.8	4,956.6	5,280.6	5,615.5	5,937.8
Russia	0.3	100.0	486.4	1,025.4	1,128.0	1,195.3	1,288.0	1,359.9	1,461.3
Serbia		51.0	399.6	1,611.2	1,717.8	1,836.3	1,995.7	2,166.2	2,306.1
Slovakia	44.3	100.0	130.2	183.0	188.0	197.8	206.0	208.4	213.7
Slovenia	7.0	100.0	148.1	207.7	221.6	241.9	252.1	261.9	268.7
Ukraine	0.0	100.0	384.1	1,149.0	1,281.7	1,729.2	1,958.7	2,159.9	2,373.9

Source: Euromonitor International from national statistics

8

Consumer Prices and Costs

Consumer Prices Statistics **Table 8.14**

Miscellaneous Goods and Services Price Indices 1990, 1995, 2000, 2006-2011

1995 = 100

	1990	1995	2000	2006	2007	2008	2009	2010	2011
Western Europe									
Austria	92.7	100.0	112.3	124.1	128.4	126.2	126.5	130.3	134.8
Belgium	92.3	100.0	94.4	105.2	115.8	113.4	106.6	106.0	109.3
Cyprus									
Denmark	84.3	100.0	105.1	108.1	105.6	105.3	109.4	112.6	115.1
Finland	91.5	100.0	122.7	115.5	125.9	126.5	123.8	131.8	136.4
France	103.7	100.0	100.9	111.7	118.3	123.0	117.0	116.9	118.7
Germany	89.8	100.0	118.5	122.2	127.1	126.5	126.8	129.3	131.4
Gibraltar									
Greece	48.5	90.5	120.2	137.3	140.9	142.7	143.5	148.3	152.0
Iceland									
Ireland	90.0	100.0	119.8	163.0	168.2	173.1	162.7	158.3	161.0
Italy	77.3	100.0	112.0	134.7	140.4	142.9	146.5	148.9	152.8
Liechtenstein									
Luxembourg									
Malta									
Monaco									
Netherlands	75.0	100.0	115.5	141.7	147.5	140.8	130.2	135.4	138.8
Norway	95.6	100.0	111.7	131.1	138.4	145.8	153.1	158.9	164.1
Portugal	67.2	100.0	124.6	154.4	159.1	163.1	163.2	164.6	167.9
Spain	67.7	100.0	118.7	133.8	140.9	141.9	127.1	128.8	132.2
Sweden	73.9	100.0	109.1	118.8	120.8	126.8	125.4	128.1	132.5
Switzerland	105.7	100.0	108.2	111.9	117.3	118.2	118.9	120.0	120.7
Turkey	5.3	100.0	1,478.2	6,145.5	6,486.6	7,111.1	8,031.8	8,594.0	9,145.8
United Kingdom	82.0	100.0	112.5	123.7	126.9	127.7	121.6	122.8	123.9
Eastern Europe									
Albania									
Belarus		100.0	4,647.0	8,121.6	3,216.2	1,940.3	2,136.3	1,633.8	1,900.0
Bosnia-Herzegovina		100.0	98.9	109.5	105.5	108.3	116.2	118.8	123.9
Bulgaria	3.6	100.0	2,620.5	2,909.7	3,212.3	3,590.7	3,982.5	4,376.2	4,567.7
Croatia		100.0	143.8	163.3	169.3	178.1	184.8	187.0	191.3
Czech Republic	49.0	100.0	118.0	135.0	133.5	137.0	134.5	134.2	135.4
Estonia	1.5	100.0	181.7	383.1	415.6	405.4	424.2	435.2	453.6
Georgia	0.0	100.0	184.8	213.2	222.1	238.3	252.5	267.2	292.9
Hungary	56.2	100.0	191.1	255.0	280.4	290.6	293.1	305.3	310.9
Latvia	6.1	100.0	121.4	160.1	181.9	213.8	216.7	253.5	268.8
Lithuania	0.2	100.0	165.3	165.9	178.4	198.4	232.5	235.8	235.9
Macedonia	0.3	100.0	121.9	149.4	155.6	163.5	164.3	167.4	174.5
Moldova									
Montenegro		100.0	84.5	143.0	147.6	161.1	166.6	167.6	172.8
Poland	16.5	100.0	180.8	190.8	194.8	194.8	204.2	209.2	216.9
Romania	0.7	100.0	1,227.2	2,876.5	2,940.3	3,073.0	3,218.4	3,411.3	3,594.5
Russia	0.2	100.0	372.2	477.8	470.7	424.3	483.1	510.6	541.7
Serbia		51.0	399.4	1,382.3	1,455.2	1,519.3	1,607.6	1,722.1	1,886.1
Slovakia	52.2	100.0	116.7	176.5	182.2	185.2	186.2	191.7	199.0
Slovenia	5.9	100.0	130.7	179.3	194.9	201.0	186.9	187.9	188.8
Ukraine	0.0	100.0	370.8	521.6	572.5	733.4	913.0	1,012.1	1,117.2

Source: Euromonitor International from national statistics

9

Economic Indicators

Economic Statistics   **Table 9.1**

GDP in National Currencies 1980, 1985, 1990, 1995, 1999-2011

National currency billion

	1980	1985	1990	1995	1999	2000	2001	2002	2003	2004
Western Europe										
Austria	76.60	103.42	136.21	174.79	199.27	208.47	214.20	220.53	225.00	234.71
Belgium	90.82	125.43	168.03	207.93	238.88	252.54	259.80	268.62	276.16	291.29
Cyprus	1.35	2.62	4.52	7.09	9.01	9.76	10.55	10.89	11.63	12.52
Denmark	392.88	648.54	840.65	1,019.55	1,213.47	1,293.96	1,335.61	1,372.74	1,400.69	1,466.18
Finland	33.26	57.31	89.32	96.06	122.32	132.20	139.29	143.65	145.53	152.27
France	444.71	744.47	1,032.78	1,196.18	1,367.01	1,439.60	1,495.55	1,542.93	1,587.90	1,655.57
Germany	854.68	1,067.01	1,416.32	1,848.50	2,000.20	2,047.50	2,101.90	2,132.20	2,147.50	2,195.70
Gibraltar				0.34	0.41	0.43	0.47	0.51	0.56	0.60
Greece	6.84	18.65	43.82	89.56	126.16	136.28	146.43	156.61	172.43	185.27
Iceland	16.14	122.42	365.05	445.11	632.40	683.75	771.89	816.45	841.49	930.14
Ireland	13.25	25.30	36.98	53.73	90.60	105.77	117.64	130.88	140.83	150.19
Italy	204.22	431.42	704.25	952.16	1,134.00	1,198.29	1,255.74	1,301.87	1,341.85	1,397.73
Liechtenstein	0.90	1.30	1.97	2.87	4.00	4.19	4.21	4.19	4.14	4.30
Luxembourg	3.78	5.84	9.18	15.11	19.89	22.00	22.57	23.99	25.83	27.46
Malta	1.01	1.23	1.90	2.96	3.63	4.04	4.11	4.34	4.50	4.53
Monaco	0.89	1.49	2.07	2.40	2.74	2.88	3.00	3.09	3.18	3.32
Netherlands	163.09	200.83	243.65	305.26	386.19	417.96	447.73	465.21	476.95	491.18
Norway	314.70	552.43	736.29	943.44	1,240.43	1,481.24	1,536.89	1,532.31	1,592.20	1,752.81
Portugal	8.10	22.74	55.23	87.84	118.66	127.32	134.47	140.57	143.47	149.31
Spain	95.34	175.63	312.42	447.21	579.94	629.91	680.40	729.26	783.08	841.29
Sweden	557.79	913.82	1,446.90	1,809.58	2,138.42	2,265.45	2,348.42	2,443.63	2,544.87	2,660.96
Switzerland	188.57	250.38	339.00	383.10	410.92	432.41	443.24	446.79	450.57	465.35
Turkey	0.01	0.05	0.53	10.43	104.60	166.66	240.22	350.48	454.78	559.03
United Kingdom	233.18	361.76	574.07	741.85	929.47	975.29	1,019.84	1,068.60	1,136.60	1,199.88
Eastern Europe										
Albania	15.53	16.86	16.81	229.79	471.58	523.04	583.37	622.71	694.10	751.02
Belarus			0.00	121.40	3,026.06	9,133.80	17,173.20	26,138.30	36,564.80	49,991.80
Bosnia-Herzegovina			0.00	2.86	8.60	11.79	12.64	13.95	14.69	15.95
Bulgaria	0.03	0.03	0.05	0.88	24.31	27.40	30.30	33.19	35.81	39.82
Croatia			0.28	115.32	164.12	178.12	192.29	208.80	228.93	247.43
Czech Republic			695.39	1,533.68	2,149.02	2,269.70	2,448.56	2,567.53	2,688.11	2,929.17
Estonia			3.59	2.77	5.36	6.16	6.97	7.78	8.72	9.69
Georgia			0.00	3.69	5.67	6.04	6.67	7.46	8.56	9.82
Hungary	721.00	1,033.70	2,089.30	5,727.83	11,443.48	13,089.05	15,103.90	17,119.42	18,738.21	20,665.02
Latvia			0.07	2.62	4.27	4.72	5.16	5.70	6.37	7.42
Lithuania			0.13	26.92	43.89	46.00	48.88	52.35	57.23	63.00
Macedonia			0.44	169.52	209.01	236.39	233.84	243.97	258.37	272.46
Moldova			0.01	6.48	12.32	16.02	19.05	22.56	27.62	32.03
Montenegro			1.77	0.89	0.79	1.07	1.30	1.36	1.51	1.67
Poland	0.25	1.04	56.03	337.22	665.69	744.38	779.56	808.58	843.16	924.54
Romania	0.06	0.08	0.09	7.26	55.19	80.98	117.95	152.02	197.43	247.37
Russia			0.64	1,428.52	4,823.23	7,305.65	8,943.58	10,819.21	13,208.23	17,027.19
Serbia				51.36	205.62	384.23	762.18	972.58	1,125.84	1,380.71
Slovakia			9.23	19.32	28.11	31.18	33.88	36.81	40.61	45.16
Slovenia			0.82	10.36	16.92	18.57	20.76	23.19	25.20	27.16
Ukraine			0.00	54.52	130.44	170.07	204.19	225.81	267.34	345.11

Source: Euromonitor International from national statistics

GDP in National Currencies 1980, 1985, 1990, 1995, 1999-2011 *(continued)*

National currency billion

	2005	2006	2007	2008	2009	2010	2011	US$ billion 2011	US$ per capita 2011
Western Europe									
Austria	245.24	259.03	274.02	282.74	276.15	286.40	300.71	418.12	49,751.03
Belgium	303.44	318.83	335.82	346.38	340.78	356.13	369.84	514.23	46,956.63
Cyprus	13.40	14.43	15.83	17.16	16.85	17.33	17.76	24.70	22,126.82
Denmark	1,545.26	1,631.66	1,695.26	1,753.15	1,667.84	1,754.65	1,782.52	332.57	59,808.44
Finland	157.43	165.77	179.83	185.67	172.32	178.80	189.37	263.30	48,984.14
France	1,718.05	1,798.12	1,886.79	1,933.20	1,885.77	1,937.26	1,996.58	2,776.11	43,976.11
Germany	2,224.40	2,313.90	2,428.50	2,473.80	2,374.50	2,496.20	2,592.60	3,604.83	44,094.96
Gibraltar	0.66	0.74	0.80	0.90	0.95	1.00	1.07	1.71	58,578.79
Greece	193.05	208.89	222.77	232.92	231.64	227.32	215.09	299.07	26,405.44
Iceland	1,025.74	1,168.60	1,308.53	1,481.99	1,495.36	1,534.23	1,630.15	14.06	43,384.56
Ireland	163.04	177.73	188.73	178.88	161.28	156.49	158.99	221.07	49,336.17
Italy	1,436.38	1,493.03	1,554.20	1,575.14	1,519.70	1,553.17	1,580.22	2,197.19	36,241.42
Liechtenstein	4.56	5.02	5.52	5.50	4.91	5.04	5.09	5.73	158,436.23
Luxembourg	30.28	33.92	37.49	39.44	37.39	40.27	42.82	59.54	115,814.19
Malta	4.82	5.07	5.44	5.84	5.83	6.15	6.43	8.94	21,369.95
Monaco	3.44	3.72	4.37	4.49	4.00	4.10	4.22	5.87	165,774.51
Netherlands	513.41	540.22	571.77	594.48	573.24	588.74	601.97	837.00	50,252.91
Norway	1,958.91	2,180.80	2,306.45	2,559.91	2,356.60	2,523.23	2,720.50	485.29	98,631.04
Portugal	154.27	160.86	169.32	171.98	168.50	172.67	170.93	237.66	22,343.21
Spain	909.30	985.55	1,053.16	1,087.79	1,048.06	1,048.88	1,063.36	1,478.52	32,035.29
Sweden	2,769.38	2,944.48	3,126.02	3,204.32	3,105.79	3,330.58	3,492.47	537.69	57,106.05
Switzerland	479.09	508.04	540.80	567.85	554.37	574.31	586.78	660.71	83,951.97
Turkey	648.93	750.39	843.18	950.53	952.56	1,098.80	1,298.06	772.77	10,540.84
United Kingdom	1,262.71	1,333.16	1,412.12	1,440.93	1,401.86	1,466.57	1,516.15	2,429.73	38,876.58
Eastern Europe									
Albania	814.80	882.21	967.67	1,089.29	1,151.02	1,242.42	1,312.11	13.00	4,045.40
Belarus	65,067.10	79,267.00	97,165.30	129,791.00	137,442.00	164,476.00	274,282.00	55.14	5,815.31
Bosnia-Herzegovina	17.16	19.27	21.78	24.72	24.00	24.86	25.67	18.25	4,747.02
Bulgaria	45.48	51.78	60.18	69.30	68.32	70.51	75.27	53.51	7,119.34
Croatia	266.65	291.04	318.31	343.41	328.67	326.98	333.96	62.49	14,163.94
Czech Republic	3,116.06	3,352.60	3,662.57	3,848.41	3,739.23	3,775.24	3,807.80	215.18	20,521.21
Estonia	11.18	13.39	16.07	16.24	13.76	14.32	15.95	22.18	16,549.35
Georgia	11.62	13.79	16.99	19.07	17.99	20.74	24.23	14.37	3,270.10
Hungary	22,018.28	23,675.85	24,991.85	26,545.65	25,622.87	26,747.66	28,080.32	139.67	13,986.49
Latvia	9.00	11.13	14.72	16.08	13.07	12.78	14.28	28.24	13,614.57
Lithuania	72.40	83.23	99.23	112.08	91.91	95.07	106.02	42.69	13,158.38
Macedonia	295.05	320.06	364.99	411.73	410.73	423.86	448.67	10.14	4,931.42
Moldova	37.65	44.75	53.43	62.92	60.43	71.89	82.17	7.00	1,968.72
Montenegro	1.81	2.15	2.68	3.09	2.98	3.10	3.26	4.53	7,310.64
Poland	983.30	1,060.03	1,176.74	1,275.43	1,344.38	1,416.45	1,524.68	514.49	13,472.07
Romania	288.95	344.65	416.01	514.70	501.14	522.56	578.55	189.78	8,858.20
Russia	21,609.77	26,917.20	33,247.51	41,276.85	38,807.22	45,172.75	54,585.62	1,857.16	12,994.91
Serbia	1,683.48	1,962.07	2,276.89	2,661.39	2,713.21	2,931.42	3,240.39	44.19	6,073.90
Slovakia	49.31	55.00	61.45	66.84	62.80	65.74	69.06	96.02	17,792.41
Slovenia	28.72	31.05	34.59	37.24	35.56	35.61	36.17	50.29	24,531.67
Ukraine	441.45	544.15	720.73	948.06	913.35	1,082.57	1,316.60	165.15	3,621.78

Source: Euromonitor International from national statistics

Economic Indicators

9

Economic Statistics

Table 9.2

GDP in US$ 1980, 1985, 1990, 1995, 1999-2011

US$ billion

	1980	1985	1990	1995	1999	2000	2001	2002	2003
Western Europe									
Austria	106.65	78.92	173.46	228.63	212.32	192.11	191.72	207.73	254.00
Belgium	126.45	95.72	213.97	271.97	254.53	232.72	232.53	253.03	311.76
Cyprus	1.87	2.00	5.76	9.27	9.60	8.99	9.44	10.26	13.13
Denmark	69.71	61.20	135.84	181.98	173.94	159.98	160.51	174.11	212.97
Finland	46.30	43.73	113.74	125.65	130.33	121.82	124.67	135.31	164.29
France	619.18	568.09	1,315.17	1,564.62	1,456.56	1,326.62	1,338.57	1,453.36	1,792.61
Germany	1,190.00	814.22	1,803.59	2,417.86	2,131.24	1,886.81	1,881.27	2,008.43	2,424.35
Gibraltar				0.53	0.66	0.66	0.68	0.76	0.91
Greece	9.52	14.23	55.80	117.14	134.42	125.58	131.06	147.52	194.66
Iceland	3.36	2.95	6.26	6.88	8.74	8.70	7.92	8.91	10.97
Ireland	18.45	19.30	47.09	70.27	96.53	97.47	105.29	123.28	158.98
Italy	284.35	329.22	896.81	1,245.43	1,208.29	1,104.25	1,123.92	1,226.30	1,514.84
Liechtenstein	0.53	0.53	1.42	2.43	2.66	2.48	2.49	2.69	3.07
Luxembourg	5.27	4.46	11.69	19.76	21.19	20.27	20.20	22.60	29.16
Malta	1.41	0.94	2.42	3.87	3.87	3.72	3.68	4.09	5.08
Monaco	1.24	1.14	2.63	3.13	2.92	2.66	2.68	2.91	3.59
Netherlands	227.08	153.25	310.27	399.28	411.49	385.16	400.73	438.21	538.43
Norway	63.71	64.26	117.62	148.92	159.05	168.29	170.93	191.92	224.89
Portugal	11.28	17.35	70.33	114.90	126.44	117.32	120.36	132.41	161.97
Spain	132.74	134.02	397.85	584.95	617.94	580.47	608.98	686.93	884.04
Sweden	131.88	106.21	244.46	253.68	258.81	247.30	227.32	251.26	314.75
Switzerland	112.53	101.90	244.03	323.98	273.56	256.04	262.64	286.81	334.59
Turkey	92.48	90.38	202.55	227.61	249.76	266.56	196.01	232.53	303.01
United Kingdom	541.92	464.24	1,019.35	1,170.72	1,503.86	1,475.80	1,467.92	1,602.92	1,856.38
Eastern Europe									
Albania	2.22	2.41	2.17	2.48	3.42	3.64	4.07	4.44	5.70
Belarus			18.83	13.85	12.14	10.42	12.35	14.59	17.83
Bosnia-Herzegovina			7.75	2.04	4.69	5.55	5.78	6.72	8.48
Bulgaria	18.62	16.42	20.73	13.11	13.24	12.90	13.87	15.98	20.67
Croatia			24.81	22.05	23.08	21.52	23.05	26.52	34.14
Czech Republic			38.73	57.79	62.17	58.80	64.38	78.43	95.29
Estonia			4.58	3.62	5.71	5.68	6.24	7.32	9.84
Georgia			8.43	2.70	2.80	3.06	3.22	3.40	3.99
Hungary	22.16	20.62	33.06	45.57	48.25	46.39	52.72	66.38	83.54
Latvia			9.81	4.96	7.29	7.78	8.22	9.22	11.15
Lithuania			9.77	6.73	10.97	11.50	12.22	14.25	18.71
Macedonia			3.85	4.47	3.67	3.59	3.44	3.79	4.76
Moldova			3.97	1.77	1.17	1.29	1.48	1.66	1.98
Montenegro			2.26	1.16	0.84	0.98	1.16	1.28	1.70
Poland	56.79	70.99	58.98	139.06	167.80	171.28	190.42	198.18	216.80
Romania	34.60	48.14	38.51	35.73	36.00	37.31	40.59	45.99	59.47
Russia			614.17	399.17	195.91	259.72	306.62	345.13	430.35
Serbia				17.50	10.86	8.73	11.39	15.10	19.55
Slovakia			11.75	25.27	29.95	28.73	30.32	34.67	45.85
Slovenia			1.05	13.55	18.03	17.11	18.59	21.85	28.44
Ukraine			90.34	48.61	31.58	31.26	38.01	42.39	50.13

Source: Euromonitor International from national statistics

GDP in US$ 1980, 1985, 1990, 1995, 1999-2011 *(continued)*

US$ billion

	2004	2005	2006	2007	2008	2009	2010	2011	US$ per capita 2011
Western Europe									
Austria	291.52	304.80	324.97	375.04	413.79	383.74	379.28	418.12	49,751.03
Belgium	361.79	377.12	399.99	459.62	506.91	473.54	471.63	514.23	46,956.63
Cyprus	15.55	16.66	18.11	21.67	25.11	23.42	22.96	24.70	22,126.82
Denmark	244.87	257.71	274.55	311.47	343.74	311.11	311.99	332.57	59,808.44
Finland	189.12	195.66	207.96	246.13	271.72	239.45	236.79	263.30	48,984.14
France	2,056.30	2,135.25	2,255.82	2,582.40	2,829.18	2,620.44	2,565.58	2,776.11	43,976.11
Germany	2,727.17	2,764.56	2,902.90	3,323.82	3,620.34	3,299.59	3,305.80	3,604.83	44,094.96
Gibraltar	1.10	1.19	1.36	1.61	1.64	1.49	1.54	1.71	58,578.79
Greece	230.11	239.93	262.07	304.90	340.87	321.89	301.04	299.07	26,405.44
Iceland	13.25	16.29	16.65	20.43	16.85	12.09	12.55	14.06	43,384.56
Ireland	186.55	202.63	222.97	258.31	261.79	224.11	207.24	221.07	49,336.17
Italy	1,736.05	1,785.18	1,873.08	2,127.19	2,305.18	2,111.76	2,056.91	2,197.19	36,241.42
Liechtenstein	3.45	3.66	4.00	4.60	5.08	4.52	4.84	5.73	158,436.23
Luxembourg	34.10	37.64	42.55	51.31	57.71	51.96	53.33	59.54	115,814.19
Malta	5.63	5.99	6.36	7.45	8.55	8.10	8.15	8.94	21,369.95
Monaco	4.12	4.28	4.66	5.97	6.58	5.56	5.42	5.87	165,774.51
Netherlands	610.07	638.08	677.73	782.57	870.01	796.56	779.69	837.00	50,252.91
Norway	260.01	304.06	340.03	393.53	453.97	374.67	417.50	485.29	98,631.04
Portugal	185.45	191.73	201.80	231.74	251.69	234.15	228.67	237.66	22,343.21
Spain	1,044.93	1,130.11	1,236.41	1,441.43	1,591.95	1,456.38	1,389.07	1,478.52	32,035.29
Sweden	362.01	370.75	399.20	462.37	486.24	405.80	462.09	537.69	57,106.05
Switzerland	374.22	384.51	405.18	450.54	524.29	510.16	550.73	660.71	83,951.97
Turkey	392.16	482.24	527.88	645.76	728.47	612.47	729.20	772.77	10,540.84
United Kingdom	2,197.08	2,295.04	2,453.29	2,825.74	2,641.48	2,185.80	2,265.09	2,429.73	38,876.58
Eastern Europe									
Albania	7.31	8.16	8.99	10.70	12.98	12.12	11.95	13.00	4,045.40
Belarus	23.14	30.21	36.96	45.28	60.75	49.21	55.22	55.14	5,815.31
Bosnia-Herzegovina	10.13	10.90	12.36	15.24	18.49	17.05	16.84	18.25	4,747.02
Bulgaria	25.28	28.89	33.21	42.12	51.82	48.57	47.73	53.51	7,119.34
Croatia	41.00	44.82	49.86	59.34	69.59	62.20	59.47	62.49	14,163.94
Czech Republic	113.98	130.07	148.37	180.48	225.43	196.13	197.68	215.18	20,521.21
Estonia	12.03	13.90	16.80	21.99	23.76	19.12	18.97	22.18	16,549.35
Georgia	5.13	6.41	7.75	10.17	12.80	10.77	11.64	14.37	3,270.10
Hungary	101.93	110.32	112.53	136.10	154.23	126.63	128.63	139.67	13,986.49
Latvia	13.73	15.94	19.85	28.65	33.45	25.90	24.09	28.24	13,614.57
Lithuania	22.66	26.06	30.24	39.33	47.51	36.99	36.47	42.69	13,158.38
Macedonia	5.51	5.99	6.56	8.16	9.83	9.31	9.12	10.14	4,931.42
Moldova	2.60	2.99	3.41	4.40	6.05	5.44	5.81	7.00	1,968.72
Montenegro	2.07	2.26	2.70	3.67	4.52	4.14	4.11	4.53	7,310.64
Poland	252.77	303.91	341.60	425.13	529.23	430.75	469.85	514.49	13,472.07
Romania	75.79	99.17	122.70	170.62	204.34	164.34	164.44	109.78	8,858.20
Russia	590.94	764.02	989.93	1,299.70	1,660.85	1,221.83	1,487.53	1,857.16	12,994.91
Serbia	23.65	25.23	29.22	38.95	47.76	40.15	37.71	44.19	6,073.90
Slovakia	56.09	61.29	69.00	84.10	97.82	87.26	87.07	96.02	17,792.41
Slovenia	33.74	35.70	38.95	47.35	54.51	49.41	47.16	50.29	24,531.67
Ukraine	64.88	86.14	107.75	142.72	179.99	117.23	136.39	165.15	3,621.78

Source: Euromonitor International from national statistics

9

Economic Indicators

Economic Statistics   **Table 9.3**

GDP Origin 2011

US$ million

	Agriculture, Hunting, Forestry and Fishing	Mining and Quarrying	Manufacturing	Electricity, Gas and Water Supply	Construction	Hotels and Restaurants
Western Europe						
Austria	6,249.4	1,381.7	73,296.9	10,955.1	26,289.7	18,277.6
Belgium	3,290.6	497.1	64,760.9	10,631.7	24,507.2	8,060.2
Cyprus						
Denmark	3,178.1	10,153.9	34,581.0	5,631.2	11,790.1	4,060.1
Finland	6,655.5	1,265.9	43,401.2	6,143.3	14,588.6	3,750.7
France	50,351.9	3,184.4	253,175.4	43,501.5	145,367.9	58,199.1
Germany	32,938.2	5,376.0	700,510.1	94,274.2	136,137.0	52,557.0
Gibraltar						
Greece	8,535.9	960.3	27,620.6	6,883.6	9,249.5	19,213.9
Iceland						
Ireland	2,697.6	992.9	54,797.8	3,687.9	6,581.9	4,210.1
Italy	37,557.7	6,330.8	323,827.4	42,960.6	117,897.1	76,474.3
Liechtenstein						
Luxembourg						
Malta						
Monaco						
Netherlands	14,355.4	25,443.0	100,655.2	15,194.0	40,462.8	12,395.4
Norway	7,332.9	104,402.3	39,061.6	11,821.0	21,324.3	6,592.7
Portugal	4,518.3	840.7	28,324.0	6,276.1	12,348.5	10,839.5
Spain	34,675.7	2,023.3	145,642.0	38,210.9	134,249.9	105,149.8
Sweden	9,252.5	6,209.4	76,042.8	16,953.9	26,991.7	7,067.6
Switzerland	6,932.4	945.5	119,160.2	12,696.0	35,603.7	13,698.3
Turkey	64,330.3	11,239.9	120,638.6	18,089.3	32,180.0	17,353.8
United Kingdom	14,903.6	34,587.6	248,560.2	34,924.5	131,741.2	59,371.2
Eastern Europe						
Albania						
Belarus	4,242.6		14,683.7	778.9	6,272.1	
Bosnia-Herzegovina	1,211.6	347.3	2,014.7	812.5	739.2	352.4
Bulgaria	3,098.4	1,988.1	8,954.9	1,583.9	2,766.7	1,172.2
Croatia	3,089.5	397.1	7,830.0	1,925.1	3,272.9	2,445.0
Czech Republic	4,748.3	2,342.9	48,176.5	9,133.7	13,871.0	3,624.3
Estonia	629.2	306.5	3,534.1	859.7	1,026.1	237.7
Georgia	1,260.2	115.1	1,539.2	370.4	665.0	281.3
Hungary	5,974.7	213.4	31,347.5	3,983.9	4,115.4	1,529.0
Latvia	1,007.4	138.7	3,325.9	928.6	1,302.5	385.0
Lithuania	1,290.1	222.8	6,960.1	1,901.3	1,744.8	409.6
Macedonia	1,004.9	125.6	1,279.5	459.0	619.5	105.8
Moldova						
Montenegro	335.5	66.4	189.9	256.6	217.8	235.1
Poland	15,510.3	9,920.4	84,535.4	18,670.6	31,111.8	5,639.9
Romania	12,579.5	1,815.1	46,442.7	4,448.9	16,530.1	2,906.6
Russia	62,522.9	181,489.6	268,965.4	73,711.9	85,784.3	14,652.5
Serbia	3,559.0	541.2	6,256.0	1,626.0	1,467.9	398.8
Slovakia	3,272.0	536.5	18,364.8	3,753.3	7,728.1	1,154.6
Slovenia	1,067.6	178.2	9,131.4	1,420.4	2,539.8	998.5
Ukraine	12,821.9	10,251.1	24,415.0	5,295.7	4,827.3	1,003.2

Source: Euromonitor International from national statistics

GDP Origin 2011 *(continued)*

US$ million

	Wholesale and Retail Trade; Repair of Motor Vehicles/Goods	Transport, Storage and Communications	Financial Intermediation, Real Estate, Renting and Business Activities	Public Administration and Defence; Compulsory Social Security	Education, Health, Social Work and Other Community Activities	Activities of Households	GDP by origin
Western Europe							
Austria	50,701.4	20,909.6	89,773.2	21,992.6	59,182.3	138.6	379,148.0
Belgium	56,355.6	34,232.6	139,480.3	34,503.5	81,695.2	731.4	458,746.2
Cyprus							
Denmark	32,184.6	22,443.3	79,429.5	18,763.5	63,712.7	491.9	286,419.9
Finland	22,554.7	17,592.3	56,470.3	11,785.1	43,364.9	205.1	227,777.5
France	257,677.4	167,339.3	844,096.7	192,475.4	460,337.1	15,365.6	2,491,071.6
Germany	322,687.7	196,866.3	897,153.1	185,216.1	599,502.8	10,334.9	3,233,553.4
Gibraltar							
Greece	43,388.2	24,911.8	53,488.5	24,965.0	39,782.0	2,322.2	261,321.5
Iceland							
Ireland	17,462.3	10,877.4	53,419.5	11,361.5	33,968.4	204.2	200,261.5
Italy	218,532.3	142,208.7	563,848.4	134,540.4	279,795.9	22,617.4	1,966,591.0
Liechtenstein							
Luxembourg							
Malta							
Monaco							
Netherlands	97,057.7	44,699.9	206,450.8	55,545.6	136,765.2	3,282.9	752,307.8
Norway	33,578.9	21,711.6	85,812.2	21,633.9	78,550.5	398.0	432,219.7
Portugal	30,139.8	14,340.8	48,282.3	18,339.1	30,914.9	1,993.3	207,157.4
Spain	140,393.3	90,860.0	328,902.5	94,990.0	229,892.0	10,872.1	1,355,869.7
Sweden	55,012.9	33,861.4	118,682.2	22,561.2	97,934.5	207.1	470,777.2
Switzerland	84,876.7	38,018.9	183,692.9	66,896.7	57,243.2	3,125.4	622,889.8
Turkey	87,683.7	100,935.3	145,327.3	32,056.9	49,941.7	1,452.3	681,229.2
United Kingdom	240,446.2	156,289.8	699,835.9	105,169.6	406,091.0	8,309.2	2,140,230.1
Eastern Europe							
Albania							
Belarus	6,147.1	5,048.2	4,824.1	2,019.5	4,293.0		48,309.2
Bosnia-Herzegovina	2,345.4	1,222.7	2,226.0	1,589.3	2,077.1		14,938.3
Bulgaria	4,462.1	4,387.0	10,507.1	3,286.9	4,042.0		46,249.3
Croatia	5,877.6	3,821.0	15,068.8	3,192.1	7,078.8	49.5	54,047.5
Czech Republic	21,986.9	19,618.4	35,857.1	10,599.3	23,251.4	40.7	193,250.4
Estonia	2,338.2	2,356.1	4,408.4	1,358.4	2,268.5	5.8	19,328.6
Georgia	2,173.2	1,320.3	1,364.9	1,438.7	1,956.9	15.0	12,500.1
Hungary	13,402.3	9,016.7	25,615.0	9,631.6	14,655.3		119,484.8
Latvia	4,307.6	3,187.7	6,003.0	1,752.3	2,951.7		25,290.3
Lithuania	6,325.4	5,947.2	6,260.9	2,604.4	4,594.5	38.2	38,299.4
Macedonia	1,401.8	789.4	701.0	688.6	1,020.3		8,195.4
Moldova							
Montenegro	556.4	438.6	573.6	362.1	546.3		3,778.3
Poland	82,916.5	34,972.4	82,321.1	26,802.6	56,732.7	2,597.6	451,731.4
Romania	19,571.4	16,886.1	25,467.9	6,179.9	14,466.7		167,294.9
Russia	275,188.4	157,216.2	247,920.9	99,800.7	132,453.1		1,599,706.0
Serbia	4,224.9	3,361.4	8,817.0	1,398.4	5,604.8	37.7	37,293.1
Slovakia	13,033.5	6,582.7	17,185.1	6,593.6	9,478.4	0.0	87,682.6
Slovenia	5,411.3	3,304.7	10,129.8	2,900.2	6,581.9	37.4	43,701.3
Ukraine	22,273.4	17,394.3	23,258.3	6,818.7	15,504.8	1.7	143,865.5

Source: Euromonitor International from national statistics

9

Economic Indicators

Economic Statistics

Table 9.4

GDP Origin (% Analysis) 2011

% of total GDP

	Agriculture, Hunting, Forestry and Fishing	Mining and Quarrying	Manufacturing	Electricity, Gas and Water Supply	Construction	Hotels and Restaurants
Western Europe						
Austria	1.65	0.36	19.33	2.89	6.93	4.82
Belgium	0.72	0.11	14.12	2.32	5.34	1.76
Cyprus						
Denmark	1.11	3.55	12.07	1.97	4.12	1.42
Finland	2.92	0.56	19.05	2.70	6.40	1.65
France	2.02	0.13	10.16	1.75	5.84	2.34
Germany	1.02	0.17	21.66	2.92	4.21	1.63
Gibraltar						
Greece	3.27	0.37	10.57	2.63	3.54	7.35
Iceland						
Ireland	1.35	0.50	27.36	1.84	3.29	2.10
Italy	1.91	0.32	16.47	2.18	5.99	3.89
Liechtenstein						
Luxembourg						
Malta						
Monaco						
Netherlands	1.91	3.38	13.38	2.02	5.38	1.65
Norway	1.70	24.15	9.04	2.73	4.93	1.53
Portugal	2.18	0.41	13.67	3.03	5.96	5.23
Spain	2.56	0.15	10.74	2.82	9.90	7.76
Sweden	1.97	1.32	16.15	3.60	5.73	1.50
Switzerland	1.11	0.15	19.13	2.04	5.72	2.20
Turkey	9.44	1.65	17.71	2.66	4.72	2.55
United Kingdom	0.70	1.62	11.61	1.63	6.16	2.77
Eastern Europe						
Albania						
Belarus	8.78		30.40	1.61	12.98	
Bosnia-Herzegovina	8.11	2.32	13.49	5.44	4.95	2.36
Bulgaria	6.70	4.30	19.36	3.42	5.98	2.53
Croatia	5.72	0.73	14.49	3.56	6.06	4.52
Czech Republic	2.46	1.21	24.93	4.73	7.18	1.88
Estonia	3.26	1.59	18.28	4.45	5.31	1.23
Georgia	10.08	0.92	12.31	2.96	5.32	2.25
Hungary	5.00	0.18	26.24	3.33	3.44	1.28
Latvia	3.98	0.55	13.15	3.67	5.15	1.52
Lithuania	3.37	0.58	18.17	4.96	4.56	1.07
Macedonia	12.26	1.53	15.61	5.60	7.56	1.29
Moldova						
Montenegro	8.88	1.76	5.03	6.79	5.77	6.22
Poland	3.43	2.20	18.71	4.13	6.89	1.25
Romania	7.52	1.08	27.76	2.66	9.88	1.74
Russia	3.91	11.35	16.81	4.61	5.36	0.92
Serbia	9.54	1.45	16.78	4.36	3.94	1.07
Slovakia	3.73	0.61	20.94	4.28	8.81	1.32
Slovenia	2.44	0.41	20.90	3.25	5.81	2.28
Ukraine	8.91	7.13	16.97	3.68	3.36	0.70

Source: Euromonitor International from national statistics

GDP Origin (% Analysis) 2011 *(continued)*

% of total GDP

	Wholesale and Retail Trade; Repair of Motor Vehicles/Goods	Transport, Storage and Communications	Financial Intermediation, Real Estate, Renting and Business Activities	Public Administration and Defence; Compulsory Social Security	Education, Health, Social Work and Other Community Activities	Activities of Households	GDP by origin
Western Europe							
Austria	13.37	5.51	23.68	5.80	15.61	0.04	100.00
Belgium	12.28	7.46	30.40	7.52	17.81	0.16	100.00
Cyprus							
Denmark	11.24	7.84	27.73	6.55	22.24	0.17	100.00
Finland	9.90	7.72	24.79	5.17	19.04	0.09	100.00
France	10.34	6.72	33.88	7.73	18.48	0.62	100.00
Germany	9.98	6.09	27.75	5.73	18.54	0.32	100.00
Gibraltar							
Greece	16.60	9.53	20.47	9.55	15.22	0.89	100.00
Iceland							
Ireland	8.72	5.43	26.67	5.67	16.96	0.10	100.00
Italy	11.11	7.23	28.67	6.84	14.23	1.15	100.00
Liechtenstein							
Luxembourg							
Malta							
Monaco							
Netherlands	12.90	5.94	27.44	7.38	18.18	0.44	100.00
Norway	7.77	5.02	19.85	5.01	18.17	0.09	100.00
Portugal	14.55	6.92	23.31	8.85	14.92	0.96	100.00
Spain	10.35	6.70	24.26	7.01	16.96	0.80	100.00
Sweden	11.69	7.19	25.21	4.79	20.80	0.04	100.00
Switzerland	13.63	6.10	29.49	10.74	9.19	0.50	100.00
Turkey	12.87	14.82	21.33	4.71	7.33	0.21	100.00
United Kingdom	11.23	7.30	32.70	4.91	18.97	0.39	100.00
Eastern Europe							
Albania							
Belarus	12.72	10.45	9.99	4.18	8.89		100.00
Bosnia-Herzegovina	15.70	8.18	14.90	10.64	13.90		100.00
Bulgaria	9.65	9.49	22.72	7.11	8.74		100.00
Croatia	10.87	7.07	27.88	5.91	13.10	0.09	100.00
Czech Republic	11.38	10.15	18.55	5.48	12.03	0.02	100.00
Estonia	12.10	12.19	22.81	7.03	11.74	0.03	100.00
Georgia	17.39	10.56	10.92	11.51	15.66	0.12	100.00
Hungary	11.22	7.55	21.44	8.06	12.27		100.00
Latvia	17.03	12.60	23.74	6.93	11.67		100.00
Lithuania	16.52	15.53	16.35	6.80	12.00	0.10	100.00
Macedonia	17.11	9.63	8.55	8.40	12.45		100.00
Moldova							
Montenegro	14.73	11.61	15.18	9.58	14.46		100.00
Poland	18.36	7.74	18.22	5.93	12.56	0.58	100.00
Romania	11.70	10.09	15.22	3.69	8.65		100.00
Russia	17.20	9.83	15.50	6.24	8.28		100.00
Serbia	11.33	9.01	23.64	3.75	15.03	0.10	100.00
Slovakia	14.86	7.51	19.60	7.52	10.81	0.00	100.00
Slovenia	12.38	7.56	23.18	6.64	15.06	0.09	100.00
Ukraine	15.48	12.09	16.17	4.74	10.78	0.00	100.00

Source: Euromonitor International from national statistics

Economic Statistics

Table 9.5

GDP Usage 2011

US$ million

	Government Final Consumption	Private Final Consumption	Increases in Stocks	Gross Fixed Capital Formation	Exports of Goods and Services	Imports of Goods and Services	Total
Western Europe							
Austria	78,698.3	227,497.2	7,413.5	89,614.2	239,548.3	225,659.2	418,120.2
Belgium	125,271.0	270,704.6	5,678.5	106,237.3	433,717.4	427,375.6	514,234.5
Cyprus	4,799.9	16,545.0	29.5	4,090.2	10,704.9	11,473.4	24,696.0
Denmark	95,051.1	161,452.2	1,013.8	57,049.7	178,923.6	160,918.0	332,572.5
Finland	63,930.7	146,030.1	3,403.8	51,575.3	107,181.4	108,959.8	263,303.3
France	680,402.2	1,600,741.5	15,133.5	557,844.0	748,316.5	826,326.7	2,776,113.8
Germany	694,896.1	2,068,489.7	5,089.0	653,294.4	1,808,687.6	1,625,623.3	3,604,833.4
Gibraltar							1,713.7
Greece	52,189.6	225,695.2	1,733.2	41,730.3	71,836.4	94,119.0	299,065.3
Iceland	3,544.7	7,350.0	36.7	1,980.9	8,207.0	7,060.7	14,058.6
Ireland	40,631.9	107,752.2	294.5	22,422.8	231,911.8	183,362.6	221,068.4
Italy	450,805.8	1,347,455.3	2,233.7	429,033.7	631,922.0	664,262.2	2,197,188.4
Liechtenstein	725.3	3,617.1	-76.6	1,271.1	3,268.4	2,598.5	5,727.3
Luxembourg	9,822.8	19,847.3	1,012.8	11,295.0	98,084.5	80,521.9	59,540.7
Malta	1,878.6	5,485.3	-207.3	1,337.7	8,847.9	8,406.8	8,935.3
Monaco	1,492.2	3,448.6	-18.8	1,104.3	1,468.2	1,621.6	5,872.9
Netherlands	233,810.8	376,961.3	3,088.1	148,345.2	694,687.5	619,890.6	837,002.4
Norway	104,496.4	201,323.3	12,536.5	98,110.0	204,282.2	137,311.5	485,294.8
Portugal	47,776.5	157,586.8	-1,495.0	42,999.1	84,448.0	93,651.6	237,664.3
Spain	309,678.4	862,084.4	7,078.7	311,405.3	447,467.4	459,191.5	1,478,522.6
Sweden	142,902.0	256,197.8	6,257.8	98,880.5	269,502.5	236,054.6	537,686.0
Switzerland	73,455.0	379,002.2	2,309.7	134,810.0	338,301.3	264,647.1	660,713.2
Turkey	107,557.2	549,860.4	15,695.6	168,381.3	183,461.4	252,188.7	772,767.1
United Kingdom	543,267.6	1,561,301.3	16,492.0	345,299.7	789,496.8	827,899.0	2,429,732.4
Eastern Europe							
Albania	1,306.4	10,285.5		4,226.0	4,385.7	7,316.4	13,004.7
Belarus	8,300.0	28,474.1	-921.1	20,939.4	48,460.3	49,621.2	55,136.2
Bosnia-Herzegovina	3,955.2	14,589.8		3,516.0	6,711.9	10,054.4	18,246.2
Bulgaria	8,320.9	32,485.5	1,152.5	11,193.1	35,594.0	35,231.8	53,514.3
Croatia	12,424.4	36,963.3	1,424.3	11,741.7	26,109.7	26,170.0	62,493.3
Czech Republic	44,786.2	108,573.9	1,191.7	51,606.7	161,283.8	152,261.5	215,180.7
Estonia	4,329.2	11,333.1	680.1	4,811.0	20,296.0	19,421.4	22,179.3
Georgia	2,901.4	10,653.5	124.9	2,258.3	5,046.4	7,099.4	14,366.4
Hungary	29,052.7	73,994.9	2,889.8	23,425.7	129,202.5	118,900.4	139,665.2
Latvia	4,543.2	17,482.2	1,557.7	6,023.6	16,605.3	17,966.7	28,244.9
Lithuania	8,057.2	27,225.8	514.9	7,510.9	33,301.4	33,916.5	42,693.7
Macedonia	1,871.4	7,809.3	400.8	2,035.2	5,694.4	7,734.7	10,143.8
Moldova	1,423.5	6,747.0	93.2	1,621.2	2,693.8	5,153.2	7,000.3
Montenegro	1,089.5	3,774.1	78.4	770.9	1,650.3	2,870.9	4,532.8
Poland	93,185.0	315,228.7	7,870.4	103,890.0	230,698.2	236,383.1	514,489.2
Romania	27,305.6	117,566.1	8,063.4	46,609.3	72,768.3	82,537.0	189,775.7
Russia	332,797.4	934,718.8	68,862.2	395,358.6	576,673.4	413,917.6	1,857,156.1
Serbia	8,474.5	35,408.1	-1,137.9	7,535.0	16,818.6	23,014.3	44,187.1
Slovakia	17,419.5	55,248.5	-607.1	21,520.0	85,538.1	83,037.0	96,020.7
Slovenia	10,474.4	29,085.3	815.6	9,307.7	36,431.3	35,820.0	50,294.6
Ukraine	29,940.9	108,689.1	4,343.0	31,088.9	88,801.5	97,716.7	165,146.7

Source: Euromonitor International from national statistics
Note: The difference between the sum of GDP by usage components and Total GDP (usually production approach measured GDP) appears due to the statistical discrepancies

Economic Statistics Table 9.6

GDP Usage (% Analysis) 2011
% of total GDP

	Government Final Consumption	Private Final Consumption	Increases in Stocks	Gross Fixed Capital Formation	Exports of Goods and Services	Imports of Goods and Services	Total
Western Europe							
Austria	18.82	54.41	1.77	21.43	57.29	53.97	100.00
Belgium	24.36	52.64	1.10	20.66	84.34	83.11	100.00
Cyprus	19.44	66.99	0.12	16.56	43.35	46.46	100.00
Denmark	28.58	48.55	0.30	17.15	53.80	48.39	100.00
Finland	24.28	55.46	1.29	19.59	40.71	41.38	100.00
France	24.51	57.66	0.55	20.09	26.96	29.77	100.00
Germany	19.28	57.38	0.14	18.12	50.17	45.10	100.00
Gibraltar							100.00
Greece	17.45	75.47	0.58	13.95	24.02	31.47	100.00
Iceland	25.21	52.28	0.26	14.09	58.38	50.22	100.00
Ireland	18.38	48.74	0.13	10.14	104.91	82.94	100.00
Italy	20.52	61.33	0.10	19.53	28.76	30.23	100.00
Liechtenstein	12.66	63.15	-1.34	22.19	57.07	45.37	100.00
Luxembourg	16.50	33.33	1.70	18.97	164.74	135.24	100.00
Malta	21.02	61.39	-2.32	14.97	99.02	94.09	100.00
Monaco	25.41	58.72	-0.32	18.80	25.00	27.61	100.00
Netherlands	27.93	45.04	0.37	17.72	83.00	74.06	100.00
Norway	21.53	41.48	2.58	20.22	42.09	28.29	100.00
Portugal	20.10	66.31	-0.63	18.09	35.53	39.40	100.00
Spain	20.95	58.31	0.48	21.06	30.26	31.06	100.00
Sweden	26.58	47.65	1.16	18.39	50.12	43.90	100.00
Switzerland	11.12	57.36	0.35	20.40	51.20	40.05	100.00
Turkey	13.92	71.15	2.03	21.79	23.74	32.63	100.00
United Kingdom	22.36	64.26	0.68	14.21	32.49	34.07	100.00
Eastern Europe							
Albania	10.05	79.09		32.50	33.72	56.26	100.00
Belarus	15.05	51.64	-1.67	37.98	87.89	90.00	100.00
Bosnia-Herzegovina	21.68	79.96		19.27	36.79	55.10	100.00
Bulgaria	15.55	60.70	2.15	20.92	66.51	65.84	100.00
Croatia	19.88	59.15	2.28	18.79	41.78	41.88	100.00
Czech Republic	20.81	50.46	0.55	23.98	74.95	70.76	100.00
Estonia	19.52	51.10	3.07	21.69	91.51	87.57	100.00
Georgia	20.20	74.16	0.87	15.72	35.13	49.42	100.00
Hungary	20.80	52.98	2.07	16.77	92.51	85.13	100.00
Latvia	16.09	61.90	5.52	21.33	58.79	63.61	100.00
Lithuania	18.87	63.77	1.21	17.59	78.00	79.44	100.00
Macedonia	18.45	76.99	3.95	20.06	56.14	76.25	100.00
Moldova	20.34	96.38	1.33	23.16	38.48	73.61	100.00
Montenegro	24.04	83.26	1.73	17.01	36.41	63.34	100.00
Poland	18.11	61.27	1.53	20.19	44.84	45.95	100.00
Romania	14.39	61.95	4.25	24.56	38.34	43.49	100.00
Russia	17.92	50.33	3.71	21.29	31.05	22.29	100.00
Serbia	19.18	80.13	-2.58	17.05	38.06	52.08	100.00
Slovakia	18.14	57.54	-0.63	22.41	89.08	86.48	100.00
Slovenia	20.83	57.83	1.62	18.51	72.44	71.22	100.00
Ukraine	18.13	65.81	2.63	18.83	53.77	59.17	100.00

Source: Euromonitor International from national statistics
Note: The difference between the sum of GDP by usage components and Total GDP (usually production approach measured GDP) appears due to the statistical discrepancies

Economic Statistics   **Table 9.7**

Gross National Income in National Currencies 1980, 1985, 1990, 1995, 1999-2011

National currency million

	1980	1985	1990	1995	1999	2000	2001	2002	2003	2004
Western Europe										
Austria	75,470	102,016	135,860	172,515	195,736	204,954	209,654	217,799	222,825	232,959
Belgium	88,334	122,081	163,855	211,663	243,515	258,312	263,966	272,256	280,359	294,510
Cyprus	1,514	3,086	4,232	6,612	8,850	9,419	10,209	10,780	11,487	12,182
Denmark	382,155	615,288	818,974	1,008,640	1,203,240	1,266,610	1,316,780	1,356,520	1,392,120	1,472,920
Finland	32,767	56,401	86,923	94,269	120,733	131,185	139,095	143,885	144,428	153,416
France	442,342	725,315	1,006,426	1,198,118	1,388,230	1,461,240	1,516,670	1,554,150	1,604,690	1,674,840
Germany	755,394	937,979	1,251,764	1,834,789	1,978,650	2,026,820	2,075,830	2,103,160	2,130,460	2,214,580
Gibraltar										
Greece	5,543	14,374	41,542	88,102	122,003	136,648	147,352	157,028	171,412	183,951
Iceland	15,675	117,211	359,053	441,303	620,011	664,837	747,638	815,123	828,135	891,145
Ireland	11,510	20,460	32,396	46,953	77,946	91,369	100,037	109,158	120,689	129,146
Italy	199,501	415,559	673,202	909,863	1,126,970	1,190,430	1,247,220	1,292,930	1,333,380	1,391,380
Liechtenstein	881	1,278	1,941	2,823	3,869	4,112	3,782	3,698	3,538	3,554
Luxembourg	3,989	6,535	9,990	14,046	17,868	19,170	20,050	19,898	20,028	23,987
Malta	1,337	1,275	1,772	3,242	3,740	3,784	3,962	4,242	4,419	4,513
Monaco										
Netherlands	154,449	193,089	241,845	309,796	390,395	426,980	451,110	469,468	482,368	504,333
Norway	305,071	542,876	715,315	931,980	1,230,020	1,461,260	1,538,260	1,537,010	1,602,110	1,756,170
Portugal	7,619	20,721	52,979	84,969	112,276	119,259	125,494	132,632	136,725	141,157
Spain	90,627	167,502	298,661	436,695	559,562	603,252	644,093	687,643	735,064	793,300
Sweden	549,779	883,312	1,396,300	1,767,190	2,118,870	2,246,400	2,331,320	2,434,050	2,576,240	2,660,470
Switzerland	191,871	256,988	339,321	384,183	428,836	453,081	450,145	448,282	470,784	482,766
Turkey	5	34	387	7,616	103,115	164,156	234,096	343,609	446,440	551,037
United Kingdom	228,084	352,581	560,449	727,497	924,729	974,483	1,027,710	1,091,500	1,155,210	1,219,760
Eastern Europe										
Albania		16,875	16,798	228,787	482,724	545,860	608,625	642,633	702,895	785,055
Belarus			4	121,351	3,028,910	9,096,100	17,113,100	26,084,300	36,616,300	49,951,600
Bosnia-Herzegovina			1	2,860	8,990	10,713	11,599	12,829	14,505	16,680
Bulgaria				852	23,997	26,744	30,372	33,969	36,399	40,361
Croatia			278	115,423	160,490	172,828	186,173	203,988	219,120	241,118
Czech Republic				1,463,500	2,031,710	2,139,690	2,273,220	2,352,130	2,466,090	2,660,120
Estonia				3,350	5,287	5,962	6,688	7,456	8,269	9,221
Georgia				2,324	5,963	6,275	6,741	7,482	8,593	9,976
Hungary	708,391	990,203	1,997,350	5,401,680	10,725,100	12,936,700	14,556,500	16,281,800	18,069,200	19,638,800
Latvia				2,631	4,225	4,739	5,233	5,775	6,372	7,274
Lithuania				26,896	42,651	45,203	48,238	51,842	55,830	61,780
Macedonia			500	168,014	206,325	233,339	231,027	242,004	249,648	263,428
Moldova				6,480	12,678	16,814	20,484	24,805	30,838	36,414
Montenegro					1,119	1,360	1,436	1,598	1,756	
Poland			52,839	332,385	662,301	741,157	777,129	804,276	833,630	894,534
Romania			85	7,165	53,943	79,759	115,949	149,958	195,224	241,216
Russia			643	1,416,320	4,633,230	7,116,120	8,819,980	10,624,100	12,839,000	16,680,200
Serbia					205,712	384,209	762,577	967,879	1,118,010	1,368,100
Slovakia	6,085	7,678	9,235	19,295	27,673	30,610	33,354	36,094	40,436	44,691
Slovenia				10,385	16,861	18,492	20,698	23,000	24,920	26,760
Ukraine				53,639	126,934	164,942	200,610	222,585	264,247	341,686

Source: Euromonitor International from national statistics

Gross National Income in National Currencies 1980, 1985, 1990, 1995, 1999-2011 *(continued)*

National currency million

	2005	2006	2007	2008	2009	2010	2011	US$ million 2011	US$ per capita 2011
Western Europe									
Austria	242,863	256,249	270,717	282,184	273,006	284,682	300,247	417,472.97	49,674.02
Belgium	305,344	321,421	338,976	351,097	338,297	360,621	375,392	521,956.96	47,661.79
Cyprus	13,174	14,081	15,606	16,948	16,097	16,858	17,156	23,853.83	21,372.26
Denmark	1,566,810	1,662,100	1,713,510	1,780,890	1,694,630	1,795,610	1,843,880	344,021.63	61,867.41
Finland	158,154	167,337	179,907	186,629	175,267	182,686	193,671	269,286.31	50,097.21
France	1,742,950	1,831,410	1,920,230	1,965,710	1,920,940	1,972,970	2,032,990	2,826,733.89	44,777.98
Germany	2,250,400	2,361,940	2,468,070	2,501,700	2,424,320	2,524,880	2,621,100	3,644,460.72	44,579.69
Gibraltar									
Greece	190,240	204,341	216,488	225,324	225,999	221,120	208,242	289,546.29	25,564.98
Iceland	989,764	1,100,400	1,236,760	1,163,730	1,221,140	1,265,180	1,389,600	11,984.06	36,982.60
Ireland	141,009	155,033	163,413	154,673	132,233	128,207	123,879	172,245.30	38,440.25
Italy	1,437,500	1,499,270	1,553,040	1,557,600	1,512,210	1,544,250	1,570,320	2,183,422.82	36,014.37
Liechtenstein	3,892	4,399	4,520	4,665	4,670	4,761	4,704	5,296.27	146,512.08
Luxembourg	26,007	25,800	30,158	29,729	25,126	28,634	30,646	42,611.73	82,885.26
Malta	4,643	4,967	5,356	5,594	5,333	5,671	5,978	8,311.78	19,878.65
Monaco									
Netherlands	515,885	554,741	581,275	581,855	559,385	579,317	607,180	844,242.36	50,687.59
Norway	1,972,360	2,182,370	2,299,170	2,548,100	2,370,060	2,553,440	2,768,190	493,802.13	100,360.06
Portugal	145,243	149,142	156,112	158,652	156,007	159,106	158,538	220,435.64	20,723.52
Spain	858,790	933,564	990,081	1,013,823	968,896	958,089	1,001,022	1,391,852.65	30,157.41
Sweden	2,789,270	2,982,310	3,197,270	3,316,060	3,164,260	3,397,530	3,568,880	549,449.58	58,355.42
Switzerland	506,163	532,171	524,368	501,415	462,878	445,765	494,243	556,512.41	70,711.94
Turkey	641,038	748,833	833,917	939,915	942,115	1,097,820	1,243,280	740,153.86	10,095.99
United Kingdom	1,275,330	1,336,830	1,425,380	1,465,150	1,413,420	1,470,160	1,526,480	2,446,282.05	39,141.38
Eastern Europe									
Albania	852,996	920,753	1,006,970	1,088,680	1,113,500	1,160,757	1,277,573	12,662.40	3,938.92
Belarus	65,186,600	79,020,900	96,283,300	128,108,000	134,332,000	161,013,000	265,550,000	53,380.85	5,630.18
Bosnia-Herzegovina	18,178	21,366	24,709	27,934	27,133	27,406	29,591	21,037.06	5,473.10
Bulgaria	45,438	50,467	55,788	66,095	66,793	69,107	73,294	52,112.45	6,932.84
Croatia	257,880	277,766	306,138	330,385	322,347	323,341	332,641	62,247.21	14,108.18
Czech Republic	2,849,950	3,062,350	3,288,160	3,668,010	3,488,770	3,521,040	3,549,350	200,575.47	19,128.35
Estonia	10,761	12,697	14,733	15,233	13,541	13,733	14,841	20,635.59	15,397.47
Georgia	11,734	14,082	17,055	18,830	17,658	19,714	22,949	13,607.55	3,097.36
Hungary	20,825,900	22,402,000	23,674,200	24,497,500	24,521,600	25,280,223	26,256,200	130,592.44	13,077.92
Latvia	8,945	10,842	14,305	16,029	14,081	13,005	14,263	28,220.13	13,602.65
Lithuania	71,301	81,541	95,506	108,610	93,938	93,860	102,953	41,458.85	12,777.80
Macedonia	283,712	310,221	348,334	394,707	396,476	411,191	441,596	9,983.89	4,853.68
Moldova	42,740	50,026	58,410	69,098	63,834	77,884	97,907	8,340.61	2,345.65
Montenegro	1,832	2,180	2,697	3,093	2,944	2,909	3,121	4,339.26	6,998.48
Poland	961,677	1,030,030	1,132,060	1,239,240	1,298,400	1,346,740	1,430,869	482,834.16	12,643.17
Romania	285,562	336,587	412,286	501,918	500,308	526,927	542,359	177,903.92	8,304.06
Russia	21,087,300	26,097,100	32,308,600	40,230,400	37,926,100	43,667,087	52,088,706	1,772,204.02	12,400.48
Serbia	1,665,240	1,941,290	2,228,760	2,586,950	2,677,400	2,817,810	3,319,945	45,271.94	6,223.02
Slovakia	47,245	52,985	58,924	65,166	60,960	64,272	66,538	92,515.88	17,142.97
Slovenia	28,506	30,683	33,828	36,232	34,593	34,894	35,050	48,734.49	23,770.73
Ukraine	436,411	535,459	717,406	939,356	894,306	1,078,920	1,297,840	162,793.51	3,570.18

Source: Euromonitor International from national statistics

9

Economic Indicators

Economic Statistics

Table 9.8

Gross National Income in US$ 1980, 1985, 1990, 1995, 1999-2011

US$ million

	1980	1985	1990	1995	1999	2000	2001	2002	2003
Western Europe									
Austria	105,079	77,847	173,009	225,652	208,559	188,869	187,647	205,156	251,551
Belgium	122,990	93,158	208,658	276,857	259,468	238,039	236,258	256,452	316,502
Cyprus	2,108	2,355	5,389	8,649	9,430	8,680	9,138	10,154	12,968
Denmark	67,807	58,066	132,337	180,038	172,477	156,603	158,251	172,054	211,665
Finland	45,623	43,039	110,690	123,304	128,642	120,890	124,494	135,533	163,047
France	615,885	553,479	1,281,612	1,567,151	1,479,176	1,346,561	1,357,466	1,463,934	1,811,564
Germany	1,051,757	715,761	1,594,033	2,399,923	2,108,275	1,867,754	1,857,932	1,981,075	2,405,115
Gibraltar									
Greece	7,717	10,968	52,900	115,238	129,996	125,924	131,885	147,913	193,510
Iceland	3,267	2,824	6,160	6,822	8,571	8,457	7,674	8,893	10,796
Ireland	16,026	15,613	41,254	61,415	83,052	84,198	89,536	102,822	136,248
Italy	277,771	317,108	857,275	1,190,110	1,200,800	1,097,004	1,116,300	1,217,877	1,505,277
Liechtenstein	526	520	1,397	2,387	2,576	2,435	2,241	2,374	2,627
Luxembourg	5,554	4,987	12,721	18,372	19,039	17,666	17,946	18,743	22,610
Malta	1,861	973	2,256	4,240	3,985	3,487	3,546	3,996	4,988
Monaco									
Netherlands	215,044	147,344	307,973	405,216	415,971	393,470	403,757	442,216	544,554
Norway	61,765	63,145	114,272	147,112	157,712	166,017	171,084	192,513	226,286
Portugal	10,608	15,812	67,465	111,141	119,631	109,899	112,321	124,933	154,351
Spain	126,183	127,819	380,324	571,202	596,220	555,908	576,483	647,726	829,827
Sweden	129,985	102,664	235,910	247,739	256,446	245,220	225,667	250,274	318,630
Switzerland	114,501	104,589	244,263	324,899	285,480	268,279	266,734	287,773	349,603
Turkey	67,651	65,682	148,168	166,117	246,225	262,558	191,007	227,974	297,451
United Kingdom	530,064	452,464	995,156	1,148,073	1,496,187	1,474,572	1,479,252	1,637,270	1,886,776
Eastern Europe									
Albania		2,411	2,169	2,468	3,506	3,798	4,242	4,585	5,768
Belarus			18,833	13,839	12,150	10,375	12,312	14,565	17,851
Bosnia-Herzegovina			7,740	2,043	4,898	5,048	5,308	6,179	8,372
Bulgaria				12,679	13,073	12,595	13,902	16,355	21,008
Croatia			24,590	22,066	22,567	20,879	22,319	25,914	32,680
Czech Republic				55,142	58,772	55,435	59,766	71,846	87,422
Estonia				4,382	5,634	5,494	5,986	7,023	9,335
Georgia			8,410	1,700	2,945	3,175	3,252	3,407	4,005
Hungary	21,775	19,757	31,601	42,979	45,226	45,846	50,810	63,135	80,556
Latvia				4,988	7,220	7,814	8,333	9,342	11,150
Lithuania				6,724	10,663	11,301	12,060	14,114	18,254
Macedonia			4,418	4,435	3,626	3,541	3,396	3,761	4,596
Moldova				1,766	1,206	1,352	1,592	1,828	2,211
Montenegro						1,032	1,217	1,353	1,804
Poland			55,620	137,067	166,948	170,535	189,826	197,125	214,352
Romania			38,105	35,236	35,181	36,741	39,899	45,366	58,802
Russia			613,135	395,756	188,190	252,980	302,380	338,903	418,317
Serbia					10,861	8,728	11,396	15,030	19,415
Slovakia	8,472	5,859	11,760	25,238	29,486	28,208	29,852	33,998	45,649
Slovenia				13,584	17,965	17,041	18,526	21,665	28,133
Ukraine				47,826	30,731	30,319	37,343	41,787	49,552

Source: Euromonitor International from national statistics

Gross National Income in US$ 1980, 1985, 1990, 1995, 1999-2011 *(continued)*

US$ million

	2004	2005	2006	2007	2008	2009	2010	2011	US$ per capita 2011
Western Europe									
Austria	289,347	301,839	321,476	370,523	412,969	379,367	377,014	417,473	49,674.02
Belgium	365,796	379,492	403,238	463,948	513,821	470,095	477,582	521,957	47,661.79
Cyprus	15,130	16,373	17,665	21,360	24,804	22,368	22,325	23,854	21,372.26
Denmark	245,997	261,305	279,673	314,823	349,181	316,111	319,272	344,022	61,867.41
Finland	190,550	196,559	209,932	246,234	273,127	243,550	241,937	269,286	50,097.21
France	2,080,235	2,166,199	2,297,589	2,628,169	2,876,766	2,669,323	2,612,868	2,826,734	44,777.98
Germany	2,750,619	2,796,876	2,963,164	3,377,983	3,661,173	3,368,815	3,343,780	3,644,461	44,579.69
Gibraltar									
Greece	228,476	236,437	256,355	296,301	329,756	314,046	292,836	289,546	25,564.98
Iceland	12,696	15,715	15,680	19,308	13,232	9,877	10,350	11,984	36,982.60
Ireland	160,406	175,251	194,496	223,659	226,360	183,750	169,789	172,245	38,440.25
Italy	1,728,163	1,786,575	1,880,904	2,125,605	2,279,507	2,101,355	2,045,100	2,183,423	36,014.37
Liechtenstein	2,858	3,124	3,508	3,766	4,307	4,298	4,565	5,296	146,512.08
Luxembourg	29,793	32,322	32,367	41,277	43,508	34,915	37,921	42,612	82,885.26
Malta	5,606	5,771	6,231	7,331	8,186	7,410	7,510	8,312	19,878.65
Monaco									
Netherlands	626,407	641,160	695,948	795,576	851,530	777,317	767,208	844,242	50,687.59
Norway	260,511	306,144	340,277	392,286	451,870	376,809	422,498	493,802	100,360.06
Portugal	175,324	180,513	187,106	213,666	232,183	216,786	210,709	220,436	20,723.52
Spain	985,317	1,067,335	1,171,199	1,355,098	1,483,704	1,346,371	1,268,828	1,391,853	30,157.41
Sweden	361,942	373,414	404,330	472,905	503,192	413,441	471,377	549,450	58,355.42
Switzerland	388,224	406,243	424,432	436,846	462,949	425,962	427,457	556,512	70,711.94
Turkey	386,547	476,373	521,229	638,670	720,329	605,751	728,549	740,154	10,095.99
United Kingdom	2,233,481	2,317,974	2,460,046	2,852,281	2,685,885	2,203,820	2,270,634	2,446,282	39,141.38
Eastern Europe									
Albania	7,638	8,541	9,386	11,136	12,977	11,724	11,168	12,662	3,938.92
Belarus	23,123	30,266	36,847	44,865	59,964	48,095	54,058	53,381	5,630.18
Bosnia-Herzegovina	10,593	11,551	13,705	17,291	20,902	19,278	18,557	21,037	5,473.10
Bulgaria	25,624	28,865	32,365	39,039	49,427	47,482	46,777	52,112	6,932.84
Croatia	39,958	43,347	47,581	57,067	66,947	61,005	58,811	62,247	14,108.18
Czech Republic	103,508	118,959	135,529	162,029	214,860	182,992	184,372	200,575	19,128.35
Estonia	11,453	13,374	15,929	20,164	22,294	18,817	18,187	20,636	15,397.47
Georgia	5,205	6,473	7,910	10,210	12,631	10,571	11,061	13,608	3,097.36
Hungary	96,864	104,347	106,478	128,926	142,334	121,189	121,572	130,592	13,077.92
Latvia	13,465	15,839	19,346	27,843	33,337	27,904	24,508	28,220	13,602.65
Lithuania	22,224	25,665	29,627	37,858	46,035	37,806	36,000	41,459	12,777.80
Macedonia	5,331	5,757	6,357	7,788	9,427	8,990	8,846	9,984	4,853.68
Moldova	2,953	3,392	3,810	4,811	6,649	5,746	6,297	8,341	2,345.65
Montenegro	2,181	2,277	2,735	3,692	4,527	4,091	3,853	4,339	6,998.48
Poland	244,566	297,228	331,930	408,989	514,213	416,015	446,723	482,834	12,643.17
Romania	73,910	98,008	119,825	169,091	199,264	164,072	165,810	177,904	8,304.06
Russia	578,897	745,544	959,771	1,263,000	1,618,742	1,194,092	1,437,951	1,772,204	12,400.48
Serbia	23,434	24,961	28,912	38,129	46,425	39,618	36,252	45,272	6,223.02
Slovakia	55,509	58,718	66,472	80,648	95,369	84,710	85,117	92,516	17,142.97
Slovenia	33,238	35,428	38,493	46,299	53,024	48,071	46,211	48,734	23,770.73
Ukraine	64,236	85,158	106,031	142,061	178,340	114,785	135,929	162,794	3,570.18

Source: Euromonitor International from national statistics

9

Economic Indicators

Economic Statistics | **Table 9.9**

Money Supply 1985, 1990, 1995, 2000, 2006-2011

National currency billion

	1985	1990	1995	2000	2006	2007	2008	2009	2010	2011	US$ billion 2011
Western Europe											
Austria				53.3	97.8	105.2	113.7	130.9	132.2	140.9	195.90
Belgium				68.5	111.8	120.4	123.7	137.6	139.8	137.4	190.98
Cyprus							9.2	10.7	11.5	12.5	17.32
Denmark			290.9	386.6	699.3	755.1	753.2	793.1	800.4	775.2	144.63
Finland				42.0	61.3	64.2	67.4	78.5	83.7	87.9	122.27
France				327.8	544.9	578.5	586.8	625.7	673.4	702.2	976.43
Germany				533.5	920.6	962.7	1,027.6	1,207.7	1,307.6	1,379.0	1,917.44
Gibraltar											
Greece				68.2	114.2	113.8	107.7	122.7	111.6	96.6	134.25
Iceland				72.5	211.5	410.8	569.1	507.3	495.8	497.3	4.29
Ireland				18.1	86.1	92.5	80.3	102.5	99.1	93.0	129.34
Italy				462.6	732.5	757.1	817.2	901.7	895.4	881.6	1,225.81
Liechtenstein											
Luxembourg				50.9	77.0	84.5	87.7	92.1	113.6	120.6	167.74
Malta							3.8	4.3	5.0	5.6	7.74
Monaco											
Netherlands				146.8	236.6	234.6	237.7	272.2	307.0	316.0	439.33
Norway				370.4	679.5	760.4	736.5	744.3	788.5	824.8	147.14
Portugal				49.2	71.2	70.6	70.2	71.9	71.7	68.9	95.85
Spain				171.2	552.8	549.1	536.3	593.6	597.9	596.3	829.16
Sweden				770.5	1,191.9	1,289.5	1,372.9	1,486.0	1,584.7	1,598.6	246.11
Switzerland	100.0	119.3	155.2	202.8	278.4	271.2	328.8	396.7	432.8	481.9	542.66
Turkey				7.3	67.2	74.7	81.5	107.3	135.2	161.2	95.97
United Kingdom		179.0	249.2	451.8	836.5	922.3	1,029.3	1,061.4	1,080.4	1,081.4	1,732.98
Eastern Europe											
Albania					242.4	242.7	282.9	284.5	275.4	276.9	2.74
Belarus				469.2	7,023.2	8,739.9	10,718.5	11,342.0	13,662.9	20,340.3	4.09
Bosnia-Herzegovina				1.4	4.7	5.7	5.7	5.5	5.9	6.2	4.40
Bulgaria				4.8	16.1	20.7	19.9	18.1	18.4	21.0	14.95
Croatia			8.2	18.0	48.5	57.9	55.2	47.2	49.2	52.9	9.89
Czech Republic				499.0	1,325.6	1,526.6	1,675.0	1,771.8	2,021.7	2,149.8	121.48
Estonia				1.5	4.6	4.9	4.3	4.1	4.9	7.2	10.04
Georgia			0.2	0.4	1.3	1.8	1.6	1.9	2.3	2.5	1.47
Hungary				2,653.8	5,833.3	6,348.3	6,162.0	6,121.6	6,635.1	7,341.6	36.52
Latvia				0.8	4.1	3.9	3.3	3.0	3.8	4.4	8.62
Lithuania			4.0	6.5	24.8	27.9	23.3	22.0	27.4	31.3	12.60
Macedonia					36.2	47.3	54.1	52.2	57.4	61.3	1.39
Moldova			0.9	2.0	8.3	10.9	11.6	13.2	15.7	17.4	1.48
Montenegro											
Poland				106.5	275.8	335.3	349.7	388.3	449.2	468.1	157.94
Romania				4.6	38.0	79.9	92.5	79.4	81.6	85.8	28.16
Russia				1,150.6	8,970.7	12,869.0	12,975.9	15,267.6	20,011.9	24,543.4	835.04
Serbia					200.1	248.9	241.0	258.4	253.3	293.7	4.00
Slovakia					18.3	20.8	19.1	23.8	25.9	26.1	36.31
Slovenia						9.8	9.8	10.7	11.9	12.2	16.98
Ukraine			4.7	20.8	123.3	181.7	225.1	233.7	289.9	311.0	39.02

Source: Euromonitor International from national statistics
Note: The money supply refers to the total amount of money held by the nonbank public at a point in time in an economy. M1: Physical currency + demand deposits, which are checking accounts

Table 9.10

Inflation Rates (Annual) 1985, 1990, 1995, 2000, 2006-2011
%

	1985	1990	1995	2000	2006	2007	2008	2009	2010	2011
Western Europe										
Austria	3.19	3.26	2.25	2.34	1.44	2.17	3.22	0.51	1.81	3.29
Belgium	4.87	3.45	1.47	2.54	1.79	1.82	4.49	-0.04	2.19	3.53
Cyprus	5.03	4.50	2.62	4.14	2.50	2.37	4.67	0.37	2.38	3.29
Denmark	4.65	2.65	2.10	2.91	1.89	1.71	3.40	1.33	2.30	2.76
Finland	5.87	6.10	0.99	3.04	1.57	2.51	4.07	0.01	1.19	3.42
France	5.83	3.38	1.78	1.69	1.68	1.49	2.82	0.09	1.53	2.12
Germany	2.10	2.70	1.72	1.47	1.58	2.29	2.63	0.32	1.14	2.30
Gibraltar	5.03	4.94	1.78	1.08	2.65	2.70	3.73	2.75	3.15	3.70
Greece	19.30	20.40	8.94	3.15	3.20	2.89	4.16	1.21	4.71	3.34
Iceland	31.69	15.51	1.65	5.12	6.68	5.06	12.68	12.00	5.40	4.00
Ireland	5.44	3.27	2.51	5.55	3.94	4.92	4.06	-4.46	-0.93	2.59
Italy	9.21	6.50	5.24	2.54	2.09	1.83	3.35	0.80	1.51	2.78
Liechtenstein	3.52	5.55	1.80	1.60	1.10	0.70	2.40	-0.50	0.70	0.23
Luxembourg	4.09	3.70	1.92	3.15	2.68	2.30	3.40	0.37	2.28	3.41
Malta	-0.24	2.98	4.43	2.37	2.77	1.25	4.26	2.09	1.52	2.72
Monaco		4.94	3.51	2.11	2.36	2.48	2.59	0.51	1.57	2.56
Netherlands	2.22	2.45	1.92	2.37	1.17	1.61	2.49	1.19	1.28	2.34
Norway	5.67	4.11	2.46	3.09	2.33	0.73	3.77	2.17	2.40	1.30
Portugal	19.65	13.37	4.12	2.86	3.10	2.45	2.57	-0.82	1.39	3.66
Spain	8.82	6.72	4.67	3.43	3.52	2.78	4.09	-0.28	1.80	3.20
Sweden	7.36	10.47	2.53	0.90	1.36	2.21	3.44	-0.48	1.16	2.96
Switzerland	3.43	5.38	1.80	1.56	1.06	0.73	2.43	-0.48	0.69	0.23
Turkey	44.96	60.31	88.11	54.92	9.59	8.78	10.43	6.28	8.58	6.45
United Kingdom	5.20	7.00	2.60	0.79	2.33	2.32	3.61	2.17	3.29	4.48
Eastern Europe										
Albania	0.57	-0.20	6.67	0.05	2.37	2.93	3.36	2.28	3.55	3.45
Belarus			709.35	168.62	7.03	8.42	14.84	12.95	7.74	53.23
Bosnia-Herzegovina			12.90	5.03	6.10	1.50	7.40	-0.38	2.12	3.70
Bulgaria	0.23	26.19	60.55	10.30	7.27	8.40	12.43	2.80	2.44	4.23
Croatia			4.04	4.62	3.21	2.87	6.08	2.39	1.05	2.26
Czech Republic	2.30	9.50	9.47	3.90	2.55	2.86	6.35	1.04	1.47	1.93
Estonia			-2.77	4.01	4.43	6.58	10.40	-0.05	2.98	4.98
Georgia			99.30	4.06	9.17	9.24	10.01	1.73	7.10	8.54
Hungary	7.01	28.97	28.30	9.80	3.92	7.97	6.06	4.21	4.90	3.90
Latvia			24.98	2.65	6.54	10.07	15.48	3.62	-1.06	4.38
Lithuania			39.66	0.98	3.74	5.72	10.94	4.51	1.33	4.13
Macedonia			16.37	6.61	3.22	2.24	8.27	-0.74	1.61	3.90
Moldova			29.86	31.30	12.78	12.37	12.77	-0.05	7.40	7.61
Montenegro			10.66	21.74	2.12	3.52	8.99	3.40	0.66	3.08
Poland	11.52	499.79	28.07	10.06	1.11	2.39	4.35	3.83	2.71	4.22
Romania	-0.20	11.23	32.24	40.71	6.62	4.82	7.85	5.57	6.07	5.84
Russia			197.47	20.78	9.69	8.99	14.10	11.73	6.88	8.47
Serbia			82.66	71.12	11.72	6.39	12.41	8.12	6.14	11.14
Slovakia			9.92	12.17	4.48	2.76	4.60	1.62	0.96	3.92
Slovenia			23.46	8.88	2.46	3.60	5.68	0.87	1.84	1.81
Ukraine			376.75	28.20	9.08	12.78	25.27	16.02	9.40	8.00

Source: Euromonitor International from national statistics

9

Economic Indicators

Economic Statistics   **Table 9.11**

Public Consumption 1985, 1990, 1995, 2000, 2006-2011
National currency billion

	1985	1990	1995	2000	2006	2007	2008	2009	2010	2011	US$ billion 2011
Western Europe											
Austria	20.1	25.6	35.5	39.6	47.3	49.4	52.8	54.6	55.5	56.6	78.70
Belgium	28.6	33.1	44.4	53.7	71.5	74.7	80.1	84.2	86.4	90.1	125.27
Cyprus	0.3	0.7	1.0	1.6	2.7	2.8	3.1	3.4	3.5	3.5	4.80
Denmark	164.3	211.2	257.2	325.1	422.6	440.0	465.4	497.0	510.2	509.5	95.05
Finland	11.8	19.4	21.9	27.2	36.9	38.7	41.7	43.4	44.2	46.0	63.93
France	171.7	224.5	282.8	329.9	421.7	435.7	449.9	467.2	481.8	489.3	680.40
Germany	218.7	269.3	358.1	389.6	424.7	434.0	451.9	475.3	487.6	499.8	694.90
Gibraltar											
Greece	3.1	6.7	13.8	24.3	35.5	39.7	42.2	47.3	41.3	37.5	52.19
Iceland	21.1	73.1	99.0	160.2	285.4	316.8	367.3	396.9	398.6	411.0	3.54
Ireland	5.0	6.3	9.0	15.5	29.3	32.5	34.4	33.0	30.0	29.2	40.63
Italy	80.3	141.2	170.2	219.2	298.2	303.3	315.4	324.7	327.4	324.2	450.81
Liechtenstein	0.1	0.2	0.3	0.5	0.6	0.6	0.6	0.6	0.6	0.6	0.73
Luxembourg	1.1	1.7	2.4	3.3	5.2	5.5	5.8	6.3	6.7	7.1	9.82
Malta	0.2	0.3	0.6	0.7	1.0	1.0	1.2	1.2	1.3	1.4	1.88
Monaco	0.3	0.4	0.6	0.7	0.9	1.0	1.0	1.0	1.0	1.1	1.49
Netherlands	47.7	56.1	72.7	91.9	135.4	143.9	152.8	164.1	167.1	168.2	233.81
Norway	102.1	155.9	203.7	286.1	411.8	444.3	488.4	530.7	556.3	585.8	104.50
Portugal			15.4	24.1	33.0	33.6	34.5	37.2	37.3	34.4	47.78
Spain	27.4	52.1	80.9	108.0	177.1	193.1	212.0	223.6	224.5	222.7	309.68
Sweden	251.1	389.8	482.1	585.5	765.3	797.4	835.2	859.7	891.3	928.2	142.90
Switzerland	26.0	38.2	45.4	48.1	56.3	58.0	58.9	62.0	63.3	65.2	73.46
Turkey	0.0	0.0	0.9	19.5	93.5	107.8	121.7	140.0	157.5	180.7	107.56
United Kingdom	75.7	112.5	143.0	181.9	285.1	295.2	315.6	327.9	335.0	339.0	543.27
Eastern Europe											
Albania	1.6	1.7	30.7	49.5	89.4	98.4	110.9	121.7	127.6	131.8	1.31
Belarus		0.0	24.9	1,779.1	15,225.1	17,998.1	21,447.9	23,001.3	27,638.1	41,289.3	8.30
Bosnia-Herzegovina		0.0	0.6	2.4	4.2	4.7	5.6	5.8	5.1	5.6	3.96
Bulgaria	0.0	0.0	0.1	5.2	9.3	10.0	11.5	11.1	11.4	11.7	8.32
Croatia			29.6	39.9	54.6	61.1	64.5	66.3	65.2	66.4	12.42
Czech Republic		161.1	308.7	460.1	694.0	725.9	759.4	809.6	808.0	792.5	44.79
Estonia		0.5	0.7	1.2	2.2	2.6	3.1	3.0	3.0	3.1	4.33
Georgia		0.0	0.3	0.5	2.1	3.7	4.9	4.4	4.4	4.9	2.90
Hungary	253.5	537.6	1,340.6	2,812.6	5,444.6	5,410.3	5,795.6	5,807.4	5,839.7	5,841.2	29.05
Latvia		0.0	0.6	1.0	1.9	2.6	3.2	2.6	2.3	2.3	4.54
Lithuania		0.0	6.6	10.4	15.9	17.6	21.5	20.2	19.5	20.0	8.06
Macedonia		0.1	31.5	43.0	58.0	62.5	75.1	78.5	83.0	82.8	1.87
Moldova		0.0	1.7	2.3	8.9	10.7	12.8	14.4	15.9	16.7	1.42
Montenegro		0.4	0.2	0.2	0.6	0.5	0.7	0.7	0.7	0.8	1.09
Poland	0.2	10.5	63.0	129.8	193.7	211.0	236.1	248.8	268.3	276.2	93.19
Romania	0.0	0.0	1.0	14.1	57.4	66.6	87.1	92.9	85.5	83.2	27.31
Russia		0.1	272.5	1,102.5	4,680.4	5,751.0	7,359.8	8,066.7	8,441.9	9,781.6	332.80
Serbia			11.8	75.2	371.6	467.9	534.4	539.9	565.0	621.5	8.47
Slovakia		2.0	4.2	6.3	10.3	10.5	11.7	12.5	12.7	12.5	17.42
Slovenia		0.1	1.9	3.5	5.8	6.0	6.8	7.2	7.4	7.5	10.47
Ukraine		0.0	11.6	31.7	100.4	129.0	169.2	184.0	220.1	238.7	29.94

Source: Euromonitor International from national statistics

Table 9.12

Private Consumption 1985, 1990, 1995, 2000, 2006-2011

National currency billion

	1985	1990	1995	2000	2006	2007	2008	2009	2010	2011	US$ billion 2011
Western Europe											
Austria	60.4	76.8	96.9	114.4	140.3	145.0	149.2	151.4	156.8	163.6	227.50
Belgium	73.1	92.7	112.3	134.4	163.6	171.1	180.2	179.8	188.5	194.7	270.70
Cyprus	1.7	2.7	4.6	6.4	9.3	10.6	12.0	11.2	11.5	11.9	16.55
Denmark	346.0	423.2	521.8	616.7	786.6	820.4	840.0	814.9	850.9	865.3	161.45
Finland	30.3	45.6	50.0	65.3	85.8	90.7	95.6	94.2	99.2	105.0	146.03
France	438.3	593.6	681.4	809.0	1,020.0	1,065.9	1,099.7	1,095.7	1,124.4	1,151.3	1,600.74
Germany	641.8	818.9	1,066.5	1,195.0	1,339.5	1,356.7	1,389.6	1,391.6	1,433.2	1,487.7	2,068.49
Gibraltar											
Greece	12.5	32.9	68.7	98.6	145.4	155.8	169.1	168.2	169.4	162.3	225.70
Iceland	77.2	218.1	258.2	414.5	679.9	751.6	789.9	764.3	787.4	852.3	7.35
Ireland	15.7	21.6	29.1	50.8	81.5	89.2	90.3	79.4	78.2	77.5	107.75
Italy	252.3	403.0	555.3	718.1	881.5	911.0	932.0	916.6	941.5	969.1	1,347.46
Liechtenstein	0.8	1.1	1.7	2.5	2.9	3.1	3.1	3.0	3.1	3.2	3.62
Luxembourg	3.5	4.8	6.5	9.0	11.4	12.0	12.8	13.0	13.5	14.3	19.85
Malta	0.9	1.3	1.9	2.6	3.3	3.4	3.7	3.7	3.8	3.9	5.49
Monaco	0.9	1.2	1.4	1.6	2.1	2.5	2.6	2.3	2.4	2.5	3.45
Netherlands	102.9	121.1	151.1	210.8	254.9	264.1	270.4	263.5	267.8	271.1	376.96
Norway	266.5	366.5	470.9	640.0	892.0	952.1	1,002.6	1,027.7	1,088.1	1,128.6	201.32
Portugal	15.6	35.5	57.3	81.0	104.7	110.6	115.0	109.8	113.9	113.3	157.59
Spain	109.0	188.1	268.4	376.1	566.2	604.7	622.4	592.4	608.1	620.0	862.08
Sweden	450.0	708.1	894.2	1,113.7	1,389.3	1,460.2	1,504.8	1,532.5	1,610.8	1,664.1	256.20
Switzerland	148.3	188.4	223.0	261.9	295.7	307.2	320.7	324.1	332.1	336.6	379.00
Turkey	0.0	0.3	7.1	117.5	534.8	601.2	663.9	680.8	787.8	923.6	549.86
United Kingdom	215.4	354.8	465.3	638.8	850.3	896.1	911.8	896.3	941.5	974.3	1,561.30
Eastern Europe											
Albania	9.9	12.2	203.1	400.4	681.7	776.6	863.6	916.4	982.9	1,037.8	10.29
Belarus		0.0	71.7	5,198.1	40,803.1	50,342.4	67,435.7	75,926.7	89,576.9	141,648.0	28.47
Bosnia-Herzegovina		0.0	3.1	11.6	18.2	20.1	22.7	21.9	20.1	20.5	14.59
Bulgaria	0.0	0.0	0.6	18.7	34.9	41.5	46.0	43.2	43.1	45.7	32.49
Croatia		0.2	77.3	110.1	171.3	187.8	201.0	192.1	192.4	197.5	36.96
Czech Republic		308.6	787.7	1,178.9	1,629.2	1,747.7	1,883.2	1,879.8	1,899.6	1,921.3	108.57
Estonia		1.6	1.5	3.4	7.4	8.7	8.9	7.5	7.5	8.2	11.33
Georgia		0.0	3.4	5.5	10.9	12.0	14.7	14.7	15.5	18.0	10.65
Hungary	509.3	1,005.9	3,121.3	7,180.8	12,732.4	13,752.9	14,380.0	13,975.8	14,246.6	14,877.0	73.99
Latvia		0.0	1.6	3.0	7.3	9.2	10.0	8.0	8.1	8.8	17.48
Lithuania		0.1	17.1	30.0	54.1	63.8	73.7	63.5	61.2	67.6	27.23
Macedonia		0.3	119.4	176.0	250.3	279.9	330.4	313.9	321.5	345.4	7.81
Moldova		0.0	3.7	14.2	42.0	50.0	58.6	54.2	67.3	79.2	6.75
Montenegro		1.3	0.7	0.7	1.7	2.4	2.8	2.5	2.6	2.7	3.77
Poland	0.6	27.2	203.8	477.4	662.3	711.9	785.1	821.0	867.8	934.2	315.23
Romania	0.0	0.1	4.9	55.4	237.5	278.4	333.8	311.4	334.4	358.4	117.57
Russia		0.3	744.1	3,374.3	13,129.3	16,217.6	20,183.6	21,202.9	23,708.0	27,473.3	934.72
Serbia			37.3	298.3	1,512.1	1,738.3	2,050.1	2,168.4	2,310.2	2,596.6	35.41
Slovakia		5.3	10.0	17.6	31.5	34.5	38.2	38.3	38.4	39.7	55.25
Slovenia		0.4	6.2	10.6	16.4	18.1	19.6	19.8	20.4	20.9	29.09
Ukraine		0.0	30.1	96.3	324.6	429.6	589.7	588.8	694.3	866.5	108.69

Source: Euromonitor International from national statistics

Economic Indicators

9

Economic Statistics

Table 9.13

Government Finance and International Liquidity 2011

US$ million / as stated

	Budget Expenditure	Budget Revenue	Budget Surplus Deficit	Foreign Debt	Foreign Exchange Reserves	Gold Reserves (million troy oz)
Western Europe						
Austria	211,401.6	200,578.2	-10,823.3	235,821.4	7,214.2	9.0
Belgium	274,015.2	254,069.4	-19,945.7	263,307.5	8,140.7	7.3
Cyprus	11,811.7	10,191.9	-1,619.9	9,846.1	163.0	0.4
Denmark	192,946.6	186,516.8	-6,429.7	20,862.4	75,501.3	2.1
Finland	143,951.4	141,658.6	-2,292.8	121,128.7	5,411.3	1.6
France	1,555,097.8	1,410,982.4	-144,115.5	1,508,860.9	26,632.1	78.3
Germany	1,632,714.5	1,597,161.2	-35,553.3	1,777,672.6	38,789.8	109.2
Gibraltar						
Greece	149,845.4	122,462.3	-27,383.2	218,290.8	30.3	3.6
Iceland	6,512.0	5,860.6	-651.5	5,718.3	7,710.5	0.1
Ireland	104,676.5	76,836.6	-27,839.9	143,701.1	27.7	0.2
Italy	1,096,682.2	1,012,702.9	-83,979.3	936,304.2	34,791.2	78.8
Liechtenstein						
Luxembourg	24,303.4	23,883.4	-419.9	6,328.4	182.1	0.1
Malta	3,837.6	3,574.8	-262.8	317.3	290.2	0.0
Monaco						
Netherlands	417,029.4	380,030.0	-36,999.4	334,029.8	9,765.6	19.7
Norway	215,778.0	282,426.3	66,648.4	51,352.1	43,600.9	0.0
Portugal	116,260.9	106,186.0	-10,075.0	137,307.9	346.6	12.3
Spain	651,424.2	524,311.0	-127,113.3	392,517.5	26,321.1	9.1
Sweden	276,041.9	276,759.0	717.1	96,642.0	38,907.0	4.0
Switzerland	220,926.1	223,658.9	2,732.8	29,076.5	271,117.9	33.4
Turkey	265,456.6	263,327.8	-2,128.9	83,974.0	76,668.0	6.3
United Kingdom	1,183,471.2	984,802.9	-198,668.3	639,164.1	49,691.3	10.0
Eastern Europe						
Albania	3,728.5	3,275.2	-453.3	3,121.8	2,312.1	0.1
Belarus	21,348.9	23,157.9	1,809.0	12,351.0	5,438.8	1.2
Bosnia-Herzegovina	8,870.1	8,317.7	-552.4		4,148.8	0.1
Bulgaria	18,838.4	17,717.9	-1,120.4	3,870.1	14,526.2	1.3
Croatia	24,878.0	23,021.6	-1,856.3	9,816.4	13,836.9	0.0
Czech Republic	93,337.8	86,700.7	-6,637.2	26,789.2	35,233.1	0.4
Estonia	8,481.1	8,710.1	229.0	733.6	102.7	0.0
Georgia	4,198.6	4,073.5	-125.1	3,674.2	2,594.9	0.0
Hungary	68,157.2	74,026.7	5,869.5	74,426.8	45,393.1	0.1
Latvia	10,951.4	9,971.2	-980.2	9,002.6	5,852.5	0.2
Lithuania	16,004.1	13,648.1	-2,356.1	12,695.0	7,850.0	0.2
Macedonia	3,264.7	3,005.1	-259.6	1,893.4	2,330.7	0.2
Moldova	2,736.0	2,569.2	-166.8	1,142.5	1,964.1	0.0
Montenegro	2,000.8	1,707.5	-293.4	1,465.8	342.4	0.0
Poland	224,425.0	198,100.9	-26,324.1	132,808.7	86,803.0	3.3
Romania	71,560.4	61,609.8	-9,950.6	16,033.2	43,144.5	3.3
Russia	680,272.4	709,559.3	29,286.8	33,208.0	453,952.0	28.4
Serbia	19,582.9	17,764.2	-1,818.8	14,979.5	14,874.6	0.5
Slovakia	36,673.9	32,048.5	-4,625.4	15,651.0	71.8	1.0
Slovenia	25,234.3	22,051.6	-3,182.7	12,828.1	336.3	0.1
Ukraine	74,520.5	70,017.4	-4,503.1	25,874.0	30,391.4	0.9

Source: Euromonitor International from national statistics

Table 9.14

Government Expenditure by Object 2011

US$ million

	General Public Services	Defence	Education	Health	Social Security and Welfare	Housing and Community Amenities	Other Community Social Services	Economic Services	Other Purposes
Western Europe									
Austria	26,666	3,412	22,829	34,218	86,653	2,387	4,386	22,594	8,256
Belgium	42,217	4,688	32,206	41,097	100,922	1,672	6,280	32,289	12,645
Cyprus	2,628	635	1,888	851	3,091	732	309	973	705
Denmark	26,396	4,617	26,168	27,881	84,294	1,131	5,294	11,885	5,280
Finland	18,479	3,872	16,740	20,318	63,328	1,385	3,095	12,055	4,680
France	180,767	59,087	165,171	217,855	670,915	48,860	40,307	96,772	75,364
Germany	201,029	35,897	145,906	245,809	702,593	19,791	53,475	173,691	54,523
Gibraltar									
Greece	35,052	5,867	10,762	22,035	55,445	1,246	1,758	10,725	6,956
Iceland	1,140	6	1,041	983	1,421	326	458	882	255
Ireland	5,949	723	9,135	13,082	26,591	2,744	1,103	40,687	4,662
Italy	167,754	32,072	96,095	165,750	455,255	16,535	17,412	84,719	61,091
Liechtenstein									
Luxembourg	2,539	346	2,956	2,787	10,525	452	989	2,450	1,260
Malta	586	74	521	504	1,319	18	69	417	329
Monaco									
Netherlands	44,978	11,141	47,248	68,962	141,670	6,070	14,813	50,968	31,179
Norway	21,410	6,527	28,035	35,120	85,592	3,385	6,394	21,359	7,955
Portugal	15,712	4,097	13,177	15,426	43,572	1,283	3,035	12,866	7,091
Spain	73,747	14,857	68,694	92,744	252,141	17,501	20,818	69,851	41,072
Sweden	34,353	8,146	36,778	37,732	114,963	3,742	6,439	24,901	8,989
Switzerland	18,087	5,331	39,466	13,656	92,469	873	5,985	28,864	16,196
Turkey									
United Kingdom	83,674	62,540	154,063	199,257	419,308	39,588	61,505	113,547	49,989
Eastern Europe									
Albania	726	137	442	360	1,101	263	208	451	41
Belarus	5,362	628	1,051	702	9,398	181	1,346	2,298	383
Bosnia-Herzegovina									
Bulgaria	1,974	952	1,826	2,344	7,338	388	330	1,963	1,723
Croatia	2,819	889	2,081	4,275	9,949	186	1,537	2,739	402
Czech Republic	10,072	2,010	10,210	17,020	29,463	1,743	3,038	13,589	6,194
Estonia	655	371	1,423	1,111	3,067	118	431	907	399
Georgia	468	396	373	282	881	327	539	658	275
Hungary	13,127	1,864	7,757	7,165	24,444	362	2,529	7,901	3,009
Latvia	1,119	149	1,360	926	3,906	346	309	2,344	491
Lithuania	1,812	382	2,361	2,095	6,075	121	333	1,497	1,328
Macedonia									
Moldova	1,691	33	293	58	138	28	148	296	52
Montenegro									
Poland	29,641	5,923	26,753	24,052	84,787	4,661	6,571	29,014	13,023
Romania	7,322	2,565	4,898	6,915	28,872	2,318	1,763	11,140	5,767
Russia	127,901	56,274	65,610	71,619	216,482	22,658	43,345	63,954	12,430
Serbia	1,754	975	1,668	2,588	7,638	537	1,023	2,816	584
Slovakia	6,749	1,033	4,304	5,240	11,458	1,007	1,142	2,344	3,397
Slovenia	2,892	750	3,259	3,502	9,573	295	1,196	2,485	1,282
Ukraine	6,583	1,611	11,381	6,561	35,213	725	4,104	6,268	2,075

Source: Euromonitor International from national statistics

9

Economic Indicators

Economic Statistics   **Table 9.15**

Government Expenditure by Object (% Analysis) 2011

% of total expenditure

	General Public Services	Defence	Education	Health	Social Security and Welfare	Housing and Community Amenities	Other Community Social Services	Economic Services	Other Purposes
Western Europe									
Austria	12.61	1.61	10.80	16.19	40.99	1.13	2.07	10.69	3.91
Belgium	15.41	1.71	11.75	15.00	36.83	0.61	2.29	11.78	4.61
Cyprus	22.25	5.37	15.98	7.20	26.17	6.20	2.62	8.23	5.97
Denmark	13.68	2.39	13.56	14.45	43.69	0.59	2.74	6.16	2.74
Finland	12.84	2.69	11.63	14.11	43.99	0.96	2.15	8.37	3.25
France	11.62	3.80	10.62	14.01	43.14	3.14	2.59	6.22	4.85
Germany	12.31	2.20	8.94	15.06	43.03	1.21	3.28	10.64	3.34
Gibraltar									
Greece	23.39	3.92	7.18	14.71	37.00	0.83	1.17	7.16	4.64
Iceland	17.50	0.09	15.98	15.10	21.82	5.01	7.03	13.55	3.91
Ireland	5.68	0.69	8.73	12.50	25.40	2.62	1.05	38.87	4.45
Italy	15.30	2.92	8.76	15.11	41.51	1.51	1.59	7.72	5.57
Liechtenstein									
Luxembourg	10.45	1.42	12.16	11.47	43.31	1.86	4.07	10.08	5.18
Malta	15.27	1.93	13.57	13.13	34.38	0.48	1.81	10.88	8.56
Monaco									
Netherlands	10.79	2.67	11.33	16.54	33.97	1.46	3.55	12.22	7.48
Norway	9.92	3.02	12.99	16.28	39.67	1.57	2.96	9.90	3.69
Portugal	13.51	3.52	11.33	13.27	37.48	1.10	2.61	11.07	6.10
Spain	11.32	2.28	10.55	14.24	38.71	2.69	3.20	10.72	6.30
Sweden	12.44	2.95	13.32	13.67	41.65	1.36	2.33	9.02	3.26
Switzerland	8.19	2.41	17.86	6.18	41.86	0.40	2.71	13.06	7.33
Turkey									
United Kingdom	7.07	5.28	13.02	16.84	35.43	3.35	5.20	9.59	4.22
Eastern Europe									
Albania	19.46	3.67	11.85	9.67	29.53	7.05	5.59	12.08	1.10
Belarus	25.12	2.94	4.92	3.29	44.02	0.85	6.31	10.76	1.79
Bosnia-Herzegovina									
Bulgaria	10.48	5.06	9.69	12.44	38.95	2.06	1.75	10.42	9.15
Croatia	11.33	3.57	8.37	17.18	39.99	0.75	6.18	11.01	1.62
Czech Republic	10.79	2.15	10.94	18.23	31.57	1.87	3.25	14.56	6.64
Estonia	7.72	4.38	16.78	13.10	36.16	1.39	5.08	10.69	4.71
Georgia	11.15	9.43	8.87	6.71	20.99	7.78	12.84	15.68	6.54
Hungary	19.26	2.73	11.38	10.51	35.86	0.53	3.71	11.59	4.41
Latvia	10.21	1.36	12.42	8.46	35.67	3.16	2.83	21.40	4.49
Lithuania	11.32	2.39	14.75	13.09	37.96	0.75	2.08	9.35	8.30
Macedonia									
Moldova	61.80	1.19	10.71	2.13	5.06	1.01	5.40	10.80	1.89
Montenegro									
Poland	13.21	2.64	11.92	10.72	37.78	2.08	2.93	12.93	5.80
Romania	10.23	3.58	6.84	9.66	40.35	3.24	2.46	15.57	8.06
Russia	18.80	8.27	9.64	10.53	31.82	3.33	6.37	9.40	1.83
Serbia	8.96	4.98	8.52	13.21	39.01	2.74	5.23	14.38	2.98
Slovakia	18.40	2.82	11.73	14.29	31.24	2.75	3.11	6.39	9.26
Slovenia	11.46	2.97	12.92	13.88	37.94	1.17	4.74	9.85	5.08
Ukraine	8.83	2.16	15.27	8.80	47.25	0.97	5.51	8.41	2.78

Source: Euromonitor International from national statistics

European Marketing Data and Statistics 2013 – © Euromonitor International Ltd 2012

Table 9.16

Current Account Balance 2000-2011

US$ million

	2000	2001	2002	2003	2004	2005	2006	2007	2008	2009	2010	2011	Current Account Balance as % of Total GDP 2011
Western Europe													
Austria	-1,334	-1,513	5,472	4,192	6,451	6,724	9,044	13,190	20,087	10,297	11,679	7,995	1.91
Belgium	9,359	7,887	11,220	10,774	11,359	7,742	7,541	7,006	-8,086	1,796	10,486	-4,860	-0.94
Cyprus	-489	-316	-393	-297	-788	-995	-1,283	-2,565	-3,943	-2,518	-2,272	-2,113	-8.56
Denmark	2,507	4,145	4,997	7,338	5,702	11,033	8,224	4,413	9,092	11,228	17,141	21,680	6.52
Finland	9,355	10,436	11,631	8,050	11,962	6,395	8,837	10,619	6,653	4,985	4,464	-3,226	-1.23
France	19,708	23,550	18,232	12,873	11,142	-10,343	-13,154	-26,638	-49,641	-35,765	-39,790	-54,497	-1.96
Germany	-32,453	-114	41,066	46,873	127,524	139,898	182,434	249,032	226,307	198,120	200,292	202,626	5.62
Gibraltar													
Greece	-9,996	-9,494	-9,584	-12,819	-13,538	-18,378	-29,705	-44,922	-50,956	-35,950	-31,061	-29,196	-9.76
Iceland	-881	-341	139	-523	-1,302	-2,631	-4,279	-3,214	-4,777	-1,425	-1,053	-915	-6.51
Ireland	33	-691	-1,106	74	-1,079	-7,134	-7,865	-13,837	-15,286	-6,291	961	164	0.07
Italy	-2,163	2,962	-5,219	-11,566	-6,192	-16,120	-27,630	-27,215	-65,009	-41,135	-72,831	-71,663	-3.26
Liechtenstein													
Luxembourg	2,688	1,770	2,386	2,378	4,046	4,353	4,415	5,186	2,946	3,381	4,100	4,016	6.74
Malta	-488	-148	104	-156	-335	-523	-635	-400	-452	-671	-521	-286	-3.20
Monaco													
Netherlands	7,915	10,465	11,716	30,222	46,819	47,464	63,101	52,531	38,015	32,946	55,379	70,699	8.45
Norway	25,097	27,542	24,263	27,708	33,007	49,010	58,149	55,470	79,135	44,527	51,444	65,302	13.46
Portugal	-12,157	-12,420	-10,863	-10,462	-15,512	-19,838	-21,531	-23,586	-31,880	-25,692	-22,728	-15,505	-6.52
Spain	-23,206	-24,022	-22,267	-30,956	-54,966	-83,307	-110,848	-144,548	-73,696	-69,783	-63,282	-51,751	-3.50
Sweden	10,243	11,366	11,693	22,024	23,712	25,128	33,655	42,864	43,229	28,445	31,841	37,943	7.06
Switzerland	30,129	20,937	24,892	43,431	48,601	52,564	58,184	38,645	10,777	54,757	79,557	94,255	14.27
Turkey	-9,920	3,760	-626	-7,515	-14,431	-22,309	-32,249	-38,434	-41,524	-13,370	-46,643	-77,141	-9.98
United Kingdom	-42,177	-34,225	-33,509	-31,889	-46,784	-46,777	-72,439	-64,188	-25,790	-27,514	-57,790	-46,406	1.91
Eastern Europe													
Albania	-134	-125	-318	-286	-292	-498	-508	-1,109	-1,966	-1,648	-1,381	-1,702	-13.09
Belarus	-338	-401	334	-426	-1,193	435	-1,448	-3,040	-4,988	-6,178	-8,278	-5,775	-10.47
Bosnia-Herzegovina	-397	-746	-1,183	-1,627	-1,639	-1,868	-984	-1,632	-2,607	-1,070	-1,016	-1,499	-8.22
Bulgaria	-711	-767	-373	-1,108	-1,672	-3,343	-5,858	-10,707	-11,883	-4,253	-796	227	0.42
Croatia	-505	-697	-1,862	-2,086	-1,784	2,460	-3,233	-4,328	-6,083	-3,067	-963	-466	-0.75
Czech Republic	-2,687	-3,274	-4,266	-5,810	-5,757	-1,204	-3,101	-7,930	-4,809	-4,923	-7,526	-6,371	-2.96
Estonia	-297	-326	-779	-1,117	-1,369	-1,387	-2,584	-3,506	-2,222	686	552	477	2.15
Georgia	-239	-205	-216	-384	-354	-709	-1,175	-2,010	-2,912	-1,212	-1,334	-1,816	-12.64
Hungary	-4,002	-3,203	-4,692	-6,721	-8,815	-8,241	-8,317	-9,918	-11,238	-81	1,557	2,012	1.44
Latvia	-371	-626	-624	-920	-1,762	-1,992	-4,522	-6,424	-4,484	2,284	722	-685	-2.42
Lithuania	-675	-574	-734	-1,281	-1,721	-1,837	-3,221	-5,700	-6,325	1,727	525	-662	-1.55
Macedonia	-68	-248	-356	-190	-451	-151	-56	-569	-1,269	-637	-199	-284	-2.80
Moldova	-98	-27	-20	-130	-46	226	-388	-671	-979	-465	-484	-743	-10.61
Montenegro				-115	-149	-192	-846	-1,451	-2,297	-1,227	-1,014	-882	-19.46
Poland	-10,352	-5,946	-5,525	-5,502	-13,237	-7,242	-13,157	-26,507	-34,914	-17,278	-21,897	-22,248	-4.32
Romania	-1,355	-2,229	-1,525	-3,311	-6,382	-8,489	-12,860	-23,095	-23,981	-6,974	-7,204	-8,432	-4.44
Russia	46,839	33,935	29,116	35,410	59,512	84,602	94,686	77,768	103,530	48,605	71,080	98,834	5.32
Serbia	-153	-285	-1,247	-1,420	-2,871	-2,194	-2,986	-6,287	-10,302	-2,859	-2,752	-4,119	-9.32
Slovakia	-668	-1,742	-1,951	-1,976	-3,296	-4,005	-4,410	-4,086	-5,730	-2,215	-2,156	27	0.03
Slovenia	-548	37	244	-215	-892	-620	-997	-2,243	-3,759	-641	-404	-227	-0.45
Ukraine	1,481	1,402	3,173	2,891	6,909	2,531	-1,617	-5,272	-12,763	-1,732	-3,018	-9,006	-5.45

Source: Euromonitor International from national statistics

9

Economic Indicators

Economic Statistics

Table 9.17

Corruption Perception Index 2000-2011

Score

	2000	2001	2002	2003	2004	2005	2006	2007	2008	2009	2010	2011
Western Europe												
Austria	7.70	7.80	7.80	8.00	8.40	8.70	8.60	8.10	8.10	7.90	7.90	7.79
Belgium	6.10	6.60	7.10	7.60	7.50	7.40	7.30	7.10	7.30	7.10	7.10	7.49
Cyprus				6.10	5.40	5.70	5.60	5.30	6.40	6.60	6.30	6.27
Denmark	9.80	9.50	9.50	9.50	9.50	9.50	9.50	9.40	9.30	9.30	9.30	9.39
Finland	10.00	9.90	9.70	9.70	9.70	9.60	9.60	9.40	9.00	8.90	9.20	9.40
France	6.70	6.70	6.30	6.90	7.10	7.50	7.40	7.30	6.90	6.90	6.80	7.01
Germany	7.60	7.40	7.30	7.70	8.20	8.20	8.00	7.80	7.90	8.00	7.90	8.05
Gibraltar												
Greece	4.90	4.20	4.20	4.30	4.30	4.30	4.40	4.60	4.70	3.80	3.50	3.39
Iceland	9.10	9.20	9.40	9.60	9.50	9.70	9.60	9.20	8.90	8.70	8.50	8.27
Ireland	7.20	7.50	6.90	7.50	7.50	7.40	7.40	7.50	7.70	8.00	8.00	7.54
Italy	4.60	5.50	5.20	5.30	4.80	5.00	4.90	5.20	4.80	4.30	3.90	3.91
Liechtenstein												
Luxembourg	8.60	8.70	9.00	8.70	8.40	8.50	8.60	8.40	8.30	8.20	8.50	8.51
Malta					6.80	6.60	6.40	5.80	5.80	5.20	5.60	5.59
Monaco												
Netherlands	8.90	8.80	9.00	8.90	8.70	8.60	8.70	9.00	8.90	8.90	8.80	8.89
Norway	9.10	8.60	8.50	8.80	8.90	8.90	8.80	8.70	7.90	8.60	8.60	8.99
Portugal	6.40	6.30	6.30	6.60	6.30	6.50	6.60	6.50	6.10	5.80	6.00	6.10
Spain	7.00	7.00	7.10	6.90	7.10	7.00	6.80	6.70	6.50	6.10	6.10	6.23
Sweden	9.40	9.00	9.30	9.30	9.20	9.20	9.20	9.30	9.30	9.20	9.20	9.30
Switzerland	8.60	8.40	8.50	8.80	9.10	9.10	9.10	9.00	9.00	9.00	8.70	8.80
Turkey	3.80	3.60	3.20	3.10	3.20	3.50	3.80	4.10	4.60	4.40	4.40	4.21
United Kingdom	8.70	8.30	8.70	8.70	8.60	8.60	8.60	8.40	7.70	7.70	7.60	7.78
Eastern Europe												
Albania			2.50	2.50	2.50	2.40	2.60	2.90	3.40	3.20	3.30	3.05
Belarus	4.10		4.80	4.20	3.30	2.60	2.10	2.10	2.00	2.40	2.50	2.42
Bosnia-Herzegovina				3.30	3.10	2.90	2.90	3.30	3.20	3.00	3.20	3.21
Bulgaria	3.50	3.90	4.00	3.90	4.10	4.00	4.00	4.10	3.60	3.80	3.60	3.33
Croatia	3.70	3.90	3.80	3.70	3.50	3.40	3.40	4.10	4.40	4.10	4.10	4.03
Czech Republic	4.30	3.90	3.70	3.90	4.20	4.30	4.80	5.20	5.20	4.90	4.60	4.37
Estonia	5.70	5.60	5.60	5.50	6.00	6.40	6.70	6.50	6.60	6.60	6.50	6.35
Georgia			2.40	1.80	2.00	2.30	2.80	3.40	3.90	4.10	3.80	4.13
Hungary	5.20	5.30	4.90	4.80	4.80	5.00	5.20	5.30	5.10	5.10	4.70	4.56
Latvia	3.40	3.40	3.70	3.80	4.00	4.20	4.70	4.80	5.00	4.50	4.30	4.19
Lithuania	4.10	4.80	4.80	4.70	4.60	4.80	4.80	4.80	4.60	4.90	5.00	4.75
Macedonia				2.30	2.70	2.70	2.70	3.30	3.60	3.80	4.10	3.94
Moldova	2.60	3.10	2.10	2.40	2.30	2.90	3.20	2.80	2.90	3.30	2.90	2.88
Montenegro								3.30	3.40	3.90	3.70	3.97
Poland	4.10	4.10	4.00	3.60	3.50	3.40	3.70	4.20	4.60	5.00	5.30	5.48
Romania	2.90	2.80	2.60	2.80	2.90	3.00	3.10	3.70	3.80	3.80	3.70	3.61
Russia	2.10	2.30	2.70	2.70	2.80	2.40	2.50	2.30	2.10	2.20	2.10	2.45
Serbia	1.30			2.30	2.70	2.80	3.00	3.40	3.40	3.50	3.50	3.31
Slovakia	3.50	3.70	3.70	3.70	4.00	4.30	4.70	4.90	5.00	4.50	4.30	3.97
Slovenia	5.50	5.20	6.00	5.90	6.00	6.10	6.40	6.60	6.70	6.60	6.40	5.87
Ukraine	1.50	2.10	2.40	2.30	2.20	2.60	2.80	2.70	2.50	2.20	2.40	2.30

Source: Euromonitor International from national statistics

Economic Statistics

Table 9.18

Minimum Wage (Monthly) 2000-2011

US$ per month

	2000	2001	2002	2003	2004	2005	2006	2007	2008	2009	2010	2011
Western Europe												
Austria												
Belgium	1,030.3	1,020.3	1,095.5	1,338.9	1,473.1	1,503.8	1,548.1	1,756.0	1,954.9	1,928.1	1,837.5	1,967.8
Cyprus												
Denmark												
Finland												
France	990.3	1,000.3	1,007.3	1,071.0	1,507.4	1,513.6	1,573.6	1,752.0	1,933.3	1,858.9	1,779.6	1,897.9
Germany												
Gibraltar												
Greece	492.1	494.1	548.2	684.7	783.5	829.8	890.4	1,050.5	1,162.0	1,199.0	1,142.7	1,199.7
Iceland												
Ireland	870.6	903.0	950.4	1,211.5	1,469.3	1,606.8	1,621.9	2,000.8	2,139.4	2,031.4	1,936.0	2,032.6
Italy												
Liechtenstein												
Luxembourg	1,125.1	1,154.8	1,245.7	1,545.2	1,742.5	1,823.0	1,886.1	2,149.2	2,355.5	2,338.3	2,284.2	2,443.8
Malta	450.0	450.6	488.5	605.4	675.5	697.9	733.0	823.8	903.3	882.2	874.0	924.6
Monaco												
Netherlands	1,023.6	1,056.5	1,160.3	1,427.9	1,570.9	1,571.9	1,611.6	1,802.5	1,985.3	1,943.5	1,875.3	1,980.5
Norway												
Portugal	342.1	349.0	382.4	469.7	529.1	543.3	564.5	643.5	727.3	729.5	733.9	786.7
Spain	456.7	452.6	486.0	594.3	711.2	743.8	791.7	911.1	1,024.4	1,011.6	978.5	1,040.5
Sweden												
Switzerland												
Turkey	190.0	137.0	166.5	203.9	311.6	363.2	369.6	448.0	489.5	445.8	504.7	474.2
United Kingdom	895.8	878.0	1,012.5	1,130.2	1,360.5	1,454.0	1,529.2	1,766.9	1,670.0	1,478.1	1,476.5	1,570.5
Eastern Europe												
Albania									202.6	189.5	182.8	198.2
Belarus	4.1	2.6	9.5	21.9	40.3	54.8	73.2	83.4	97.7	82.0	134.3	116.1
Bosnia-Herzegovina												
Bulgaria	35.3	39.8	48.1	63.5	76.2	95.3	102.6	126.0	164.5	170.6	162.5	192.0
Croatia	205.4	203.8	228.7	277.2	323.4	349.8	371.7	428.4	556.6	532.6	511.8	526.6
Czech Republic	110.1	131.5	174.1	219.8	260.7	299.9	352.1	394.2	468.6	419.6	418.9	452.1
Estonia	82.5	91.5	111.4	155.8	196.9	213.7	240.5	314.9	406.9	386.3	368.2	386.6
Georgia												
Hungary	90.4	139.6	193.9	222.9	261.4	285.6	297.1	356.7	400.9	353.4	353.5	388.0
Latvia	82.4	95.6	97.1	122.5	148.1	141.7	160.6	233.6	332.8	356.7	339.2	395.7
Lithuania	107.5	107.5	117.1	140.6	179.9	198.0	218.0	277.5	339.1	322.0	306.8	322.2
Macedonia												
Moldova									38.5	69.0	88.9	93.7
Montenegro												
Poland	161.1	185.6	186.3	205.7	225.3	262.4	289.7	338.2	467.2	408.8	436.9	467.7
Romania	32.2	48.2	52.9	75.3	85.8	106.4	117.5	160.0	198.5	196.8	188.8	219.8
Russia	4.7	15.4	14.4	19.5	25.0	28.3	40.5	89.9	92.5	136.3	142.6	156.9
Serbia												
Slovakia	122.4	130.7	153.8	208.7	250.7	268.2	287.3	345.3	393.5	410.6	407.5	440.8
Slovenia	296.1	315.3	372.1	488.2	577.8	609.4	641.8	714.2	829.1	818.7	972.3	1,040.2
Ukraine	21.7	22.0	26.3	30.9	49.3	64.4	79.2	91.1	114.9	95.5	116.2	115.7

Source: Euromonitor International from national statistics

Economic Statistics   **Table 9.19**

Foreign Direct Investment Intensity 2000-2011

% of total GDP

	2000	2001	2002	2003	2004	2005	2006	2007	2008	2009	2010	2011
Western Europe												
Austria	4.6	3.1	0.2	2.8	1.3	3.5	2.4	8.3	1.7	2.4	1.1	3.4
Belgium	38.1	37.9	6.4	10.7	12.0	9.1	14.7	20.3	38.3	13.0	17.2	17.3
Cyprus	9.5	9.8	10.1	6.8	7.0	7.0	10.1	10.3	5.6	14.8	3.3	1.1
Denmark	21.1	7.2	3.8	1.3	-4.3	5.0	1.0	3.8	0.5	1.3	-2.4	4.4
Finland	7.3	3.0	5.9	2.0	1.5	2.4	3.7	5.1	-0.4	0.2	2.8	0.0
France	3.3	3.8	3.4	2.4	1.6	4.0	3.2	3.7	2.3	0.9	1.2	1.5
Germany	10.5	1.4	2.7	1.3	-0.4	1.7	1.9	2.4	0.2	0.7	1.4	1.1
Gibraltar	21.0	1.8	10.8	6.8	16.6	10.3	10.1	10.3	9.7	11.6	10.7	9.7
Greece	0.9	1.2	0.0	0.7	0.9	0.3	2.0	0.7	1.3	0.8	0.1	0.6
Iceland	2.0	2.2	1.0	3.0	5.6	18.9	23.1	33.4	5.4	0.7	2.0	7.2
Ireland	26.4	9.2	23.8	14.3	-5.7	-15.6	-2.5	9.6	-6.3	11.6	12.7	5.9
Italy	1.2	1.3	1.4	1.3	1.2	1.3	2.3	2.1	-0.5	1.0	0.4	1.3
Liechtenstein												
Luxembourg	437.7	436.6	18.0	10.0	15.2	17.4	74.8	-55.1	19.4	43.1	17.3	29.4
Malta	15.6	6.4	-10.2	18.9	7.0	11.3	28.9	10.8	9.4	9.2	13.0	6.0
Monaco												
Netherlands	16.6	13.0	5.7	6.1	2.0	6.1	2.1	15.3	0.5	4.5	-1.1	2.0
Norway	4.2	1.2	0.4	1.5	1.0	1.8	2.1	1.5	2.3	3.6	4.2	0.7
Portugal	5.7	5.2	1.4	4.4	1.0	2.0	5.4	1.3	1.9	1.2	1.2	4.4
Spain	6.8	4.7	5.7	2.9	2.4	2.2	2.5	4.5	4.8	0.7	2.9	2.0
Sweden	9.5	4.8	4.9	1.6	3.3	3.2	7.2	6.0	7.6	2.5	-0.3	2.2
Switzerland	7.5	3.4	2.2	4.9	0.2	-0.2	10.8	7.2	2.9	5.6	3.7	0.0
Turkey	0.4	1.7	0.5	0.6	0.7	2.1	3.8	3.4	2.7	1.4	1.2	2.1
United Kingdom	8.0	3.6	1.5	0.9	2.5	7.7	6.4	7.0	3.5	3.3	2.2	2.2
Eastern Europe												
Albania	4.0	5.1	3.0	3.1	4.7	3.2	3.6	6.2	7.5	8.2	8.8	7.9
Belarus	1.1	0.8	1.7	1.0	0.7	1.0	1.0	4.0	3.6	3.8	2.5	7.2
Bosnia-Herzegovina	2.6	2.1	3.9	4.5	5.0	3.2	4.5	11.9	5.4	1.5	1.4	2.4
Bulgaria	7.9	5.8	5.8	10.1	13.4	13.6	23.5	29.4	19.0	7.0	3.4	3.5
Croatia	4.9	5.7	4.0	5.8	2.9	4.1	7.0	8.4	8.9	5.4	0.7	2.4
Czech Republic	8.5	8.8	10.8	2.2	4.4	9.0	3.7	5.8	2.9	1.5	3.1	2.5
Estonia	6.9	8.6	3.9	9.4	8.0	20.6	10.7	12.4	7.3	9.6	8.1	1.2
Georgia	4.3	3.4	4.7	8.4	9.6	7.1	15.1	17.2	12.2	6.1	7.0	6.8
Hungary	6.0	7.5	4.5	2.6	4.2	7.0	6.1	2.9	4.1	1.6	1.8	3.4
Latvia	5.3	1.6	2.7	2.7	4.6	4.4	8.4	8.1	3.8	0.4	1.6	5.5
Lithuania	3.3	3.6	5.1	1.0	3.4	3.9	6.0	5.1	4.1	0.2	2.1	2.9
Macedonia	6.0	13.0	2.8	2.4	5.9	1.6	6.6	8.5	6.0	2.2	2.3	4.2
Moldova	9.9	7.0	5.1	3.7	5.6	6.4	7.6	12.3	11.8	2.7	3.4	3.9
Montenegro							23.1	25.5	21.3	36.9	18.5	12.3
Poland	5.5	3.0	2.1	2.1	5.1	3.4	5.7	5.5	2.8	3.0	1.9	2.9
Romania	2.8	2.9	2.5	3.7	8.5	6.5	9.3	5.8	6.8	2.9	1.8	1.4
Russia	1.0	0.9	1.0	1.8	2.6	1.7	3.0	4.2	4.5	3.0	2.9	2.8
Serbia	0.6	1.6	3.7	7.8	4.3	8.2	14.6	8.8	6.2	4.9	3.5	6.1
Slovakia	6.7	5.2	11.9	4.7	5.4	4.0	6.8	4.3	4.8	0.0	0.6	2.2
Slovenia	0.8	2.0	7.4	1.1	2.4	1.6	1.7	3.2	3.6	-1.3	0.8	2.0
Ukraine	1.9	2.1	1.6	2.8	2.6	9.1	5.2	6.9	6.1	4.1	4.8	4.4

Source: Euromonitor International from national statistics

Table 9.20

Exchange Rates Against the US$ 1985, 1990, 1995, 2000, 2006-2011

National currency per US$

	1985	1990	1995	2000	2006	2007	2008	2009	2010	2011
Western Europe										
Austria	1.31	0.79	0.76	1.09	0.80	0.73	0.68	0.72	0.76	0.72
Belgium	1.31	0.79	0.76	1.09	0.80	0.73	0.68	0.72	0.76	0.72
Cyprus	1.31	0.79	0.76	1.09	0.80	0.73	0.68	0.72	0.76	0.72
Denmark	10.60	6.19	5.60	8.09	5.94	5.44	5.10	5.36	5.62	5.36
Finland	1.31	0.79	0.76	1.09	0.80	0.73	0.68	0.72	0.76	0.72
France	1.31	0.79	0.76	1.09	0.80	0.73	0.68	0.72	0.76	0.72
Germany	1.31	0.79	0.76	1.09	0.80	0.73	0.68	0.72	0.76	0.72
Gibraltar	0.78	0.56	0.63	0.66	0.54	0.50	0.55	0.64	0.65	0.62
Greece	1.31	0.79	0.76	1.09	0.80	0.73	0.68	0.72	0.76	0.72
Iceland	41.51	58.28	64.69	78.62	70.18	64.06	87.95	123.64	122.24	115.95
Ireland	1.31	0.79	0.76	1.09	0.80	0.73	0.68	0.72	0.76	0.72
Italy	1.31	0.79	0.76	1.09	0.80	0.73	0.68	0.72	0.76	0.72
Liechtenstein	2.46	1.39	1.18	1.69	1.25	1.20	1.08	1.09	1.04	0.89
Luxembourg	1.31	0.79	0.76	1.09	0.80	0.73	0.68	0.72	0.76	0.72
Malta	1.31	0.79	0.76	1.09	0.80	0.73	0.68	0.72	0.76	0.72
Monaco	1.31	0.79	0.76	1.09	0.80	0.73	0.68	0.72	0.76	0.72
Netherlands	1.31	0.79	0.76	1.09	0.80	0.73	0.68	0.72	0.76	0.72
Norway	8.60	6.26	6.34	8.80	6.41	5.86	5.64	6.29	6.04	5.61
Portugal	1.31	0.79	0.76	1.09	0.80	0.73	0.68	0.72	0.76	0.72
Spain	1.31	0.79	0.76	1.09	0.80	0.73	0.68	0.72	0.76	0.72
Sweden	8.60	5.92	7.13	9.16	7.38	6.76	6.59	7.65	7.21	6.50
Switzerland	2.46	1.39	1.18	1.69	1.25	1.20	1.08	1.09	1.04	0.89
Turkey	0.00	0.00	0.05	0.63	1.44	1.31	1.30	1.56	1.51	1.68
United Kingdom	0.78	0.56	0.63	0.66	0.54	0.50	0.55	0.64	0.65	0.62
Eastern Europe										
Albania	7.00	7.75	92.70	143.71	98.10	90.43	83.89	94.98	103.94	100.90
Belarus		0.00	8.77	876.75	2,144.56	2,146.08	2,136.40	2,793.05	2,978.51	4,974.63
Bosnia-Herzegovina		0.00	1.40	2.12	1.56	1.43	1.34	1.41	1.48	1.41
Bulgaria	0.00	0.00	0.07	2.12	1.56	1.43	1.34	1.41	1.48	1.41
Croatia		0.01	5.23	8.28	5.84	5.36	4.94	5.28	5.50	5.34
Czech Republic		17.95	26.54	38.60	22.60	20.29	17.07	19.07	19.10	17.70
Estonia	1.31	0.79	0.76	1.09	0.80	0.73	0.68	0.72	0.76	0.72
Georgia		0.00	1.37	1.98	1.78	1.67	1.49	1.67	1.78	1.69
Hungary	50.12	63.21	125.68	282.18	210.39	183.63	172.11	202.34	207.94	201.05
Latvia		0.01	0.53	0.61	0.56	0.51	0.48	0.50	0.53	0.51
Lithuania		0.01	4.00	4.00	2.75	2.52	2.36	2.48	2.61	2.48
Macedonia		0.11	37.88	65.90	48.80	44.73	41.87	44.10	46.49	44.23
Moldova		0.00	3.67	12.43	13.13	12.14	10.39	11.11	12.37	11.74
Montenegro	1.31	0.79	0.76	1.09	0.80	0.73	0.68	0.72	0.76	0.72
Poland	0.01	0.95	2.42	4.35	3.10	2.77	2.41	3.12	3.01	2.96
Romania	0.00	0.00	0.20	2.17	2.81	2.44	2.52	3.05	3.18	3.05
Russia		0.00	3.58	28.13	27.19	25.58	24.85	31.76	30.37	29.39
Serbia		0.00	2.93	44.02	67.15	58.45	55.72	67.58	77.73	73.33
Slovakia	1.31	0.79	0.76	1.09	0.80	0.73	0.68	0.72	0.76	0.72
Slovenia	1.31	0.79	0.76	1.09	0.80	0.73	0.68	0.72	0.76	0.72
Ukraine		0.00	1.12	5.44	5.05	5.05	5.27	7.79	7.94	7.97

Source: Euromonitor International from national statistics
Note: Annual average market exchange rates

Economic Indicators

9

Economic Statistics | **Table 9.21**

Exchange Rates Against the Euro 1985, 1990, 1995, 2000, 2006-2011

National currency per Euro

	1985	1990	1995	2000	2006	2007	2008	2009	2010	2011
Western Europe										
Austria	1.00	1.00	1.00	1.00	1.00	1.00	1.00	1.00	1.00	1.00
Belgium	1.00	1.00	1.00	1.00	1.00	1.00	1.00	1.00	1.00	1.00
Cyprus	1.00	1.00	1.00	1.00	1.00	1.00	1.00	1.00	1.00	1.00
Denmark	8.09	7.88	7.33	7.45	7.46	7.45	7.46	7.45	7.45	7.45
Finland	1.00	1.00	1.00	1.00	1.00	1.00	1.00	1.00	1.00	1.00
France	1.00	1.00	1.00	1.00	1.00	1.00	1.00	1.00	1.00	1.00
Germany	1.00	1.00	1.00	1.00	1.00	1.00	1.00	1.00	1.00	1.00
Gibraltar	0.59	0.72	0.83	0.61	0.68	0.68	0.80	0.89	0.86	0.87
Greece	1.00	1.00	1.00	1.00	1.00	1.00	1.00	1.00	1.00	1.00
Iceland	31.67	74.22	84.62	72.45	88.04	87.67	128.71	171.81	161.89	161.23
Ireland	1.00	1.00	1.00	1.00	1.00	1.00	1.00	1.00	1.00	1.00
Italy	1.00	1.00	1.00	1.00	1.00	1.00	1.00	1.00	1.00	1.00
Liechtenstein	1.88	1.77	1.55	1.56	1.57	1.64	1.59	1.51	1.38	1.23
Luxembourg	1.00	1.00	1.00	1.00	1.00	1.00	1.00	1.00	1.00	1.00
Malta	1.00	1.00	1.00	1.00	1.00	1.00	1.00	1.00	1.00	1.00
Monaco	1.00	1.00	1.00	1.00	1.00	1.00	1.00	1.00	1.00	1.00
Netherlands	1.00	1.00	1.00	1.00	1.00	1.00	1.00	1.00	1.00	1.00
Norway	6.56	7.97	8.29	8.11	8.05	8.02	8.25	8.74	8.00	7.79
Portugal	1.00	1.00	1.00	1.00	1.00	1.00	1.00	1.00	1.00	1.00
Spain	1.00	1.00	1.00	1.00	1.00	1.00	1.00	1.00	1.00	1.00
Sweden	6.57	7.54	9.33	8.44	9.25	9.25	9.64	10.64	9.55	9.03
Switzerland	1.88	1.77	1.55	1.56	1.57	1.64	1.59	1.51	1.38	1.23
Turkey	0.00	0.00	0.06	0.58	1.80	1.79	1.91	2.16	2.00	2.34
United Kingdom	0.59	0.72	0.83	0.61	0.68	0.68	0.80	0.89	0.86	0.87
Eastern Europe										
Albania	5.34	9.86	121.25	132.43	123.08	123.77	122.78	131.98	137.65	140.29
Belarus		0.00	11.47	807.94	2,690.45	2,937.28	3,126.57	3,881.20	3,944.54	6,916.88
Bosnia-Herzegovina		0.00	1.83	1.96	1.96	1.96	1.96	1.96	1.96	1.96
Bulgaria	0.00	0.00	0.09	1.96	1.96	1.96	1.96	1.95	1.96	1.96
Croatia		0.01	6.84	7.63	7.32	7.34	7.22	7.34	7.28	7.43
Czech Republic		22.86	34.72	35.57	28.35	27.78	24.98	26.49	25.29	24.60
Estonia	1.00	1.00	1.00	1.00	1.00	1.00	1.00	1.00	1.00	1.00
Georgia		0.00	1.79	1.82	2.23	2.29	2.18	2.32	2.36	2.34
Hungary	38.25	80.49	164.39	260.03	263.94	251.32	251.88	281.17	275.39	279.55
Latvia		0.01	0.69	0.56	0.70	0.70	0.70	0.70	0.70	0.70
Lithuania		0.02	5.23	3.69	3.45	3.45	3.45	3.45	3.45	3.45
Macedonia		0.14	49.55	60.73	61.22	61.22	61.27	61.28	61.56	61.50
Moldova		0.00	4.80	11.46	16.47	16.62	15.21	15.44	16.38	16.32
Montenegro	1.00	1.00	1.00	1.00	1.00	1.00	1.00	1.00	1.00	1.00
Poland	0.01	1.21	3.17	4.00	3.89	3.79	3.53	4.34	3.99	4.12
Romania	0.00	0.00	0.27	2.00	3.52	3.34	3.69	4.24	4.21	4.24
Russia		0.00	4.68	25.92	34.11	35.01	36.37	44.14	40.22	40.87
Serbia		0.00	3.84	40.57	84.24	80.00	81.55	93.91	102.94	101.97
Slovakia	1.00	1.00	1.00	1.00	1.00	1.00	1.00	1.00	1.00	1.00
Slovenia	1.00	1.00	1.00	1.00	1.00	1.00	1.00	1.00	1.00	1.00
Ukraine		0.00	1.47	5.01	6.34	6.91	7.71	10.83	10.51	11.08

Source: Euromonitor International from national statistics
Note: Annual average market exchange rates

10

CHAPTER TEN

Education

Education Statistics

Table 10.1

Education Statistics 2011

As stated

	Adult Literacy Rate (% of population aged 15+)	Compulsory Education Commencement (years)	School Leaving Age (years)
Western Europe			
Austria	100	6	14
Belgium	100	6	18
Cyprus	98	6	14
Denmark	100	7	16
Finland	100	7	16
France	100	6	16
Germany	100	6	18
Gibraltar		4	15
Greece	97	6	14
Iceland		6	16
Ireland	100	6	15
Italy	99	6	14
Liechtenstein		6	14
Luxembourg		6	15
Malta	94	5	15
Monaco		6	16
Netherlands	100	5	17
Norway	100	6	16
Portugal	95	6	14
Spain	98	6	16
Sweden	100	7	16
Switzerland	100	7	15
Turkey	92	6	14
United Kingdom	100	5	16
Eastern Europe			
Albania	95	6	13
Belarus	100	6	14
Bosnia-Herzegovina	98	6	15
Bulgaria	98	7	14
Croatia	99	7	14
Czech Republic	100	6	15
Estonia	100	7	15
Georgia	100	6	15
Hungary	99	7	16
Latvia	100	7	15
Lithuania	100	7	15
Macedonia	97	7	14
Moldova	99	7	15
Montenegro	98	6	14
Poland	100	7	15
Romania	98	6	16
Russia	100	6	15
Serbia	98	7	14
Slovakia	100	6	14
Slovenia	100	6	14
Ukraine	100	6	17

Source: Euromonitor International from national statistics

Table 10.2

Pre-primary Education 2011
As stated

	Pre-Primary Schools	Staff ('000)	Pupils ('000)	Pupil to Staff Ratio
Western Europe				
Austria	5,083.0	19.8	241.4	12.2
Belgium	2,248.0	32.3	443.9	13.7
Cyprus	682.0	1.3	21.3	16.0
Denmark	1,964.0	41.7	254.5	6.1
Finland		14.8	161.4	
France	16,067.0	135.5	2,551.5	18.8
Germany	1,515.0	224.6	2,378.4	10.6
Gibraltar				
Greece	6,617.0	12.7	158.0	12.4
Iceland	278.0	2.2	13.1	6.0
Ireland				
Italy	24,419.0	146.3	1,680.9	11.5
Liechtenstein		0.1	0.7	
Luxembourg		1.5	15.7	
Malta	102.0	0.5	8.1	15.9
Monaco			0.9	
Netherlands			394.1	
Norway	6,529.0		181.9	
Portugal	7,154.0	17.5	280.4	16.0
Spain	21,131.0	192.3	1,986.7	10.3
Sweden	9,917.0	76.6	416.0	5.4
Switzerland		11.4	146.7	
Turkey	27,606.0	48.3	1,115.8	23.1
United Kingdom	3,095.0	59.0	1,242.1	21.1
Eastern Europe				
Albania	1,860.0	4.1	74.4	18.3
Belarus	4,033.0	45.5	281.0	6.2
Bosnia-Herzegovina	130.0	0.8	10.6	14.1
Bulgaria	2,138.0	18.5	223.2	12.0
Croatia	1,497.0	7.9	101.6	12.9
Czech Republic	4,829.0	22.6	330.4	14.7
Estonia	642.0	8.1	56.3	7.0
Georgia	1,147.0	6.8	86.2	12.7
Hungary	4,358.0	30.4	330.2	11.1
Latvia	591.0	7.4	72.0	9.7
Lithuania	621.0	12.4	87.4	7.1
Macedonia	55.0	3.7	38.6	10.3
Moldova	1,381.0	12.5	121.0	9.7
Montenegro	91.0	0.8	10.4	13.6
Poland	19,418.0	57.1	1,061.5	18.6
Romania	1,680.0	38.9	672.6	17.3
Russia	45,155.0	642.7	5,359.7	8.3
Serbia	2,552.0	11.6	154.9	13.4
Slovakia	2,671.0	11.3	144.5	12.8
Slovenia	912.0	2.7	49.8	18.6
Ukraine	15,691.0	139.1	1,264.3	9.1

Source: Euromonitor International from national statistics

10

Education

Education Statistics

Table 10.3

Primary Education 2011

As stated

	Primary Schools	Staff ('000)	Pupils ('000)	Pupil to Staff Ratio
Western Europe				
Austria	3,177.0	30.3	329.5	10.9
Belgium	4,862.0	65.9	729.2	11.1
Cyprus	370.0	4.2	54.8	12.9
Denmark	2,430.0	45.0	401.4	8.9
Finland	2,140.0	27.8	346.8	12.5
France	37,569.0	221.4	4,136.4	18.7
Germany	16,099.0	239.2	2,974.3	12.4
Gibraltar		0.2	3.6	
Greece	5,977.0	65.4	659.6	10.1
Iceland		4.5	29.4	
Ireland	3,332.0	32.8	509.6	15.5
Italy	17,966.0	275.2	2,817.3	10.2
Liechtenstein		0.2	2.1	
Luxembourg		2.7	35.1	
Malta	117.0	2.7	22.0	8.1
Monaco			1.8	
Netherlands	7,186.0	146.0	1,270.5	8.7
Norway	1,742.0	46.1	421.9	9.2
Portugal	6,056.0	64.4	732.2	11.4
Spain	13,906.0	231.4	2,818.4	12.2
Sweden	4,529.0	64.7	578.9	9.0
Switzerland		42.3	491.3	
Turkey	32,797.0	503.3	6,292.3	12.5
United Kingdom	21,301.0	234.6	4,472.3	19.1
Eastern Europe				
Albania	1,577.0	11.7	230.8	19.6
Belarus	312.0	24.1	354.1	14.7
Bosnia-Herzegovina	1,091.0	15.6	233.2	14.9
Bulgaria	1,585.0	13.7	251.4	18.4
Croatia	2,128.0	12.0	159.6	13.3
Czech Republic	4,105.0	24.0	469.8	19.6
Estonia	63.0	5.6	73.2	13.0
Georgia	2,421.0	39.9	302.9	7.6
Hungary	3,306.0	35.6	390.5	11.0
Latvia	395.0	12.5	113.7	9.1
Lithuania	182.0	9.4	115.6	12.3
Macedonia	1,044.0	6.1	89.1	14.6
Moldova	83.0	9.4	142.0	15.1
Montenegro	441.0	5.1	34.1	6.7
Poland	13,728.0	251.2	2,175.2	8.7
Romania	4,449.0	53.7	817.1	15.2
Russia	2,327.0	292.7	5,275.5	18.0
Serbia	3,491.0	17.4	271.6	15.6
Slovakia	2,180.0	13.6	208.0	15.3
Slovenia	869.0	6.4	113.5	17.8
Ukraine	24,814.0	103.9	1,532.2	14.7

Source: Euromonitor International from national statistics

Table 10.4

Secondary Education 2011

As stated

	Staff ('000)	Total Pupils ('000)	Pupils in Technical Colleges ('000)	Pupil to Staff Ratio
Western Europe				
Austria	73.7	729.3	294.0	9.9
Belgium	82.3	803.6	333.0	9.8
Cyprus	6.7	62.2	3.8	9.3
Denmark	76.9	499.7	129.7	6.5
Finland	42.2	415.6	128.4	9.9
France	457.6	5,887.4	1,417.1	12.9
Germany	580.2	7,455.9	1,448.7	12.9
Gibraltar	0.4	1.6		4.5
Greece	87.9	643.7	75.2	7.3
Iceland	3.6	34.9	7.1	9.6
Ireland	25.2	336.5	114.3	13.4
Italy	486.2	4,591.0	1,691.9	9.4
Liechtenstein	0.3	3.3	1.2	10.2
Luxembourg	4.2	42.9	12.8	10.1
Malta	4.7	35.7	6.7	7.6
Monaco	0.5	3.0	0.6	5.5
Netherlands	110.4	1,486.6	711.3	13.5
Norway	48.6	425.3	119.4	8.7
Portugal	101.3	744.6	224.4	7.4
Spain	298.1	3,055.3	482.1	10.2
Sweden	75.7	721.5	243.5	9.5
Switzerland	50.1	602.5	213.5	12.0
Turkey	374.3	7,686.3	1,928.9	20.5
United Kingdom	362.7	5,044.7	592.2	13.9
Eastern Europe				
Albania	24.9	345.1	20.4	13.9
Belarus	85.2	614.8	3.7	7.2
Bosnia-Herzegovina	7.4	90.0	44.7	12.1
Bulgaria	41.4	500.7	146.9	12.1
Croatia	47.9	387.7	128.0	8.1
Czech Republic	70.4	795.7	313.5	11.3
Estonia	9.8	93.6	17.5	9.6
Georgia	46.6	354.3	5.3	7.6
Hungary	87.5	914.9	273.6	10.5
Latvia	16.5	155.3	35.8	9.4
Lithuania	36.9	378.1	37.6	10.3
Macedonia	17.3	199.7	56.4	11.5
Moldova	27.5	292.6	39.7	10.6
Montenegro	2.2	70.1		32.0
Poland	271.0	2,804.9	810.9	10.4
Romania	147.6	1,796.8	593.2	12.2
Russia	1,092.3	8,574.3	1,404.7	7.8
Serbia	65.3	596.9	219.3	9.1
Slovakia	43.3	516.3	181.9	11.9
Slovenia	15.2	128.5	46.3	8.5
Ukraine	337.7	3,013.7	274.9	8.9

Source: Euromonitor International from national statistics

10

Education

Education Statistics **Table 10.5**

Higher and University Education 2011

As stated

	Establishments	Teaching Staff ('000)	Students ('000)	Student to Staff Ratio	University Teachers ('000)	University Teachers (% of total)	University Students ('000)	University Teachers (% of total)	University Students to Staff Ratio
Western Europe									
Austria	64.0	34.8	347.7	10.0			308.6	88.8	
Belgium	29.0	27.6	452.9	16.4			223.7	49.4	
Cyprus	43.0	2.8	35.3	12.6	0.5	16.7	26.8	76.1	57.5
Denmark	180.0	22.7	236.5	10.4			199.2	84.2	
Finland	51.0	13.5	291.3	21.5	5.7	42.2	271.0	93.0	47.4
France	321.0	139.4	2,155.4	15.5			1,521.2	70.6	
Germany	413.0	358.0	2,487.7	6.9	266.5	74.4	1,982.9	79.7	7.4
Gibraltar									
Greece	26.0	28.1	653.7	23.3	17.3	61.8	348.4	53.3	20.1
Iceland		2.4	17.8	7.5	2.4	100.0	17.1	96.2	7.2
Ireland	45.0	13.5	182.8	13.5			128.2	70.2	
Italy		110.5	1,998.5	18.1	110.2	99.8	1,947.8	97.5	17.7
Liechtenstein			0.8				0.8	94.3	
Luxembourg		0.5	2.6	5.3			2.2	82.9	
Malta	7.0	1.1	10.1	8.9	1.1	100.0	8.7	86.0	7.7
Monaco									
Netherlands	66.0	54.4	647.6	11.9	54.4	100.0	638.1	98.5	11.7
Norway	71.0	23.1	222.9	9.7	12.7	54.9	213.9	96.0	16.9
Portugal	289.0	34.9	381.3	10.9			370.2	97.1	
Spain	77.0	156.1	1,817.8	11.6	125.6	80.5	1,478.3	81.3	11.8
Sweden	36.0	35.5	422.8	11.9			375.0	88.7	
Switzerland		40.8	261.2	6.4	40.8	100.0	181.6	69.5	4.4
Turkey	1,709.0	111.2	3,174.3	28.5	105.1	94.5	2,053.6	64.7	19.5
United Kingdom	164.0	142.6	2,411.1	16.9			1,817.7	75.4	
Eastern Europe									
Albania	33.0	3.3	100.3	30.4					
Belarus	56.0	41.0	581.3	14.2	26.8	65.2	425.4	73.2	15.9
Bosnia-Herzegovina	91.0	1.4	73.1	51.1					
Bulgaria	53.0	19.3	278.8	14.4	18.2	94.3	247.4	88.7	13.6
Croatia	137.0	17.0	155.2	9.2			109.1	70.2	
Czech Republic	262.0	26.5	455.0	17.1	19.9	75.1	397.5	87.4	19.9
Estonia	32.0	6.1	67.7	11.1	3.3	53.8	43.3	63.9	13.2
Georgia	129.0	9.6	74.9	7.8	8.9	92.9	60.7	81.1	6.8
Hungary	69.0	23.2	372.5	16.1	20.9	90.2	329.3	88.4	15.8
Latvia	58.0	8.2	116.5	14.2	7.2	87.9	92.6	79.4	12.8
Lithuania	62.0	14.4	208.3	14.5	10.7	74.7	143.8	69.0	13.4
Macedonia		4.4	73.4	16.7	3.9	88.5	71.0	96.7	18.3
Moldova	34.0	6.8	120.8	17.6	6.1	89.0	101.6	84.0	16.7
Montenegro	4.0	1.4	23.0	16.0			22.5	97.6	
Poland	455.0	100.5	2,096.1	20.9			2,044.7	97.5	
Romania	110.0	30.2	1,163.5	38.6	30.2	100.0	1,148.5	98.7	38.1
Russia	1,123.0	688.4	9,271.3	13.5	502.6	73.0	7,252.1	78.2	14.4
Serbia		15.9	238.8	15.0	9.3	58.6	198.9	83.3	21.4
Slovakia	34.0	11.9	249.4	21.0	11.0	92.2	237.7	95.3	21.7
Slovenia	89.0	6.7	111.7	16.7			82.8	74.1	
Ukraine	841.0	192.9	2,679.9	13.9			2,320.4	86.6	

Source: Euromonitor International from national statistics

Table 10.6

Foreign Students in Higher and University Education 1985, 1990, 1995, 2000, 2006-2011

'000

	1985	1990	1995	2000	2006	2007	2008	2009	2010	2011
Western Europe										
Austria		17.9	26.3	30.4	39.3	43.6	53.4	59.7	63.9	70.3
Belgium		20.7	32.4	38.8	24.9	25.2	29.8	34.0	37.1	40.9
Cyprus				2.0	5.3	5.6	7.2	9.8	11.3	13.1
Denmark		6.1	8.8	12.9	12.2	12.7	6.4	12.6	12.7	12.6
Finland		1.6	3.4	5.6	11.5	10.1	11.3	12.6	12.9	13.9
France		136.0	129.2	137.1	247.5	246.6	243.4	249.1	250.2	250.1
Germany			159.9	187.0	208.0	206.9	189.3	197.9	193.0	186.6
Gibraltar										
Greece		2.3	3.8	4.8	16.6	21.2	26.2	29.1	32.5	35.9
Iceland				0.4	0.7	0.7	0.7	0.8	0.8	0.8
Ireland		3.3	5.8	7.4	12.7	16.8	12.8	12.9	13.1	12.2
Italy		21.4	22.4	24.9	49.1	57.3	68.3	75.9	84.1	92.2
Liechtenstein					0.6	0.6	0.7	0.6	0.6	0.6
Luxembourg				0.7	1.1	1.2	1.2	1.2	1.2	1.2
Malta				0.4	0.6	0.5	0.4	0.4	0.4	0.3
Monaco										
Netherlands		8.9	9.7	14.0	27.0	27.5	30.1	23.7	22.8	21.2
Norway		6.9	11.2	8.7	14.3	15.6	16.1	17.5	17.8	18.4
Portugal		3.8	7.2	11.2	17.1	18.0	8.1	9.1	7.5	5.4
Spain					18.2	32.3	37.7	48.5	56.8	63.7
Sweden					21.3	22.1	22.7	27.0	29.1	31.3
Switzerland		22.6	24.1	26.0	36.7	38.3	31.7	34.8	34.2	32.7
Turkey		7.7	14.1	17.7	19.1	19.3	20.2	21.0	21.3	21.9
United Kingdom		80.2	197.2	222.9	330.1	351.5	341.8	369.0	378.1	382.7
Eastern Europe										
Albania										
Belarus			1.8	2.7	3.5	4.4	5.9	6.2	6.5	6.9
Bosnia-Herzegovina										
Bulgaria		7.3	8.2	8.1	9.4	9.1	9.3	9.4	9.3	9.2
Croatia			0.3	1.6	3.4	3.5	4.7	5.1	5.6	6.4
Czech Republic			3.3	5.5	21.4	24.5	28.0	30.6	33.1	35.3
Estonia			0.4	0.9	1.1	1.0	1.0	1.1	1.1	1.1
Georgia				0.2	0.1	0.4	0.6	0.5	0.6	0.6
Hungary		3.3	6.9	9.9	14.5	15.1	15.5	14.5	14.6	14.4
Latvia			0.6	6.0	1.6	1.4	1.5	1.6	1.6	1.6
Lithuania			0.3	0.5	1.2	1.9	3.0	2.8	3.3	3.6
Macedonia				0.2	0.2	0.9	1.3	1.4	1.8	2.1
Moldova				2.0	1.9	1.9	1.6	1.5	1.3	1.1
Montenegro										
Poland		4.3	5.6	6.1	11.4	13.0	15.0	17.0	18.3	19.5
Romania		8.1	12.9	12.6	8.6	9.4	13.9	10.4	10.5	10.6
Russia			22.3	41.2	77.4	60.3	136.8	146.4	161.3	183.8
Serbia						7.0	11.3	10.4	13.3	15.0
Slovakia			1.8	1.6	1.6	1.9	5.2	6.3	7.6	9.1
Slovenia			0.4	0.8	1.1	1.2	1.4	2.0	2.3	2.5
Ukraine			19.1	15.6	26.6	29.6	32.6	35.8	37.5	39.0

Source: Euromonitor International from national statistics

Education Statistics

Table 10.7

Foreign Students' Share of All Higher and University Education Students 1985, 1990, 1995, 2000, 2006-2011

%

	1985	1990	1995	2000	2006	2007	2008	2009	2010	2011
Western Europe										
Austria		9.0	11.2	11.6	15.5	16.7	18.7	19.4	19.6	20.2
Belgium		7.6	9.2	10.9	6.3	6.4	7.4	8.0	8.5	9.0
Cyprus				19.5	25.8	25.1	27.9	31.8	35.1	37.1
Denmark		4.5	5.2	6.8	5.3	5.5	2.8	5.4	5.4	5.3
Finland		1.0	1.7	2.1	3.7	3.3	3.6	4.2	4.4	4.8
France		8.6	6.7	6.8	11.2	11.3	11.2	11.5	11.5	11.6
Germany			7.4	9.1	9.1	9.1	8.4	8.1	7.8	7.5
Gibraltar										
Greece		0.8	1.3	1.1	2.5	3.5	4.1	4.5	5.1	5.5
Iceland				3.8	4.3	4.7	4.1	4.6	4.7	4.7
Ireland		3.9	4.8	4.6	6.8	8.8	7.2	7.1	7.1	6.7
Italy		1.6	1.3	1.4	2.4	2.8	3.4	3.8	4.2	4.6
Liechtenstein					89.1	86.6	81.3	74.4	70.7	66.7
Luxembourg				26.6	42.4	43.2	44.3	44.4	45.0	45.6
Malta				5.5	6.7	5.5	4.6	3.9	3.6	3.3
Monaco										
Netherlands		2.0	1.9	2.9	4.7	4.7	5.0	3.8	3.6	3.3
Norway		5.3	6.5	4.6	6.7	7.3	7.6	8.0	8.0	8.3
Portugal		2.4	2.4	3.0	4.7	4.9	2.1	2.4	2.0	1.4
Spain					1.0	1.8	2.1	2.7	3.1	3.5
Sweden					5.0	5.4	5.6	6.4	6.9	7.4
Switzerland		17.0	16.3	16.6	17.9	18.0	14.1	14.9	13.7	12.5
Turkey		1.1	1.2	1.1	0.8	0.8	0.8	0.7	0.7	0.7
United Kingdom		6.8	10.9	11.0	14.1	14.9	14.7	15.3	15.6	15.9
Eastern Europe										
Albania										
Belarus		0.6	0.7	0.7	0.8	1.0	1.1	1.1	1.2	
Bosnia-Herzegovina										
Bulgaria	4.6	3.7	3.1	3.8	3.5	3.5	3.4	3.3	3.3	
Croatia		0.3	1.6	2.5	2.5	3.3	3.7	3.8	4.1	
Czech Republic		1.8	2.2	6.3	6.7	7.1	7.3	7.6	7.8	
Estonia		1.6	1.6	1.6	1.4	1.5	1.5	1.5	1.6	
Georgia			0.1	0.1	0.3	0.5	0.5	0.7	0.9	
Hungary	3.3	4.1	3.2	3.3	3.5	3.7	3.7	3.8	3.9	
Latvia		1.5	6.6	1.2	1.1	1.2	1.3	1.3	1.3	
Lithuania		0.4	0.4	0.6	1.0	1.4	1.3	1.5	1.7	
Macedonia			0.7	0.4	1.5	2.0	2.2	2.6	2.8	
Moldova			1.9	1.3	1.3	1.1	1.1	1.0	0.9	
Montenegro										
Poland	0.8	0.6	0.4	0.5	0.6	0.7	0.8	0.9	0.9	
Romania	4.9	5.0	2.8	1.0	1.0	1.3	0.9	0.9	0.9	
Russia		0.5	0.7	0.8	0.6	1.4	1.5	1.7	2.0	
Serbia					2.9	4.7	4.4	5.5	6.3	
Slovakia		2.2	1.2	0.8	0.9	2.3	2.7	3.1	3.7	
Slovenia		1.0	0.9	0.9	1.0	1.2	1.8	2.0	2.3	
Ukraine		1.2	0.9	1.0	1.1	1.1	1.3	1.4	1.5	

Source: Euromonitor International from national statistics

11

Energy Resources and Output

Energy Statistics

Table 11.1

Refinery Product Consumption 2011

'000 metric tonnes

	Motor Gasoline	Liquefied Gases	Aviation Fuels	Diesel/Gasoil	Biofuels
Western Europe					
Austria	1,817.5	144.1	717.6	7,617.0	686.0
Belgium	1,010.9	665.7	1,939.1	11,514.1	497.5
Cyprus	406.0	53.8	280.8	468.4	
Denmark	1,670.7	59.3	886.7	3,858.3	14.7
Finland	1,734.6	376.5	679.1	4,217.2	322.7
France	7,578.8	3,986.8	7,013.2	46,278.2	3,276.6
Germany	16,978.2	2,641.5	9,101.9	45,192.6	5,445.5
Gibraltar	26.6		4.0	75.6	
Greece	3,795.6	314.8	1,030.9	6,327.5	147.5
Iceland	154.1	2.2	53.9	259.6	
Ireland	1,669.1	88.6	478.7	3,518.5	135.6
Italy	8,317.3	3,099.0	3,849.9	29,163.4	1,743.9
Liechtenstein					
Luxembourg	352.5	10.6	430.3	2,100.1	62.6
Malta	76.4	22.7	103.9	126.3	
Monaco					
Netherlands	4,067.9	1,966.7	3,686.0	7,922.2	763.7
Norway	1,229.6	1,409.8	751.5	3,913.9	158.9
Portugal	1,508.6	809.9	962.4	5,202.8	385.8
Spain	5,401.4	1,930.8	5,416.4	32,197.1	1,739.5
Sweden	3,195.0	1,037.9	924.4	3,867.6	546.9
Switzerland	3,296.6	193.1	1,375.7	6,589.2	11.3
Turkey	2,062.7	3,467.5	2,425.7	16,052.4	18.6
United Kingdom	15,279.5	4,374.5	12,234.7	26,250.2	1,586.7
Eastern Europe					
Albania	116.6	75.7	19.4	548.9	
Belarus	1,151.8	265.6		2,549.6	
Bosnia-Herzegovina	315.0	28.0	5.0	558.6	
Bulgaria	594.6	393.5	200.8	1,763.5	
Croatia	692.3	264.5	100.8	1,798.8	
Czech Republic	2,018.1	187.7	405.3	4,283.6	358.7
Estonia	311.8	7.5	33.9	564.0	
Georgia	339.2	50.6	50.0	373.1	
Hungary	1,523.4	303.7	265.9	3,206.7	230.9
Latvia	310.0	44.0	105.0	787.0	
Lithuania	379.2	247.0	60.1	957.2	
Macedonia	121.2	76.3	0.5	378.1	
Moldova	250.7	55.8	16.2	403.5	
Montenegro					
Poland	3,811.5	2,685.3	565.4	12,817.2	1,058.1
Romania	1,607.4	520.1	200.3	3,872.8	
Russia	33,627.4	15,459.0	10,891.7	28,750.5	
Serbia	626.3	446.2	44.4	1,524.9	
Slovakia	591.1	166.8	53.2	1,272.3	208.8
Slovenia	597.1	83.2	25.8	1,822.4	111.0
Ukraine	5,306.8	839.5	313.1	5,391.6	

Source: Euromonitor International from national statistics

Table 11.2

Motor Gasoline Consumption 1985, 1990, 1995, 2000, 2006-2011

'000 metric tonnes

	1985	1990	1995	2000	2006	2007	2008	2009	2010	2011
Western Europe										
Austria	2,430.0	2,552.0	2,394.0	1,981.0	2,007.0	1,926.0	1,665.0	1,744.0	1,797.1	1,817.5
Belgium	2,502.0	2,727.0	2,833.0	2,245.0	1,465.0	1,394.0	1,439.0	1,346.0	1,239.2	1,010.9
Cyprus	124.0	163.0	183.0	206.0	323.0	352.0	373.0	383.0	389.5	406.0
Denmark	1,530.0	1,581.0	1,893.0	1,966.0	1,834.0	1,817.0	1,730.0	1,642.0	1,731.3	1,670.7
Finland	1,521.0	1,986.0	1,897.0	1,785.0	1,861.0	1,857.0	1,662.0	1,601.0	1,688.7	1,734.6
France	18,006.0	18,231.0	15,613.0	13,803.0	10,033.0	9,302.0	8,284.0	7,973.0	8,244.1	7,578.8
Germany	26,212.0	31,274.0	30,134.0	28,806.0	22,092.0	20,828.0	20,162.0	19,543.0	18,901.9	16,978.2
Gibraltar	5.0	12.0	16.0	20.0	23.0	24.0	25.0	26.0	26.1	26.6
Greece	1,795.0	2,423.0	2,774.0	3,280.0	3,959.0	4,137.0	4,059.0	4,070.0	3,936.5	3,795.6
Iceland	99.0	134.0	136.0	143.0	161.0	160.0	152.0	157.0	152.9	154.1
Ireland	841.0	885.0	1,037.0	1,493.0	1,877.0	1,821.0	1,706.0	1,548.0	1,665.9	1,669.1
Italy	11,820.0	14,055.0	18,496.0	16,863.0	13,090.0	12,321.0	11,223.0	10,688.0	9,079.9	8,317.3
Liechtenstein										
Luxembourg	303.0	412.0	516.0	582.0	450.0	432.0	410.0	376.0	384.7	352.5
Malta	20.0	65.0	120.0	71.0	76.0	64.0	70.0	73.0	73.8	76.4
Monaco										
Netherlands	3,395.0	3,445.0	4,023.0	4,031.0	4,169.0	4,053.0	4,151.0	3,962.0	4,061.4	4,067.9
Norway	1,587.0	1,785.0	1,664.0	1,619.0	1,519.0	1,440.0	1,351.0	1,269.0	1,299.5	1,229.6
Portugal	855.0	1,369.0	1,890.0	2,123.0	1,672.0	1,587.0	1,488.0	1,462.0	1,495.0	1,508.6
Spain	5,894.0	8,145.0	8,534.0	8,524.0	6,928.0	6,669.0	6,143.0	5,765.0	5,666.7	5,401.4
Sweden	3,750.0	4,166.0	4,251.0	3,977.0	3,741.0	3,654.0	3,363.0	3,323.0	3,402.6	3,195.0
Switzerland	3,058.0	3,724.0	3,590.0	3,983.0	3,484.0	3,450.0	3,374.0	3,282.0	3,240.0	3,296.6
Turkey	1,916.0	3,196.0	4,330.0	3,619.0	2,723.0	2,463.0	2,344.0	2,449.0	2,140.1	2,062.7
United Kingdom	20,403.0	24,312.0	21,953.0	21,603.0	18,144.0	17,591.0	16,663.0	15,762.0	15,589.4	15,279.5
Eastern Europe										
Albania	121.0	60.0	133.0	103.0	176.0	160.0	99.0	56.0	119.0	116.6
Belarus		2,363.0	1,154.0	987.0	1,121.0	1,094.0	1,137.0	1,095.0	1,088.9	1,151.8
Bosnia-Herzegovina		349.0	118.0	321.0	280.0	299.0	315.0	306.0	311.4	315.0
Bulgaria	1,213.0	1,391.0	1,083.0	659.0	605.0	597.0	598.0	616.0	602.5	594.6
Croatia		764.0	575.0	784.0	710.0	724.0	695.0	691.0	695.8	692.3
Czech Republic	1,069.0	1,161.0	1,637.0	1,858.0	2,010.0	2,098.0	1,965.0	1,950.0	1,995.6	2,018.1
Estonia		523.0	247.0	282.0	308.0	323.0	320.0	294.0	308.3	311.8
Georgia		894.0	134.0	272.0	328.0	409.0	351.0	350.0	340.6	339.2
Hungary	1,336.0	1,790.0	1,427.0	1,336.0	1,510.0	1,533.0	1,492.0	1,492.0	1,507.7	1,523.4
Latvia		608.0	412.0	337.0	381.0	416.0	379.0	317.0	302.8	310.0
Lithuania		980.0	603.0	381.0	355.0	418.0	412.0	345.0	374.1	379.2
Macedonia		161.0	207.0	144.0	107.0	114.0	118.0	121.0	120.1	121.2
Moldova		774.0	223.0	117.0	198.0	203.0	238.0	206.0	237.0	250.7
Montenegro										
Poland	2,944.0	3,079.0	4,372.0	5,001.0	4,058.0	4,049.0	3,999.0	4,007.0	3,844.7	3,811.5
Romania	1,405.0	2,083.0	1,022.0	1,326.0	1,552.0	1,607.0	1,532.0	1,486.0	1,602.3	1,607.4
Russia		30,436.0	24,836.0	23,259.0	27,893.0	28,757.0	31,573.0	31,279.0	31,998.7	33,627.4
Serbia		647.0	396.0	340.0	1,110.0	608.0	563.0	522.0	605.5	626.3
Slovakia	408.0	438.0	504.0	592.0	604.0	613.0	623.0	568.0	591.9	591.1
Slovenia		565.0	821.0	807.0	640.0	618.0	643.0	591.0	609.7	597.1
Ukraine		10,960.0	4,355.0	3,825.0	4,742.0	5,231.0	5,292.0	4,706.0	5,195.7	5,306.8

Source: Euromonitor International from national statistics

Energy Statistics

Table 11.3

Aviation Fuel Consumption 1990, 1995, 2000, 2006-2011

'000 metric tonnes

	1990	1995	2000	2006	2007	2008	2009	2010	2011
Western Europe									
Austria	302.0	449.0	571.0	686.0	726.0	729.0	636.0	690.5	717.6
Belgium	927.0	920.0	1,481.0	1,146.0	986.0	1,988.0	1,878.0	1,887.2	1,939.1
Cyprus	236.0	260.0	268.0	300.0	287.0	286.0	266.0	282.7	280.8
Denmark	662.0	694.0	823.0	893.0	934.0	914.0	812.0	865.0	886.7
Finland	447.0	397.0	492.0	592.0	658.0	701.0	626.0	643.4	679.1
France	3,735.0	4,565.0	6,507.0	6,866.0	7,052.0	7,102.0	6,576.0	6,787.7	7,013.2
Germany	5,417.0	5,804.0	7,142.0	8,497.0	8,808.0	8,924.0	8,683.0	8,612.6	9,101.9
Gibraltar	7.0	4.0	4.0	4.0	4.0	4.0	4.0	4.0	4.0
Greece	1,231.0	1,213.0	1,290.0	1,261.0	1,277.0	1,300.0	1,113.0	1,063.3	1,030.9
Iceland	80.0	73.0	137.0	181.0	168.0	120.0	77.0	56.9	53.9
Ireland	355.0	380.0	597.0	841.0	992.0	924.0	569.0	514.6	478.7
Italy	2,238.0	2,692.0	3,579.0	4,014.0	4,231.0	4,069.0	3,692.0	3,795.3	3,849.9
Liechtenstein									
Luxembourg	128.0	184.0	312.0	394.0	423.0	426.0	407.0	423.7	430.3
Malta	70.0	72.0	84.0	75.0	87.0	125.0	89.0	102.6	103.9
Monaco									
Netherlands	1,561.0	2,529.0	3,255.0	3,603.0	3,627.0	3,668.0	3,411.0	3,613.9	3,686.0
Norway	489.0	551.0	636.0	723.0	725.0	724.0	717.0	727.8	751.5
Portugal	565.0	604.0	769.0	898.0	974.0	998.0	936.0	962.1	962.4
Spain	2,391.0	3,023.0	4,368.0	5,422.0	5,704.0	5,631.0	5,133.0	5,347.1	5,416.4
Sweden	740.0	827.0	904.0	843.0	911.0	963.0	832.0	899.5	924.4
Switzerland	1,115.0	1,273.0	1,576.0	1,239.0	1,321.0	1,414.0	1,356.0	1,375.9	1,375.7
Turkey	467.0	1,120.0	1,228.0	1,723.0	2,119.0	2,033.0	2,097.0	2,289.2	2,425.7
United Kingdom	6,590.0	7,716.0	10,838.0	12,641.0	12,633.0	12,142.0	11,514.0	12,064.8	12,234.7
Eastern Europe									
Albania	27.4	31.2	41.0	38.0	10.0	18.0	18.0	21.0	19.4
Belarus									
Bosnia-Herzegovina	25.0	37.0	10.0	5.0	5.0	5.0	5.0	5.0	5.0
Bulgaria	269.0	322.0	98.0	199.0	217.0	218.0	170.0	196.9	200.8
Croatia	160.0	85.0	72.0	96.0	100.0	113.0	97.0	98.1	100.8
Czech Republic	169.0	180.0	192.0	339.0	368.0	387.0	358.0	389.7	405.3
Estonia	35.0	18.0	19.0	28.0	49.0	27.0	33.0	30.6	33.9
Georgia	197.0	4.0	15.0	37.0	47.0	40.0	40.0	46.9	50.0
Hungary	160.0	177.0	224.0	264.0	242.0	269.0	230.0	259.0	265.9
Latvia	71.0	27.0	26.0	66.0	79.0	95.0	99.0	101.4	105.0
Lithuania	131.0	40.0	26.0	55.0	70.0	79.0	39.0	54.3	60.1
Macedonia	5.0	31.0	28.0	4.0	7.0	6.0	3.0	1.2	0.5
Moldova	72.0	12.0	21.0	17.0	20.0	17.0	14.0	15.7	16.2
Montenegro									
Poland	215.0	262.0	269.0	417.0	434.0	520.0	471.0	527.0	565.4
Romania	227.0	179.0	123.0	135.0	174.0	184.0	195.0	188.2	200.3
Russia	17,323.0	9,189.0	8,717.0	10,602.0	10,699.0	11,394.0	10,445.0	10,720.8	10,891.7
Serbia	101.6	25.4	21.0	52.0	47.0	47.0	39.0	44.6	44.4
Slovakia	26.4	39.0	26.0	39.0	48.0	61.0	44.0	51.5	53.2
Slovenia	26.0	19.0	24.0	24.0	31.0	34.0	26.0	25.8	25.8
Ukraine	2,009.0	155.0	255.0	325.0	348.0	252.0	239.0	311.4	313.1

Source: Euromonitor International from national statistics

Table 11.4

Biofuel Consumption 2000-2011

'000 metric tonnes

	2000	2001	2002	2003	2004	2005	2006	2007	2008	2009	2010	2011
Western Europe												
Austria	20.0	22.0	23.0	23.0	25.0	64.0	323.0	408.0	510.0	643.0	616.5	686.0
Belgium						1.0	13.0	111.0	132.0	358.0	398.0	497.5
Cyprus												
Denmark							6.0	9.0	9.0	13.0	14.1	14.7
Finland			1.0	6.0	7.0		1.0	2.0	110.0	182.0	242.5	322.7
France	399.0	393.0	411.0	378.0	412.0	474.0	852.0	1,727.0	2,725.0	2,920.0	2,889.2	3,276.6
Germany	250.0	350.0	550.0	800.0	1,115.0	2,256.0	4,040.0	5,277.0	4,574.0	3,989.0	4,388.2	5,445.5
Gibraltar												
Greece							51.0	94.0	76.0	86.0	120.4	147.5
Iceland												
Ireland						1.0	3.0	27.0	70.0	97.0	108.3	135.6
Italy					286.0	200.0	223.0	202.0	884.0	1,373.0	1,358.4	1,743.9
Liechtenstein												
Luxembourg						1.0	1.0	1.0	40.0	43.0	47.0	53.8	62.6
Malta												
Monaco												
Netherlands						11.0	12.0	82.0	442.0	404.0	516.0	644.7	763.7
Norway							6.0	34.0	92.0	107.0	132.0	158.9
Portugal							79.0	153.0	150.0	254.0	327.6	385.8
Spain	80.0	80.0	187.0	257.0	229.0	339.0	242.0	480.0	732.0	1,264.0	1,424.6	1,739.5
Sweden		22.0	49.0	102.0	194.0	207.0	273.0	398.0	487.0	490.0	516.1	546.9
Switzerland						3.0	8.0	9.0	14.0	14.0	10.0	10.7	11.3
Turkey							22.0	14.0	20.0	10.0	15.4	18.6
United Kingdom			3.0	17.0	18.0	96.0	224.0	426.0	943.0	1,169.0	1,354.0	1,586.7
Eastern Europe												
Albania												
Belarus												
Bosnia-Herzegovina												
Bulgaria												
Croatia												
Czech Republic	63.5	46.0	66.3	70.0	36.0	3.0	21.0	34.0	139.0	245.0	297.3	358.7
Estonia												
Georgia												
Hungary						4.0	17.0	44.0	205.0	210.0	184.8	230.9
Latvia												
Lithuania												
Macedonia												
Moldova												
Montenegro												
Poland				44.0	21.0	70.0	126.0	140.0	548.0	775.0	828.6	1,058.1
Romania												
Russia												
Serbia												
Slovakia		33.0	3.0	2.0	1.0	11.0	46.0	102.0	155.0	201.0	182.1	208.8
Slovenia							2.0	16.0	29.0	35.0	87.3	111.0
Ukraine												

Source: Euromonitor International from national statistics

Energy Statistics

Table 11.5

Energy Intensity 2000-2011

US$ per tonne of energy consumed

	2000	2001	2002	2003	2004	2005	2006	2007	2008	2009	2010	2011
Western Europe												
Austria	6,117.9	5,790.9	6,338.6	7,452.1	8,752.4	9,054.2	9,894.4	11,727.5	12,560.1	11,866.1	11,751.1	13,786.1
Belgium	3,725.9	3,781.1	4,088.7	4,813.0	5,611.4	5,895.1	6,262.3	7,179.7	7,683.0	7,737.3	7,294.6	8,399.0
Cyprus												
Denmark	8,510.0	8,622.1	9,473.5	10,881.8	13,389.2	14,642.7	13,862.6	16,820.6	19,361.6	18,855.4	18,660.8	21,791.7
Finland	4,725.0	4,737.1	5,168.4	5,817.8	6,736.0	7,552.4	7,722.4	9,080.4	10,336.9	9,687.6	8,980.2	10,487.0
France	5,233.2	5,195.4	5,710.1	6,937.4	7,828.6	8,209.1	8,750.6	10,133.5	11,072.8	10,863.8	10,327.9	11,635.0
Germany	5,726.3	5,612.5	6,103.7	7,325.4	8,285.9	8,542.9	8,855.4	10,749.0	11,667.5	11,356.6	10,890.6	12,727.7
Gibraltar												
Greece	3,941.2	4,106.1	4,494.2	5,997.3	6,778.9	7,147.5	7,605.6	8,859.2	10,029.3	9,897.5	9,706.4	10,115.5
Iceland	3,623.9	3,169.2	3,425.8	4,219.2	4,907.9	6,032.0	5,947.0	6,383.8	4,320.7	3,101.2	3,218.1	3,604.8
Ireland	7,132.5	7,226.2	8,544.9	11,296.8	12,909.0	13,677.1	14,773.9	16,708.2	17,265.6	16,337.8	15,098.6	17,709.8
Italy	6,343.3	6,423.4	7,077.4	8,489.6	9,554.7	9,809.2	10,339.3	11,947.5	13,077.3	12,913.5	12,297.2	13,662.2
Liechtenstein												
Luxembourg												
Malta												
Monaco												
Netherlands	4,425.6	4,452.7	4,856.7	5,914.7	6,499.5	6,679.3	7,097.0	8,084.9	9,131.1	8,539.0	7,956.5	8,992.7
Norway	3,643.2	4,083.3	4,408.5	5,766.4	6,552.1	6,640.3	8,069.9	8,592.7	9,707.6	8,592.0	9,993.1	11,279.2
Portugal	4,722.8	4,816.4	5,296.8	6,408.7	7,477.6	7,745.2	8,258.8	9,669.8	11,295.9	10,478.4	10,051.4	11,028.6
Spain	4,489.1	4,570.3	5,103.0	6,236.4	7,114.9	7,628.3	8,300.3	9,450.2	10,832.7	10,833.3	10,162.1	11,095.1
Sweden	5,000.0	4,279.6	5,059.9	6,672.9	7,194.6	7,143.4	8,203.7	9,382.8	9,986.1	9,210.3	9,791.2	11,582.6
Switzerland	8,812.4	8,437.1	9,862.5	11,593.3	13,111.1	13,997.2	14,139.9	15,881.4	17,837.1	17,357.6	19,191.7	24,230.0
Turkey	3,637.2	2,882.4	3,183.9	3,884.3	4,732.6	5,614.1	5,494.0	6,275.3	7,115.7	5,985.4	6,757.2	6,579.0
United Kingdom	6,621.7	6,513.0	7,276.0	8,296.3	9,755.7	10,178.4	11,030.2	13,143.5	12,513.8	10,973.7	11,105.1	12,686.6
Eastern Europe												
Albania												
Belarus	489.1	573.7	671.6	835.2	989.5	1,271.0	1,464.8	1,854.2	2,361.3	2,046.2	2,193.9	2,156.5
Bosnia-Herzegovina												
Bulgaria	712.7	740.1	880.9	1,076.4	1,338.0	1,489.6	1,677.6	2,198.6	2,694.8	2,881.5	2,710.7	2,826.5
Croatia												
Czech Republic	1,469.8	1,551.3	1,891.2	2,188.0	2,523.1	2,875.6	3,234.5	3,988.5	5,109.4	4,754.4	4,623.7	5,019.6
Estonia												
Georgia												
Hungary	2,017.3	2,191.1	2,842.6	3,494.7	4,270.8	4,359.6	4,471.6	5,509.9	6,341.9	5,703.5	5,653.8	6,359.6
Latvia												
Lithuania	1,654.3	1,509.7	1,655.7	2,057.0	2,472.5	3,097.8	3,735.0	4,515.2	5,500.0	4,657.0	4,305.1	4,873.7
Macedonia												
Moldova												
Montenegro												
Poland	1,936.2	2,143.3	2,263.0	2,410.0	2,761.8	3,333.9	3,617.4	4,468.5	5,552.3	4,742.6	4,802.5	5,118.3
Romania	1,008.1	1,088.6	1,191.5	1,573.5	1,945.1	2,494.1	3,024.7	4,545.3	5,308.0	4,839.1	4,826.4	5,480.5
Russia	423.1	491.9	551.5	667.4	907.3	1,174.4	1,477.1	1,929.3	2,445.2	1,896.4	2,225.0	2,709.1
Serbia												
Slovakia	1,585.1	1,632.9	1,855.4	2,532.9	3,188.7	3,270.7	3,885.3	4,923.4	5,572.2	5,487.9	5,164.9	5,672.2
Slovenia												
Ukraine	231.4	281.4	318.8	367.0	471.8	633.0	783.7	1,054.1	1,364.2	1,044.5	1,128.3	1,306.3

Source: Euromonitor International from national statistics

Table 11.6

Biofuel Production 2000-2011

Million tonnes of oil equivalent

	2000	2001	2002	2003	2004	2005	2006	2007	2008	2009	2010	2011
Western Europe												
Austria	17.5	19.2	20.1	20.1	30.5	41.5	140.2	260.4	277.8	304.7	253.5	300.5
Belgium						16.8	29.2	165.4	288.6	352.5	352.5	454.6
Cyprus									6.2	6.2	8.2	10.9
Denmark		22.5	35.9	40.4	58.4	62.9	62.9	62.9	88.9	78.1	78.1	82.9
Finland									73.0	192.5	250.5	334.0
France	330.8	329.6	354.1	388.5	407.3	462.9	683.9	1,127.2	1,952.0	2,213.7	2,135.1	2,471.0
Germany	225.0	318.0	499.0	738.0	1,007.0	2,236.0	3,842.1	3,986.7	3,878.6	3,843.3	4,079.2	4,632.9
Gibraltar												
Greece							43.4	83.3	62.6	70.8	112.5	143.2
Iceland												
Ireland						0.9	3.2	15.4	21.3	57.0	51.6	64.0
Italy					255.5	178.7	199.2	180.4	702.3	1,119.2	1,346.2	1,704.8
Liechtenstein												
Luxembourg												
Malta												
Monaco												
Netherlands						18.2	67.9	129.1	120.4	121.6	289.8	362.2	445.1
Norway												
Portugal							69.8	162.6	153.7	228.9	288.1	329.9
Spain	72.0	72.0	139.2	191.2	175.9	259.1	171.7	381.7	368.6	1,041.6	993.6	1,214.6
Sweden		14.9	32.2	66.5	143.7	218.3	318.9	430.0	455.4	557.7	576.4	640.1
Switzerland					2.3	6.0	6.7	10.3	10.3	4.6	5.4	5.8
Turkey							19.5	12.4	15.2	6.7	11.8	15.1
United Kingdom						7.9	225.0	384.3	283.1	210.7	210.7	241.1
Eastern Europe												
Albania												
Belarus									7.0	20.2	33.4	46.6
Bosnia-Herzegovina												
Bulgaria							7.9	3.5	10.5	19.8	25.5	33.6
Croatia								3.5	3.5	5.3	7.0	9.4
Czech Republic	70.0	52.0	73.0	103.5	77.1	112.5	98.8	90.1	105.2	195.3	236.7	285.6
Estonia												
Georgia												
Hungary						2.6	10.9	17.0	162.1	153.3	141.5	173.1
Latvia						1.8	9.4	15.6	32.3	48.5	61.6	76.9
Lithuania					3.1	10.7	15.2	31.6	68.0	107.7	138.5	174.1
Macedonia							2.6	0.9	0.9	1.2	1.7
Moldova												
Montenegro												
Poland				28.2	13.5	116.2	166.0	110.8	296.4	428.4	461.4	578.2
Romania								19.3	81.7	74.6	99.5	126.2
Russia												
Serbia												
Slovakia		35.7	2.9	1.9	11.0	33.4	42.4	58.7	138.7	149.7	128.3	151.5
Slovenia							1.8	4.4	7.1	6.2	16.7	20.9
Ukraine												

Source: Euromonitor International from national statistics
Note: Million tonnes of oil equivalent = the amount of oil required to fuel an oil-fired plant in order to generate the same amount of electricity

Energy Resources and Output

11

Energy Statistics

Table 11.7

Crude Oil Production 2000-2011

Million metric tonnes

	2000	2001	2002	2003	2004	2005	2006	2007	2008	2009	2010	2011
Western Europe												
Austria												
Belgium												
Cyprus												
Denmark	17.7	17.0	18.1	17.9	19.1	18.4	16.7	15.2	14.0	12.9	12.2	10.9
Finland												
France												
Germany												
Gibraltar												
Greece												
Iceland												
Ireland												
Italy	4.6	4.1	5.5	5.6	5.5	6.1	5.8	5.9	5.2	4.6	5.1	5.3
Liechtenstein												
Luxembourg												
Malta												
Monaco												
Netherlands												
Norway	160.2	162.0	157.3	153.0	149.9	138.2	128.7	118.6	114.2	108.8	98.6	93.4
Portugal												
Spain												
Sweden												
Switzerland												
Turkey												
United Kingdom	126.2	116.7	115.9	106.1	95.4	84.7	76.6	76.8	71.7	68.2	63.0	52.0
Eastern Europe												
Albania												
Belarus	2.0	2.0	2.3	2.4	2.8	3.0	3.2	3.4	3.5	3.7	3.9	4.1
Bosnia-Herzegovina												
Bulgaria												
Croatia												
Czech Republic												
Estonia												
Georgia												
Hungary												
Latvia												
Lithuania												
Macedonia												
Moldova												
Montenegro												
Poland												
Romania	6.3	6.2	6.1	5.9	5.7	5.4	5.0	4.7	4.7	4.5	4.3	4.2
Russia	323.3	348.1	379.6	421.4	458.8	470.0	480.5	491.3	488.5	494.2	505.1	511.4
Serbia												
Slovakia												
Slovenia												
Ukraine												

Source: Euromonitor International from national statistics

Table 11.8

Electricity Production 2011

GWh / % shares

	Net Total Production	% Fossil Fuels	% Combustible Renewables and Waste	% Geothermal	% Hydroelectric	% Nuclear	% Wind-Powered
Western Europe							
Austria	71,588.0	31.4	12.3	0.0	53.4		2.8
Belgium	98,194.0	41.2	5.8		1.7	49.0	1.4
Cyprus	5,425.0	98.9					
Denmark	40,274.0	64.5	14.4		0.0		21.0
Finland	81,710.0	40.5	13.9		15.8	28.3	0.4
France	584,887.0	10.4	1.1		12.0	74.4	1.8
Germany	642,814.0	57.7	6.8	0.0	4.1	22.7	5.8
Gibraltar	187.0						
Greece	61,760.0	82.5	0.4		13.3		3.6
Iceland	17,194.0	0.0		25.6	74.4		
Ireland	29,092.0	86.4	0.8		2.4		10.4
Italy	301,711.0	71.2	4.1	1.8	19.0		3.1
Liechtenstein							
Luxembourg	5,053.0	62.1	2.9		33.5		1.1
Malta	2,397.0						
Monaco							
Netherlands	114,586.0	84.9	7.9		0.1	3.4	3.5
Norway	128,778.0	4.7	0.4		94.2		0.7
Portugal	53,632.0	42.7	5.2	0.4	32.7		18.6
Spain	311,651.0	42.9	1.6		16.1	21.1	15.6
Sweden	167,077.0	7.9	6.3		47.3	35.9	2.6
Switzerland	68,970.0	1.3	4.2		55.7	38.6	0.0
Turkey	226,777.0	72.3	0.2	0.4	25.5		1.6
United Kingdom	390,566.0	75.4	3.7		1.7	16.4	2.8
Eastern Europe							
Albania	6,090.0	1.5			98.5		
Belarus	35,882.0	99.3	0.6		0.2		0.0
Bosnia-Herzegovina	16,738.0	58.4			41.6		
Bulgaria	43,903.0	55.2	0.0		9.7	34.4	0.7
Croatia	12,584.0	42.2	0.2		57.0		0.5
Czech Republic	86,899.0	58.8	2.7		4.1	33.1	0.4
Estonia	14,255.0	90.8	6.6		0.2		2.4
Georgia	9,159.0	12.1			87.9		
Hungary	37,979.0	47.7	7.1		0.5	43.1	1.6
Latvia	5,992.0	34.0	0.9		64.2		0.9
Lithuania	9,820.0	61.3	3.0		29.1	0.0	6.5
Macedonia	7,265.0	81.6			18.4		
Moldova	3,642.0	98.5			1.5		
Montenegro	3,528.0						
Poland	161,678.0	92.1	4.5		2.3		1.2
Romania	65,081.0	49.1	0.0		27.1	23.7	0.0
Russia	1,035,401.0	65.1	0.3	0.0	17.8	16.8	0.0
Serbia	40,690.0	70.8			29.2		
Slovakia	28,700.0	23.6	2.0		21.7	52.6	0.0
Slovenia	16,475.0	34.9	1.4		29.7	33.9	
Ukraine	186,433.0	45.8			6.6	47.6	0.0

Source: Euromonitor International from national statistics

11

Energy Resources and Output

Energy Statistics

Table 11.9

Natural Gas Production 1985, 1990, 1995, 2000, 2006-2011

Million tonnes of oil equivalent

	1985	1990	1995	2000	2006	2007	2008	2009	2010	2011
Western Europe										
Austria										
Belgium										
Cyprus										
Denmark	1.0	2.8	4.8	7.3	9.4	8.3	9.1	7.6	7.4	6.4
Finland										
France			2.4	2.0	1.0	0.8	0.6	0.5	0.3	0.3
Germany	15.7	14.3	14.5	15.2	14.1	12.9	11.7	11.0	9.6	9.0
Gibraltar										
Greece										
Iceland										
Ireland										
Italy	11.5	14.0	16.3	13.7	9.1	8.0	7.6	6.6	6.8	6.9
Liechtenstein										
Luxembourg										
Malta										
Monaco										
Netherlands	61.6	54.9	61.0	52.3	55.4	54.5	60.0	56.4	63.5	57.8
Norway	23.6	22.9	25.0	44.8	78.9	80.7	89.4	93.4	95.7	91.3
Portugal										
Spain										
Sweden										
Switzerland										
Turkey										
United Kingdom	35.7	40.9	63.7	97.5	72.0	64.9	62.7	53.7	51.4	40.7
Eastern Europe										
Albania										
Belarus										
Bosnia-Herzegovina										
Bulgaria										
Croatia			1.7	1.4	1.3	1.3	1.3	1.4	1.4	1.4
Czech Republic										
Estonia										
Georgia										
Hungary	5.8	3.8	3.7	2.4	2.3	2.3	2.2	2.1	2.1	2.0
Latvia										
Lithuania										
Macedonia										
Moldova										
Montenegro										
Poland	4.1	2.4	3.1	3.3	3.9	3.9	3.7	3.7	3.7	3.9
Romania	31.3	25.5	16.2	12.4	10.7	10.4	10.3	10.1	9.8	9.9
Russia	376.3	531.0	479.3	475.7	535.6	532.8	541.5	474.9	530.0	546.3
Serbia										
Slovakia			3.0	2.8	2.9	2.7	2.5	2.3	2.1	1.9
Slovenia										
Ukraine	34.9	22.9	14.8	14.6	16.9	16.9	17.1	17.3	16.3	16.4

Source: Euromonitor International from national statistics
Note: Million tonnes of oil equivalent = the amount of oil required to fuel an oil-fired plant in order to generate the same amount of electricity

    Table 11.10

Refinery Output 1990, 1995, 2000, 2006-2011

'000 tonnes of oil

	1990	1995	2000	2006	2007	2008	2009	2010	2011
Western Europe									
Austria	8,779.0	9,271.0	8,770.0	8,988.0	8,964.0	9,165.0	8,549.0	8,092.0	8,632.4
Belgium	29,372.1	29,643.0	38,092.0	36,386.0	38,196.0	37,901.0	33,401.0	35,174.0	36,039.6
Cyprus	638.2	829.7	1,181.0						
Denmark	7,848.0	9,778.0	8,231.0	7,813.0	7,622.0	7,326.0	7,523.0	6,899.0	7,246.3
Finland	10,344.1	11,533.0	12,893.0	13,827.0	14,503.0	14,985.0	14,790.0	13,886.0	14,268.5
France	81,320.4	83,693.7	88,576.0	86,839.0	86,060.0	88,475.0	78,298.0	71,908.0	76,655.2
Germany	3,480.0	114,414.0	115,973.0	120,571.0	118,486.0	115,984.0	107,727.0	101,472.0	105,972.5
Gibraltar									
Greece	16,678.2	17,650.9	22,232.0	22,245.0	23,047.0	21,823.0	21,293.0	22,156.0	22,208.2
Iceland									
Ireland	1,525.8	2,273.0	3,286.0	3,232.0	3,261.0	3,216.0	2,737.0	2,879.0	3,041.7
Italy	91,019.6	91,171.2	94,771.0	99,199.0	100,714.0	94,663.0	86,403.0	89,936.0	92,929.2
Liechtenstein									
Luxembourg									
Malta									
Monaco									
Netherlands	67,904.5	80,123.1	80,185.0	80,881.0	57,262.0	57,502.0	57,349.0	58,340.0	59,077.3
Norway	13,018.1	13,109.0	15,196.0	16,691.0	16,518.0	15,084.0	14,970.0	14,131.0	14,776.2
Portugal	11,144.0	13,346.0	12,308.0	13,664.0	12,621.0	12,397.0	10,807.0	11,450.0	12,066.8
Spain	52,954.1	55,312.2	59,830.0	61,350.0	59,855.0	60,543.0	57,224.0	57,644.0	58,468.3
Sweden	17,239.0	19,105.0	22,712.0	19,861.0	17,953.0	20,879.0	20,248.0	20,766.0	21,291.7
Switzerland	3,047.0	4,638.0	4,647.0	5,500.0	4,740.0	5,095.0	4,816.0	4,518.0	4,703.3
Turkey	22,884.0	27,140.1	23,745.0	26,235.0	25,554.0	24,390.0	18,637.0	19,932.0	21,537.5
United Kingdom	88,120.3	92,617.2	86,341.0	82,841.0	81,210.0	80,436.0	74,857.0	71,451.0	71,399.6
Eastern Europe									
Albania	675.0	501.0	311.0	474.0	509.0	333.0	306.0	401.1	409.8
Belarus	913.2	12,974.0	13,352.0	20,879.0	20,966.0	20,933.0	21,310.0	23,573.4	24,499.0
Bosnia-Herzegovina			512.0	154.0	164.0	169.0	986.0	1,031.3	1,068.8
Bulgaria	6,973.8	7,255.2	5,181.0	7,136.0	7,051.0	7,149.0	6,367.0	6,644.9	6,785.4
Croatia		5,233.9	5,214.0	4,823.0	5,242.0	4,460.0	4,716.0	4,873.8	4,884.6
Czech Republic		7,260.0	6,131.0	8,179.0	7,753.0	8,583.0	7,657.0	8,160.0	8,388.2
Estonia									
Georgia		40.0	19.0	12.0	39.0	50.0	13.0	25.6	37.5
Hungary	8,316.0	7,837.0	7,483.0	8,512.0	8,623.0	8,439.0	7,549.0	8,280.0	8,387.2
Latvia									
Lithuania		3,269.0	4,903.0	8,257.0	5,776.0	9,473.0	8,646.0	8,868.2	9,319.8
Macedonia		111.0	936.0	1,026.0	1,049.0	1,037.0	965.0	934.7	944.6
Moldova									
Montenegro									
Poland	12,686.3	13,859.9	18,480.0	20,947.0	21,599.0	21,864.0	21,879.0	23,768.0	23,805.8
Romania	22,708.7	14,558.9	10,990.0	14,407.0	13,835.0	14,015.0	12,196.0	13,001.9	13,506.2
Russia	267,723.0	178,148.0	176,803.0	216,548.0	223,731.0	229,924.0	232,225.0	241,117.5	254,984.9
Serbia	4,674.0	1,155.0	1,215.0	2,661.0	3,426.0	3,058.0	2,926.0	3,155.7	3,310.1
Slovakia		4,954.0	5,810.0	6,276.0	6,628.0	6,415.0	6,355.0	6,099.0	6,284.9
Slovenia		593.0	184.0						
Ukraine		16,554.0	9,788.0	15,177.0	14,726.0	11,232.0	11,580.0	12,514.3	12,892.6

Source: Euromonitor International from national statistics

11

Energy Resources and Output

Energy Statistics

Table 11.11

Primary Energy Consumption: Selected Materials 2011

Million tonnes of oil equivalent

	Crude Oil	Hydroelectricity	Natural Gas	Nuclear Energy	Coal	Total
Western Europe						
Austria	12.5	6.9	8.5		2.5	30.3
Belgium	33.7	0.0	14.4	10.9	2.1	61.2
Cyprus						
Denmark	8.3	0.0	3.8		3.2	15.3
Finland	10.5	2.8	3.2	5.3	3.3	25.1
France	82.9	10.3	36.3	100.0	9.0	238.6
Germany	111.5	4.4	65.3	24.4	77.6	283.2
Gibraltar						
Greece	17.2	1.0	4.1		7.3	29.6
Iceland						
Ireland	6.8	0.2	4.2		1.3	12.5
Italy	71.1	10.1	64.2		15.4	160.8
Liechtenstein						
Luxembourg						
Malta						
Monaco						
Netherlands	50.1	0.0	34.3	0.9	7.8	93.1
Norway	11.1	27.6	3.6		0.6	43.0
Portugal	11.6	2.8	4.6		2.6	21.5
Spain	69.5	6.9	28.9	13.0	14.9	133.3
Sweden	14.5	15.0	1.1	13.8	2.0	46.4
Switzerland	11.0	7.4	2.6	6.1	0.1	27.3
Turkey	32.0	11.8	41.2		32.4	117.5
United Kingdom	71.6	1.3	72.2	15.6	30.8	191.5
Eastern Europe						
Albania						
Belarus	9.0	0.0	16.5		0.1	25.6
Bosnia-Herzegovina						
Bulgaria	3.5	0.6	2.6	3.7	8.4	18.9
Croatia						
Czech Republic	9.1	0.6	7.6	6.4	19.2	42.9
Estonia						
Georgia						
Hungary	6.5	0.1	9.1	3.5	2.7	22.0
Latvia						
Lithuania	2.7	0.2	3.1	2.5	0.2	8.8
Macedonia						
Moldova						
Montenegro						
Poland	26.3	0.6	13.8		59.8	100.5
Romania	9.0	3.4	12.5	2.7	7.1	34.6
Russia	136.0	37.3	382.1	39.2	90.9	685.5
Serbia						
Slovakia	3.7	0.9	5.6	3.4	3.3	16.9
Slovenia						
Ukraine	12.9	2.4	48.3	20.4	42.4	126.4

Source: Euromonitor International from national statistics
Note: Million tonnes of oil equivalent = the amount of oil required to fuel an oil-fired plant in order to generate the same amount of electricity

Energy Statistics   **Table 11.12**

Coal Consumption 1985, 1990, 1995, 2000, 2006-2011

Million tonnes of oil equivalent

	1985	1990	1995	2000	2006	2007	2008	2009	2010	2011
Western Europe										
Austria	3.5	3.6	2.8	2.8	3.1	3.0	2.8	2.3	2.6	2.5
Belgium	10.7	10.7	8.2	7.3	4.8	4.4	3.9	3.1	3.3	2.1
Cyprus										
Denmark	7.1	6.0	6.6	4.0	5.6	4.7	4.1	4.0	3.8	3.2
Finland	3.5	3.3	4.1	3.3	4.7	4.4	3.0	3.3	4.3	3.3
France	20.0	19.1	14.5	13.0	12.1	12.3	11.9	9.9	10.7	9.0
Germany	147.6	129.6	90.6	84.9	83.5	85.7	80.1	71.7	76.6	77.6
Gibraltar										
Greece	6.0	8.0	8.2	9.2	8.1	8.5	8.1	8.1	7.4	7.3
Iceland										
Ireland	1.1	2.1	1.8	1.8	1.6	1.6	1.4	1.2	1.2	1.3
Italy	15.1	14.1	12.0	12.2	16.4	16.6	16.4	12.9	14.3	15.4
Liechtenstein										
Luxembourg										
Malta										
Monaco										
Netherlands	7.0	9.5	9.8	8.6	8.5	9.0	8.5	7.9	7.9	7.8
Norway	1.2	0.8	1.0	1.0	0.6	0.7	0.7	0.5	0.6	0.6
Portugal	0.8	2.8	4.2	4.5	3.8	3.3	2.9	3.3	1.9	2.6
Spain	19.1	19.0	18.7	22.3	19.8	21.9	15.5	11.8	9.8	14.9
Sweden	2.9	2.2	2.1	1.9	2.3	2.2	2.0	1.6	2.1	2.0
Switzerland	0.4	0.3	0.2	0.1	0.1	0.2	0.1	0.1	0.1	0.1
Turkey	11.7	15.9	16.5	22.5	25.9	28.9	29.2	30.4	30.9	32.4
United Kingdom	62.9	64.9	47.5	36.7	40.9	38.4	35.6	29.9	31.0	30.8
Eastern Europe										
Albania										
Belarus	1.1	1.2	0.3	0.1	0.1	0.1	0.1	0.1	0.1	0.1
Bosnia-Herzegovina										
Bulgaria	10.1	8.8	7.6	6.4	6.9	7.7	7.5	6.4	6.8	8.4
Croatia										
Czech Republic	38.2	33.5	23.5	21.0	21.1	21.2	19.9	17.4	18.2	19.2
Estonia										
Georgia										
Hungary	7.6	5.6	3.6	3.2	2.9	2.9	2.8	2.5	2.6	2.7
Latvia										
Lithuania	0.6	0.6	0.1	0.1	0.2	0.2	0.2	0.1	0.2	0.2
Macedonia										
Moldova										
Montenegro										
Poland	99.9	80.2	71.7	57.6	58.0	57.9	56.0	51.9	56.4	59.8
Romania	16.9	11.7	9.7	7.0	8.5	7.4	7.4	6.6	6.1	7.1
Russia	195.6	180.6	119.4	105.2	96.7	93.4	100.4	91.9	90.2	90.9
Serbia										
Slovakia	7.2	6.9	5.1	4.0	3.8	3.8	3.7	3.5	3.4	3.3
Slovenia										
Ukraine	76.5	74.8	42.1	39.1	39.7	39.7	40.2	35.1	37.9	42.4

Source: Euromonitor International from national statistics
Note: Million tonnes of oil equivalent = the amount of oil required to fuel an oil-fired plant in order to generate the same amount of electricity

11

Energy Resources and Output

Energy Statistics

Table 11.13

Crude Oil Consumption 1985, 1990, 1995, 2000, 2006-2011

Million metric tonnes

	1985	1990	1995	2000	2006	2007	2008	2009	2010	2011
Western Europe										
Austria	9.8	10.8	11.3	11.8	14.1	13.4	13.3	12.8	12.9	12.5
Belgium	19.7	23.8	27.8	30.8	33.4	33.7	36.8	32.2	33.5	33.7
Cyprus										
Denmark	10.7	9.0	10.5	10.4	9.6	9.7	9.5	8.5	8.4	8.3
Finland	10.8	11.0	9.9	10.7	10.6	10.6	10.5	9.9	10.4	10.5
France	84.3	89.4	89.0	94.9	93.0	91.4	90.8	87.5	84.4	82.9
Germany	126.3	127.3	135.1	129.8	123.6	112.5	118.9	113.9	115.4	111.5
Gibraltar										
Greece	12.0	15.7	17.6	19.9	22.1	21.7	21.3	20.1	18.7	17.2
Iceland										
Ireland	3.9	4.4	5.7	8.2	9.3	9.4	9.0	8.0	7.6	6.8
Italy	84.4	93.6	95.5	93.5	86.7	84.0	80.4	75.1	73.1	71.1
Liechtenstein										
Luxembourg										
Malta										
Monaco										
Netherlands	29.6	35.7	38.8	42.5	52.0	53.5	51.1	49.4	49.9	50.1
Norway	9.0	9.3	9.4	9.4	10.5	10.7	10.4	10.6	10.8	11.1
Portugal	8.8	11.1	13.0	15.5	14.4	14.4	13.6	12.8	12.5	11.6
Spain	42.9	46.4	57.5	69.9	79.4	80.4	78.0	73.6	72.1	69.5
Sweden	19.2	17.4	17.1	16.1	16.5	16.0	15.7	14.6	15.3	14.5
Switzerland	12.0	12.8	11.8	12.2	12.6	11.3	12.1	12.3	11.4	11.0
Turkey	16.8	22.0	28.3	30.7	32.7	33.5	31.9	31.6	30.2	32.0
United Kingdom	77.4	82.9	81.9	78.6	82.3	79.2	77.9	74.4	73.5	71.6
Eastern Europe										
Albania										
Belarus	25.4	24.9	10.5	7.0	8.1	7.3	8.3	9.4	7.3	9.0
Bosnia-Herzegovina										
Bulgaria	10.4	6.8	4.9	4.1	4.7	4.6	4.6	4.2	3.8	3.5
Croatia										
Czech Republic	10.6	8.4	8.0	7.9	9.8	9.7	9.9	9.7	9.1	9.1
Estonia										
Georgia										
Hungary	10.3	9.3	7.7	6.8	7.8	7.7	7.5	7.1	6.7	6.5
Latvia										
Lithuania	8.7	7.5	3.2	2.4	2.8	2.8	3.1	2.6	2.7	2.7
Macedonia										
Moldova										
Montenegro										
Poland	16.4	15.8	14.9	20.0	23.3	24.2	25.3	25.3	26.7	26.3
Romania	15.0	18.7	13.5	10.0	10.3	10.3	10.4	9.2	8.7	9.0
Russia	247.4	251.7	152.2	123.1	130.8	123.6	129.8	124.8	128.9	136.0
Serbia										
Slovakia	6.2	5.0	3.2	3.4	3.4	3.6	3.9	3.7	3.9	3.7
Slovenia										
Ukraine	64.3	63.8	19.0	12.1	14.2	15.6	14.9	13.4	13.0	12.9

Source: Euromonitor International from national statistics

Table 11.14

Natural Gas Consumption 1985, 1990, 1995, 2000, 2006-2011

Million tonnes of oil equivalent

	1985	1990	1995	2000	2006	2007	2008	2009	2010	2011
Western Europe										
Austria	5.0	5.8	7.1	7.3	8.5	8.0	8.6	8.4	9.1	8.5
Belgium	7.4	8.2	10.6	13.4	15.0	14.9	14.8	15.1	17.0	14.4
Cyprus										
Denmark	0.6	1.8	3.2	4.4	4.6	4.1	4.1	4.0	4.5	3.8
Finland	0.8	2.3	2.9	3.4	3.8	3.5	3.6	3.2	3.6	3.2
France	23.3	26.4	29.7	35.4	37.9	38.2	39.4	38.0	42.2	36.3
Germany	49.2	53.9	67.0	71.5	78.5	74.6	73.1	70.2	75.0	65.3
Gibraltar										
Greece	0.1	0.1	0.1	1.8	2.8	3.4	3.6	3.0	3.3	4.1
Iceland										
Ireland	2.0	1.9	2.3	3.4	4.0	4.3	4.5	4.3	4.7	4.2
Italy	27.2	39.1	44.9	58.4	69.7	70.0	70.0	64.4	68.5	64.2
Liechtenstein										
Luxembourg										
Malta										
Monaco										
Netherlands	32.9	31.1	34.6	35.0	34.3	33.3	34.7	35.0	39.2	34.3
Norway	1.1	1.9	2.7	3.6	4.0	3.8	3.9	3.7	3.7	3.6
Portugal				2.1	3.7	3.9	4.2	4.2	4.5	4.6
Spain	2.1	5.0	7.5	15.2	30.3	31.6	34.8	31.1	31.2	28.9
Sweden	0.1	0.6	0.7	0.7	0.8	0.9	0.8	1.0	1.4	1.1
Switzerland	1.3	1.6	2.2	2.4	2.7	2.6	2.8	2.7	3.0	2.6
Turkey		3.0	6.1	13.1	27.4	32.5	33.8	32.1	35.1	41.2
United Kingdom	46.6	47.2	63.5	87.2	81.1	81.9	84.5	78.0	84.6	72.2
Eastern Europe										
Albania										
Belarus	8.1	12.1	10.8	14.2	17.1	17.0	17.3	14.5	17.7	16.5
Bosnia-Herzegovina										
Bulgaria	4.6	5.3	4.5	2.9	2.9	2.9	2.9	2.1	2.3	2.6
Croatia										
Czech Republic	3.7	4.9	6.5	7.5	8.4	7.8	7.8	7.4	8.4	7.6
Estonia										
Georgia										
Hungary	8.6	8.7	9.2	9.7	11.5	10.7	10.6	9.1	9.8	9.1
Latvia										
Lithuania	3.8	5.0	2.1	2.5	2.9	3.3	2.9	2.5	2.8	3.1
Macedonia										
Moldova										
Montenegro										
Poland	8.9	8.9	9.0	10.0	12.4	12.4	13.5	13.0	14.0	13.8
Romania	31.9	27.7	21.6	15.4	16.3	14.5	14.3	11.9	12.2	12.5
Russia	315.4	366.8	329.9	318.6	367.7	379.9	374.4	350.7	372.7	382.1
Serbia										
Slovakia	4.2	5.3	5.1	5.8	5.4	5.1	5.2	4.4	5.0	5.6
Slovenia										
Ukraine	78.4	111.6	66.5	63.9	60.3	56.9	54.0	42.3	46.9	48.3

Source: Euromonitor International from national statistics
Note: Million tonnes of oil equivalent = the amount of oil required to fuel an oil-fired plant in order to generate the same amount of electricity

Energy Statistics

Table 11.15

Nuclear Energy Consumption 1985, 1990, 1995, 2000, 2006-2011

Million tonnes of oil equivalent

	1985	1990	1995	2000	2006	2007	2008	2009	2010	2011
Western Europe										
Austria										
Belgium	7.8	9.7	9.4	10.9	10.6	10.9	10.3	10.7	10.8	10.9
Cyprus										
Denmark										
Finland	4.3	4.3	4.3	5.1	5.2	5.4	5.3	5.4	5.2	5.3
France	50.7	71.1	85.4	94.0	102.1	99.7	99.6	92.8	96.9	100.0
Germany	31.4	34.5	34.9	38.4	37.9	31.8	33.7	30.5	31.8	24.4
Gibraltar										
Greece										
Iceland										
Ireland										
Italy										
Liechtenstein										
Luxembourg										
Malta										
Monaco										
Netherlands	0.9	0.8	0.9	0.9	0.8	1.0	0.9	1.0	0.9	0.9
Norway										
Portugal										
Spain	6.3	12.3	12.5	14.1	13.6	12.5	13.3	11.9	14.0	13.0
Sweden	13.3	15.4	15.8	13.0	15.2	15.2	14.5	11.9	13.2	13.8
Switzerland	5.1	5.3	5.6	6.0	6.3	6.3	6.2	6.2	6.0	6.1
Turkey										
United Kingdom	13.8	14.9	20.1	19.3	17.1	14.3	11.9	15.6	14.1	15.6
Eastern Europe										
Albania										
Belarus										
Bosnia-Herzegovina										
Bulgaria	3.0	3.3	3.9	4.1	4.4	3.3	3.6	3.4	3.5	3.7
Croatia										
Czech Republic	0.5	2.8	2.8	3.1	5.9	5.9	6.0	6.2	6.3	6.4
Estonia										
Georgia										
Hungary	1.5	3.1	3.2	3.2	3.0	3.3	3.4	3.5	3.6	3.5
Latvia										
Lithuania	2.1	3.9	2.7	1.9	2.0	2.2	2.2	2.5	2.5	2.5
Macedonia										
Moldova										
Montenegro										
Poland										
Romania				1.2	1.3	1.7	2.5	2.7	2.6	2.7
Russia	22.5	26.8	22.5	29.5	35.4	36.2	36.9	37.0	38.5	39.2
Serbia										
Slovakia	2.1	2.7	2.6	3.7	4.1	3.5	3.8	3.2	3.3	3.4
Slovenia										
Ukraine	12.1	17.2	16.0	17.5	20.4	20.9	20.3	18.8	20.2	20.4

Source: Euromonitor International from national statistics
Note: Million tonnes of oil equivalent = the amount of oil required to fuel an oil-fired plant in order to generate the same amount of electricity

Table 11.16

Hydroelectricity Consumption 1985, 1990, 1995, 2000, 2006-2011

Million tonnes of oil equivalent

	1985	1990	1995	2000	2006	2007	2008	2009	2010	2011
Western Europe										
Austria	7.0	7.1	8.4	9.5	7.2	7.7	8.3	8.9	7.7	6.9
Belgium	0.1	0.1	0.1	0.1	0.1	0.1	0.1	0.1	0.1	0.0
Cyprus										
Denmark	0.0	0.0	0.0	0.0	0.0	0.0	0.0	0.0	0.0	0.0
Finland	2.8	2.5	2.9	3.3	2.6	3.2	3.9	2.9	2.9	2.8
France	14.1	12.2	16.5	15.3	12.7	13.2	13.7	13.0	14.2	10.3
Germany	3.9	3.9	4.5	4.9	4.4	4.6	4.5	4.2	4.8	4.4
Gibraltar										
Greece	0.6	0.5	0.9	0.9	1.5	0.8	0.9	1.3	1.7	1.0
Iceland										
Ireland	0.2	0.2	0.2	0.2	0.2	0.2	0.2	0.2	0.1	0.2
Italy	9.3	7.2	8.6	10.0	8.4	7.4	9.4	11.1	11.5	10.1
Liechtenstein										
Luxembourg										
Malta										
Monaco										
Netherlands		0.0	0.0	0.0	0.0	0.0	0.0	0.0	0.0	0.0
Norway	23.3	27.5	27.7	32.2	27.1	30.6	31.8	28.8	26.7	27.6
Portugal	2.4	2.1	1.9	2.7	2.6	2.3	1.7	2.0	3.8	2.8
Spain	7.1	5.8	5.2	7.7	5.8	6.2	5.3	6.0	9.6	6.9
Sweden	16.2	16.5	15.3	17.8	14.0	15.0	15.7	14.9	15.1	15.0
Switzerland	7.3	6.7	8.0	8.3	7.0	8.0	8.2	8.1	8.2	7.4
Turkey	2.7	5.2	8.0	7.0	10.0	8.1	7.5	8.1	11.7	11.8
United Kingdom	0.9	1.2	1.1	1.2	1.0	1.2	1.2	1.2	0.8	1.3
Eastern Europe										
Albania										
Belarus	0.0	0.0	0.0	0.0	0.0	0.0	0.0	0.0	0.0	0.0
Bosnia-Herzegovina										
Bulgaria	0.5	0.4	0.5	0.5	0.9	0.6	0.6	0.8	1.3	0.6
Croatia										
Czech Republic	0.4	0.3	0.5	0.5	0.7	0.6	0.5	0.7	0.8	0.6
Estonia										
Georgia										
Hungary	0.0	0.0	0.0	0.0	0.0	0.0	0.0	0.1	0.0	0.1
Latvia										
Lithuania	0.1	0.1	0.2	0.1	0.2	0.2	0.2	0.3	0.3	0.2
Macedonia										
Moldova										
Montenegro										
Poland	0.9	0.8	0.9	0.9	0.7	0.7	0.6	0.7	0.8	0.6
Romania	2.7	2.5	3.8	3.3	4.2	3.6	3.9	3.6	4.5	3.4
Russia	36.1	37.8	40.1	37.4	39.6	40.5	37.7	39.9	38.1	37.3
Serbia										
Slovakia	0.6	0.6	1.2	1.1	1.0	1.0	1.0	1.0	1.3	0.9
Slovenia										
Ukraine	2.4	2.4	2.3	2.6	2.9	2.3	2.6	2.7	2.9	2.4

Source: Euromonitor International from national statistics
Note: Million tonnes of oil equivalent = the amount of oil required to fuel an oil-fired plant in order to generate the same amount of electricity

Energy Resources and Output

11

Energy Statistics

Table 11.17

Electricity Residential Consumption 1985, 1990, 1995, 2000, 2006-2011

'000 GWh

	1985	1990	1995	2000	2006	2007	2008	2009	2010	2011
Western Europe										
Austria	8.3	11.9	13.6	14.2	17.5	17.1	17.3	17.4	17.6	17.9
Belgium	15.5	18.4	22.1	23.7	22.7	21.9	20.0	20.2	20.9	21.0
Cyprus	0.3	0.4	0.8	1.1	1.5	1.6	1.7	1.7	1.8	1.8
Denmark	9.1	9.7	10.3	10.2	10.6	10.3	10.3	10.1	10.3	10.4
Finland	12.2	14.6	16.3	18.1	21.1	21.5	21.2	22.0	22.7	23.0
France	85.8	96.9	108.8	128.7	147.1	145.8	155.6	170.2	163.5	165.4
Germany	132.6	137.1	127.2	128.9	141.5	140.1	139.5	139.2	141.5	143.0
Gibraltar										
Greece	7.7	9.1	11.5	14.2	17.7	18.0	18.1	18.1	17.4	16.7
Iceland	0.5	0.6	0.6	0.6	0.8	0.8	0.9	0.9	0.9	0.9
Ireland	4.0	4.1	5.0	6.4	8.1	8.1	8.5	8.0	8.1	7.9
Italy	44.5	52.7	57.2	61.1	67.6	67.2	68.4	68.9	68.7	69.5
Liechtenstein										
Luxembourg	0.6	0.6	0.7	0.8	0.8	0.8	0.9	0.9	0.9	0.9
Malta	0.2	0.3	0.4	0.6	0.7	0.7	0.6	0.6	0.6	0.6
Monaco										
Netherlands	16.0	16.5	19.7	21.8	24.8	24.3	24.8	24.2	24.9	25.2
Norway	28.9	30.3	34.6	34.6	33.6	34.9	34.9	36.4	36.0	36.2
Portugal	4.5	5.9	7.9	10.1	13.4	13.9	13.4	14.2	14.3	14.1
Spain	23.3	30.2	36.0	43.6	70.7	71.3	73.1	69.5	68.6	69.6
Sweden	39.7	38.1	42.4	42.0	41.5	39.6	38.9	40.9	41.8	41.9
Switzerland	12.0	13.6	15.2	15.7	17.7	17.5	17.9	17.9	18.2	18.4
Turkey	5.0	9.1	14.5	23.9	34.5	36.5	39.6	39.1	41.8	46.0
United Kingdom	88.2	93.8	102.2	111.8	124.4	122.8	125.8	122.5	122.4	123.3
Eastern Europe										
Albania		0.7	0.9	2.5	2.0	2.1	2.3	2.8	3.1	3.7
Belarus		3.5	4.9	5.6	5.7	6.0	6.3	6.5	6.7	6.9
Bosnia-Herzegovina		3.0	2.5	3.7	4.1	4.1	4.2	4.5	4.7	4.8
Bulgaria	9.6	10.5	11.0	9.9	9.3	9.4	10.0	10.3	10.9	11.3
Croatia		4.5	4.6	5.7	6.5	6.4	6.7	6.5	6.4	6.4
Czech Republic	8.0	9.6	14.8	13.8	15.2	14.6	14.7	14.7	14.9	14.9
Estonia		0.9	1.1	1.5	1.7	1.8	1.8	1.9	1.9	1.8
Georgia		2.9	4.6	2.7	2.7	2.8	2.9	2.9	2.9	3.0
Hungary	7.4	9.2	9.8	9.8	11.5	11.3	11.5	11.2	11.1	11.3
Latvia		1.3	1.2	1.2	1.7	1.8	2.0	2.0	2.0	2.0
Lithuania		1.8	1.5	1.8	2.4	2.5	2.7	2.7	2.7	2.7
Macedonia		1.7	2.4	2.7	3.0	3.0	3.1	3.3	3.3	3.4
Moldova		1.7	1.9	1.2	1.8	1.3	1.4	1.5	1.6	1.6
Montenegro										
Poland	14.9	20.2	18.1	21.0	26.5	26.4	27.1	27.5	28.8	29.4
Romania	4.8	5.4	7.1	7.7	10.0	10.4	10.4	11.0	10.9	11.2
Russia		106.9	126.1	140.7	112.5	115.9	117.1	123.8	122.6	119.7
Serbia		8.5	12.8	13.0	14.1	13.9	14.1	14.4	14.5	14.8
Slovakia	2.9	3.7	5.0	5.4	4.6	4.6	4.5	4.4	4.4	4.4
Slovenia		2.2	2.6	2.6	3.1	3.0	3.2	3.1	3.1	3.2
Ukraine		17.2	36.0	30.1	27.7	28.3	31.1	28.0	30.8	33.6

Source: Euromonitor International from national statistics

Table 11.18

Gas Residential Consumption 1985, 1990, 1995, 2000, 2006-2011

'000 TJ

	1985	1990	1995	2000	2006	2007	2008	2009	2010	2011
Western Europe										
Austria	32.6	36.2	47.5	63.3	56.4	52.8	53.6	54.6	52.8	51.7
Belgium		115.5	145.5	153.2	160.8	152.5	153.5	154.1	155.2	155.7
Cyprus										
Denmark		19.3	29.9	30.6	31.8	29.5	29.5	29.8	30.4	31.0
Finland		1.3	0.8	1.0	1.6	1.7	1.7	2.0	2.1	2.3
France		306.5	365.0	589.0	679.8	602.0	651.4	679.1	690.5	695.3
Germany		671.9	978.4	1,090.5	1,340.4	1,310.2	1,350.2	1,340.0	1,264.4	1,294.8
Gibraltar										
Greece		0.1	0.1	0.2	6.5	8.2	9.7	11.9	11.7	11.6
Iceland										
Ireland	1.4	5.4	11.7	20.4	29.3	27.5	31.1	29.0	29.5	29.1
Italy		534.9	636.8	696.6	791.6	741.6	745.0	782.5	787.8	789.3
Liechtenstein										
Luxembourg		6.5	8.5	7.3	8.8	7.6	8.0	9.4	9.0	8.5
Malta										
Monaco										
Netherlands		365.8	400.9	370.7	342.9	308.6	330.6	347.1	350.1	347.7
Norway				0.0	0.2	0.2	0.1	0.1	0.2	0.2
Portugal		1.9	1.9	4.6	9.4	10.2	10.7	12.3	12.2	12.3
Spain		29.6	46.6	94.0	170.4	175.8	169.3	146.8	161.6	163.7
Sweden		2.4	4.1	4.8	2.6	2.5	2.4	3.5	2.9	2.5
Switzerland		28.1	36.4	38.7	44.1	42.4	46.1	46.2	46.8	47.2
Turkey		2.4	52.2	125.4	287.6	321.1	303.6	204.6	280.4	317.0
United Kingdom	1,021.5	1,081.4	1,173.6	1,331.7	1,320.9	1,270.3	1,294.4	1,205.4	1,146.9	1,216.1
Eastern Europe										
Albania										
Belarus		35.0	42.6	46.7	55.4	55.8	55.7	60.3	61.4	61.4
Bosnia-Herzegovina		1.4	1.1	1.5	2.1	2.1	2.1	1.8	2.1	2.1
Bulgaria				0.0	1.1	1.5	1.8	2.4	2.5	2.8
Croatia		8.4	14.7	19.1	25.1	23.9	25.7	26.6	25.9	26.0
Czech Republic		50.0	76.2	95.3	105.9	94.7	95.2	95.8	98.5	99.4
Estonia		2.6	2.2	2.0	2.1	2.3	2.3	2.4	2.3	2.3
Georgia		52.0	2.7	11.2	8.4	8.8	9.0	9.3	9.2	10.5
Hungary		76.4	134.5	140.7	169.5	147.7	153.3	148.0	141.2	133.5
Latvia		4.4	4.6	3.0	4.8	5.1	5.2	4.8	4.8	4.9
Lithuania		10.3	8.6	4.8	6.5	6.8	6.8	6.8	6.7	6.7
Macedonia										
Moldova		10.2	12.8	8.9	11.4	11.7	10.6	16.0	16.7	17.5
Montenegro										
Poland		139.2	177.6	142.0	154.2	147.4	146.1	149.9	151.2	152.1
Romania		105.0	83.3	103.1	118.5	96.2	101.8	99.9	104.8	104.6
Russia		2,192.7	2,011.8	2,006.1	1,840.6	1,806.0	1,856.7	1,939.0	1,996.9	2,026.2
Serbia			6.7	8.7	10.0	3.8	8.5	9.3	7.8	6.9
Slovakia		50.8	47.5	76.4	59.7	51.6	55.0	56.1	52.4	50.0
Slovenia		1.3	2.5	2.7	4.3	4.0	4.8	4.9	5.3	5.4
Ukraine		406.4	524.6	596.3	692.4	621.7	643.2	628.1	641.4	648.1

Source: Euromonitor International from national statistics

Energy Resources and Output

11

12

Environmental Data

Environmental Statistics

Table 12.1

Carbon Dioxide Emissions 2011

'000 metric tonnes / as stated

	Fossil Fuels	Natural Gases	Coal	Petroleum	CO2 emissions per unit of output (kg per US$)
Western Europe					
Austria	69,355.20	19,322.84	12,005.68	38,026.67	0.17
Belgium	125,284.71	40,567.03	6,042.61	78,675.07	0.24
Cyprus	9,164.24		11.35	9,152.89	0.37
Denmark	44,961.61	10,333.24	10,127.36	24,501.00	0.14
Finland	53,969.01	8,887.04	15,239.05	29,842.93	0.20
France	397,672.72	97,897.76	45,249.34	254,525.62	0.14
Germany	795,538.23	185,028.26	300,741.46	309,768.51	0.22
Gibraltar	3,730.62			3,730.62	2.18
Greece	84,235.53	6,910.42	25,144.85	52,180.26	0.28
Iceland	3,417.65		302.66	3,114.99	0.24
Ireland	41,658.76	11,840.69	3,996.51	25,821.56	0.19
Italy	410,661.84	157,654.15	49,212.49	203,795.19	0.19
Liechtenstein					
Luxembourg	10,483.89	2,742.23	265.32	7,476.35	0.18
Malta	3,166.30			3,166.30	0.35
Monaco					
Netherlands	263,602.56	92,798.63	48,259.91	122,544.03	0.31
Norway	40,621.36	12,301.16	3,401.56	24,918.64	0.08
Portugal	50,922.53	10,643.44	6,240.61	34,038.49	0.21
Spain	305,657.20	71,380.20	31,630.24	202,646.74	0.21
Sweden	65,804.54	3,811.29	9,275.05	52,718.20	0.12
Switzerland	45,580.78	7,090.33	394.52	38,095.93	0.07
Turkey	285,632.68	80,402.31	141,354.01	63,876.37	0.37
United Kingdom	524,015.19	189,054.50	112,086.32	222,874.37	0.22
Eastern Europe					
Albania	5,255.02	62.80	42.05	5,150.16	0.40
Belarus	68,659.80	42,731.83	188.31	25,739.66	1.25
Bosnia-Herzegovina	21,596.09	391.17	16,878.37	4,326.54	1.18
Bulgaria	40,410.32	3,640.43	25,630.86	11,139.02	0.76
Croatia	22,132.36	5,088.11	4,365.00	12,679.25	0.35
Czech Republic	89,384.18	17,545.96	46,656.33	25,181.89	0.42
Estonia	21,474.13	1,261.35	15,235.02	4,977.75	0.97
Georgia	5,590.08	3,397.78	441.24	1,751.06	0.39
Hungary	49,833.99	22,465.44	10,934.23	16,434.32	0.36
Latvia	8,775.49	2,699.74	214.80	5,860.95	0.31
Lithuania	17,048.17	6,188.51	811.47	10,048.19	0.40
Macedonia	8,152.88	148.01	5,170.19	2,834.66	0.80
Moldova	7,683.81	4,347.35	278.19	3,058.27	1.10
Montenegro	2,047.72		1,326.09	721.62	0.45
Poland	306,803.20	30,250.15	207,859.63	68,693.42	0.60
Romania	75,112.13	22,778.96	26,334.12	25,999.05	0.40
Russia	1,648,721.79	854,679.48	447,783.53	346,258.78	0.89
Serbia	50,060.32	4,286.26	34,414.22	11,359.85	1.13
Slovakia	34,915.29	12,076.22	12,654.59	10,184.49	0.36
Slovenia	17,215.85	1,969.43	6,358.50	8,887.90	0.34
Ukraine	280,091.13	104,251.73	136,448.49	39,390.93	1.70

Source: Euromonitor International from national statistics

Table 12.2

Air and Water Pollutant Emissions 2011

'000 metric tonnes / as stated

	Carbon Monoxide	Nitrogen Oxide	Daily Organic Water Pollutants (kg)	Particulate Matter	Sulphur Oxide
Western Europe					
Austria	593	173	82,787	24	19
Belgium	263	197	88,766	20	61
Cyprus	50	19	7,934	24	13
Denmark	378	113	52,175	15	11
Finland	426	139	35,717	14	53
France	3,347	1,005	509,280	12	244
Germany	2,828	1,285	878,497	15	411
Gibraltar					
Greece	528	363	66,154	28	389
Iceland	17	21	9,960	16	91
Ireland	141	83	15,679	11	25
Italy	2,283	886	472,295	19	157
Liechtenstein				14	
Luxembourg	39	24	4,342	12	4
Malta	31	8	4,185	1	6
Monaco	1				
Netherlands	565	251	134,377	28	32
Norway	307	170	39,693	14	13
Portugal	452	221	58,103	18	64
Spain	1,548	936	386,669	24	360
Sweden	520	140	88,545	9	28
Switzerland	293	75	97,092	21	12
Turkey	3,475	831	366,126	34	1,210
United Kingdom	1,776	918	473,170	12	320
Eastern Europe					
Albania			4,817	32	
Belarus	159	201		8	123
Bosnia-Herzegovina			18,972	19	640
Bulgaria	1,059	157	104,330	39	550
Croatia	221	70	44,841	22	49
Czech Republic	355	232	156,342	15	156
Estonia	169	26	14,201	7	45
Georgia				58	
Hungary	282	158	81,513	13	70
Latvia	107	25	25,559	10	3
Lithuania	195	67	40,190	13	34
Macedonia	131	44	20,682	16	80
Moldova			14,400	31	
Montenegro					
Poland	2,587	814	364,819	32	745
Romania	1,441	211	196,404	13	440
Russia	20,311	5,337	1,282,206	15	650
Serbia					
Slovakia	180	80	48,100	11	58
Slovenia	113	44	32,709	24	10
Ukraine	3,265	1,013	442,220	14	1,626

Source: Euromonitor International from national statistics

12

Environmental Data

Environmental Statistics

Table 12.3

Waste Generation 2011

'000 tonnes / kg per capita

	Municipal Waste	Municipal Waste per capita	Nuclear Waste: Spent Fuel Arising	Nuclear Waste: Spent Fuel Arising per capita	Hazardous Industrial Waste	Hazardous Industrial Waste per capita
Western Europe						
Austria	4,963	591			1,469	175
Belgium	4,872	445	119	11	6,377	582
Cyprus	619	555			31	28
Denmark	3,538	636			383	69
Finland	2,467	459	87	16	1,876	349
France	34,503	547	1,143	18	11,344	180
Germany	47,626	583	279	3	23,629	289
Gibraltar						
Greece	5,233	462			220	19
Iceland	185	570			10	31
Ireland	2,662	594			780	174
Italy	31,939	527			7,348	121
Liechtenstein						
Luxembourg	348	676			195	380
Malta	239	572			63	151
Monaco						
Netherlands	9,746	585	10	1	5,177	311
Norway	2,289	465			1,616	328
Portugal	5,597	526			4,691	441
Spain	24,167	524	143	3	3,462	75
Sweden	4,367	464	243	26	2,281	242
Switzerland	5,684	722	58	7	1,433	182
Turkey	29,646	404			1,016	14
United Kingdom	31,673	507	318	5	6,026	96
Eastern Europe						
Albania						
Belarus						
Bosnia-Herzegovina	1,642	427				
Bulgaria	3,017	401			14,312	1,904
Croatia	1,600	363			272	62
Czech Republic	3,437	328	96	9	1,688	161
Estonia	386	288			8,212	6,127
Georgia						
Hungary	3,974	398	62	6	611	61
Latvia	673	325			80	38
Lithuania	1,219	376			135	42
Macedonia	725	352				
Moldova					1	
Montenegro						
Poland	12,418	325			1,570	41
Romania	7,892	368			392	18
Russia	71,569	501			147,821	1,034
Serbia						
Slovakia	1,856	344	29	5	519	96
Slovenia	857	418			187	91
Ukraine					1,109	24

Source: Euromonitor International from national statistics

Table 12.4

Recycling Levels of Packaging Waste 2011

% of total consumption

	Glass	Paper and Cardboard
Western Europe		
Austria	90	71
Belgium	94	68
Cyprus	30	84
Denmark	97	64
Finland	108	90
France	70	62
Germany	83	80
Gibraltar		
Greece	6	41
Iceland	94	15
Ireland	115	118
Italy	79	60
Liechtenstein	61	77
Luxembourg		
Malta	29	7
Monaco		
Netherlands	95	103
Norway	84	65
Portugal	65	87
Spain	68	69
Sweden	94	79
Switzerland	95	87
Turkey	33	44
United Kingdom	75	75
Eastern Europe		
Albania		
Belarus		
Bosnia-Herzegovina		
Bulgaria	43	55
Croatia		
Czech Republic	74	57
Estonia	40	38
Georgia		
Hungary	38	53
Latvia		
Lithuania	64	86
Macedonia		
Moldova		
Montenegro		
Poland	56	80
Romania	54	71
Russia		
Serbia		
Slovakia	61	65
Slovenia	94	59
Ukraine		

Source: Euromonitor International from national statistics

12

Environmental Data

13

External Trade

External Trade Statistics   **Table 13.1**

Imports (cif) 1980, 1985, 1990, 1995, 1999-2011

US$ million

	1980	1985	1990	1995	1999	2000	2001	2002
Western Europe								
Austria	24,444	20,986	49,088	66,386	69,555	68,987	70,493	72,839
Belgium			120,068	159,683	164,607	177,008	178,721	198,225
Cyprus	1,202	1,247	2,568	3,694	3,618	3,846	3,923	3,863
Denmark	19,340	18,245	33,248	45,728	44,519	44,329	44,136	48,956
Finland	15,635	13,232	27,001	28,114	31,617	33,900	32,115	33,661
France	134,889	108,337	234,447	281,440	294,921	310,834	306,281	316,140
Germany	188,002	158,488	346,153	464,271	473,539	495,457	486,069	490,528
Gibraltar	110	91	362	411	484	482	438	382
Greece	10,548	10,134	19,777	26,795	28,720	28,323	28,256	31,284
Iceland	999	905	1,680	1,756	2,503	2,591	2,252	2,274
Ireland	11,153	10,015	20,682	33,064	47,194	51,475	51,444	52,281
Italy	100,741	87,692	181,968	206,040	220,323	230,726	229,363	239,486
Liechtenstein								
Luxembourg	3,612	3,144	7,596	9,748	11,045	10,716	11,151	11,597
Malta	938	759	1,961	2,943	2,846	3,400	2,726	2,839
Monaco								
Netherlands	88,419	73,123	126,475	176,874	190,279	198,929	195,574	194,235
Norway	16,926	15,556	27,221	32,968	34,167	34,391	32,954	34,873
Portugal	9,309	7,652	25,264	33,306	39,825	42,129	41,666	42,627
Spain	34,078	29,963	87,554	113,319	144,436	152,903	153,638	163,672
Sweden	33,438	28,548	54,245	64,741	68,755	73,329	64,313	67,740
Switzerland	36,342	30,696	69,681	76,985	75,438	76,092	77,070	82,426
Turkey	7,910	11,343	22,303	35,710	40,226	54,503	41,399	51,554
United Kingdom	115,559	109,643	224,416	265,176	317,970	334,186	331,142	351,429
Eastern Europe								
Albania		261	423	714	1,140	1,091	1,331	1,504
Belarus				5,564	6,674	8,646	8,286	9,092
Bosnia-Herzegovina				1,082	4,128	3,894	4,095	4,416
Bulgaria		3,237	3,097	5,661	5,453	6,504	7,263	7,987
Croatia			5,188	7,352	7,799	7,922	9,054	10,722
Czech Republic				26,385	29,482	32,104	36,453	40,735
Estonia				2,546	4,110	4,237	4,300	4,810
Georgia				489	690	709	753	796
Hungary	9,245	8,224	8,671	15,380	27,923	31,955	33,724	37,787
Latvia				1,818	2,945	3,184	3,505	4,053
Lithuania				3,013	4,627	5,219	6,060	7,535
Macedonia				1,719	1,776	2,094	1,694	1,995
Moldova				841	586	776	893	1,039
Montenegro						322	459	585
Poland	16,690	11,855	8,413	29,050	45,903	48,197	49,314	53,987
Romania	13,843	11,267	9,843	10,278	10,392	13,055	15,552	17,862
Russia				68,863	43,588	44,862	53,765	60,967
Serbia						3,330	4,261	5,614
Slovakia				9,648	12,453	16,306	18,846	21,227
Slovenia			4,727	9,492	10,083	10,120	10,152	10,939
Ukraine				15,484	11,846	14,943	16,893	16,977

Source: Euromonitor International from national statistics
Note: US$ totals in this table may differ from the totals given for Imports (cif) by Origin and Imports (cif) by Commodity

Imports (cif) 1980, 1985, 1990, 1995, 1999-2011 *(continued)*
US$ million

	2003	2004	2005	2006	2007	2008	2009	2010	2011
Western Europe									
Austria	91,600	113,344	119,873	130,945	156,761	176,063	136,118	150,586	182,381
Belgium	234,968	285,611	318,547	351,570	412,011	467,379	353,348	393,465	461,101
Cyprus	4,288	5,659	6,304	6,917	8,696	10,791	7,907	8,632	8,703
Denmark	56,310	66,926	74,265	85,343	97,341	109,111	82,334	84,521	98,047
Finland	41,603	50,679	58,433	69,449	81,757	92,108	60,884	68,769	84,249
France	376,283	447,645	490,269	546,510	631,448	715,339	560,409	606,713	704,244
Germany	604,780	715,919	779,961	922,389	1,055,997	1,185,913	926,399	1,056,085	1,255,690
Gibraltar	469	531	551	679	852	827	747	746	867
Greece	44,218	52,768	54,487	63,639	78,639	92,893	69,393	63,227	60,090
Iceland	2,789	3,553	4,557	5,084	6,107	5,649	3,604	3,920	4,704
Ireland	54,174	63,605	71,455	76,433	87,049	84,878	62,613	60,680	67,158
Italy	297,919	355,281	384,577	442,603	511,871	563,100	414,836	486,926	557,557
Liechtenstein									
Luxembourg	13,691	16,826	17,564	19,433	22,301	25,514	18,652	21,738	25,698
Malta	3,398	3,824	3,807	4,079	4,508	5,354	4,382	4,957	6,732
Monaco									
Netherlands	234,027	283,969	310,325	358,518	421,092	494,749	382,383	439,991	507,870
Norway	40,057	48,533	55,480	64,276	80,389	90,308	68,952	77,333	90,833
Portugal	50,329	61,287	63,879	70,712	82,280	94,668	71,776	75,584	80,410
Spain	208,566	257,676	287,456	326,049	384,954	416,789	290,821	315,521	362,913
Sweden	84,207	100,837	111,618	127,703	153,412	168,999	120,057	148,764	175,974
Switzerland	95,584	110,318	119,697	132,021	153,173	173,312	147,777	167,233	196,776
Turkey	69,340	97,540	116,774	139,576	170,063	201,964	140,928	185,544	240,842
United Kingdom	386,925	461,057	509,246	588,849	622,843	643,052	486,799	562,970	639,633
Eastern Europe									
Albania	1,864	2,309	2,618	3,058	4,188	5,251	4,550	4,406	5,395
Belarus	11,558	16,491	16,708	22,351	28,693	39,381	28,569	34,884	45,743
Bosnia-Herzegovina	4,835	5,964	7,122	7,301	9,720	12,189	8,364	9,223	11,051
Bulgaria	10,902	14,467	18,162	23,269	30,087	37,015	23,552	25,473	32,579
Croatia	14,209	16,590	18,560	21,488	25,839	30,728	21,205	20,054	22,717
Czech Republic	51,239	68,245	76,340	93,430	118,467	142,172	105,242	126,606	152,123
Estonia	6,480	8,333	10,208	13,465	15,689	16,062	10,147	12,257	17,603
Georgia	1,141	1,846	2,490	3,678	5,217	6,066	4,386	5,097	6,948
Hungary	47,602	59,637	65,783	77,206	94,888	108,685	77,369	87,448	101,418
Latvia	5,242	7,048	8,592	11,430	15,182	15,775	9,362	11,141	15,262
Lithuania	9,675	12,389	15,488	19,413	24,456	31,267	18,339	23,381	31,780
Macedonia	2,306	2,932	3,228	3,763	5,216	6,843	5,038	5,449	7,003
Moldova	1,403	1,773	2,292	2,693	3,690	4,899	3,278	3,855	5,191
Montenegro	603	967	1,080	1,842	2,867	3,731	2,313	2,182	2,544
Poland	66,712	87,801	99,550	124,820	164,411	209,430	149,713	177,683	208,086
Romania	24,003	32,664	40,463	51,114	69,787	82,936	54,469	61,834	76,247
Russia	76,070	97,382	125,433	164,280	223,488	291,861	191,804	248,636	323,832
Serbia	7,477	10,753	10,461	13,172	18,554	22,875	16,047	16,734	20,139
Slovakia	28,874	38,808	43,793	54,950	66,096	74,081	54,203	62,958	75,141
Slovenia	13,858	17,585	19,618	23,065	29,531	33,987	23,887	26,347	30,847
Ukraine	23,020	28,997	36,136	45,040	60,619	85,533	45,487	60,911	82,594

Source: Euromonitor International from national statistics
Note: US$ totals in this table may differ from the totals given for Imports (cif) by Origin and Imports (cif) by Commodity

13

External Trade

External Trade Statistics

Table 13.2

Imports (cif) by Origin 2011

US$ million

	France	Germany	Italy	Netherlands	Poland	Sweden	United Kingdom	Total EU	Norway	Switzerland
Western Europe										
Austria	5,216	78,140	12,319	7,382	2,958	1,926	2,786	142,185	651	10,114
Belgium	49,673	69,276	13,562	91,864	4,439	9,042	27,819	318,503	6,115	5,021
Cyprus	496	720	720	399	49	56	782	6,054	40	74
Denmark	3,381	20,490	3,454	7,061	3,032	13,271	6,208	70,783	5,660	897
Finland	2,542	11,749	2,105	6,587	1,618	11,801	2,618	52,383	2,440	557
France		134,271	54,434	52,842	11,315	8,986	36,135	484,316	6,618	18,238
Germany	96,449		68,274	175,436	47,904	19,918	60,584	807,452	26,964	49,593
Gibraltar										
Greece	3,031	6,379	5,553	3,276	461	455	1,721	31,490	130	828
Iceland	87	370	149	347	90	184	243	2,164	751	94
Ireland	2,579	5,242	1,132	3,901	355	642	26,726	45,664	1,509	1,143
Italy	49,355	92,245		30,831	11,203	5,325	15,921	315,588	1,131	14,789
Liechtenstein										
Luxembourg	2,773	6,691	545	1,480	217	98	462	20,983	3	422
Malta	563	465	2,152	198	39	186	538	4,987	6	227
Monaco										
Netherlands	20,523	73,837	9,723		6,342	7,599	31,113	237,604	16,104	2,803
Norway	2,960	10,921	2,356	3,776	2,386	12,197	5,080	57,119		1,058
Portugal	5,569	9,968	4,331	3,851	544	847	2,694	58,986	589	505
Spain	42,884	47,057	24,315	18,199	4,464	3,820	16,473	206,709	1,997	2,932
Sweden	8,059	32,444	5,266	10,647	5,028		10,393	121,427	13,750	1,391
Switzerland	16,922	63,575	20,473	8,577	1,465	1,695	6,782	153,592	327	
Turkey	9,230	22,985	13,452	4,005	3,496	2,284	5,840	91,131	796	5,021
United Kingdom	36,380	80,296	22,453	45,341	11,361	12,282		320,498	30,159	10,169
Eastern Europe										
Albania	82	234	1,781	55	23	11	33	3,535	1	46
Belarus	431	2,556	968	400	1,289	217	356	8,683	98	273
Bosnia-Herzegovina	161	1,442	1,053	187	216	77	46	6,951	5	94
Bulgaria	1,068	3,622	2,353	834	630	207	513	19,473	19	231
Croatia	692	2,859	3,713	440	473	184	336	14,049	55	399
Czech Republic	4,778	45,099	5,680	8,634	10,860	1,432	3,691	113,223	85	1,328
Estonia	313	1,927	418	672	1,275	1,993	650	14,789	160	145
Georgia	90	475	180	121	59	17	80	2,006	7	45
Hungary	3,767	25,015	4,390	4,456	4,788	1,197	2,092	70,430	25	647
Latvia	482	1,806	682	557	1,176	583	494	11,953	114	183
Lithuania	779	3,128	1,013	1,584	2,930	1,073	498	17,920	84	82
Macedonia	86	925	380	173	64	18	559	5,110	4	73
Moldova	71	546	339	98	223	31	76	3,005	7	29
Montenegro	66	223	293	99	29	14	31	1,805	1	29
Poland	9,175	59,787	11,133	12,244		4,950	5,962	150,246	1,759	1,002
Romania	4,422	13,104	8,720	2,456	3,037	461	1,781	55,687	30	568
Russia	9,835	32,386	13,866	5,683	6,538	3,287	5,488	114,058	2,077	2,974
Serbia	400	2,234	1,780	457	416		170	13,178	15	193
Slovakia	2,787	14,529	3,064	1,795	4,132	504	1,087	55,604	27	343
Slovenia	1,279	5,071	4,930	883	568	156	432	20,903	28	243
Ukraine	1,447	7,445	2,316	1,439	4,393	482	878	29,365	272	746

Source: Euromonitor International from national statistics
Note: US$ totals in this table may differ from the totals given for Imports (cif) by Commodity and Total Imports (cif)

Imports (cif) by Origin 2011 *(continued)*

US$ million

	Russia	Africa and the Middle East	Asia Pacific	Japan	China	Australasia	Latin America	Brazil	USA	Canada	Total, including others
Western Europe											
Austria	4,054	4,088	11,607	1,306	5,149	100	613	329	3,066	267	182,381
Belgium	11,958	22,422	49,372	8,675	19,332	2,329	11,924	3,626	24,360	2,606	461,101
Cyprus	33	1,191	769	71	418	26	77	19	117	11	8,703
Denmark	1,459	1,382	9,937	460	6,143	364	1,979	499	2,564	303	98,047
Finland	15,204	878	6,872	511	3,624	396	1,780	724	2,001	685	84,249
France	18,274	50,220	76,962	6,882	34,161	1,549	10,746	4,693	23,310	2,804	704,244
Germany	52,701	34,316	176,450	23,310	89,240	3,431	25,286	9,277	44,140	5,148	1,255,690
Gibraltar											867
Greece	5,626	8,549	8,306	444	3,416	92	848	211	987	69	60,090
Iceland	41	47	501	74	295	7	460	273	511	55	4,704
Ireland	143	1,031	5,692	846	2,509	144	892	232	8,761	341	67,158
Italy	14,237	59,737	90,218	6,098	43,108	1,941	17,609	6,103	17,115	2,267	557,557
Liechtenstein											
Luxembourg	16	46	2,149	180	1,784	2	577	10	1,345	44	25,698
Malta	4	47	713	56	210	31	165	6	244	9	6,732
Monaco											
Netherlands	30,337	36,672	109,606	14,072	60,242	2,493	26,894	10,520	30,075	3,411	507,870
Norway	1,887	1,899	15,424	1,992	8,211	150	2,554	1,356	4,922	3,606	90,833
Portugal	736	7,778	6,041	467	2,087	58	3,502	2,044	1,285	306	80,410
Spain	11,349	51,802	40,996	3,410	21,057	1,301	21,916	4,740	12,097	1,315	362,913
Sweden	9,986	1,574	15,707	2,013	8,223	541	2,550	729	5,315	474	175,974
Switzerland	967	4,796	21,575	4,424	6,724	621	2,572	983	9,773	585	196,776
Turkey	23,953	26,628	51,381	4,264	21,693	807	5,394	2,074	16,043	1,312	240,842
United Kingdom	11,246	37,719	106,504	12,925	52,286	8,939	16,820	5,138	44,704	18,243	639,633
Eastern Europe											
Albania	65	85	463	2	317	7	100	72	54	69	5,395
Belarus	24,920	402	4,204	246	2,193	11	1,759	365	558	42	45,743
Bosnia-Herzegovina	830	13	109	1	60	9	17	4	31	7	11,051
Bulgaria	5,793	700	1,693	94	939	14	326	135	277	45	32,579
Croatia	1,635	309	3,381	235	1,606	13	402	220	524	33	22,717
Czech Republic	7,355	741	22,330	1,718	11,514	29	412	125	1,868	149	152,123
Estonia	667	40	1,065	45	822	14	44	18	153	101	17,603
Georgia	392	383	1,669	147	530	20	173	143	251	14	6,948
Hungary	8,769	371	14,144	1,578	8,495	26	877	140	1,796	183	101,418
Latvia	1,262	40	704	22	388	4	35	14	99	8	15,262
Lithuania	10,477	384	1,007	51	636	13	140	27	279	18	31,780
Macedonia	40	38	210	8	117	2	97	33	47	23	7,003
Moldova	474	26	191	4	116		39	17	47	1	5,191
Montenegro	100	38	327	32	219	2	104	90	35	4	2,544
Poland	21,375	1,675	19,718	1,482	10,979	114	1,665	490	2,444	202	208,086
Romania	2,935	860	9,076	359	3,527	17	994	555	841	162	76,247
Russia		4,877	85,466	7,357	50,447	1,328	9,825	4,783	12,181	1,720	323,832
Serbia	568	102	945	25	444	2	170	27	141	11	20,139
Slovakia	8,592	227	7,069	583	3,024	33	80	32	376	70	75,141
Slovenia	489	627	2,975	98	1,265	7	621	307	614	34	30,847
Ukraine	25,257	1,362	14,077	883	7,341	184	1,013	494	2,645	212	82,594

Source: Euromonitor International from national statistics
Note: US$ totals in this table may differ from the totals given for Imports (cif) by Commodity and Total Imports (cif)

External Trade Statistics

Table 13.3

Imports (cif) by Origin (% Analysis) 2011

% of total imports

	France	Germany	Italy	Netherlands	Poland	Sweden	United Kingdom	Total EU	Norway	Switzerland
Western Europe										
Austria	2.86	42.84	6.75	4.05	1.62	1.06	1.53	77.96	0.36	5.55
Belgium	10.77	15.02	2.94	19.92	0.96	1.96	6.03	69.07	1.33	1.09
Cyprus	5.70	8.27	8.27	4.58	0.56	0.64	8.99	69.56	0.46	0.85
Denmark	3.45	20.90	3.52	7.20	3.09	13.54	6.33	72.19	5.77	0.91
Finland	3.02	13.95	2.50	7.82	1.92	14.01	3.11	62.18	2.90	0.66
France		19.07	7.73	7.50	1.61	1.28	5.13	68.77	0.94	2.59
Germany	7.68		5.44	13.97	3.81	1.59	4.82	64.30	2.15	3.95
Gibraltar										
Greece	5.04	10.62	9.24	5.45	0.77	0.76	2.86	52.41	0.22	1.38
Iceland	1.85	7.86	3.17	7.38	1.92	3.92	5.17	46.01	15.97	2.00
Ireland	3.84	7.81	1.69	5.81	0.53	0.96	39.80	67.99	2.25	1.70
Italy	8.85	16.54		5.53	2.01	0.96	2.86	56.60	0.20	2.65
Liechtenstein										
Luxembourg	10.79	26.04	2.12	5.76	0.85	0.38	1.80	81.65	0.01	1.64
Malta	8.37	6.91	31.97	2.95	0.58	2.76	7.99	74.08	0.09	3.38
Monaco										
Netherlands	4.04	14.54	1.91		1.25	1.50	6.13	46.78	3.17	0.55
Norway	3.26	12.02	2.59	4.16	2.63	13.43	5.59	62.88		1.16
Portugal	6.93	12.40	5.39	4.79	0.68	1.05	3.35	73.36	0.73	0.63
Spain	11.82	12.97	6.70	5.01	1.23	1.05	4.54	56.96	0.55	0.81
Sweden	4.58	18.44	2.99	6.05	2.86		5.91	69.00	7.81	0.79
Switzerland	8.60	32.31	10.40	4.36	0.74	0.86	3.45	78.05	0.17	
Turkey	3.83	9.54	5.59	1.66	1.45	0.95	2.42	37.84	0.33	2.08
United Kingdom	5.69	12.55	3.51	7.09	1.78	1.92		50.11	4.72	1.59
Eastern Europe										
Albania	1.53	4.33	33.01	1.01	0.43	0.21	0.62	65.51	0.03	0.85
Belarus	0.94	5.59	2.12	0.88	2.82	0.48	0.78	18.98	0.21	0.60
Bosnia-Herzegovina	1.46	13.05	9.53	1.69	1.95	0.70	0.42	62.90	0.04	0.85
Bulgaria	3.28	11.12	7.22	2.56	1.93	0.64	1.57	59.77	0.06	0.71
Croatia	3.04	12.59	16.35	1.93	2.08	0.81	1.48	61.84	0.24	1.76
Czech Republic	3.14	29.65	3.73	5.68	7.14	0.94	2.43	74.43	0.06	0.87
Estonia	1.78	10.94	2.37	3.82	7.24	11.32	3.69	84.01	0.91	0.82
Georgia	1.29	6.84	2.59	1.74	0.85	0.25	1.16	28.88	0.10	0.65
Hungary	3.71	24.67	4.33	4.39	4.72	1.18	2.06	69.45	0.02	0.64
Latvia	3.16	11.83	4.47	3.65	7.71	3.82	3.24	78.32	0.75	1.20
Lithuania	2.45	9.84	3.19	4.98	9.22	3.38	1.57	56.39	0.26	0.26
Macedonia	1.23	13.21	5.42	2.47	0.92	0.26	7.99	72.97	0.05	1.05
Moldova	1.38	10.52	6.52	1.89	4.29	0.60	1.47	57.89	0.14	0.56
Montenegro	2.61	8.75	11.52	3.88	1.13	0.54	1.23	70.95	0.05	1.14
Poland	4.41	28.73	5.35	5.88		2.38	2.87	72.20	0.85	0.48
Romania	5.80	17.19	11.44	3.22	3.98	0.60	2.34	73.04	0.04	0.74
Russia	3.04	10.00	4.28	1.76	2.02	1.01	1.69	35.22	0.64	0.92
Serbia	1.98	11.09	8.84	2.27	2.06	0.00	0.84	65.43	0.07	0.96
Slovakia	3.71	19.34	4.08	2.39	5.50	0.67	1.45	74.00	0.04	0.46
Slovenia	4.15	16.44	15.98	2.86	1.84	0.50	1.40	67.76	0.09	0.79
Ukraine	1.75	9.01	2.80	1.74	5.32	0.58	1.06	35.55	0.33	0.90

Source: Euromonitor International from national statistics

External Trade Statistics

Imports (cif) by Origin (% Analysis) 2011 *(continued)*
% of total imports

	Russia	Africa and the Middle East	Asia Pacific	Japan	China	Australasia	Latin America	Brazil	USA	Canada	Total, including others
Western Europe											
Austria	2.22	2.24	6.36	0.72	2.82	0.05	0.34	0.18	1.68	0.15	100.00
Belgium	2.59	4.86	10.71	1.88	4.19	0.51	2.59	0.79	5.28	0.57	100.00
Cyprus	0.38	13.69	8.83	0.81	4.80	0.30	0.88	0.21	1.34	0.13	100.00
Denmark	1.49	1.41	10.14	0.47	6.27	0.37	2.02	0.51	2.62	0.31	100.00
Finland	18.05	1.04	8.16	0.61	4.30	0.47	2.11	0.86	2.37	0.81	100.00
France	2.59	7.13	10.93	0.98	4.85	0.22	1.53	0.67	3.31	0.40	100.00
Germany	4.20	2.73	14.05	1.86	7.11	0.27	2.01	0.74	3.52	0.41	100.00
Gibraltar											100.00
Greece	9.36	14.23	13.82	0.74	5.68	0.15	1.41	0.35	1.64	0.11	100.00
Iceland	0.87	1.01	10.66	1.56	6.27	0.15	9.79	5.81	10.87	1.17	100.00
Ireland	0.21	1.54	8.48	1.26	3.74	0.21	1.33	0.35	13.05	0.51	100.00
Italy	2.55	10.71	16.18	1.09	7.73	0.35	3.16	1.09	3.07	0.41	100.00
Liechtenstein											
Luxembourg	0.06	0.18	8.36	0.70	6.94	0.01	2.25	0.04	5.23	0.17	100.00
Malta	0.06	0.70	10.60	0.82	3.13	0.45	2.45	0.09	3.63	0.14	100.00
Monaco											
Netherlands	5.97	7.22	21.58	2.77	11.86	0.49	5.30	2.07	5.92	0.67	100.00
Norway	2.08	2.09	16.98	2.19	9.04	0.16	2.81	1.49	5.42	3.97	100.00
Portugal	0.92	9.67	7.51	0.58	2.60	0.07	4.36	2.54	1.60	0.38	100.00
Spain	3.13	14.27	11.30	0.94	5.80	0.36	6.04	1.31	3.33	0.36	100.00
Sweden	5.67	0.89	8.93	1.14	4.67	0.31	1.45	0.41	3.02	0.27	100.00
Switzerland	0.49	2.44	10.96	2.25	3.42	0.32	1.31	0.50	4.97	0.30	100.00
Turkey	9.95	11.06	21.33	1.77	9.01	0.34	2.24	0.86	6.66	0.54	100.00
United Kingdom	1.76	5.90	16.65	2.02	8.17	1.40	2.63	0.80	6.99	2.85	100.00
Eastern Europe											
Albania	1.20	1.58	8.59	0.05	5.87	0.12	1.85	1.34	0.99	1.29	100.00
Belarus	54.48	0.88	9.19	0.54	4.80	0.02	3.85	0.80	1.22	0.09	100.00
Bosnia-Herzegovina	7.51	0.12	0.99	0.01	0.55	0.08	0.16	0.04	0.28	0.06	100.00
Bulgaria	17.78	2.15	5.20	0.29	2.88	0.04	1.00	0.41	0.85	0.14	100.00
Croatia	7.20	1.36	14.88	1.04	7.07	0.06	1.77	0.97	2.31	0.15	100.00
Czech Republic	4.84	0.49	14.68	1.13	7.57	0.02	0.27	0.08	1.23	0.10	100.00
Estonia	3.79	0.23	6.05	0.26	4.67	0.08	0.25	0.10	0.87	0.58	100.00
Georgia	5.64	5.51	24.01	2.12	7.63	0.29	2.50	2.06	3.62	0.21	100.00
Hungary	8.65	0.37	13.95	1.56	8.38	0.03	0.86	0.14	1.77	0.18	100.00
Latvia	8.27	0.26	4.61	0.15	2.54	0.03	0.23	0.09	0.65	0.06	100.00
Lithuania	32.97	1.21	3.17	0.16	2.00	0.04	0.44	0.09	0.88	0.06	100.00
Macedonia	0.58	0.55	3.00	0.12	1.67	0.03	1.38	0.47	0.68	0.32	100.00
Moldova	9.13	0.50	3.69	0.08	2.23	0.00	0.76	0.32	0.90	0.03	100.00
Montenegro	3.91	1.50	12.87	1.24	8.61	0.06	4.08	3.54	1.37	0.15	100.00
Poland	10.27	0.81	9.48	0.71	5.28	0.05	0.80	0.24	1.17	0.10	100.00
Romania	3.85	1.13	11.90	0.47	4.63	0.02	1.30	0.73	1.10	0.21	100.00
Russia		1.51	26.39	2.27	15.58	0.41	3.03	1.48	3.76	0.53	100.00
Serbia	2.82	0.51	4.69	0.12	2.21	0.01	0.85	0.13	0.70	0.05	100.00
Slovakia	11.44	0.30	9.41	0.78	4.02	0.04	0.11	0.04	0.50	0.09	100.00
Slovenia	1.58	2.03	9.65	0.32	4.10	0.02	2.01	0.99	1.99	0.11	100.00
Ukraine	30.58	1.65	17.04	1.07	8.89	0.22	1.23	0.60	3.20	0.26	100.00

Source: Euromonitor International from national statistics

External Trade Statistics

Table 13.4

Imports (cif) by Commodity: SITC Classification 2011

US$ million

	Food and live animals	Beverages and tobacco	Crude materials excluding fuels	Mineral fuels etc	Oils and fats	Chemicals
Western Europe						
Austria	10,808	1,427	9,193	19,676	652	23,093
Belgium	30,575	4,452	19,665	65,351	2,228	117,669
Cyprus	961	302	82	1,801	38	857
Denmark	11,131	1,331	3,102	7,581	756	11,463
Finland	4,796	819	7,344	15,916	537	9,788
France	50,385	6,521	17,716	97,513	2,531	100,110
Germany	73,402	9,628	43,250	147,901	4,694	157,424
Gibraltar						
Greece	5,883	963	1,435	11,639	285	9,144
Iceland	415	65	667	594	24	464
Ireland	6,419	1,128	925	7,478	269	11,452
Italy	41,093	5,638	21,304	97,095	4,424	75,203
Liechtenstein						
Luxembourg	2,116	711	1,821	2,841	23	2,511
Malta	859	133	60	819	17	689
Monaco						
Netherlands	39,090	4,768	18,124	72,724	4,491	56,238
Norway	5,456	921	6,058	6,138	667	8,882
Portugal	8,992	691	2,628	11,841	592	10,224
Spain	28,441	4,523	14,197	63,819	1,732	47,326
Sweden	13,139	1,564	5,480	24,014	818	19,152
Switzerland	8,910	2,180	3,094	14,699	353	42,451
Turkey	5,996	593	20,245	34,747	1,378	32,695
United Kingdom	49,356	9,496	16,796	73,556	2,117	78,126
Eastern Europe						
Albania	686	227	197	740	63	551
Belarus	2,966	417	1,680	15,685	214	4,776
Bosnia-Herzegovina	1,530	358	380	2,190	70	1,348
Bulgaria	2,545	443	2,763	7,302	155	3,812
Croatia	2,084	212	382	4,353	91	3,273
Czech Republic	6,947	862	3,909	14,744	269	15,361
Estonia	1,570	399	487	2,962	35	1,835
Georgia	945	171	158	1,247	66	713
Hungary	4,164	497	1,467	9,076	230	9,932
Latvia	1,803	341	504	2,353	98	1,947
Lithuania	3,194	563	1,072	9,353	194	4,290
Macedonia	704	61	259	954	66	698
Moldova	565	186	114	620	12	710
Montenegro	515	100	112	315	20	256
Poland	12,575	1,180	5,901	21,477	785	27,448
Romania	4,829	454	2,295	7,588	361	10,051
Russia	40,458	5,106	9,007	5,128	2,399	44,796
Serbia	934	137	784	3,598	49	2,480
Slovakia	3,952	555	2,909	9,485	248	6,320
Slovenia	2,029	269	1,862	4,141	100	4,305
Ukraine	6,071	1,014	3,042	27,152	555	11,896

Source: Euromonitor International from national statistics
Note: US$ totals in this table may differ from the totals given for Imports (cif) by Origin and Total Imports (cif)

Imports (cif) by Commodity: SITC Classification 2011 (continued)

US$ million

	Basic manufactures	Machinery and Transport Equipment	Miscellaneous Manufactured Goods	Others	Total
Western Europe					
Austria	28,589	58,626	26,295	4,022	182,381
Belgium	66,503	106,152	42,158	6,349	461,101
Cyprus	1,101	2,167	1,220	174	8,703
Denmark	13,741	30,414	16,542	1,987	98,047
Finland	10,340	23,549	8,350	2,809	84,249
France	89,011	239,660	99,940	856	704,244
Germany	155,470	416,818	138,573	108,529	1,255,690
Gibraltar					867
Greece	6,747	16,396	7,539	60	60,090
Iceland	557	1,368	546	5	4,704
Ireland	5,387	20,447	8,890	4,764	67,158
Italy	78,223	152,488	61,246	20,843	557,557
Liechtenstein					
Luxembourg	4,430	7,569	2,605	1,070	25,698
Malta	668	2,627	799	63	6,732
Monaco					
Netherlands	47,192	145,313	51,125	68,804	507,870
Norway	13,184	34,655	13,607	1,266	90,833
Portugal	11,882	24,247	9,022	292	80,410
Spain	43,254	115,263	42,859	1,501	362,913
Sweden	23,257	62,615	19,145	6,790	175,974
Switzerland	28,974	52,673	41,533	1,909	196,776
Turkey	40,854	69,882	15,056	19,397	240,842
United Kingdom	78,001	197,948	97,477	36,760	639,633
Eastern Europe					
Albania	1,306	1,016	605	4	5,395
Belarus	6,827	8,751	1,847	2,579	45,743
Bosnia-Herzegovina	2,139	1,992	1,038	4	11,051
Bulgaria	5,239	6,958	2,271	1,091	32,579
Croatia	4,050	5,675	2,592	6	22,717
Czech Republic	25,395	64,302	14,824	5,509	152,123
Estonia	2,802	4,864	1,701	949	17,603
Georgia	1,036	1,739	663	211	6,948
Hungary	12,535	46,093	6,408	11,016	101,418
Latvia	2,300	3,409	1,450	1,057	15,262
Lithuania	3,716	6,543	2,186	669	31,780
Macedonia	1,802	1,449	489	521	7,003
Moldova	981	1,080	479	445	5,191
Montenegro	404	504	318		2,544
Poland	37,559	72,887	19,682	8,592	208,086
Romania	16,027	26,033	6,475	2,133	76,247
Russia	41,280	131,442	38,617	5,599	323,832
Serbia	3,580	3,387	1,432	3,758	20,139
Slovakia	11,598	31,965	7,832	277	75,141
Slovenia	5,915	9,001	3,059	165	30,847
Ukraine	11,819	15,182	5,033	830	82,594

Source: Euromonitor International from national statistics
Note: US$ totals in this table may differ from the totals given for Imports (cif) by Origin and Total Imports (cif)

13

External Trade

External Trade Statistics

Table 13.5

Imports (cif) by Commodity: SITC Classification (% Analysis) 2011
% of total imports

	Food and live animals	Beverages and tobacco	Crude materials excluding fuels	Mineral fuels etc	Oils and fats	Chemicals
Western Europe						
Austria	5.93	0.78	5.04	10.79	0.36	12.66
Belgium	6.63	0.97	4.26	14.17	0.48	25.52
Cyprus	11.04	3.47	0.94	20.69	0.44	9.85
Denmark	11.35	1.36	3.16	7.73	0.77	11.69
Finland	5.69	0.97	8.72	18.89	0.64	11.62
France	7.15	0.93	2.52	13.85	0.36	14.22
Germany	5.85	0.77	3.44	11.78	0.37	12.54
Gibraltar						
Greece	9.79	1.60	2.39	19.37	0.47	15.22
Iceland	8.83	1.38	14.19	12.63	0.51	9.85
Ireland	9.56	1.68	1.38	11.13	0.40	17.05
Italy	7.37	1.01	3.82	17.41	0.79	13.49
Liechtenstein						
Luxembourg	8.23	2.77	7.09	11.05	0.09	9.77
Malta	12.75	1.98	0.89	12.17	0.25	10.23
Monaco						
Netherlands	7.70	0.94	3.57	14.32	0.88	11.07
Norway	6.01	1.01	6.67	6.76	0.73	9.78
Portugal	11.18	0.86	3.27	14.73	0.74	12.72
Spain	7.84	1.25	3.91	17.59	0.48	13.04
Sweden	7.47	0.89	3.11	13.65	0.46	10.88
Switzerland	4.53	1.11	1.57	7.47	0.18	21.57
Turkey	2.49	0.25	8.41	14.43	0.57	13.58
United Kingdom	7.72	1.48	2.63	11.50	0.33	12.21
Eastern Europe						
Albania	12.71	4.22	3.65	13.72	1.17	10.22
Belarus	6.48	0.91	3.67	34.29	0.47	10.44
Bosnia-Herzegovina	13.85	3.24	3.44	19.82	0.63	12.20
Bulgaria	7.81	1.36	8.48	22.41	0.48	11.70
Croatia	9.17	0.93	1.68	19.16	0.40	14.41
Czech Republic	4.57	0.57	2.57	9.69	0.18	10.10
Estonia	8.92	2.26	2.77	16.83	0.20	10.42
Georgia	13.60	2.45	2.27	17.95	0.95	10.27
Hungary	4.11	0.49	1.45	8.95	0.23	9.79
Latvia	11.82	2.23	3.30	15.42	0.64	12.76
Lithuania	10.05	1.77	3.37	29.43	0.61	13.50
Macedonia	10.06	0.87	3.70	13.62	0.94	9.97
Moldova	10.89	3.58	2.21	11.93	0.22	13.67
Montenegro	20.23	3.92	4.41	12.37	0.79	10.04
Poland	6.04	0.57	2.84	10.32	0.38	13.19
Romania	6.33	0.60	3.01	9.95	0.47	13.18
Russia	12.49	1.58	2.78	1.58	0.74	13.83
Serbia	4.64	0.68	3.89	17.87	0.25	12.31
Slovakia	5.26	0.74	3.87	12.62	0.33	8.41
Slovenia	6.58	0.87	6.04	13.43	0.32	13.96
Ukraine	7.35	1.23	3.68	32.87	0.67	14.40

Source: Euromonitor International from national statistics

Imports (cif) by Commodity: SITC Classification (% Analysis) 2011 *(continued)*

% of total imports

	Basic manufactures	Machinery and Transport Equipment	Miscellaneous Manufactured Goods	Others	Total
Western Europe					
Austria	15.68	32.15	14.42	2.21	100.00
Belgium	14.42	23.02	9.14	1.38	100.00
Cyprus	12.65	24.90	14.02	2.00	100.00
Denmark	14.01	31.02	16.87	2.03	100.00
Finland	12.27	27.95	9.91	3.33	100.00
France	12.64	34.03	14.19	0.12	100.00
Germany	12.38	33.19	11.04	8.64	100.00
Gibraltar					100.00
Greece	11.23	27.29	12.55	0.10	100.00
Iceland	11.83	29.07	11.61	0.10	100.00
Ireland	8.02	30.45	13.24	7.09	100.00
Italy	14.03	27.35	10.98	3.74	100.00
Liechtenstein					
Luxembourg	17.24	29.45	10.14	4.17	100.00
Malta	9.92	39.02	11.86	0.94	100.00
Monaco					
Netherlands	9.29	28.61	10.07	13.55	100.00
Norway	14.51	38.15	14.98	1.39	100.00
Portugal	14.78	30.15	11.22	0.36	100.00
Spain	11.92	31.76	11.81	0.41	100.00
Sweden	13.22	35.58	10.88	3.86	100.00
Switzerland	14.72	26.77	21.11	0.97	100.00
Turkey	16.96	29.02	6.25	8.05	100.00
United Kingdom	12.19	30.95	15.24	5.75	100.00
Eastern Europe					
Albania	24.20	18.84	11.21	0.07	100.00
Belarus	14.93	19.13	4.04	5.64	100.00
Bosnia-Herzegovina	19.36	18.03	9.39	0.04	100.00
Bulgaria	16.08	21.36	6.97	3.35	100.00
Croatia	17.83	24.98	11.41	0.03	100.00
Czech Republic	16.69	42.27	9.74	3.62	100.00
Estonia	15.92	27.63	9.66	5.39	100.00
Georgia	14.90	25.02	9.55	3.04	100.00
Hungary	12.36	45.45	6.32	10.86	100.00
Latvia	15.07	22.34	9.50	6.93	100.00
Lithuania	11.69	20.59	6.88	2.10	100.00
Macedonia	25.74	20.69	6.98	7.43	100.00
Moldova	18.90	20.81	9.22	8.57	100.00
Montenegro	15.90	19.83	12.51		100.00
Poland	18.05	35.03	9.46	4.13	100.00
Romania	21.02	34.14	8.49	2.80	100.00
Russia	12.75	40.59	11.93	1.73	100.00
Serbia	17.78	16.82	7.11	18.66	100.00
Slovakia	15.43	42.54	10.42	0.37	100.00
Slovenia	19.18	29.18	9.92	0.54	100.00
Ukraine	14.31	18.38	6.09	1.00	100.00

Source: Euromonitor International from national statistics

13

External Trade

External Trade Statistics

Table 13.6

Exports (fob) 1980, 1985, 1990, 1995, 1999-2011

US$ million

	1980	1985	1990	1995	1999	2000	2001	2002
Western Europe								
Austria	17,489	17,239	41,135	57,643	64,124	64,170	66,494	73,156
Belgium			118,296	175,849	178,972	187,890	190,356	215,972
Cyprus	532	476	957	1,229	995	951	976	770
Denmark	16,749	17,090	37,037	51,478	50,399	50,349	51,083	56,385
Finland	14,150	13,617	26,571	39,573	41,841	45,482	42,803	44,702
France	116,030	101,671	216,591	286,738	302,493	298,768	297,859	311,289
Germany	192,860	183,933	410,104	523,802	542,870	550,229	571,476	616,073
Gibraltar	10	14	83	117	120	127	121	147
Greece	5,153	4,539	8,105	10,961	10,475	10,964	10,254	10,322
Iceland	918	815	1,592	1,804	2,005	1,892	2,022	2,227
Ireland	8,398	10,357	23,747	44,635	71,219	77,098	82,985	88,237
Italy	78,104	76,717	170,486	233,998	235,175	240,389	244,804	252,932
Liechtenstein								
Luxembourg	3,005	2,831	6,305	7,750	7,895	7,946	8,238	8,495
Malta	483	400	1,130	1,914	1,983	2,443	1,958	2,225
Monaco								
Netherlands	84,948	77,873	131,775	196,276	200,778	213,427	216,186	219,974
Norway	18,543	19,985	34,049	41,992	45,455	60,058	59,218	59,661
Portugal	4,640	5,685	16,422	23,207	25,227	25,089	24,930	26,897
Spain	20,720	24,247	55,521	91,046	109,964	113,349	115,179	123,636
Sweden	30,906	30,461	57,538	79,801	84,812	87,738	78,192	83,035
Switzerland	29,632	27,433	63,784	78,040	76,122	74,856	78,067	87,413
Turkey	2,910	7,957	12,959	21,599	26,587	27,775	31,334	36,059
United Kingdom	110,144	101,299	185,107	241,976	268,178	284,404	272,218	280,071
Eastern Europe								
Albania		198	224	202	264	261	305	330
Belarus				4,803	5,909	7,326	7,451	8,021
Bosnia-Herzegovina				152	749	1,069	1,032	1,010
Bulgaria		1,773	1,708	5,359	3,964	4,822	5,115	5,749
Croatia			4,020	4,517	4,303	4,422	4,659	4,903
Czech Republic				21,686	26,241	28,996	33,358	38,504
Estonia				1,840	3,018	3,167	3,312	3,444
Georgia				155	238	323	318	346
Hungary	8,671	8,538	9,598	12,801	24,950	28,016	30,530	34,512
Latvia				1,305	1,723	1,865	2,001	2,284
Lithuania				2,039	2,754	3,548	4,279	5,238
Macedonia				1,204	1,191	1,323	1,158	1,116
Moldova				739	474	472	568	644
Montenegro						228	253	303
Poland	14,191	11,489	13,627	22,895	27,397	35,895	41,651	46,732
Romania	11,209	12,167	5,775	7,910	8,505	10,367	11,385	13,876
Russia				82,913	75,665	105,036	101,886	107,302
Serbia						1,558	1,721	2,075
Slovakia				8,579	10,234	15,894	16,899	19,352
Slovenia			4,118	8,316	8,546	8,741	9,261	10,360
Ukraine				13,128	11,582	15,722	17,091	17,957

Source: Euromonitor International from national statistics
Note: US$ totals in this table may differ from the totals given for Exports (fob) by Destination and Exports (fob) by Commodity

Exports (fob) 1980, 1985, 1990, 1995, 1999-2011 *(continued)*
US$ million

	2003	2004	2005	2006	2007	2008	2009	2010	2011
Western Europe									
Austria	89,264	111,723	117,647	130,376	157,316	173,302	130,826	144,875	169,558
Belgium	255,637	306,807	335,625	366,758	431,119	473,348	370,612	409,281	476,163
Cyprus	834	1,081	1,528	1,395	1,482	1,744	1,348	1,506	1,954
Denmark	65,376	75,665	83,570	91,635	101,973	116,018	93,102	96,500	112,621
Finland	52,518	60,920	65,193	77,288	90,092	96,837	62,888	69,488	79,145
France	367,292	422,385	443,313	490,706	550,460	608,554	476,036	515,544	582,201
Germany	751,878	909,533	977,265	1,122,124	1,323,823	1,450,554	1,120,964	1,261,469	1,475,600
Gibraltar	148	197	200	242	304	283	264	258	246
Greece	13,472	15,453	17,247	20,774	23,606	26,428	20,456	21,322	30,999
Iceland	2,385	2,896	2,942	3,239	4,350	5,216	4,057	4,604	5,395
Ireland	92,929	104,963	107,848	109,006	122,253	126,961	119,296	118,941	127,553
Italy	299,878	353,554	372,728	417,224	500,241	544,631	406,799	446,810	523,304
Liechtenstein									
Luxembourg	9,979	12,175	12,696	14,174	16,144	17,590	12,786	14,293	16,718
Malta	2,467	2,627	2,376	2,707	2,983	3,066	2,314	2,994	5,027
Monaco									
Netherlands	264,864	317,835	349,349	400,677	472,660	545,558	431,812	492,702	569,638
Norway	68,324	82,524	103,750	122,119	136,392	171,792	116,747	130,681	159,220
Portugal	33,104	38,452	38,720	44,782	52,515	57,535	44,262	48,737	58,923
Spain	156,035	182,161	190,991	213,352	248,917	277,527	220,910	246,253	298,523
Sweden	102,429	123,279	130,961	147,947	168,923	183,912	130,851	158,393	187,130
Switzerland	100,726	117,814	126,003	141,669	164,799	191,404	166,682	186,025	223,210
Turkey	47,253	63,167	73,476	85,535	107,272	132,027	102,143	113,883	134,907
United Kingdom	307,712	349,731	384,385	447,861	441,649	468,109	357,397	410,629	479,329
Eastern Europe									
Albania	448	605	658	798	1,078	1,355	1,091	1,545	1,951
Belarus	9,946	13,774	15,979	19,734	24,275	32,571	21,304	25,284	41,192
Bosnia-Herzegovina	1,401	1,913	2,406	3,312	4,154	5,029	3,954	4,803	5,850
Bulgaria	7,540	9,931	11,739	15,101	18,575	22,484	16,378	20,571	28,222
Croatia	6,187	8,025	8,806	10,376	12,364	14,112	10,492	11,807	13,364
Czech Republic	48,709	67,194	77,985	95,143	122,760	146,406	113,161	133,026	162,898
Estonia	4,539	5,933	7,695	9,700	11,020	12,475	9,063	11,592	16,753
Georgia	461	647	865	993	1,240	1,507	1,140	1,581	2,188
Hungary	42,532	54,892	62,179	74,216	94,745	108,220	82,663	94,768	111,293
Latvia	2,893	3,982	5,108	5,893	7,892	9,278	7,185	8,849	11,889
Lithuania	6,975	9,311	11,764	14,154	17,170	23,746	16,493	20,721	28,050
Macedonia	1,367	1,676	2,041	2,401	3,356	3,920	2,692	3,291	4,433
Moldova	789	980	1,091	1,050	1,340	1,591	1,283	1,542	2,217
Montenegro	405	506	562	556	626	617	388	437	628
Poland	60,977	81,849	96,450	117,418	145,300	178,701	142,071	165,901	193,908
Romania	17,618	23,485	27,730	32,335	40,234	49,622	40,671	49,331	62,662
Russia	135,930	183,209	243,800	303,551	354,403	471,606	303,388	400,630	522,013
Serbia	2,756	3,523	4,482	6,428	8,825	10,972	8,345	9,795	11,775
Slovakia	29,340	36,738	40,765	51,487	65,039	73,005	55,568	64,007	78,513
Slovenia	12,768	15,892	17,891	21,055	26,615	29,229	22,348	24,168	28,514
Ukraine	23,067	32,666	34,231	38,368	49,296	66,954	39,782	51,478	68,460

Source: Euromonitor International from national statistics
Note: US$ totals in this table may differ from the totals given for Exports (fob) by Destination and Exports (fob) by Commodity

13

External Trade

External Trade Statistics

Table 13.7

Exports (fob) by Destination 2011

US$ million

	France	Germany	Italy	Netherlands	Poland	Sweden	United Kingdom	Total EU	Norway	Switzerland
Western Europe										
Austria	7,155.0	54,760.6	13,317.2	2,789.0	5,162.5	2,011.8	5,164.4	123,377.7	563.1	7,551.4
Belgium	80,769.2	89,215.4	21,937.2	59,717.2	7,956.4	6,972.6	34,231.2	354,106.9	2,256.6	7,244.1
Cyprus	19.6	107.9	67.2	28.2	6.0	26.3	199.0	1,144.9	3.3	12.3
Denmark	4,910.2	19,112.2	3,409.8	5,481.5	3,023.4	14,912.8	11,138.8	76,385.6	6,460.5	981.0
Finland	2,525.0	8,060.4	1,928.7	5,501.9	2,259.1	9,570.8	4,170.7	44,895.6	2,217.6	1,051.0
France		97,371.8	48,285.8	25,314.6	9,461.5	7,895.7	39,022.2	361,057.9	2,131.3	17,695.1
Germany	149,707.8		91,627.6	102,311.8	64,204.7	32,494.5	96,686.5	925,706.1	10,872.1	69,676.7
Gibraltar										
Greece	902.6	2,437.5	2,943.8	633.0	363.2	173.5	1,232.7	15,736.0	40.3	186.2
Iceland	210.4	811.6	137.2	1,750.8	65.1	34.5	486.0	4,227.4	238.8	35.4
Ireland	7,256.8	8,978.9	4,385.6	4,521.0	890.7	1,266.4	20,602.0	76,865.5	533.6	5,352.5
Italy	61,773.1	69,787.8		12,891.7	13,305.1	5,510.4	24,754.1	296,766.4	1,869.5	28,099.8
Liechtenstein										
Luxembourg	2,602.7	3,713.8	910.4	681.8	299.5	369.6	1,222.4	13,437.4	62.0	720.8
Malta	527.8	702.8	372.1	56.3	34.1	17.5	320.5	2,681.8	10.4	54.9
Monaco										
Netherlands	53,181.2	149,470.9	27,439.8		11,697.8	10,690.4	43,743.5	449,074.6	4,444.7	6,567.0
Norway	11,399.2	17,646.5	3,603.5	18,394.8	2,827.2	10,393.9	43,294.1	128,862.8		1,302.8
Portugal	7,156.8	8,005.4	2,179.5	2,340.9	566.7	610.1	3,021.7	43,281.3	126.3	513.2
Spain	53,263.4	31,661.3	24,811.0	9,011.6	5,018.8	2,894.2	20,117.3	199,818.1	1,632.0	5,738.9
Sweden	9,131.0	19,686.2	5,023.7	9,771.3	5,192.1		13,886.0	110,849.7	17,480.8	1,882.8
Switzerland	15,917.6	45,094.0	17,445.5	5,521.1	2,116.8	1,717.2	10,657.6	127,058.5	913.8	
Turkey	6,801.9	13,935.8	7,846.0	3,239.6	1,756.4	1,181.8	8,142.7	62,286.9	379.1	1,492.4
United Kingdom	35,277.4	52,225.7	16,088.1	37,823.9	6,938.9	10,061.8		255,238.9	4,775.5	33,880.6
Eastern Europe										
Albania	10.0	67.9	884.6	12.5	1.2	2.1	1.1	1,266.8	3.5	3.1
Belarus	67.4	1,867.0	565.6	6,295.2	1,148.2	93.5	416.0	16,078.0	155.4	8.2
Bosnia-Herzegovina	65.8	808.6	857.9	56.6	68.1	49.0	26.8	4,212.8	18.3	51.6
Bulgaria	1,219.4	3,433.0	2,443.8	509.8	514.0	139.1	538.3	17,969.8	50.5	117.7
Croatia	380.9	1,349.2	2,109.3	179.1	143.5	63.8	199.5	7,987.3	204.1	124.6
Czech Republic	8,979.3	52,786.9	6,802.3	5,736.6	10,314.6	2,686.7	7,433.1	136,179.6	814.0	2,645.3
Estonia	479.6	829.1	293.8	486.9	282.6	2,846.7	364.1	11,832.3	497.0	59.7
Georgia	26.8	51.4	62.8	16.4	9.3	0.3	13.6	431.7	22.3	1.6
Hungary	5,311.3	27,909.5	5,596.2	2,937.0	4,353.5	1,114.9	5,102.3	84,499.7	209.6	1,005.3
Latvia	159.8	926.2	169.6	257.7	650.7	695.0	334.7	7,966.2	246.9	48.3
Lithuania	1,173.8	2,657.0	512.2	1,740.6	1,996.4	1,017.3	1,183.5	17,516.3	466.9	53.3
Macedonia	12.9	1,247.8	318.0	100.4	21.2	17.7	53.7	2,652.2	7.5	50.2
Moldova	31.7	136.1	308.2	32.2	79.3	6.0	55.7	1,135.4	1.7	3.5
Montenegro	6.3	33.4	83.3	7.6	7.8	1.9	8.8	517.9	0.3	11.0
Poland	12,294.6	52,344.7	10,792.4	8,751.5		5,713.5	12,884.9	156,088.9	1,674.3	1,741.5
Romania	4,760.0	11,860.3	8,179.5	1,981.7	1,513.2	501.7	2,044.8	45,257.4	100.1	406.8
Russia	11,411.1	23,932.1	29,241.4	64,212.1	22,204.0	5,388.6	10,850.7	237,804.8	1,122.3	9,441.6
Serbia	232.1	1,123.3	1,155.0	130.4	118.7	0.0	134.5	6,459.7	8.0	71.6
Slovakia	5,294.3	16,823.9	4,117.5	1,994.5	6,222.4	1,452.4	2,985.2	70,618.6	150.6	760.6
Slovenia	1,634.4	5,688.5	3,410.3	555.8	967.1	256.1	570.2	20,273.5	54.1	297.0
Ukraine	562.9	2,023.9	3,171.0	884.3	2,628.1	67.9	432.6	18,897.3	121.6	67.1

Source: Euromonitor International from national statistics
Note: US$ totals in this table may differ from the totals given for Exports (fob) by Commodity and Total Exports (fob)

Exports (fob) by Destination 2011 *(continued)*
US$ million

	Russia	Africa and the Middle East	Asia Pacific	Japan	China	Australasia	Latin America	Brazil	USA	Canada	Total, including others
Western Europe											
Austria	4,789.1	4,560.9	10,949.8	1,438.3	3,682.1	851.9	2,668.0	1,194.9	6,707.9	741.3	169,557.5
Belgium	6,126.7	23,785.4	33,958.3	4,143.3	8,043.9	2,315.0	6,993.3	3,013.9	21,321.1	2,342.2	476,163.2
Cyprus	29.5	238.8	145.7	0.4	29.4	12.8	5.0	0.8	28.6	2.8	1,954.5
Denmark	2,046.8	3,397.5	9,411.3	1,955.1	2,773.8	1,096.0	2,114.0	815.0	6,224.6	889.0	112,620.6
Finland	7,475.7	3,281.3	9,201.3	1,357.7	3,774.0	949.0	2,047.5	749.1	4,001.3	1,281.8	79,145.3
France	8,886.6	58,372.3	60,631.7	8,525.3	18,128.1	5,890.3	14,917.2	5,340.9	29,400.2	3,908.6	582,201.0
Germany	45,527.3	63,018.9	163,027.3	15,847.2	75,611.7	10,279.0	39,629.5	14,641.5	82,448.6	7,431.0	1,475,599.9
Gibraltar											246.4
Greece	450.1	3,264.7	1,654.8	31.4	384.4	162.4	272.2	43.3	1,607.8	211.3	30,999.4
Iceland	169.1	118.8	225.5	134.7	47.5	13.1	22.1	5.5	201.3	23.1	5,395.2
Ireland	688.0	2,768.0	8,093.0	2,481.1	2,133.1	1,073.7	1,513.2	406.9	28,476.1	817.7	127,553.4
Italy	13,005.9	45,954.9	47,047.9	6,459.2	13,978.5	4,717.3	19,680.2	6,613.0	30,862.9	3,736.5	523,304.2
Liechtenstein											
Luxembourg	235.3	452.8	538.2	44.1	178.0	34.2	143.5	32.8	421.4	78.6	16,718.0
Malta	1.2	262.8	188.0	73.8	35.3	9.4	48.8	8.3	102.5	25.2	5,026.6
Monaco											
Netherlands	8,423.0	22,233.9	28,357.4	3,679.2	7,803.7	2,449.3	9,116.8	2,773.8	18,953.7	1,925.0	569,637.6
Norway	1,374.2	1,882.5	9,169.9	1,845.9	2,905.3	304.4	2,045.5	853.8	8,985.4	2,587.1	159,220.2
Portugal	196.4	6,536.0	1,409.2	242.3	548.1	112.6	1,983.8	787.3	1,928.6	271.5	58,923.3
Spain	3,409.9	23,791.0	14,253.0	2,527.7	4,498.9	2,004.3	15,096.4	3,289.2	10,216.9	1,563.9	298,522.5
Sweden	3,359.6	11,032.4	16,873.2	2,131.7	5,843.2	2,252.7	4,956.3	2,048.9	10,358.2	1,388.9	187,130.3
Switzerland	3,239.0	12,311.7	38,635.1	7,149.9	9,505.6	2,900.3	6,447.3	2,396.2	22,910.0	2,973.6	223,209.5
Turkey	5,986.2	35,021.8	12,121.5	296.1	2,463.7	623.0	2,394.8	882.5	4,598.8	874.3	134,906.9
United Kingdom	4,418.0	32,729.0	50,359.7	6,030.3	9,885.4	6,288.1	8,037.3	2,515.2	47,418.9	7,188.1	479,329.5
Eastern Europe											
Albania	7.6	33.8	249.3	2.7	152.5	0.7	5.6	2.8	27.1	6.7	1,951.1
Belarus	13,990.1	710.6	3,452.2	12.5	651.3	30.9	1,775.1	1,251.4	88.0	12.7	41,192.2
Bosnia-Herzegovina	64.2	89.9	100.2	8.3	39.3	4.3	11.7	7.6	65.5	16.2	5,850.0
Bulgaria	722.5	1,678.3	985.8	32.4	386.9	29.2	141.0	41.6	352.2	120.2	28,221.7
Croatia	320.1	810.9	297.5	73.8	54.6	35.0	236.1	29.3	363.5	16.0	13,364.0
Czech Republic	4,776.0	3,446.3	5,230.1	571.4	1,663.2	441.0	1,212.8	439.9	3,025.9	260.4	162,897.7
Estonia	1,990.2	267.2	507.4	70.1	193.1	36.8	95.8	70.8	601.8	32.4	16,752.9
Georgia	41.5	135.8	863.2	2.8	28.5	1.8	51.3	0.0	120.4	112.3	2,188.4
Hungary	3,574.8	4,445.3	5,344.9	594.4	1,715.3	373.8	771.9	266.7	2,371.3	226.2	111,293.2
Latvia	2,097.3	234.3	571.4	43.5	60.1	8.6	38.8	3.9	108.9	14.2	11,888.7
Lithuania	4,684.1	446.8	989.5	26.3	81.9	20.2	76.4	3.4	729.7	324.7	28,049.8
Macedonia	75.6	22.5	192.0	10.8	150.6	5.3	3.3	2.1	52.4	8.8	4,432.7
Moldova	455.8	40.8	94.4	13.1	12.5	1.1	5.3	2.7	16.9	2.2	2,216.8
Montenegro	6.3	11.2	23.8	3.5	18.9	0.4	0.0	0.0	4.2	0.5	627.5
Poland	8,184.6	3,162.4	5,675.9	554.8	1,951.3	428.4	1,245.1	377.2	3,103.0	451.1	193,908.0
Romania	1,429.0	3,910.5	1,988.9	239.9	533.0	36.2	419.0	166.4	1,062.9	203.2	62,662.2
Russia		15,064.5	92,074.5	15,004.7	33,703.8	121.5	6,571.2	2,210.0	16,486.6	563.9	522,013.0
Serbia	854.3	135.9	327.8	12.3	77.6	7.0	31.4	24.4	133.7	16.2	11,775.4
Slovakia	1,874.5	456.9	867.9	32.9	339.2	55.7	318.3	86.4	557.1	53.9	78,513.5
Slovenia	1,102.6	786.8	690.5	33.0	126.8	45.7	178.8	44.2	367.4	66.5	28,514.0
Ukraine	18,542.8	9,104.6	10,355.9	129.6	2,535.7	36.8	1,571.4	607.0	1,296.6	134.6	68,460.0

Source: Euromonitor International from national statistics
Note: US$ totals in this table may differ from the totals given for Exports (fob) by Commodity and Total Exports (fob)

13

External Trade

External Trade Statistics

Table 13.8

Exports (fob) by Destination (% Analysis) 2011

% of total exports

	France	Germany	Italy	Netherlands	Poland	Sweden	United Kingdom	Total EU	Norway	Switzerland
Western Europe										
Austria	4.22	32.30	7.85	1.64	3.04	1.19	3.05	72.76	0.33	4.45
Belgium	16.96	18.74	4.61	12.54	1.67	1.46	7.19	74.37	0.47	1.52
Cyprus	1.00	5.52	3.44	1.44	0.31	1.35	10.18	58.58	0.17	0.63
Denmark	4.36	16.97	3.03	4.87	2.68	13.24	9.89	67.83	5.74	0.87
Finland	3.19	10.18	2.44	6.95	2.85	12.09	5.27	56.73	2.80	1.33
France		16.72	8.29	4.35	1.63	1.36	6.70	62.02	0.37	3.04
Germany	10.15		6.21	6.93	4.35	2.20	6.55	62.73	0.74	4.72
Gibraltar										
Greece	2.91	7.86	9.50	2.04	1.17	0.56	3.98	50.76	0.13	0.60
Iceland	3.90	15.04	2.54	32.45	1.21	0.64	9.01	78.36	4.43	0.66
Ireland	5.69	7.04	3.44	3.54	0.70	0.99	16.15	60.26	0.42	4.20
Italy	11.80	13.34		2.46	2.54	1.05	4.73	56.71	0.36	5.37
Liechtenstein										
Luxembourg	15.57	22.21	5.45	4.08	1.79	2.21	7.31	80.38	0.37	4.31
Malta	10.50	13.98	7.40	1.12	0.68	0.35	6.38	53.35	0.21	1.09
Monaco										
Netherlands	9.34	26.24	4.82		2.05	1.88	7.68	78.84	0.78	1.15
Norway	7.16	11.08	2.26	11.55	1.78	6.53	27.19	80.93		0.82
Portugal	12.15	13.59	3.70	3.97	0.96	1.04	5.13	73.45	0.21	0.87
Spain	17.84	10.61	8.31	3.02	1.68	0.97	6.74	66.94	0.55	1.92
Sweden	4.88	10.52	2.68	5.22	2.77		7.42	59.24	9.34	1.01
Switzerland	7.13	20.20	7.82	2.47	0.95	0.77	4.77	56.92	0.41	
Turkey	5.04	10.33	5.82	2.40	1.30	0.88	6.04	46.17	0.28	1.11
United Kingdom	7.36	10.90	3.36	7.89	1.45	2.10		53.25	1.00	7.07
Eastern Europe										
Albania	0.51	3.48	45.34	0.64	0.06	0.11	0.05	64.93	0.18	0.16
Belarus	0.16	4.53	1.37	15.28	2.79	0.23	1.01	39.03	0.38	0.02
Bosnia-Herzegovina	1.12	13.82	14.66	0.97	1.16	0.84	0.46	72.01	0.31	0.88
Bulgaria	4.32	12.16	8.66	1.81	1.82	0.49	1.91	63.67	0.18	0.42
Croatia	2.85	10.10	15.78	1.34	1.07	0.48	1.49	59.77	1.53	0.93
Czech Republic	5.51	32.40	4.18	3.52	6.33	1.65	4.56	83.60	0.50	1.62
Estonia	2.86	4.95	1.75	2.91	1.69	16.99	2.17	70.63	2.97	0.36
Georgia	1.22	2.35	2.87	0.75	0.42	0.01	0.62	19.72	1.02	0.07
Hungary	4.77	25.08	5.03	2.64	3.91	1.00	4.58	75.93	0.19	0.90
Latvia	1.34	7.79	1.43	2.17	5.47	5.85	2.82	67.01	2.08	0.41
Lithuania	4.18	9.47	1.83	6.21	7.12	3.63	4.22	62.45	1.66	0.19
Macedonia	0.29	28.15	7.17	2.27	0.48	0.40	1.21	59.83	0.17	1.13
Moldova	1.43	6.14	13.90	1.45	3.58	0.27	2.51	51.22	0.08	0.16
Montenegro	1.00	5.32	13.27	1.21	1.25	0.31	1.41	82.53	0.04	1.75
Poland	6.34	26.99	5.57	4.51		2.95	6.64	80.50	0.86	0.90
Romania	7.60	18.93	13.05	3.16	2.41	0.80	3.26	72.22	0.16	0.65
Russia	2.19	4.58	5.60	12.30	4.25	1.03	2.08	45.56	0.22	1.81
Serbia	1.97	9.54	9.81	1.11	1.01	0.00	1.14	54.86	0.07	0.61
Slovakia	6.74	21.43	5.24	2.54	7.93	1.85	3.80	89.94	0.19	0.97
Slovenia	5.73	19.95	11.96	1.95	3.39	0.90	2.00	71.10	0.19	1.04
Ukraine	0.82	2.96	4.63	1.29	3.84	0.10	0.63	27.60	0.18	0.10

Source: Euromonitor International from national statistics

Exports (fob) by Destination (% Analysis) 2011 *(continued)*

% of total exports

	Russia	Africa and the Middle East	Asia Pacific	Japan	China	Australasia	Latin America	Brazil	USA	Canada	Total, including others
Western Europe											
Austria	2.82	2.69	6.46	0.85	2.17	0.50	1.57	0.70	3.96	0.44	100.00
Belgium	1.29	5.00	7.13	0.87	1.69	0.49	1.47	0.63	4.48	0.49	100.00
Cyprus	1.51	12.22	7.45	0.02	1.51	0.65	0.25	0.04	1.46	0.15	100.00
Denmark	1.82	3.02	8.36	1.74	2.46	0.97	1.88	0.72	5.53	0.79	100.00
Finland	9.45	4.15	11.63	1.72	4.77	1.20	2.59	0.95	5.06	1.62	100.00
France	1.53	10.03	10.41	1.46	3.11	1.01	2.56	0.92	5.05	0.67	100.00
Germany	3.09	4.27	11.05	1.07	5.12	0.70	2.69	0.99	5.59	0.50	100.00
Gibraltar											100.00
Greece	1.45	10.53	5.34	0.10	1.24	0.52	0.88	0.14	5.19	0.68	100.00
Iceland	3.13	2.20	4.18	2.50	0.88	0.24	0.41	0.10	3.73	0.43	100.00
Ireland	0.54	2.17	6.34	1.95	1.67	0.84	1.19	0.32	22.32	0.64	100.00
Italy	2.49	8.78	8.99	1.23	2.67	0.90	3.76	1.26	5.90	0.71	100.00
Liechtenstein											
Luxembourg	1.41	2.71	3.22	0.26	1.06	0.20	0.86	0.20	2.52	0.47	100.00
Malta	0.02	5.23	3.74	1.47	0.70	0.19	0.97	0.16	2.04	0.50	100.00
Monaco											
Netherlands	1.48	3.90	4.98	0.65	1.37	0.43	1.60	0.49	3.33	0.34	100.00
Norway	0.86	1.18	5.76	1.16	1.82	0.19	1.28	0.54	5.64	1.62	100.00
Portugal	0.33	11.09	2.39	0.41	0.93	0.19	3.37	1.34	3.27	0.46	100.00
Spain	1.14	7.97	4.77	0.85	1.51	0.67	5.06	1.10	3.42	0.52	100.00
Sweden	1.80	5.90	9.02	1.14	3.12	1.20	2.65	1.09	5.54	0.74	100.00
Switzerland	1.45	5.52	17.31	3.20	4.26	1.30	2.89	1.07	10.26	1.33	100.00
Turkey	4.44	25.96	8.99	0.22	1.83	0.46	1.78	0.65	3.41	0.65	100.00
United Kingdom	0.92	6.83	10.51	1.26	2.06	1.31	1.68	0.52	9.89	1.50	100.00
Eastern Europe											
Albania	0.39	1.73	12.78	0.14	7.82	0.04	0.29	0.14	1.39	0.35	100.00
Belarus	33.96	1.73	8.38	0.03	1.58	0.07	4.31	3.04	0.21	0.03	100.00
Bosnia-Herzegovina	1.10	1.54	1.71	0.14	0.67	0.07	0.20	0.13	1.12	0.28	100.00
Bulgaria	2.56	5.95	3.49	0.11	1.37	0.10	0.50	0.15	1.25	0.43	100.00
Croatia	2.40	6.07	2.23	0.55	0.41	0.26	1.77	0.22	2.72	0.12	100.00
Czech Republic	2.93	2.12	3.21	0.35	1.02	0.27	0.74	0.27	1.86	0.16	100.00
Estonia	11.88	1.60	3.03	0.42	1.15	0.22	0.57	0.42	3.59	0.19	100.00
Georgia	1.90	6.21	39.44	0.13	1.30	0.08	2.34	0.00	5.50	5.13	100.00
Hungary	3.21	3.99	4.80	0.53	1.54	0.34	0.69	0.24	2.13	0.20	100.00
Latvia	17.64	1.97	4.81	0.37	0.51	0.07	0.33	0.03	0.92	0.12	100.00
Lithuania	16.70	1.59	3.53	0.09	0.29	0.07	0.27	0.01	2.60	1.16	100.00
Macedonia	1.71	0.51	4.33	0.24	3.40	0.12	0.08	0.05	1.18	0.20	100.00
Moldova	20.56	1.84	4.26	0.59	0.56	0.05	0.24	0.12	0.76	0.10	100.00
Montenegro	1.01	1.79	3.80	0.56	3.01	0.06	0.00	0.00	0.66	0.08	100.00
Poland	4.22	1.63	2.93	0.29	1.01	0.22	0.64	0.19	1.60	0.23	100.00
Romania	2.28	6.24	3.17	0.38	0.85	0.06	0.67	0.27	1.70	0.32	100.00
Russia		2.89	17.64	2.87	6.46	0.02	1.26	0.42	3.16	0.11	100.00
Serbia	7.25	1.15	2.78	0.10	0.66	0.06	0.27	0.21	1.14	0.14	100.00
Slovakia	2.39	0.58	1.11	0.04	0.43	0.07	0.41	0.11	0.71	0.07	100.00
Slovenia	3.87	2.76	2.42	0.12	0.44	0.16	0.63	0.15	1.29	0.23	100.00
Ukraine	27.09	13.30	15.13	0.19	3.70	0.05	2.30	0.89	1.89	0.20	100.00

Source: Euromonitor International from national statistics

External Trade Statistics

Table 13.9

Exports (fob) by Commodity: SITC Classification 2011

US$ million

	Food and live animals	Beverages and tobacco	Crude materials excluding fuels	Mineral fuels etc	Oils and fats	Chemicals
Western Europe						
Austria	8,826.5	2,465.7	4,700.8	5,535.5	285.0	19,881.5
Belgium	36,995.7	3,677.9	13,041.5	43,010.2	1,423.8	146,388.8
Cyprus	311.8	126.1	125.6	274.7	1.9	474.9
Denmark	18,779.2	1,287.9	4,608.3	9,270.8	704.8	12,648.5
Finland	1,699.9	208.8	5,451.0	6,575.6	157.7	9,080.0
France	50,341.0	17,085.2	13,755.9	21,190.0	1,645.1	104,806.7
Germany	62,662.7	11,740.2	25,155.5	30,768.4	2,884.1	220,215.1
Gibraltar						
Greece	5,644.0	1,127.1	1,611.7	3,221.2	586.3	4,427.9
Iceland	2,136.5	9.1	66.4	59.6	97.0	152.4
Ireland	9,872.4	1,696.4	1,770.4	1,192.6	39.8	71,939.0
Italy	29,469.7	8,306.4	6,145.5	22,484.5	2,437.2	57,405.5
Liechtenstein						
Luxembourg	1,014.3	306.8	383.0	173.8	2.2	1,241.6
Malta	289.3	17.6	30.0	90.9	0.5	564.6
Monaco						
Netherlands	61,088.6	9,732.5	23,738.7	53,559.0	5,786.4	78,875.2
Norway	11,417.7	89.4	2,018.4	102,071.0	242.7	5,601.6
Portugal	4,252.8	2,070.9	3,045.1	4,103.2	457.4	4,961.7
Spain	35,697.8	4,670.0	6,153.2	16,246.0	4,054.3	38,581.0
Sweden	7,512.8	1,121.2	12,660.2	13,464.4	335.9	21,454.1
Switzerland	5,882.3	2,578.0	2,408.0	6,231.2	40.0	86,129.3
Turkey	12,696.6	1,068.1	4,101.0	5,088.2	414.1	7,391.4
United Kingdom	18,570.3	10,998.8	11,905.0	61,879.5	777.4	86,581.5
Eastern Europe						
Albania	79.8	5.3	262.8	370.8	1.3	9.6
Belarus	5,238.4	78.1	1,040.7	11,305.5	94.1	6,282.8
Bosnia-Herzegovina	350.3	43.7	716.7	924.5	44.8	301.8
Bulgaria	3,074.2	635.1	2,491.2	3,715.0	196.6	2,214.7
Croatia	1,149.1	286.2	902.5	1,656.1	32.3	1,547.9
Czech Republic	4,766.3	1,050.3	4,774.8	6,166.3	290.2	10,231.9
Estonia	1,292.7	231.6	1,324.4	2,691.9	78.4	891.0
Georgia	252.0	213.8	397.5	85.7	1.6	197.7
Hungary	7,042.2	315.3	2,055.8	3,017.5	339.0	9,352.2
Latvia	1,433.8	426.3	1,789.4	574.5	24.8	1,039.8
Lithuania	4,140.1	514.8	1,129.7	6,404.6	79.0	3,716.1
Macedonia	416.2	306.0	176.5	110.9	9.8	189.8
Moldova	600.7	291.3	218.2	11.1	64.4	117.2
Montenegro	48.5	40.5	88.1	68.5	2.7	25.7
Poland	16,928.4	2,187.1	3,894.2	7,124.9	405.6	14,879.5
Romania	3,285.7	786.5	4,075.6	3,179.6	245.3	3,592.1
Russia	9,161.9	950.0	17,330.4	364,442.8	888.5	23,145.8
Serbia	2,157.5	283.2	559.9	631.0	181.0	1,035.3
Slovakia	2,887.6	110.1	2,242.2	3,855.8	126.6	3,680.4
Slovenia	941.2	113.9	1,123.4	1,281.8	16.5	4,667.9
Ukraine	7,833.6	840.5	7,328.5	4,995.9	3,504.8	4,412.9

Source: Euromonitor International from national statistics
Note: US$ totals in this table may differ from the totals given for Exports (fob) by Destination and Total Exports (fob)

Exports (fob) by Commodity: SITC Classification 2011 *(continued)*

US$ million

	Basic manufactures	Machinery and Transport Equipment	Miscellaneous Manufactured Goods	Others	Total
Western Europe					
Austria	36,973.5	63,506.9	19,245.9	8,136.2	169,557.5
Belgium	81,804.1	95,262.6	42,498.0	12,060.5	476,163.2
Cyprus	86.5	320.0	212.7	20.3	1,954.5
Denmark	9,724.8	27,870.6	17,735.9	9,989.9	112,620.6
Finland	25,101.3	24,860.5	4,475.2	1,535.3	79,145.3
France	68,499.9	226,603.9	62,249.4	16,023.9	582,201.0
Germany	193,060.5	670,573.4	150,197.9	108,342.1	1,475,599.9
Gibraltar					246.4
Greece	6,324.5	4,038.8	3,270.7	747.1	30,999.4
Iceland	2,290.6	446.5	108.6	28.5	5,395.2
Ireland	2,068.2	19,957.8	14,294.8	4,721.9	127,553.4
Italy	99,957.1	190,204.5	90,272.0	16,621.8	523,304.2
Liechtenstein					
Luxembourg	7,632.7	3,955.0	1,579.3	429.2	16,718.0
Malta	272.0	2,886.4	819.4	55.9	5,026.6
Monaco					
Netherlands	45,349.5	156,030.2	45,503.3	89,974.2	569,637.6
Norway	13,351.8	14,633.7	4,035.4	5,758.7	159,220.2
Portugal	13,194.4	15,737.0	9,718.6	1,382.2	58,923.3
Spain	51,651.0	106,940.0	27,028.4	7,500.8	298,522.5
Sweden	34,467.5	68,198.1	16,343.7	11,572.3	187,130.3
Switzerland	23,133.3	45,803.7	49,609.2	1,394.4	223,209.5
Turkey	39,472.6	37,120.7	23,034.0	4,514.0	134,906.9
United Kingdom	51,699.5	150,204.6	56,729.7	29,983.1	479,329.5
Eastern Europe					
Albania	441.6	80.6	693.0	6.3	1,951.1
Belarus	6,125.5	6,920.4	2,594.0	1,512.6	41,192.2
Bosnia-Herzegovina	1,410.1	668.2	1,221.2	168.8	5,850.0
Bulgaria	6,308.5	4,690.6	3,972.3	923.5	28,221.7
Croatia	1,872.3	4,251.0	1,655.5	11.0	13,364.0
Czech Republic	26,850.1	86,837.3	17,446.9	4,483.6	162,897.7
Estonia	2,440.8	4,594.0	2,382.9	825.2	16,752.9
Georgia	443.8	358.2	65.5	172.7	2,188.4
Hungary	10,176.8	63,630.9	8,585.5	6,778.0	111,293.2
Latvia	2,671.7	2,300.4	1,172.0	456.0	11,888.7
Lithuania	2,770.5	4,918.7	3,947.7	428.5	28,049.8
Macedonia	1,112.0	221.5	1,149.5	740.5	4,432.7
Moldova	145.2	279.1	489.1	0.4	2,216.8
Montenegro	282.1	54.4	17.2		627.5
Poland	39,815.8	81,312.2	24,219.8	3,140.4	193,908.0
Romania	10,290.9	26,802.5	9,200.3	1,203.7	62,662.2
Russia	62,492.6	16,221.6	3,563.3	23,816.1	522,013.0
Serbia	3,345.6	1,938.2	1,460.8	182.9	11,775.4
Slovakia	14,757.9	43,025.6	7,717.9	109.4	78,513.5
Slovenia	6,245.1	11,031.5	3,015.6	77.2	28,514.0
Ukraine	24,802.5	11,885.3	2,381.1	474.8	68,460.0

Source: Euromonitor International from national statistics
Note: US$ totals in this table may differ from the totals given for Exports (fob) by Destination and Total Exports (fob)

13

External Trade

External Trade Statistics   **Table 13.10**

Exports (fob) by Commodity: SITC Classification (% Analysis) 2011
% of total exports

	Food and live animals	Beverages and tobacco	Crude materials excluding fuels	Mineral fuels etc	Oils and fats	Chemicals
Western Europe						
Austria	5.21	1.45	2.77	3.26	0.17	11.73
Belgium	7.77	0.77	2.74	9.03	0.30	30.74
Cyprus	15.96	6.45	6.43	14.06	0.10	24.30
Denmark	16.67	1.14	4.09	8.23	0.63	11.23
Finland	2.15	0.26	6.89	8.31	0.20	11.47
France	8.65	2.93	2.36	3.64	0.28	18.00
Germany	4.25	0.80	1.70	2.09	0.20	14.92
Gibraltar						
Greece	18.21	3.64	5.20	10.39	1.89	14.28
Iceland	39.60	0.17	1.23	1.10	1.80	2.83
Ireland	7.74	1.33	1.39	0.94	0.03	56.40
Italy	5.63	1.59	1.17	4.30	0.47	10.97
Liechtenstein						
Luxembourg	6.07	1.84	2.29	1.04	0.01	7.43
Malta	5.76	0.35	0.60	1.81	0.01	11.23
Monaco						
Netherlands	10.72	1.71	4.17	9.40	1.02	13.85
Norway	7.17	0.06	1.27	64.11	0.15	3.52
Portugal	7.22	3.51	5.17	6.96	0.78	8.42
Spain	11.96	1.56	2.06	5.44	1.36	12.92
Sweden	4.01	0.60	6.77	7.20	0.18	11.46
Switzerland	2.64	1.15	1.08	2.79	0.02	38.59
Turkey	9.41	0.79	3.04	3.77	0.31	5.48
United Kingdom	3.87	2.29	2.48	12.91	0.16	18.06
Eastern Europe						
Albania	4.09	0.27	13.47	19.01	0.06	0.49
Belarus	12.72	0.19	2.53	27.45	0.23	15.25
Bosnia-Herzegovina	5.99	0.75	12.25	15.80	0.77	5.16
Bulgaria	10.89	2.25	8.83	13.16	0.70	7.85
Croatia	8.60	2.14	6.75	12.39	0.24	11.58
Czech Republic	2.93	0.64	2.93	3.79	0.18	6.28
Estonia	7.72	1.38	7.91	16.07	0.47	5.32
Georgia	11.51	9.77	18.16	3.91	0.07	9.03
Hungary	6.33	0.28	1.85	2.71	0.30	8.40
Latvia	12.06	3.59	15.05	4.83	0.21	8.75
Lithuania	14.76	1.84	4.03	22.83	0.28	13.25
Macedonia	9.39	6.90	3.98	2.50	0.22	4.28
Moldova	27.10	13.14	9.84	0.50	2.91	5.29
Montenegro	7.72	6.46	14.04	10.91	0.43	4.09
Poland	8.73	1.13	2.01	3.67	0.21	7.67
Romania	5.24	1.26	6.50	5.07	0.39	5.73
Russia	1.76	0.18	3.32	69.81	0.17	4.43
Serbia	18.32	2.40	4.75	5.36	1.54	8.79
Slovakia	3.68	0.14	2.86	4.91	0.16	4.69
Slovenia	3.30	0.40	3.94	4.50	0.06	16.37
Ukraine	11.44	1.23	10.70	7.30	5.12	6.45

Source: Euromonitor International from national statistics

Exports (fob) by Commodity: SITC Classification (% Analysis) 2011 *(continued)*

% of total exports

	Basic manufactures	Machinery and Transport Equipment	Miscellaneous Manufactured Goods	Others	Total
Western Europe					
Austria	21.81	37.45	11.35	4.80	100.00
Belgium	17.18	20.01	8.93	2.53	100.00
Cyprus	4.43	16.37	10.88	1.04	100.00
Denmark	8.64	24.75	15.75	8.87	100.00
Finland	31.72	31.41	5.65	1.94	100.00
France	11.77	38.92	10.69	2.75	100.00
Germany	13.08	45.44	10.18	7.34	100.00
Gibraltar					100.00
Greece	20.40	13.03	10.55	2.41	100.00
Iceland	42.46	8.28	2.01	0.53	100.00
Ireland	1.62	15.65	11.21	3.70	100.00
Italy	19.10	36.35	17.25	3.18	100.00
Liechtenstein					
Luxembourg	45.66	23.66	9.45	2.57	100.00
Malta	5.41	57.42	16.30	1.11	100.00
Monaco					
Netherlands	7.96	27.39	7.99	15.79	100.00
Norway	8.39	9.19	2.53	3.62	100.00
Portugal	22.39	26.71	16.49	2.35	100.00
Spain	17.30	35.82	9.05	2.51	100.00
Sweden	18.42	36.44	8.73	6.18	100.00
Switzerland	10.36	20.52	22.23	0.62	100.00
Turkey	29.26	27.52	17.07	3.35	100.00
United Kingdom	10.79	31.34	11.84	6.26	100.00
Eastern Europe					
Albania	22.63	4.13	35.52	0.33	100.00
Belarus	14.87	16.80	6.30	3.67	100.00
Bosnia-Herzegovina	24.10	11.42	20.87	2.88	100.00
Bulgaria	22.35	16.62	14.08	3.27	100.00
Croatia	14.01	31.81	12.39	0.08	100.00
Czech Republic	16.48	53.31	10.71	2.75	100.00
Estonia	14.57	27.42	14.22	4.93	100.00
Georgia	20.28	16.37	2.99	7.89	100.00
Hungary	9.14	57.17	7.71	6.09	100.00
Latvia	22.47	19.35	9.86	3.84	100.00
Lithuania	9.88	17.54	14.07	1.53	100.00
Macedonia	25.09	5.00	25.93	16.71	100.00
Moldova	6.55	12.59	22.06	0.02	100.00
Montenegro	44.95	8.66	2.74		100.00
Poland	20.53	41.93	12.49	1.62	100.00
Romania	16.42	42.77	14.68	1.92	100.00
Russia	11.97	3.11	0.68	4.56	100.00
Serbia	28.41	16.46	12.41	1.55	100.00
Slovakia	18.80	54.80	9.83	0.14	100.00
Slovenia	21.90	38.69	10.58	0.27	100.00
Ukraine	36.23	17.36	3.48	0.69	100.00

Source: Euromonitor International from national statistics

13

External Trade

External Trade Statistics   **Table 13.11**

Trade Balance 1980, 1985, 1990, 1995, 1999-2011

US$ million

	1980	1985	1990	1995	1999	2000	2001	2002
Western Europe								
Austria	-6,955	-3,747	-7,953	-8,743	-5,431	-4,817	-3,999	317
Belgium			-1,772	16,166	14,365	10,882	11,635	17,747
Cyprus	-671	-771	-1,611	-2,465	-2,623	-2,895	-2,947	-3,094
Denmark	-2,591	-1,155	3,789	5,750	5,880	6,021	6,946	7,429
Finland	-1,484	385	-430	11,459	10,224	11,582	10,688	11,041
France	-18,859	-6,666	-17,856	5,298	7,572	-12,066	-8,422	-4,851
Germany	4,858	25,445	63,951	59,531	69,331	54,772	85,407	125,544
Gibraltar	-100	-77	-279	-294	-364	-355	-317	-235
Greece	-5,395	-5,596	-11,672	-15,834	-18,244	-17,359	-18,003	-20,962
Iceland	-81	-90	-89	48	-499	-699	-231	-47
Ireland	-2,755	342	3,065	11,571	24,025	25,623	31,541	35,957
Italy	-22,637	-10,976	-11,482	27,958	14,852	9,663	15,441	13,446
Liechtenstein								
Luxembourg	-607	-314	-1,291	-1,998	-3,150	-2,769	-2,913	-3,102
Malta	-455	-359	-831	-1,029	-863	-957	-768	-614
Monaco								
Netherlands	-3,472	4,750	5,300	19,402	10,499	14,499	20,612	25,739
Norway	1,616	4,430	6,828	9,024	11,289	25,666	26,264	24,788
Portugal	-4,670	-1,967	-8,843	-10,100	-14,598	-17,040	-16,735	-15,730
Spain	-13,358	-5,716	-32,033	-22,273	-34,472	-39,554	-38,460	-40,037
Sweden	-2,533	1,913	3,293	15,061	16,057	14,409	13,879	15,295
Switzerland	-6,709	-3,264	-5,897	1,055	684	-1,237	996	4,987
Turkey	-4,999	-3,386	-9,344	-14,111	-13,639	-26,728	-10,065	-15,495
United Kingdom	-5,415	-8,344	-39,309	-23,200	-49,792	-49,782	-58,924	-71,359
Eastern Europe								
Albania		-63	-199	-511	-876	-829	-1,026	-1,173
Belarus				-760	-765	-1,320	-836	-1,071
Bosnia-Herzegovina				-930	-3,379	-2,825	-3,063	-3,406
Bulgaria		-1,464	-1,389	-302	-1,490	-1,683	-2,148	-2,238
Croatia			-1,168	-2,834	-3,496	-3,500	-4,395	-5,819
Czech Republic				-4,699	-3,241	-3,109	-3,095	-2,231
Estonia				-706	-1,092	-1,070	-988	-1,366
Georgia				-334	-452	-387	-436	-450
Hungary	-573	314	927	-2,578	-2,973	-3,939	-3,194	-3,276
Latvia				-513	-1,222	-1,318	-1,504	-1,769
Lithuania				-974	-1,873	-1,671	-1,781	-2,297
Macedonia				-515	-585	-771	-536	-880
Moldova				-102	-112	-305	-325	-395
Montenegro						-94	-205	-282
Poland	-2,499	-366	5,214	-6,155	-18,506	-12,302	-7,663	-7,255
Romania	-2,634	900	-4,068	-2,368	-1,887	-2,688	-4,167	-3,986
Russia				14,050	32,078	60,174	48,121	46,335
Serbia						-1,772	-2,540	-3,539
Slovakia				-1,068	-2,220	-413	-1,947	-1,875
Slovenia			-609	-1,175	-1,537	-1,379	-891	-580
Ukraine				-2,356	-264	779	198	980

Source: Euromonitor International from national statistics

Trade Balance 1980, 1985, 1990, 1995, 1999-2011 *(continued)*

US$ million

	2003	2004	2005	2006	2007	2008	2009	2010	2011
Western Europe									
Austria	-2,336	-1,621	-2,226	-570	556	-2,760	-5,291	-5,711	-12,823
Belgium	20,669	21,196	17,079	15,189	19,108	5,969	17,264	15,816	15,062
Cyprus	-3,455	-4,577	-4,776	-5,522	-7,214	-9,047	-6,559	-7,126	-6,748
Denmark	9,066	8,738	9,305	6,292	4,632	6,907	10,768	11,979	14,574
Finland	10,915	10,240	6,760	7,839	8,334	4,730	2,004	719	-5,104
France	-8,991	-25,260	-46,956	-55,804	-80,989	-106,784	-84,372	-91,168	-122,043
Germany	147,098	193,615	197,304	199,734	267,826	264,641	194,565	205,383	219,910
Gibraltar	-321	-334	-351	-436	-548	-544	-483	-487	-621
Greece	-30,745	-37,315	-37,240	-42,864	-55,033	-66,465	-48,937	-41,905	-29,091
Iceland	-404	-657	-1,614	-1,845	-1,757	-433	453	685	691
Ireland	38,755	41,358	36,393	32,573	35,204	42,083	56,683	58,261	60,395
Italy	1,959	-1,727	-11,849	-25,379	-11,630	-18,470	-8,037	-40,115	-34,253
Liechtenstein									
Luxembourg	-3,712	-4,651	-4,868	-5,259	-6,157	-7,924	-5,866	-7,445	-8,980
Malta	-931	-1,197	-1,432	-1,371	-1,525	-2,288	-2,069	-1,962	-1,705
Monaco									
Netherlands	30,837	33,866	39,024	42,159	51,568	50,809	49,428	52,711	61,768
Norway	28,267	33,991	48,271	57,842	56,003	81,483	47,795	53,348	68,387
Portugal	-17,225	-22,835	-25,159	-25,930	-29,764	-37,132	-27,515	-26,847	-21,486
Spain	-52,531	-75,515	-96,465	-112,698	-136,037	-139,262	-69,911	-69,268	-64,391
Sweden	18,222	22,443	19,343	20,245	15,511	14,913	10,794	9,629	11,157
Switzerland	5,143	7,495	6,306	9,648	11,626	18,091	18,906	18,791	26,434
Turkey	-22,087	-34,373	-43,298	-54,041	-62,791	-69,936	-38,786	-71,661	-105,935
United Kingdom	-79,213	-111,326	-124,861	-140,988	-181,194	-174,943	-129,402	-152,342	-160,303
Eastern Europe									
Albania	-1,416	-1,704	-1,960	-2,261	-3,110	-3,896	-3,459	-2,861	-3,444
Belarus	-1,612	-2,717	-729	-2,618	-4,418	-6,811	-7,265	-9,601	-4,551
Bosnia-Herzegovina	-3,434	-4,051	-4,716	-3,988	-5,566	-7,160	-4,410	-4,420	-5,201
Bulgaria	-3,361	-4,536	-6,423	-8,168	-11,511	-14,531	-7,175	-4,902	-4,357
Croatia	-8,022	-8,565	-9,754	-11,112	-13,475	-16,617	-10,713	-8,247	-9,353
Czech Republic	-2,530	-1,051	1,645	1,713	4,293	4,234	7,919	6,420	10,775
Estonia	-1,942	-2,400	-2,513	-3,765	-4,669	-3,587	-1,083	-664	-850
Georgia	-680	-1,199	-1,624	-2,685	-3,977	-4,559	-3,246	-3,516	-4,760
Hungary	-5,070	-4,744	-3,605	-2,990	-143	-465	5,293	7,319	9,875
Latvia	-2,350	-3,066	-3,483	-5,538	-7,290	-6,497	2,177	-2,292	-3,373
Lithuania	-2,700	-3,079	-3,724	-5,260	-7,286	-7,521	-1,846	-2,659	-3,731
Macedonia	-939	-1,256	-1,187	-1,362	-1,860	-2,923	-2,346	-2,159	-2,570
Moldova	-614	-793	-1,201	-1,643	-2,350	-3,308	-1,995	-2,314	-2,975
Montenegro	-198	-461	-518	-1,285	-2,241	-3,115	-1,926	-1,745	-1,917
Poland	-5,735	-5,952	-3,100	-7,402	-19,111	-30,729	-7,642	-11,782	-14,178
Romania	-6,385	-9,179	-12,733	-18,780	-29,552	-33,314	-13,798	-12,503	-13,585
Russia	59,860	85,827	118,367	139,271	130,915	179,745	111,584	151,994	198,181
Serbia	-4,721	-7,230	-5,980	-6,744	-9,729	-11,903	-7,702	-6,940	-8,364
Slovakia	467	-2,069	-3,027	-3,463	-1,058	-1,076	1,365	1,050	3,373
Slovenia	-1,090	-1,693	-1,728	-2,011	-2,916	-4,758	-1,540	-2,179	-2,333
Ukraine	47	3,669	-1,905	-6,672	-11,323	-18,579	-5,705	-9,433	-14,134

Source: Euromonitor International from national statistics

13

External Trade

CHAPTER FOURTEEN

Health

Health Statistics

Table 14.1

Hospitals and Hospital Beds 2011

As stated

	In-Patient Beds ('000)	Hospitals and Clinics	Beds per '000 Inhabitants
Western Europe			
Austria	65	269	8
Belgium	71	196	6
Cyprus	3	96	3
Denmark	18	44	3
Finland	34	284	6
France	433	2,960	7
Germany	658	3,289	8
Gibraltar			
Greece	54	311	5
Iceland	2	20	5
Ireland	20	173	5
Italy	221	1,207	4
Liechtenstein			
Luxembourg	3		5
Malta	2	8	4
Monaco			
Netherlands	69	185	4
Norway	15	65	3
Portugal	34	186	3
Spain	149	784	3
Sweden		87	
Switzerland	38	301	5
Turkey	193	1,366	3
United Kingdom	189		3
Eastern Europe			
Albania	9	42	3
Belarus	106	645	11
Bosnia-Herzegovina		41	
Bulgaria	49	377	7
Croatia	24	60	5
Czech Republic	74	255	7
Estonia	8	61	6
Georgia	13	263	3
Hungary	68	171	7
Latvia	14	57	7
Lithuania	22	114	7
Macedonia	9	67	5
Moldova	21	81	6
Montenegro	2	11	4
Poland	258	925	7
Romania	138	559	6
Russia	1,343	5,018	9
Serbia	37	103	5
Slovakia	35	137	7
Slovenia	10	29	5
Ukraine	393	2,352	9

Source: Euromonitor International from national statistics

Table 14.2

Healthcare Professionals 2011

Number

	Doctors	Dentists	Nurses	Active Pharmacists
Western Europe				
Austria	40,853	4,741	66,039	5,680
Belgium	52,363	7,620	201,881	12,721
Cyprus	2,447	769	3,906	175
Denmark	19,820	4,221	85,617	2,527
Finland	14,790	3,813	72,379	6,183
France	212,335	41,785	562,361	73,236
Germany	306,708	65,364	926,280	50,779
Gibraltar				
Greece	75,899	15,375	38,918	10,753
Iceland	1,160	302	5,279	366
Ireland	19,776	2,785	68,942	4,690
Italy	259,917	29,125	370,038	54,737
Liechtenstein				
Luxembourg	1,441	428	5,723	365
Malta	1,254	187	2,798	284
Monaco				
Netherlands	50,833	8,955	189,774	3,529
Norway	20,687	4,242	71,152	4,154
Portugal	41,648	8,336	65,686	8,292
Spain	177,843	29,328	228,767	35,357
Sweden	37,283	7,468	105,827	6,859
Switzerland	31,147	4,155	122,643	4,223
Turkey	126,281	21,902	112,056	26,490
United Kingdom	170,727	32,364	580,784	40,654
Eastern Europe				
Albania	3,710	749	12,265	1,348
Belarus	51,413	5,544	122,384	3,135
Bosnia-Herzegovina	6,954	715	19,236	396
Bulgaria	28,055	6,500	31,912	747
Croatia	11,891	3,333	23,219	2,769
Czech Republic	37,853	7,191	85,366	5,982
Estonia	4,439	1,199	8,178	871
Georgia	20,642	1,024	14,520	251
Hungary	30,929	5,037	62,916	5,967
Latvia	6,729	1,527	9,800	1,329
Lithuania	12,107	2,459	22,765	2,920
Macedonia	5,982	1,493	7,826	1,053
Moldova	11,158	1,692	27,063	2,840
Montenegro	1,366	30	3,265	85
Poland	83,462	12,047	203,779	25,401
Romania	49,472	13,605	123,124	12,357
Russia	624,711	45,235	1,145,894	11,749
Serbia	21,558	2,160	43,674	2,162
Slovakia	16,015	2,888	32,870	2,481
Slovenia	5,032	1,257	16,978	1,158
Ukraine	145,974	19,426	357,611	20,712

Source: Euromonitor International from national statistics

14

Health

Health Statistics

Table 14.3

Causes of Death: Male 2011

Per 100,000 inhabitants

	Tuberculosis	HIV	Cancer	Diabetes	Mental and Behavioural Disorders	Diseases of Circulatory System	Diseases of Respiratory System	Diseases of Digestive System
Western Europe								
Austria	0.4	0.8	265.0	33.1	14.8	346.2	53.8	44.2
Belgium	0.8	0.6	296.8	13.8	20.7	293.9	128.7	44.4
Cyprus	0.0	0.0	176.4	36.9	5.4	261.3	57.8	19.4
Denmark	0.8	0.9	290.2	26.9	50.9	258.1	112.6	54.5
Finland	0.4	0.0	231.7	8.5	29.5	394.0	52.6	62.6
France	1.0	1.6	317.2	20.0	27.9	242.5	61.3	45.9
Germany	0.4	0.7	296.8	23.1	26.2	378.2	86.5	52.5
Gibraltar								
Greece	1.1	0.2	304.1	8.5	0.6	407.4	104.5	27.0
Iceland	1.1	0.0	196.6	9.8	13.6	236.4	43.8	14.4
Ireland	0.8	0.6	235.2	12.0	9.5	236.2	90.3	30.2
Italy	0.8	2.5	344.5	31.7	19.7	365.5	78.3	42.7
Liechtenstein								
Luxembourg	1.1	2.8	222.7	4.9	4.9	245.3	63.2	37.7
Malta	0.0	0.0	230.3	34.1	28.7	295.1	91.9	27.6
Monaco								
Netherlands	0.3	0.5	285.8	16.8	28.5	221.3	80.6	29.6
Norway	0.7	0.5	234.9	12.2	26.7	250.2	82.0	23.1
Portugal	3.5	9.5	296.7	41.5	3.5	298.1	130.6	54.4
Spain	1.1	3.7	297.2	19.8	24.2	254.4	118.1	48.6
Sweden	0.2	0.1	243.0	21.5	37.8	363.7	54.2	29.5
Switzerland	0.5	0.9	233.4	16.6	28.4	261.2	50.5	29.3
Turkey	11.2		102.6	8.8	3.1	383.0	45.1	32.1
United Kingdom	0.8	0.6	290.9	10.0	27.2	300.7	127.0	47.9
Eastern Europe								
Albania	0.3	0.2	119.8	6.0	3.6	321.7	37.2	12.1
Belarus	22.3		232.8	2.5	11.0	866.6	57.2	54.0
Bosnia-Herzegovina	6.9		247.3	16.6	9.2	449.9	56.3	37.9
Bulgaria	3.8		269.4	22.5	1.4	932.9	68.0	60.1
Croatia	4.1	0.4	366.0	29.6	21.0	514.4	60.5	70.3
Czech Republic	0.3	0.0	299.2	17.5	2.0	464.4	70.6	52.2
Estonia	4.3	7.4	303.6	14.8	11.4	583.9	46.1	58.7
Georgia	6.0	0.0	136.9	12.8	0.5	606.0	19.9	43.1
Hungary	2.2	0.2	388.9	22.7	22.9	618.9	77.1	104.8
Latvia	6.2	6.1	305.4	17.7	11.7	668.1	35.7	49.4
Lithuania	12.8	0.6	305.4	7.6	3.1	660.9	67.0	79.4
Macedonia	2.7		258.9	18.4	1.0	564.8	81.3	33.0
Moldova	28.5	3.4	203.1	11.5	9.5	700.2	99.6	146.9
Montenegro	0.1	0.0	153.4	8.8	5.6	474.4	55.2	28.7
Poland	3.3	0.4	286.0	16.0	8.3	462.1	68.1	52.9
Romania	11.6	0.7	268.5	10.4	1.3	700.0	76.4	98.5
Russia	32.9	3.8	223.3	4.3	6.3	784.2	77.0	77.5
Serbia	2.5	0.8	344.4	37.6	14.9	720.8	75.6	58.0
Slovakia	1.2	0.1	258.9	12.0	0.1	489.2	73.0	69.2
Slovenia	1.0	0.3	321.6	9.0	6.2	288.8	58.8	63.1
Ukraine	37.6	19.0	224.8	4.4	9.7	989.0	75.5	111.5

Source: Euromonitor International from national statistics

Table 14.4

Causes of Death: Female 2011

Per 100,000 inhabitants

	Tuberculosis	HIV	Cancer	Diabetes	Mental and Behavioural Disorders	Diseases of Circulatory System	Diseases of Respiratory System	Diseases of Digestive System
Western Europe								
Austria	0.4	0.2	223.3	40.1	7.1	465.4	48.3	31.6
Belgium	0.2	0.2	206.9	16.9	37.7	344.0	115.5	46.1
Cyprus	0.0	0.0	131.2	40.4	8.1	235.8	48.1	14.5
Denmark	0.3	0.2	266.1	23.3	68.9	269.8	123.6	47.3
Finland	0.6	0.0	199.6	7.7	57.5	401.9	34.2	40.3
France	0.8	0.4	211.8	19.8	33.0	261.1	51.3	36.5
Germany	0.2	0.2	241.3	33.5	36.7	496.1	76.2	51.5
Gibraltar								
Greece	0.2	0.1	185.5	8.3	1.2	434.9	93.5	18.9
Iceland	2.9	0.0	158.0	6.9	17.3	220.1	69.6	27.4
Ireland	0.6	0.3	183.4	10.1	18.6	233.3	90.0	27.7
Italy	0.5	0.7	251.4	41.5	40.0	442.0	59.0	42.0
Liechtenstein								
Luxembourg	0.0	2.7	195.3	9.1	8.6	259.3	62.2	32.6
Malta	0.0	0.0	182.8	36.2	42.2	296.7	58.7	22.9
Monaco								
Netherlands	0.1	0.1	232.9	19.0	65.7	246.9	76.0	33.8
Norway	0.2	0.3	201.8	15.1	52.4	292.0	89.2	31.0
Portugal	1.5	3.1	194.3	52.5	0.7	352.2	114.8	38.3
Spain	0.7	1.0	177.6	26.4	46.0	296.0	85.3	42.0
Sweden	0.1	0.0	220.1	19.9	71.1	399.2	52.0	27.7
Switzerland	0.3	0.3	183.3	19.0	55.1	312.1	40.5	37.0
Turkey	2.9		70.0	9.8	1.6	367.2	28.4	20.7
United Kingdom	0.5	0.3	252.8	11.0	51.6	307.6	136.7	51.3
Eastern Europe								
Albania	0.2	0.2	72.9	5.9	4.1	294.5	24.3	7.5
Belarus	2.2		134.4	5.5	2.6	765.1	14.9	28.8
Bosnia-Herzegovina	2.2		148.9	18.8	9.5	449.0	29.6	26.3
Bulgaria	0.9		176.3	27.1	0.5	916.8	40.7	26.6
Croatia	1.4	0.0	249.9	34.2	18.8	650.7	37.4	41.7
Czech Republic	0.1	0.0	224.8	20.0	0.8	566.5	55.4	39.4
Estonia	2.4	1.2	226.1	14.3	7.2	695.8	20.2	34.2
Georgia	1.1	0.0	108.1	14.5	0.6	572.3	15.0	15.6
Hungary	1.0	0.0	279.1	27.3	31.8	673.6	53.9	59.2
Latvia	1.6	1.2	230.7	32.1	11.7	713.6	16.7	38.4
Lithuania	2.7	0.3	206.6	10.9	1.2	762.3	27.6	54.7
Macedonia	0.9		164.6	18.4	0.9	570.4	68.0	20.0
Moldova	3.4	1.8	138.2	9.9	2.7	764.9	46.3	114.5
Montenegro	0.1	0.0	118.5	13.4	8.5	515.9	34.3	15.8
Poland	0.8	0.1	209.0	20.6	1.4	488.2	44.8	36.5
Romania	2.0	0.4	172.6	12.3	0.7	739.5	41.7	58.5
Russia	6.4	1.1	167.3	9.0	2.7	833.4	27.5	50.2
Serbia	1.2	0.2	246.8	50.0	13.6	836.5	44.6	45.0
Slovakia	0.4	0.1	190.3	13.4	0.0	561.4	49.4	43.3
Slovenia	1.1	0.0	246.6	10.1	1.3	429.5	67.0	47.9
Ukraine	7.6	6.9	150.0	5.3	3.0	1,057.0	22.4	53.2

Source: Euromonitor International from national statistics

Health Statistics

Table 14.5

Food Supply: Average Daily Consumption of Calories, Protein and Fat 2011

Daily averages, calories / grams per inhabitant

	Calories (number)	Protein (grams)	Fat (grams)
Western Europe			
Austria	3,836	110	172
Belgium	3,727	98	165
Cyprus	2,675	83	119
Denmark	3,395	110	139
Finland	3,258	112	131
France	3,564	111	163
Germany	3,555	102	144
Gibraltar			
Greece	3,660	116	156
Iceland	3,409	135	152
Ireland	3,628	113	130
Italy	3,626	112	161
Liechtenstein			
Luxembourg	3,608	114	153
Malta	3,436	113	112
Monaco			
Netherlands	3,266	106	139
Norway	3,479	107	142
Portugal	3,621	118	142
Spain	3,229	106	148
Sweden	3,121	106	125
Switzerland	3,466	93	152
Turkey	3,674	105	104
United Kingdom	3,429	103	141
Eastern Europe			
Albania	2,935	98	95
Belarus	3,202	92	121
Bosnia-Herzegovina	3,116	90	76
Bulgaria	2,773	80	102
Croatia	3,143	85	121
Czech Republic	3,315	94	142
Estonia	3,137	93	91
Georgia	2,866	78	69
Hungary	3,506	90	150
Latvia	2,952	84	113
Lithuania	3,492	128	111
Macedonia	2,969	76	108
Moldova	2,731	70	79
Montenegro	2,932	82	127
Poland	3,398	100	115
Romania	3,500	111	107
Russia	3,172	95	88
Serbia	2,842	82	89
Slovakia	2,894	75	102
Slovenia	3,286	102	118
Ukraine	3,266	89	92

Source: Euromonitor International from national statistics

Table 14.6

Government Health Expenditure 2011

As stated

	Government Health Spend as a % of Total Central Government Spend	Per Capita Health Spend (US$)	Government Spend on Drugs (US$ million)
Western Europe			
Austria	9.5	4,709.7	3,631.1
Belgium	9.4	4,400.0	5,363.1
Cyprus	8.2	1,823.5	
Denmark	8.3	4,953.0	1,422.4
Finland	7.0	3,415.8	1,829.3
France	9.9	4,354.0	34,892.6
Germany	10.5	4,648.6	48,701.3
Gibraltar			
Greece	12.1	3,189.8	11,133.9
Iceland	7.9	3,410.9	111.9
Ireland	8.0	3,930.7	2,964.5
Italy	9.3	3,364.3	16,345.9
Liechtenstein			
Luxembourg	4.4	5,088.4	312.8
Malta	7.2	1,549.2	
Monaco	4.5	7,514.9	
Netherlands	11.1	5,553.5	8,109.6
Norway	5.8	5,697.2	1,585.2
Portugal	11.5	2,570.7	2,986.2
Spain	10.3	3,311.4	20,585.1
Sweden	7.0	4,022.6	3,634.2
Switzerland	6.6	5,543.4	5,036.0
Turkey	8.3	879.6	1,469.1
United Kingdom	9.8	3,806.7	22,489.6
Eastern Europe			
Albania	7.4	298.7	
Belarus	5.5	321.1	
Bosnia-Herzegovina	69.8	3,311.4	
Bulgaria	7.4	525.2	
Croatia	8.5	1,200.8	
Czech Republic	11.3	2,322.5	2,291.7
Estonia	9.7	1,605.1	155.1
Georgia	8.6	281.0	
Hungary	11.1	1,549.6	1,767.8
Latvia	6.1	833.8	
Lithuania	6.3	822.8	
Macedonia	6.8	334.8	
Moldova	10.3	202.4	
Montenegro	9.4	690.2	
Poland	11.6	1,564.7	3,235.0
Romania	5.1	450.8	
Russia	3.9	511.7	
Serbia	7.6	460.9	
Slovakia	13.4	2,381.3	1,607.4
Slovenia	11.3	2,769.2	524.0
Ukraine	5.3	192.0	

Source: Euromonitor International from national statistics

14

Health

Health Statistics   **Table 14.7**

Obese Population (BMI 30kg/sq m or More) 1985, 1990, 1995, 2000, 2006-2011

% of population aged 15+

	1985	1990	1995	2000	2006	2007	2008	2009	2010	2011
Western Europe										
Austria	7.2	8.3	9.4	10.9	11.7	11.9	12.1	12.3	12.5	12.7
Belgium	9.4	10.1	10.7	11.0	13.3	13.6	13.9	14.2	14.5	14.9
Cyprus										
Denmark	4.8	6.5	7.7	9.4	11.2	11.7	12.4	13.1	13.4	14.0
Finland	6.7	8.4	10.5	11.2	14.3	15.0	15.7	15.0	15.6	16.0
France	4.6	5.8	6.9	9.0	10.4	10.5	10.6	10.6	10.7	10.9
Germany	8.3	9.4	10.5	11.9	14.2	14.8	15.4	16.0	16.1	16.2
Gibraltar										
Greece	7.0	7.6	8.7	10.1	16.4	16.8	18.1	18.8	19.6	20.2
Iceland	6.2	7.5	10.6	12.0	18.5	20.1	20.3	20.9	21.0	21.5
Ireland	4.9	6.0	7.3	8.6	10.0	10.2	10.5	10.8	11.0	11.3
Italy	3.5	5.0	7.6	8.6	10.2	9.9	9.9	10.3	10.3	10.6
Liechtenstein										
Luxembourg	8.9	9.4	12.8	15.4	20.2	19.8	20.1	21.7	22.3	23.3
Malta										
Monaco										
Netherlands	5.0	6.1	6.9	9.4	11.3	11.2	11.2	11.8	11.4	11.6
Norway	2.1	3.0	4.9	7.2	8.8	9.1	9.5	9.9	10.4	10.7
Portugal	4.1	5.6	7.8	10.6	15.3	15.6	16.0	16.3	16.6	17.0
Spain	6.5	7.4	10.4	12.4	14.9	15.3	16.4	17.1	17.3	17.5
Sweden	4.4	5.8	7.3	9.2	10.1	10.2	10.6	11.2	12.9	13.3
Switzerland	3.5	4.8	6.4	7.4	8.9	9.0	9.2	9.3	9.5	9.7
Turkey	11.2	12.7	15.2	14.5	14.2	14.8	15.4	16.2	17.1	17.3
United Kingdom	7.2	11.9	15.1	20.5	24.0	24.0	24.5	25.3	26.1	26.6
Eastern Europe										
Albania										
Belarus	19.6	20.8	22.0	23.3	24.9	25.1	25.3	25.6	25.8	25.9
Bosnia-Herzegovina	16.3	16.6	17.1	17.6	18.2	18.3	18.4	18.5	18.6	18.7
Bulgaria	10.2	10.6	11.2	12.2	17.0	17.3	17.6	17.9	18.2	18.6
Croatia	8.6	9.0	10.0	13.3	17.5	17.8	18.1	18.5	18.8	19.2
Czech Republic	10.2	10.9	11.3	14.5	15.9	16.2	16.6	16.9	17.2	17.5
Estonia	10.1	10.7	11.4	13.7	15.9	16.8	18.0	17.4	16.9	16.9
Georgia	5.9	6.5	7.5	8.7	10.5	10.9	11.2	11.5	11.9	12.2
Hungary	14.9	16.0	17.3	18.3	19.1	19.3	19.4	19.5	19.4	19.4
Latvia	14.5	14.8	14.1	11.8	17.0	17.4	17.7	17.9	18.2	18.3
Lithuania	10.0	12.2	15.9	20.4	19.9	19.7	19.9	20.4	20.9	21.4
Macedonia	5.2	6.1	8.0	11.4	15.8	16.5	17.1	17.8	18.5	19.0
Moldova										
Montenegro										
Poland	5.6	7.4	10.5	14.1	18.1	18.7	19.2	19.7	20.2	20.6
Romania	7.7	8.0	8.3	8.6	9.0	9.1	9.1	9.2	9.2	9.3
Russia	15.6	17.0	19.3	20.4	22.0	22.3	22.6	22.8	23.1	23.4
Serbia										
Slovakia	10.5	10.5	10.8	12.4	15.3	15.3	15.3	15.1	15.5	15.8
Slovenia	11.5	11.6	12.4	14.6	17.2	17.6	17.9	18.3	18.7	19.0
Ukraine	12.1	12.4	12.8	13.3	13.9	14.0	14.1	14.1	14.2	14.3

Source: Euromonitor International from national statistics

15

Home Ownership

Home Ownership Statistics

Table 15.1

Housing Stock 1980, 1985, 1990, 1995, 1999-2011

'000 units

	1980	1985	1990	1995	1999	2000	2001	2002
Western Europe								
Austria	3,008	3,214	3,398	3,590	3,783	3,827	3,858	3,890
Belgium	3,614	3,733	3,845	3,992	4,127	4,152	4,177	4,198
Cyprus	151	187	222	251	268			
Denmark	2,177	2,294	2,399	2,477	2,531	2,546	2,559	2,574
Finland	1,838	2,015	2,210	2,389	2,491	2,520	2,552	2,583
France	22,863	24,693	26,471	28,098	29,321	29,646	29,991	30,337
Germany	31,597	33,141	34,192	35,954	37,958	38,384	38,682	38,925
Gibraltar								
Greece	3,940	4,262	4,588	4,964	5,298	5,387	5,476	5,584
Iceland								
Ireland	879	961	1,031	1,115	1,251	1,293	1,337	1,387
Italy	23,572	24,676	25,543	26,463	27,001	27,142	27,292	27,447
Liechtenstein								
Luxembourg								
Malta								
Monaco								
Netherlands	4,918	5,415	5,802	6,192	6,522	6,590	6,651	6,710
Norway	1,581	1,751	1,887	1,985	2,059	2,079	2,098	2,121
Portugal	3,796	3,995	4,196	4,474	4,774	4,881	4,993	5,106
Spain	15,289	16,384	17,450	18,674	19,762	20,117	20,531	21,034
Sweden	3,585	3,807	3,987	4,222	4,271	4,282	4,294	4,308
Switzerland	2,752	2,961	3,160	3,375	3,526	3,569	3,607	3,645
Turkey	10,055	11,122	12,344	13,584	14,604	14,817	15,060	15,300
United Kingdom	21,448	22,383	23,510	24,341	25,097	25,283	25,456	25,617
Eastern Europe								
Albania								
Belarus	2,665	2,936	3,285	3,619	3,800	3,819	3,851	3,877
Bosnia-Herzegovina	921	989	1,061	623	771	809	835	852
Bulgaria	2,839	3,162	3,387	3,474	3,642	3,669	3,686	3,692
Croatia	1,382	1,514	1,589	1,607	1,645	1,653	1,661	1,671
Czech Republic	3,987	4,127	4,217	4,263	4,326	4,346	4,366	4,384
Estonia	469	536	596	617	620	621	622	623
Georgia								
Hungary	3,542	3,826	3,888	3,989	4,061	4,065	4,076	4,104
Latvia	854	902	953	957	958	958	958	958
Lithuania	999	1,077	1,159	1,247	1,324	1,309	1,292	1,295
Macedonia	560	578	613	648	677	684	691	698
Moldova								
Montenegro	129	143	163	212	238	242	245	247
Poland	10,053	10,883	11,609	12,073	12,301	12,368	12,438	12,517
Romania	6,986	7,523	7,809	7,945	8,044	8,066	8,087	8,107
Russia	32,175	35,776	40,798	45,399	47,913	48,349	48,707	49,073
Serbia	2,333	2,429	2,534	2,643	2,707	2,719	2,730	2,740
Slovakia	1,635	1,702	1,759	1,834	1,862	1,872	1,885	1,895
Slovenia	618	672	715	746	769	773	779	785
Ukraine	15,207	16,459	17,783	18,597	18,866	18,921	18,960	19,023

Source: Euromonitor International from national statistics

Housing Stock 1980, 1985, 1990, 1995, 1999-2011 *(continued)*

'000 units

	2003	2004	2005	2006	2007	2008	2009	2010	2011
Western Europe									
Austria	3,917	3,945	3,972	3,997	4,026	4,061	4,093	4,123	4,151
Belgium	4,219	4,239	4,257	4,278	4,300	4,325	4,350	4,373	4,394
Cyprus									
Denmark	2,590	2,611	2,634	2,658	2,684	2,710	2,735	2,749	2,745
Finland	2,610	2,638	2,667	2,698	2,732	2,762	2,789	2,808	2,831
France	30,669	31,014	31,424	31,857	32,302	32,708	33,035	33,289	33,566
Germany	39,142	39,362	39,551	39,754	39,918	40,057	40,184	40,271	40,339
Gibraltar									
Greece	5,712	5,839	5,938	6,044	6,143	6,225	6,288	6,350	6,403
Iceland									
Ireland	1,437	1,494	1,555	1,616	1,682	1,742	1,791	1,815	1,828
Italy	27,613	27,779	27,959	28,153	28,375	28,601	28,809	29,004	29,197
Liechtenstein									
Luxembourg									
Malta									
Monaco									
Netherlands	6,764	6,810	6,859	6,912	6,967	7,043	7,105	7,172	7,218
Norway	2,142	2,163	2,186	2,215	2,243	2,274	2,301	2,324	2,343
Portugal	5,232	5,323	5,395	5,470	5,533	5,590	5,663	5,722	5,751
Spain	21,551	22,059	22,623	23,210	23,859	24,496	25,118	25,536	25,809
Sweden	4,329	4,351	4,380	4,404	4,436	4,470	4,503	4,527	4,508
Switzerland	3,689	3,736	3,778	3,825	3,873	3,930	4,008	4,079	4,126
Turkey	15,460	15,641	15,844	16,091	16,383	16,706	17,059	17,459	17,835
United Kingdom	25,798	25,985	26,197	26,419	26,656	26,911	27,109	27,249	27,363
Eastern Europe									
Albania									
Belarus	3,899	3,922	3,951	3,982	4,012	4,047	4,083	4,116	4,155
Bosnia-Herzegovina	864	874	883	895	906	916	926	936	947
Bulgaria	3,697	3,705	3,716	3,729	3,747	3,767	3,789	3,804	3,819
Croatia	1,683	1,693	1,704	1,715	1,728	1,742	1,756	1,766	1,775
Czech Republic	4,404	4,423	4,446	4,470	4,492	4,522	4,549	4,577	4,603
Estonia	624	626	629	633	638	645	651	654	656
Georgia									
Hungary	4,119	4,134	4,173	4,209	4,238	4,270	4,303	4,331	4,349
Latvia	967	987	998	1,018	1,036	1,042	1,035	1,039	1,044
Lithuania	1,296	1,300	1,300	1,299	1,305	1,308	1,310	1,312	1,314
Macedonia	703	708	714	719	725	731	736	740	746
Moldova									
Montenegro	249	251	253	255	258	261	265	269	272
Poland	12,596	12,683	12,776	12,877	12,994	13,150	13,302	13,422	13,540
Romania	8,129	8,152	8,176	8,201	8,231	8,270	8,329	8,385	8,428
Russia	49,453	49,863	50,321	50,790	51,318	51,911	52,511	53,032	53,431
Serbia	2,750	2,763	2,778	2,794	2,811	2,829	2,847	2,866	2,884
Slovakia	1,909	1,922	1,935	1,949	1,963	1,979	1,996	2,012	2,029
Slovenia	791	798	805	812	820	830	838	844	849
Ukraine	19,049	19,075	19,132	19,107	19,183	19,255	19,288	19,322	19,360

Source: Euromonitor International from national statistics

15

Home Ownership

Home Ownership Statistics

Table 15.2

New Dwellings Completed 1980, 1985, 1990, 1995, 1999-2011

'000 units

	1980	1985	1990	1995	1999	2000	2001	2002
Western Europe								
Austria	51.0	41.2	36.6	53.4	59.5	53.8	45.9	41.9
Belgium	48.6	30.3	43.1	65.6	45.0	44.0	37.4	36.5
Cyprus								
Denmark	30.3	22.7	27.2	13.5	17.5	16.3	17.4	18.8
Finland	49.6	50.3	65.4	25.0	28.9	32.3	30.1	26.7
France	430.0	412.6	400.0	362.7	374.7	398.8	399.4	383.2
Germany	379.3	280.9	256.5	602.8	473.0	423.1	326.2	289.6
Gibraltar								
Greece	136.0	88.5	120.2	70.9	88.5	89.3	108.0	128.2
Iceland								
Ireland	27.8	23.9	19.5	30.6	46.5	49.4	52.2	57.3
Italy	287.0	180.7	194.9	145.3	151.7	162.4	167.5	182.6
Liechtenstein								
Luxembourg								
Malta								
Monaco								
Netherlands	116.4	98.1	97.4	93.8	78.6	70.7	73.0	66.7
Norway	38.1	26.1	27.1	19.2	19.9	19.4	23.2	21.2
Portugal	40.9	39.1	46.8	68.8	108.1	112.4	114.8	125.1
Spain	262.9	188.7	281.1	221.3	356.3	415.8	505.1	519.8
Sweden	51.4	32.9	58.4	12.7	11.7	13.0	15.4	19.9
Switzerland	40.9	44.2	40.0	46.2	33.1	32.2	28.9	28.6
Turkey	196.3	236.3	232.0	248.9	215.6	245.2	243.5	161.5
United Kingdom	242.0	207.5	203.4	199.7	184.0	176.9	174.1	182.0
Eastern Europe								
Albania								
Belarus	80.4	88.5	86.1	52.8	46.1	39.4	32.5	28.8
Bosnia-Herzegovina							4.1	4.9
Bulgaria	74.3	64.9	26.0	6.8	9.8	8.8	6.1	6.2
Croatia	31.0	22.8	18.6	7.4	12.2	16.0	12.9	18.0
Czech Republic	80.7	66.7	44.6	12.7	23.7	25.2	24.8	27.3
Estonia	14.4	13.5	7.6	1.1	0.8	0.7	0.6	1.1
Georgia								
Hungary	89.1	72.5	43.8	24.7	19.3	21.6	28.1	31.5
Latvia	19.9	19.9	13.3	1.8	1.1	0.9	0.8	0.8
Lithuania	28.3	28.8	22.1	5.6	4.4	4.4	3.7	4.5
Macedonia	4.8	5.0	7.4	7.2	7.3	7.2	6.9	5.5
Moldova								
Montenegro	2.5	3.5	7.4	9.3	4.4	3.4	1.9	2.4
Poland	217.1	189.6	134.2	67.1	82.0	87.8	105.8	97.6
Romania	197.8	105.6	48.6	35.8	29.5	26.4	27.0	27.7
Russia	602.8	927.1	1,104.0	830.8	454.2	373.0	382.0	396.0
Serbia	20.1	21.4	24.2	18.9	13.6	11.8	10.5	10.7
Slovakia	48.2	38.0	24.7	6.2	10.7	12.9	10.3	14.2
Slovenia	13.6	10.8	8.1	6.1	5.4	5.1	5.0	4.9
Ukraine	329.0	341.0	289.0	119.0	73.5	62.9	65.6	64.4

Source: Euromonitor International from national statistics

New Dwellings Completed 1980, 1985, 1990, 1995, 1999-2011 *(continued)*

'000 units

	2003	2004	2005	2006	2007	2008	2009	2010	2011
Western Europe									
Austria	41.0	39.2	38.5	43.4	51.7	47.0	44.3	43.7	43.9
Belgium	33.9	31.3	35.9	38.2	41.9	43.8	38.7	34.7	37.1
Cyprus									
Denmark	23.8	26.3	27.4	29.0	31.5	27.1	18.9	11.7	11.9
Finland	27.7	30.4	33.8	33.6	35.0	30.0	21.4	25.1	31.1
France	406.0	492.8	547.5	592.9	567.7	483.4	394.0	453.5	534.8
Germany	268.1	278.0	242.3	249.4	210.7	176.0	159.0	145.0	141.7
Gibraltar									
Greece	127.0	122.2	195.2	125.4	103.9	79.6	61.5	52.3	31.4
Iceland									
Ireland	68.4	76.6	80.6	93.0	77.6	51.3	26.4	14.6	10.5
Italy	187.1	207.1	227.2	265.7	275.8	258.8	247.8	249.9	252.0
Liechtenstein									
Luxembourg									
Malta									
Monaco									
Netherlands	59.6	65.3	67.0	72.4	80.2	78.8	82.9	56.0	57.7
Norway	21.2	23.5	29.5	28.5	31.1	28.6	21.7	18.1	20.0
Portugal	91.2	74.1	76.0	68.6	67.2	58.8	47.0	38.0	31.0
Spain	506.3	563.6	590.8	658.0	646.8	632.2	424.5	276.9	179.4
Sweden	20.0	25.3	23.1	29.8	30.5	32.0	22.8	19.5	20.1
Switzerland	32.1	36.9	38.0	42.0	42.9	41.0	38.7	41.0	46.0
Turkey	162.9	165.0	249.8	295.4	325.3	356.4	468.1	414.2	549.9
United Kingdom	190.5	203.5	209.6	212.8	226.4	188.3	158.6	137.3	142.0
Eastern Europe									
Albania									
Belarus	32.0	40.4	43.3	45.6	53.1	59.8	69.6	84.7	87.0
Bosnia-Herzegovina	4.4	4.2	5.9	5.5	6.5	5.7	5.8	5.0	5.2
Bulgaria	6.3	8.3	12.1	13.3	18.9	20.9	22.1	15.8	14.0
Croatia	18.5	18.8	20.0	22.1	25.6	25.4	18.7	15.0	13.9
Czech Republic	27.1	32.3	32.9	30.2	41.6	38.4	38.5	36.4	26.6
Estonia	2.4	3.1	3.9	5.1	7.1	5.3	3.0	2.3	1.9
Georgia									
Hungary	35.5	43.9	41.1	33.9	36.2	36.1	32.0	20.8	12.7
Latvia	0.8	2.8	3.8	5.9	9.3	8.1	4.2	1.9	2.7
Lithuania	4.5	6.8	5.9	7.3	9.3	11.8	9.4	3.7	5.1
Macedonia	4.2	6.4	5.0	6.5	5.8	5.1	4.7	5.2	4.4
Moldova									
Montenegro	1.9	3.2	2.1	2.7	3.4	4.7	5.8	4.1	3.6
Poland	162.7	108.1	114.1	115.4	133.7	165.2	160.0	135.8	131.0
Romania	29.1	30.1	32.9	39.6	47.3	67.3	62.5	48.9	37.8
Russia	427.0	477.0	515.0	609.0	721.0	768.0	702.0	717.0	744.9
Serbia	13.9	16.4	16.4	18.2	19.0	19.8	19.1	20.1	21.4
Slovakia	14.0	12.6	14.9	14.4	16.5	17.2	18.8	17.1	14.6
Slovenia	5.9	6.9	7.1	8.4	10.1	8.3	5.9	4.7	3.7
Ukraine	63.2	71.2	76.0	82.0	95.0	94.0	66.0	77.0	83.2

Source: Euromonitor International from national statistics

15

Home Ownership

Home Ownership Statistics   **Table 15.3**

Households by Tenure 2011

'000 / % of total

	Home Owner, with Mortgage	Home Owner without mortgage	Rented	Other	Home Owner, with Mortgage (% of total)	Home Owner without mortgage (% of total)	Rented (% of total)	Other (% of total)
Western Europe								
Austria	676.0	1,336.9	1,489.4	161.0	18.5	36.5	40.7	4.4
Belgium	1,301.0	1,790.2	1,495.5	119.2	27.6	38.0	31.8	2.5
Cyprus								
Denmark	847.4	467.2	1,198.2	76.7	32.7	18.0	46.3	3.0
Finland	599.6	797.9	879.8	296.3	23.3	31.0	34.2	11.5
France	5,617.2	10,140.6	10,803.4	879.6	20.5	37.0	39.4	3.2
Germany	9,820.6	5,690.1	24,496.1		24.5	14.2	61.2	
Gibraltar								
Greece	678.9	2,354.6	793.3	258.4	16.6	57.6	19.4	6.3
Iceland								
Ireland	701.6	558.4	412.9	21.6	41.4	33.0	24.4	1.3
Italy	5,672.3	12,391.0	4,216.7	2,451.8	22.9	50.1	17.0	9.9
Liechtenstein								
Luxembourg								
Malta								
Monaco								
Netherlands	3,787.0	507.6	2,865.8	202.5	51.4	6.9	38.9	2.8
Norway	1,150.4	515.6	531.9		52.3	23.5	24.2	
Portugal	985.4	2,166.5	705.9	342.8	23.5	51.6	16.8	8.2
Spain	7,915.2	7,157.8	1,679.3	1,134.4	44.3	40.0	9.4	6.3
Sweden	1,176.5	1,659.7	1,339.0	419.7	25.6	36.1	29.1	9.1
Switzerland	830.6	1,454.4	1,110.4	162.5	23.3	40.9	31.2	4.6
Turkey	2,064.4	13,010.4	2,646.7	1,214.4	10.9	68.7	14.0	6.4
United Kingdom	8,746.3	10,343.3	8,540.5		31.7	37.4	30.9	
Eastern Europe								
Albania								
Belarus	345.3	3,099.2	304.5	362.8	8.4	75.4	7.4	8.8
Bosnia-Herzegovina								
Bulgaria	236.3	2,447.2	210.8	21.2	8.1	83.9	7.2	0.7
Croatia	119.0	1,263.6	94.5	35.0	7.9	83.6	6.2	2.3
Czech Republic	448.4	1,796.9	1,165.8	1,209.0	9.7	38.9	25.2	26.2
Estonia	99.3	408.8	66.8	12.4	16.9	69.6	11.4	2.1
Georgia								
Hungary	779.7	3,185.5	232.0	39.7	18.4	75.2	5.5	0.9
Latvia	123.2	567.2	120.2		15.2	70.0	14.8	
Lithuania	133.1	1,063.0	76.5	119.6	9.6	76.4	5.5	8.6
Macedonia								
Moldova								
Montenegro								
Poland	913.4	8,783.8	2,738.7	2,256.8	6.2	59.8	18.6	15.4
Romania	574.0	6,669.2	214.1	26.0	7.7	89.1	2.9	0.3
Russia	3,254.5	30,210.0	19,099.5		6.2	57.5	36.3	
Serbia								
Slovakia	178.1	1,653.0	152.9	307.3	7.8	72.1	6.7	13.4
Slovenia	39.2	615.2	32.3	61.6	5.2	82.2	4.3	8.2
Ukraine	710.8	15,853.2	3,052.8	350.5	3.6	79.4	15.3	1.8

Source: Euromonitor International from national statistics

Table 15.4

Households by Type of Dwelling 2011

'000 / % of total

	Detached House	Semi-Detached and Terraced House	Apartment	Other	Detached House (% of total)	Semi-Detached and Terraced House (% of total)	Apartment (% of total)	Other (% of total)
Western Europe								
Austria	1,167.9	656.4	1,763.9	75.1	31.9	17.9	48.2	2.0
Belgium	1,706.1	2,129.4	763.5	106.9	36.3	45.2	16.2	2.3
Cyprus								
Denmark	1,007.5	324.2	1,243.8	14.0	38.9	12.5	48.0	0.5
Finland	957.2	403.5	1,094.0	118.8	37.2	15.7	42.5	4.6
France	11,206.8	3,851.1	11,159.1	1,223.8	40.8	14.0	40.7	4.5
Germany	9,771.2	7,759.8	21,511.0	964.9	24.4	19.4	53.8	2.4
Gibraltar								
Greece	1,605.2	1,183.3	1,267.4	29.4	39.3	29.0	31.0	0.7
Iceland								
Ireland	671.1	822.5	113.2	87.7	39.6	48.5	6.7	5.2
Italy	3,414.0	2,981.4	18,336.3	0.0	13.8	12.1	74.1	0.0
Liechtenstein								
Luxembourg								
Malta								
Monaco								
Netherlands	1,280.2	3,892.0	2,042.1	148.5	17.4	52.9	27.7	2.0
Norway	1,140.5	456.7	500.0	100.7	51.9	20.8	22.7	4.6
Portugal	2,008.8	1,132.8	1,007.2	51.6	47.8	27.0	24.0	1.2
Spain	4,194.5	3,855.0	9,837.1		23.5	21.6	55.0	
Sweden	1,854.5	1,277.0	1,220.3	243.1	40.4	27.8	26.6	5.3
Switzerland	811.4	776.3	1,520.0	450.3	22.8	21.8	42.7	12.7
Turkey			9,800.0	352.6			51.8	1.9
United Kingdom	6,616.2	16,537.0	3,760.3	716.7	23.9	59.9	13.6	2.6
Eastern Europe								
Albania								
Belarus			2,674.9	126.2			65.1	3.1
Bosnia-Herzegovina								
Bulgaria			1,320.6	14.9			45.3	0.5
Croatia			1,093.8	18.7			72.3	1.2
Czech Republic	853.0	930.4	2,545.1	291.6	18.5	20.1	55.1	6.3
Estonia	154.4	33.5	383.6	15.7	26.3	5.7	65.3	2.7
Georgia								
Hungary			2,444.3	18.9			57.7	0.4
Latvia	164.9	53.4	572.5	19.9	20.3	6.6	70.6	2.5
Lithuania	316.4	130.9	855.5	89.4	22.7	9.4	61.5	6.4
Macedonia								
Moldova								
Montenegro								
Poland			7,116.2	381.3			48.4	2.6
Romania			2,742.7	125.1			36.7	1.7
Russia	7,437.6	3,297.2	40,502.9	1,326.2	14.1	6.3	77.1	2.5
Serbia								
Slovakia			1,293.9	44.6			56.5	1.9
Slovenia			368.7				49.3	
Ukraine	9,411.6	1,925.0	8,367.7	263.0	47.1	9.6	41.9	1.3

Source: Euromonitor International from national statistics

15

Home Ownership

16

Household Profiles

Household Statistics **Table 16.1**

Households 1985, 1990, 1995, 2000, 2006-2011
'000

	1985	1990	1995	2000	2006	2007	2008	2009	2010	2011
Western Europe										
Austria	2,887.0	2,996.1	3,131.0	3,303.0	3,512.0	3,545.8	3,577.6	3,607.8	3,636.6	3,663.3
Belgium	3,765.7	3,958.8	4,094.6	4,237.8	4,481.8	4,523.4	4,569.5	4,606.5	4,651.1	4,705.9
Cyprus	183.4	205.6	231.4	255.9	282.4	286.6	290.7	294.9	299.1	303.4
Denmark	2,159.5	2,265.0	2,357.6	2,434.1	2,516.3	2,532.0	2,547.4	2,562.1	2,575.8	2,589.5
Finland	1,910.1	2,036.7	2,180.9	2,295.4	2,453.8	2,481.6	2,507.5	2,530.9	2,553.2	2,573.6
France	20,283.0	21,542.0	22,830.0	24,107.7	25,991.7	26,296.0	26,592.9	26,883.1	27,165.7	27,440.8
Germany	32,967.0	34,775.0	36,938.0	38,124.0	39,767.0	39,824.7	39,886.5	39,942.6	39,982.2	40,006.9
Gibraltar	7.2	7.5	7.9	8.2	9.2	9.3	9.3	9.4	9.4	9.5
Greece	3,062.2	3,168.2	3,402.9	3,627.5	3,870.4	3,914.2	3,957.8	4,000.9	4,043.5	4,085.2
Iceland	54.4	70.2	94.9	106.8	125.6	128.9	132.5	136.0	139.2	142.1
Ireland	966.5	1,011.8	1,104.1	1,220.3	1,469.5	1,522.0	1,571.3	1,616.5	1,656.8	1,694.5
Italy	18,916.0	19,687.6	20,822.0	21,645.0	23,611.8	23,885.9	24,126.2	24,345.7	24,548.0	24,731.6
Liechtenstein	9.5	10.5	11.9	13.2	14.8	15.0	15.2	15.3	15.5	15.7
Luxembourg	133.9	142.9	157.4	173.7	192.8	195.7	198.6	201.4	204.2	206.9
Malta	104.4	110.4	119.1	128.1	138.1	139.4	140.5	141.6	142.9	144.2
Monaco	13.1	14.1	14.8	15.0	15.4	15.5	15.6	15.7	15.8	15.9
Netherlands	5,613.0	6,061.0	6,516.0	6,819.0	7,146.1	7,190.5	7,233.3	7,278.9	7,321.2	7,362.9
Norway	1,634.9	1,751.4	1,859.3	1,947.6	2,051.4	2,064.8	2,104.5	2,137.5	2,168.7	2,197.9
Portugal	3,038.9	3,129.1	3,294.1	3,577.8	3,992.7	4,043.8	4,089.6	4,130.3	4,167.1	4,200.5
Spain	10,439.0	11,626.9	12,784.9	13,934.1	16,323.2	16,735.4	17,081.0	17,376.5	17,641.7	17,886.7
Sweden	3,670.0	3,830.0	4,234.1	4,363.0	4,465.2	4,499.6	4,523.3	4,547.4	4,570.9	4,594.9
Switzerland	2,602.0	2,859.8	3,098.0	3,181.6	3,345.0	3,372.8	3,416.5	3,470.9	3,514.5	3,558.0
Turkey	8,962.8	11,188.6	13,232.3	15,070.1	17,119.0	17,474.6	17,834.8	18,198.5	18,565.6	18,935.8
United Kingdom	21,960.4	23,206.6	24,281.8	25,193.1	26,488.3	26,721.7	26,951.8	27,179.5	27,405.6	27,630.2
Eastern Europe										
Albania	589.4	709.7	713.7	725.4	767.9	775.4	783.0	790.9	799.4	808.3
Belarus	3,292.0	3,535.4	3,733.7	3,898.7	4,052.0	4,068.3	4,082.5	4,094.4	4,104.1	4,111.8
Bosnia-Herzegovina	1,124.4	1,236.1	1,016.9	1,149.6	1,211.1	1,216.6	1,221.1	1,224.6	1,227.0	1,228.3
Bulgaria	3,030.3	3,000.4	2,913.9	2,914.1	2,936.7	2,934.8	2,931.7	2,927.4	2,922.0	2,915.5
Croatia	1,480.9	1,536.4	1,527.5	1,474.6	1,500.5	1,503.8	1,506.5	1,508.7	1,510.5	1,512.1
Czech Republic	3,962.0	4,032.4	4,147.4	4,250.6	4,401.4	4,437.2	4,496.5	4,552.3	4,588.9	4,620.1
Estonia	479.0	521.0	572.0	582.1	588.9	588.9	588.7	588.3	587.8	587.2
Georgia	1,279.9	1,339.1	1,260.2	1,177.5	1,181.5	1,181.5	1,179.7	1,182.1	1,184.5	1,187.0
Hungary	3,882.4	3,889.5	3,869.2	3,846.6	4,046.6	4,090.6	4,132.9	4,171.9	4,206.6	4,236.9
Latvia	778.8	833.8	809.6	802.2	809.5	810.0	810.3	810.6	810.7	810.7
Lithuania	1,184.0	1,292.3	1,335.8	1,352.7	1,386.8	1,389.5	1,391.2	1,392.3	1,392.5	1,392.1
Macedonia	430.0	470.0	509.9	549.5	591.5	597.7	603.8	609.8	615.5	621.0
Moldova	1,117.6	1,283.5	1,428.9	1,534.1	1,648.7	1,679.6	1,714.6	1,752.4	1,792.0	1,833.4
Montenegro	150.8	161.3	170.4	177.3	182.8	183.5	184.2	184.9	185.6	186.2
Poland	11,683.5	12,112.6	12,501.0	13,031.1	13,982.7	14,135.4	14,288.5	14,435.0	14,570.2	14,692.7
Romania	7,162.9	7,377.5	7,202.2	7,269.1	7,404.7	7,424.3	7,441.7	7,457.5	7,471.2	7,483.3
Russia	33,552.5	42,280.2	48,871.9	52,196.8	52,947.2	52,914.3	52,858.7	52,781.0	52,681.7	52,564.0
Serbia	2,367.7	2,408.6	2,460.0	2,508.1	2,540.1	2,544.6	2,549.2	2,553.9	2,558.6	2,563.4
Slovakia	1,734.9	1,814.9	1,918.9	2,045.3	2,199.0	2,220.4	2,240.3	2,258.6	2,275.6	2,291.3
Slovenia	607.9	636.3	651.5	675.4	713.5	720.9	728.0	734.9	741.6	748.3
Ukraine	14,097.0	14,559.0	15,774.7	17,684.2	19,821.3	19,933.3	19,997.4	20,020.0	20,007.8	19,967.3

Source: Euromonitor International from national statistics

Table 16.2

Household Average Number of Occupants at January 1st 1985, 1990, 1995, 2000, 2006-2011

Number

	1985	1990	1995	2000	2006	2007	2008	2009	2010	2011	Average number of children per houseold 2011
Western Europe											
Austria	2.62	2.55	2.54	2.42	2.35	2.34	2.33	2.32	2.30	2.29	0.42
Belgium	2.62	2.51	2.47	2.42	2.35	2.34	2.33	2.33	2.33	2.33	0.47
Cyprus	3.84	3.73	3.70	3.69	3.70	3.70	3.70	3.69	3.69	3.68	0.80
Denmark	2.37	2.27	2.21	2.19	2.16	2.15	2.15	2.15	2.15	2.15	0.47
Finland	2.56	2.44	2.34	2.25	2.14	2.13	2.11	2.10	2.10	2.09	0.42
France	2.72	2.63	2.53	2.44	2.36	2.35	2.34	2.32	2.31	2.30	0.50
Germany	2.36	2.27	2.21	2.16	2.07	2.07	2.06	2.05	2.05	2.04	0.33
Gibraltar	3.70	3.57	3.45	3.32	3.18	3.16	3.15	3.13	3.11	3.09	0.54
Greece	3.24	3.19	3.11	3.01	2.87	2.85	2.83	2.81	2.80	2.77	0.48
Iceland	4.44	3.63	2.82	2.63	2.40	2.37	2.34	2.32	2.30	2.28	0.57
Ireland	3.67	3.47	3.26	3.10	2.86	2.83	2.80	2.75	2.70	2.64	0.67
Italy	2.99	2.88	2.73	2.63	2.49	2.48	2.47	2.47	2.46	2.45	0.41
Liechtenstein	2.80	2.70	2.58	2.46	2.36	2.35	2.33	2.32	2.31	2.31	0.37
Luxembourg	2.74	2.67	2.59	2.51	2.42	2.43	2.45	2.47	2.49	2.48	0.53
Malta	3.35	3.33	3.25	3.10	2.97	2.96	2.94	2.93	2.92	2.90	0.54
Monaco	2.18	2.19	2.23	2.34	2.28	2.27	2.26	2.25	2.23	2.22	0.31
Netherlands	2.58	2.46	2.37	2.33	2.29	2.27	2.27	2.26	2.26	2.26	0.48
Norway	2.54	2.42	2.34	2.30	2.26	2.27	2.25	2.25	2.24	2.24	0.51
Portugal	3.30	3.19	3.04	2.85	2.65	2.62	2.60	2.57	2.55	2.53	0.46
Spain	3.67	3.34	3.08	2.87	2.68	2.66	2.65	2.64	2.61	2.58	0.46
Sweden	2.27	2.23	2.08	2.03	2.03	2.03	2.03	2.04	2.04	2.05	0.42
Switzerland	2.48	2.33	2.27	2.25	2.23	2.23	2.22	2.22	2.22	2.21	0.41
Turkey	5.58	4.89	4.40	4.23	4.02	3.99	3.96	3.93	3.90	3.87	1.18
United Kingdom	2.57	2.46	2.39	2.33	2.28	2.27	2.27	2.27	2.26	2.26	0.48
Eastern Europe											
Albania	5.02	4.64	4.40	4.23	4.10	4.08	4.05	4.03	4.01	3.98	1.08
Belarus	3.02	2.88	2.73	2.57	2.38	2.35	2.34	2.32	2.31	2.31	0.42
Bosnia-Herzegovina	3.78	3.64	3.46	3.26	3.17	3.16	3.15	3.14	3.13	3.13	0.58
Bulgaria	2.95	2.92	2.85	2.74	2.63	2.62	2.61	2.60	2.59	2.58	0.43
Croatia	3.17	3.11	3.06	3.01	2.96	2.95	2.94	2.94	2.93	2.92	0.54
Czech Republic	2.60	2.55	2.49	2.41	2.33	2.32	2.30	2.29	2.28	2.27	0.40
Estonia	3.18	3.01	2.53	2.36	2.28	2.28	2.28	2.28	2.28	2.28	0.42
Georgia	3.88	3.84	3.80	3.77	3.73	3.72	3.71	3.71	3.71	3.70	0.77
Hungary	2.75	2.67	2.67	2.66	2.49	2.46	2.43	2.40	2.38	2.36	0.43
Latvia	3.30	3.20	3.09	2.97	2.74	2.70	2.67	2.64	2.60	2.56	0.43
Lithuania	2.98	2.86	2.73	2.60	2.45	2.44	2.42	2.41	2.39	2.33	0.44
Macedonia	4.21	4.03	3.82	3.64	3.45	3.42	3.39	3.36	3.34	3.31	0.72
Moldova	3.77	3.40	3.04	2.68	2.26	2.20	2.13	2.06	1.99	1.94	0.40
Montenegro	3.89	3.66	3.53	3.47	3.40	3.39	3.38	3.36	3.34	3.33	0.77
Poland	3.17	3.14	3.06	2.94	2.73	2.70	2.67	2.64	2.62	2.60	0.49
Romania	3.17	3.15	3.09	3.02	2.92	2.90	2.89	2.88	2.87	2.86	0.53
Russia	4.25	3.49	3.04	2.81	2.71	2.70	2.70	2.71	2.71	2.72	0.50
Serbia	3.22	3.14	3.10	3.00	2.92	2.91	2.89	2.87	2.86	2.84	0.53
Slovakia	2.96	2.90	2.79	2.63	2.44	2.42	2.40	2.38	2.37	2.36	0.45
Slovenia	3.19	3.14	3.05	2.94	2.81	2.79	2.78	2.77	2.76	2.74	0.47
Ukraine	3.59	3.54	3.25	2.78	2.36	2.33	2.31	2.30	2.29	2.28	0.40

Source: Euromonitor International from national statistics

16

Household Profiles

Household Statistics
Table 16.3

Households by Urban/Rural Split 2011

% of total households

	Urban	Rural
Western Europe		
Austria	74.4	25.6
Belgium	97.7	2.3
Cyprus		
Denmark	86.2	13.8
Finland	86.9	13.1
France	79.6	20.4
Germany	85.7	14.3
Gibraltar		
Greece	77.0	23.0
Iceland		
Ireland	63.4	36.6
Italy	71.1	28.9
Liechtenstein		
Luxembourg		
Malta		
Monaco		
Netherlands	75.9	24.1
Norway	81.8	18.2
Portugal	63.0	37.0
Spain	83.0	17.0
Sweden	87.1	12.9
Switzerland	76.6	23.4
Turkey	73.2	26.8
United Kingdom	91.5	8.5
Eastern Europe		
Albania		
Belarus	74.0	26.0
Bosnia-Herzegovina	51.6	48.4
Bulgaria	71.3	28.7
Croatia	60.0	40.0
Czech Republic	75.7	24.3
Estonia	70.5	29.5
Georgia	53.7	46.3
Hungary	70.3	29.7
Latvia	68.8	31.2
Lithuania	69.1	30.9
Macedonia	71.9	28.1
Moldova		
Montenegro	65.1	34.9
Poland	66.8	33.2
Romania	55.6	44.4
Russia	74.3	25.7
Serbia	59.3	40.7
Slovakia	54.9	45.1
Slovenia	52.9	47.1
Ukraine	69.2	30.8

Source: Euromonitor International from national statistics

Table 16.4

Households by Number of Persons 2011

% of total households

	One Person	Two Persons	Three Persons	Four Persons	Five Persons	Six or More Persons
Western Europe						
Austria	36.3	28.5	15.7	13.0	4.5	2.1
Belgium	33.3	32.9	14.7	12.3	5.1	1.7
Cyprus						
Denmark	39.6	33.1	11.0	11.2	3.9	1.4
Finland	39.4	35.4	11.2	9.1	3.6	1.4
France	34.3	32.6	14.7	12.1	4.6	1.8
Germany	38.7	35.4	12.7	9.6	3.4	0.3
Gibraltar						
Greece	23.0	30.6	20.2	17.3	5.4	3.5
Iceland						
Ireland	24.1	31.3	17.3	15.1	8.1	4.2
Italy	29.3	30.0	19.4	16.4	4.1	0.9
Liechtenstein						
Luxembourg						
Malta						
Monaco						
Netherlands	36.4	32.6	12.1	13.2	4.1	1.5
Norway	40.0	28.8	12.1	11.3	5.8	2.1
Portugal	21.0	33.4	22.7	16.8	4.7	1.4
Spain	25.1	28.4	19.4	18.9	5.6	2.4
Sweden	47.1	26.0	11.1	11.1	3.4	1.4
Switzerland	37.9	31.6	11.7	12.3	4.5	2.0
Turkey	6.0	16.0	19.3	25.8	14.8	18.1
United Kingdom	34.2	32.4	15.9	12.9	3.6	1.0
Eastern Europe						
Albania						
Belarus	27.9	33.2	26.1	8.4	3.3	1.2
Bosnia-Herzegovina	14.9	22.4	18.4	29.0	10.0	5.3
Bulgaria	25.6	30.6	20.3	15.5	5.1	2.9
Croatia	23.0	24.7	18.1	18.3	9.1	6.8
Czech Republic	33.4	29.9	17.5	14.9	3.4	0.9
Estonia	35.4	29.7	17.2	12.2	3.9	1.6
Georgia	17.0	17.6	17.2	21.8	12.9	13.4
Hungary	32.9	31.1	17.1	12.4	4.5	2.1
Latvia	22.7	33.3	18.6	14.1	5.8	5.5
Lithuania	33.0	28.4	17.6	13.9	4.4	2.7
Macedonia	14.5	19.4	19.8	25.8	11.1	9.4
Moldova						
Montenegro	17.6	23.0	16.3	19.0	11.0	13.1
Poland	30.2	26.6	16.4	14.7	6.7	5.5
Romania	20.5	27.9	23.1	16.5	6.8	5.1
Russia	24.8	26.6	23.0	16.4	6.1	2.9
Serbia	22.0	26.3	18.1	19.8	7.3	6.5
Slovakia	36.9	23.6	16.6	16.3	4.4	2.2
Slovenia	24.8	25.2	19.4	21.0	6.4	3.3
Ukraine	33.4	33.7	16.1	10.3	3.6	2.9

Source: Euromonitor International from national statistics

16

Household Profiles

Household Statistics   **Table 16.5**

Households by Number of Rooms 2011

% of total households

	1	2	3	4	5+
Western Europe					
Austria	8.8	19.0	32.6	20.3	19.3
Belgium	6.0	5.9	5.8	15.7	66.6
Cyprus					
Denmark	7.1	22.0	23.3	17.8	29.7
Finland	13.9	32.7	19.8	20.1	13.5
France	6.8	12.4	21.1	26.0	33.7
Germany	2.2	6.3	21.7	29.4	40.4
Gibraltar					
Greece	3.5	16.2	28.6	38.8	13.0
Iceland					
Ireland	0.3	2.4	6.4	15.7	75.2
Italy	0.7	9.6	26.5	35.1	28.2
Liechtenstein					
Luxembourg					
Malta					
Monaco					
Netherlands	3.0	7.0	22.1	33.5	34.4
Norway	4.4	13.0	18.2	21.3	43.1
Portugal	0.7	1.6	11.6	29.4	56.7
Spain	0.6	2.4	8.6	16.7	71.6
Sweden	7.5	22.3	25.6	21.7	22.8
Switzerland	1.3	4.3	12.0	26.9	55.5
Turkey	4.2	15.5	27.3	37.8	15.2
United Kingdom	0.2	2.0	7.3	18.1	72.3
Eastern Europe					
Albania					
Belarus	16.8	38.8	33.2	8.8	2.4
Bosnia-Herzegovina					
Bulgaria	8.9	38.3	39.3	9.7	3.7
Croatia	25.4	50.6	18.5	3.4	2.1
Czech Republic	9.6	25.7	37.3	15.3	12.1
Estonia	16.9	50.0	30.5	1.5	1.2
Georgia					
Hungary	17.8	40.3	30.9	6.4	4.5
Latvia	17.0	50.3	22.2	5.7	4.9
Lithuania	13.7	46.6	32.0	5.6	2.0
Macedonia					
Moldova					
Montenegro					
Poland	2.1	14.6	33.1	39.2	10.9
Romania	9.7	36.3	38.9	10.6	4.5
Russia	13.6	39.2	26.1	14.2	6.9
Serbia					
Slovakia	16.3	40.9	30.2	7.4	5.2
Slovenia	14.0	29.0	25.9	16.1	15.0
Ukraine	10.3	28.2	31.0	19.9	10.6

Source: Euromonitor International from national statistics

Table 16.6

Households by Sex of Head of Household 2011

% of total households

	Male	Female
Western Europe		
Austria	60.2	39.8
Belgium	68.0	32.0
Cyprus		
Denmark	55.2	44.8
Finland	61.3	38.7
France	71.8	28.2
Germany	67.3	32.7
Gibraltar		
Greece	74.7	25.3
Iceland		
Ireland	56.0	44.0
Italy	71.3	28.7
Liechtenstein		
Luxembourg		
Malta		
Monaco		
Netherlands	67.4	32.6
Norway	60.9	39.1
Portugal	74.9	25.1
Spain	76.0	24.0
Sweden	61.6	38.4
Switzerland	57.7	42.3
Turkey	86.8	13.2
United Kingdom	57.5	42.5
Eastern Europe		
Albania		
Belarus	49.3	50.7
Bosnia-Herzegovina		
Bulgaria	69.2	30.8
Croatia	57.9	42.1
Czech Republic	62.8	37.2
Estonia	48.2	51.8
Georgia		
Hungary	63.5	36.5
Latvia	51.8	48.2
Lithuania	49.8	50.2
Macedonia		
Moldova		
Montenegro		
Poland	59.7	40.3
Romania	70.3	29.7
Russia	51.0	49.0
Serbia		
Slovakia	66.6	33.4
Slovenia	50.0	50.0
Ukraine	49.2	50.8

Source: Euromonitor International from national statistics

16

Household Profiles

Household Statistics   **Table 16.7**

Households by Age of Head of Household 2011

% of total households

	29	30-39	40-49	50-59	60+
Western Europe					
Austria	9.40	15.89	22.29	18.21	34.20
Belgium	10.34	15.55	20.47	18.59	35.05
Cyprus					
Denmark	15.20	17.40	18.57	17.54	31.28
Finland	15.81	14.42	15.98	18.79	34.99
France	11.18	16.18	18.90	17.78	35.96
Germany	13.28	11.79	18.33	19.57	37.03
Gibraltar					
Greece	5.58	15.60	19.88	19.22	39.73
Iceland					
Ireland	10.78	21.83	20.60	18.05	28.73
Italy	5.25	12.94	21.32	18.17	42.31
Liechtenstein					
Luxembourg					
Malta					
Monaco					
Netherlands	10.88	16.69	20.50	18.26	33.67
Norway	11.70	16.35	20.22	20.17	31.56
Portugal	6.32	17.71	19.85	18.91	37.21
Spain	3.79	14.67	22.50	21.32	37.72
Sweden	13.63	14.44	17.58	15.96	38.40
Switzerland	10.96	17.62	21.76	19.06	30.59
Turkey	14.06	27.98	23.32	16.53	18.11
United Kingdom	11.71	17.64	20.62	17.53	32.50
Eastern Europe					
Albania					
Belarus	8.65	17.29	20.56	24.05	29.45
Bosnia-Herzegovina	4.96	14.13	21.10	24.44	35.37
Bulgaria	7.13	15.17	17.93	19.98	39.79
Croatia	4.05	13.40	18.97	23.25	40.33
Czech Republic	8.36	20.55	17.43	18.62	35.04
Estonia	14.80	16.44	17.19	18.30	33.28
Georgia	4.19	9.39	15.90	26.43	44.09
Hungary	8.06	19.36	17.53	19.97	35.08
Latvia	9.90	15.13	18.26	19.63	37.08
Lithuania	11.97	16.76	19.47	18.13	33.67
Macedonia	6.98	16.33	21.29	23.03	32.37
Moldova					
Montenegro					
Poland	8.67	17.96	17.82	22.78	32.76
Romania	6.37	16.29	18.72	21.02	37.59
Russia	11.80	15.85	18.35	23.27	30.73
Serbia	4.33	12.79	17.52	24.22	41.15
Slovakia	4.44	17.74	20.31	24.12	33.39
Slovenia	5.21	16.56	20.57	21.94	35.73
Ukraine	9.40	16.10	18.53	22.29	33.69

Source: Euromonitor International from national statistics

Table 16.8

Households by Education of Head of Household 2011

% of total households

	Primary and No Education	Secondary	Higher
Western Europe			
Austria	23.0	48.2	28.8
Belgium	18.4	65.2	16.4
Cyprus			
Denmark	27.5	47.3	25.2
Finland	34.1	46.0	19.9
France	13.3	57.0	23.9
Germany	11.5	60.6	26.5
Gibraltar			
Greece	46.8	40.3	12.9
Iceland			
Ireland	19.6	44.5	35.8
Italy	18.2	71.4	10.5
Liechtenstein			
Luxembourg			
Malta			
Monaco			
Netherlands	18.8	54.2	27.1
Norway	16.6	53.8	27.2
Portugal	58.0	23.9	18.1
Spain	45.8	35.8	18.4
Sweden	28.5	46.6	24.9
Switzerland	20.1	64.1	15.8
Turkey	65.8	18.7	15.5
United Kingdom	13.0	56.0	31.0
Eastern Europe			
Albania			
Belarus	21.8	59.2	19.0
Bosnia-Herzegovina			
Bulgaria	42.5	39.9	17.6
Croatia	39.1	47.5	13.4
Czech Republic	20.1	67.3	12.7
Estonia	21.7	60.2	18.1
Georgia			
Hungary	39.5	49.1	11.4
Latvia	38.9	40.3	20.9
Lithuania	16.1	67.8	16.1
Macedonia			
Moldova			
Montenegro			
Poland	24.9	64.1	11.0
Romania	27.1	63.1	9.8
Russia	20.2	63.9	16.0
Serbia			
Slovakia	18.0	66.1	16.0
Slovenia	24.3	58.9	16.8
Ukraine	26.4	50.7	22.9

Source: Euromonitor International from national statistics

16

Household Profiles

Household Statistics **Table 16.9**

Households by Status of Head of Household 2011

% of total households

	Employee	Employer Self-Employed	Unemployed	Other
Western Europe				
Austria	54.5	8.8	1.3	35.5
Belgium	51.0	8.8	6.3	34.0
Cyprus				
Denmark	57.5	2.6	1.3	38.5
Finland	45.0	8.6	4.2	42.2
France	55.8	6.6	7.2	30.4
Germany	54.4	5.2	3.0	37.4
Gibraltar				
Greece	35.1	17.6	2.0	45.3
Iceland				
Ireland	38.5	13.4	9.3	38.8
Italy	37.6	13.8	2.7	45.8
Liechtenstein				
Luxembourg				
Malta				
Monaco				
Netherlands	51.4	12.5	2.2	33.9
Norway	56.8	5.7	1.4	36.2
Portugal	52.7	5.6	4.2	37.6
Spain	41.3	10.7	7.5	40.4
Sweden	57.6	3.0	4.0	35.4
Switzerland	62.4	7.3	3.2	27.1
Turkey	52.6	20.8	1.4	25.3
United Kingdom	52.4	7.9	2.9	36.8
Eastern Europe				
Albania				
Belarus	65.2	2.0	0.4	32.4
Bosnia-Herzegovina	37.5	11.9	9.4	41.3
Bulgaria	35.3	3.5	9.8	51.4
Croatia	29.8	11.8	4.7	53.8
Czech Republic	47.5	13.4	6.4	32.7
Estonia	54.9	7.4	6.7	31.0
Georgia	29.4	34.9	5.8	29.9
Hungary	51.8	7.1	1.2	39.9
Latvia	58.2	10.6	4.4	26.8
Lithuania	55.2	6.6	5.4	32.8
Macedonia	46.5	15.5	13.9	24.1
Moldova				
Montenegro				
Poland	49.0	12.1	2.8	36.2
Romania	37.6	14.1	3.4	44.9
Russia	60.8	4.9	3.5	30.8
Serbia	42.0	16.5	6.4	35.0
Slovakia	52.8	10.9	3.9	32.5
Slovenia	53.8	6.9	2.7	36.6
Ukraine	43.1	28.1	2.9	26.0

Source: Euromonitor International from national statistics

Table 16.10

Households by Type 2011
% of total households

	Single Person	Couple Without Children	Couple With Children	Single Parent Family	Other
Western Europe					
Austria	36.3	19.8	25.4	9.1	9.4
Belgium	33.3	21.2	25.5	13.2	6.9
Cyprus					
Denmark	39.6	33.5	14.5	5.0	7.3
Finland	39.4	25.4	22.4	8.5	4.3
France	34.3	26.4	26.6	8.0	4.7
Germany	38.7	29.9	24.7	5.5	1.3
Gibraltar					
Greece	23.0	20.4	35.9	8.1	12.6
Iceland					
Ireland	24.1	19.7	33.2	10.5	12.5
Italy	29.3	21.9	37.5	9.2	2.2
Liechtenstein					
Luxembourg					
Malta					
Monaco					
Netherlands	36.4	27.7	29.4	6.2	0.3
Norway	40.0	21.2	27.8	8.3	2.7
Portugal	21.0	22.9	39.9	7.6	8.5
Spain	25.1	19.4	36.3	9.4	9.7
Sweden	47.1	30.1	16.5	4.2	2.1
Switzerland	37.9	26.5	26.3	5.0	4.3
Turkey	6.0	15.9	38.8	2.4	37.0
United Kingdom	34.2	26.4	19.4	7.7	12.2
Eastern Europe					
Albania					
Belarus	27.9	18.3	29.3	11.0	13.5
Bosnia-Herzegovina	14.9	18.5	34.2	8.5	23.9
Bulgaria	25.6	20.6	30.0	6.9	16.8
Croatia	23.0	22.5	41.0	12.5	1.1
Czech Republic	33.4	22.1	28.7	14.7	1.0
Estonia	35.4	19.0	25.6	14.0	6.0
Georgia	17.0	17.3	36.1	11.9	17.7
Hungary	32.9	22.0	30.4	10.6	4.1
Latvia	22.7	16.6	27.4	20.9	12.4
Lithuania	33.0	17.6	33.9	12.8	2.7
Macedonia	14.5	21.1	44.5	8.2	11.7
Moldova					
Montenegro					
Poland	30.2	18.2	35.4	11.0	5.3
Romania	20.5	19.7	33.0	9.4	17.4
Russia	24.8	15.1	26.4	12.7	21.0
Serbia	22.0	17.5	31.7	9.6	19.2
Slovakia	36.9	18.4	30.3	12.5	1.9
Slovenia	24.8	15.3	42.6	11.9	5.5
Ukraine	33.4	17.0	23.6	5.1	20.9

Source: Euromonitor International from national statistics

16

Household Profiles

Household Statistics   **Table 16.11**

Households by Annual Disposable Income Band 2011

% of total households

	Over $500	Over $750	Over $1,000	Over $1,750	Over $2,500	Over $5,000	Over $7,500	Over $10,000	Over $15,000	Over $25,000
Western Europe										
Austria	100.0	100.0	100.0	100.0	100.0	100.0	99.9	99.8	99.2	95.3
Belgium	100.0	100.0	100.0	100.0	99.9	99.7	99.3	98.7	96.7	89.8
Cyprus										
Denmark	100.0	100.0	100.0	99.9	99.8	99.2	98.3	97.0	93.4	83.2
Finland	100.0	100.0	100.0	100.0	100.0	99.9	99.8	99.5	98.3	91.7
France	100.0	100.0	100.0	99.9	99.8	99.2	98.3	97.2	94.2	86.3
Germany	100.0	100.0	100.0	99.9	99.9	99.5	98.8	97.7	94.6	84.9
Gibraltar										
Greece	100.0	100.0	100.0	99.9	99.9	99.4	98.5	97.2	93.4	81.9
Iceland										
Ireland	100.0	100.0	99.9	99.8	99.7	99.0	97.9	96.6	93.2	84.3
Italy	100.0	100.0	100.0	100.0	100.0	99.8	99.3	98.5	95.6	84.9
Liechtenstein										
Luxembourg										
Malta										
Monaco										
Netherlands	100.0	100.0	100.0	100.0	99.9	99.5	98.7	97.5	93.8	81.7
Norway	100.0	100.0	100.0	100.0	100.0	100.0	100.0	100.0	99.9	99.3
Portugal	100.0	100.0	100.0	100.0	99.9	99.4	98.1	96.0	88.7	66.1
Spain	100.0	100.0	100.0	100.0	99.9	99.7	99.1	98.1	95.1	84.2
Sweden	100.0	100.0	100.0	100.0	100.0	100.0	100.0	99.9	99.2	93.4
Switzerland	100.0	100.0	100.0	100.0	100.0	99.9	99.8	99.6	99.0	96.8
Turkey	100.0	100.0	100.0	99.8	99.6	97.9	94.4	89.1	74.6	44.6
United Kingdom	100.0	100.0	100.0	100.0	99.9	99.7	99.1	98.2	95.1	84.5
Eastern Europe										
Albania										
Belarus	100.0	100.0	99.9	98.9	95.9	64.9	33.6	18.4	7.7	3.0
Bosnia-Herzegovina	99.9	99.7	99.5	98.1	95.7	81.3	61.9	44.4	22.2	7.3
Bulgaria	99.8	99.6	99.1	96.7	92.4	68.5	43.6	26.7	11.2	3.7
Croatia	99.9	99.7	99.6	98.9	97.9	93.6	87.8	81.1	66.7	40.6
Czech Republic	100.0	100.0	100.0	100.0	100.0	99.9	99.5	97.7	85.7	39.2
Estonia	100.0	100.0	100.0	99.9	99.8	97.9	93.2	84.8	61.6	25.4
Georgia	98.6	97.4	95.9	90.6	84.3	62.3	44.2	31.2	16.4	5.9
Hungary	100.0	100.0	100.0	100.0	99.9	98.4	93.4	83.1	53.5	17.7
Latvia	100.0	99.9	99.8	99.4	98.8	95.1	89.0	81.1	63.1	32.4
Lithuania	99.9	99.8	99.6	98.9	97.8	92.3	84.5	75.4	56.5	27.6
Macedonia	99.8	99.6	99.4	98.0	96.0	85.0	70.3	55.3	31.9	10.9
Moldova										
Montenegro										
Poland	100.0	99.9	99.9	99.6	99.1	95.7	89.5	81.1	61.4	30.2
Romania	100.0	100.0	100.0	100.0	99.8	96.3	82.5	60.9	29.0	9.6
Russia	100.0	99.9	99.8	99.3	98.5	92.9	83.7	72.5	50.6	23.8
Serbia	100.0	99.9	99.8	99.2	98.1	90.2	76.9	61.5	35.5	12.2
Slovakia	100.0	100.0	100.0	100.0	100.0	99.8	98.9	96.7	85.7	45.6
Slovenia	100.0	100.0	100.0	99.9	99.8	99.0	97.7	95.8	90.5	75.4
Ukraine	99.7	99.2	98.3	93.7	86.0	50.8	25.5	13.3	5.1	2.2

Source: Euromonitor International from national statistics

Households by Annual Disposable Income Band 2011 *(continued)*

% of total households

	Over $35,000	Over $45,000	Over $55,000	Over $65,000	Over $75,000	Over $100,000	Over $125,000	Over $150,000	Over $200,000	Over $250,000	Over $300,000
Western Europe											
Austria	85.6	70.6	54.1	39.7	28.9	14.1	8.1	5.4	3.4	2.5	2.0
Belgium	79.8	67.9	55.7	44.4	34.7	18.2	10.0	6.1	3.4	2.6	2.0
Cyprus											
Denmark	70.9	58.3	46.7	36.9	29.0	16.0	9.3	5.9	3.2	2.3	1.8
Finland	78.9	62.3	46.3	33.3	24.0	11.5	6.6	4.5	3.0	2.2	1.8
France	76.7	66.4	56.3	46.8	38.3	22.4	12.9	7.7	3.7	2.7	2.1
Germany	72.2	58.7	46.3	35.7	27.4	14.2	8.1	5.2	3.0	2.2	1.8
Gibraltar											
Greece	67.7	53.8	41.7	32.1	24.7	13.5	8.1	5.4	3.0	2.2	1.7
Iceland											
Ireland	73.8	63.1	53.0	43.9	36.1	21.9	13.4	8.6	4.3	2.7	2.1
Italy	69.7	54.0	40.7	30.6	23.2	12.5	7.6	5.2	3.0	2.2	1.8
Liechtenstein											
Luxembourg											
Malta											
Monaco											
Netherlands	66.1	50.7	37.7	27.8	20.6	10.4	6.1	4.1	2.6	1.9	1.5
Norway	97.4	93.3	86.4	76.7	65.3	38.5	21.8	13.1	6.3	4.2	3.4
Portugal	44.2	29.1	19.8	14.0	10.3	5.7	3.7	2.7	1.8	1.4	1.1
Spain	69.2	53.6	40.1	29.5	21.8	10.9	6.3	4.3	2.7	2.0	1.6
Sweden	77.8	57.0	39.3	27.3	19.5	9.9	6.1	4.4	2.9	2.2	1.7
Switzerland	93.1	88.1	81.9	74.8	67.4	49.2	34.2	23.3	11.3	6.2	4.0
Turkey	25.4	15.2	9.9	6.9	5.1	3.0	2.1	1.7	1.2	0.9	0.7
United Kingdom	69.7	54.2	40.6	29.8	21.9	10.9	6.3	4.2	2.7	2.0	1.6
Eastern Europe											
Albania											
Belarus	2.0	1.4	1.1	0.9	0.7	0.5	0.4	0.3	0.2	0.2	0.1
Bosnia-Herzegovina	3.6	2.4	1.9	1.5	1.3	0.9	0.7	0.5	0.4	0.3	0.2
Bulgaria	2.2	1.6	1.2	1.0	0.8	0.6	0.4	0.4	0.2	0.2	0.1
Croatia	23.0	12.8	7.5	4.8	3.4	2.3	1.7	1.4	0.9	0.7	0.6
Czech Republic	16.7	8.9	5.8	4.3	3.6	2.5	1.8	1.5	1.0	0.8	0.6
Estonia	11.5	6.4	4.2	3.2	2.7	1.9	1.4	1.1	0.8	0.6	0.5
Georgia	3.0	1.9	1.4	1.1	1.0	0.7	0.5	0.4	0.3	0.2	0.2
Hungary	7.7	4.6	3.4	2.7	2.3	1.6	1.2	0.9	0.6	0.5	0.4
Latvia	15.8	8.4	5.1	3.6	2.8	2.0	1.5	1.2	0.8	0.6	0.5
Lithuania	13.1	6.9	4.2	3.0	2.5	1.7	1.3	1.0	0.7	0.5	0.4
Macedonia	4.9	3.0	2.2	1.8	1.5	1.1	0.8	0.6	0.4	0.3	0.3
Moldova											
Montenegro											
Poland	15.1	8.4	5.3	3.8	2.9	2.0	1.5	1.2	0.8	0.6	0.5
Romania	4.9	3.2	2.5	2.0	1.7	1.2	0.9	0.7	0.5	0.4	0.3
Russia	12.6	7.6	5.1	3.7	2.9	1.8	1.4	1.1	0.8	0.6	0.5
Serbia	5.6	3.4	2.5	2.0	1.7	1.2	0.9	0.7	0.5	0.4	0.3
Slovakia	20.0	10.1	6.3	4.6	3.7	2.6	1.9	1.5	1.0	0.8	0.6
Slovenia	57.9	41.6	28.7	19.4	13.2	5.8	3.6	2.8	2.0	1.5	1.2
Ukraine	1.5	1.1	0.8	0.7	0.6	0.4	0.3	0.2	0.2	0.1	0.1

Source: Euromonitor International from national statistics

16

Household Profiles

Household Statistics

Table 16.12

Household Durable Ownership 2011

% of total households

	Air Conditioner	Bicycle	Black/White TV	Broadband Internet Enabled Computer	Cable TV	Camera	Cassette Radio Player	CD Player	Colour TV Set	Cooker
Western Europe										
Austria	6.6	78.3	0.7	72.0	36.9	98.3	63.0	66.8	95.5	95.8
Belgium	7.9	69.9	1.2	74.0	71.5	79.3	18.9	31.5	96.3	96.4
Cyprus										
Denmark	5.4	63.1	1.0	84.0	57.5	99.0	54.0	84.0	98.0	97.9
Finland	3.6	85.0	0.7	81.3	51.0	86.3	47.0	60.4	95.2	99.2
France	8.2	74.6	0.5	70.0	13.7	78.0	63.2	22.5	97.8	97.8
Germany	7.0	81.0	0.6	72.0	46.4	88.1	72.1	79.0	96.2	96.4
Gibraltar										
Greece	18.1	44.3	1.3	45.4	0.9	92.0	62.3	17.9	98.7	95.9
Iceland										
Ireland	8.3	62.4	0.0	65.4	32.0	87.4	40.8	38.6	98.2	98.6
Italy	36.9	50.3	1.3	51.7	1.0	64.2	50.4	11.5	97.0	95.7
Liechtenstein										
Luxembourg										
Malta										
Monaco										
Netherlands	7.3	92.4	2.3	82.9	70.6	91.2	61.6	84.4	99.4	96.2
Norway	3.5	81.3	1.3	80.4	42.3	89.9	56.1	84.5	96.1	99.1
Portugal	10.4	24.9	2.2	56.6	54.1	41.8	63.7	41.3	99.3	99.9
Spain	19.8	38.8	1.2	61.9	13.7	71.1	79.5	40.8	99.5	97.9
Sweden	3.8	85.1	0.7	85.5	55.8	90.4	58.2	79.2	98.1	98.6
Switzerland	10.5	66.2	1.6	82.0	85.8	99.0	54.0	56.7	94.8	96.1
Turkey	12.0	27.9	4.8	39.3	13.2	30.8	91.1	8.0	95.1	62.4
United Kingdom	8.9	65.0	0.2	74.8	14.2	83.1	48.2	87.7	99.0	96.0
Eastern Europe										
Albania										
Belarus	2.0	31.2	3.1	34.0	54.0	29.8	13.5	5.9	98.3	92.0
Bosnia-Herzegovina	6.4	24.3	1.0	26.0	24.5		23.1		92.8	92.5
Bulgaria	23.6	41.6	5.3	29.3	43.7	45.6	28.7	7.1	92.4	79.3
Croatia	23.9	41.5	1.2	55.6	19.7	63.5	26.8	21.5	97.3	96.5
Czech Republic	5.9	48.7	1.6	63.4	24.0	59.6	65.2	23.6	98.9	98.6
Estonia	4.7	79.4	1.0	66.2	45.8	52.7	31.8	13.1	98.0	98.5
Georgia	6.4	14.7	4.7	20.6	12.0		6.3		91.5	65.2
Hungary	4.3	78.8	0.8	60.8	55.1	75.1	72.7	35.6	97.4	98.2
Latvia	4.7	58.8	2.1	59.4	40.1	32.1	45.9	8.2	96.7	98.1
Lithuania	4.7	45.9	1.3	48.4	50.9	35.8	56.0	7.6	98.5	98.1
Macedonia	24.0	37.5	1.8	42.1	42.7		41.0		97.1	85.9
Moldova										
Montenegro	38.0		3.2	38.4	35.0		27.2		98.4	96.5
Poland	5.3	64.6	0.2	61.1	33.8	52.4	47.0	12.7	97.5	97.9
Romania	3.0	28.7	0.0	31.0	44.1	43.7	28.5	2.9	95.7	94.2
Russia	8.1	37.6	2.4	33.8	36.6	45.1	25.1	10.8	97.6	94.1
Serbia	20.3	38.4	3.1	31.0	41.9		27.2		96.8	88.2
Slovakia	5.2	68.3	1.6	55.3	42.6	47.0	44.7	10.2	99.4	98.4
Slovenia	16.3	64.6	4.2	67.0	68.3	70.1	83.9	25.3	97.8	97.1
Ukraine	5.8	35.2	3.4	16.4	21.4	22.7	10.7	9.0	95.5	89.3

Source: Euromonitor International from national statistics

Household Durable Ownership 2011 *(continued)*
% of total households

	Dishwasher	DVD Player Recorder	Freezer	Hi-Fi Stereo	Internet Enabled Computer	Microwave Oven	Mobile Phone	Motorcycle	Passenger Car	Personal Computer
Western Europe										
Austria	78.9	76.1	88.1	63.6	75.4	75.1	99.9	8.5	85.2	78.1
Belgium	57.4	77.3	62.9	65.9	76.5	88.7	94.6	4.7	85.6	81.9
Cyprus										
Denmark	67.0	85.3	98.5	91.7	90.1	75.0	97.0	24.2	73.9	91.0
Finland	55.5	84.6	90.0	91.7	84.2	93.5	98.0	14.1	75.2	86.6
France	55.9	91.5	54.0	65.7	75.9	87.8	82.9	18.9	82.0	81.2
Germany	67.0	71.3	78.9	75.8	75.9	72.0	90.0	10.8	77.9	82.0
Gibraltar										
Greece	37.9	68.0	26.8	64.3	50.2	54.7	88.8	12.4	67.3	57.2
Iceland										
Ireland	65.8	86.1	35.1	72.8	78.1	92.2	98.4	1.7	81.9	82.3
Italy	46.8	90.0	48.5	56.0	61.6	38.8	89.4	7.6	61.4	66.4
Liechtenstein										
Luxembourg										
Malta										
Monaco										
Netherlands	62.3	92.1	87.4	92.8	93.6	94.4	95.1	13.3	78.9	94.2
Norway	77.8	90.9	91.1	92.6	92.2	85.8	99.3	13.0	79.5	93.6
Portugal	58.3	88.7	71.8	50.9	58.0	88.6	88.3	20.1	69.5	63.7
Spain	45.4	77.9	41.2	61.0	63.9	85.4	95.1	22.8	78.7	72.6
Sweden	73.4	88.3	99.4	89.4	90.6	81.5	98.9	4.3	86.3	91.5
Switzerland	71.3	74.4	69.9	73.1	88.9	68.1	93.1	33.8	89.7	90.0
Turkey	28.5	29.0	2.2	45.5	42.9	9.7	90.9	12.5	29.9	48.5
United Kingdom	41.2	87.3	51.0	77.5	75.2	94.0	80.0	3.6	78.3	78.9
Eastern Europe										
Albania										
Belarus	5.0	27.2	19.0	33.8	40.3	40.9	82.0	4.3	61.4	46.4
Bosnia-Herzegovina	12.8	57.2	66.8	71.3	32.0	45.1	78.0		56.4	36.5
Bulgaria	5.4	30.8	27.3	31.5	35.8	38.1	84.3	5.7	45.3	38.0
Croatia	27.9	49.2	80.2	37.5	61.4	40.3	96.7	5.3	59.5	64.0
Czech Republic	29.6	70.5	30.2	48.6	66.6	83.2	90.3	0.9	77.4	69.0
Estonia	14.2	53.8	41.9	59.9	70.8	69.3	94.1	2.6	53.9	75.3
Georgia	0.6	24.2	11.8	15.1	23.3	17.6	88.6		31.4	23.8
Hungary	12.3	54.1	45.8	34.8	65.2	87.4	94.7	15.9	49.0	69.7
Latvia	3.1	42.2	16.8	56.6	63.6	43.5	98.2	0.8	54.2	64.3
Lithuania	4.2	42.0	19.1	47.5	55.8	78.4	91.0	2.7	62.9	63.1
Macedonia	12.4	45.6	27.1	26.4	51.6	42.2	82.0	6.0	51.5	64.8
Moldova										
Montenegro	21.3	39.7	83.7	33.9	44.5	37.7	95.7		51.6	46.6
Poland	17.6	56.6	29.9	41.1	64.8	55.1	90.5	6.3	61.3	68.3
Romania	5.8	30.2	23.7	19.1	47.4	34.4	82.2	0.8	29.0	52.9
Russia	3.1	49.5	12.6	41.3	46.0	49.3	95.3	17.2	48.9	57.1
Serbia	7.2	29.6	29.3	25.8	43.9	16.1	76.2		41.6	55.8
Slovakia	11.6	44.2	42.5	20.6	70.8	76.2	88.7	6.7	60.7	75.4
Slovenia	52.7	65.1	79.7	46.6	72.6	57.7	91.9	5.3	80.9	75.1
Ukraine	0.4	27.5	10.7	12.3	26.0	34.9	87.4	2.1	21.0	30.7

Source: Euromonitor International from national statistics

16

Household Profiles

Household Statistics

Household Durable Ownership 2011 *(continued)*

% of total households

	Refrigerator	Satellite TV	Telephone	Tumble Drier	Vacuum Cleaner	Video Camera	Video Game Console	Video Recorder	Washing Machine
Western Europe									
Austria	99.7	51.7	53.7	25.8	98.3	21.9	17.3	63.3	98.8
Belgium	99.3	5.4	71.8	62.8	94.7	18.4	16.8	51.5	88.7
Cyprus									
Denmark	99.3	11.2	58.0	54.0	96.9	28.0	40.0	51.1	80.0
Finland	97.5	25.5	25.8	60.5	97.6	24.8	18.3	74.1	89.4
France	99.8	29.2	90.1	46.4	90.4	9.2	19.4	58.6	95.6
Germany	99.1	42.1	92.7	39.7	96.1	21.6	23.9	61.7	95.0
Gibraltar									
Greece	96.2	12.8	82.5	13.8	87.5	6.2	10.0	45.9	94.2
Iceland									
Ireland	99.8	46.4	65.5	66.9	94.4	12.3	41.4	80.4	96.9
Italy	99.3	31.1	71.2	18.5	81.0	26.6	15.5	70.0	97.1
Liechtenstein									
Luxembourg									
Malta									
Monaco									
Netherlands	99.5	9.6	93.4	61.8	97.4	26.7	12.8	75.7	97.9
Norway	99.1	33.1	86.8	43.4	96.2	21.3	19.9	38.7	88.4
Portugal	99.9	19.5	66.9	26.1	87.6	16.1	15.1	45.0	93.6
Spain	100.0	14.4	80.6	17.2	84.6	10.8	10.5	58.7	99.1
Sweden	99.3	18.6	91.4	45.8	97.1	25.3	15.3	77.1	76.9
Switzerland	100.0	14.6	99.2	42.5	99.2	20.3	24.0	32.9	99.8
Turkey	98.5	43.9	51.4	1.5	85.1	3.8	3.8	16.1	94.0
United Kingdom	99.6	39.0	86.3	56.6	96.1	12.3	17.1	50.6	96.0
Eastern Europe									
Albania									
Belarus	98.7	12.1	87.3	1.6	60.6	0.7	5.7	23.8	52.6
Bosnia-Herzegovina	97.8	15.4	70.0		81.5				88.3
Bulgaria	88.3	26.4	66.6	4.3	83.9	0.3	4.1	37.7	82.5
Croatia	98.2	27.5	87.0	9.4	84.0	8.0	9.6	18.1	93.3
Czech Republic	82.0	26.2	23.4	3.0	90.2	16.4	10.5	51.3	97.8
Estonia	98.5	16.1	50.8	6.2	85.0	10.3	6.4	41.2	90.7
Georgia	94.6	0.8	43.5		65.7				50.8
Hungary	61.0	26.6	39.5	3.0	93.7	15.0	10.6	36.9	93.6
Latvia	99.2	12.1	32.7	3.6	84.0	7.7	7.0	32.0	90.2
Lithuania	97.8	11.6	44.4	4.0	83.6	8.5	7.2	22.0	92.4
Macedonia	98.6	9.0	62.0		86.5				91.6
Moldova									
Montenegro	99.0	35.0	59.5		85.4				78.1
Poland	99.1	67.5	58.5	1.7	94.9	11.1	8.5	22.1	90.8
Romania	78.9	35.3	42.3	0.6	65.7	0.7	3.4	5.0	76.7
Russia	96.8	7.8	69.5	1.4	94.3	8.8	4.1	16.6	97.1
Serbia	97.2	4.3	86.7		83.1			5.8	88.2
Slovakia	83.8	53.3	39.6	2.0	89.4	7.0	8.7	48.8	82.0
Slovenia	98.5	9.3	79.6	27.9	92.9	15.0	10.7	47.7	96.5
Ukraine	97.2	13.9	51.8	1.6	75.1	4.3	3.8	9.2	84.6

Source: Euromonitor International from national statistics

17

Income and Deductions

Income Statistics **Table 17.1**

Gross Income (Annual) 1990, 1995, 2000, 2006-2011

National currency billion / US$ per capita

	1990	1995	2000	2006	2007	2008	2009	2010	2011	US$ per capita
Western Europe										
Austria	122.6	155.9	179.4	220.1	230.6	242.0	240.7	249.2	258.8	42,818.38
Belgium	165.8	211.6	246.6	296.6	311.0	328.3	332.1	339.4	353.1	44,832.66
Cyprus										
Denmark	644.0	757.8	902.3	1,137.2	1,180.7	1,201.3	1,208.0	1,273.3	1,299.3	43,594.50
Finland	76.2	84.5	106.3	135.1	143.2	151.3	152.4	157.2	163.8	42,383.10
France	978.3	1,165.6	1,376.0	1,733.6	1,811.1	1,869.9	1,876.4	1,912.2	1,962.3	43,221.06
Germany	1,141.4	1,442.2	1,605.2	1,762.9	1,828.4	1,904.6	1,858.3	1,898.3	1,987.6	33,805.86
Gibraltar										
Greece	40.4	83.6	127.7	190.4	215.2	221.4	227.6	229.0	219.3	26,925.96
Iceland										
Ireland	30.3	39.8	71.1	116.2	125.2	128.0	121.1	119.1	117.8	36,542.68
Italy	742.2	955.1	1,137.1	1,424.0	1,480.9	1,523.0	1,488.3	1,505.2	1,529.8	35,086.05
Liechtenstein										
Luxembourg										
Malta										
Monaco										
Netherlands	239.1	288.4	363.3	463.0	485.4	501.2	498.2	503.1	509.1	42,498.33
Norway	562.1	723.3	1,022.4	1,363.7	1,484.9	1,607.5	1,689.0	1,774.0	1,882.2	68,239.43
Portugal	49.9	82.1	114.6	147.0	154.0	160.8	160.6	166.8	166.1	21,709.26
Spain	305.0	425.9	586.3	886.7	953.1	1,001.2	995.3	981.0	997.2	30,043.67
Sweden	1,283.6	1,559.9	1,938.8	2,404.2	2,546.9	2,604.0	2,642.9	2,721.7	2,794.5	45,693.44
Switzerland	259.3	304.5	342.4	381.7	403.8	418.0	416.9	433.2	440.2	62,986.36
Turkey	0.4	7.0	144.8	644.4	720.4	795.6	809.3	937.9	1,101.7	8,946.58
United Kingdom	515.2	700.0	917.4	1,216.5	1,257.1	1,307.0	1,313.4	1,360.6	1,402.3	35,956.02
Eastern Europe										
Albania										
Belarus	0.0	88.7	6,650.4	57,511.2	71,256.8	91,498.9	103,609.4	123,158.3	194,924.9	4,132.79
Bosnia-Herzegovina	0.0	3.4	12.8	20.7	23.1	26.1	25.1	23.6	24.3	4,489.98
Bulgaria	0.0	0.8	19.4	32.5	37.7	42.3	39.9	40.5	43.4	4,105.32
Croatia	0.2	84.7	136.8	234.0	252.8	272.0	260.8	260.9	268.5	11,386.01
Czech Republic	460.7	1,247.3	1,838.8	2,599.0	2,801.0	2,953.5	2,949.2	2,977.5	3,008.6	16,213.97
Estonia	2.7	2.7	4.6	9.1	11.2	12.1	11.0	10.9	11.9	12,342.45
Georgia	0.0	3.0	5.8	12.3	13.6	16.2	16.2	17.1	20.0	2,697.78
Hungary	1,618.0	5,141.6	11,086.5	19,589.0	20,880.5	21,818.5	21,195.1	20,967.3	22,015.4	10,965.62
Latvia	0.1	2.1	4.0	9.0	11.3	13.3	10.9	10.3	11.4	10,878.56
Lithuania	0.1	21.1	39.8	68.0	77.3	90.1	81.9	76.3	84.1	10,441.96
Macedonia	0.4	145.7	215.0	295.2	331.6	390.7	375.2	383.7	409.7	4,502.59
Moldova										
Montenegro										
Poland	42.0	315.8	680.5	912.9	994.3	1,081.0	1,147.3	1,180.2	1,268.8	11,210.70
Romania	0.1	6.2	71.2	252.7	304.9	395.6	375.4	385.4	412.8	6,320.29
Russia	0.4	1,084.9	4,384.5	17,912.2	22,198.1	27,235.8	29,627.0	33,143.8	38,409.1	9,143.84
Serbia		48.3	365.9	1,925.4	2,213.7	2,529.9	2,734.6	2,903.7	3,224.4	6,043.87
Slovakia	7.8	15.2	26.0	43.3	48.4	53.7	54.2	56.0	58.4	15,058.31
Slovenia	0.7	9.7	16.8	26.8	29.2	32.0	31.7	32.0	32.6	22,138.58
Ukraine	0.0	37.2	121.7	464.0	604.8	826.6	843.4	978.8	1,212.0	3,333.99

Source: Euromonitor International from national statistics

Gross Income by Source 2011

% of gross income

	Benefits	Employment	Investments	Other Sources	Total
Western Europe					
Austria	21.18	50.15	14.35	14.32	100.00
Belgium	20.73	55.38	22.26	1.63	100.00
Cyprus					
Denmark	23.97	63.35	9.90	2.78	100.00
Finland	21.90	59.18	11.37	7.55	100.00
France	21.81	54.40	14.00	0.16	100.00
Germany	20.46	52.37	17.31	9.87	100.00
Gibraltar					
Greece	22.79	38.85	15.28	23.08	100.00
Iceland					
Ireland	24.45	56.41	14.94	4.20	100.00
Italy	21.66	42.84	19.05	16.45	100.00
Liechtenstein					
Luxembourg					
Malta					
Monaco					
Netherlands	22.20	61.86	11.44	4.50	100.00
Norway	20.92	63.63	14.20	1.26	100.00
Portugal	20.70	52.71	22.45	4.14	100.00
Spain	17.03	51.92	8.37	22.68	100.00
Sweden	20.25	62.03	8.67	9.05	100.00
Switzerland	21.99	61.05	12.64	4.33	100.00
Turkey	10.89	54.32	13.44	21.35	100.00
United Kingdom	20.85	57.34	13.60	8.20	100.00
Eastern Europe					
Albania					
Belarus	14.09	65.19	9.18	11.54	100.00
Bosnia-Herzegovina					
Bulgaria	14.47	57.47	12.89	15.18	100.00
Croatia	17.81	69.98	1.01	11.20	100.00
Czech Republic	18.67	58.74	5.05	17.54	100.00
Estonia	17.25	64.39	5.08	13.29	100.00
Georgia	14.81	52.76	1.25	31.18	100.00
Hungary	21.74	56.72	10.04	11.49	100.00
Latvia	15.68	60.52	5.99	17.82	100.00
Lithuania	16.41	48.19	23.67	11.74	100.00
Macedonia	20.05	68.83	8.28	2.84	100.00
Moldova					
Montenegro					
Poland	18.40	44.99	6.19	30.42	100.00
Romania	15.23	52.56	23.87	8.34	100.00
Russia	16.17	62.81	8.39	12.63	100.00
Serbia	18.27	45.29	10.27	26.17	100.00
Slovakia	16.32	48.09	31.75	3.83	100.00
Slovenia	20.64	59.88	7.23	12.25	100.00
Ukraine	23.09	57.83	14.83	4.25	100.00

Source: Euromonitor International from national statistics

Income Statistics **Table 17.3**

Tax and Social Security Contributions 1990, 1995, 2000, 2006-2011

National currency billion / US$ per capita

	1990	1995	2000	2006	2007	2008	2009	2010	2011	US$ per capita
Western Europe										
Austria	39.2	50.0	60.9	71.9	75.7	80.1	79.3	82.2	85.7	14,183.46
Belgium	58.0	74.2	89.4	108.4	112.9	119.3	119.2	124.0	129.0	16,381.35
Cyprus										
Denmark	216.4	261.2	319.2	388.8	406.8	407.0	414.8	435.8	443.7	14,886.25
Finland	27.6	30.7	39.5	47.6	50.1	52.6	50.8	51.6	53.6	13,876.70
France	315.1	380.8	462.6	574.2	592.4	610.7	609.3	620.1	636.4	14,016.79
Germany	176.3	208.3	229.7	210.9	239.0	265.0	234.2	236.2	249.7	4,246.43
Gibraltar										
Greece	6.7	14.2	26.4	40.5	45.5	48.3	48.4	48.6	46.7	5,729.78
Iceland										
Ireland	8.4	11.1	19.4	33.4	36.3	35.1	31.1	30.7	30.4	9,433.43
Italy	206.8	275.2	340.3	425.5	449.3	474.4	467.1	473.2	476.7	10,933.20
Liechtenstein										
Luxembourg										
Malta										
Monaco										
Netherlands	99.6	123.2	155.4	199.1	209.6	222.5	221.9	222.9	225.5	18,827.02
Norway	193.1	240.2	356.8	484.8	536.8	594.4	611.7	634.2	681.0	24,690.14
Portugal	11.7	19.1	27.9	37.3	38.8	40.7	40.8	42.3	42.1	5,496.70
Spain	87.7	125.4	170.5	261.0	288.0	295.9	283.9	287.2	292.0	8,796.48
Sweden	579.1	639.1	886.4	1,044.5	1,089.7	1,070.0	1,034.5	1,068.3	1,069.0	17,479.88
Switzerland	55.2	59.8	66.0	67.8	74.5	79.5	74.8	82.8	84.2	12,045.77
Turkey	0.1	1.5	27.4	110.8	120.5	133.0	130.0	151.7	179.4	1,457.20
United Kingdom	163.3	208.3	277.4	399.2	411.3	422.9	430.5	435.8	450.2	11,543.54
Eastern Europe										
Albania										
Belarus	0.0	18.5	1,465.1	13,971.1	16,566.4	21,866.7	23,802.7	28,293.8	44,781.1	949.45
Bosnia-Herzegovina	0.0	0.3	1.7	3.1	3.6	4.1	4.0	4.4	4.6	852.77
Bulgaria	0.0	0.2	4.7	6.7	7.9	9.3	8.4	8.5	9.1	859.06
Croatia	0.1	21.6	37.4	57.2	64.0	69.3	66.4	66.0	67.8	2,873.62
Czech Republic	126.9	354.3	538.3	827.7	910.1	928.1	889.9	903.1	918.2	4,948.46
Estonia	0.8	0.7	1.1	2.5	3.2	3.4	3.0	2.9	3.2	3,337.85
Georgia	0.0	-0.1	0.2	1.0	1.0	0.8	0.9	0.9	1.3	181.98
Hungary	423.1	1,366.9	3,183.3	5,760.1	6,498.9	6,977.9	6,543.4	6,355.9	6,674.6	3,324.53
Latvia	0.0	0.5	0.9	2.1	2.8	3.1	2.4	2.3	2.5	2,394.78
Lithuania	0.0	3.7	8.0	14.2	17.1	19.8	16.1	14.8	16.4	2,040.96
Macedonia	0.0	13.7	20.5	29.7	34.4	41.7	41.9	43.9	46.9	515.72
Moldova										
Montenegro										
Poland	6.7	74.4	156.4	219.9	251.9	277.6	291.4	290.8	313.9	2,773.59
Romania	0.0	1.2	13.7	52.2	63.2	76.5	76.5	84.6	90.6	1,387.34
Russia	0.1	178.5	854.4	3,069.3	3,881.7	4,951.4	5,224.7	5,835.1	6,766.8	1,610.94
Serbia		12.8	101.1	495.7	474.9	525.2	518.5	549.7	609.5	1,142.46
Slovakia	2.0	4.2	6.5	11.2	12.5	14.1	13.7	14.1	14.8	3,805.52
Slovenia	0.2	2.7	4.5	7.5	8.2	9.2	9.1	9.1	9.2	6,270.43
Ukraine	0.0	9.3	24.7	100.0	133.1	190.7	179.7	208.7	259.9	714.90

Source: Euromonitor International from national statistics

Income Statistics

Table 17.4

Disposable Income (Annual) 1990, 1995, 2000, 2006-2011

National currency billion / US$ per capita

	1990	1995	2000	2006	2007	2008	2009	2010	2011	US$ per capita
Western Europe										
Austria	83.4	106.0	118.5	148.2	154.9	161.9	161.3	167.0	173.1	28,634.92
Belgium	107.8	137.4	157.2	188.2	198.1	209.0	212.9	215.3	224.1	28,451.31
Cyprus										
Denmark	427.7	496.7	583.1	748.3	774.0	794.3	793.1	837.5	855.6	28,708.26
Finland	48.6	53.8	66.8	87.6	93.1	98.7	101.7	105.6	110.2	28,506.40
France	663.2	784.8	913.3	1,159.4	1,218.7	1,259.3	1,267.1	1,292.1	1,325.9	29,204.27
Germany	965.1	1,233.9	1,375.5	1,552.0	1,589.4	1,639.6	1,624.1	1,662.1	1,738.0	29,559.43
Gibraltar										
Greece	33.7	69.4	101.3	149.9	169.7	173.2	179.2	180.4	172.7	21,196.18
Iceland										
Ireland	21.9	28.7	51.8	82.8	88.9	93.0	90.0	88.4	87.4	27,109.25
Italy	535.4	680.0	796.8	998.4	1,031.7	1,048.6	1,021.3	1,032.0	1,053.1	24,152.84
Liechtenstein										
Luxembourg										
Malta										
Monaco										
Netherlands	139.4	165.2	207.9	263.9	275.9	278.7	276.3	280.2	283.6	23,671.31
Norway	369.0	483.1	665.7	878.9	948.1	1,013.1	1,077.3	1,139.8	1,201.2	43,549.29
Portugal	38.2	63.1	86.7	109.8	115.2	120.1	119.7	124.5	124.0	16,212.56
Spain	217.3	300.6	415.9	625.8	665.2	705.2	711.4	693.7	705.3	21,247.19
Sweden	704.6	920.8	1,052.5	1,359.7	1,457.2	1,534.0	1,608.4	1,653.5	1,725.5	28,213.56
Switzerland	204.2	244.8	276.4	314.0	329.4	338.5	342.1	350.4	356.1	50,940.60
Turkey	0.3	5.5	117.4	533.6	600.0	662.5	679.3	786.2	922.3	7,489.38
United Kingdom	351.9	491.7	640.0	817.2	845.8	884.1	882.9	924.8	952.1	24,412.47
Eastern Europe										
Albania										
Belarus	0.0	70.2	5,185.3	43,540.1	54,690.4	69,632.2	79,806.7	94,864.6	150,143.9	3,183.34
Bosnia-Herzegovina	0.0	3.0	11.1	17.6	19.5	21.9	21.0	19.2	19.7	3,637.21
Bulgaria	0.0	0.6	14.7	25.8	29.7	33.1	31.5	31.9	34.3	3,246.26
Croatia	0.2	63.1	99.4	176.8	188.8	202.7	194.4	194.9	200.7	8,512.39
Czech Republic	333.7	893.0	1,300.6	1,771.3	1,890.9	2,025.4	2,059.3	2,074.4	2,090.4	11,265.51
Estonia	2.0	2.0	3.5	6.6	8.0	8.7	8.1	8.0	8.7	9,004.60
Georgia	0.0	3.1	5.6	11.3	12.6	15.3	15.3	16.1	18.6	2,515.80
Hungary	1,194.8	3,774.7	7,903.2	13,829.0	14,381.8	14,840.6	14,651.8	14,611.4	15,340.0	7,641.09
Latvia	0.0	1.6	3.0	6.9	8.4	10.2	8.5	8.1	8.9	8,483.77
Lithuania	0.1	17.3	31.8	53.8	60.2	70.3	65.8	61.4	67.7	8,401.00
Macedonia	0.4	132.0	194.4	265.4	297.2	348.9	333.3	339.8	362.7	3,986.87
Moldova										
Montenegro										
Poland	35.2	241.3	524.1	693.0	742.4	803.4	856.0	889.5	954.9	8,437.11
Romania	0.1	5.0	57.5	200.5	241.6	319.1	298.9	300.8	322.2	4,932.95
Russia	0.3	906.5	3,530.1	14,842.9	18,316.4	22,284.4	24,402.2	27,308.7	31,642.3	7,532.90
Serbia		35.5	264.8	1,429.7	1,738.8	2,004.7	2,216.1	2,354.0	2,614.9	4,901.42
Slovakia	5.8	11.0	19.5	32.1	35.9	39.6	40.4	41.9	43.7	11,252.79
Slovenia	0.5	7.0	12.2	19.3	21.0	22.8	22.7	22.9	23.4	15,868.15
Ukraine	0.0	27.9	97.0	364.1	471.7	635.9	663.7	770.1	952.1	2,619.10

Source: Euromonitor International from national statistics

17

Income and Deductions

Income Statistics **Table 17.5**

Net Savings 1990, 1995, 2000, 2006-2011

National currency billion / US$ per capita

	1990	1995	2000	2006	2007	2008	2009	2010	2011	US$ per capita
Western Europe										
Austria	8.5	11.6	7.0	11.4	13.7	16.5	14.0	14.4	13.9	2,292.71
Belgium	16.6	26.9	25.1	28.0	30.5	32.6	37.3	31.3	34.1	4,334.97
Cyprus										
Denmark	10.8	-16.9	-23.7	-27.1	-34.4	-33.2	-8.2	0.6	4.8	161.63
Finland	4.7	5.8	4.1	5.5	6.3	7.2	11.8	11.1	10.3	2,654.40
France	84.2	123.9	131.2	172.8	188.2	195.6	209.3	207.1	215.4	4,745.12
Germany	164.6	195.4	211.7	246.5	267.1	285.3	269.9	268.5	291.1	4,951.41
Gibraltar										
Greece	1.3	1.9	4.4	7.8	17.3	7.2	14.5	14.6	13.8	1,689.69
Iceland										
Ireland	1.3	1.3	3.1	5.3	4.1	7.3	15.3	14.9	14.7	4,546.66
Italy	135.0	127.9	82.6	122.7	126.5	122.6	110.8	97.0	90.7	2,079.29
Liechtenstein										
Luxembourg										
Malta										
Monaco										
Netherlands	19.7	15.9	0.6	13.7	16.6	13.3	17.8	17.6	17.8	1,487.39
Norway	22.1	33.5	51.8	25.5	36.7	55.0	98.0	102.2	125.5	4,549.57
Portugal	3.3	7.3	7.9	8.1	8.0	8.7	13.5	14.2	14.3	1,870.82
Spain	30.8	35.5	45.2	68.3	70.1	92.9	129.2	96.3	96.0	2,893.53
Sweden	13.8	49.5	-25.2	17.5	43.6	77.2	125.4	94.1	114.7	1,875.05
Switzerland	21.8	29.0	22.4	28.3	32.5	28.8	29.1	29.7	31.1	4,447.34
Turkey	-0.1	-1.6	-0.1	-1.2	-1.3	-1.4	-1.4	-1.5	-1.3	-10.93
United Kingdom	8.9	43.0	24.6	-0.7	-16.0	7.9	22.6	20.8	17.4	446.13
Eastern Europe										
Albania										
Belarus	0.0	2.2	173.4	3,949.4	5,788.7	4,057.8	5,937.3	7,649.7	12,107.2	256.70
Bosnia-Herzegovina	0.0	-0.1	-0.4	-0.4	-0.4	-0.5	-0.6	-0.6	-0.6	-109.11
Bulgaria	0.0	0.0	-3.9	-9.0	-11.6	-12.7	-11.4	-10.9	-11.1	-1,046.83
Croatia	0.0	-13.0	-8.7	6.7	2.3	3.1	3.9	4.0	4.8	203.13
Czech Republic	27.7	116.3	137.7	166.8	171.2	168.8	206.8	202.6	197.1	1,062.01
Estonia	0.4	0.5	0.1	-0.6	-0.5	0.0	0.8	0.7	0.8	796.95
Georgia	0.0	0.1	0.2	0.5	0.7	0.8	0.7	0.7	0.8	103.63
Hungary	200.0	716.2	914.9	1,459.2	1,018.0	855.1	1,083.5	757.2	860.0	428.34
Latvia	0.0	0.0	0.1	-0.3	-0.6	0.3	0.6	0.1	0.2	179.02
Lithuania	0.0	0.3	2.0	-0.1	-3.4	-3.1	2.5	0.5	0.3	38.48
Macedonia	0.0	12.6	19.9	15.8	19.4	21.1	21.9	20.9	20.6	226.65
Moldova										
Montenegro										
Poland	8.5	40.6	54.3	40.1	40.5	29.0	45.9	33.1	32.7	289.33
Romania	0.0	0.1	3.0	-32.6	-31.8	-8.8	-5.5	-25.9	-27.7	-424.84
Russia	0.0	186.7	234.9	1,868.2	2,284.7	2,317.0	3,431.4	3,856.9	4,460.9	1,061.98
Serbia		-1.4	-27.8	-63.0	24.8	-18.9	72.9	71.2	48.1	90.11
Slovakia	0.6	1.1	2.2	1.2	2.0	2.0	2.8	4.2	4.7	1,205.49
Slovenia	0.1	0.9	1.8	3.2	3.2	3.5	3.1	2.8	2.8	1,874.56
Ukraine	0.0	0.8	3.9	43.8	47.5	52.4	80.8	82.3	93.2	256.30

Source: Euromonitor International from national statistics

Table 17.6

Savings Ratio 1990, 1995, 2000, 2006-2011

% of personal disposable income

	1990	1995	2000	2006	2007	2008	2009	2010	2011
Western Europe									
Austria	10.1	10.9	5.9	7.7	8.8	10.2	8.7	8.6	8.0
Belgium	15.4	19.6	16.0	14.9	15.4	15.6	17.5	14.5	15.2
Cyprus									
Denmark	2.5	-3.4	-4.1	-3.6	-4.4	-4.2	-1.0	0.1	0.6
Finland	9.7	10.8	6.2	6.2	6.8	7.3	11.6	10.5	9.3
France	12.7	15.8	14.4	14.9	15.4	15.5	16.5	16.0	16.2
Germany	17.1	15.8	15.4	15.9	16.8	17.4	16.6	16.2	16.8
Gibraltar									
Greece	4.0	2.8	4.3	5.2	10.2	4.2	8.1	8.1	8.0
Iceland									
Ireland	6.1	4.4	6.1	6.4	4.6	7.9	17.0	16.9	16.8
Italy	25.2	18.8	10.4	12.3	12.3	11.7	10.9	9.4	8.6
Liechtenstein									
Luxembourg									
Malta									
Monaco									
Netherlands	14.1	9.6	0.3	5.2	6.0	4.8	6.5	6.3	6.3
Norway	6.0	6.9	7.8	2.9	3.9	5.4	9.1	9.0	10.4
Portugal	8.6	11.6	9.2	7.4	6.9	7.3	11.3	11.4	11.5
Spain	14.2	11.8	10.9	10.9	10.5	13.2	18.2	13.9	13.6
Sweden	2.0	5.4	-2.4	1.3	3.0	5.0	7.8	5.7	6.6
Switzerland	10.7	11.8	8.1	9.0	9.9	8.5	8.5	8.5	8.7
Turkey	-27.8	-29.1	-0.1	-0.2	-0.2	-0.2	-0.2	-0.2	-0.1
United Kingdom	2.5	8.7	3.8	-0.1	-1.9	0.9	2.6	2.2	1.8
Eastern Europe									
Albania									
Belarus	16.8	3.2	3.3	9.1	10.6	5.8	7.4	8.1	8.1
Bosnia-Herzegovina	-3.6	-1.7	-3.8	-2.4	-2.2	-2.4	-2.7	-3.1	-3.0
Bulgaria	17.3	-2.7	-26.6	-34.7	-38.9	-38.4	-36.2	-34.1	-32.2
Croatia	-23.4	-20.6	-8.8	3.8	1.2	1.5	2.0	2.1	2.4
Czech Republic	8.3	13.0	10.6	9.4	9.1	8.3	10.0	9.8	9.4
Estonia	20.1	24.6	3.6	-9.3	-6.2	0.2	9.7	9.0	8.9
Georgia	0.8	2.5	4.1	4.7	5.3	4.9	4.5	4.3	4.1
Hungary	16.7	19.0	11.6	10.6	7.1	5.8	7.4	5.2	5.6
Latvia	1.6	-0.9	2.4	-4.5	-7.5	2.7	7.1	1.7	2.1
Lithuania	2.0	1.5	6.2	-0.2	-5.6	-4.4	3.8	0.7	0.5
Macedonia	7.8	9.5	10.2	5.9	6.5	6.0	6.6	6.2	5.7
Moldova									
Montenegro									
Poland	24.0	16.8	10.4	5.8	5.5	3.6	5.4	3.7	3.4
Romania	0.6	2.7	5.2	-16.3	-13.2	-2.8	-1.8	-8.6	-8.6
Russia	8.9	20.6	6.7	12.6	12.5	10.4	14.1	14.1	14.1
Serbia		-4.1	-10.5	-4.4	1.4	-0.9	3.3	3.0	1.8
Slovakia	9.9	10.1	11.3	3.8	5.7	5.0	6.9	10.0	10.7
Slovenia	12.0	12.9	14.5	16.4	15.1	15.4	13.8	12.3	11.8
Ukraine	15.5	3.0	4.0	12.0	10.1	8.2	12.2	10.7	9.8

Source: Euromonitor International from national statistics

17

Income and Deductions

18

Industry

Industry Statistics   **Table 18.1**

General Industrial Production Indices 1980, 1985, 1990, 1995, 1999-2011

1995 = 100

	1980	1985	1990	1995	1999	2000	2001	2002
Western Europe								
Austria	68.1	74.2	89.0	100.0	123.1	134.1	138.8	140.2
Belgium	80.9	84.1	99.4	100.0	109.8	115.5	120.9	121.3
Cyprus	63.0	73.3	97.2	100.0	100.9	105.4	105.1	105.2
Denmark	66.3	80.2	86.2	100.0	107.8	115.5	117.3	118.8
Finland	65.7	76.2	87.3	100.0	133.4	144.5	144.9	147.2
France	87.9	86.1	100.4	100.0	110.7	114.4	115.4	113.8
Germany			100.0	100.0	108.8	114.5	114.6	113.5
Gibraltar								
Greece	91.9	98.4	101.8	100.0	114.2	122.5	118.4	118.8
Iceland								
Ireland	34.4	44.0	63.1	100.0	174.9	199.7	223.8	242.6
Italy	82.0	79.5	93.5	100.0	104.2	107.7	106.8	105.3
Liechtenstein								
Luxembourg	68.1	82.4	98.0	100.0	116.3	122.1	126.4	129.4
Malta								
Monaco								
Netherlands	79.1	83.9	92.2	100.0	106.5	110.0	111.3	112.5
Norway	49.7	60.1	78.6	100.0	107.2	110.7	109.8	109.2
Portugal	62.3	73.5	100.6	100.0	110.2	118.1	120.4	121.0
Spain	81.0	83.4	97.2	100.0	114.6	119.3	118.1	118.1
Sweden	73.6	81.0	89.2	100.0	113.5	119.9	119.0	119.2
Switzerland	79.9	82.3	97.0	100.0	111.3	121.7	120.5	114.3
Turkey		60.0	85.5	100.0	114.3	121.2	109.0	119.3
United Kingdom	76.5	82.6	94.1	100.0	105.0	107.2	105.7	104.1
Eastern Europe								
Albania				100.0	59.7	121.3	91.3	75.6
Belarus			169.2	100.0	152.4	164.3	174.0	181.9
Bosnia-Herzegovina								
Bulgaria	143.4	177.8	166.1	100.0	72.2	78.2	80.0	83.8
Croatia			178.3	100.0	112.7	114.5	121.4	127.5
Czech Republic			131.8	100.0	102.0	105.7	113.9	118.6
Estonia			207.0	100.0	118.6	135.9	148.0	160.7
Georgia								
Hungary	111.7	122.9	113.8	100.0	143.9	168.4	175.4	181.3
Latvia			260.4	100.0	107.6	104.9	116.1	124.2
Lithuania			197.2	100.0	102.5	110.1	123.8	132.3
Macedonia			207.5	100.0	106.7	110.4	99.3	94.0
Moldova								
Montenegro								
Poland	99.9	98.9	80.8	100.0	133.4	143.5	145.0	147.2
Romania	148.6	183.5	152.7	100.0	77.7	83.2	86.6	86.3
Russia			202.4	100.0	96.7	105.2	108.3	111.8
Serbia				100.0	91.7	102.1	102.2	104.1
Slovakia			125.3	100.0	112.5	117.4	121.7	130.4
Slovenia			124.7	100.0	105.2	111.8	115.2	118.1
Ukraine			190.8	100.0	95.9	109.0	123.1	131.1

Source: Euromonitor International from national statistics
Note: Indices based on value of production (or contribution to GDP) at constant prices

General Industrial Production Indices 1980, 1985, 1990, 1995, 1999-2011 *(continued)*

1995 = 100

	2003	2004	2005	2006	2007	2008	2009	2010	2011
Western Europe									
Austria	142.8	152.9	158.9	170.4	180.6	185.0	163.4	174.9	188.1
Belgium	125.3	131.4	134.3	138.7	146.2	148.3	131.0	142.3	148.3
Cyprus	113.6	115.7	116.8	117.7	123.2	127.4	117.3	116.4	107.8
Denmark	119.1	117.4	120.3	125.3	123.0	122.0	103.8	105.8	107.8
Finland	147.4	155.2	153.8	169.7	177.7	180.2	148.2	156.3	158.0
France	112.4	114.8	114.8	115.4	117.0	114.1	99.7	104.8	107.4
Germany	114.1	119.0	122.6	129.3	136.8	138.0	115.7	128.7	138.6
Gibraltar									
Greece	119.4	120.2	118.4	119.5	122.2	117.0	106.6	99.5	90.7
Iceland									
Ireland	257.2	261.2	272.1	281.4	297.3	291.0	278.2	300.1	300.8
Italy	104.1	105.4	103.6	106.9	109.8	106.0	86.8	93.1	92.7
Liechtenstein									
Luxembourg	136.2	143.7	146.9	149.7	149.0	141.5	118.8	131.3	128.1
Malta									
Monaco									
Netherlands	110.9	116.2	116.7	119.1	124.2	125.4	115.9	125.0	124.3
Norway	106.7	106.4	106.7	104.5	103.3	103.8	99.8	94.1	89.6
Portugal	119.7	115.0	110.9	114.4	114.8	110.2	100.9	102.7	100.5
Spain	119.8	122.4	122.8	127.3	130.4	121.3	102.5	103.5	101.8
Sweden	121.0	127.8	131.1	135.1	140.0	136.7	112.4	123.2	130.8
Switzerland	114.6	119.7	123.5	133.7	147.1	149.3	136.8	145.6	147.8
Turkey	129.7	142.4	162.7	174.8	187.6	187.1	169.9	192.4	210.2
United Kingdom	103.8	104.8	104.0	104.0	104.5	101.7	92.6	94.3	93.1
Eastern Europe									
Albania	70.5	72.2	72.1	75.0	65.5	85.0	84.0	101.6	86.8
Belarus	194.8	225.8	249.7	277.6	301.6	335.8	325.3	363.5	396.4
Bosnia-Herzegovina									
Bulgaria	94.7	106.9	114.3	121.4	133.1	134.3	111.0	112.0	119.0
Croatia	131.7	136.0	142.2	148.3	155.8	157.9	143.2	141.4	139.6
Czech Republic	120.7	133.4	138.5	150.1	166.3	163.8	142.1	156.6	167.1
Estonia	178.5	197.1	218.7	240.7	256.3	244.0	186.9	230.6	272.0
Georgia									
Hungary	193.6	208.9	223.0	245.2	264.9	265.7	219.7	242.8	256.7
Latvia	133.9	143.8	154.0	164.3	166.2	161.4	132.5	152.1	166.0
Lithuania	150.6	168.3	180.5	193.0	198.1	209.3	179.1	190.9	206.0
Macedonia	98.4	96.2	103.0	109.1	113.3	119.1	108.8	103.6	107.0
Moldova									
Montenegro									
Poland	160.0	180.9	187.5	210.1	229.9	236.8	228.3	253.6	271.3
Romania	85.7	88.0	85.4	93.2	103.0	105.8	100.3	105.8	112.0
Russia	122.4	132.3	139.0	147.8	158.1	159.6	144.9	157.1	164.7
Serbia	101.0	107.6	108.2	112.8	117.4	119.1	104.0	106.6	108.9
Slovakia	150.7	156.3	155.0	179.3	209.6	217.2	188.1	222.9	239.3
Slovenia	119.7	125.7	130.0	137.5	147.5	151.2	126.0	134.0	137.0
Ukraine	151.9	170.3	175.4	189.7	204.3	194.8	155.1	172.5	186.1

Source: Euromonitor International from national statistics
Note: Indices based on value of production (or contribution to GDP) at constant prices

Industry Statistics

Table 18.2

Manufacturing Production Indices 1980, 1985, 1990, 1995, 1999-2011

1995 = 100

	1980	1985	1990	1995	1999	2000	2001	2002
Western Europe								
Austria	66.5	72.5	88.7	100.0	124.9	137.3	139.9	139.9
Belgium	74.4	77.4	94.0	100.0	109.7	116.2	116.1	117.1
Cyprus		79.7	103.3	100.0	96.3	100.1	98.2	95.8
Denmark	64.8	79.1	86.2	100.0	109.7	115.6	117.9	119.1
Finland	66.1	76.7	87.0	100.0	130.9	147.9	147.2	150.1
France	93.7	91.9	102.2	100.0	111.5	116.3	117.6	116.0
Germany			100.0	100.0	109.4	116.3	116.8	115.5
Gibraltar								
Greece	99.4	100.3	102.2	100.0	109.2	114.8	111.9	111.8
Iceland								
Ireland	31.6	41.4	61.6	100.0	180.4	208.8	230.5	247.8
Italy	83.1	79.8	93.9	100.0	103.6	106.7	105.8	103.8
Liechtenstein								
Luxembourg	69.4	84.7	99.0	100.0	117.7	123.6	126.7	128.9
Malta								
Monaco								
Netherlands	73.3	79.9	92.9	100.0	109.2	113.8	113.6	113.7
Norway	80.8	88.9	89.7	100.0	106.2	103.0	101.9	96.7
Portugal	69.5	81.3	104.3	100.0	114.4	114.8	117.4	117.9
Spain	81.3	82.2	96.8	100.0	115.8	119.7	117.3	117.8
Sweden	73.7	81.0	89.1	100.0	114.6	121.8	120.6	121.8
Switzerland	79.2	81.6	97.0	100.0	112.8	123.2	121.8	115.4
Turkey		65.2	90.5	100.0	113.9	121.3	109.8	121.8
United Kingdom	80.7	83.9	97.7	100.0	104.1	106.6	105.2	102.4
Eastern Europe								
Albania				100.0	77.7	116.0	77.6	53.6
Belarus			170.9	100.0	154.2	167.0	176.4	184.3
Bosnia-Herzegovina								
Bulgaria				100.0	69.7	74.7	75.7	81.3
Croatia			188.0	100.0	105.4	108.5	115.4	120.5
Czech Republic			162.9	100.0	107.9	108.2	116.2	118.6
Estonia			215.5	100.0	124.7	145.3	160.1	174.1
Georgia								
Hungary	115.4	126.9	116.4	100.0	154.7	186.8	194.6	201.6
Latvia			261.8	100.0	103.6	108.4	116.5	123.8
Lithuania			216.0	100.0	102.8	111.9	129.6	133.3
Macedonia								
Moldova								
Montenegro								
Poland	93.8	90.9	75.7	100.0	142.4	153.7	153.5	156.3
Romania			159.7	100.0	78.5	85.1	93.7	99.7
Russia			230.4	100.0	96.9	107.5	109.7	110.8
Serbia				100.0	94.7	108.4	109.3	112.5
Slovakia			127.9	100.0	106.7	116.6	128.1	138.8
Slovenia			126.1	100.0	105.3	112.7	115.9	118.1
Ukraine			201.2	100.0	97.1	113.2	132.7	144.5

Source: Euromonitor International from national statistics
Note: Indices based on value of production (or contribution to GDP) at constant prices

Manufacturing Production Indices 1980, 1985, 1990, 1995, 1999-2011 *(continued)*

1995 = 100

	2003	2004	2005	2006	2007	2008	2009	2010	2011
Western Europe									
Austria	143.0	154.5	160.6	172.0	182.8	186.5	161.7	173.6	186.0
Belgium	117.7	126.0	127.6	131.9	138.9	141.3	121.8	133.2	139.9
Cyprus	94.3	95.9	95.2	94.6	99.2	103.5	91.6	88.8	81.6
Denmark	117.4	115.0	118.6	125.1	126.4	126.1	104.4	106.8	111.8
Finland	150.6	160.5	162.3	176.2	186.6	190.2	151.6	159.0	162.3
France	114.0	116.3	116.2	117.0	119.0	115.4	99.1	103.8	107.6
Germany	115.9	121.1	125.1	132.4	140.6	142.0	117.5	131.6	143.3
Gibraltar									
Greece	111.2	111.9	109.9	112.1	114.5	109.1	97.1	92.1	83.4
Iceland									
Ireland	261.9	265.5	276.3	285.4	301.2	292.3	281.0	304.2	305.6
Italy	101.9	102.6	100.1	103.4	106.4	102.8	82.9	88.6	88.0
Liechtenstein									
Luxembourg	136.3	145.3	148.7	151.2	150.8	143.3	118.5	131.1	129.1
Malta									
Monaco									
Netherlands	112.6	116.8	119.3	123.5	130.9	129.0	117.9	126.1	130.2
Norway	92.9	94.3	96.6	101.8	107.4	110.9	104.1	106.8	108.3
Portugal	115.7	112.3	105.1	108.2	109.3	105.0	94.4	96.4	95.4
Spain	119.3	121.2	120.8	125.6	128.8	118.7	98.5	99.1	97.7
Sweden	124.9	131.0	133.8	140.3	145.0	140.1	112.8	123.1	131.8
Switzerland	115.4	120.9	124.8	135.2	148.8	150.8	138.0	146.9	148.8
Turkey	133.1	146.9	153.9	165.0	176.1	173.2	153.8	175.9	192.0
United Kingdom	102.1	104.7	104.5	106.3	107.1	104.3	94.3	97.7	99.4
Eastern Europe									
Albania	54.7	56.5	62.5	66.0	70.6	82.5	95.2	107.7	120.7
Belarus	197.2	229.4	253.5	285.1	313.8	352.1	342.4	381.7	423.0
Bosnia-Herzegovina									
Bulgaria	95.6	111.3	119.9	130.3	142.7	143.8	111.6	116.0	121.8
Croatia	124.4	128.7	136.2	141.6	149.8	151.4	135.3	132.5	132.3
Czech Republic	119.6	134.9	141.8	155.3	174.5	171.9	145.7	162.4	175.9
Estonia	192.6	214.9	240.1	265.3	281.2	268.4	200.0	239.9	296.3
Georgia									
Hungary	217.0	235.8	253.9	281.5	305.1	303.1	247.5	277.0	292.9
Latvia	134.6	143.5	154.5	164.4	164.9	159.1	127.0	147.9	165.2
Lithuania	148.1	167.0	181.3	195.1	200.0	213.1	179.9	194.6	214.9
Macedonia									
Moldova									
Montenegro									
Poland	172.8	198.0	207.0	236.6	262.3	270.4	261.3	294.0	316.1
Romania	98.6	101.7	98.1	110.3	123.7	127.6	119.3	126.4	133.5
Russia	120.4	133.2	143.2	155.2	171.6	172.4	146.2	163.4	174.0
Serbia	107.4	116.2	115.1	120.3	125.9	127.3	106.8	110.9	110.5
Slovakia	168.7	174.6	172.2	208.3	252.5	259.6	219.1	263.0	286.3
Slovenia	120.1	125.3	130.2	138.3	150.0	153.9	125.3	133.5	134.9
Ukraine	171.0	194.4	199.6	211.0	232.5	218.1	160.3	182.6	197.4

Source: Euromonitor International from national statistics
Note: Indices based on value of production (or contribution to GDP) at constant prices

Industry Statistics   **Table 18.3**

Mining Production Indices 1980, 1985, 1990, 1995, 1999-2011
1995 = 100

	1980	1985	1990	1995	1999	2000	2001	2002
Western Europe								
Austria	107.0	117.7	111.5	100.0	107.4	112.3	109.6	113.1
Belgium			69.0	100.0	125.2	138.1	139.5	182.2
Cyprus			82.2	100.0	130.2	135.3	128.9	143.6
Denmark			103.1	100.0	93.5	93.8	92.3	88.2
Finland			94.9	100.0	128.1	99.4	120.0	131.1
France			116.0	100.0	86.8	88.4	87.4	83.0
Germany	57.2	104.7	100.0	100.0	85.5	79.6	74.3	73.2
Gibraltar								
Greece	155.3	153.7	120.9	100.0	96.4	109.3	111.9	122.7
Iceland								
Ireland	65.6	65.6	85.7	100.0	92.9	114.7	114.6	109.0
Italy			87.6	100.0	107.8	98.4	90.8	106.2
Liechtenstein								
Luxembourg			103.4	100.0	107.8	108.8	109.9	100.0
Malta								
Monaco								
Netherlands			89.1	100.0	99.5	97.2	104.1	104.5
Norway			94.1	100.0	109.8	115.7	119.2	117.2
Portugal			114.3	100.0	102.2	103.8	105.8	100.2
Spain			101.9	100.0	90.1	91.1	88.2	87.7
Sweden			95.0	100.0	96.4	97.8	95.5	96.9
Switzerland				100.0	93.5	94.2	94.7	93.3
Turkey			95.5	100.0	109.6	106.6	98.0	90.0
United Kingdom			73.3	100.0	108.6	105.1	99.3	99.7
Eastern Europe								
Albania				100.0	41.4	36.4	32.1	31.8
Belarus				100.0	123.9	117.5	130.6	134.7
Bosnia-Herzegovina								
Bulgaria				100.0	78.6	80.7	73.7	73.3
Croatia			132.1	100.0	96.1	97.8	99.8	116.8
Czech Republic	125.0	137.5	144.7	100.0	81.6	88.2	88.9	89.7
Estonia	268.8	236.5	195.7	100.0	87.0	91.7	95.0	109.7
Georgia								
Hungary			192.3	100.0	75.3	68.2	79.4	71.9
Latvia	579.9	168.2	257.7	100.0	123.9	134.9	141.4	154.2
Lithuania				100.0	177.1	198.1	263.1	250.8
Macedonia								
Moldova								
Montenegro								
Poland			108.8	100.0	83.2	82.1	77.9	75.5
Romania			120.5	100.0	76.1	79.8	84.4	80.0
Russia			141.2	100.0	98.7	105.0	111.3	118.8
Serbia				100.0	86.0	93.8	81.9	83.6
Slovakia			233.6	100.0	103.8	101.4	88.1	113.3
Slovenia			132.3	100.0	97.8	95.2	87.7	94.4
Ukraine			201.2	100.0	98.3	104.6	108.0	110.5

Source: Euromonitor International from national statistics
Note: Indices based on value of production (or contribution to GDP) at constant prices

Mining Production Indices 1980, 1985, 1990, 1995, 1999-2011 *(continued)*

1995 = 100

	2003	2004	2005	2006	2007	2008	2009	2010	2011
Western Europe									
Austria	112.9	107.2	105.1	116.3	116.3	124.3	115.9	121.2	113.4
Belgium	173.8	173.2	184.5	191.1	202.2	208.6	177.3	187.1	190.4
Cyprus	149.9	156.9	162.9	162.0	174.0	188.7	153.5	168.5	154.6
Denmark	86.9	91.3	95.4	89.6	80.7	79.4	71.5	68.3	62.3
Finland	125.1	98.1	119.3	152.5	118.8	121.4	107.5	111.7	118.8
France	81.3	81.3	79.0	81.3	81.9	80.2	70.8	70.3	70.4
Germany	72.7	71.1	69.7	66.5	86.4	76.8	64.7	59.5	54.8
Gibraltar									
Greece	118.4	117.8	109.2	106.1	105.7	101.0	89.1	83.3	83.3
Iceland									
Ireland	134.5	134.8	136.5	139.1	134.6	125.9	109.8	102.4	83.6
Italy	108.2	105.9	114.0	112.0	104.8	96.5	84.7	83.5	84.8
Liechtenstein									
Luxembourg	88.9	89.9	86.9	68.7	70.4	69.1	61.7	48.8	59.1
Malta									
Monaco									
Netherlands	101.3	112.3	92.3	89.9	89.8	97.2	90.1	100.6	92.4
Norway	116.0	114.4	110.8	105.8	101.0	100.3	97.4	89.0	82.0
Portugal	95.7	105.7	100.7	90.1	101.2	106.6	85.3	79.4	80.1
Spain	87.8	83.6	80.3	82.6	83.2	71.8	54.4	56.8	48.5
Sweden	96.1	104.7	110.3	111.6	118.9	119.4	100.6	128.8	134.1
Switzerland	92.6	96.5	91.5	100.3	106.5	99.1	101.8	115.3	111.0
Turkey	86.9	90.4	102.9	110.7	119.6	129.5	128.5	131.2	135.2
United Kingdom	94.6	87.7	80.1	74.0	72.2	67.5	61.5	58.3	49.5
Eastern Europe									
Albania	28.7	27.2	25.9	30.2	35.3	40.5	39.6	62.5	104.3
Belarus	147.4	160.8	173.5	178.8	181.8	183.9	189.4	208.0	211.3
Bosnia-Herzegovina									
Bulgaria	77.8	91.4	90.5	91.2	84.0	79.4	67.5	68.4	74.0
Croatia	119.5	115.7	112.2	123.7	127.3	125.0	111.5	101.3	96.2
Czech Republic	89.2	87.3	84.5	84.5	83.6	81.1	80.3	80.1	81.1
Estonia	115.6	105.3	116.9	127.8	141.2	130.0	116.7	132.2	142.9
Georgia									
Hungary	70.7	77.5	74.6	85.9	71.0	96.0	85.3	66.6	77.2
Latvia	162.8	181.2	214.5	235.5	265.1	258.9	210.8	239.6	259.7
Lithuania	270.1	240.7	214.0	210.6	210.4	192.8	125.0	137.0	151.1
Macedonia									
Moldova									
Montenegro									
Poland	74.1	76.4	74.2	74.9	72.6	73.2	63.6	64.8	66.2
Romania	79.7	80.4	78.7	80.6	79.3	79.3	69.8	65.0	67.9
Russia	129.3	138.2	140.1	144.0	148.8	149.4	148.5	153.8	156.8
Serbia	84.3	85.0	88.0	91.7	91.9	96.8	93.1	98.4	108.7
Slovakia	103.8	111.4	95.3	92.3	106.5	95.1	96.6	97.0	93.4
Slovenia	99.8	87.8	89.9	96.7	102.1	107.7	104.6	116.1	107.4
Ukraine	116.4	121.3	125.5	132.9	136.2	130.3	116.5	120.8	129.6

Source: Euromonitor International from national statistics
Note: Indices based on value of production (or contribution to GDP) at constant prices

19

CHAPTER NINETEEN

IT and
Telecommunications

IT and Telecommunications Statistics

Table 19.1

Internet Users 1990, 1995, 2000, 2006-2011

'000

	1990	1995	2000	2006	2007	2008	2009	2010	2011
Western Europe									
Austria	10.0	150.1	2,699.1	5,249.7	5,745.9	6,061.8	6,136.9	6,295.7	6,706.6
Belgium	0.1	100.5	3,013.5	6,277.4	6,820.7	7,040.1	7,527.2	8,129.9	8,542.0
Cyprus		3.5	143.9	374.8	432.2	454.7	542.6	584.8	643.8
Denmark	5.0	199.5	2,087.9	4,702.9	4,631.7	4,655.5	4,786.1	4,910.4	4,995.9
Finland	20.0	708.7	1,926.2	4,186.6	4,262.7	4,434.9	4,393.7	4,649.9	4,805.8
France	29.9	946.0	8,420.1	28,668.9	40,670.7	43,896.4	44,701.0	50,280.3	50,179.6
Germany	99.6	1,498.5	24,826.8	59,487.3	61,867.9	64,129.9	64,781.9	67,011.6	67,579.2
Gibraltar			5.2	13.2	15.1	17.0	19.0	19.0	19.0
Greece	0.0	79.4	996.5	3,587.9	4,008.4	4,283.7	4,774.4	5,019.5	6,002.7
Iceland	0.0	30.0	125.1	269.6	277.1	282.6	293.3	304.1	307.9
Ireland	0.0	39.9	674.3	2,306.9	2,611.2	2,875.8	2,998.4	3,120.8	3,442.2
Italy	9.9	298.1	13,155.5	22,319.8	24,119.7	26,548.5	29,324.1	32,423.3	34,459.8
Liechtenstein			11.8	22.4	22.9	24.7	26.7	28.7	30.7
Luxembourg		6.5	99.7	338.4	376.1	400.1	433.9	459.8	467.3
Malta		0.9	52.1	165.8	193.2	207.1	244.3	262.4	289.4
Monaco	0.1	7.6	14.8	21.7	22.7	23.8	24.8	26.6	27.3
Netherlands	49.8	998.4	6,977.7	13,671.7	14,038.4	14,341.6	14,776.2	15,036.8	15,372.1
Norway	29.9	279.3	2,328.8	3,830.5	4,069.3	4,290.5	4,419.2	4,537.1	4,623.6
Portugal	0.0	149.7	1,675.1	4,017.5	4,199.4	4,448.8	4,941.7	5,435.9	5,882.2
Spain	5.0	149.8	5,456.8	22,041.0	24,510.0	26,988.8	28,596.8	30,260.8	31,199.4
Sweden	49.8	449.5	4,048.6	7,940.3	7,473.8	8,264.6	8,423.3	8,406.6	8,568.2
Switzerland	39.8	249.3	3,374.5	5,646.6	5,796.7	6,014.0	6,261.6	6,532.3	6,704.6
Turkey		48.4	2,397.7	12,560.2	19,952.0	24,260.5	26,032.2	28,859.0	30,864.2
United Kingdom	49.9	1,098.1	15,767.2	41,562.5	45,667.3	47,963.7	48,057.6	48,333.3	51,053.6
Eastern Europe									
Albania		0.4	3.5	302.6	475.2	757.4	1,314.1	1,441.9	1,575.2
Belarus		0.3	186.4	1,579.6	1,913.7	2,228.7	2,653.0	3,069.6	3,812.0
Bosnia-Herzegovina			40.6	965.4	1,073.2	1,332.3	1,450.9	1,999.1	2,306.2
Bulgaria		9.9	428.8	2,091.0	2,583.3	3,030.9	3,422.9	3,496.7	3,833.5
Croatia		24.0	295.1	1,687.4	1,840.4	2,244.8	2,495.6	2,669.6	3,119.8
Czech Republic		150.0	1,001.2	4,913.3	5,342.1	6,524.4	6,715.2	7,198.4	7,651.5
Estonia		40.2	392.1	854.0	888.5	946.4	971.8	993.0	1,025.2
Georgia		0.6	21.5	331.3	363.0	438.6	880.1	1,180.7	1,606.2
Hungary	0.0	70.0	715.5	4,742.0	5,365.3	5,625.4	4,814.9	5,307.6	5,891.6
Latvia			150.5	1,189.3	1,294.8	1,370.9	1,427.9	1,441.9	1,487.1
Lithuania			225.7	1,494.0	1,689.1	1,858.9	2,001.9	2,068.0	2,110.6
Macedonia		0.8	49.7	583.4	741.2	941.6	1,060.6	1,065.4	1,166.3
Moldova		0.2	52.7	731.4	754.3	853.9	993.5	1,154.0	1,351.2
Montenegro				179.8	191.6	204.6	218.1	232.8	248.0
Poland	0.0	247.9	2,787.6	17,010.4	18,529.0	20,250.8	22,488.7	23,785.9	24,777.2
Romania		16.7	792.5	5,329.1	6,102.9	6,979.6	7,868.5	8,569.9	9,430.7
Russia		219.9	2,904.4	25,845.4	35,278.4	38,349.0	41,446.5	61,473.8	70,027.9
Serbia				2,019.7	2,452.3	2,622.1	2,794.6	2,988.4	3,070.0
Slovakia		28.0	507.0	3,011.7	3,319.2	3,549.7	3,767.1	4,081.0	4,017.3
Slovenia		57.7	300.4	1,082.0	1,140.7	1,175.0	1,300.7	1,432.9	1,476.1
Ukraine		22.1	351.8	2,106.6	3,043.5	5,081.2	8,227.4	10,667.3	13,953.0

Source: Euromonitor International from national statistics

Table 19.2

Dial-Up Internet Subscribers 2000-2011

'000

	2000	2001	2002	2003	2004	2005	2006	2007	2008	2009	2010	2011
Western Europe												
Austria	258.8	858.3	750.0	896.4	763.6	597.6	472.7	377.8	318.0	303.0	246.3	187.3
Belgium	1,006.0	964.5	879.0	666.2	412.8	272.8	107.4	146.4	93.3	71.0	42.6	32.2
Cyprus	52.0	62.5	73.1	66.5	64.3	59.1	42.7	33.0	12.4	14.9	12.1	8.5
Denmark	1,617.2	1,785.5	2,129.7	964.3	665.0	465.0	308.3	197.5	128.3	90.3	74.6	49.6
Finland	581.0	816.0	783.5	827.3	600.0	538.1	467.6	363.7	295.4	225.1	154.5	93.4
France	5,248.0	6,385.0	7,405.0	7,047.6	5,378.0	3,746.0	2,541.0	1,500.0	980.0	600.0	500.0	329.8
Germany	12,735.0	11,900.0	11,795.0	12,530.0	12,000.0	9,213.2	8,429.6	7,193.3	5,753.9	4,713.2	3,599.3	2,527.3
Gibraltar												
Greece	271.3	288.0	394.0	520.0	648.6	722.1	466.6	244.2	237.5	63.4	25.5	18.2
Iceland	44.6	39.6	26.6	10.2	10.3	9.1	10.5	8.0	6.9	6.4	7.1	6.4
Ireland	550.0	829.0	1,097.4	1,158.2	664.3	603.0	475.1	449.3	359.1	233.5	133.2	66.9
Italy	5,685.0	11,610.0	12,150.0	14,550.0	12,425.5	10,877.8	3,281.0	2,077.0	7.0	16.6	340.0	13.4
Liechtenstein												
Luxembourg	24.5	41.0	64.2	92.3	76.5	48.9	31.6	27.9	0.0	0.0	0.0	0.0
Malta												
Monaco												
Netherlands	5,651.0	4,033.8	3,329.0	3,012.0	2,094.0	1,500.0	777.8	111.0	0.0	0.0	0.0	0.0
Norway	1,152.4	1,146.9	1,197.9	888.7	746.6	429.4	268.0	166.0	31.8	15.1	10.2	2.7
Portugal	627.2	560.3	406.3	403.0	394.9	271.0	156.4	99.3	29.9	96.8	94.7	88.7
Spain	3,146.0	3,207.4	2,677.0	2,558.9	1,851.7	1,199.1	768.2	601.2	340.3	153.2	124.7	83.6
Sweden	1,999.0	2,232.0	2,192.0	2,148.0	1,883.0	1,562.0	1,106.0	801.8	490.3	340.0	244.1	168.4
Switzerland	1,609.0	2,059.7	1,881.8	1,947.1	1,023.0	916.1	776.9	419.5	204.0	108.0	82.0	59.1
Turkey	460.2	669.4	918.6	995.9	933.2	663.3	406.4	124.9	79.3	0.0	0.0	0.0
United Kingdom	8,368.0	11,029.1	10,929.3	11,327.7	9,376.8	6,421.7	3,943.0	2,694.0	1,299.3	1,016.2	1,398.0	1,088.9
Eastern Europe												
Albania												
Belarus	4.7	8.1	18.1	22.6	29.8	36.0	396.0	827.8	1,120.1	538.2	378.2	257.5
Bosnia-Herzegovina	14.9	15.7	86.8	126.5	162.3	167.6	197.9	189.1	147.7	142.4	127.6	111.1
Bulgaria	5.5	6.5	7.4	6.2	12.4	18.6	24.7	13.2	6.6	1.0	0.9	0.1
Croatia	187.0	331.4	538.0	566.6	828.7	837.6	817.9	790.3	835.9	813.3	759.4	632.3
Czech Republic	415.9	1,250.5	1,629.1	2,113.9	1,893.1	1,643.4	295.4	94.9	34.5	14.5	8.1	2.2
Estonia	79.6	69.1	74.5	47.0	32.6	17.8	11.9	6.4	6.6	3.6	1.3	0.7
Georgia	2.7	2.7	2.7	2.7	89.2	175.6	135.0	41.0	34.3	26.5	0.2	0.1
Hungary	217.0	290.3	334.4	391.4	369.6	325.1	92.9	63.0	24.7	23.4	14.1	7.6
Latvia	33.2	40.3	27.7	27.5	18.1	12.3	6.4	0.0	0.0	0.0	0.0	0.0
Lithuania	53.2	56.1	59.2	47.2	44.6	23.3	11.4	5.8	3.8	0.6	0.4	0.3
Macedonia	30.0	45.6	61.1	76.7	92.2	95.4	129.5	173.1	107.4	3.0	1.7	1.1
Moldova												
Montenegro	7.8	13.6	22.8	33.8	53.3	73.3	62.8	69.6	61.5	53.5	45.8	39.4
Poland	930.0	1,128.1	1,484.2	2,531.5	1,635.3	1,741.3	333.1	296.2	379.6	238.2	2.5	1.5
Romania	99.9	300.1	350.0	448.6	823.6	412.9	340.0	201.9	0.0	0.0	0.0	0.0
Russia	492.2	1,027.5	1,879.5	7,269.4	12,659.3	17,467.2	21,878.1	31,518.7	38,779.4	46,800.0	50,147.9	52,616.9
Serbia	228.1	298.1	385.4	503.4	583.9	723.2	883.4	685.9	392.7	252.2	59.7	39.0
Slovakia	68.0	100.1	130.0	159.7	151.9	112.6	90.7	71.9	56.1	46.4	36.9	31.0
Slovenia	138.5	274.5	205.4	186.4	231.5	201.1	127.4	72.7	29.4	28.9	20.7	15.4
Ukraine	67.3	120.2	229.0	1,402.7	2,576.3	3,620.0	2,042.3	574.6	305.1	742.7	706.6	657.1

Source: Euromonitor International from national statistics

19

IT and Telecommunications

IT and Telecommunications Statistics

Table 19.3

Broadband Internet Subscribers 2000-2011

'000

	2000	2001	2002	2003	2004	2005	2006	2007	2008	2009	2010	2011
Western Europe												
Austria	190.5	320.6	451.0	601.0	870.0	1,174.0	1,432.0	1,622.0	1,729.0	1,846.0	2,076.0	2,229.0
Belgium	144.2	460.0	815.4	1,242.9	1,619.9	2,010.6	2,451.6	2,715.3	2,962.5	3,134.1	3,373.1	3,543.8
Cyprus	0.0	2.5	5.9	10.0	17.1	31.9	63.1	97.6	147.3	176.0	194.5	201.8
Denmark	67.0	238.0	451.3	718.3	1,017.6	1,343.9	1,735.3	1,882.0	1,984.9	2,040.9	2,092.4	2,129.6
Finland	35.0	134.0	273.5	491.1	800.0	1,174.2	1,429.0	1,617.0	1,591.9	1,533.8	1,572.7	1,588.7
France	196.6	601.5	1,655.0	3,569.4	6,561.0	9,471.0	12,711.0	15,750.0	17,830.0	19,900.0	21,300.0	22,800.0
Germany	265.0	2,100.0	3,205.0	4,470.0	7,000.0	10,786.8	14,977.2	19,687.0	22,643.6	24,891.8	26,089.8	26,679.4
Gibraltar												
Greece	0.0	0.0	0.0	10.5	51.5	160.1	488.2	1,017.5	1,506.6	1,916.6	2,257.1	2,464.3
Iceland	2.4	10.4	24.3	41.6	55.8	78.0	87.7	97.9	103.7	107.1	107.0	110.0
Ireland	0.0	0.0	10.6	41.8	152.1	322.5	561.7	636.2	769.7	870.6	941.4	999.3
Italy	115.0	390.0	850.0	2,250.0	4,724.5	6,822.2	8,497.4	10,122.1	11,276.3	12,283.4	13,060.0	13,886.0
Liechtenstein												
Luxembourg	0.0	1.2	5.8	15.4	36.5	70.1	98.9	128.7	143.2	156.1	168.4	169.8
Malta												
Monaco												
Netherlands	260.0	466.2	1,171.0	1,988.0	3,206.0	4,100.0	5,192.2	5,507.0	5,805.0	6,129.0	6,329.0	6,456.0
Norway	23.3	88.5	205.3	398.8	671.7	991.3	1,244.5	1,436.0	1,577.9	1,668.8	1,723.7	1,800.0
Portugal	25.2	99.3	260.6	502.0	838.4	1,165.4	1,423.7	1,512.4	1,613.7	1,911.8	2,126.7	2,239.7
Spain	76.4	466.6	1,247.5	2,121.9	3,401.4	5,035.2	6,739.1	7,990.4	9,054.2	9,706.7	10,534.5	10,925.8
Sweden	249.0	587.0	840.0	1,095.0	1,410.0	2,522.0	2,489.0	2,775.6	2,898.9	2,941.6	2,987.0	2,999.0
Switzerland	56.4	140.0	455.2	783.9	1,227.4	1,669.2	2,050.2	2,380.5	2,556.2	2,739.1	2,911.5	3,019.0
Turkey	0.0	10.9	21.2	199.3	577.9	1,589.8	2,773.7	4,753.8	5,749.9	6,456.4	7,079.8	7,575.9
United Kingdom	52.9	331.0	1,356.5	3,113.7	6,123.9	9,898.7	13,013.0	15,606.0	17,274.0	18,222.0	19,130.0	20,438.0
Eastern Europe												
Albania												
Belarus	0.0	0.0	0.0	0.1	0.8	1.6	11.4	169.8	477.8	1,092.3	1,665.9	2,097.3
Bosnia-Herzegovina	0.0	0.1	0.2	1.5	6.6	13.7	40.0	84.7	188.5	236.2	307.5	430.2
Bulgaria	0.0	0.0	0.0	0.0	6.7	165.5	384.7	629.1	818.6	958.2	1,088.3	1,154.8
Croatia	0.0	0.0	0.0	3.4	26.2	116.2	251.8	387.1	524.7	685.0	803.8	858.0
Czech Republic	2.5	6.2	15.3	34.7	236.0	709.1	1,112.5	1,496.7	1,759.6	1,355.0	1,521.0	1,650.0
Estonia	3.0	26.7	46.5	90.3	138.7	179.2	246.8	277.8	317.9	339.3	336.3	363.9
Georgia	0.0	0.4	0.9	1.4	1.9	2.4	27.0	46.7	112.1	150.0	253.9	329.2
Hungary	3.4	31.4	111.5	264.3	411.1	651.7	1,199.2	1,381.8	1,681.1	1,879.2	2,057.8	2,208.1
Latvia	0.3	3.2	10.0	19.5	49.1	60.8	109.7	320.7	395.6	437.0	434.9	457.4
Lithuania	0.1	2.4	20.0	66.8	129.1	234.1	368.7	507.6	590.1	564.3	684.1	732.0
Macedonia	0.0	0.0	0.0	0.0	0.0	12.4	36.5	100.5	181.0	218.7	256.9	271.8
Moldova												
Montenegro	0.0	0.0	0.0	0.0	0.0	7.7	25.8	16.1	34.2	53.1	52.4	65.0
Poland	0.0	12.0	121.7	195.8	875.9	945.2	2,911.2	4,174.0	3,985.4	4,798.1	4,960.5	5,500.0
Romania	1.0	6.0	15.8	196.1	104.3	377.1	1,090.0	1,920.0	2,490.0	2,800.0	3,000.0	3,300.0
Russia	0.0	0.0	11.0	343.0	675.0	1,589.0	2,900.0	4,900.0	9,280.0	12,900.0	15,700.0	17,423.1
Serbia	0.0	0.0	0.0	0.0	16.1	33.5	121.7	325.7	457.2	590.6	858.2	879.1
Slovakia	0.0	0.0	4.1	22.5	78.8	181.5	304.6	472.0	519.9	627.7	694.4	746.7
Slovenia	1.5	5.5	56.7	58.0	115.1	196.7	279.8	344.7	425.3	452.0	481.8	503.8
Ukraine	0.0	0.0	0.0	0.0	0.0	130.0	520.0	800.0	1,600.0	1,906.7	2,954.6	3,168.3

Source: Euromonitor International from national statistics

Table 19.4

Personal Computers in Use 1990, 1995, 2000, 2006-2011

'000

	1990	1995	2000	2006	2007	2008	2009	2010	2011
Western Europe									
Austria	500	1,300	2,900	5,389	5,783	6,115	6,405	6,653	6,866
Belgium	876	1,800	2,300	4,241	4,527	4,811	5,092	5,372	5,651
Cyprus	5	35	150	324	353	383	413	443	474
Denmark	590	1,400	2,700	3,962	4,150	4,333	4,511	4,659	4,797
Finland	500	1,200	2,050	2,776	2,927	3,081	3,237	3,393	3,549
France	4,000	8,500	17,920	40,000	43,333	46,508	49,248	51,450	53,382
Germany	6,500	14,600	27,640	54,000	58,009	61,811	65,237	68,279	70,949
Gibraltar			15	19	20	20	21	22	23
Greece	175	350	750	1,045	1,121	1,203	1,291	1,386	1,487
Iceland	10	55	110	160	174	185	197	210	228
Ireland	300	660	1,360	2,480	2,702	2,826	2,932	3,045	3,164
Italy	2,100	4,800	10,300	24,050	26,647	29,222	31,566	33,843	36,024
Liechtenstein									
Luxembourg			200	318	330	342	354	366	379
Malta	5	30	80	135	144	153	163	172	181
Monaco									
Netherlands	1,400	3,100	6,300	14,900	16,308	17,657	18,922	19,633	20,157
Norway		1,193	2,200	2,931	3,159	3,326	3,495	3,659	3,817
Portugal	260	550	1,050	1,719	1,831	1,965	2,057	2,221	2,398
Spain	1,100	2,400	7,000	16,000	18,083	20,032	22,088	24,099	26,039
Sweden	900	2,200	4,500	8,000	8,372	8,670	8,919	9,125	9,296
Switzerland	600	2,000	4,700	6,630	6,924	7,191	7,589	7,790	7,963
Turkey	300	920	2,500	4,400	4,806	5,237	5,690	6,167	6,655
United Kingdom	6,200	11,800	20,190	48,600	53,008	56,574	58,848	60,983	62,644
Eastern Europe									
Albania			25	120	130	145	158	172	187
Belarus				85	91	98	105	113	121
Bosnia-Herzegovina				242	254	274	295	316	336
Bulgaria		140	361	604	707	791	854	980	1,069
Croatia		100	499	1,051	1,110	1,190	1,270	1,350	1,430
Czech Republic	120	550	1,250	3,416	3,748	4,079	4,389	4,689	4,981
Estonia			220	321	341	342	363	386	410
Georgia			112	225	251	271	293	315	337
Hungary	100	400	870	1,845	2,153	2,290	2,435	2,590	2,755
Latvia		20	340	748	784	848	912	976	1,040
Lithuania		24	240	620	677	772	875	938	1,003
Macedonia				540	806	850	900	954	994
Moldova		9	64	424	518	631	710	789	864
Montenegro									
Poland	300	1,100	2,670	6,456	6,967	7,531	8,113	8,713	9,333
Romania	50	300	713	3,200	3,712	3,967	4,240	4,531	4,842
Russia	500	2,600	9,300	19,000	21,277	23,766	26,448	29,310	32,312
Serbia				1,700	2,053	2,152	2,286	2,429	2,580
Slovakia		220	740	2,320	2,698	3,146	3,483	3,786	4,041
Slovenia		200	548	816	885	942	999	1,056	1,114
Ukraine	100	430	890	2,121	2,318	2,530	2,761	3,013	3,279

Source: Euromonitor International from national statistics

IT and Telecommunications Statistics

Table 19.5

ISDN Subscribers 1990, 1995, 2000, 2006-2011

'000

	1990	1995	2000	2006	2007	2008	2009	2010	2011
Western Europe									
Austria		17	347	418	393	363	344	318	293
Belgium		28	430	399	391	378	357	342	328
Cyprus			7	26	26	25	23	21	20
Denmark		14	376	283	249	214	175	161	148
Finland		6	208	105	101	83	77	70	65
France	7	284	1,700	2,911	2,764	2,664	2,591	2,519	2,429
Germany	16	961	7,465	12,800	13,000	12,570	12,056	11,753	11,491
Gibraltar				1	1	1	1	1	1
Greece			101	604	586	554	523	495	468
Iceland			17	15	13	12	11	10	9
Ireland			43	108	107	104	95	88	84
Italy		49	1,954	3,092	3,191	3,275	3,349	3,408	3,459
Liechtenstein		1	6	8	8	9	9	9	9
Luxembourg		2	41	80	83	81	80	79	79
Malta				2	2	2	3	3	3
Monaco			4	5	5	5	5	5	5
Netherlands		24	1,185	1,297	1,207	1,116	1,041	998	976
Norway		12	704	514	445	389	338	305	273
Portugal		8	195	268	259	244	215	199	182
Spain		11	646	1,129	1,134	1,133	1,119	1,110	1,105
Sweden		13	273	160	146	133	115	105	96
Switzerland		69	726	863	822	784	742	699	658
Turkey			7	15	15	17	17	17	17
United Kingdom	2	117	860	872	822	740	705	650	592
Eastern Europe									
Albania				1	1	1	1	1	1
Belarus			1	3	4	4	4	5	5
Bosnia-Herzegovina			1	26	31	33	33	35	38
Bulgaria			4	20	22	24	24	25	27
Croatia			27	127	116	105	96	90	83
Czech Republic			26	161	161	159	144	138	132
Estonia			9	51	42	33	29	26	25
Georgia									
Hungary			104	200	196	190	173	165	157
Latvia			6	28	32	33	34	36	38
Lithuania			3	16	17	17	15	15	14
Macedonia			3	16	15	15	13	13	12
Moldova			1	5	11	12	15	16	18
Montenegro				32	32	32	32	32	32
Poland			57	1,231	1,358	1,187	1,134	1,073	1,033
Romania				17	18	19	17	17	17
Russia			64	101	105	109	112	115	118
Serbia				68	79	84	87	90	93
Slovakia			12	47	80	72	67	62	61
Slovenia		1	55	231	210	182	153	143	133
Ukraine									

Source: Euromonitor International from national statistics

Table 19.6

Capital Investment in Telecommunications 1985, 1990, 1995, 2000, 2006-2011

National currency million / US$ million

	1985	1990	1995	2000	2006	2007	2008	2009	2010	2011	US$ million (latest year)
Western Europe											
Austria				918	750	878	713	518	674	657	892.60
Belgium				1,574	1,051	1,167	1,123	1,155	1,265	1,298	1,675.37
Cyprus	43	30	39	118	67	63	110	113	123	130	162.64
Denmark	2,596	3,254	3,078	9,015	7,957	8,141	8,027	8,038	7,116	6,600	1,266.27
Finland				888	444	436	437	580	630	676	834.33
France				7,841	7,015	6,140	6,529	5,965	6,400	6,246	8,475.73
Germany				9,650	6,500	7,100	7,200	6,000	5,900	5,750	7,813.56
Gibraltar											
Greece	324	296	515	2,114	805	1,294	1,371	1,347	1,088	1,019	1,440.87
Iceland	400	838	1,958	5,459	5,494	8,483	8,303	4,296	5,264	5,206	43.06
Ireland				410	408	458	516	442	443	460	586.68
Italy				7,113	6,837	7,163	6,689	6,222	6,156	5,986	8,152.59
Liechtenstein											
Luxembourg				63	93	95	88	98	92	91	121.51
Malta	4	22	14	27	43	38	41	39	37	36	48.92
Monaco											
Netherlands				3,353	4,011	4,183	4,344	4,498	4,644	4,783	6,150.64
Norway	3,581	2,747	5,129	18,718	25,725	26,563	27,350	28,067	28,692	29,260	4,747.46
Portugal				1,249	971	1,315	1,000	1,054	1,077	1,104	1,426.51
Spain				7,332	5,686	5,788	4,765	3,954	4,095	3,811	5,422.90
Sweden	5,061	6,286	7,783	22,621	10,198	10,698	9,689	9,101	7,022	6,387	974.24
Switzerland	1,814	3,077	2,156	3,794	6,487	2,762	2,278	2,292	2,178	2,022	2,088.55
Turkey		2	20	393	2,500	2,479	3,761	6,383	3,761	4,076	2,495.79
United Kingdom	1,879	2,758	4,557	10,971	6,879	6,349	5,819	5,133	3,680	3,385	5,603.69
Eastern Europe											
Albania		30	476	2,640	5,402	6,106	9,045	11,984	14,922	16,209	143.57
Belarus			482	39,390	789,080	1,039,200	1,023,200	1,140,200	1,464,267	1,577,618	491.61
Bosnia-Herzegovina			20	111	246	167	273	292	250	251	169.28
Bulgaria			3	115	815	1,053	792	571	800	779	541.30
Croatia		2	2,079	1,515	2,056	1,781	2,433	2,069	2,106	2,119	383.09
Czech Republic			20,000	46,430	14,171	16,153	14,879	14,546	14,970	15,217	783.87
Estonia			37	55	81	95	95	65	69	66	91.21
Georgia			17	124	281	315	364	297	229	209	128.68
Hungary	4,715	13,334	85,651	152,784	86,801	89,746	97,812	99,414	100,991	102,252	485.66
Latvia			62	44	53	77	101	126	139	151	261.74
Lithuania			120	517	526	547	454	328	359	334	137.54
Macedonia			1,604	3,033	2,199	9,898	7,823	3,496	3,131	2,898	67.36
Moldova			64	425	1,184	1,927	1,963	1,750	1,725	1,658	139.47
Montenegro											
Poland		160	2,149	5,953	7,586	7,479	7,372	8,003	7,210	7,116	2,391.63
Romania				2,794	3,040	3,690	2,760	2,400	2,302	755.22	
Russia		3	4,491	16,698	78,712	310,400	234,157	147,893	192,066	210,094	6,324.72
Serbia			294	3,554	15,010	36,633	45,792	26,992	27,728	29,606	356.72
Slovakia			144	193	352	387	403	391	359	350	475.53
Slovenia			75	371	249	325	283	181	150	137	199.20
Ukraine			270	1,458	9,808	10,299	10,791	9,466	5,885	5,364	741.36

Source: Euromonitor International from national statistics

IT and Telecommunications Statistics | **Table 19.7**

Mobile Telephone Subscriptions 1990, 1995, 2000, 2006-2011

'000

	1990	1995	2000	2006	2007	2008	2009	2010	2011
Western Europe									
Austria	73.7	383.5	6,117.0	9,281.0	9,912.0	10,816.0	11,434.0	12,241.0	13,022.6
Belgium	42.9	235.3	5,629.0	9,847.4	10,738.1	11,341.7	11,775.2	12,154.0	12,540.6
Cyprus	3.2	44.5	218.3	867.8	988.3	1,016.7	977.5	1,034.1	1,090.9
Denmark	148.2	822.3	3,363.6	5,828.2	6,308.0	6,557.0	6,833.7	6,981.0	7,047.0
Finland	257.9	1,039.1	3,728.6	5,670.0	6,080.0	6,830.0	7,700.0	8,390.0	8,940.0
France	283.2	1,302.5	29,052.4	51,662.0	55,358.1	57,972.0	59,600.0	63,200.0	66,300.0
Germany	272.6	3,725.0	48,202.0	85,652.0	96,232.9	105,523.1	105,000.0	104,560.0	108,700.0
Gibraltar		0.7	5.6	22.0	24.0	26.0	28.6	30.0	32.5
Greece		273.0	5,932.4	10,979.8	12,294.9	13,799.3	13,295.1	12,292.7	12,128.0
Iceland	10.0	30.9	214.9	301.9	326.1	336.9	339.7	341.1	344.1
Ireland	25.0	158.0	2,461.0	4,690.1	4,970.7	5,048.1	4,704.5	4,701.5	4,906.4
Italy	266.0	3,923.0	42,246.0	80,418.0	89,801.0	90,341.0	88,024.0	90,600.0	92,300.0
Liechtenstein	0.6	9.5	10.0	28.8	32.0	34.0	35.0	35.5	37.0
Luxembourg	0.8	26.8	303.3	713.0	684.5	707.0	720.0	727.0	765.0
Malta	1.1	10.8	114.4	346.8	368.5	385.6	422.1	455.6	521.7
Monaco	0.4	3.0	13.9	18.3	20.4	22.0	23.0	23.4	30.4
Netherlands	79.0	539.0	10,755.0	17,296.0	19,285.0	20,627.0	20,149.0	19,179.0	19,835.0
Norway	196.8	981.3	3,224.0	4,868.9	5,037.7	5,211.2	5,359.6	5,648.7	5,750.0
Portugal	6.5	340.8	6,665.0	12,226.4	13,477.4	14,049.2	11,795.1	12,210.4	12,284.6
Spain	54.7	945.0	24,265.1	45,695.1	48,422.5	49,623.3	51,083.9	51,601.0	53,066.8
Sweden	461.2	2,008.0	6,372.3	9,607.0	10,116.9	10,014.0	10,440.0	10,885.4	11,194.0
Switzerland	125.0	447.2	4,638.5	7,436.2	8,208.9	8,896.7	9,322.6	9,644.2	10,017.0
Turkey	31.8	437.1	16,133.4	52,662.7	61,975.8	65,824.1	62,779.6	61,769.6	65,321.7
United Kingdom	1,114.0	5,735.8	43,452.0	70,077.9	73,836.2	76,735.4	80,255.4	81,115.5	81,612.0
Eastern Europe									
Albania		1.8	29.8	1,909.9	2,322.4	1,859.6	2,463.7	2,692.4	3,100.0
Belarus		5.9	49.4	5,960.0	6,960.0	8,128.0	9,686.2	10,332.9	10,694.9
Bosnia-Herzegovina			93.4	1,887.8	2,450.4	3,179.0	3,257.2	3,110.2	3,171.3
Bulgaria		20.9	738.0	8,253.4	9,897.5	10,429.0	10,454.8	10,199.9	10,475.1
Croatia	0.2	33.7	1,033.0	4,395.2	5,034.6	4,554.8	4,675.0	4,928.4	5,115.1
Czech Republic		48.9	4,346.0	12,406.2	13,228.6	13,780.2	14,258.4	12,775.1	12,810.0
Estonia		30.5	557.0	1,658.7	1,681.8	1,624.5	1,570.5	1,652.8	1,863.1
Georgia		0.2	194.7	1,703.9	2,599.7	2,755.1	2,837.0	3,980.0	4,430.6
Hungary	2.6	265.0	3,076.3	9,965.7	11,029.9	12,224.2	11,792.5	12,011.8	11,689.9
Latvia		15.0	401.3	2,183.7	2,217.0	2,298.6	2,303.6	2,306.1	2,309.0
Lithuania		14.8	524.0	4,718.2	4,912.1	5,022.6	4,961.5	4,891.0	5,004.2
Macedonia			115.7	1,263.8	1,794.4	1,967.5	1,943.2	2,153.4	2,257.1
Moldova		0.0	139.0	1,358.2	1,882.8	2,423.4	2,784.8	3,165.1	3,715.0
Montenegro				643.7	703.0	1,158.0	1,294.2	1,170.0	1,213.6
Poland		75.0	6,747.0	36,745.5	41,388.8	43,926.4	44,806.6	46,952.1	49,200.0
Romania		9.1	2,499.0	15,991.0	20,400.0	24,470.0	25,100.0	24,400.0	23,400.0
Russia		88.5	3,263.2	150,674.0	171,200.0	199,522.3	230,499.5	237,689.2	256,116.6
Serbia				6,643.7	8,452.6	9,618.8	9,912.3	9,915.3	10,182.0
Slovakia		12.3	1,243.7	4,893.2	6,068.1	5,520.0	5,497.7	5,925.0	5,983.1
Slovenia		27.3	1,215.6	1,819.6	1,928.4	2,054.9	2,100.4	2,122.0	2,168.5
Ukraine		14.0	818.5	49,076.2	55,240.4	55,681.5	54,942.8	53,919.5	55,566.9

Source: Euromonitor International from national statistics

Table 19.8

Mobile Telecommunications Revenues 1990, 1995, 2000, 2006-2011

% of telecom revenue

	1990	1995	2000	2006	2007	2008	2009	2010	2011
Western Europe									
Austria			47	59	60	63	64	64	66
Belgium	2	10	48	44	42	37	36	33	31
Cyprus			32	45	51	49	46	46	44
Denmark		14	24	39	40	40	41	42	42
Finland	9	20	36	50	46	48	44	45	44
France	3	7	26	41	41	42	43	44	44
Germany			31	35	40	41	42	44	45
Gibraltar									
Greece		11	33	54	54	55	55	62	63
Iceland		10	27	47	41	37	36	34	33
Ireland			42	46	45	46	45	44	43
Italy			38	36	52	52	52	53	53
Liechtenstein									
Luxembourg	1	5	18	52	51	50	48	52	51
Malta		5	44	47	57	49	50	51	52
Monaco									
Netherlands	3	10	26	32	33	47	47	46	45
Norway		15	35	46	48	49	50	52	54
Portugal		14	41	37	40	35	36	33	32
Spain	1	5	41	46	48	48	48	48	49
Sweden	14	25	21	34	37	41	44	47	50
Switzerland		6	23	29	28	29	27	28	27
Turkey	2	7	43	56	61	54	54	64	65
United Kingdom		13	18	24	25	25	23	23	22
Eastern Europe									
Albania			27	77	82	82	79	73	72
Belarus				55	56	50	49	43	39
Bosnia-Herzegovina			22	42	43	48	47	50	51
Bulgaria				59	58	62	62	70	73
Croatia		4	28	56	56	58	57	58	58
Czech Republic		7	45	64	58	83	60	59	58
Estonia		29	47	62	60	57	52	43	38
Georgia			51	65	64	64	65	72	73
Hungary		33	30	37	40	40	42	43	45
Latvia		6	53	64	66	68	69	71	73
Lithuania			29	46	47	44	39	38	35
Macedonia			32	54	56	56	60	59	60
Moldova				42	44	44	52	56	62
Montenegro				63	61	63	64	64	65
Poland		8	24	48	50	42	43	43	44
Romania				56	45	48	45	43	42
Russia			26	47	47	48	47	47	48
Serbia				47	57	63	56	53	52
Slovakia		12	35	65	65	66	64	65	65
Slovenia			63	48	43	42	42	40	38
Ukraine			20	64	68	69	67	66	66

Source: Euromonitor International from national statistics

IT and Telecommunications Statistics   **Table 19.9**

Mobile Telephone Calls 1990, 1995, 2000, 2006-2011

Million minutes

	1990	1995	2000	2006	2007	2008	2009	2010	2011
Western Europe									
Austria			6,000	13,410	16,339	18,795	20,179	22,138	24,025
Belgium				10,498	12,242	13,685	14,105	14,581	15,212
Cyprus				1,812	2,865	3,256	3,251	3,346	3,656
Denmark	180	564	2,695	7,316	8,718	9,747	10,367	11,362	11,732
Finland		316	5,294	12,492	13,546	14,548	15,412	16,745	17,658
France			35,524	92,933	100,891	103,345	102,911	105,817	110,182
Germany			24,347	55,052	71,468	88,114	93,610	101,000	108,512
Gibraltar			5	10	11	12	14	15	17
Greece				13,478	16,182	19,926	23,023	22,061	22,453
Iceland			247	440	510	652	704	744	776
Ireland			2,228	6,112	6,672	7,900	8,648	9,127	9,837
Italy			35,719	82,131	94,454	111,829	117,239	127,560	133,522
Liechtenstein									
Luxembourg			128	386	399	569	629	798	882
Malta			33	192	223	250	308	383	454
Monaco									
Netherlands			6,739	16,075	16,383	19,386	21,107	21,453	22,562
Norway			2,880	7,579	8,945	9,625	10,911	11,570	12,060
Portugal		436	6,176	11,869	13,646	15,272	17,753	19,734	20,647
Spain			17,026	54,424	63,548	66,895	66,079	66,876	69,333
Sweden			4,742	12,642	15,631	18,078	19,760	22,036	23,454
Switzerland			3,245	5,812	4,604	5,505	6,051	7,335	7,597
Turkey				47,788	57,367	74,482	108,065	125,863	140,484
United Kingdom		5,059	35,384	82,498	101,274	112,651	120,260	126,589	130,493
Eastern Europe									
Albania				471	671	1,304	2,600	4,174	5,211
Belarus		6	87	5,009	9,040	17,275	19,626	22,417	24,624
Bosnia-Herzegovina				1,060	862	1,507	1,369	4,302	4,647
Bulgaria			136	4,749	7,659	10,578	12,118	13,547	14,701
Croatia			788	3,982	4,887	5,547	5,877	6,334	6,768
Czech Republic			2,334	9,598	10,463	12,351	13,536	14,649	15,167
Estonia				1,758	2,153	2,238	2,221	2,498	2,900
Georgia									
Hungary			2,773	11,637	13,353	15,425	16,333	17,108	16,949
Latvia				2,431	2,536	2,757	2,938	3,013	3,062
Lithuania			429	3,716	4,606	5,383	5,906	6,077	6,446
Macedonia			77	667	1,015	1,770	2,279	2,677	2,967
Moldova				659	1,129	2,277	3,035	3,667	4,554
Montenegro									
Poland				26,238	34,162	42,529	49,484	57,714	63,012
Romania			609	14,066	20,466	30,537	42,334	52,007	52,805
Russia									
Serbia				2,685	3,772	5,985	8,203	8,840	9,574
Slovakia		31	992	5,175	6,029	6,637	7,403	8,297	8,583
Slovenia			1,075	2,506	2,764	3,005	3,381	3,756	3,923
Ukraine									

Source: Euromonitor International from national statistics

Table 19.10

Mobile Telephone Calls per Mobile Telephone Subscriber 1990, 1995, 2000, 2006-2011

Minutes

	1990	1995	2000	2006	2007	2008	2009	2010	2011
Western Europe									
Austria			980.9	1,444.9	1,648.4	1,737.7	1,764.8	1,808.5	1,844.9
Belgium				1,066.1	1,140.0	1,206.6	1,197.8	1,199.7	1,213.0
Cyprus				2,088.2	2,898.7	3,202.8	3,325.4	3,236.1	3,350.9
Denmark	1,215.9	686.1	801.1	1,255.2	1,382.1	1,486.4	1,517.0	1,627.5	1,664.8
Finland		304.2	1,419.7	2,203.2	2,228.0	2,130.0	2,001.6	1,995.9	1,975.1
France			1,222.8	1,798.9	1,822.5	1,782.7	1,726.7	1,674.3	1,661.9
Germany			505.1	642.7	742.7	835.0	891.5	966.0	998.3
Gibraltar			899.2	437.9	438.8	450.7	473.6	507.5	514.5
Greece				1,227.5	1,316.2	1,444.0	1,731.7	1,794.6	1,851.4
Iceland			1,147.1	1,457.5	1,564.8	1,934.7	2,071.4	2,182.5	2,255.0
Ireland			905.3	1,303.3	1,342.2	1,564.9	1,838.2	1,941.2	2,005.0
Italy			845.5	1,021.3	1,051.8	1,237.9	1,331.9	1,407.9	1,446.6
Liechtenstein									
Luxembourg			420.8	541.4	582.6	804.1	873.3	1,097.9	1,153.5
Malta			284.5	554.3	604.5	647.1	730.8	841.5	870.2
Monaco									
Netherlands			626.6	929.4	849.5	939.8	1,047.5	1,118.6	1,137.5
Norway			893.4	1,556.7	1,775.6	1,847.0	2,035.8	2,048.3	2,097.5
Portugal		1,277.9	926.6	970.8	1,012.5	1,087.0	1,505.1	1,616.2	1,680.7
Spain			701.7	1,191.0	1,312.4	1,348.1	1,293.5	1,296.0	1,306.5
Sweden			744.2	1,315.9	1,545.0	1,805.3	1,892.7	2,024.4	2,095.3
Switzerland			699.6	781.6	560.9	618.8	649.1	760.5	758.4
Turkey				907.4	925.6	1,131.5	1,721.3	2,037.6	2,150.6
United Kingdom		882.0	814.3	1,177.2	1,371.6	1,468.0	1,498.5	1,560.6	1,598.9
Eastern Europe									
Albania				246.4	288.9	701.0	1,055.1	1,550.5	1,680.9
Belarus		1,051.4	1,768.7	840.4	1,298.9	2,125.3	2,026.1	2,169.5	2,302.4
Bosnia-Herzegovina				561.5	351.9	474.0	420.3	1,383.3	1,465.4
Bulgaria			183.8	575.3	773.9	1,014.3	1,159.1	1,328.1	1,403.4
Croatia			762.6	905.9	970.8	1,217.8	1,257.2	1,285.1	1,323.1
Czech Republic			537.1	773.7	790.9	896.3	949.3	1,146.7	1,184.0
Estonia				1,059.9	1,280.0	1,377.8	1,414.4	1,511.5	1,556.6
Georgia									
Hungary			901.4	1,167.7	1,210.6	1,261.8	1,385.1	1,424.2	1,449.9
Latvia				1,113.4	1,143.8	1,199.6	1,275.3	1,306.7	1,326.1
Lithuania			819.3	787.7	937.8	1,071.8	1,190.4	1,242.5	1,288.0
Macedonia			667.0	527.7	565.8	899.4	1,172.6	1,242.9	1,314.4
Moldova				484.9	599.7	939.7	1,089.7	1,158.6	1,225.9
Montenegro									
Poland				714.0	825.4	968.2	1,104.4	1,229.2	1,280.7
Romania			243.6	879.6	1,003.2	1,247.9	1,686.6	2,131.4	2,256.6
Russia									
Serbia				404.2	446.2	622.2	827.5	891.5	940.2
Slovakia		2,509.6	797.7	1,057.5	993.5	1,202.3	1,346.5	1,400.3	1,434.6
Slovenia			884.3	1,377.5	1,433.3	1,462.5	1,609.7	1,769.9	1,809.1
Ukraine									

Source: Euromonitor International from national statistics

IT and Telecommunications Statistics | **Table 19.11**

Telephone Lines in Use 1990, 1995, 2000, 2006-2011
'000

	1990	1995	2000	2006	2007	2008	2009	2010	2011
Western Europe									
Austria	3,223	3,797	3,997	3,605	3,407	3,285	3,253	3,398	3,388
Belgium	3,913	4,682	5,036	4,728	4,847	4,735	4,636	4,640	4,631
Cyprus	246	347	440	408	409	413	415	413	405
Denmark	2,911	3,193	3,835	3,099	2,825	2,975	2,774	2,614	2,515
Finland	2,670	2,810	2,849	1,910	1,740	1,650	1,430	1,250	1,080
France	28,085	32,400	33,987	34,125	34,800	35,100	35,400	35,300	35,300
Germany	31,887	42,000	50,220	54,400	53,100	50,300	53,700	52,800	51,800
Gibraltar	11	17	24	24	24	24	24	24	24
Greece	3,949	5,163	5,659	6,170	5,469	5,254	5,980	5,876	5,685
Iceland	130	149	196	189	187	200	190	194	190
Ireland	983	1,310	1,832	2,177	2,259	2,223	2,132	2,078	2,047
Italy	22,350	24,845	27,153	26,890	22,417	22,039	21,683	21,480	21,060
Liechtenstein	17	20	20	20	20	20	20	20	20
Luxembourg	184	229	249	248	248	261	264	272	279
Malta	128	171	204	208	230	241	243	245	229
Monaco	24	31	30	34	35	35	34	34	34
Netherlands	6,940	8,124	9,889	7,450	7,404	7,317	7,256	7,232	7,135
Norway	2,132	2,444	2,401	2,055	1,988	1,900	1,771	2,215	2,104
Portugal	2,379	3,643	4,321	4,242	4,204	4,160	4,343	4,477	4,525
Spain	12,603	15,095	17,104	19,865	20,193	20,576	20,235	20,206	19,667
Sweden	5,849	6,013	6,056	5,547	5,500	5,338	5,140	4,924	4,600
Switzerland	3,943	4,480	5,236	5,022	4,927	4,828	5,132	4,908	4,684
Turkey	6,861	13,127	18,395	18,832	18,201	17,502	16,534	16,201	15,211
United Kingdom	25,368	29,411	35,228	33,849	33,462	34,192	33,540	33,409	33,230
Eastern Europe									
Albania	40	42	153	256	300	344	363	333	339
Belarus	1,574	1,968	2,752	3,368	3,672	3,718	3,983	4,139	4,208
Bosnia-Herzegovina		238	780	989	1,064	1,031	999	999	956
Bulgaria	2,175	2,563	2,882	2,399	2,300	2,190	2,205	2,223	2,311
Croatia	823	1,287	1,721	1,831	1,847	1,878	1,859	1,866	1,761
Czech Republic	1,624	2,444	3,872	2,888	2,403	2,478	2,527	2,406	2,202
Estonia	320	412	523	452	495	498	493	482	471
Georgia	540	554	509	553	556	618	620	1,106	1,342
Hungary	996	2,157	3,798	3,360	3,251	3,094	3,069	2,977	2,933
Latvia	620	705	735	657	644	593	562	532	516
Lithuania	781	941	1,188	792	799	785	747	734	723
Macedonia	286	351	507	491	464	457	437	413	413
Moldova	462	566	584	1,018	1,080	1,115	1,139	1,161	1,180
Montenegro				168	176	174	172	170	169
Poland	3,293	5,728	10,946	11,476	10,491	9,454	8,493	7,667	6,921
Romania	2,366	2,968	3,899	4,198	4,416	4,750	4,700	4,500	4,700
Russia	20,700	25,019	32,070	43,900	45,218	45,539	45,380	44,916	44,181
Serbia				2,719	2,993	3,085	3,106	3,110	3,030
Slovakia	711	1,118	1,698	1,167	1,310	1,289	1,220	1,099	1,056
Slovenia	422	615	785	1,029	1,006	978	939	911	873
Ukraine	7,028	8,311	10,417	12,397	12,906	13,177	13,026	12,941	12,681

Source: Euromonitor International from national statistics

European Marketing Data and Statistics 2013 – © Euromonitor International Ltd 2012

Table 19.12

National Telephone Calls 1990, 1995, 2000, 2006-2011

Million minutes

	1990	1995	2000	2006	2007	2008	2009	2010	2011
Western Europe									
Austria		5,682	9,758	6,406	5,676	5,100	4,585	4,410	4,249
Belgium	6,057	7,912	22,000	11,650	11,528	10,623	9,698	8,027	6,468
Cyprus		1,783	2,026	3,410	2,905	2,421	2,193	1,665	1,561
Denmark	10,920	12,657	22,438	11,498	9,547	8,115	6,741	5,766	5,276
Finland		14,305	17,977	3,144	2,278	2,255	2,321	2,149	1,910
France	104,670	104,400	104,838	90,540	85,200	87,067	88,060	88,130	88,740
Germany	35,400	83,789	291,550	201,699	191,800	185,613	172,064	158,780	154,488
Gibraltar									
Greece	21,920	32,271	22,375	17,649	17,184	17,150	16,954	16,590	16,326
Iceland	620	864	1,923	575	520	532	510	443	396
Ireland				5,778	5,291	5,065	4,583	4,290	3,957
Italy		99,464	125,510	122,510	149,134	142,303	158,122	170,067	184,807
Liechtenstein	56	57	71	51	48	46	44	43	40
Luxembourg	208	384	1,579	907	838	640	580	547	529
Malta				518	504	542	612	734	792
Monaco									
Netherlands	7,413	31,708	57,553	20,633	20,794	19,441	17,900	17,423	16,294
Norway	8,173	11,625	22,801	8,112	6,946	5,909	4,978	4,522	4,215
Portugal	11,127	11,104	8,958	6,351	6,298	6,340	6,477	6,453	6,478
Spain	46,025	45,587	75,613	63,596	51,276	51,899	53,365	52,131	52,000
Sweden	26,620	30,711	37,101	23,838	22,255	19,513	16,692	16,223	15,585
Switzerland	14,080	14,831	17,213	12,823	12,722	11,341	10,974	9,723	9,140
Turkey				39,880	27,860	24,274	19,907	15,599	13,361
United Kingdom		116,632	132,343	105,560	96,721	89,971	83,060	75,279	68,263
Eastern Europe									
Albania		123	235	636	580	534	558	556	536
Belarus									
Bosnia-Herzegovina					2,058	1,960	1,862	1,764	1,666
Bulgaria			7,455	3,331	3,085	2,402	2,148	1,976	1,851
Croatia				3,991	3,531	4,633	4,492	3,622	3,412
Czech Republic			10,629	4,390	3,861	2,848	2,315	1,906	1,535
Estonia		119	2,302	918	951	905	831	613	542
Georgia			2,440	3,348	3,523	2,438	2,389	2,317	2,214
Hungary		6,450	11,600	6,305	5,608	5,209	4,860	4,524	3,960
Latvia		805	1,719	1,109	1,032	960	905	859	790
Lithuania		2,273	4,138	1,547	1,478	1,506	1,454	1,409	1,376
Macedonia		2,274	2,225	1,390	1,287	1,126	896	934	820
Moldova		229	2,049	3,534	3,617	3,885	4,095	4,282	4,486
Montenegro									
Poland		10,042	31,487	25,394	21,537	16,944	14,828	12,097	9,284
Romania				6,068	5,478	5,670	4,871	4,430	4,020
Russia									
Serbia				10,870	10,673	13,464	10,323	10,151	10,065
Slovakia		2,295	3,193	1,464	1,469	1,438	1,270	1,206	1,139
Slovenia				1,783	1,583	1,494	1,188	1,041	897
Ukraine									

Source: Euromonitor International from national statistics

IT and Telecommunications Statistics | **Table 19.13**

International Outgoing Telephone Calls 1990, 1995, 2000, 2006-2011

Million minutes

	1990	1995	2000	2006	2007	2008	2009	2010	2011
Western Europe									
Austria	559	901	1,087	1,236	1,192	1,110	957	900	852
Belgium	731	1,106	1,543	1,599	1,452	1,408	1,380	1,389	1,374
Cyprus	57	117	193	253	291	290	292	208	196
Denmark	368	529	707	596	527	485	462	430	404
Finland	186	314	468	155	296	437	494	539	576
France	2,126	2,850	4,952	4,823	6,650	7,980	8,800	9,700	10,513
Germany	3,146	5,238	9,223	12,262	13,380	13,080	13,773	14,467	15,018
Gibraltar	9	12	18	15	15	15	15	15	14
Greece	213	463	793	1,018	1,165	1,091	1,337	1,478	1,570
Iceland	19	29	60	40	43	28	31	26	24
Ireland	261	407	1,250	1,279	1,279	1,257	1,094	973	911
Italy	1,043	1,839	4,138	3,739	4,730	4,710	3,810	3,490	3,242
Liechtenstein	11	16	55	33	32	31	31	30	30
Luxembourg	151	232	356	351	340	340	336	307	296
Malta	13	29	43	48	44	48	58	52	53
Monaco									
Netherlands	905	1,459	2,550	1,385	1,798	1,210	1,114	1,089	1,014
Norway	281	437	559	622	629	637	622	628	630
Portugal	156	300	505	550	566	558	545	540	537
Spain	611	1,063	2,956	5,441	5,477	4,719	4,023	3,454	3,183
Sweden	631	875	1,086	869	1,083	1,125	961	898	884
Switzerland	1,332	1,733	2,624	2,256	2,411	2,030	1,922	1,804	1,695
Turkey	159	374	732	515	490	520	599	2,588	2,812
United Kingdom	2,530	4,068	7,981	5,715	5,891	7,130	6,990	7,195	7,398
Eastern Europe									
Albania	20	23	72	46	43	37	29	18	16
Belarus		132	179	330	353	409	346	419	441
Bosnia-Herzegovina		10	93	211	174	120	136	125	114
Bulgaria	62	84	110	85	126	99	96	137	150
Croatia	69	211	222	310	308	364	298	284	278
Czech Republic	83	259	360	260	207	200	189	200	198
Estonia		53	78	69	60	62	48	44	41
Georgia			60	106	195	50	90	78	71
Hungary	122	247	211	169	154	133	140	138	134
Latvia		44	58	49	49	51	54	56	57
Lithuania	17	55	39	53	51	50	47	52	52
Macedonia		45	73	28	26	26	26	24	23
Moldova		66	43	109	140	140	96	81	80
Montenegro				47	51	54	56	59	62
Poland	81	381	676	399	430	402	390	372	366
Romania	25	88	169	318	339	347	301	336	341
Russia	72	898	944	1,349	1,527	1,705	1,567	1,204	1,168
Serbia				368	323	303	269	198	181
Slovakia		59	162	250	293	386	452	509	548
Slovenia		101	102	108	114	115	111	107	105
Ukraine		422	383	389	383	362	349	331	318

Source: Euromonitor International from national statistics

20

Labour

Labour Statistics

Table 20.1

Employed Population 1980, 1990, 2000, 2005-2011

'000

	1980	1990	2000	2005	2006	2007	2008	2009	2010	2011
Western Europe										
Austria	3,085	3,421	3,773	3,824	3,928	4,027	4,090	4,077	4,097	4,172
Belgium	3,699	3,623	4,098	4,161	4,264	4,379	4,446	4,421	4,488	4,560
Cyprus	229	266	296	348	357	378	383	381	385	384
Denmark	2,321	2,631	2,733	2,764	2,815	2,802	2,849	2,775	2,718	2,729
Finland	2,232	2,494	2,354	2,419	2,464	2,492	2,531	2,458	2,447	2,474
France	21,599	22,504	23,862	25,068	25,053	25,468	25,811	25,578	25,619	25,767
Germany		36,056	36,288	36,575	37,351	38,191	38,852	38,763	38,734	39,339
Gibraltar	12	14	12	13	13	13	13	13	13	13
Greece	3,504	3,453	3,980	4,370	4,446	4,509	4,559	4,508	4,387	4,137
Iceland			156	160	168	175	177	166	166	174
Ireland	1,262	1,133	1,662	1,951	2,043	2,116	2,094	1,914	1,840	1,830
Italy	20,626	21,275	21,338	22,569	22,985	23,219	23,409	23,022	22,871	23,029
Liechtenstein			27	30	31	32	33	35	35	36
Luxembourg			173	193	196	203	202	217	221	220
Malta	120	127	141	147	152	156	160	161	164	165
Monaco			12							
Netherlands	5,754	6,581	7,813	7,871	8,093	8,306	8,446	8,451	8,265	8,345
Norway	1,904	2,031	2,273	2,290	2,362	2,443	2,516	2,498	2,498	2,531
Portugal	4,160	4,519	5,016	5,123	5,160	5,170	5,198	5,054	4,978	4,866
Spain	11,557	12,579	15,905	18,969	19,745	20,356	20,261	18,885	18,454	18,269
Sweden	3,933	4,575	4,242	4,353	4,429	4,538	4,591	4,496	4,547	4,625
Switzerland		3,575	3,858	3,959	4,031	4,099	4,202	4,234	4,260	4,329
Turkey	18,959	19,309	21,719	20,925	19,967	20,363	20,799	20,815	22,180	22,791
United Kingdom		26,784	27,320	28,655	28,927	29,111	29,358	28,916	28,939	29,071
Eastern Europe										
Albania			1,067	1,136	1,140	1,150	1,160	1,160	1,173	1,179
Belarus			4,443	4,359	4,418	4,474	4,573	4,604	4,633	4,679
Bosnia-Herzegovina				812	811	849	890	858	844	835
Bulgaria			2,919	2,975	3,096	3,197	3,274	3,174	2,963	2,933
Croatia	2,066	2,107	1,574	1,564	1,576	1,605	1,627	1,597	1,533	1,505
Czech Republic		5,225	4,726	4,763	4,825	4,915	4,995	4,927	4,876	4,930
Estonia	814	790	609	608	646	655	657	596	571	602
Georgia			1,758	1,745	1,747	1,704	1,602	1,656	1,628	1,638
Hungary	5,069	4,537	3,854	3,904	3,930	3,925	3,880	3,782	3,781	3,765
Latvia			977	1,026	1,081	1,113	1,118	970	928	967
Lithuania	1,796	1,622	1,397	1,474	1,497	1,532	1,518	1,414	1,342	1,371
Macedonia		518	553	545	570	589	608	629	637	644
Moldova			1,514	1,318	1,257	1,247	1,251	1,182	1,143	1,117
Montenegro			205	178	182	214	222	214	209	208
Poland	18,505	17,857	14,520	14,109	14,588	15,237	15,799	15,862	15,954	15,865
Romania	10,341	10,913	9,972	9,137	9,310	9,355	9,370	9,242	9,238	9,197
Russia	76,222	76,453	62,567	67,862	68,838	70,556	70,940	69,321	69,788	70,465
Serbia			3,094	2,733	2,624	2,656	2,822	2,616	2,396	2,214
Slovakia	2,460	2,430	2,104	2,213	2,300	2,356	2,431	2,364	2,314	2,340
Slovenia	897	956	904	943	956	985	996	981	966	959
Ukraine	21,998	22,393	20,163	20,677	20,739	20,899	20,970	20,196	20,265	20,217

Source: Euromonitor International from national statistics

Table 20.2

Employment by Activity 2011

% of total employed population

	Agriculture, Forestry & Fishing	Community, Social & Personal Services	Construction	Electricity, Gas & Water Supply	Finance, Insurance, Real Estate & Business	Manufacturing
Western Europe						
Austria	5.3	27.1	8.4	1.1	13.5	14.8
Belgium	1.6	36.5	7.3	1.4	12.7	14.4
Cyprus	3.7	28.4	12.3	1.0	14.2	8.2
Denmark	2.4	37.5	6.5	1.1	12.7	12.4
Finland	4.2	32.7	7.4	1.0	13.4	14.8
France	2.5	37.0	7.4	1.4	13.4	13.1
Germany	1.6	30.6	6.1	1.4	14.7	20.0
Gibraltar						
Greece	10.4	27.1	8.3	1.4	9.8	10.7
Iceland	4.5	35.2	8.0	0.9	13.6	9.7
Ireland	4.3	30.6	9.7	1.2	14.3	10.3
Italy	3.3	26.0	8.7	1.3	14.6	18.6
Liechtenstein						
Luxembourg	1.3	35.0	6.7	0.5	22.1	5.4
Malta	1.3	29.5	7.3	2.5	11.3	13.5
Monaco						
Netherlands	2.7	34.2	5.6	0.9	13.4	9.6
Norway	2.3	38.7	7.4	1.2	12.7	9.4
Portugal	10.7	26.6	9.8	1.0	9.0	16.0
Spain	3.6	28.2	10.6	1.0	12.9	12.4
Sweden	2.1	37.2	6.9	0.9	15.9	11.7
Switzerland	2.5	39.0	7.2	1.2	12.6	9.4
Turkey	20.0	17.3	6.6	0.6	6.9	19.6
United Kingdom	1.1	36.1	8.5	1.3	15.8	9.0
Eastern Europe						
Albania	43.6	15.6	9.0	1.1		10.6
Belarus						
Bosnia-Herzegovina						
Bulgaria	6.6	20.2	10.4	2.2	7.8	21.1
Croatia	13.5	21.5	9.0	2.4	8.0	16.7
Czech Republic	2.7	23.0	9.7	2.1	9.9	26.3
Estonia	3.3	26.5	11.4	1.2	9.9	19.1
Georgia	53.5	16.1	5.3	0.9	3.5	4.8
Hungary	3.9	26.8	8.1	2.1	10.2	20.2
Latvia	6.8	25.5	10.0	2.6	10.1	13.2
Lithuania	6.4	26.1	10.1	1.9	9.4	15.8
Macedonia	18.2	21.8	6.7	2.5	4.2	20.0
Moldova	23.8	24.9	7.9	1.9	4.5	11.4
Montenegro						
Poland	11.9	23.0	8.1	2.0	9.2	19.8
Romania	25.8	15.9	8.7	2.2	5.5	19.3
Russia	7.6	26.9	8.3	3.1	9.2	15.5
Serbia	25.4	19.1	6.8	1.6	5.8	16.6
Slovakia	2.8	23.3	11.6	2.4	9.0	24.2
Slovenia	8.9	23.7	6.4	1.7	9.9	23.5
Ukraine	14.0	23.5	5.3		8.2	14.3

Source: Euromonitor International from national statistics

Labour Statistics

Employment by Activity 2011 *(continued)*
% of total employed population

	Mining & Quarrying	Transport, Storage & Communications	Wholesale & Retail Trade, Restaurants & Hotels	Undefined Sectors	Total
Western Europe					
Austria	0.3	7.3	22.2	0.1	100.0
Belgium	0.1	9.0	16.0	1.0	100.0
Cyprus	0.1	6.4	24.6	1.1	100.0
Denmark	0.2	8.6	18.4	0.1	100.0
Finland	0.3	10.0	15.8	0.5	100.0
France	0.1	8.0	16.9	0.1	100.0
Germany	0.2	7.7	17.5	0.2	100.0
Gibraltar					100.0
Greece	0.3	6.6	25.3	0.2	100.0
Iceland	0.0	10.0	16.9	1.1	100.0
Ireland	0.5	8.3	20.5	0.4	100.0
Italy	0.1	7.0	20.0	0.3	100.0
Liechtenstein					100.0
Luxembourg	0.1	8.3	12.0	8.5	100.0
Malta	0.6	9.2	23.8	1.0	100.0
Monaco					100.0
Netherlands	0.1	8.6	17.1	7.9	100.0
Norway	1.8	8.9	16.7	0.8	100.0
Portugal	0.4	5.6	20.8	0.1	100.0
Spain	0.2	7.5	23.2	0.4	100.0
Sweden	0.2	9.1	15.6	0.4	100.0
Switzerland	1.8	9.1	16.5	0.8	100.0
Turkey	0.5	5.4	21.8	1.3	100.0
United Kingdom	0.4	8.6	18.5	0.7	100.0
Eastern Europe					
Albania	0.2	3.5	16.3		100.0
Belarus					100.0
Bosnia-Herzegovina					100.0
Bulgaria	0.8	7.5	23.0	0.5	100.0
Croatia	0.6	8.3	19.7	0.3	100.0
Czech Republic	0.9	9.0	16.2	0.0	100.0
Estonia	1.0	9.9	17.2	0.5	100.0
Georgia	0.3	4.2	10.5	1.0	100.0
Hungary	0.3	9.1	19.3	0.0	100.0
Latvia	0.5	11.7	19.5	0.1	100.0
Lithuania	0.3	8.5	21.1	0.4	100.0
Macedonia	1.2	6.3	18.9	0.3	100.0
Moldova	0.4	6.1	18.7	0.4	100.0
Montenegro					100.0
Poland	1.3	7.7	17.0	0.1	100.0
Romania	1.0	6.3	15.4	0.0	100.0
Russia	1.8	9.4	18.2	0.1	100.0
Serbia	1.1	5.7	17.8	0.2	100.0
Slovakia	0.4	8.3	17.9	0.1	100.0
Slovenia	0.4	8.6	16.4	0.4	100.0
Ukraine	3.1	7.1	24.5		100.0

Source: Euromonitor International from national statistics

Table 20.3

Paid Employment in Manufacturing 1980, 1990, 2000, 2005-2011

'000

	1980	1990	2000	2005	2006	2007	2008	2009	2010	2011
Western Europe										
Austria	1,259	1,098	717	668	701	689	610	583	600	590
Belgium	1,008	856	731	682	667	676	668	613	612	602
Cyprus	30	37	27	31	30	30	30	28	26	25
Denmark	374	401	486	425	411	419	403	338	329	314
Finland	567	495	437	412	416	420	392	356	341	329
France	6,102	4,410	3,900	3,791	3,766	3,740	3,526	3,313	3,193	3,084
Germany	8,717	8,876	8,141	7,638	7,761	8,023	7,804	7,575	7,422	7,372
Gibraltar	3	1	1		1	1	1	1	1	1
Greece	496	457	413	415	407	411	398	377	345	333
Iceland	25	23	21	19	18	17	17	17	16	15
Ireland	243	210	277	250	248	248	227	199	190	179
Italy	4,745	4,081	4,060	4,086	4,075	4,114	3,989	3,832	3,674	3,608
Liechtenstein										
Luxembourg	38	34	33	17	16	16	13	12	12	11
Malta	40	36	31	26	25	24	22	21	22	22
Monaco										
Netherlands	1,121	1,143	1,030	996	985	955	869	798	750	708
Norway	371	301	284	257	261	269	252	239	229	225
Portugal	921	1,037	961	853	867	842	806	768	745	724
Spain	2,723	2,557	2,578	2,719	2,716	2,712	2,595	2,215	2,102	2,001
Sweden	1,002	903	721	616	652	652	649	575	565	552
Switzerland	692	728	698	640	657	680	698	677	669	675
Turkey	1,986	2,582	2,845	3,366	3,478	3,346	3,469	3,281	3,592	3,670
United Kingdom	6,935	4,756	4,361	3,544	3,461	3,462	3,113	2,609	2,664	2,506
Eastern Europe										
Albania			32	38	38	32	36	37	38	39
Belarus		1,437	1,208	1,111	1,101	1,095	1,088	1,072	1,084	1,077
Bosnia-Herzegovina				83	117	151	145	143	134	142
Bulgaria	1,308	1,588	639	697	716	736	741	685	609	600
Croatia		546	278	267	280	288	282	259	233	225
Czech Republic	1,540	1,543	1,195	1,199	1,255	1,296	1,285	1,157	1,141	1,135
Estonia		206	125	133	131	129	131	110	104	99
Georgia			86	65	60	60	56	54	54	52
Hungary	1,386	1,118	861	812	814	827	813	751	741	726
Latvia		236	149	149	153	156	156	129	122	116
Lithuania		652	243	255	255	255	244	215	201	193
Macedonia		187	99	121	123	126	93	127	107	106
Moldova		365	98	106	104	97	93	85	79	74
Montenegro										
Poland	4,126	3,014	2,684	2,625	2,765	2,952	3,036	2,866	2,772	2,812
Romania	3,031	3,452	1,986	1,902	1,925	1,924	1,858	1,708	1,598	1,532
Russia	23,812	18,884	12,335	12,278	12,233	12,089	11,358	11,020	10,582	10,271
Serbia				454	419	389	368	336	312	284
Slovakia			516	556	574	597	603	529	489	480
Slovenia		373	258	261	251	254	248	224	216	209
Ukraine		5,975	2,916	2,371	2,329	2,268	2,192	2,103	2,047	1,996

Source: Euromonitor International from national statistics

Labour Statistics **Table 20.4**

Unemployed Population 1980, 1990, 2000, 2005-2011
'000

	1980	1990	2000	2005	2006	2007	2008	2009	2010	2011
Western Europe										
Austria		115	142	208	196	186	163	205	189	180
Belgium	453	286	303	383	383	354	333	379	407	352
Cyprus	6	7	15	19	17	17	15	21	25	31
Denmark	241	239	124	141	114	111	102	178	219	224
Finland	106	82	255	221	206	183	172	220	224	209
France	1,381	2,049	2,365	2,568	2,554	2,330	2,178	2,690	2,760	2,742
Germany		2,019	3,159	4,652	4,277	3,620	3,169	3,260	2,949	2,489
Gibraltar				1	1	1	1	1		
Greece	215	281	504	479	434	407	378	472	631	890
Iceland			4	4	5	4	6	13	14	12
Ireland		172	73	89	95	102	142	258	292	309
Italy	1,645	2,618	2,384	1,883	1,677	1,508	1,688	1,948	2,104	2,107
Liechtenstein				1	1	1	1	1	1	1
Luxembourg			12	9	9	9	11	12	10	14
Malta	4	5	10	12	11	11	10	12	12	12
Monaco			1							
Netherlands		332	247	438	367	306	268	327	386	389
Norway	33	111	76	109	84	63	66	82	93	86
Portugal	299	224	211	422	428	449	427	529	603	711
Spain	1,488	2,441	2,097	1,916	1,840	1,834	2,588	4,153	4,635	5,046
Sweden	80	74	252	361	336	299	305	408	416	376
Switzerland			107	185	170	157	149	192	203	183
Turkey		1,566	1,516	2,477	2,285	2,319	2,562	3,391	3,001	2,481
United Kingdom		2,006	1,549	1,445	1,646	1,629	1,758	2,370	2,443	2,539
Eastern Europe										
Albania			216	186	182	175	169	173	166	163
Belarus			94	68	52	44	37	40	33	33
Bosnia-Herzegovina				363	366	347	272	272	315	318
Bulgaria			574	336	306	238	195	234	340	373
Croatia			297	226	199	170	149	159	205	234
Czech Republic		227	448	410	371	276	230	351	383	355
Estonia		5	96	52	41	32	38	95	116	86
Georgia			203	279	275	261	316	336	317	317
Hungary			258	302	317	313	328	421	475	465
Latvia			155	109	86	77	98	216	229	187
Lithuania		273	275	133	89	69	94	225	291	249
Macedonia		159	260	324	321	317	310	299	300	293
Moldova			141	104	100	67	52	81	92	100
Montenegro			65	78	77	51	45	50	51	52
Poland			2,791	3,053	2,350	1,623	1,212	1,417	1,706	1,698
Romania			726	704	730	640	575	682	727	737
Russia			7,416	5,570	5,308	4,603	4,817	6,336	5,652	5,006
Serbia			426	720	692	585	445	503	569	659
Slovakia		202	490	433	358	298	258	326	392	369
Slovenia			65	66	61	50	46	61	76	86
Ukraine			2,678	1,604	1,525	1,423	1,428	1,955	1,786	1,728

Source: Euromonitor International from national statistics

Table 20.5

Unemployment Rate 1980, 1990, 2000, 2005-2011

% of economically active population

	1980	1990	2000	2005	2006	2007	2008	2009	2010	2011
Western Europe										
Austria		3.2	3.6	5.2	4.8	4.4	3.8	4.8	4.4	4.1
Belgium	10.9	7.3	6.9	8.4	8.3	7.5	7.0	7.9	8.3	7.2
Cyprus	2.5	2.6	4.9	5.3	4.5	4.2	3.7	5.3	6.2	7.4
Denmark	9.4	8.3	4.3	4.8	3.9	3.8	3.4	6.0	7.5	7.6
Finland	4.6	3.2	9.8	8.4	7.7	6.9	6.4	8.2	8.4	7.8
France	6.0	8.3	9.0	9.3	9.3	8.4	7.8	9.5	9.7	9.6
Germany		5.3	8.0	11.3	10.3	8.7	7.5	7.8	7.1	6.0
Gibraltar	1.7	2.7	3.2	3.7	3.8	3.9	4.0	4.0	3.0	2.7
Greece	5.8	7.5	11.2	9.9	8.9	8.3	7.7	9.5	12.6	17.7
Iceland			2.3	2.6	2.8	2.5	3.3	7.2	7.6	6.6
Ireland		13.2	4.2	4.4	4.5	4.6	6.3	11.9	13.7	14.4
Italy	7.4	11.0	10.1	7.7	6.8	6.1	6.7	7.8	8.4	8.4
Liechtenstein		0.0	1.1	2.6	2.5	2.1	1.5	1.5	1.6	1.5
Luxembourg			6.7	4.6	4.6	4.0	5.1	5.2	4.4	5.8
Malta	3.3	3.9	6.7	7.3	6.9	6.5	6.0	6.9	6.9	6.6
Monaco			4.7							
Netherlands		4.8	3.1	5.3	4.3	3.6	3.1	3.7	4.5	4.5
Norway	1.7	5.2	3.2	4.5	3.5	2.5	2.6	3.2	3.6	3.3
Portugal	6.7	4.7	4.0	7.6	7.7	8.0	7.6	9.5	10.8	12.7
Spain	11.4	16.3	11.7	9.2	8.5	8.3	11.3	18.0	20.1	21.6
Sweden	2.0	1.6	5.6	7.7	7.1	6.2	6.2	8.3	8.4	7.5
Switzerland			2.7	4.5	4.1	3.7	3.4	4.3	4.5	4.1
Turkey		7.5	6.5	10.6	10.3	10.2	11.0	14.0	11.9	9.8
United Kingdom		7.0	5.4	4.8	5.4	5.3	5.7	7.6	7.8	8.0
Eastern Europe										
Albania			16.8	14.1	13.8	13.2	12.7	13.0	12.4	12.1
Belarus			2.1	1.5	1.2	1.0	0.8	0.9	0.7	0.7
Bosnia-Herzegovina				30.9	31.1	29.0	23.4	24.1	27.2	27.6
Bulgaria			16.4	10.1	9.0	6.9	5.6	6.9	10.3	11.3
Croatia			15.9	12.7	11.2	9.6	8.4	9.1	11.8	13.5
Czech Republic		4.2	8.7	7.9	7.1	5.3	4.4	6.7	7.3	6.7
Estonia		0.7	13.7	7.9	5.9	4.7	5.5	13.8	16.9	12.5
Georgia			10.3	13.8	13.6	13.3	16.5	16.9	16.3	16.2
Hungary			6.3	7.2	7.5	7.4	7.8	10.0	11.2	11.0
Latvia			13.7	9.6	7.4	6.5	8.0	18.2	19.8	16.2
Lithuania		14.4	16.4	8.3	5.6	4.3	5.8	13.7	17.8	15.4
Macedonia		23.5	31.9	37.3	36.0	35.0	33.8	32.2	32.0	31.2
Moldova			8.5	7.3	7.4	5.1	4.0	6.4	7.4	8.2
Montenegro			24.0	30.3	29.6	19.4	16.8	19.1	19.7	19.9
Poland			16.1	17.8	13.9	9.6	7.1	8.2	9.7	9.7
Romania			6.8	7.2	7.3	6.4	5.8	6.9	7.3	7.4
Russia			10.6	7.6	7.2	6.1	6.4	8.4	7.5	6.6
Serbia			12.1	20.8	20.9	18.1	13.6	16.1	19.2	23.0
Slovakia		7.7	18.9	16.4	13.5	11.2	9.6	12.1	14.5	13.6
Slovenia			6.7	6.5	6.0	4.9	4.4	5.9	7.3	8.2
Ukraine			11.7	7.2	6.9	6.4	6.4	8.8	8.1	7.9

Source: Euromonitor International from national statistics

Labour Statistics   **Table 20.6**

Average Working Week in Non-Agricultural Activities 1980, 1990, 2000, 2005-2011

Hours

	1980	1990	2000	2005	2006	2007	2008	2009	2010	2011
Western Europe										
Austria		38.3	39.2	38.7	38.5	38.0	37.7	36.7	36.5	36.7
Belgium	33.8	33.7	37.1	36.7	36.8	37.0	36.8	36.7	37.0	36.8
Cyprus	42.0	42.0	40.0	39.9	39.9	39.8	40.4	40.6	40.6	40.7
Denmark	35.1	33.9	35.6	35.1	34.9	34.9	34.7	34.3	34.6	34.9
Finland		35.5	37.7	37.1	36.9	36.8	36.8	36.1	36.4	36.4
France	40.8	39.0	38.4	36.8	36.8	36.8	36.8	36.5	36.8	36.8
Germany	41.6	39.7	38.0	36.9	36.0	36.0	35.9	35.3	35.6	35.6
Gibraltar	43.2	45.1	43.0	41.6	41.9	41.7	41.7	41.3	41.7	41.7
Greece			42.1	41.9	41.5	41.2	41.1	40.8	40.9	40.9
Iceland	49.3	46.4	40.9	41.4	41.2	40.9	40.4	38.6	38.9	39.4
Ireland			38.9	37.3	37.1	36.8	36.3	35.1	35.0	34.9
Italy	39.0	38.8	39.3	38.1	38.0	38.0	37.7	37.3	37.3	37.1
Liechtenstein										
Luxembourg	38.1	38.2	37.6	36.6	36.2	35.8	35.9	36.4	35.9	36.8
Malta	40.0	39.3	38.0	38.3	38.1	38.7	38.6	38.7	38.5	38.9
Monaco										
Netherlands	32.1	31.7	32.3	31.6	31.9	31.8	31.7	31.5	31.5	31.7
Norway	35.5	35.3	36.1	34.5	34.2	34.1	34.1	33.8	33.7	34.0
Portugal	38.4	41.1	39.1	38.4	38.3	38.0	37.9	38.0	38.1	38.0
Spain	43.8	40.1	38.7	38.6	38.6	38.4	38.3	37.8	37.7	37.6
Sweden	35.6	37.5	36.4	35.6	35.5	35.5	35.5	35.1	35.8	35.7
Switzerland	36.5	34.8	35.6	35.7	35.7	35.2	35.4	34.8	35.2	35.2
Turkey		50.1	51.6	54.0	52.3	51.0	50.5	49.3	49.2	48.9
United Kingdom		38.4	36.2	35.8	35.7	35.8	35.5	35.4	35.3	35.3
Eastern Europe										
Albania										
Belarus			38.3	38.8	38.8	38.8	38.8	38.8	38.8	38.8
Bosnia-Herzegovina										
Bulgaria			39.6	40.6	41.1	41.1	41.0	40.4	40.5	40.3
Croatia		44.5	41.8	39.7	39.7	39.8	39.5	39.2	39.0	38.9
Czech Republic			43.4	41.7	41.4	41.3	41.3	40.5	40.4	40.3
Estonia			40.6	39.9	39.9	39.6	39.2	37.6	38.4	38.6
Georgia										
Hungary			41.5	40.3	40.2	39.9	40.0	39.6	39.6	39.1
Latvia			42.2	41.4	41.3	40.5	39.4	38.9	38.4	38.6
Lithuania			38.4	38.1	38.1	38.6	39.2	38.6	38.5	38.3
Macedonia										
Moldova			29.7	32.2	31.5	32.2	32.2	32.2	32.2	32.2
Montenegro										
Poland	37.5	37.0	40.6	40.3	40.3	40.3	40.1	39.7	39.7	39.5
Romania			38.5	40.1	39.8	39.7	39.6	39.4	39.3	39.2
Russia			33.9	35.7	35.7	35.7	35.5	35.5	35.5	35.5
Serbia										
Slovakia			41.7	41.0	40.1	40.3	39.9	39.3	39.5	39.4
Slovenia		36.0	41.3	40.2	39.5	39.6	39.5	38.9	38.6	38.4
Ukraine			38.3	42.1	41.7	41.4	42.8	38.9	36.4	37.5

Source: Euromonitor International from national statistics
Note: Hours actually worked by wage earners, unless otherwise stated

Table 20.7

Average Working Week in Manufacturing 1980, 1990, 2000, 2005-2011

Hours

	1980	1990	2000	2005	2006	2007	2008	2009	2010	2011
Western Europe										
Austria	39.1	37.4	39.3	38.9	39.0	38.9	38.7	37.2	37.8	38.6
Belgium	33.4	33.4	37.3	37.4	37.8	37.8	37.5	37.1	37.7	38.0
Cyprus	41.0	41.0	40.2	39.7	39.1	39.1	39.1	38.8	39.1	38.3
Denmark	36.3	35.0	36.3	36.1	36.2	36.3	36.4	35.9	36.4	37.4
Finland	33.2	38.2	37.1	38.0	38.0	37.8	38.2	37.5	37.5	38.2
France	40.0	30.7	30.7	37.0	37.2	37.1	37.3	36.7	37.3	38.3
Germany	41.8	39.9	37.5	37.6	38.2	37.3	37.6	38.0	36.6	37.5
Gibraltar	45.8	46.9	45.1	49.1	47.7	47.1	46.6	46.1	45.3	44.6
Greece	40.7	41.1	42.0	41.6	41.7	41.6	41.5	41.1	41.2	41.0
Iceland			43.5	42.8	43.1	42.5	43.8	41.9	42.3	42.5
Ireland			38.8	38.7	38.5	38.6	38.3	37.2	37.5	37.8
Italy	38.5	39.0	40.1	39.5	39.4	39.6	39.3	38.6	38.9	39.1
Liechtenstein										
Luxembourg	39.6	39.4	39.6	39.2	39.5	39.1	38.6	40.5	39.5	40.8
Malta	40.0	39.9	41.0	40.4	39.3	40.1	40.8	39.8	39.1	39.3
Monaco										
Netherlands	37.2	36.2	35.7	33.5	34.6	34.9	34.7	35.4	35.2	34.9
Norway	38.1	37.0	36.5	36.7	36.7	36.6	36.7	36.6	36.4	36.2
Portugal	39.0	40.7	39.3	39.5	39.5	39.2	39.1	39.4	39.7	40.7
Spain	41.4	39.1	38.5	40.0	40.1	39.8	39.7	39.1	39.3	39.8
Sweden	37.7	38.5	36.2	37.0	36.7	36.9	37.0	36.2	37.4	37.6
Switzerland	41.5	39.4	41.1	40.3	40.6	40.5	40.4	40.4	40.3	40.1
Turkey		48.8	51.3	53.7	53.9	51.9	51.8	52.0	50.4	51.7
United Kingdom		40.5	39.6	39.6	39.5	39.6	39.4	39.1	39.5	40.0
Eastern Europe										
Albania										
Belarus										
Bosnia-Herzegovina										
Bulgaria			40.4	40.7	41.0	40.8	40.6	39.7	40.1	40.1
Croatia		45.4	41.6	41.4	41.0	41.0	41.1	40.9	40.8	40.4
Czech Republic	43.5	40.1	40.7	40.3	40.2	40.1	39.9	39.2	39.6	40.4
Estonia			39.6	40.4	40.2	40.2	39.5	37.6	39.0	39.8
Georgia										
Hungary	44.9	40.1	39.9	40.0	39.8	39.5	39.7	39.3	39.6	39.2
Latvia			43.2	41.9	41.7	40.2	39.0	38.8	38.9	39.4
Lithuania			38.6	39.6	39.3	39.4	39.9	39.3	39.3	39.2
Macedonia				44.4	44.2	44.0	43.6	43.3	43.0
Moldova		34.5	24.4	30.4	29.5	31.3	31.4	31.7	32.0	32.3
Montenegro										
Poland	40.3	37.5	41.2	41.3	41.6	41.4	41.3	40.8	40.4	40.6
Romania			40.6	41.7	41.7	41.5	41.6	41.4	41.1	41.2
Russia			31.2	34.5	34.5	35.0	34.0	34.0	34.1	34.0
Serbia										
Slovakia			40.1	40.3	39.3	39.5	39.2	38.0	39.0	39.6
Slovenia		37.8	39.8	40.3	39.5	39.9	39.6	38.5	39.0	39.0
Ukraine			36.0	37.4	37.5	37.5	36.7	35.1	35.4	35.4

Source: Euromonitor International from national statistics
Note: Hours actually worked by wage earners, unless otherwise stated

Labour Statistics

Table 20.8

Economically Active Population by Age Group 2011

'000

	0-14	15-19	20-24	25-29	30-34	35-39
Western Europe						
Austria	214.7	377.0	486.3	455.0		509.5
Belgium	62.4	361.4	624.8	619.3		666.1
Cyprus	11.4	33.9	59.5	54.8		50.5
Denmark	211.4	265.1	250.5	313.2		348.4
Finland	93.9	214.6	289.7	299.8		266.8
France	595.8	2,389.7	3,398.5	3,389.3		3,856.3
Germany	1,272.9	3,392.5	4,126.3	4,084.9		4,184.9
Gibraltar						
Greece	43.4	295.3	636.5	711.3		709.4
Iceland	14.2	17.2	19.1	19.5		19.0
Ireland	50.5	192.6	327.7	315.4		279.7
Italy	268.1	1,483.7	2,450.2	3,353.2		3,886.8
Liechtenstein						
Luxembourg	3.0	12.3	29.1	33.4		35.0
Malta	7.6	22.5	25.6	25.3		19.1
Monaco						
Netherlands	597.0	792.2	874.5	886.5		976.8
Norway	140.5	226.7	261.9	285.9		326.4
Portugal	64.8	341.1	626.6	783.8		769.9
Spain	411.6	1,714.5	2,926.2	3,596.0		3,500.3
Sweden	204.6	441.6	489.9	535.5		585.7
Switzerland	253.5	377.9	457.1	477.3		495.3
Turkey	1,658.4	2,722.0	4,034.5	3,930.9		3,545.1
United Kingdom	1,463.9	3,137.5	3,705.6	3,201.7		3,463.1
Eastern Europe						
Albania						
Belarus	33.8	492.7	672.6	609.2		602.5
Bosnia-Herzegovina	26.3	106.1	138.2	146.7		150.5
Bulgaria	33.5	239.0	309.3	397.4		494.6
Croatia	32.6	145.3	186.4	162.8		173.5
Czech Republic	43.1	364.1	609.2	753.0		764.3
Estonia	10.0	64.3	85.4	78.3		83.1
Georgia	39.5	162.2	184.0	185.4		186.4
Hungary	21.8	276.1	531.3	644.5		646.6
Latvia	15.1	118.5	147.5	136.9		143.1
Lithuania	11.6	147.6	199.0	193.0		202.9
Macedonia	21.3	87.1	129.1	126.9		120.5
Moldova	19.1	101.1	129.5	138.5		150.2
Montenegro	5.8	15.9	37.9	35.6		32.0
Poland	194.2	1,560.2	2,616.4	2,575.6		2,299.0
Romania	152.2	776.7	1,210.9	1,447.9		1,403.7
Russia	1,141.8	7,967.4	10,317.5	9,532.7		9,008.3
Serbia	30.3	196.5	280.3	321.2		344.5
Slovakia	24.8	225.9	373.6	395.6		364.5
Slovenia	18.5	79.3	126.8	150.5		137.8
Ukraine	567.4	2,290.5	2,945.3	2,666.5		2,699.5

Source: Euromonitor International from national statistics

Economically Active Population by Age Group 2011 *(continued)*

'000

	40-44	45-49	50-54	55-59	60-64	Over 65	Total
Western Europe							
Austria	635.0	643.1	512.8	318.2	112.6	87.6	4,351.9
Belgium	698.6	714.8	609.2	387.2	134.8	32.8	4,911.6
Cyprus	48.8	48.6	42.1	34.3	18.1	12.5	414.5
Denmark	376.7	371.5	325.8	280.8	147.7	62.0	2,953.0
Finland	319.5	341.9	326.9	300.8	189.9	39.1	2,682.9
France	3,912.5	3,900.2	3,579.3	2,615.8	710.9	160.7	28,508.9
Germany	6,116.0	6,241.9	5,287.9	4,329.8	2,072.4	718.8	41,828.2
Gibraltar							
Greece	762.5	621.6	565.0	384.9	212.2	84.3	5,026.2
Iceland	19.8	20.6	20.1	17.4	12.4	6.7	185.9
Ireland	247.5	234.7	200.1	152.6	93.5	44.5	2,139.0
Italy	3,959.9	3,618.5	2,953.7	2,005.9	773.0	383.5	25,136.4
Liechtenstein							
Luxembourg	36.7	34.3	26.9	16.4	4.8	2.2	234.0
Malta	18.7	17.4	19.8	13.7	4.6	2.0	176.3
Monaco							
Netherlands	1,137.5	1,135.5	990.3	778.0	430.0	135.5	8,733.8
Norway	329.3	297.3	278.3	238.1	176.5	56.7	2,617.6
Portugal	687.8	695.0	588.3	439.0	267.3	312.8	5,576.4
Spain	3,218.3	2,887.0	2,347.4	1,668.0	887.9	158.0	23,315.1
Sweden	624.2	578.5	530.4	489.3	410.5	110.7	5,000.9
Switzerland	564.7	599.4	509.7	397.9	272.1	107.1	4,511.9
Turkey	3,117.6	2,445.7	1,676.8	1,039.6	611.5	490.0	25,272.1
United Kingdom	3,985.4	4,003.2	3,346.1	2,589.2	1,830.3	884.4	31,610.5
Eastern Europe							
Albania							
Belarus	530.1	644.5	660.6	346.1	99.4	20.3	4,711.7
Bosnia-Herzegovina	151.4	148.0	130.2	94.3	41.1	21.2	1,153.9
Bulgaria	472.6	499.2	350.2	318.3	146.1	45.7	3,305.9
Croatia	207.2	260.1	258.3	178.6	81.9	52.7	1,739.4
Czech Republic	662.4	642.1	630.2	548.0	192.9	76.6	5,285.8
Estonia	79.4	85.8	79.9	66.7	34.9	20.1	687.9
Georgia	195.4	230.2	217.1	180.3	136.1	238.3	1,955.0
Hungary	532.1	508.1	554.9	403.1	79.6	31.2	4,229.2
Latvia	135.4	149.2	135.2	106.3	40.7	26.1	1,153.9
Lithuania	206.3	233.5	196.9	139.6	61.6	27.6	1,619.6
Macedonia	120.1	114.6	103.7	74.1	31.5	8.1	937.0
Moldova	146.9	185.5	137.2	146.8	35.1	26.9	1,216.8
Montenegro	37.8	32.9	31.5	20.8	7.7	1.4	259.3
Poland	2,019.9	2,080.9	2,185.5	1,357.0	428.3	245.4	17,562.4
Romania	1,390.8	990.4	1,053.3	747.8	334.4	425.3	9,933.3
Russia	8,713.6	10,535.8	9,505.2	5,943.5	1,812.5	993.1	75,471.4
Serbia	350.4	401.7	367.4	320.4	140.0	120.9	2,873.6
Slovakia	338.6	346.3	340.8	239.7	48.8	10.5	2,709.2
Slovenia	132.5	152.9	126.1	73.9	22.1	24.7	1,045.2
Ukraine	2,578.6	2,867.0	2,555.2	1,603.3	737.4	434.3	21,945.1

Source: Euromonitor International from national statistics

Labour Statistics   **Table 20.9**

Economically Active Population by Age Group (% Analysis) 2011

% of economically active population

	0-14	15-19	20-24	25-29	30-34	35-39
Western Europe						
Austria	4.9	8.7	11.2	10.5	11.7
Belgium	1.3	7.4	12.7	12.6	13.6
Cyprus	2.8	8.2	14.4	13.2	12.2
Denmark	7.2	9.0	8.5	10.6	11.8
Finland	3.5	8.0	10.8	11.2	9.9
France	2.1	8.4	11.9	11.9	13.5
Germany	3.0	8.1	9.9	9.8	10.0
Gibraltar					
Greece	0.9	5.9	12.7	14.2	14.1
Iceland	7.6	9.3	10.2	10.5	10.2
Ireland	2.4	9.0	15.3	14.7	13.1
Italy	1.1	5.9	9.7	13.3	15.5
Liechtenstein					
Luxembourg	1.3	5.3	12.4	14.3	15.0
Malta	4.3	12.7	14.5	14.4	10.8
Monaco					
Netherlands	6.8	9.1	10.0	10.2	11.2
Norway	5.4	8.7	10.0	10.9	12.5
Portugal	1.2	6.1	11.2	14.1	13.8
Spain	1.8	7.4	12.6	15.4	15.0
Sweden	4.1	8.8	9.8	10.7	11.7
Switzerland	5.6	8.4	10.1	10.6	11.0
Turkey	6.6	10.8	16.0	15.6	14.0
United Kingdom	4.6	9.9	11.7	10.1	11.0
Eastern Europe						
Albania					
Belarus	0.7	10.5	14.3	12.9	12.8
Bosnia-Herzegovina	2.3	9.2	12.0	12.7	13.0
Bulgaria	1.0	7.2	9.4	12.0	15.0
Croatia	1.9	8.4	10.7	9.4	10.0
Czech Republic	0.8	6.9	11.5	14.2	14.5
Estonia	1.5	9.4	12.4	11.4	12.1
Georgia	2.0	8.3	9.4	9.5	9.5
Hungary	0.5	6.5	12.6	15.2	15.3
Latvia	1.3	10.3	12.8	11.9	12.4
Lithuania	0.7	9.1	12.3	11.9	12.5
Macedonia	2.3	9.3	13.8	13.5	12.9
Moldova	1.6	8.3	10.6	11.4	12.3
Montenegro	2.2	6.1	14.6	13.7	12.3
Poland	1.1	8.9	14.9	14.7	13.1
Romania	1.5	7.8	12.2	14.6	14.1
Russia	1.5	10.6	13.7	12.6	11.9
Serbia	1.1	6.8	9.8	11.2	12.0
Slovakia	0.9	8.3	13.8	14.6	13.5
Slovenia	1.8	7.6	12.1	14.4	13.2
Ukraine	2.6	10.4	13.4	12.2	12.3

Source: Euromonitor International from national statistics

Economically Active Population by Age Group (% Analysis) 2011 *(continued)*

% of economically active population

	40-44	45-49	50-54	55-59	60-64	Over 65	Total
Western Europe							
Austria	14.6	14.8	11.8	7.3	2.6	2.0	100.0
Belgium	14.2	14.6	12.4	7.9	2.7	0.7	100.0
Cyprus	11.8	11.7	10.1	8.3	4.4	3.0	100.0
Denmark	12.8	12.6	11.0	9.5	5.0	2.1	100.0
Finland	11.9	12.7	12.2	11.2	7.1	1.5	100.0
France	13.7	13.7	12.6	9.2	2.5	0.6	100.0
Germany	14.6	14.9	12.6	10.4	5.0	1.7	100.0
Gibraltar							
Greece	15.2	12.4	11.2	7.7	4.2	1.7	100.0
Iceland	10.7	11.1	10.8	9.3	6.7	3.6	100.0
Ireland	11.6	11.0	9.4	7.1	4.4	2.1	100.0
Italy	15.8	14.4	11.8	8.0	3.1	1.5	100.0
Liechtenstein							
Luxembourg	15.7	14.6	11.5	7.0	2.1	0.9	100.0
Malta	10.6	9.9	11.2	7.8	2.6	1.2	100.0
Monaco							
Netherlands	13.0	13.0	11.3	8.9	4.9	1.6	100.0
Norway	12.6	11.4	10.6	9.1	6.7	2.2	100.0
Portugal	12.3	12.5	10.5	7.9	4.8	5.6	100.0
Spain	13.8	12.4	10.1	7.2	3.8	0.7	100.0
Sweden	12.5	11.6	10.6	9.8	8.2	2.2	100.0
Switzerland	12.5	13.3	11.3	8.8	6.0	2.4	100.0
Turkey	12.3	9.7	6.6	4.1	2.4	1.9	100.0
United Kingdom	12.6	12.7	10.6	8.2	5.8	2.8	100.0
Eastern Europe							
Albania							
Belarus	11.3	13.7	14.0	7.3	2.1	0.4	100.0
Bosnia-Herzegovina	13.1	12.8	11.3	8.2	3.6	1.8	100.0
Bulgaria	14.3	15.1	10.6	9.6	4.4	1.4	100.0
Croatia	11.9	15.0	14.8	10.3	4.7	3.0	100.0
Czech Republic	12.5	12.1	11.9	10.4	3.6	1.4	100.0
Estonia	11.5	12.5	11.6	9.7	5.1	2.9	100.0
Georgia	10.0	11.8	11.1	9.2	7.0	12.2	100.0
Hungary	12.6	12.0	13.1	9.5	1.9	0.7	100.0
Latvia	11.7	12.9	11.7	9.2	3.5	2.3	100.0
Lithuania	12.7	14.4	12.2	8.6	3.8	1.7	100.0
Macedonia	12.8	12.2	11.1	7.9	3.4	0.9	100.0
Moldova	12.1	15.2	11.3	12.1	2.9	2.2	100.0
Montenegro	14.6	12.7	12.2	8.0	3.0	0.5	100.0
Poland	11.5	11.8	12.4	7.7	2.4	1.4	100.0
Romania	14.0	10.0	10.6	7.5	3.4	4.3	100.0
Russia	11.5	14.0	12.6	7.9	2.4	1.3	100.0
Serbia	12.2	14.0	12.8	11.1	4.9	4.2	100.0
Slovakia	12.5	12.8	12.6	8.8	1.8	0.4	100.0
Slovenia	12.7	14.6	12.1	7.1	2.1	2.4	100.0
Ukraine	11.8	13.1	11.6	7.3	3.4	2.0	100.0

Source: Euromonitor International from national statistics

Labour Statistics **Table 20.10**

Economically Active Population by Sex 2011

As stated

	Total ('000)	EAP as % Total Population	Males ('000)	Males as % Total EAP	Females ('000)	Females as % Total EAP
Western Europe						
Austria	4,352	52	2,326	53	2,026	47
Belgium	4,912	45	2,687	55	2,224	45
Cyprus	414	37	225	54	189	46
Denmark	2,953	53	1,558	53	1,395	47
Finland	2,683	50	1,384	52	1,299	48
France	28,509	45	14,923	52	13,586	48
Germany	41,828	51	22,570	54	19,258	46
Gibraltar	13	46	8	58	6	42
Greece	5,026	44	2,929	58	2,098	42
Iceland	186	57	100	54	86	46
Ireland	2,139	48	1,193	56	946	44
Italy	25,136	41	14,857	59	10,280	41
Liechtenstein	36	101				
Luxembourg	234	46	132	56	102	44
Malta	176	42	116	66	60	34
Monaco						
Netherlands	8,734	52	4,715	54	4,019	46
Norway	2,618	53	1,386	53	1,232	47
Portugal	5,576	52	2,922	52	2,655	48
Spain	23,315	51	12,996	56	10,319	44
Sweden	5,001	53	2,641	53	2,360	47
Switzerland	4,512	57	2,438	54	2,074	46
Turkey	25,272	34	18,105	72	7,167	28
United Kingdom	31,611	51	17,054	54	14,557	46
Eastern Europe						
Albania	1,342	42	665	50	677	50
Belarus	4,712	50	2,258	48	2,454	52
Bosnia-Herzegovina	1,154	30	713	62	441	38
Bulgaria	3,306	44	1,740	53	1,565	47
Croatia	1,739	39	933	54	806	46
Czech Republic	5,286	50	2,997	57	2,289	43
Estonia	688	51	343	50	345	50
Georgia	1,955	45	1,044	53	911	47
Hungary	4,229	42	2,278	54	1,951	46
Latvia	1,154	56	580	50	573	50
Lithuania	1,620	50	803	50	816	50
Macedonia	937	46	575	61	362	39
Moldova	1,217	34	632	52	585	48
Montenegro	259	42	146	56	113	44
Poland	17,562	46	9,595	55	7,967	45
Romania	9,933	46	5,529	56	4,404	44
Russia	75,471	53	38,559	51	36,913	49
Serbia	2,874	40	1,631	57	1,242	43
Slovakia	2,709	50	1,500	55	1,209	45
Slovenia	1,045	51	567	54	478	46
Ukraine	21,945	48	11,303	52	10,642	48

Source: Euromonitor International from national statistics

21

Media and Leisure

Media and Leisure Statistics

Table 21.1

Cinema Statistics 2011
As stated

	Seating Capacity of Fixed Cinemas ('000)	Number of Cinema Screens	Box Office Revenues (US$ million)	Annual Cinema Trips per Capita
Western Europe				
Austria	104.8	586.0	186.2	2.2
Belgium	113.6	517.0	310.6	2.2
Cyprus		38.0	9.6	0.8
Denmark	58.6	399.0	185.9	2.4
Finland	47.7	279.0	98.2	1.5
France	1,083.9	5,523.0	1,859.3	3.4
Germany	803.4	4,662.0	1,309.8	1.6
Gibraltar				
Greece		338.0	144.9	1.0
Iceland	6.5	41.0	14.3	5.8
Ireland	77.7	444.0	159.3	3.9
Italy		3,888.0	1,117.8	2.1
Liechtenstein				
Luxembourg	6.6	35.0	12.3	2.4
Malta		36.0	2.7	2.2
Monaco				
Netherlands	127.5	797.0	316.1	1.7
Norway	79.0	429.0	172.3	2.3
Portugal	110.9	566.0	119.9	1.6
Spain	913.2	4,062.0	928.7	2.1
Sweden	124.0	795.0	212.8	1.7
Switzerland	110.5	561.0	249.8	1.9
Turkey	268.8	1,918.0	261.7	0.6
United Kingdom	791.5	3,692.0	1,643.5	2.8
Eastern Europe				
Albania				
Belarus				1.6
Bosnia-Herzegovina			2.8	0.2
Bulgaria	31.6	148.0	25.2	0.6
Croatia	39.8	122.0	17.1	0.8
Czech Republic	145.7	685.0	88.1	1.3
Estonia	7.9	76.0	11.0	1.7
Georgia	4.2	32.0	1.4	0.1
Hungary	74.2	385.0	57.1	1.0
Latvia	16.6	67.0	12.1	1.1
Lithuania	20.5	82.0	12.5	0.7
Macedonia	5.1	21.0		0.1
Moldova				
Montenegro				0.4
Poland	250.0	1,060.0	251.2	1.0
Romania	53.2	216.0	38.7	0.3
Russia		2,614.0	1,244.4	1.3
Serbia	35.4	90.0	7.1	0.3
Slovakia	46.9	248.0	25.5	0.8
Slovenia	22.3	109.0	19.1	1.5
Ukraine	470.7	1,606.0	26.9	0.2

Source: Euromonitor International from national statistics

Table 21.2

Cinema Attendances 1990, 1995, 2000, 2006-2011

Million

	1990	1995	2000	2006	2007	2008	2009	2010	2011
Western Europe									
Austria	10.2	11.5	16.3	17.3	15.7	15.6	18.4	17.3	18.9
Belgium	17.1	19.2	23.5	23.9	22.7	21.9	22.6	23.7	24.0
Cyprus			0.9	0.8	0.9	0.9	0.9	0.9	0.9
Denmark	9.6	8.8	10.7	12.6	12.1	13.3	14.1	13.0	13.5
Finland	6.2	5.3	7.1	6.7	6.5	6.9	6.8	7.6	8.3
France	121.0	130.2	166.0	188.8	178.4	190.2	201.4	206.8	213.0
Germany	91.0	123.9	152.5	136.7	125.4	129.4	146.4	126.6	129.2
Gibraltar									
Greece	13.0	8.2	13.5	12.8	13.8	11.8	12.3	11.7	11.3
Iceland			1.6	1.5	1.5	1.6	1.7	1.8	1.9
Ireland	7.5	9.8	14.9	17.9	18.4	18.2	17.7	16.5	17.4
Italy	90.7	90.7	104.2	106.1	116.4	111.6	111.5	120.6	124.7
Liechtenstein									
Luxembourg	0.6	0.7	1.4	1.3	1.2	1.1	1.3	1.2	1.2
Malta			1.0	0.9	1.0	1.0	1.0	0.9	0.9
Monaco									
Netherlands	14.6	17.2	21.5	23.4	23.1	23.5	27.3	28.2	29.1
Norway	10.8	11.0	11.6	12.0	10.8	11.9	12.7	11.0	11.1
Portugal		12.0	17.9	16.4	16.3	16.0	15.7	16.6	17.2
Spain	78.5	96.7	135.4	121.7	116.9	107.8	110.0	101.6	97.0
Sweden	15.7	15.2	17.0	15.3	14.9	15.3	17.4	15.8	16.1
Switzerland	13.6	15.0	15.6	16.4	13.8	14.3	15.3	14.8	15.1
Turkey			25.3	34.9	31.2	38.5	36.9	41.1	44.1
United Kingdom	97.4	114.9	142.5	156.6	162.4	164.2	173.5	169.3	173.9
Eastern Europe									
Albania									
Belarus				14.0	14.2	14.2	14.8	15.1	15.4
Bosnia-Herzegovina				0.5	0.5	0.2	0.5	0.7	0.8
Bulgaria		3.4	2.2	2.4	2.5	2.8	3.2	4.0	4.4
Croatia		3.7	2.7	2.7	2.5	3.3	3.5	3.4	3.6
Czech Republic		9.3	8.7	11.5	12.8	12.9	12.5	13.5	13.8
Estonia	1.1	1.0	1.1	1.6	1.6	1.6	1.8	2.1	2.3
Georgia					0.3	0.3	0.3	0.3	0.3
Hungary	14.1	14.0	14.3	11.7	11.1	10.4	10.6	11.0	9.5
Latvia	0.4	1.0	1.5	2.1	2.4	2.4	1.9	2.1	2.2
Lithuania		0.7	2.1	2.5	3.3	3.4	2.8	2.5	2.3
Macedonia			0.6	0.1	0.1	0.1	0.1	0.2	0.2
Moldova									
Montenegro				0.0	0.0	0.0	0.2	0.3	0.3
Poland	16.0	22.0	18.7	32.0	32.6	33.8	39.2	37.5	38.0
Romania			5.1	2.8	2.9	3.8	5.3	6.5	6.7
Russia	10.3	13.3	42.8	91.8	106.6	123.9	138.5	165.5	184.5
Serbia					1.4	1.5	1.7	2.0	2.1
Slovakia		5.6	2.6	3.4	2.8	3.4	4.1	3.9	4.3
Slovenia		2.9	2.2	2.7	2.4	2.4	2.7	2.9	3.0
Ukraine				11.1	11.5	10.2	10.6	11.2	11.2

Source: Euromonitor International from national statistics

21

Media and Leisure

Media and Leisure Statistics

Table 21.3

DVD Rentals 2011

Number / as stated

	DVD Rental Transactions (million)	DVD Rental Turnover (US$ million)	New DVD Rental Releases	Video and DVD Rental Outlets
Western Europe				
Austria	3.4	14.5	392.0	338.0
Belgium	4.7	22.3	767.0	520.0
Cyprus				
Denmark	8.3	57.8	538.0	1,880.0
Finland	7.6	30.8	538.0	718.0
France	11.3	43.2	445.0	1,300.0
Germany	90.2	296.9	392.0	4,137.0
Gibraltar				
Greece	3.0	7.1	500.0	530.0
Iceland	2.0	7.7	413.0	100.0
Ireland	11.3	70.6	356.0	650.0
Italy	24.3	96.3	275.0	1,808.0
Liechtenstein				
Luxembourg				
Malta				
Monaco				
Netherlands	6.0	38.6	666.0	446.0
Norway	6.3	43.8	538.0	1,261.0
Portugal	6.3	26.5	365.0	470.0
Spain	31.0	127.5	168.0	1,314.0
Sweden	26.4	178.9	525.0	575.0
Switzerland	1.2	9.5	373.0	273.0
Turkey				
United Kingdom	60.8	291.6	378.0	1,574.0
Eastern Europe				
Albania				
Belarus				
Bosnia-Herzegovina				
Bulgaria				
Croatia	1.4	3.0	153.0	800.0
Czech Republic	0.4	2.1	148.0	775.0
Estonia				
Georgia				
Hungary	0.8	1.9	190.0	209.0
Latvia				
Lithuania				
Macedonia				
Moldova				
Montenegro				
Poland	1.3	2.6	139.0	1,083.0
Romania				
Russia				3,000.0
Serbia				
Slovakia				
Slovenia				
Ukraine				

Source: Euromonitor International from national statistics

Media and Leisure Statistics

Table 21.4

Newspapers 2011

Number / as stated

	Total Number	Dailies	Non-Dailies	Total Circulation ('000)	Daily Circulation ('000)	Non-Daily Circulation ('000)
Western Europe						
Austria	264	17	247	2,945	2,945	
Belgium	26	23	3	2,457	1,639	818
Cyprus	33	22	11	149	102	47
Denmark	284	36	248	7,919	1,360	6,559
Finland	236	52	184	2,734	1,901	833
France	170	125	45	14,015	9,376	4,639
Germany	1,763	347	1,416	110,862	18,761	92,101
Gibraltar	7	2	5	8	8	
Greece	55	42	13	1,422	1,250	172
Iceland	21	1	20	169	104	65
Ireland	154	9	145	1,888	708	1,179
Italy	561	95	466	9,073	8,570	503
Liechtenstein	2	2		20	20	
Luxembourg	19	8	11	508	255	253
Malta	11	4	7	101	101	
Monaco	2		2			
Netherlands	493	28	465	18,767	4,140	14,627
Norway	230	70	160	2,457	1,716	741
Portugal	55	17	38	5,386	953	4,433
Spain	324	126	198	9,162	2,449	6,713
Sweden	222	85	137	5,357	3,450	1,907
Switzerland	488	76	412	2,610	2,185	425
Turkey	2,630	65	2,565	4,692	4,692	
United Kingdom	1,160	113	1,047	37,294	17,333	19,962
Eastern Europe						
Albania	111	28	83	70	70	
Belarus	663	33	630	14,775	1,818	12,957
Bosnia-Herzegovina	126	11	115	245	245	
Bulgaria	457	72	385	6,374	1,094	5,280
Croatia	305	17	288	3,294	526	2,768
Czech Republic	529	79	450	13,512	1,477	12,035
Estonia	132	13	119	406	228	178
Georgia	71	9	62	44	44	
Hungary	242	29	213	2,715	1,550	1,166
Latvia	99	16	83	1,507	278	1,229
Lithuania	288	22	266	2,099	616	1,484
Macedonia	24	13	11	325	292	33
Moldova	248	6	242	1,546	520	1,026
Montenegro	52	4	48	66	66	
Poland	51	34	17	3,861	3,297	563
Romania	61	43	18	4,484	1,178	3,306
Russia	26,004	581	25,423	966		
Serbia	431	11	420	1,202	1,202	
Slovakia	9	8	1	406	348	58
Slovenia	238	7	231	1,548	424	1,124
Ukraine	2,286	28	2,258	3,032	3,032	

Source: Euromonitor International from national statistics

Media and Leisure Statistics   **Table 21.5**

Colour TV Households 2006-2011
'000

	2006	2007	2008	2009	2010	2011
Western Europe						
Austria	3,343.5	3,379.2	3,415.4	3,447.0	3,473.3	3,499.2
Belgium	4,302.5	4,353.8	4,409.6	4,431.5	4,476.6	4,531.5
Cyprus						
Denmark	2,465.9	2,481.4	2,496.4	2,510.8	2,524.3	2,537.7
Finland	2,331.1	2,359.4	2,385.2	2,408.3	2,429.9	2,449.7
France	25,212.0	25,586.0	25,821.7	26,211.0	26,549.7	26,836.0
Germany	37,858.2	38,191.9	37,533.2	38,305.0	38,462.9	38,486.6
Gibraltar						
Greece	3,821.1	3,863.8	3,906.3	3,948.9	3,991.0	4,032.1
Iceland						
Ireland	1,440.1	1,492.5	1,541.7	1,586.8	1,626.9	1,664.3
Italy	22,714.6	23,032.0	23,310.7	23,561.8	23,791.9	23,997.1
Liechtenstein						
Luxembourg						
Malta						
Monaco						
Netherlands	7,049.7	7,106.2	7,160.5	7,216.6	7,268.4	7,317.5
Norway	1,948.9	1,968.7	2,012.4	2,048.4	2,081.4	2,111.3
Portugal	3,972.8	4,019.5	4,061.5	4,100.5	4,137.3	4,170.9
Spain	16,257.9	16,651.7	17,029.7	17,307.0	17,553.5	17,801.7
Sweden	4,344.6	4,387.7	4,419.1	4,449.9	4,479.1	4,508.0
Switzerland	3,158.5	3,187.3	3,230.9	3,284.9	3,329.0	3,372.9
Turkey	15,995.8	16,399.0	16,804.0	17,208.4	17,611.7	18,015.1
United Kingdom	26,223.4	26,454.5	26,682.3	26,907.7	27,131.5	27,353.9
Eastern Europe						
Albania						
Belarus	3,841.3	3,913.7	3,972.2	4,003.4	4,026.5	4,042.7
Bosnia-Herzegovina	1,103.3	1,111.8	1,122.0	1,129.5	1,135.8	1,139.9
Bulgaria	2,571.9	2,609.3	2,639.2	2,662.4	2,680.9	2,694.2
Croatia	1,424.0	1,446.7	1,467.3	1,493.6	1,462.2	1,471.9
Czech Republic	4,290.5	4,344.0	4,413.7	4,480.8	4,527.4	4,567.4
Estonia	559.4	565.3	570.2	573.0	574.5	575.2
Georgia	1,055.4	1,060.7	1,064.9	1,072.9	1,080.1	1,086.2
Hungary	3,924.1	3,974.0	4,020.6	4,062.3	4,098.2	4,127.9
Latvia	767.5	772.2	776.6	779.8	782.1	783.8
Lithuania	1,331.3	1,347.8	1,363.4	1,368.5	1,370.9	1,371.9
Macedonia	569.6	576.8	582.7	592.7	592.7	602.9
Moldova						
Montenegro	182.1	179.3	180.1	182.6	182.1	183.2
Poland	13,549.2	13,725.5	13,931.3	14,117.4	14,220.5	14,328.9
Romania	6,515.6	6,730.8	6,892.4	7,002.2	7,084.3	7,164.3
Russia	49,717.4	50,337.3	50,781.4	51,102.6	51,253.3	51,323.5
Serbia	2,438.5	2,442.8	2,449.8	2,480.1	2,477.3	2,480.6
Slovakia	2,153.8	2,192.6	2,218.5	2,240.8	2,259.9	2,276.9
Slovenia	689.2	695.7	707.1	716.0	724.2	732.0
Ukraine	17,581.5	18,199.1	18,777.5	18,908.9	19,007.4	19,067.9

Source: Euromonitor International from national statistics

Table 21.6

Cable TV Households 2006-2011
'000 / %

	2006	2007	2008	2009	2010	2011	Cable TV households as % of colour TV households 2011
Western Europe							
Austria	1,353.3	1,346.7	1,347.4	1,359.8	1,344.0	1,352.6	38.65
Belgium	3,854.4	3,792.9	3,733.3	3,445.7	3,330.1	3,365.5	74.27
Cyprus							
Denmark	1,562.6	1,591.4	1,577.7	1,633.0	1,513.6	1,489.1	58.68
Finland	1,284.7	1,314.0	1,352.4	1,397.0	1,283.5	1,313.1	53.60
France	3,389.0	3,658.8	3,834.9	3,823.5	3,772.9	3,760.1	14.01
Germany	20,519.8	19,912.4	19,065.8	19,372.2	19,191.5	18,563.2	48.23
Gibraltar							
Greece	14.7	20.8	25.6	29.6	32.8	35.8	0.89
Iceland							
Ireland	607.4	606.1	540.5	548.8	545.9	542.5	32.59
Italy	207.1	208.3	218.5	229.0	239.5	249.9	1.04
Liechtenstein							
Luxembourg							
Malta							
Monaco							
Netherlands	6,204.0	6,154.7	5,717.8	5,518.7	5,323.3	5,195.4	71.00
Norway	922.5	928.5	952.6	921.6	921.9	928.7	43.99
Portugal	1,584.9	1,713.0	1,916.4	2,049.6	2,169.8	2,272.3	54.48
Spain	2,546.4	2,359.7	2,562.1	2,589.1	2,487.5	2,445.6	13.74
Sweden	2,412.5	2,416.5	2,557.8	2,630.1	2,577.3	2,562.6	56.85
Switzerland	2,875.6	2,932.1	2,936.8	2,971.2	3,017.4	3,053.3	90.52
Turkey	1,951.6	2,027.0	2,140.2	2,271.2	2,389.4	2,495.7	13.85
United Kingdom	3,381.0	3,514.9	3,686.2	3,762.0	3,839.6	3,931.8	14.37
Eastern Europe							
Albania							
Belarus	1,809.4	1,969.3	2,071.0	2,143.5	2,191.6	2,219.2	54.89
Bosnia-Herzegovina	140.4	167.0	198.5	235.1	276.5	300.8	26.39
Bulgaria	1,360.2	1,339.0	1,292.6	1,221.0	1,247.7	1,274.7	47.31
Croatia	229.6	246.6	262.9	277.6	288.5	298.3	20.27
Czech Republic	937.5	958.4	1,034.2	1,069.8	1,101.3	1,108.8	24.28
Estonia	301.0	298.4	277.1	271.1	270.0	268.9	46.74
Georgia	103.5	112.6	120.9	128.9	136.0	142.5	13.12
Hungary	2,262.4	2,330.8	2,348.3	2,404.5	2,352.4	2,332.4	56.50
Latvia	360.6	422.6	336.3	317.5	320.7	325.0	41.46
Lithuania	443.8	486.3	584.3	642.6	682.0	708.4	51.64
Macedonia	87.2	168.6	205.2	228.1	246.6	265.2	43.98
Moldova							
Montenegro	51.7	54.5	57.3	60.2	62.8	65.1	35.55
Poland	4,484.5	4,490.9	4,861.0	4,860.8	4,910.7	4,966.0	34.66
Romania	3,817.8	3,426.9	3,517.3	3,519.0	3,363.2	3,297.3	46.02
Russia	19,003.7	19,112.4	19,183.3	19,224.0	19,239.8	19,236.0	37.48
Serbia	904.0	932.6	979.0	1,015.5	1,046.7	1,073.0	43.26
Slovakia	1,081.9	1,003.6	990.7	957.7	966.6	975.7	42.85
Slovenia	378.1	389.3	444.1	477.2	496.9	511.2	69.84
Ukraine	2,893.7	3,337.6	3,633.3	3,897.1	4,103.8	4,282.3	22.46

Source: Euromonitor International from national statistics

21

Media and Leisure

Media and Leisure Statistics | **Table 21.7**

Satellite TV Households 2006-2011
'000 / %

	2006	2007	2008	2009	2010	2011	Satellite TV households as % of colour TV households 2011
Western Europe							
Austria	1,766.8	1,830.9	1,815.9	1,881.8	1,879.0	1,892.8	54.09
Belgium	224.1	242.0	260.5	244.1	242.9	256.0	5.65
Cyprus							
Denmark	469.4	471.4	425.9	389.2	316.1	289.5	11.41
Finland	532.5	567.5	596.0	618.5	637.8	655.9	26.77
France	5,683.2	5,961.0	6,504.8	7,191.4	7,626.1	8,017.3	29.87
Germany	16,026.1	15,571.5	15,595.6	15,937.1	16,392.7	16,842.9	43.76
Gibraltar							
Greece	406.5	450.8	418.6	444.5	495.9	523.4	12.98
Iceland							
Ireland	525.6	611.3	628.7	704.4	751.0	786.5	47.26
Italy	6,300.0	6,900.0	7,250.0	7,302.0	7,490.8	7,681.7	32.01
Liechtenstein							
Luxembourg							
Malta							
Monaco							
Netherlands	671.8	761.1	694.7	685.1	687.8	706.3	9.65
Norway	795.6	821.3	788.0	768.4	737.2	727.1	34.44
Portugal	570.0	600.0	692.4	746.0	787.3	819.9	19.66
Spain	3,248.3	3,497.7	3,655.3	3,405.8	2,858.0	2,573.1	14.45
Sweden	951.8	893.1	906.4	898.2	865.5	856.7	19.00
Switzerland	417.1	499.2	536.4	506.7	500.7	517.8	15.35
Turkey	5,820.5	6,488.0	7,077.3	7,545.1	7,949.8	8,311.1	46.13
United Kingdom	8,839.8	9,169.7	9,520.8	10,268.1	10,536.4	10,766.9	39.36
Eastern Europe							
Albania							
Belarus	324.2	367.8	406.6	443.4	473.2	499.2	12.35
Bosnia-Herzegovina	182.3	184.9	186.8	188.1	189.0	189.5	16.62
Bulgaria	548.7	575.5	622.5	632.7	731.8	768.6	28.53
Croatia	514.2	518.0	468.0	428.0	416.7	416.0	28.26
Czech Republic	506.2	585.7	809.4	1,010.6	1,179.3	1,210.5	26.50
Estonia	68.2	90.5	95.4	93.7	93.6	94.3	16.40
Georgia	3.6	5.4	6.7	7.6	8.5	9.4	0.86
Hungary	670.7	786.9	803.7	931.6	1,054.2	1,126.8	27.30
Latvia	87.7	88.0	101.2	93.9	96.5	98.4	12.56
Lithuania	127.6	140.3	148.0	153.7	157.6	160.9	11.73
Macedonia	45.9	47.9	49.7	52.0	54.0	55.7	9.24
Moldova							
Montenegro	35.9	37.2	54.3	58.9	62.6	65.1	35.56
Poland	6,837.5	7,322.1	7,987.3	8,704.3	9,397.8	9,917.2	69.21
Romania	808.3	1,839.2	2,368.7	2,544.1	2,591.8	2,641.5	36.87
Russia	3,278.0	3,526.1	3,717.4	3,894.5	4,008.7	4,120.9	8.03
Serbia	157.5	147.6	170.8	107.8	109.3	109.4	4.41
Slovakia	486.0	590.6	854.3	950.8	1,149.0	1,222.0	53.67
Slovenia	100.0	93.7	87.2	82.1	73.0	69.7	9.52
Ukraine	555.0	1,186.0	1,819.8	2,152.1	2,481.0	2,765.6	14.50

Source: Euromonitor International from national statistics

Table 21.8

Digital Satellite Pay-TV Subscribers 2006-2011

'000 / %

	2006	2007	2008	2009	2010	2011	Digital satellite pay-TV households as % of colour TV households 2011
Western Europe							
Austria							
Belgium	30.0	55.0	73.0	100.0	115.0	122.5	2.70
Cyprus	22.0	23.2	14.4	13.9	11.5	10.0	
Denmark	424.2	414.5	385.6	358.6	322.2	323.8	12.76
Finland	79.0	76.0	76.1	70.4	83.4	85.4	3.49
France	3,174.0	3,486.6	3,771.0	4,423.2	5,105.1	5,527.4	20.60
Germany	1,307.3	1,143.2	1,133.9	1,208.8	1,300.0	1,367.6	3.55
Gibraltar							
Greece	260.0	292.4	307.4	318.6	363.7	389.8	9.67
Iceland							
Ireland	465.0	535.0	573.0	601.0	628.0	649.2	39.01
Italy	4,030.0	4,430.0	4,700.0	4,737.0	4,877.0	5,132.4	21.39
Liechtenstein							
Luxembourg							
Malta							
Monaco							
Netherlands	507.8	750.0	760.0	770.0	795.0	835.4	11.42
Norway	700.4	722.5	715.6	694.9	665.9	673.9	31.92
Portugal	436.0	484.0	586.4	645.0	670.0	726.2	17.41
Spain	2,044.0	2,065.0	2,035.0	1,845.8	1,784.6	1,749.5	9.83
Sweden	768.4	720.0	680.7	666.0	639.5	626.3	13.89
Switzerland	6.2	6.4	10.0	10.0	10.3	10.9	0.32
Turkey	1,546.7	1,850.0	2,294.0	2,531.0	2,645.0	2,813.8	15.62
United Kingdom	7,976.0	8,297.0	8,665.0	9,107.0	9,468.0	9,828.4	35.93
Eastern Europe							
Albania							
Belarus							
Bosnia-Herzegovina							
Bulgaria	215.0	327.0	405.0	445.0	545.0	593.2	22.02
Croatia				77.0	114.0	135.0	9.17
Czech Republic	194.2	389.4	494.4	514.8	611.2	695.8	15.23
Estonia	25.0	40.0	49.0	47.5	49.0	52.0	9.03
Georgia							
Hungary	370.9	542.0	590.0	717.6	838.2	892.9	21.63
Latvia	25.0	58.0	71.0	66.0	68.5	73.5	9.37
Lithuania	36.0	69.0	84.0	74.5	78.9	82.9	6.04
Macedonia							
Moldova							
Montenegro							
Poland	2,251.0	3,436.0	4,754.0	5,928.3	6,541.2	7,122.5	49.71
Romania	610.3	1,695.3	2,150.3	2,333.1	2,382.8	2,617.5	36.53
Russia	482.1	1,480.0	3,780.0	5,472.0	6,300.0	6,692.5	13.04
Serbia							
Slovakia	119.6	256.9	321.5	357.5	483.5	556.0	24.42
Slovenia		3.0	15.7	21.4	30.4	36.5	4.99
Ukraine							

Source: Euromonitor International from national statistics

21

Media and Leisure

22

Population

Population Statistics

Table 22.1

Population: National Estimates at Mid-Year 1980, 1985, 1990, 1995, 1999-2011
'000 / % growth

	1980	1985	1990	1995	1999	2000	2001	2002	2003
Western Europe									
Austria	7,549	7,565	7,678	7,948	7,992	8,012	8,042	8,082	8,121
Belgium	9,859	9,858	9,967	10,137	10,226	10,251	10,287	10,333	10,376
Cyprus	688	710	775	865	935	952	970	987	1,005
Denmark	5,123	5,114	5,141	5,233	5,322	5,340	5,359	5,376	5,391
Finland	4,780	4,902	4,986	5,108	5,165	5,176	5,188	5,201	5,213
France	53,880	55,284	56,709	57,844	58,677	59,062	59,476	59,894	60,304
Germany	78,289	77,685	79,433	81,678	82,100	82,212	82,350	82,488	82,534
Gibraltar	27	27	27	27	27	27	28	28	29
Greece	9,643	9,934	10,157	10,634	10,883	10,917	10,950	10,988	11,024
Iceland	229	243	256	269	280	283	286	289	292
Ireland	3,413	3,546	3,514	3,609	3,755	3,805	3,866	3,932	3,997
Italy	56,434	56,593	56,719	56,844	56,916	56,942	56,977	57,157	57,605
Liechtenstein	26	27	29	31	32	33	33	34	34
Luxembourg	364	368	384	410	433	438	442	446	450
Malta	329	351	370	388	397	399	401	404	406
Monaco	26	29	31	33	35	35	35	35	35
Netherlands	14,150	14,492	14,952	15,459	15,812	15,926	16,046	16,149	16,225
Norway	4,086	4,153	4,241	4,359	4,462	4,491	4,514	4,538	4,565
Portugal	9,766	10,024	9,983	10,030	10,172	10,226	10,293	10,368	10,441
Spain	37,527	38,419	38,850	39,387	39,926	40,263	40,720	41,314	42,005
Sweden	8,310	8,350	8,559	8,827	8,858	8,872	8,896	8,925	8,958
Switzerland	6,319	6,470	6,716	7,041	7,144	7,184	7,230	7,285	7,339
Turkey	45,530	50,510	55,139	59,728	63,298	64,175	65,043	65,905	66,761
United Kingdom	56,314	56,550	57,248	58,019	58,682	58,893	59,108	59,326	59,566
Eastern Europe									
Albania	2,699	2,989	3,280	3,137	3,083	3,082	3,100	3,113	3,123
Belarus	9,627	9,958	10,189	10,194	10,024	9,980	9,929	9,866	9,797
Bosnia-Herzegovina	4,059	4,279	4,444	3,482	3,721	3,771	3,801	3,822	3,834
Bulgaria	8,851	8,952	8,718	8,269	8,011	7,961	7,914	7,868	7,824
Croatia	4,600	4,712	4,781	4,581	4,498	4,440	4,441	4,443	4,442
Czech Republic	10,285	10,302	10,303	10,308	10,245	10,228	10,213	10,205	10,207
Estonia	1,477	1,529	1,569	1,437	1,376	1,370	1,364	1,359	1,354
Georgia	4,787	4,984	5,159	4,734	4,453	4,418	4,386	4,357	4,329
Hungary	10,713	10,628	10,374	10,329	10,238	10,211	10,188	10,159	10,130
Latvia	2,512	2,579	2,663	2,485	2,390	2,370	2,345	2,316	2,288
Lithuania	3,413	3,545	3,698	3,629	3,524	3,500	3,481	3,469	3,454
Macedonia	1,785	1,819	1,899	1,953	1,995	2,004	2,013	2,020	2,027
Moldova	4,026	4,232	4,368	4,315	4,134	4,079	4,019	3,951	3,878
Montenegro	586	586	591	603	614	616	618	620	621
Poland	35,574	37,202	38,031	38,275	38,270	38,258	38,248	38,230	38,205
Romania	22,207	22,733	23,202	22,239	21,953	21,908	21,860	21,803	21,742
Russia	138,483	143,033	147,969	148,376	147,215	146,597	145,976	145,306	144,652
Serbia	7,743	7,619	7,574	7,625	7,540	7,516	7,503	7,497	7,481
Slovakia	4,980	5,156	5,278	5,353	5,377	5,379	5,377	5,374	5,371
Slovenia	1,901	1,942	1,998	1,990	1,983	1,989	1,992	1,995	1,996
Ukraine	49,866	50,752	51,590	51,087	49,330	48,889	48,452	48,032	47,633

Source: Euromonitor International from national statistics

Population: National Estimates at Mid-Year 1980, 1985, 1990, 1995, 1999-2011 *(continued)*

'000 / % growth

	2004	2005	2006	2007	2008	2009	2010	2011	% growth
Western Europe									
Austria	8,172	8,228	8,269	8,301	8,337	8,365	8,390	8,424	11.58
Belgium	10,421	10,479	10,548	10,626	10,710	10,796	10,896	10,996	11.53
Cyprus	1,024	1,039	1,053	1,067	1,082	1,096	1,110	1,122	63.20
Denmark	5,405	5,419	5,437	5,461	5,494	5,523	5,548	5,571	8.74
Finland	5,228	5,246	5,266	5,289	5,313	5,339	5,363	5,388	12.74
France	60,734	61,181	61,597	61,965	62,300	62,628	62,959	63,294	17.47
Germany	82,516	82,469	82,376	82,266	82,110	81,902	81,777	81,796	4.48
Gibraltar	29	29	29	29	29	29	29	29	10.00
Greece	11,062	11,104	11,148	11,193	11,237	11,283	11,316	11,336	17.56
Iceland	295	299	304	308	313	318	322	326	42.11
Ireland	4,070	4,160	4,260	4,357	4,426	4,459	4,474	4,479	31.25
Italy	58,175	58,607	58,941	59,375	59,832	60,193	60,483	60,739	7.63
Liechtenstein	34	35	35	35	35	36	36	36	42.24
Luxembourg	455	462	472	482	492	502	511	518	42.01
Malta	408	410	411	413	414	416	417	419	27.28
Monaco	35	35	35	35	35	35	35	35	34.90
Netherlands	16,282	16,320	16,346	16,382	16,446	16,530	16,615	16,693	17.97
Norway	4,592	4,623	4,661	4,709	4,768	4,829	4,889	4,953	21.23
Portugal	10,502	10,549	10,584	10,608	10,622	10,632	10,637	10,636	8.90
Spain	42,692	43,398	44,116	44,879	45,556	45,909	46,071	46,175	23.04
Sweden	8,994	9,030	9,081	9,148	9,220	9,299	9,378	9,449	13.70
Switzerland	7,390	7,437	7,484	7,551	7,648	7,744	7,828	7,911	25.19
Turkey	67,608	68,445	69,275	70,138	71,052	71,995	72,893	73,684	61.83
United Kingdom	59,868	60,224	60,596	60,987	61,394	61,811	62,263	62,745	11.42
Eastern Europe									
Albania	3,135	3,145	3,155	3,167	3,182	3,197	3,209	3,221	19.32
Belarus	9,730	9,664	9,605	9,561	9,528	9,507	9,491	9,473	-1.60
Bosnia-Herzegovina	3,840	3,843	3,843	3,844	3,844	3,844	3,844	3,843	-5.31
Bulgaria	7,781	7,740	7,699	7,660	7,623	7,585	7,540	7,496	-15.31
Croatia	4,443	4,443	4,442	4,439	4,436	4,430	4,419	4,407	-4.20
Czech Republic	10,216	10,236	10,269	10,324	10,392	10,441	10,473	10,495	2.05
Estonia	1,349	1,346	1,344	1,342	1,341	1,340	1,340	1,340	-9.31
Georgia	4,318	4,361	4,398	4,388	4,384	4,387	4,391	4,396	-8.17
Hungary	10,107	10,087	10,071	10,056	10,038	10,023	10,000	9,973	-6.91
Latvia	2,260	2,232	2,203	2,175	2,149	2,122	2,091	2,057	-10.11
Lithuania	3,436	3,414	3,394	3,376	3,358	3,339	3,287	3,221	-5.62
Macedonia	2,033	2,037	2,040	2,044	2,047	2,051	2,055	2,059	15.36
Moldova	3,804	3,747	3,708	3,670	3,632	3,593	3,564	3,544	-11.98
Montenegro	622	622	622	622	622	621	620	620	5.81
Poland	38,182	38,165	38,141	38,121	38,126	38,152	38,178	38,200	7.38
Romania	21,685	21,634	21,588	21,547	21,514	21,480	21,443	21,405	-3.61
Russia	144,112	143,642	143,230	142,996	142,926	142,941	142,938	142,888	3.18
Serbia	7,463	7,441	7,412	7,382	7,350	7,321	7,291	7,257	-6.27
Slovakia	5,370	5,370	5,371	5,373	5,378	5,386	5,394	5,401	8.45
Slovenia	1,997	2,000	2,007	2,018	2,029	2,040	2,049	2,053	7.96
Ukraine	47,271	46,925	46,607	46,329	46,078	45,873	45,690	45,526	-8.70

Source: Euromonitor International from national statistics

Population Statistics | **Table 22.2**

Population: National Estimates at January 1st 1980, 1985, 1990, 1995, 1999-2011

'000

	1980	1985	1990	1995	1999	2000	2001	2002	2003
Western Europe									
Austria	7,546	7,563	7,645	7,943	7,982	8,002	8,021	8,064	8,100
Belgium	9,855	9,858	9,948	10,131	10,214	10,239	10,263	10,310	10,356
Cyprus	686	704	767	855	926	943	961	979	996
Denmark	5,122	5,111	5,135	5,216	5,314	5,330	5,349	5,368	5,384
Finland	4,771	4,894	4,974	5,099	5,160	5,171	5,181	5,195	5,206
France	53,731	55,157	56,577	57,753	58,497	58,858	59,267	59,686	60,102
Germany	78,180	77,709	79,113	81,539	82,037	82,163	82,260	82,440	82,537
Gibraltar	27	27	27	27	27	27	28	28	28
Greece	9,584	9,920	10,121	10,595	10,861	10,904	10,931	10,969	11,006
Iceland	228	241	255	267	279	281	284	287	290
Ireland	3,393	3,544	3,507	3,598	3,732	3,778	3,833	3,900	3,964
Italy	56,388	56,588	56,694	56,844	56,909	56,924	56,961	56,994	57,321
Liechtenstein	26	27	28	31	32	32	33	34	34
Luxembourg	364	367	381	408	430	435	440	444	448
Malta	327	349	368	387	396	397	400	403	405
Monaco	26	29	31	33	35	35	35	35	35
Netherlands	14,091	14,454	14,893	15,424	15,760	15,864	15,987	16,105	16,193
Norway	4,079	4,146	4,233	4,348	4,445	4,478	4,503	4,524	4,552
Portugal	9,714	10,017	9,996	10,018	10,149	10,195	10,257	10,329	10,407
Spain	37,418	38,353	38,826	39,343	39,803	40,050	40,477	40,964	41,664
Sweden	8,303	8,343	8,527	8,816	8,854	8,861	8,883	8,909	8,941
Switzerland	6,304	6,456	6,674	7,019	7,124	7,164	7,204	7,256	7,314
Turkey	45,032	50,034	54,675	59,274	62,855	63,741	64,610	65,477	66,334
United Kingdom	56,285	56,482	57,157	57,943	58,580	58,785	59,000	59,216	59,435
Eastern Europe									
Albania	2,671	2,957	3,289	3,141	3,095	3,072	3,093	3,107	3,118
Belarus	9,592	9,929	10,189	10,210	10,045	10,002	9,957	9,900	9,831
Bosnia-Herzegovina	4,040	4,246	4,498	3,523	3,689	3,753	3,790	3,813	3,830
Bulgaria	8,835	8,954	8,767	8,308	8,038	7,984	7,937	7,891	7,846
Croatia	4,598	4,702	4,778	4,669	4,554	4,442	4,437	4,444	4,442
Czech Republic	10,277	10,302	10,301	10,317	10,253	10,236	10,220	10,206	10,203
Estonia	1,472	1,523	1,571	1,448	1,379	1,372	1,367	1,361	1,356
Georgia	4,770	4,961	5,145	4,794	4,470	4,435	4,401	4,372	4,343
Hungary	10,709	10,657	10,375	10,337	10,253	10,222	10,200	10,175	10,142
Latvia	2,509	2,570	2,668	2,501	2,399	2,382	2,359	2,331	2,301
Lithuania	3,404	3,529	3,694	3,643	3,536	3,512	3,487	3,476	3,463
Macedonia	1,779	1,812	1,893	1,948	1,990	2,000	2,009	2,017	2,024
Moldova	4,010	4,215	4,364	4,339	4,160	4,107	4,051	3,987	3,916
Montenegro	586	586	590	601	612	615	617	619	620
Poland	35,413	37,063	37,988	38,265	38,277	38,263	38,254	38,242	38,219
Romania	22,133	22,687	23,211	22,285	21,976	21,929	21,887	21,833	21,773
Russia	138,127	142,539	147,665	148,460	147,539	146,890	146,304	145,649	144,963
Serbia	7,756	7,628	7,572	7,625	7,553	7,528	7,505	7,502	7,491
Slovakia	4,963	5,140	5,270	5,349	5,376	5,379	5,379	5,376	5,372
Slovenia	1,893	1,937	1,996	1,989	1,978	1,988	1,990	1,994	1,995
Ukraine	49,781	50,648	51,557	51,300	49,545	49,115	48,664	48,241	47,823

Source: Euromonitor International from national statistics

Population: National Estimates at January 1st 1980, 1985, 1990, 1995, 1999-2011 *(continued)*

'000

	2004	2005	2006	2007	2008	2009	2010	2011	% growth
Western Europe									
Austria	8,143	8,201	8,254	8,283	8,319	8,355	8,375	8,404	11.38
Belgium	10,396	10,446	10,511	10,585	10,667	10,753	10,840	10,951	11.12
Cyprus	1,014	1,033	1,046	1,060	1,075	1,089	1,104	1,116	62.81
Denmark	5,398	5,411	5,427	5,447	5,476	5,511	5,535	5,561	8.56
Finland	5,220	5,237	5,256	5,277	5,300	5,326	5,351	5,375	12.66
France	60,505	60,963	61,400	61,795	62,135	62,466	62,791	63,128	17.49
Germany	82,532	82,501	82,438	82,315	82,218	82,002	81,802	81,752	4.57
Gibraltar	29	29	29	29	29	29	29	29	10.12
Greece	11,041	11,083	11,125	11,172	11,214	11,260	11,305	11,326	18.17
Iceland	293	297	301	306	311	315	320	324	42.03
Ireland	4,029	4,112	4,208	4,313	4,401	4,450	4,468	4,481	32.07
Italy	57,888	58,462	58,752	59,131	59,619	60,045	60,340	60,626	7.52
Liechtenstein	34	35	35	35	35	36	36	36	40.07
Luxembourg	453	457	467	477	487	497	507	514	41.18
Malta	407	409	410	412	414	415	417	418	27.98
Monaco	35	35	35	35	35	35	35	35	35.85
Netherlands	16,258	16,306	16,334	16,358	16,405	16,486	16,575	16,656	18.20
Norway	4,577	4,606	4,640	4,681	4,737	4,799	4,858	4,920	20.63
Portugal	10,475	10,529	10,570	10,599	10,618	10,627	10,638	10,637	9.51
Spain	42,345	43,038	43,758	44,475	45,283	45,828	45,989	46,153	23.35
Sweden	8,976	9,011	9,048	9,113	9,183	9,256	9,341	9,416	13.40
Switzerland	7,364	7,415	7,459	7,509	7,593	7,702	7,786	7,870	24.85
Turkey	67,188	68,029	68,861	69,689	70,586	71,517	72,474	73,312	62.80
United Kingdom	59,697	60,039	60,410	60,781	61,192	61,595	62,027	62,499	11.04
Eastern Europe									
Albania	3,129	3,142	3,149	3,160	3,174	3,190	3,204	3,215	20.34
Belarus	9,763	9,697	9,630	9,579	9,542	9,514	9,500	9,481	-1.15
Bosnia-Herzegovina	3,837	3,843	3,843	3,844	3,844	3,844	3,844	3,844	-4.86
Bulgaria	7,801	7,761	7,719	7,679	7,640	7,607	7,564	7,517	-14.92
Croatia	4,442	4,444	4,443	4,441	4,436	4,435	4,426	4,412	-4.04
Czech Republic	10,211	10,221	10,251	10,287	10,361	10,423	10,460	10,486	2.04
Estonia	1,351	1,348	1,345	1,342	1,341	1,340	1,340	1,340	-8.97
Georgia	4,315	4,322	4,401	4,395	4,382	4,385	4,389	4,393	-7.91
Hungary	10,117	10,098	10,077	10,066	10,045	10,031	10,014	9,986	-6.76
Latvia	2,274	2,245	2,218	2,188	2,162	2,136	2,107	2,075	-17.31
Lithuania	3,446	3,425	3,403	3,385	3,366	3,350	3,329	3,245	-4.69
Macedonia	2,030	2,035	2,039	2,042	2,045	2,049	2,053	2,057	15.60
Moldova	3,841	3,767	3,728	3,689	3,651	3,613	3,573	3,556	-11.33
Montenegro	621	622	622	622	622	621	621	620	5.87
Poland	38,191	38,174	38,157	38,125	38,116	38,136	38,167	38,189	7.84
Romania	21,711	21,659	21,610	21,565	21,529	21,499	21,462	21,424	-3.20
Russia	144,340	143,885	143,400	143,059	142,933	142,919	142,962	142,914	3.47
Serbia	7,470	7,456	7,425	7,398	7,366	7,335	7,307	7,275	-6.21
Slovakia	5,369	5,370	5,370	5,371	5,374	5,382	5,390	5,397	8.73
Slovenia	1,996	1,998	2,003	2,010	2,026	2,032	2,047	2,050	8.30
Ukraine	47,442	47,100	46,749	46,466	46,192	45,963	45,783	45,598	-8.40

Source: Euromonitor International from national statistics

22

Population

Population Statistics

Table 22.3

Population by Sex and Age at January 1st 2011

'000

	Total	Male	Female	0-14	15-64	65+
Western Europe						
Austria	8,404	4,095	4,309	1,235	5,689	1,480
Belgium	10,951	5,370	5,581	1,857	7,212	1,883
Cyprus	1,116	570	546	195	789	132
Denmark	5,561	2,757	2,804	995	3,632	934
Finland	5,375	2,638	2,737	888	3,547	941
France	63,128	30,579	32,548	11,594	40,852	10,682
Germany	81,752	40,112	41,639	10,941	53,966	16,844
Gibraltar	29	15	15	5	19	5
Greece	11,326	5,606	5,720	1,624	7,517	2,185
Iceland	324	163	161	67	217	40
Ireland	4,481	2,220	2,261	977	2,984	520
Italy	60,626	29,413	31,213	8,513	39,812	12,302
Liechtenstein	36	18	18	6	25	5
Luxembourg	514	256	258	90	352	72
Malta	418	207	211	62	296	61
Monaco	35	17	19	5	23	8
Netherlands	16,656	8,243	8,412	2,907	11,154	2,595
Norway	4,920	2,461	2,459	922	3,256	742
Portugal	10,637	5,147	5,490	1,608	7,098	1,931
Spain	46,153	22,725	23,428	6,965	31,310	7,878
Sweden	9,416	4,690	4,725	1,565	6,113	1,737
Switzerland	7,870	3,877	3,993	1,191	5,350	1,330
Turkey	73,312	36,784	36,528	18,542	49,373	5,397
United Kingdom	62,499	30,773	31,726	10,915	41,178	10,406
Eastern Europe						
Albania	3,215	1,608	1,606	710	2,189	317
Belarus	9,481	4,408	5,073	1,414	6,767	1,299
Bosnia-Herzegovina	3,844	1,849	1,994	573	2,731	540
Bulgaria	7,517	3,635	3,882	1,035	5,152	1,329
Croatia	4,412	2,130	2,282	669	2,986	757
Czech Republic	10,486	5,146	5,340	1,511	7,346	1,629
Estonia	1,340	618	722	206	906	228
Georgia	4,393	2,082	2,311	733	3,030	630
Hungary	9,986	4,744	5,242	1,461	6,854	1,671
Latvia	2,075	958	1,117	285	1,429	360
Lithuania	3,245	1,507	1,737	488	2,221	536
Macedonia	2,057	1,031	1,026	359	1,458	241
Moldova	3,556	1,688	1,868	592	2,564	400
Montenegro	620	306	314	118	424	78
Poland	38,189	18,435	19,755	5,749	27,253	5,188
Romania	21,424	10,430	10,994	3,247	14,992	3,184
Russia	142,914	66,086	76,828	21,989	103,062	17,863
Serbia	7,275	3,539	3,736	1,099	4,960	1,217
Slovakia	5,397	2,628	2,769	825	3,904	668
Slovenia	2,050	1,015	1,036	291	1,420	339
Ukraine	45,598	21,033	24,566	6,496	32,137	6,965

Source: Euromonitor International from national statistics

Table 22.4

Population by Sex and Age at January 1st (% Analysis) 2011

% of total population

	Total	Male	Female	0-14	15-64	65+
Western Europe						
Austria	100.00	48.73	51.27	14.69	67.70	17.61
Belgium	100.00	49.04	50.96	16.95	65.85	17.19
Cyprus	100.00	51.04	48.96	17.51	70.71	11.79
Denmark	100.00	49.57	50.43	17.90	65.31	16.79
Finland	100.00	49.08	50.92	16.51	65.98	17.51
France	100.00	48.44	51.50	10.07	64.71	16.02
Germany	100.00	49.07	50.93	13.38	66.01	20.60
Gibraltar	100.00	50.20	49.80	17.61	65.27	17.12
Greece	100.00	49.50	50.50	14.34	66.37	19.29
Iceland	100.00	50.38	49.62	20.76	67.04	12.20
Ireland	100.00	49.55	50.45	21.80	66.59	11.62
Italy	100.00	48.52	51.48	14.04	65.67	20.29
Liechtenstein	100.00	49.48	50.52	15.98	70.13	13.89
Luxembourg	100.00	49.73	50.27	17.59	68.44	13.97
Malta	100.00	49.62	50.38	14.71	70.72	14.56
Monaco	100.00	47.64	52.36	13.85	63.57	22.58
Netherlands	100.00	49.49	50.51	17.45	66.97	15.58
Norway	100.00	50.01	49.99	18.73	66.18	15.09
Portugal	100.00	48.38	51.62	15.11	66.73	18.16
Spain	100.00	49.24	50.76	15.09	67.84	17.07
Sweden	100.00	49.81	50.19	16.62	64.93	18.45
Switzerland	100.00	49.27	50.73	15.13	67.97	16.90
Turkey	100.00	50.17	49.83	25.29	67.35	7.36
United Kingdom	100.00	49.24	50.76	17.46	65.89	16.65
Eastern Europe						
Albania	100.00	50.03	49.97	22.07	68.08	9.85
Belarus	100.00	46.49	53.51	14.92	71.38	13.70
Bosnia-Herzegovina	100.00	48.12	51.88	14.91	71.05	14.04
Bulgaria	100.00	48.35	51.65	13.77	68.55	17.68
Croatia	100.00	48.27	51.73	15.15	67.68	17.16
Czech Republic	100.00	49.07	50.93	14.41	70.06	15.53
Estonia	100.00	46.09	53.91	15.35	67.64	17.01
Georgia	100.00	47.39	52.61	16.69	68.97	14.34
Hungary	100.00	47.50	52.50	14.63	68.64	16.74
Latvia	100.00	46.17	53.83	13.75	68.89	17.36
Lithuania	100.00	46.45	53.55	15.04	68.45	16.51
Macedonia	100.00	50.11	49.89	17.44	70.87	11.69
Moldova	100.00	47.46	52.54	16.65	72.11	11.24
Montenegro	100.00	49.39	50.61	19.10	68.32	12.57
Poland	100.00	48.27	51.73	15.05	71.36	13.58
Romania	100.00	48.68	51.32	15.16	69.98	14.86
Russia	100.00	46.24	53.76	15.39	72.11	12.50
Serbia	100.00	48.64	51.36	15.10	68.18	16.72
Slovakia	100.00	48.69	51.31	15.28	72.35	12.37
Slovenia	100.00	49.49	50.51	14.19	69.28	16.53
Ukraine	100.00	46.13	53.87	14.25	70.48	15.28

Source: Euromonitor International from national statistics

Population Statistics | | | | | | | | | | **Table 22.5**

Live Births 1985, 1990, 1995, 2000, 2006-2011
'000

	1985	1990	1995	2000	2006	2007	2008	2009	2010	2011
Western Europe										
Austria	87.4	90.5	88.7	78.3	77.9	76.3	77.8	76.3	78.7	78.1
Belgium	114.1	123.8	115.5	116.4	122.5	124.1	127.2	127.3	129.2	131.0
Cyprus	14.5	14.7	14.0	12.5	12.4	12.5	12.7	12.8	12.9	12.9
Denmark	53.7	63.4	69.8	67.1	65.0	64.1	65.0	62.8	63.4	59.0
Finland	62.8	65.5	63.1	56.7	58.8	58.7	59.5	60.4	61.0	60.0
France	768.4	762.4	729.6	774.8	796.9	786.0	796.0	793.4	802.2	827.0
Germany	813.8	905.7	765.2	767.0	672.7	684.9	682.5	665.1	677.9	662.7
Gibraltar	0.5	0.5	0.4	0.4	0.4	0.4	0.4	0.4	0.4	0.4
Greece	116.5	102.2	101.5	103.3	112.0	111.9	118.3	117.9	110.0	109.6
Iceland	4.3	4.5	4.4	4.1	4.4	4.5	4.6	4.7	4.7	4.8
Ireland	62.4	53.0	48.8	54.8	65.4	70.6	74.0	74.3	73.7	71.7
Italy	577.3	569.3	525.6	543.1	560.0	563.9	576.7	568.9	561.9	555.6
Liechtenstein	0.4	0.4	0.4	0.4	0.4	0.4	0.4	0.4	0.3	0.3
Luxembourg	4.3	4.8	5.4	5.4	5.4	5.5	5.6	5.7	5.8	5.9
Malta	6.1	5.8	5.1	4.2	3.8	3.8	3.8	3.8	3.8	3.8
Monaco		0.8	0.8	0.8	0.9	0.9	0.9	0.9	0.9	0.9
Netherlands	178.1	198.0	190.5	206.6	185.1	181.3	184.6	184.9	184.4	180.1
Norway	51.1	60.9	60.3	59.2	58.5	58.5	60.5	61.8	61.4	60.2
Portugal	130.5	116.4	107.2	120.0	105.4	102.5	104.6	99.5	101.3	100.1
Spain	456.3	401.4	363.5	397.6	483.0	492.5	519.8	493.7	485.3	475.1
Sweden	98.5	123.9	103.4	90.4	105.9	107.4	109.3	111.8	115.6	111.8
Switzerland	74.7	83.9	82.2	78.5	73.4	74.5	76.7	78.3	80.3	80.8
Turkey	1,437.4	1,395.0	1,468.0	1,494.0	1,362.0	1,361.0	1,272.0	1,238.3	1,236.1	1,230.8
United Kingdom	750.5	798.4	731.6	679.0	748.6	772.2	794.4	790.2	807.3	812.0
Eastern Europe										
Albania	78.0	78.8	68.0	52.3	41.8	41.2	41.0	40.9	40.9	41.0
Belarus	165.0	142.2	101.1	93.7	96.7	103.6	107.9	109.3	108.1	109.1
Bosnia-Herzegovina	72.7	67.0	47.9	39.6	34.0	33.8	34.6	34.7	34.6	34.5
Bulgaria	119.0	105.2	72.0	73.7	74.0	75.3	77.7	81.0	80.9	80.4
Croatia	62.7	55.4	50.2	43.7	41.4	41.9	43.8	44.6	43.4	43.5
Czech Republic	135.9	130.6	96.1	90.9	105.8	114.6	119.6	118.3	117.2	108.7
Estonia	23.6	22.3	13.5	13.1	14.9	15.8	16.0	15.8	15.8	15.9
Georgia	97.7	92.8	56.3	48.8	47.8	49.3	56.6	56.7	56.7	56.6
Hungary	130.2	125.7	112.1	97.6	99.9	97.6	99.1	96.4	90.3	89.8
Latvia	39.8	37.9	21.6	20.2	22.3	23.3	23.9	21.7	19.2	18.6
Lithuania	58.5	56.9	41.2	34.1	31.3	32.3	35.1	36.7	35.6	35.3
Macedonia	36.3	33.2	29.9	26.2	22.6	22.7	22.9	23.7	24.1	24.4
Moldova	92.6	80.4	59.3	48.3	44.7	44.7	44.7	44.5	44.1	43.5
Montenegro	9.9	9.6	9.5	9.2	7.5	7.8	8.3	8.6	7.4	7.3
Poland	680.1	547.7	433.1	378.3	374.2	387.9	414.5	417.6	410.6	409.7
Romania	358.8	314.7	236.6	234.5	219.5	214.7	221.9	222.4	220.5	218.1
Russia	2,375.1	1,988.9	1,363.8	1,266.8	1,479.6	1,610.1	1,713.9	1,761.7	1,788.9	1,796.8
Serbia	99.7	94.0	86.2	73.8	71.0	68.1	69.1	70.3	68.3	68.0
Slovakia	90.2	80.0	61.4	55.2	53.9	54.4	57.4	61.2	60.4	60.8
Slovenia	25.9	22.4	19.0	18.2	18.9	19.8	21.8	21.9	22.3	22.4
Ukraine	762.8	657.2	492.9	385.1	460.4	472.7	510.6	512.5	497.7	502.6

Source: Euromonitor International from national statistics

| Table 22.6

Deaths 1985, 1990, 1995, 2000, 2006-2011

'000

	1985	1990	1995	2000	2006	2007	2008	2009	2010	2011
Western Europe										
Austria	89.6	83.0	81.2	76.8	74.3	74.6	75.1	77.4	77.2	76.5
Belgium	111.6	104.1	104.9	104.9	101.6	100.7	104.6	104.5	105.1	106.0
Cyprus	5.2	5.4	5.9	6.5	7.1	7.2	7.3	7.4	7.5	7.6
Denmark	58.4	60.9	63.1	58.0	55.5	55.6	54.6	54.9	54.4	52.5
Finland	48.2	50.1	49.3	49.3	48.1	49.1	49.1	49.9	50.9	50.6
France	552.5	526.2	531.6	530.9	516.4	521.0	532.1	538.1	540.5	555.0
Germany	929.6	921.4	884.6	838.8	821.6	827.2	844.4	854.5	858.8	852.4
Gibraltar	0.3	0.3	0.2	0.3	0.2	0.2	0.2	0.2	0.2	0.2
Greece	92.9	94.2	100.2	105.2	105.5	109.9	108.0	108.3	106.7	107.3
Iceland	1.7	1.7	1.8	1.9	1.9	1.9	2.0	2.0	2.0	2.1
Ireland	33.2	31.4	32.3	31.4	27.5	28.1	28.3	28.9	27.1	31.1
Italy	547.4	541.7	554.3	555.5	558.6	572.9	578.2	585.2	587.5	591.9
Liechtenstein		0.2	0.2	0.2	0.2	0.2	0.2	0.2	0.2	0.2
Luxembourg	4.0	3.9	3.9	3.9	3.9	3.9	4.0	4.0	4.1	4.1
Malta	2.8	2.9	2.9	3.1	3.3	3.3	3.4	3.4	3.4	3.5
Monaco		0.6	0.6	0.5	0.5	0.5	0.5	0.5	0.5	0.5
Netherlands	122.7	128.8	135.7	140.5	135.4	133.0	135.1	134.2	136.1	135.5
Norway	44.4	46.0	45.2	44.0	41.3	42.0	41.7	41.4	41.5	41.4
Portugal	97.1	103.1	103.9	105.4	102.0	103.5	104.3	104.4	105.9	106.6
Spain	312.5	333.1	346.2	360.4	371.5	385.4	386.3	383.2	380.2	388.5
Sweden	94.0	95.2	94.0	93.5	91.2	91.7	91.4	90.1	90.5	89.9
Switzerland	59.6	63.7	63.4	62.5	60.3	61.1	61.2	62.5	62.6	62.1
Turkey	422.5	404.0	436.0	477.0	456.0	464.0	454.0	461.8	470.9	479.0
United Kingdom	670.7	641.8	645.5	608.4	572.2	574.7	579.7	559.6	561.7	560.0
Eastern Europe										
Albania	17.2	18.9	20.1	18.6	18.5	18.7	19.0	19.3	19.7	20.1
Belarus	105.7	109.6	133.8	134.9	138.4	133.0	133.9	135.1	137.1	135.1
Bosnia-Herzegovina	29.0	29.1	26.8	30.5	33.2	35.0	34.0	34.8	35.6	36.2
Bulgaria	107.5	108.6	114.7	115.1	113.4	113.0	110.5	108.1	107.5	106.9
Croatia	52.1	52.2	50.5	50.2	50.4	52.4	52.2	52.4	52.1	52.4
Czech Republic	131.6	129.2	117.9	109.0	104.4	104.6	104.9	107.4	106.8	106.8
Estonia	19.3	19.5	20.8	18.4	17.3	17.4	16.7	16.1	15.8	15.8
Georgia	46.2	50.7	49.1	47.4	42.3	41.2	43.0	43.8	44.5	45.1
Hungary	147.6	145.7	145.4	135.6	131.6	132.9	130.0	130.4	130.5	130.0
Latvia	34.2	34.8	38.9	32.2	33.1	33.0	31.0	29.9	30.0	28.5
Lithuania	39.2	39.8	45.3	38.9	44.8	45.6	43.8	42.0	42.1	41.5
Macedonia	14.3	14.5	16.2	17.1	18.6	19.6	19.0	19.1	19.3	19.6
Moldova	45.6	45.4	49.1	49.4	49.6	49.4	49.0	48.5	47.8	47.1
Montenegro	3.5	3.8	4.9	5.4	6.0	6.0	5.7	5.9	5.6	5.7
Poland	384.0	390.3	386.1	368.0	369.7	377.2	379.4	384.9	388.2	391.2
Romania	246.7	247.1	271.7	255.8	258.1	252.0	253.2	257.2	256.6	256.0
Russia	1,625.3	1,656.0	2,203.8	2,225.3	2,166.7	2,080.4	2,076.0	2,010.5	2,028.5	2,014.1
Serbia	86.0	88.3	93.9	104.0	102.9	102.8	102.7	104.0	103.2	104.4
Slovakia	52.5	54.6	52.7	52.7	53.3	53.9	53.2	52.9	53.4	51.9
Slovenia	19.9	18.6	19.0	18.6	18.2	18.6	18.3	18.8	18.6	18.9
Ukraine	617.5	629.6	792.6	758.1	758.1	762.9	754.5	706.7	698.2	664.6

Source: Euromonitor International from national statistics

Population Statistics

Table 22.7

Birth Rates 1985, 1990, 1995, 2000, 2006-2011

Per '000 inhabitants

	1985	1990	1995	2000	2006	2007	2008	2009	2010	2011
Western Europe										
Austria	11.6	11.8	11.2	9.8	9.4	9.2	9.3	9.1	9.4	9.3
Belgium	11.6	12.4	11.4	11.4	11.6	11.7	11.9	11.8	11.9	11.9
Cyprus	20.3	19.0	16.4	13.2	11.9	11.8	11.8	11.7	11.7	11.6
Denmark	10.5	12.3	13.3	12.6	12.0	11.7	11.8	11.4	11.4	10.6
Finland	12.8	13.1	12.3	11.0	11.2	11.1	11.2	11.3	11.4	11.1
France	13.9	13.4	12.6	13.1	12.9	12.7	12.8	12.7	12.7	13.1
Germany	10.5	11.4	9.4	9.3	8.2	8.3	8.3	8.1	8.3	8.1
Gibraltar	18.7	19.8	15.9	14.9	12.8	13.7	13.7	13.4	13.6	13.6
Greece	11.7	10.1	9.5	9.5	10.0	10.0	10.5	10.5	9.7	9.7
Iceland	17.7	17.5	16.5	14.8	14.6	14.7	14.8	14.8	14.8	14.8
Ireland	17.6	15.1	13.5	14.4	15.4	16.2	16.7	16.7	16.5	16.0
Italy	10.2	10.0	9.2	9.5	9.5	9.5	9.6	9.5	9.3	9.1
Liechtenstein	14.0	13.4	13.9	12.9	10.3	10.0	9.9	11.4	9.1	8.9
Luxembourg	11.8	12.6	13.3	12.5	11.4	11.4	11.4	11.5	11.5	11.6
Malta	17.5	15.8	13.3	10.6	9.1	9.1	9.2	9.2	9.2	9.1
Monaco		25.6	25.1	21.6	25.0	25.2	25.6	25.6	25.8	25.9
Netherlands	12.3	13.2	12.3	13.0	11.3	11.1	11.2	11.2	11.1	10.8
Norway	12.3	14.4	13.8	13.2	12.6	12.4	12.7	12.8	12.6	12.2
Portugal	13.0	11.7	10.7	11.7	10.0	9.7	9.8	9.4	9.5	9.4
Spain	11.9	10.3	9.2	9.9	10.9	11.0	11.4	10.8	10.5	10.3
Sweden	11.8	14.5	11.7	10.2	11.7	11.7	11.9	12.0	12.3	11.8
Switzerland	11.5	12.5	11.7	10.9	9.8	9.9	10.0	10.1	10.3	10.2
Turkey	28.5	25.3	24.6	23.3	19.7	19.4	17.9	17.2	17.0	16.7
United Kingdom	13.3	13.9	12.6	11.5	12.4	12.7	12.9	12.8	13.0	12.9
Eastern Europe										
Albania	26.1	24.6	21.4	16.9	13.3	13.0	12.9	12.8	12.8	12.7
Belarus	16.6	14.0	9.9	9.4	10.1	10.8	11.3	11.5	11.4	11.5
Bosnia-Herzegovina	17.0	15.1	13.8	10.5	8.9	8.8	9.0	9.0	9.0	9.0
Bulgaria	13.3	12.1	8.7	9.3	9.6	9.8	10.2	10.7	10.7	10.7
Croatia	13.3	11.6	11.0	9.9	9.3	9.4	9.9	10.1	9.8	9.9
Czech Republic	13.2	12.7	9.3	8.9	10.3	11.1	11.5	11.3	11.2	10.4
Estonia	15.5	14.2	9.4	9.5	11.1	11.8	12.0	11.8	11.8	11.8
Georgia	19.6	18.0	11.9	11.0	10.9	11.2	12.9	12.9	12.9	12.9
Hungary	12.3	12.1	10.8	9.6	9.9	9.7	9.9	9.6	9.0	9.0
Latvia	15.4	14.2	8.7	8.5	9.7	10.2	10.6	9.6	8.9	9.0
Lithuania	16.5	15.4	11.4	9.8	9.2	9.6	10.4	11.0	10.8	11.0
Macedonia	20.0	17.5	15.2	12.9	11.1	11.1	11.2	11.5	11.7	11.8
Moldova	22.0	18.5	13.7	11.8	12.0	12.1	12.2	12.3	12.3	12.3
Montenegro	16.9	16.2	15.8	14.9	12.1	12.6	13.3	13.9	12.0	11.9
Poland	18.3	14.4	11.3	9.9	9.8	10.2	10.9	10.9	10.8	10.7
Romania	15.8	13.6	10.6	10.7	10.2	10.0	10.3	10.4	10.3	10.2
Russia	16.6	13.4	9.2	8.6	10.3	11.3	12.0	12.3	12.5	12.6
Serbia	13.1	12.4	11.3	9.8	9.6	9.2	9.4	9.6	9.5	9.4
Slovakia	17.5	15.2	11.5	10.3	10.0	10.1	10.7	11.4	11.2	11.3
Slovenia	13.4	11.2	9.5	9.1	9.4	9.8	10.8	10.7	10.9	10.9
Ukraine	15.0	12.7	9.6	7.9	9.9	10.2	11.1	11.2	10.9	11.0

Source: Euromonitor International from national statistics

Table 22.8

Death Rates 1985, 1990, 1995, 2000, 2006-2011

Per '000 inhabitants

	1985	1990	1995	2000	2006	2007	2008	2009	2010	2011
Western Europe										
Austria	11.8	10.8	10.2	9.6	9.0	9.0	9.0	9.3	9.2	9.1
Belgium	11.3	10.4	10.3	10.2	9.6	9.5	9.8	9.7	9.6	9.6
Cyprus	7.2	7.0	6.9	6.8	6.8	6.8	6.8	6.8	6.8	6.8
Denmark	11.4	11.9	12.1	10.9	10.2	10.2	9.9	9.9	9.8	9.4
Finland	9.8	10.0	9.6	9.5	9.1	9.3	9.2	9.3	9.5	9.4
France	10.0	9.3	9.2	9.0	8.4	8.4	8.5	8.6	8.6	8.8
Germany	12.0	11.6	10.8	10.2	10.0	10.1	10.3	10.6	10.7	10.8
Gibraltar	10.4	10.4	7.5	9.6	7.9	6.9	7.8	7.7	7.7	7.7
Greece	9.4	9.3	9.4	9.6	9.5	9.8	9.6	9.6	9.4	9.5
Iceland	6.9	6.8	6.9	6.6	6.3	6.3	6.4	6.4	6.4	6.4
Ireland	9.4	8.9	8.9	8.2	6.4	6.4	6.4	6.5	6.1	6.9
Italy	9.7	9.6	9.8	9.8	9.5	9.7	9.7	9.9	10.2	10.2
Liechtenstein		6.9	7.3	7.3	6.3	6.4	5.8	6.4	6.6	6.7
Luxembourg	10.9	10.2	9.6	8.9	8.2	8.2	8.1	8.1	8.0	8.0
Malta	8.0	7.7	7.7	7.7	8.1	8.1	8.2	8.2	8.2	8.3
Monaco		19.0	17.0	15.6	15.2	14.7	14.6	14.1	13.9	13.7
Netherlands	8.5	8.6	8.8	8.8	8.3	8.1	8.2	8.1	8.2	8.1
Norway	10.7	10.9	10.4	9.8	8.9	8.9	8.7	8.6	8.5	8.4
Portugal	9.7	10.3	10.4	10.3	9.6	9.8	9.8	9.8	10.0	10.0
Spain	8.1	8.6	8.8	9.0	8.4	8.6	8.5	8.3	8.3	8.4
Sweden	11.3	11.1	10.6	10.5	10.0	10.0	9.9	9.7	9.6	9.5
Switzerland	9.2	9.5	9.0	8.7	8.1	8.1	8.0	8.1	8.0	7.8
Turkey	8.4	7.3	7.3	7.4	6.6	6.6	6.4	6.4	6.5	6.5
United Kingdom	11.9	11.2	11.1	10.3	9.4	9.4	9.3	9.4	9.5	9.5
Eastern Europe										
Albania	5.8	5.9	6.3	6.0	5.9	5.9	6.0	6.1	6.1	6.2
Belarus	10.6	10.8	13.1	13.5	14.4	13.9	14.1	14.2	14.4	14.3
Bosnia-Herzegovina	6.8	6.5	7.7	8.1	8.6	9.1	8.8	9.1	9.2	9.4
Bulgaria	12.0	12.5	13.9	14.5	14.7	14.8	14.5	14.2	14.3	14.3
Croatia	11.1	10.9	11.0	11.3	11.3	11.8	11.8	11.8	11.8	11.9
Czech Republic	12.8	12.5	11.4	10.7	10.2	10.1	10.1	10.3	10.2	10.2
Estonia	12.7	12.4	14.5	13.4	12.9	13.0	12.4	12.0	11.8	11.8
Georgia	9.3	9.8	10.4	10.7	9.6	9.4	9.8	10.0	10.1	10.3
Hungary	13.9	14.0	14.1	13.3	13.1	13.2	13.0	13.0	13.0	13.0
Latvia	13.2	13.1	15.7	13.6	14.5	14.5	13.7	13.3	13.9	13.9
Lithuania	11.1	10.8	12.5	11.1	13.2	13.5	13.1	12.6	12.8	12.9
Macedonia	7.9	7.6	8.2	8.4	9.1	9.6	9.3	9.3	9.4	9.5
Moldova	10.9	10.4	11.4	12.1	13.3	13.4	13.4	13.4	13.4	13.3
Montenegro	6.0	6.5	8.2	8.8	9.6	9.6	9.2	9.4	9.1	9.1
Poland	10.3	10.3	10.1	9.6	9.7	9.9	10.0	10.1	10.2	10.2
Romania	10.9	10.6	12.2	11.7	12.0	11.7	11.8	12.0	12.0	12.0
Russia	11.4	11.2	14.9	15.2	15.1	14.5	14.5	14.1	14.2	14.1
Serbia	11.3	11.7	12.3	13.8	13.9	13.9	14.0	14.2	14.3	14.4
Slovakia	10.2	10.3	9.8	9.8	9.9	10.0	9.9	9.8	9.9	9.6
Slovenia	10.2	9.3	9.5	9.3	9.1	9.2	9.0	9.2	9.1	9.2
Ukraine	12.2	12.2	15.5	15.5	16.3	16.5	16.4	15.4	15.3	14.6

Source: Euromonitor International from national statistics

22

Population

Population Statistics

Table 22.9

Infant Mortality Rates 1985, 1990, 1995, 2000, 2006-2011

Deaths per '000 live births

	1985	1990	1995	2000	2006	2007	2008	2009	2010	2011
Western Europe										
Austria	11.2	7.8	5.4	4.8	3.6	3.7	3.7	3.8	3.9	3.8
Belgium	9.8	8.0	6.1	4.8	4.0	4.0	3.8	3.5	3.5	3.5
Cyprus	13.7	10.8	8.4	6.6	4.9	4.7	4.6	4.5	4.4	4.4
Denmark	7.9	7.5	5.1	5.3	3.5	4.0	4.0	3.1	3.4	3.4
Finland	6.3	5.6	3.9	3.8	2.8	2.7	2.6	2.6	2.3	2.3
France	8.3	7.3	4.9	4.4	3.6	3.6	3.6	3.7	3.7	3.6
Germany	9.1	7.0	5.3	4.4	3.8	3.9	3.5	3.5	3.4	3.4
Gibraltar										
Greece	14.1	9.7	8.1	5.9	3.7	3.5	2.7	3.1	2.8	2.8
Iceland	5.8	5.2	4.4	3.3	2.1	2.1	2.0	2.0	2.0	2.0
Ireland	8.8	8.2	6.4	6.2	3.6	3.1	3.8	3.2	3.8	3.8
Italy	10.5	8.1	6.1	4.3	3.6	3.5	3.3	3.9	3.4	3.4
Liechtenstein										
Luxembourg	10.4	8.0	5.9	4.9	3.2	2.7	2.4	2.2	2.1	2.1
Malta	14.1	11.6	9.5	7.8	6.1	5.9	5.8	5.6	5.5	5.5
Monaco	7.3	6.7	5.0	3.9	3.5	3.5	3.4	3.4	3.4	3.3
Netherlands	8.0	7.1	5.5	5.1	4.4	4.1	3.8	3.8	3.8	3.8
Norway	8.5	6.9	4.0	3.8	3.2	3.1	2.7	3.1	2.8	2.8
Portugal	17.8	10.9	7.4	5.5	3.3	3.4	3.3	3.6	2.4	2.4
Spain	8.9	7.6	5.5	4.4	3.5	3.5	3.3	3.3	3.2	3.2
Sweden	6.8	6.0	4.1	3.4	2.8	2.5	2.5	2.5	2.5	2.5
Switzerland	6.9	6.8	5.1	4.9	4.4	3.9	4.0	4.3	3.8	3.8
Turkey	93.2	54.0	44.7	26.4	22.6	15.6	16.0	15.7	13.7	12.7
United Kingdom	11.1	7.9	6.2	5.6	4.9	4.7	4.6	4.7	4.3	4.3
Eastern Europe										
Albania	41.2	36.9	32.8	24.7	18.6	18.3	17.9	17.6	17.3	17.0
Belarus	14.6	12.1	13.5	9.3	6.1	5.2	4.5	4.7	4.1	4.0
Bosnia-Herzegovina	25.1	15.3	14.8	9.7	7.5	6.8	6.9	6.5	5.9	5.8
Bulgaria	15.4	14.8	14.8	13.3	9.7	9.2	8.6	9.0	9.4	9.2
Croatia	16.6	10.7	8.9	7.4	5.2	5.6	4.5	5.3	4.4	4.4
Czech Republic	12.5	10.8	7.7	4.1	3.3	3.1	2.8	2.9	2.7	2.7
Estonia	14.1	12.3	14.9	8.4	4.4	5.0	5.0	3.6	3.3	3.3
Georgia	20.8	15.8	13.1	22.5	15.8	13.3	17.0	16.7	12.4	12.0
Hungary	20.4	14.8	10.7	9.2	5.7	5.9	5.6	5.1	5.3	5.2
Latvia	13.0	13.7	18.8	10.4	7.6	8.7	6.7	7.8	5.7	5.6
Lithuania	14.2	10.2	12.5	8.6	6.8	5.9	4.9	4.9	4.3	4.2
Macedonia	46.3	33.7	24.3	13.2	11.5	10.3	9.7	11.7	7.7	7.5
Moldova	32.5	30.2	27.0	21.6	16.3	15.8	15.3	15.0	14.7	14.5
Montenegro	19.8	15.2	12.8	11.9	10.3	7.3	7.9	6.3	6.1	6.0
Poland	22.1	19.4	13.6	8.1	6.0	6.0	5.6	5.6	5.0	4.9
Romania	25.6	26.9	21.2	18.6	13.9	12.0	11.0	10.1	9.8	9.6
Russia	20.8	17.6	18.2	15.2	10.2	9.2	8.4	8.1	7.5	7.4
Serbia	26.5	18.6	12.0	10.6	7.4	7.1	6.7	7.0	6.7	6.6
Slovakia	16.3	12.0	11.0	8.6	6.6	6.1	5.9	5.7	5.7	5.6
Slovenia	13.0	8.4	5.5	4.9	3.4	2.8	2.4	2.4	2.5	2.5
Ukraine	15.9	13.0	14.8	12.0	9.6	11.0	9.9	9.4	9.1	9.0

Source: Euromonitor International from national statistics
Note: Rates refer to deaths of infants under one year

Population Statistics

Table 22.10

Marriage Rates 1985, 1990, 1995, 2000, 2006-2011

Per '000 inhabitants

	1985	1990	1995	2000	2006	2007	2008	2009	2010	2011
Western Europe										
Austria	5.9	5.9	5.4	4.9	4.5	4.4	4.2	4.3	4.5	4.6
Belgium	5.8	6.5	5.1	4.4	4.3	4.3	4.3	4.0	4.0	4.0
Cyprus	8.0	7.3	7.8	9.8	4.7	6.0	5.7	5.8	6.2	6.2
Denmark	5.7	6.1	6.7	7.2	6.7	6.7	6.8	6.0	5.6	5.1
Finland	5.3	5.0	4.7	5.1	5.4	5.6	5.9	5.6	5.6	5.6
France	4.9	5.1	4.4	5.1	4.4	4.4	4.3	4.0	4.1	4.1
Germany	6.4	6.6	5.3	5.1	4.5	4.5	4.6	4.6	4.6	4.6
Gibraltar				5.4	5.5	4.5	5.4	5.2	5.2	5.3
Greece	6.4	5.8	6.0	4.4	5.2	5.5	4.7	5.2	5.2	5.1
Iceland	5.2	4.5	4.6	6.3	5.8	5.9	5.5	4.7	4.5	4.2
Ireland	5.3	5.1	4.3	5.1	5.3	5.3	5.1	4.9	4.9	4.9
Italy	5.3	5.5	5.1	5.0	4.2	4.2	4.2	3.9	3.6	3.6
Liechtenstein	12.7	11.5	13.4	7.3	4.3	5.2	5.8	4.3	5.0	5.0
Luxembourg	5.4	6.1	5.1	4.9	4.2	4.1	3.9	3.5	3.4	3.2
Malta	7.3	6.8	6.0	6.4	6.2	6.0	6.0	5.7	6.2	6.3
Monaco		6.0	5.0	4.9	4.7	4.6	4.5	4.5	4.4
Netherlands	5.7	6.4	5.3	5.6	4.4	4.4	4.5	4.4	4.4	4.4
Norway	4.9	5.2	5.0	5.7	4.7	5.0	5.3	5.2	4.9	4.8
Portugal	6.8	7.2	6.6	6.3	4.5	4.4	4.1	3.8	3.7	3.7
Spain	5.2	5.7	5.1	5.4	4.7	4.6	4.3	3.8	3.7	3.7
Sweden	4.6	4.8	3.8	4.5	5.0	5.3	5.5	5.2	5.5	5.5
Switzerland	6.0	7.0	5.8	5.6	5.4	5.4	5.5	5.5	5.5	5.5
Turkey	7.4	8.5	7.9	7.3	9.3	9.2	9.2	8.3	8.1	8.0
United Kingdom	7.0	6.6	5.6	5.2	5.2	4.5	4.4	5.2	5.1	5.0
Eastern Europe										
Albania	8.5	8.8	8.6	8.4	6.8	7.1	6.7	6.6	6.6	6.4
Belarus	10.0	9.8	7.5	6.2	8.1	9.3	8.0	8.1	8.2	8.3
Bosnia-Herzegovina	7.8	6.7	6.0	5.9	5.6	6.1	5.8	5.4	5.4	5.5
Bulgaria	7.5	6.8	4.4	4.4	4.2	3.8	3.6	3.4	3.2	3.2
Croatia	6.9	6.2	5.2	4.9	5.0	5.2	5.3	5.1	5.1	5.1
Czech Republic	7.8	8.8	5.3	5.4	5.2	5.6	5.1	4.6	4.7	4.7
Estonia	8.5	7.5	4.8	4.0	5.2	5.2	4.6	4.0	3.8	3.8
Georgia	8.9	6.8	4.4	2.9	5.0	5.7	7.2	7.2	7.9	7.5
Hungary	6.9	6.4	5.2	4.7	4.4	4.1	4.0	3.7	3.5	3.5
Latvia	9.4	8.9	4.4	3.9	6.4	6.8	5.7	4.4	4.1	4.1
Lithuania	9.7	9.9	6.1	4.8	6.2	6.8	7.1	6.1	5.6	5.6
Macedonia	9.0	8.3	8.1	7.1	7.3	7.6	7.2	7.3	6.9	6.9
Moldova	9.7	9.4	7.6	5.3	7.3	7.9	7.3	7.4	7.4	7.3
Montenegro	7.1	6.3	5.9	6.1	5.5	6.4	5.5	6.1	6.1	6.1
Poland	7.2	6.7	5.4	5.5	5.9	6.5	6.8	6.6	6.0	6.1
Romania	7.1	8.3	6.9	6.2	6.8	8.8	6.9	6.2	6.3	6.4
Russia	9.8	9.0	7.2	6.1	7.8	8.9	8.3	8.4	8.6	8.6
Serbia	6.4	6.1	5.5	5.6	5.3	5.5	5.2	5.0	5.0	5.0
Slovakia	7.6	7.7	5.1	4.8	4.8	5.1	5.2	4.9	4.9	4.9
Slovenia	5.5	4.3	4.1	3.6	3.2	3.2	3.3	3.2	3.2	3.2
Ukraine	9.7	9.4	8.4	5.6	7.6	8.9	7.0	6.9	7.0	7.1

Source: Euromonitor International from national statistics
Note: Rates refer to legal marriages (recognised marriages performed and registered)

Population Statistics **Table 22.11**

Divorce Rates 1985, 1990, 1995, 2000, 2006-2011

Per '000 inhabitants

	1985	1990	1995	2000	2006	2007	2008	2009	2010	2011
Western Europe										
Austria	2.0	2.1	2.3	2.4	2.5	2.5	2.4	2.3	2.3	2.4
Belgium	1.9	2.0	3.5	2.6	2.8	2.9	3.3	3.0	3.1	3.2
Cyprus	0.4	0.5	0.9	1.3	1.7	1.6	1.5	1.6	1.6	1.6
Denmark	2.8	2.7	2.5	2.7	2.6	2.6	2.7	2.7	2.6	2.7
Finland	1.9	2.6	2.8	2.7	2.5	2.5	2.5	2.5	2.6	2.6
France	2.0	1.9	2.1	1.9	2.2	2.1	2.1	2.1	2.1	2.1
Germany	2.3	2.0	2.1	2.4	2.3	2.3	2.3	2.3	2.3	2.3
Gibraltar				3.5	4.1	3.3	2.7	2.5	2.2	2.0
Greece	0.8	0.6	1.0	1.0	1.2	1.2	1.2	1.2	1.2	1.2
Iceland	2.2	1.9	1.8	1.9	1.7	1.7	1.8	1.7	1.8	1.8
Ireland				0.7	0.8	0.9	0.8	0.8	0.8	0.8
Italy	0.3	0.5	0.5	0.7	0.8	0.9	0.9	0.9	0.9	0.9
Liechtenstein		1.0	1.2	3.9	2.3	2.8	2.8	2.8	2.4	2.3
Luxembourg	1.8	2.0	1.8	2.4	2.5	2.3	2.0	2.1	2.1	2.1
Malta										
Monaco			2.5	2.6	2.1	2.1	2.0	1.9	1.9	1.8
Netherlands	2.4	1.9	2.2	2.2	1.9	2.0	2.0	1.9	1.9	1.9
Norway	2.0	2.4	2.4	2.3	2.3	2.2	2.2	2.1	2.1	2.1
Portugal	0.9	0.9	1.2	1.9	2.3	2.4	2.5	2.5	2.5	2.6
Spain	0.5	0.6	0.8	0.9	2.9	2.8	2.4	2.2	2.1	2.1
Sweden	2.4	2.3	2.6	2.4	2.2	2.3	2.3	2.4	2.5	2.6
Switzerland	1.8	2.0	2.2	1.5	2.8	2.7	2.6	2.5	2.5	2.5
Turkey	0.4	0.5	0.5	0.6	1.4	1.4	1.4	1.6	1.6	1.6
United Kingdom	3.1	2.9	2.9	2.6	2.5	2.4	2.2	2.4	2.4	2.4
Eastern Europe										
Albania	0.8	0.8	0.7	0.7	1.3	1.0	1.1	1.1	1.0	1.0
Belarus	3.2	3.4	4.1	4.3	3.3	3.7	3.8	3.6	3.6	3.5
Bosnia-Herzegovina	0.4	0.4	0.5	0.5	0.4	0.5	0.4	0.4	0.4	0.4
Bulgaria	1.6	1.3	1.3	1.3	1.9	2.1	1.8	1.5	1.5	1.4
Croatia	1.2	1.2	0.9	1.0	1.0	1.1	1.1	1.2	1.2	1.2
Czech Republic	3.0	3.1	3.0	2.9	3.1	3.0	3.0	2.8	2.9	3.0
Estonia	4.0	3.7	5.1	3.1	2.8	2.8	2.6	2.4	2.2	2.2
Georgia	1.3	1.3	0.6	0.4	0.5	0.5	0.7	0.9	1.1	1.0
Hungary	2.7	2.4	2.4	2.3	2.5	2.5	2.5	2.4	2.4	2.4
Latvia	4.6	4.0	3.1	2.6	3.2	3.2	2.7	2.3	2.2	2.2
Lithuania	3.3	3.5	2.8	3.1	3.3	3.3	3.1	2.8	3.0	3.0
Macedonia	0.5	0.4	0.4	0.7	0.7	0.7	0.6	0.6	0.8	0.8
Moldova	2.7	3.0	3.4	2.4	3.4	3.8	3.5	3.3	3.2	3.1
Montenegro	0.6	0.5	0.6	0.7	0.7	0.7	0.7	0.7	0.7	0.7
Poland	1.3	1.1	1.0	1.1	1.9	1.7	1.7	1.7	1.6	1.6
Romania	1.4	1.4	1.6	1.4	1.5	1.7	1.7	1.5	1.5	1.6
Russia	4.0	3.8	4.5	4.3	4.5	4.8	4.9	4.9	4.5	4.6
Serbia	1.2	1.1	1.0	1.0	1.1	1.2	1.2	1.2	1.2	1.1
Slovakia	1.5	1.7	1.7	1.7	2.4	2.3	2.3	2.3	2.3	2.3
Slovenia	1.3	0.9	0.8	1.1	1.2	1.3	1.1	1.1	1.1	1.2
Ukraine	3.6	3.7	3.8	4.0	3.8	3.8	3.6	3.2	3.2	3.3

Source: Euromonitor International from national statistics
Note: Rates refer to final divorce decrees granted under civil law

Table 22.12

Fertility Rates 1985, 1990, 1995, 2000, 2006-2011

Children born per female

	1985	1990	1995	2000	2006	2007	2008	2009	2010	2011
Western Europe										
Austria	1.5	1.5	1.4	1.4	1.4	1.4	1.4	1.4	1.4	1.4
Belgium	1.5	1.6	1.6	1.7	1.8	1.8	1.9	1.8	1.8	1.8
Cyprus	2.5	2.4	2.1	1.7	1.5	1.5	1.5	1.5	1.5	1.5
Denmark	1.4	1.7	1.8	1.8	1.9	1.8	1.9	1.8	1.9	1.8
Finland	1.6	1.8	1.8	1.7	1.8	1.8	1.9	1.9	1.9	1.8
France	1.8	1.8	1.7	1.9	2.0	2.0	2.0	2.0	2.0	2.0
Germany	1.4	1.5	1.2	1.4	1.3	1.4	1.4	1.4	1.4	1.4
Gibraltar										
Greece	1.7	1.4	1.3	1.3	1.4	1.4	1.5	1.5	1.6	1.6
Iceland	2.2	2.2	2.1	2.0	2.1	2.1	2.1	2.1	2.1	2.1
Ireland	2.6	2.1	1.9	1.9	1.9	1.9	2.0	2.1	2.0	1.9
Italy	1.4	1.4	1.2	1.3	1.3	1.4	1.4	1.4	1.4	1.4
Liechtenstein										
Luxembourg	1.5	1.6	1.7	1.7	1.6	1.6	1.6	1.6	1.6	1.7
Malta	2.1	2.1	1.9	1.6	1.3	1.3	1.3	1.3	1.3	1.3
Monaco										
Netherlands	1.5	1.6	1.5	1.7	1.7	1.7	1.8	1.8	1.8	1.8
Norway	1.7	1.9	1.9	1.9	1.9	1.9	2.0	2.0	2.0	1.9
Portugal	1.7	1.6	1.4	1.6	1.4	1.3	1.4	1.3	1.3	1.3
Spain	1.6	1.4	1.2	1.2	1.4	1.4	1.5	1.4	1.4	1.4
Sweden	1.7	2.1	1.7	1.6	1.9	1.9	1.9	1.9	2.0	2.0
Switzerland	1.5	1.6	1.5	1.5	1.4	1.5	1.5	1.5	1.5	1.5
Turkey	3.6	3.1	2.8	2.3	2.2	2.2	2.1	2.1	2.1	2.1
United Kingdom	1.8	1.8	1.7	1.6	1.8	1.9	2.0	1.9	2.0	2.0
Eastern Europe										
Albania	3.8	3.2	2.6	2.2	1.7	1.6	1.6	1.6	1.5	1.5
Belarus	2.1	1.9	1.4	1.3	1.3	1.4	1.4	1.4	1.5	1.5
Bosnia-Herzegovina	2.0	1.7	1.6	1.3	1.2	1.2	1.2	1.2	1.2	1.2
Bulgaria	2.0	1.8	1.2	1.3	1.4	1.4	1.5	1.6	1.6	1.6
Croatia	1.8	1.7	1.6	1.4	1.4	1.4	1.5	1.5	1.5	1.5
Czech Republic	2.0	1.9	1.3	1.1	1.3	1.4	1.5	1.5	1.5	1.4
Estonia	2.1	2.1	1.4	1.4	1.6	1.6	1.7	1.6	1.6	1.6
Georgia	2.3	2.2	1.5	1.5	1.4	1.5	1.7	1.7	1.7	1.7
Hungary	1.9	1.9	1.6	1.3	1.4	1.3	1.4	1.3	1.3	1.3
Latvia	2.1	2.0	1.3	1.2	1.4	1.4	1.5	1.3	1.2	1.2
Lithuania	2.1	2.0	1.6	1.4	1.3	1.4	1.5	1.6	1.6	1.6
Macedonia	2.3	2.2	2.0	1.7	1.4	1.5	1.5	1.5	1.5	1.5
Moldova	2.6	2.4	1.9	1.6	1.5	1.5	1.5	1.5	1.5	1.5
Montenegro	2.1	1.9	1.8	1.8	1.7	1.7	1.7	1.7	1.7	1.6
Poland	2.3	2.0	1.6	1.4	1.3	1.3	1.4	1.4	1.4	1.4
Romania	2.3	1.8	1.3	1.3	1.3	1.3	1.4	1.4	1.4	1.4
Russia	2.1	1.9	1.3	1.2	1.3	1.4	1.5	1.5	1.6	1.6
Serbia	2.3	2.1	1.8	1.7	1.7	1.6	1.6	1.6	1.6	1.6
Slovakia	2.3	2.1	1.5	1.3	1.2	1.3	1.3	1.4	1.4	1.4
Slovenia	1.7	1.5	1.3	1.3	1.3	1.3	1.5	1.5	1.6	1.6
Ukraine	2.0	1.8	1.4	1.1	1.3	1.3	1.5	1.5	1.4	1.5

Source: Euromonitor International from national statistics

22

Population

Population Statistics   **Table 22.13**

Life Expectancy at Birth 2011
Years

	Male	Female
Western Europe		
Austria	78.0	83.6
Belgium	77.8	83.3
Cyprus	77.4	81.7
Denmark	77.3	81.6
Finland	77.1	83.6
France	78.5	85.4
Germany	78.1	83.1
Gibraltar	74.8	79.9
Greece	78.5	83.0
Iceland	79.9	84.2
Ireland	78.8	83.3
Italy	79.3	84.5
Liechtenstein	81.1	85.4
Luxembourg	78.1	83.6
Malta	79.3	83.7
Monaco	79.0	85.6
Netherlands	79.0	83.1
Norway	79.2	83.4
Portugal	76.9	82.9
Spain	79.3	85.5
Sweden	79.8	83.7
Switzerland	80.4	84.9
Turkey	71.6	76.2
United Kingdom	78.9	82.7
Eastern Europe		
Albania	74.0	80.2
Belarus	64.9	76.6
Bosnia-Herzegovina	73.0	78.2
Bulgaria	70.5	77.6
Croatia	73.7	80.1
Czech Republic	74.4	80.7
Estonia	70.9	81.0
Georgia	70.1	77.1
Hungary	70.9	78.8
Latvia	68.9	78.6
Lithuania	68.3	79.0
Macedonia	73.1	77.3
Moldova	65.4	72.9
Montenegro	73.8	78.6
Poland	72.4	80.9
Romania	70.1	77.5
Russia	63.4	75.1
Serbia	71.5	76.7
Slovakia	71.9	79.5
Slovenia	76.6	83.3
Ukraine	65.5	75.6

Source: Euromonitor International from national statistics

Table 22.14

Population Density 1985, 1990, 1995, 2000, 2006-2011

Persons per sq km

	1985	1990	1995	2000	2006	2007	2008	2009	2010	2011
Western Europe										
Austria	91.7	92.7	96.3	97.1	100.1	100.5	100.9	101.4	101.6	102.0
Belgium	325.6	328.5	334.6	338.1	347.1	349.6	352.3	355.1	358.0	361.7
Cyprus	76.2	83.0	92.6	102.1	113.2	114.7	116.3	117.9	119.4	120.8
Denmark	120.6	121.1	122.9	125.6	127.9	128.4	129.1	129.9	130.4	131.1
Finland	16.1	16.3	16.7	17.0	17.3	17.4	17.4	17.5	17.6	17.7
France	100.7	103.3	105.5	107.5	112.1	112.8	113.5	114.1	114.7	115.3
Germany	222.6	226.6	233.6	235.5	236.4	236.1	235.8	235.2	234.7	234.5
Gibraltar	2,660.8	2,683.0	2,728.3	2,734.8	2,923.7	2,929.6	2,928.7	2,925.7	2,924.4	2,925.4
Greece	77.0	78.5	82.2	84.6	86.3	86.7	87.0	87.4	87.7	87.9
Iceland	2.4	2.5	2.7	2.8	3.0	3.1	3.1	3.1	3.2	3.2
Ireland	51.4	50.9	52.2	54.8	61.1	62.6	63.9	64.6	64.9	65.0
Italy	192.4	192.8	193.3	193.5	199.7	201.0	202.7	204.1	205.1	206.1
Liechtenstein	166.8	177.8	191.4	202.7	218.2	219.8	221.0	222.4	224.3	225.9
Luxembourg	141.9	147.5	157.6	168.1	180.2	184.0	187.9	191.9	195.9	198.5
Malta	1,091.0	1,148.5	1,208.1	1,241.9	1,282.5	1,287.1	1,292.2	1,297.2	1,301.6	1,306.6
Monaco	14,266.5	15,448.0	16,507.0	17,563.0	17,633.5	17,647.5	17,668.0	17,688.5	17,703.5	17,713.5
Netherlands	428.1	441.1	456.9	469.9	483.8	484.5	485.9	488.8	491.4	493.8
Norway	13.6	13.9	14.3	14.7	15.2	15.4	15.5	15.7	15.9	16.1
Portugal	109.5	109.2	109.5	111.4	115.6	115.9	116.1	116.2	116.3	116.3
Spain	76.8	77.7	78.8	80.3	87.7	89.1	90.8	91.9	92.2	92.5
Sweden	20.3	20.8	21.5	21.6	22.0	22.2	22.4	22.6	22.8	22.9
Switzerland	161.4	166.8	175.5	179.1	186.5	187.7	189.8	192.5	194.6	196.8
Turkey	65.0	71.0	77.0	82.8	89.5	90.5	91.7	92.9	94.2	95.3
United Kingdom	233.5	236.3	239.5	243.0	249.7	251.2	252.9	254.6	256.4	258.3
Eastern Europe										
Albania	107.9	120.1	114.6	112.1	114.9	115.3	115.8	116.4	116.9	117.3
Belarus			50.3	49.3	47.5	47.2	47.0	46.9	46.8	46.7
Bosnia-Herzegovina	83.1	88.0	69.1	73.6	75.3	75.4	75.4	75.4	75.4	75.4
Bulgaria	80.9	79.2	75.1	72.2	71.1	70.7	70.3	70.1	69.7	69.3
Croatia			83.5	79.4	79.4	79.4	79.3	79.3	79.1	78.8
Czech Republic	133.3	133.3	133.5	132.5	132.7	133.2	134.1	134.9	135.4	135.7
Estonia	36.0	37.2	34.2	32.4	31.7	31.7	31.6	31.6	31.6	31.6
Georgia	71.4	74.0	69.0	63.8	63.3	63.2	63.1	63.1	63.2	63.2
Hungary	118.6	115.4	115.0	114.1	112.4	112.3	112.1	110.8	110.6	110.3
Latvia	41.4	43.0	40.2	38.3	35.7	35.2	34.8	34.4	33.9	33.4
Lithuania	54.5	57.0	58.1	56.0	54.3	54.0	53.7	53.4	53.1	51.8
Macedonia	71.3	74.4	76.6	78.6	80.2	80.9	81.1	81.2	81.4	81.6
Moldova			131.8	124.9	113.3	112.1	111.0	109.8	108.6	108.1
Montenegro	43.1	43.4	44.2	45.2	46.3	46.2	46.2	46.2	46.1	46.1
Poland	121.7	124.8	125.7	125.7	125.4	125.3	125.3	125.4	125.5	125.5
Romania	98.5	101.2	97.1	95.5	94.0	93.8	93.6	93.4	93.3	93.1
Russia	8.7	9.0	9.1	9.0	8.8	8.7	8.7	8.7	8.7	8.7
Serbia	86.3	85.7	86.3	85.2	84.0	83.7	83.4	83.0	82.7	82.3
Slovakia	106.9	109.6	111.2	111.8	111.7	111.7	111.7	111.9	112.1	112.2
Slovenia	96.3	99.2	98.8	98.7	99.5	99.8	100.6	100.9	101.6	101.8
Ukraine	87.4	89.0	88.5	84.8	80.7	80.2	79.7	79.3	79.0	78.7

Source: Euromonitor International from national statistics

22

Population

Population Statistics

Table 22.15

Urban Population 1985, 1990, 1995, 2000, 2006-2011

% of total population

	1985	1990	1995	2000	2006	2007	2008	2009	2010	2011
Western Europe										
Austria	65.6	65.8	65.8	65.8	66.7	67.0	67.2	67.4	67.6	67.9
Belgium	95.9	96.4	96.8	97.1	97.3	97.4	97.5	97.5	97.4	97.6
Cyprus	64.7	66.8	68.0	68.6	69.8	70.0	70.1	70.2	70.3	70.5
Denmark	84.4	84.8	85.0	85.1	86.1	86.4	86.7	86.9	87.2	87.4
Finland	75.8	79.4	81.0	82.2	83.9	84.2	84.6	84.8	85.1	85.4
France	73.7	74.1	74.9	76.9	82.4	83.2	84.0	84.6	85.3	85.9
Germany	72.7	73.1	73.3	73.1	73.5	73.7	73.7	73.8	73.8	74.0
Gibraltar	100.0	100.0	100.0	100.0	100.0	100.0	100.0	100.0	100.0	100.0
Greece	58.4	58.8	59.3	59.7	60.6	60.8	61.0	61.2	61.4	61.7
Iceland	89.6	90.8	91.6	92.4	93.0	93.1	93.3	93.4	93.4	93.6
Ireland	56.3	56.9	57.9	59.1	60.9	61.3	61.5	61.7	61.9	62.2
Italy	66.8	66.7	66.9	67.2	67.8	68.0	68.1	68.3	68.4	68.7
Liechtenstein	17.6	16.9	16.5	15.1	14.5	14.5	14.5	14.4	14.4	14.4
Luxembourg	80.7	80.9	82.9	83.8	84.0	84.3	84.7	85.1	85.2	85.7
Malta	89.8	90.4	90.9	92.4	94.0	94.3	94.4	94.5	94.7	94.8
Monaco	100.0	100.0	100.0	100.0	100.0	100.0	100.0	100.0	100.0	100.0
Netherlands	66.7	68.7	72.8	76.8	80.8	81.3	81.9	82.4	82.9	83.3
Norway	71.3	72.0	73.8	76.1	77.8	78.3	78.7	79.1	79.4	79.9
Portugal	45.3	47.9	51.1	54.4	58.3	58.9	59.5	60.1	60.7	61.4
Spain	74.2	75.4	75.9	76.3	77.0	77.3	77.4	77.4	77.4	77.7
Sweden	83.1	83.1	83.8	84.0	84.2	84.3	84.5	84.6	84.7	84.9
Switzerland	65.2	73.2	73.6	73.3	73.4	73.5	73.6	73.6	73.6	73.8
Turkey	52.4	59.2	62.1	64.7	67.8	68.2	68.7	69.2	69.6	70.1
United Kingdom	78.4	78.1	78.4	78.7	79.2	79.3	79.4	79.5	79.6	79.8
Eastern Europe										
Albania	35.1	36.4	38.9	41.7	47.9	49.0	50.0	51.0	51.9	52.9
Belarus	62.0	66.0	67.8	69.8	72.6	73.0	73.5	73.9	74.3	74.7
Bosnia-Herzegovina	37.6	39.2	41.1	43.2	46.3	46.9	47.4	48.0	48.6	49.2
Bulgaria	64.6	66.4	67.8	68.9	70.5	70.8	71.1	71.4	71.7	72.0
Croatia	52.3	54.0	54.9	55.6	56.7	57.0	57.2	57.4	57.7	58.0
Czech Republic	75.4	75.3	74.7	74.0	73.7	73.7	73.8	73.7	73.5	73.7
Estonia	70.8	71.1	70.0	69.4	69.4	69.4	69.4	69.4	69.5	69.6
Georgia	54.0	55.3	53.6	52.0	52.5	52.5	52.6	52.7	52.8	53.0
Hungary	65.1	65.8	65.2	64.6	66.6	67.0	67.3	67.7	68.1	68.5
Latvia	40.6	40.9	40.8	40.5	41.3	41.5	41.6	41.8	41.9	42.1
Lithuania	65.0	67.6	67.3	67.0	66.8	66.8	66.9	66.9	67.0	67.0
Macedonia	55.7	57.8	60.3	62.9	65.9	66.4	66.9	67.4	67.9	68.4
Moldova	44.2	46.8	46.3	44.6	43.8	44.5	45.2	46.1	47.0	47.6
Montenegro	42.7	48.5	53.8	59.1	62.6	62.8	63.1	63.5	64.0	64.4
Poland	59.9	61.3	61.5	61.7	61.3	61.3	61.2	61.2	61.2	61.2
Romania	49.6	53.2	54.0	53.5	53.8	54.0	54.2	54.4	54.6	54.9
Russia	72.0	73.6	73.0	73.1	72.9	73.0	73.1	73.1	73.1	73.1
Serbia	48.3	50.4	51.7	53.0	54.6	54.9	55.3	55.7	56.1	56.5
Slovakia	54.1	56.4	56.4	56.1	55.3	55.1	54.9	54.7	54.6	54.6
Slovenia	49.6	50.4	50.6	50.8	50.1	49.9	49.7	49.6	49.5	49.4
Ukraine	64.2	66.7	67.4	67.0	67.6	67.8	68.0	68.2	68.3	68.4

Source: Euromonitor International from national statistics

Table 22.16

Rural Population 1985, 1990, 1995, 2000, 2006-2011
% of total population

	1985	1990	1995	2000	2006	2007	2008	2009	2010	2011
Western Europe										
Austria	34.4	34.2	34.2	34.2	33.3	33.0	32.8	32.6	32.4	32.1
Belgium	4.1	3.6	3.2	2.9	2.7	2.6	2.5	2.5	2.6	2.4
Cyprus	35.3	33.2	32.0	31.4	30.2	30.0	29.9	29.8	29.7	29.5
Denmark	15.6	15.2	15.0	14.9	13.9	13.6	13.3	13.1	12.8	12.6
Finland	24.2	20.6	19.0	17.8	16.1	15.8	15.4	15.2	14.9	14.6
France	26.0	26.0	25.1	23.1	17.6	16.8	16.0	15.4	14.7	14.1
Germany	27.3	26.9	26.7	26.9	26.5	26.3	26.3	26.2	26.2	26.0
Gibraltar										
Greece	41.6	41.2	40.7	40.3	39.4	39.2	39.0	38.8	38.6	38.3
Iceland	10.4	9.2	8.4	7.6	7.0	6.9	6.7	6.6	6.6	6.4
Ireland	43.7	43.1	42.1	40.9	39.1	38.7	38.5	38.3	38.1	37.8
Italy	33.2	33.3	33.1	32.8	32.2	32.0	31.9	31.7	31.6	31.3
Liechtenstein	82.4	83.1	83.5	84.9	85.5	85.5	85.5	85.6	85.6	85.6
Luxembourg	19.3	19.1	17.1	16.2	16.0	15.7	15.3	14.9	14.8	14.3
Malta	10.2	9.6	9.1	7.6	6.0	5.7	5.6	5.5	5.3	5.2
Monaco										
Netherlands	33.3	31.3	27.2	23.2	19.2	18.7	18.1	17.6	17.1	16.7
Norway	28.7	28.0	26.2	23.9	22.2	21.7	21.3	20.9	20.6	20.1
Portugal	54.7	52.1	48.9	45.6	41.7	41.1	40.5	39.9	39.3	38.6
Spain	25.8	24.6	24.1	23.7	23.0	22.7	22.6	22.6	22.6	22.3
Sweden	16.9	16.9	16.2	16.0	15.8	15.7	15.5	15.4	15.3	15.1
Switzerland	34.8	26.8	26.4	26.7	26.6	26.5	26.4	26.4	26.4	26.2
Turkey	47.6	40.8	37.9	35.3	32.2	31.8	31.3	30.8	30.4	29.9
United Kingdom	21.6	21.9	21.6	21.3	20.8	20.7	20.6	20.5	20.4	20.2
Eastern Europe										
Albania	64.9	63.6	61.1	58.3	52.1	51.0	50.0	49.0	48.1	47.1
Belarus	38.0	34.0	32.2	30.2	27.4	27.0	26.5	26.1	25.7	25.3
Bosnia-Herzegovina	62.4	60.8	58.9	56.8	53.7	53.1	52.6	52.0	51.4	50.8
Bulgaria	35.4	33.6	32.2	31.1	29.5	29.2	28.9	28.6	28.3	28.0
Croatia	47.7	46.0	45.1	44.4	43.3	43.0	42.8	42.6	42.3	42.0
Czech Republic	24.6	24.7	25.3	26.0	26.3	26.3	26.2	26.3	26.5	26.3
Estonia	29.2	28.9	30.0	30.6	30.6	30.6	30.6	30.6	30.5	30.4
Georgia	46.0	44.7	46.4	48.0	47.5	47.5	47.4	47.3	47.2	47.0
Hungary	34.9	34.2	34.8	35.4	33.4	33.0	32.7	32.3	31.9	31.5
Latvia	59.4	59.1	59.2	59.5	58.7	58.5	58.4	58.2	58.1	57.9
Lithuania	35.0	32.4	32.7	33.0	33.2	33.2	33.1	33.1	33.0	33.0
Macedonia	44.3	42.2	39.7	37.1	34.1	33.6	33.1	32.6	32.1	31.6
Moldova	55.8	53.2	53.7	55.4	56.2	55.5	54.8	53.9	53.0	52.4
Montenegro	57.3	51.5	46.2	40.9	37.4	37.2	36.9	36.5	36.0	35.6
Poland	40.1	38.7	38.5	38.3	38.7	38.7	38.8	38.8	38.8	38.8
Romania	50.4	46.8	46.0	46.5	46.2	46.0	45.8	45.6	45.4	45.1
Russia	28.0	26.4	27.0	26.9	27.1	27.0	26.9	26.9	26.9	26.9
Serbia	51.7	49.6	48.3	47.0	45.4	45.1	44.7	44.3	43.9	43.5
Slovakia	45.9	43.6	43.6	43.9	44.7	44.9	45.1	45.3	45.4	45.4
Slovenia	50.4	49.6	49.4	49.2	49.9	50.1	50.3	50.4	50.5	50.6
Ukraine	35.8	33.3	32.6	33.0	32.4	32.2	32.0	31.8	31.7	31.6

Source: Euromonitor International from national statistics

Population Statistics

Table 22.17

Pensioners 1990, 1995, 2000, 2006-2011

'000

	1990	1995	2000	2006	2007	2008	2009	2010	2011
Western Europe									
Austria	1,361	1,393	1,438	1,590	1,621	1,652	1,682	1,709	1,725
Belgium	1,649	1,776	1,875	1,853	1,857	1,873	1,840	1,864	1,885
Cyprus	76	87	96	113	117	120	124	128	132
Denmark	800	799	790	823	835	853	875	903	934
Finland	662	720	767	841	869	875	892	910	942
France	10,764	11,599	12,132	12,803	13,137	13,562	13,929	14,282	14,627
Germany	11,794	12,542	13,351	15,870	16,299	16,519	16,699	16,837	16,745
Gibraltar									
Greece	1,699	1,927	2,137	2,351	2,387	2,420	2,446	2,484	2,533
Iceland	23	26	29	31	32	32	33	33	34
Ireland	399	411	424	461	469	479	492	506	520
Italy	10,073	11,117	12,085	13,234	13,498	13,724	13,956	14,152	14,264
Liechtenstein									
Luxembourg	51	56	61	66	67	68	69	71	72
Malta	36	41	45	55	56	56	57	59	61
Monaco									
Netherlands	1,906	2,034	2,152	2,330	2,368	2,415	2,472	2,538	2,594
Norway	606	622	618	606	610	614	617	624	635
Portugal	1,322	1,475	1,635	1,810	1,829	1,850	1,874	1,901	1,931
Spain	5,215	5,946	6,706	7,308	7,407	7,520	7,629	7,746	7,878
Sweden	1,518	1,540	1,533	1,565	1,581	1,608	1,645	1,691	1,737
Switzerland	1,007	1,067	1,129	1,232	1,258	1,288	1,320	1,353	1,389
Turkey	6,310	6,957	7,168	7,437	7,485	7,657	7,693	8,102	8,397
United Kingdom	10,499	10,616	10,767	11,282	11,437	11,669	11,868	11,865	11,853
Eastern Europe									
Albania	218	243	281	330	340	349	358	366	374
Belarus	2,000	2,143	2,145	2,070	2,074	2,087	2,093	2,118	2,132
Bosnia-Herzegovina	274	287	415	523	528	530	532	535	540
Bulgaria	1,806	1,858	1,843	1,733	1,710	1,688	1,671	1,691	1,704
Croatia	702	795	840	873	879	886	892	897	892
Czech Republic	1,973	1,988	2,038	2,156	2,184	2,204	2,231	2,258	2,283
Estonia	250	258	270	280	278	275	274	273	273
Georgia	639	669	698	726	728	730	737	745	753
Hungary	1,920	1,980	2,028	2,053	2,011	2,020	1,970	1,994	2,020
Latvia	408	431	446	470	467	456	454	455	456
Lithuania	697	738	719	659	658	657	659	661	663
Macedonia	183	202	234	262	266	268	271	275	280
Moldova	590	607	618	595	596	599	604	610	623
Montenegro	62	68	80	92	93	93	94	94	95
Poland	4,792	5,181	5,564	5,888	5,983	6,082	6,196	6,317	6,449
Romania	3,518	3,840	4,053	4,129	4,140	4,122	4,098	4,069	4,055
Russia	27,621	29,876	30,138	29,240	29,524	29,954	30,312	30,927	31,348
Serbia	1,264	1,469	1,595	1,593	1,595	1,599	1,561	1,521	1,477
Slovakia	912	934	965	986	977	967	960	956	953
Slovenia	409	440	467	460	459	460	456	461	467
Ukraine	10,957	11,533	11,621	11,120	11,108	11,106	11,111	11,198	11,253

Source: Euromonitor International from national statistics

Table 22.18

Population by Marital Status 2011

'000 / % analysis

	Married	Divorced	Widowed	Single	Married (% analysis)	Divorced (% analysis)	Widowed (% analysis)	Single (% analysis)
Western Europe								
Austria	3,612	615	554	3,623	43	7	7	43
Belgium	4,450	928	714	4,859	41	8	7	44
Cyprus								
Denmark	2,191	309	448	2,614	39	6	8	47
Finland	2,007	526	291	2,552	37	10	5	47
France	23,985	4,036	3,947	31,160	38	6	6	49
Germany	35,079	6,464	5,858	34,351	43	8	7	42
Gibraltar								
Greece	5,639	369	851	4,465	50	3	8	39
Iceland								
Ireland	1,669	199	187	2,426	37	4	4	54
Italy	29,967	2,115	5,017	23,527	49	3	8	39
Liechtenstein								
Luxembourg								
Malta								
Monaco								
Netherlands	6,865	1,151	866	7,773	41	7	5	47
Norway	1,741	437	247	2,495	35	9	5	51
Portugal	5,833	322	705	3,776	55	3	7	36
Spain	22,044	1,969	2,851	19,290	48	4	6	42
Sweden	3,191	465	899	4,860	34	5	10	52
Switzerland	3,502	575	407	3,387	44	7	5	43
Turkey	34,972	1,516	2,942	33,720	48	2	4	46
United Kingdom	23,472	6,352	3,770	28,904	38	10	6	46
Eastern Europe								
Albania								
Belarus	4,604	753	963	3,161	49	8	10	33
Bosnia-Herzegovina								
Bulgaria	3,829	437	770	2,439	51	6	10	33
Croatia	2,087	134	432	1,744	47	3	10	40
Czech Republic	4,507	1,061	745	4,172	43	10	7	40
Estonia	538	170	111	502	41	13	8	38
Georgia	2,598	132	494	1,167	59	3	11	27
Hungary	3,885	915	966	4,219	39	9	10	42
Latvia	781	248	185	860	38	12	9	41
Lithuania	1,327	324	247	1,345	41	10	8	41
Macedonia	985	23	107	942	48	1	5	46
Moldova								
Montenegro	354	17	57	191	57	3	9	31
Poland	17,746	1,643	3,028	15,375	47	4	8	41
Romania	9,767	1,018	2,089	8,534	46	5	10	40
Russia	67,358	11,958	14,047	45,556	48	9	10	33
Serbia	3,654	269	708	2,644	50	4	10	36
Slovakia	2,329	282	398	2,277	44	5	8	43
Slovenia	847	96	143	874	43	5	7	45
Ukraine	21,225	3,879	4,846	15,464	47	9	11	34

Source: Euromonitor International from national statistics

Population Statistics **Table 22.19**

Population by Educational Attainment 2011

'000 / % analysis

	Primary	Secondary	Higher	No Education	Other/ Unknown	Primary (% analysis)	Secondary (% analysis)	Higher (% analysis)	No Education (% analysis)	Other/ Unknown (% analysis)
Western Europe										
Austria	798	4,993	733		646	11	70	10		9
Belgium	1,446	4,628	2,288	62	670	16	51	25	1	7
Cyprus										
Denmark	282	3,282	864		138	6	72	19		3
Finland	509	2,835	1,144			11	63	25		
France	5,981	31,886	13,004	664		12	62	25	1	
Germany	8,383	43,081	18,244		1,102	12	61	26		2
Gibraltar										
Greece	2,153	5,614	1,812	123		22	58	19	1	
Iceland										
Ireland	560	1,789	1,000		155	16	51	29		4
Italy	8,445	35,113	6,131	2,425		16	67	12	5	
Liechtenstein										
Luxembourg										
Malta										
Monaco										
Netherlands	1,478	8,526	3,745			11	62	27		
Norway	54	2,702	1,013		230	1	68	25		6
Portugal	3,571	3,316	1,492	651		40	37	17	7	
Spain	6,574	22,319	7,687	501	2,106	17	57	20	1	5
Sweden	497	5,136	2,061		157	6	65	26		2
Switzerland	831	3,975	1,873			12	60	28		
Turkey	26,322	19,098	4,724	4,616	9	48	35	9	8	
United Kingdom	6,301	29,482	15,489	312		12	57	30	1	
Eastern Europe										
Albania										
Belarus	1,462	5,014	1,216	376		18	62	15	5	
Bosnia-Herzegovina										
Bulgaria	418	4,745	1,293		25	6	73	20		
Croatia	573	2,591	513	49	17	15	69	14	1	
Czech Republic	1,236	6,254	1,318	42	123	14	70	15		1
Estonia	94	830	202	8		8	73	18	1	
Georgia	840	1,558	888		374	23	43	24		10
Hungary	827	6,355	1,250	93		10	75	15	1	
Latvia	260	1,237	275	18		15	69	15	1	
Lithuania	242	1,620	863	5	26	9	59	31		1
Macedonia	598	654	198	248		35	39	12	15	
Moldova										
Montenegro	145	259	68	18	11	29	52	13	4	2
Poland	4,916	22,298	4,646	189	392	15	69	14	1	1
Romania	3,925	11,953	1,916	375	8	22	66	11	2	
Russia	21,326	75,243	18,206	6,150		18	62	15	5	
Serbia	2,344	2,823	757	242	10	38	46	12	4	
Slovakia	684	3,175	639	18	56	15	69	14		1
Slovenia	201	1,265	283	11		11	72	16	1	
Ukraine	8,659	23,543	4,971	1,929		22	60	13	5	

Source: Euromonitor International from national statistics

Table 22.20

Males and Females by Age at January 1st 2011

'000

	Males 0-14	Males 15-64	Males 65+	Females 0-14	Females 15-64	Females 65+
Western Europe						
Austria	633	2,846	616	602	2,843	864
Belgium	949	3,625	797	908	3,587	1,086
Cyprus	101	409	59	95	380	72
Denmark	510	1,830	417	485	1,802	517
Finland	454	1,793	392	434	1,753	549
France	5,933	20,220	4,426	5,661	20,632	6,256
Germany	5,612	27,299	7,201	5,329	26,667	9,643
Gibraltar						
Greece	837	3,807	962	787	3,710	1,223
Iceland	34	111	18	33	107	21
Ireland	501	1,485	235	476	1,499	286
Italy	4,377	19,845	5,191	4,136	19,967	7,111
Liechtenstein						
Luxembourg	46	178	31	44	174	41
Malta	32	150	26	30	146	35
Monaco						
Netherlands	1,487	5,616	1,141	1,420	5,538	1,454
Norway	472	1,663	326	450	1,594	416
Portugal	823	3,518	806	784	3,580	1,126
Spain	3,582	15,787	3,356	3,383	15,523	4,522
Sweden	804	3,107	780	761	3,007	957
Switzerland	611	2,695	572	580	2,655	758
Turkey	9,530	24,911	2,342	9,012	24,461	3,055
United Kingdom	5,586	20,597	4,590	5,329	20,580	5,817
Eastern Europe						
Albania	370	1,091	147	339	1,098	169
Belarus	727	3,268	414	688	3,499	886
Bosnia-Herzegovina	296	1,323	231	277	1,408	309
Bulgaria	532	2,564	539	503	2,588	791
Croatia	343	1,491	295	325	1,495	462
Czech Republic	776	3,715	655	736	3,631	973
Estonia	106	437	75	100	469	153
Georgia	392	1,444	247	342	1,586	383
Hungary	749	3,383	611	711	3,471	1,060
Latvia	146	695	117	139	734	243
Lithuania	250	1,077	180	238	1,144	355
Macedonia	185	739	107	174	719	133
Moldova	302	1,238	148	290	1,326	252
Montenegro	62	211	33	57	212	45
Poland	2,952	13,526	1,956	2,797	13,726	3,231
Romania	1,667	7,477	1,286	1,580	7,515	1,899
Russia	11,279	49,250	5,557	10,710	53,812	12,306
Serbia	565	2,463	511	534	2,497	705
Slovakia	423	1,954	250	401	1,950	418
Slovenia	150	731	134	141	690	205
Ukraine	3,338	15,391	2,303	3,158	16,746	4,662

Source: Euromonitor International from national statistics

Population Statistics

Table 22.21

Males at January 1st 1990, 1995, 2000, 2006-2011

'000

	1990	1995	2000	2006	2007	2008	2009	2010	2011
Western Europe									
Austria	3,655	3,831	3,868	4,014	4,030	4,049	4,068	4,079	4,095
Belgium	4,860	4,955	5,006	5,144	5,181	5,224	5,269	5,312	5,370
Cyprus	389	432	475	530	538	547	555	563	570
Denmark	2,531	2,573	2,634	2,686	2,697	2,713	2,732	2,743	2,757
Finland	2,413	2,482	2,523	2,572	2,584	2,597	2,612	2,625	2,638
France	27,544	28,078	28,567	29,714	29,918	30,085	30,247	30,412	30,579
Germany	38,110	39,645	40,091	40,340	40,301	40,274	40,184	40,104	40,112
Gibraltar	14	14	14	15	15	15	15	15	15
Greece	4,982	5,243	5,400	5,508	5,532	5,554	5,577	5,597	5,606
Iceland	128	134	141	151	154	156	159	161	163
Ireland	1,743	1,787	1,877	2,103	2,158	2,197	2,215	2,216	2,220
Italy	27,528	27,569	27,563	28,527	28,718	28,950	29,152	29,287	29,413
Liechtenstein	14	15	16	17	17	17	18	18	18
Luxembourg	187	200	215	231	236	241	247	252	256
Malta	181	191	197	203	204	205	206	207	207
Monaco	14	16	17	17	17	17	17	17	17
Netherlands	7,358	7,627	7,846	8,077	8,089	8,112	8,156	8,203	8,243
Norway	2,093	2,150	2,217	2,302	2,326	2,360	2,395	2,427	2,461
Portugal	4,819	4,827	4,918	5,116	5,130	5,139	5,143	5,148	5,147
Spain	19,025	19,269	19,607	21,561	21,943	22,357	22,628	22,672	22,725
Sweden	4,212	4,356	4,380	4,487	4,524	4,564	4,604	4,649	4,690
Switzerland	3,258	3,428	3,501	3,653	3,679	3,727	3,787	3,831	3,877
Turkey	27,539	29,816	32,024	34,535	34,940	35,377	35,901	36,372	36,784
United Kingdom	27,774	28,156	28,634	29,591	29,805	30,036	30,264	30,509	30,773
Eastern Europe									
Albania	1,687	1,583	1,533	1,573	1,579	1,587	1,596	1,605	1,608
Belarus	4,777	4,780	4,694	4,489	4,461	4,441	4,425	4,418	4,408
Bosnia-Herzegovina	2,223	1,708	1,809	1,849	1,849	1,849	1,850	1,850	1,849
Bulgaria	4,324	4,071	3,890	3,743	3,721	3,700	3,681	3,659	3,635
Croatia	2,315	2,244	2,138	2,139	2,140	2,138	2,139	2,135	2,130
Czech Republic	4,998	5,013	4,981	5,003	5,026	5,073	5,114	5,134	5,146
Estonia	735	671	633	619	618	617	617	617	618
Georgia	2,440	2,268	2,093	2,084	2,080	2,078	2,081	2,081	2,082
Hungary	4,985	4,942	4,865	4,785	4,779	4,770	4,763	4,757	4,744
Latvia	1,241	1,154	1,097	1,022	1,008	997	985	972	958
Lithuania	1,747	1,717	1,644	1,587	1,577	1,567	1,559	1,548	1,507
Macedonia	954	979	1,005	1,022	1,024	1,025	1,027	1,029	1,031
Moldova	2,080	2,073	1,960	1,771	1,752	1,733	1,715	1,695	1,688
Montenegro	305	307	306	305	305	305	306	306	306
Poland	18,516	18,602	18,550	18,454	18,427	18,412	18,415	18,429	18,435
Romania	11,451	10,938	10,724	10,535	10,511	10,491	10,473	10,451	10,430
Russia	69,115	69,659	68,698	66,463	66,237	66,145	66,111	66,124	66,086
Serbia	3,707	3,729	3,662	3,611	3,597	3,581	3,567	3,554	3,539
Slovakia	2,578	2,605	2,614	2,607	2,607	2,610	2,616	2,623	2,628
Slovenia	968	964	971	981	987	1,001	1,004	1,014	1,015
Ukraine	23,826	23,792	22,755	21,575	21,435	21,298	21,185	21,107	21,033

Source: Euromonitor International from national statistics

Table 22.22

Females at January 1st 1990, 1995, 2000, 2006-2011

'000

	1990	1995	2000	2006	2007	2008	2009	2010	2011
Western Europe									
Austria	3,990	4,112	4,134	4,240	4,253	4,270	4,287	4,296	4,309
Belgium	5,088	5,176	5,233	5,368	5,403	5,443	5,484	5,528	5,581
Cyprus	378	424	468	516	522	528	534	540	546
Denmark	2,605	2,642	2,696	2,742	2,750	2,763	2,779	2,791	2,804
Finland	2,562	2,617	2,648	2,683	2,693	2,704	2,715	2,726	2,737
France	20,003	20,674	20,291	31,685	31,878	32,050	32,218	32,379	32,548
Germany	41,003	41,894	42,073	42,098	42,014	41,944	41,818	41,699	41,639
Gibraltar	13	14	14	15	15	15	15	15	15
Greece	5,139	5,352	5,504	5,617	5,640	5,660	5,684	5,708	5,720
Iceland	127	133	140	150	152	154	157	159	161
Ireland	1,764	1,810	1,901	2,105	2,155	2,204	2,235	2,251	2,261
Italy	29,167	29,275	29,361	30,225	30,413	30,670	30,893	31,053	31,213
Liechtenstein	15	16	17	18	18	18	18	18	18
Luxembourg	194	207	221	236	241	245	250	255	258
Malta	186	195	200	207	208	208	209	210	211
Monaco	16	18	19	19	19	19	19	19	19
Netherlands	7,534	7,797	8,018	8,257	8,269	8,293	8,329	8,372	8,412
Norway	2,140	2,198	2,261	2,338	2,355	2,377	2,404	2,431	2,459
Portugal	5,177	5,191	5,277	5,454	5,469	5,479	5,485	5,490	5,490
Spain	19,802	20,075	20,443	22,197	22,532	22,926	23,200	23,317	23,428
Sweden	4,315	4,460	4,481	4,561	4,590	4,619	4,653	4,692	4,725
Switzerland	3,416	3,591	3,664	3,807	3,829	3,866	3,915	3,955	3,993
Turkey	27,136	29,458	31,717	34,326	34,749	35,210	35,616	36,102	36,528
United Kingdom	29,383	29,787	30,151	30,819	30,976	31,156	31,331	31,518	31,726
Eastern Europe									
Albania	1,602	1,558	1,539	1,576	1,581	1,587	1,593	1,600	1,606
Belarus	5,411	5,431	5,309	5,141	5,118	5,102	5,088	5,082	5,073
Bosnia-Herzegovina	2,276	1,815	1,944	1,994	1,995	1,994	1,995	1,995	1,994
Bulgaria	4,444	4,237	4,094	3,975	3,958	3,941	3,925	3,904	3,882
Croatia	2,463	2,425	2,304	2,303	2,301	2,298	2,296	2,291	2,282
Czech Republic	5,302	5,304	5,256	5,248	5,261	5,288	5,308	5,326	5,340
Estonia	836	777	739	725	724	724	723	723	722
Georgia	2,706	2,527	2,342	2,317	2,315	2,304	2,305	2,308	2,311
Hungary	5,390	5,395	5,356	5,292	5,287	5,276	5,268	5,257	5,242
Latvia	1,428	1,346	1,285	1,196	1,180	1,165	1,151	1,135	1,117
Lithuania	1,946	1,926	1,868	1,817	1,808	1,799	1,791	1,781	1,737
Macedonia	939	969	995	1,016	1,018	1,020	1,022	1,024	1,026
Moldova	2,284	2,266	2,146	1,957	1,937	1,917	1,898	1,878	1,868
Montenegro	285	294	309	317	317	316	316	315	314
Poland	19,472	19,663	19,713	19,703	19,699	19,704	19,721	19,739	19,755
Romania	11,761	11,347	11,205	11,075	11,054	11,038	11,026	11,011	10,994
Russia	78,550	78,801	78,192	76,937	76,822	76,788	76,808	76,838	76,828
Serbia	3,864	3,896	3,866	3,815	3,801	3,784	3,768	3,753	3,736
Slovakia	2,692	2,743	2,764	2,764	2,764	2,764	2,765	2,768	2,769
Slovenia	1,028	1,025	1,017	1,022	1,023	1,025	1,028	1,033	1,036
Ukraine	27,730	27,508	26,360	25,175	25,031	24,895	24,778	24,676	24,566

Source: Euromonitor International from national statistics

Population Statistics

Table 22.23

Children Aged 0-14 Years at January 1st 1990, 1995, 2000, 2006-2011
'000

	1990	1995	2000	2006	2007	2008	2009	2010	2011
Western Europe									
Austria	1,340	1,417	1,372	1,313	1,295	1,278	1,262	1,245	1,235
Belgium	1,801	1,827	1,805	1,796	1,798	1,800	1,815	1,832	1,857
Cyprus	195	209	211	205	203	201	199	196	195
Denmark	881	901	981	1,016	1,014	1,010	1,008	1,001	995
Finland	962	972	943	907	901	895	891	888	888
France	11,389	11,330	11,114	11,259	11,321	11,370	11,462	11,534	11,594
Germany	12,639	13,294	12,897	11,650	11,441	11,282	11,139	11,023	10,941
Gibraltar	5	5	5	5	5	5	5	5	5
Greece	1,978	1,861	1,695	1,594	1,597	1,601	1,613	1,624	1,624
Iceland	64	65	65	66	66	66	66	67	67
Ireland	959	883	829	862	879	905	931	954	977
Italy	9,521	8,395	8,145	8,284	8,322	8,367	8,429	8,478	8,513
Liechtenstein	6	6	6	6	6	6	6	6	6
Luxembourg	66	75	83	86	87	88	89	90	90
Malta	89	88	81	68	67	65	64	62	62
Monaco	4	4	5	5	5	5	5	5	5
Netherlands	2,715	2,838	2,946	2,985	2,959	2,936	2,923	2,913	2,907
Norway	801	845	895	907	906	907	912	918	922
Portugal	2,081	1,796	1,655	1,644	1,638	1,629	1,623	1,617	1,608
Spain	7,856	6,657	5,965	6,342	6,459	6,620	6,761	6,872	6,965
Sweden	1,522	1,663	1,640	1,561	1,550	1,542	1,542	1,549	1,565
Switzerland	1,137	1,237	1,249	1,194	1,183	1,177	1,180	1,181	1,191
Turkey	18,004	18,588	18,619	18,684	18,698	18,642	18,789	18,639	18,542
United Kingdom	10,833	11,292	11,244	10,766	10,729	10,735	10,773	10,834	10,915
Eastern Europe									
Albania	1,078	1,020	918	795	771	754	740	727	710
Belarus	2,351	2,246	1,894	1,477	1,439	1,414	1,406	1,407	1,414
Bosnia-Herzegovina	1,090	777	743	621	608	599	591	582	573
Bulgaria	1,801	1,506	1,268	1,047	1,032	1,023	1,022	1,026	1,035
Croatia	952	858	760	703	693	687	681	676	669
Czech Republic	2,239	1,945	1,700	1,501	1,480	1,474	1,474	1,488	1,511
Estonia	350	302	251	202	200	199	200	203	206
Georgia	1,267	1,157	972	792	771	753	742	735	733
Hungary	2,131	1,892	1,729	1,553	1,530	1,509	1,493	1,477	1,461
Latvia	572	522	428	318	305	297	293	290	285
Lithuania	834	798	710	560	538	517	505	499	488
Macedonia	481	483	451	397	386	378	370	364	359
Moldova	1,218	1,154	974	680	650	627	610	596	592
Montenegro	151	141	134	122	121	120	120	119	118
Poland	9,600	8,849	7,480	6,189	6,022	5,901	5,829	5,780	5,749
Romania	5,508	4,694	4,126	3,360	3,319	3,280	3,264	3,252	3,247
Russia	34,031	32,050	27,066	21,340	21,004	20,960	21,243	21,559	21,989
Serbia	1,505	1,389	1,248	1,166	1,151	1,135	1,121	1,109	1,099
Slovakia	1,341	1,224	1,065	891	867	847	831	826	825
Slovenia	418	369	320	283	281	283	284	287	291
Ukraine	11,084	10,529	8,781	6,765	6,606	6,501	6,476	6,484	6,496

Source: Euromonitor International from national statistics

Table 22.24

Persons of Working Age (15-64 Years) at January 1st 1990, 1995, 2000, 2006-2011

'000

	1990	1995	2000	2006	2007	2008	2009	2010	2011
Western Europe									
Austria	5,165	5,330	5,397	5,584	5,589	5,616	5,643	5,654	5,689
Belgium	6,673	6,707	6,719	6,906	6,977	7,047	7,101	7,148	7,212
Cyprus	495	560	636	728	741	754	767	780	789
Denmark	3,454	3,516	3,558	3,589	3,598	3,613	3,628	3,631	3,632
Finland	3,350	3,407	3,461	3,508	3,507	3,531	3,543	3,553	3,547
France	37,317	37,736	38,314	39,978	40,266	40,464	40,583	40,706	40,852
Germany	54,680	55,702	55,915	54,918	54,574	54,417	54,134	53,878	53,966
Gibraltar	18	18	18	19	19	19	19	19	19
Greece	6,760	7,147	7,414	7,471	7,501	7,523	7,545	7,540	7,517
Iceland	164	172	183	200	204	208	211	215	217
Ireland	2,148	2,304	2,525	2,884	2,965	3,017	3,027	3,008	2,984
Italy	38,829	39,081	38,469	38,875	39,017	39,306	39,531	39,656	39,812
Liechtenstein	20	21	23	25	25	25	25	25	25
Luxembourg	264	276	292	314	322	331	339	347	352
Malta	243	257	271	287	289	292	294	296	296
Monaco	20	21	23	23	23	23	23	23	23
Netherlands	10,272	10,552	10,766	11,019	11,031	11,055	11,091	11,124	11,154
Norway	2,741	2,809	2,901	3,051	3,090	3,136	3,182	3,218	3,256
Portugal	6,593	6,747	6,905	7,115	7,133	7,139	7,130	7,120	7,098
Spain	25,755	26,740	27,379	30,108	30,609	31,143	31,439	31,371	31,310
Sweden	5,488	5,614	5,689	5,922	5,982	6,033	6,069	6,100	6,113
Switzerland	4,565	4,750	4,821	5,073	5,109	5,172	5,246	5,296	5,350
Turkey	32,954	36,263	40,137	45,177	46,028	46,944	47,835	48,636	49,373
United Kingdom	37,340	37,477	38,248	39,979	40,319	40,600	40,803	40,988	41,178
Eastern Europe									
Albania	2,036	1,925	1,925	2,081	2,106	2,129	2,149	2,168	2,189
Belarus	6,764	6,717	6,778	6,736	6,724	6,732	6,751	6,765	6,767
Bosnia-Herzegovina	3,135	2,459	2,595	2,699	2,708	2,715	2,722	2,727	2,731
Bulgaria	5,830	5,568	5,425	5,343	5,323	5,294	5,261	5,212	5,152
Croatia	3,276	3,175	2,984	2,987	2,990	2,985	2,986	2,985	2,986
Czech Republic	6,777	7,018	7,124	7,293	7,325	7,377	7,399	7,380	7,346
Estonia	1,039	953	916	917	913	912	911	909	906
Georgia	3,396	3,101	2,907	2,975	2,990	2,998	3,014	3,024	3,030
Hungary	6,870	6,987	6,961	6,932	6,931	6,913	6,898	6,874	6,854
Latvia	1,781	1,642	1,600	1,527	1,509	1,493	1,474	1,452	1,429
Lithuania	2,461	2,402	2,319	2,321	2,319	2,316	2,309	2,295	2,221
Macedonia	1,259	1,299	1,352	1,416	1,427	1,435	1,443	1,451	1,458
Moldova	2,784	2,794	2,723	2,626	2,621	2,612	2,598	2,579	2,564
Montenegro	391	407	418	421	422	423	424	424	424
Poland	24,607	25,230	26,164	26,892	26,987	27,083	27,160	27,221	27,253
Romania	15,319	14,912	14,873	15,053	15,044	15,045	15,038	15,005	14,992
Russia	99,056	99,008	101,761	102,097	101,983	102,257	102,642	102,978	103,062
Serbia	5,220	5,207	5,079	4,983	4,973	4,963	4,957	4,955	4,960
Slovakia	3,387	3,547	3,700	3,849	3,867	3,884	3,900	3,904	3,904
Slovenia	1,367	1,381	1,392	1,407	1,410	1,414	1,414	1,421	1,420
Ukraine	34,298	33,811	33,515	32,417	32,256	32,185	32,170	32,130	32,137

Source: Euromonitor International from national statistics

22

Population

Population Statistics | | | | | | | | **Table 22.25**

Persons Aged 65 Years and Over at January 1st 1990, 1995, 2000, 2006-2011

'000

	1990	1995	2000	2006	2007	2008	2009	2010	2011
Western Europe									
Austria	1,140	1,197	1,234	1,358	1,399	1,425	1,451	1,476	1,480
Belgium	1,474	1,597	1,715	1,809	1,810	1,820	1,837	1,860	1,883
Cyprus	76	87	96	113	117	120	124	128	132
Denmark	800	799	790	823	835	853	875	903	934
Finland	662	720	767	841	869	875	892	910	941
France	7,872	8,686	9,431	10,163	10,208	10,301	10,421	10,551	10,682
Germany	11,794	12,542	13,351	15,870	16,299	16,519	16,729	16,902	16,844
Gibraltar	3	4	4	5	5	5	5	5	5
Greece	1,382	1,587	1,796	2,061	2,074	2,090	2,103	2,142	2,185
Iceland	27	30	33	35	36	37	38	38	40
Ireland	399	411	424	461	469	479	492	506	520
Italy	8,344	9,369	10,310	11,592	11,793	11,946	12,085	12,206	12,302
Liechtenstein	3	3	3	4	4	4	5	5	5
Luxembourg	51	56	61	66	67	68	69	71	72
Malta	36	41	45	55	56	56	57	59	61
Monaco	7	7	8	8	8	8	8	8	8
Netherlands	1,906	2,034	2,152	2,330	2,368	2,415	2,472	2,538	2,595
Norway	691	695	683	682	686	693	705	723	742
Portugal	1,322	1,475	1,635	1,810	1,829	1,850	1,874	1,901	1,931
Spain	5,215	5,946	6,706	7,308	7,407	7,520	7,629	7,746	7,878
Sweden	1,518	1,540	1,533	1,565	1,581	1,608	1,645	1,691	1,737
Switzerland	972	1,032	1,094	1,192	1,217	1,245	1,276	1,309	1,330
Turkey	3,717	4,423	4,985	5,000	4,964	5,000	4,893	5,198	5,397
United Kingdom	8,984	9,175	9,293	9,664	9,734	9,857	10,019	10,205	10,406
Eastern Europe									
Albania	175	196	228	273	282	292	301	310	317
Belarus	1,074	1,248	1,331	1,417	1,416	1,396	1,357	1,328	1,299
Bosnia-Herzegovina	274	287	415	523	528	530	532	535	540
Bulgaria	1,136	1,234	1,291	1,328	1,325	1,323	1,324	1,326	1,329
Croatia	550	636	697	753	759	765	767	764	757
Czech Republic	1,285	1,354	1,412	1,456	1,482	1,510	1,549	1,592	1,629
Estonia	182	193	205	225	229	230	229	229	228
Georgia	482	537	557	634	634	631	630	629	630
Hungary	1,374	1,458	1,531	1,591	1,605	1,624	1,640	1,663	1,671
Latvia	315	336	353	373	374	372	369	366	360
Lithuania	399	443	483	522	527	533	536	534	536
Macedonia	152	166	197	226	229	233	236	239	241
Moldova	362	391	410	422	417	411	404	398	400
Montenegro	48	54	63	79	79	78	77	77	78
Poland	3,781	4,186	4,619	5,076	5,117	5,131	5,146	5,166	5,188
Romania	2,383	2,679	2,930	3,197	3,202	3,204	3,196	3,204	3,184
Russia	14,578	17,402	18,063	19,963	20,072	19,716	19,034	18,426	17,863
Serbia	847	1,030	1,201	1,277	1,274	1,267	1,257	1,243	1,217
Slovakia	541	578	613	630	637	644	651	661	668
Slovenia	212	240	275	313	320	329	334	338	339
Ukraine	6,175	6,961	6,819	7,567	7,603	7,507	7,317	7,169	6,965

Source: Euromonitor International from national statistics

Table 22.26

Population by Age Group at January 1st 2011

'000

	0-4	5-9	10-14	15-19	20-24	25-29	30-34	35-39
Western Europe								
Austria	393.4	405.1	436.3	495.8	524.1	556.9	532.8	584.6
Belgium	641.3	603.8	611.5	644.8	677.9	692.7	715.6	736.1
Cyprus	64.6	62.1	68.7	84.3	92.5	102.5	93.0	81.9
Denmark	325.5	327.9	341.7	356.5	337.5	311.5	342.6	389.8
Finland	301.6	289.3	296.7	332.1	327.8	346.1	339.3	313.9
France	2,806.9	3,847.6	3,849.4	3,806.2	3,974.0	3,898.0	3,877.0	4,265.7
Germany	3,409.1	3,568.3	3,963.7	4,140.4	4,996.0	4,950.6	4,842.6	4,966.8
Gibraltar								
Greece	570.8	531.0	522.3	563.8	608.9	745.9	860.4	875.3
Iceland	24.1	21.7	21.5	23.9	23.4	24.5	23.1	22.0
Ireland	363.7	315.3	297.8	270.2	256.0	371.0	385.7	348.0
Italy	2,846.4	2,842.2	2,824.6	2,934.6	3,134.6	3,471.3	4,062.2	4,788.2
Liechtenstein								
Luxembourg	29.1	29.9	31.4	31.1	30.7	35.5	38.2	38.9
Malta	19.7	18.9	23.0	27.2	31.0	31.8	31.6	27.8
Monaco								
Netherlands	923.1	985.2	998.7	1,006.7	1,034.7	1,001.5	1,004.8	1,121.6
Norway	308.8	297.8	315.1	323.6	319.0	313.1	320.5	356.0
Portugal	511.1	553.8	542.9	558.0	604.8	714.6	818.9	840.0
Spain	2,484.3	2,336.5	2,144.2	2,208.5	2,538.8	3,211.3	3,951.2	3,988.7
Sweden	561.8	515.7	487.5	618.6	632.0	581.9	581.9	633.9
Switzerland	390.6	383.1	417.1	451.6	485.0	521.4	534.8	558.9
Turkey	5,889.0	6,072.6	6,580.4	6,275.5	6,236.5	6,398.8	6,206.2	5,557.9
United Kingdom	3,897.3	3,480.4	3,537.1	3,874.7	4,332.8	4,296.0	3,939.6	4,134.4
Eastern Europe								
Albania	203.2	236.0	270.4	280.7	310.8	286.4	215.4	204.1
Belarus	518.8	440.8	454.8	587.2	763.2	761.7	688.3	664.9
Bosnia-Herzegovina	175.0	181.2	216.9	228.6	285.2	300.5	280.2	274.2
Bulgaria	375.2	340.7	319.1	386.4	507.7	530.5	567.7	558.9
Croatia	215.6	206.6	246.5	254.9	276.3	309.1	312.3	298.2
Czech Republic	576.9	482.9	451.5	580.1	688.9	743.2	892.4	885.0
Estonia	77.9	66.5	61.4	74.4	105.7	103.4	93.9	92.3
Georgia	260.6	236.4	236.1	323.4	367.5	322.5	289.5	281.5
Hungary	486.3	482.1	492.3	588.0	642.4	685.6	822.3	789.0
Latvia	103.8	94.4	87.1	121.0	166.8	162.8	144.3	146.6
Lithuania	167.2	146.9	173.8	223.1	252.9	233.6	207.0	220.1
Macedonia	114.5	115.5	128.8	151.4	161.8	164.8	157.3	150.0
Moldova	223.4	177.8	190.8	269.3	345.5	307.2	250.1	220.1
Montenegro	38.2	39.5	40.8	40.3	47.6	48.3	45.7	41.8
Poland	1,995.4	1,776.2	1,977.5	2,419.1	2,848.3	3,285.1	3,080.3	2,727.2
Romania	1,086.7	1,055.5	1,105.0	1,193.2	1,682.6	1,600.3	1,773.1	1,666.7
Russia	8,342.2	7,130.5	6,516.4	7,900.6	11,955.4	12,525.1	11,092.5	10,261.5
Serbia	347.3	383.5	367.7	421.2	462.3	508.0	516.6	497.0
Slovakia	284.2	258.5	281.9	347.9	407.0	446.7	469.9	427.0
Slovenia	106.6	90.9	93.4	102.5	127.3	145.5	158.1	150.9
Ukraine	2,429.6	2,001.1	2,065.3	2,688.1	3,564.4	3,766.4	3,397.1	3,260.6

Source: Euromonitor International from national statistics

Population Statistics

Population by Age Group at January 1st 2011 *(continued)*
'000

	40-44	45-49	50-54	55-59	60-64	65-69	70-74	75-79	80+
Western Europe									
Austria	693.4	709.7	614.7	503.0	474.5	422.7	383.0	264.8	409.6
Belgium	786.6	826.2	779.9	701.6	650.5	480.0	448.2	401.5	553.0
Cyprus	75.2	72.8	70.8	62.6	53.7	43.3	34.1	24.7	29.5
Denmark	403.3	409.9	367.2	349.5	363.9	318.8	223.8	162.6	228.5
Finland	349.7	377.1	374.9	384.1	401.7	282.0	223.5	179.6	255.9
France	4,350.2	4,381.5	4,198.3	4,067.8	4,033.4	2,625.7	2,378.2	2,228.8	3,449.2
Germany	6,627.6	7,097.7	6,231.0	5,464.0	4,649.4	4,381.9	4,915.6	3,240.1	4,306.7
Gibraltar									
Greece	895.1	800.0	789.5	708.4	669.5	532.9	574.2	501.5	576.3
Iceland	21.4	22.2	21.7	19.0	16.1	11.9	8.7	7.8	11.1
Ireland	319.2	302.5	271.4	242.7	217.1	168.4	126.7	97.8	127.5
Italy	4,940.4	4,784.8	4,143.2	3,727.3	3,825.1	3,052.2	3,102.2	2,533.6	3,613.5
Liechtenstein									
Luxembourg	42.9	41.4	36.3	31.0	25.8	20.1	17.4	14.8	19.6
Malta	24.6	28.9	31.2	30.4	31.2	18.4	17.0	11.9	13.6
Monaco									
Netherlands	1,295.9	1,298.3	1,196.3	1,090.2	1,103.7	790.6	637.5	499.3	667.5
Norway	369.5	342.5	320.9	298.8	292.4	226.8	163.8	130.5	221.2
Portugal	782.0	779.5	721.4	666.5	612.1	531.3	484.1	422.8	493.2
Spain	3,744.4	3,486.4	3,098.7	2,640.5	2,441.5	2,103.0	1,742.8	1,712.6	2,319.4
Sweden	652.2	642.5	584.7	571.4	614.1	547.7	389.6	303.0	496.9
Switzerland	634.1	650.9	566.3	486.8	459.8	397.2	303.4	256.1	372.9
Turkey	4,581.6	4,697.5	3,684.9	3,262.2	2,471.5	1,807.7	1,413.1	1,123.5	1,052.9
United Kingdom	4,610.8	4,598.6	4,037.4	3,588.0	3,765.1	2,994.4	2,464.4	2,010.9	2,936.5
Eastern Europe									
Albania	201.5	203.9	213.2	155.2	117.4	109.0	91.5	62.9	53.1
Belarus	651.7	739.7	772.1	631.2	507.5	304.9	407.4	279.6	307.4
Bosnia-Herzegovina	281.9	300.8	296.6	271.2	211.8	154.9	160.0	126.6	98.1
Bulgaria	528.1	509.9	522.1	517.6	523.5	400.5	336.9	296.8	295.2
Croatia	299.9	318.2	328.0	317.8	271.7	204.6	213.0	174.5	165.1
Czech Republic	701.7	693.6	669.5	751.0	740.6	549.7	382.1	312.0	384.8
Estonia	88.2	90.8	93.2	87.1	77.4	59.4	64.0	47.5	57.1
Georgia	276.5	331.6	331.9	283.0	222.6	154.2	195.9	141.0	139.0
Hungary	697.0	593.2	669.4	750.5	616.5	512.6	417.2	335.0	406.4
Latvia	142.5	149.5	151.6	129.9	114.0	100.2	102.9	72.1	85.0
Lithuania	236.1	251.0	239.1	192.6	165.4	153.5	142.0	115.0	125.3
Macedonia	147.0	145.6	142.3	130.2	107.2	80.5	69.3	52.3	38.5
Moldova	211.6	256.7	269.8	252.2	181.6	121.2	115.3	81.8	81.4
Montenegro	39.7	41.5	43.7	41.0	33.8	21.8	23.5	17.3	15.3
Poland	2,348.5	2,442.9	2,914.2	2,857.7	2,329.3	1,356.8	1,357.2	1,144.7	1,329.0
Romania	1,795.5	1,187.6	1,448.6	1,442.5	1,202.3	865.6	922.3	708.6	687.6
Russia	9,304.1	10,670.1	11,550.3	9,974.8	7,827.6	3,857.3	6,315.0	3,520.1	4,170.5
Serbia	472.8	489.0	524.1	578.7	490.2	320.4	347.6	288.4	260.2
Slovakia	358.6	376.9	386.9	382.7	300.7	215.4	168.4	134.1	149.8
Slovenia	150.7	157.0	153.6	151.2	123.5	94.0	87.5	72.4	85.1
Ukraine	3,041.9	3,325.9	3,485.6	3,039.9	2,567.2	1,709.2	2,424.4	1,231.3	1,600.4

Source: Euromonitor International from national statistics

Table 22.27

Population by Age Group at January 1st (% Analysis) 2011

% of total

	0-4	5-9	10-14	15-19	20-24	25-29	30-34	35-39
Western Europe								
Austria	4.68	4.82	5.19	5.90	6.24	6.63	6.34	6.96
Belgium	5.86	5.51	5.58	5.89	6.19	6.32	6.53	6.72
Cyprus	5.79	5.56	6.16	7.55	8.29	9.18	8.33	7.34
Denmark	5.85	5.90	6.15	6.41	6.07	5.60	6.16	7.01
Finland	5.61	5.38	5.52	6.18	6.10	6.44	6.31	5.84
France	6.17	6.09	6.10	6.03	6.30	6.17	6.14	6.76
Germany	4.17	4.36	4.85	5.06	6.11	6.06	5.92	6.08
Gibraltar								
Greece	5.04	4.69	4.61	4.98	5.38	6.59	7.60	7.73
Iceland	7.43	6.69	6.64	7.38	7.21	7.55	7.12	6.79
Ireland	8.12	7.04	6.65	6.03	5.71	8.28	8.61	7.77
Italy	4.70	4.69	4.66	4.84	5.17	5.73	6.70	7.90
Liechtenstein								
Luxembourg	5.67	5.82	6.10	6.04	5.97	6.90	7.44	7.57
Malta	4.70	4.52	5.49	6.51	7.41	7.61	7.56	6.66
Monaco								
Netherlands	5.54	5.92	6.00	6.04	6.21	6.01	6.03	6.73
Norway	6.28	6.05	6.40	6.58	6.48	6.36	6.51	7.24
Portugal	4.80	5.21	5.10	5.25	5.69	6.72	7.70	7.90
Spain	5.38	5.06	4.65	4.79	5.50	6.96	8.56	8.64
Sweden	5.97	5.48	5.18	6.57	6.71	6.18	6.18	6.73
Switzerland	4.96	4.87	5.30	5.74	6.16	6.62	6.80	7.10
Turkey	8.03	8.28	8.98	8.56	8.51	8.73	8.47	7.58
United Kingdom	6.24	5.57	5.66	6.20	6.93	6.87	6.30	6.62
Eastern Europe								
Albania	6.32	7.34	8.41	8.73	9.67	8.91	6.70	6.35
Belarus	5.47	4.65	4.80	6.19	8.05	8.03	7.26	7.01
Bosnia-Herzegovina	4.55	4.71	5.64	5.95	7.42	7.82	7.29	7.13
Bulgaria	4.99	4.53	4.25	5.14	6.75	7.06	7.55	7.44
Croatia	4.89	4.68	5.59	5.78	6.26	7.01	7.08	6.76
Czech Republic	5.50	4.61	4.31	5.53	6.57	7.09	8.51	8.44
Estonia	5.81	4.96	4.58	5.55	7.88	7.71	7.01	6.89
Georgia	5.93	5.38	5.38	7.36	8.37	7.34	6.59	6.41
Hungary	4.87	4.83	4.93	5.89	6.43	6.87	8.23	7.90
Latvia	5.00	4.55	4.20	5.83	8.04	7.85	6.96	7.07
Lithuania	5.15	4.53	5.36	6.88	7.79	7.20	6.38	6.78
Macedonia	5.57	5.61	6.26	7.36	7.87	8.01	7.65	7.29
Moldova	6.28	5.00	5.37	7.57	9.72	8.64	7.03	6.19
Montenegro	6.16	6.37	6.58	6.51	7.68	7.79	7.37	6.74
Poland	5.22	4.65	5.18	6.33	7.46	8.60	8.07	7.14
Romania	5.07	4.93	5.16	5.57	7.85	7.47	8.28	7.78
Russia	5.84	4.99	4.56	5.53	8.37	8.76	7.76	7.18
Serbia	4.77	5.27	5.05	5.79	6.35	6.98	7.10	6.83
Slovakia	5.27	4.79	5.22	6.45	7.54	8.28	8.71	7.91
Slovenia	5.20	4.43	4.56	5.00	6.21	7.10	7.71	7.36
Ukraine	5.33	4.39	4.53	5.90	7.82	8.26	7.45	7.15

Source: Euromonitor International from national statistics

22

Population

Population Statistics

Population by Age Group at January 1st (% Analysis) 2011 *(continued)*
% of total

	40-44	45-49	50-54	55-59	60-64	65-69	70-74	75-79	80+
Western Europe									
Austria	8.25	8.44	7.31	5.98	5.65	5.03	4.56	3.15	4.87
Belgium	7.18	7.54	7.12	6.41	5.94	4.38	4.09	3.67	5.05
Cyprus	6.73	6.52	6.34	5.61	4.81	3.88	3.05	2.21	2.64
Denmark	7.25	7.37	6.60	6.29	6.54	5.73	4.03	2.92	4.11
Finland	6.51	7.02	6.97	7.15	7.47	5.25	4.16	3.34	4.76
France	6.89	6.94	6.65	6.44	6.39	4.16	3.77	3.53	5.46
Germany	8.11	8.68	7.62	6.68	5.69	5.36	6.01	3.96	5.27
Gibraltar									
Greece	7.90	7.06	6.97	6.25	5.91	4.71	5.07	4.43	5.09
Iceland	6.60	6.85	6.70	5.87	4.96	3.68	2.69	2.39	3.44
Ireland	7.12	6.75	6.06	5.42	4.84	3.76	2.83	2.18	2.85
Italy	8.15	7.89	6.83	6.15	6.31	5.03	5.12	4.18	5.96
Liechtenstein									
Luxembourg	8.35	8.05	7.07	6.02	5.03	3.90	3.38	2.88	3.80
Malta	5.88	6.90	7.47	7.26	7.46	4.41	4.07	2.83	3.25
Monaco									
Netherlands	7.78	7.79	7.18	6.55	6.63	4.75	3.83	3.00	4.01
Norway	7.51	6.96	6.52	6.07	5.94	4.61	3.33	2.65	4.49
Portugal	7.35	7.33	6.78	6.27	5.75	4.99	4.55	3.98	4.64
Spain	8.11	7.55	6.71	5.72	5.29	4.56	3.78	3.71	5.03
Sweden	6.93	6.82	6.21	6.07	6.52	5.82	4.14	3.22	5.28
Switzerland	8.06	8.27	7.20	6.19	5.84	5.05	3.86	3.25	4.74
Turkey	6.25	6.41	5.03	4.45	3.37	2.47	1.93	1.53	1.44
United Kingdom	7.38	7.36	6.46	5.74	6.02	4.79	3.94	3.22	4.70
Eastern Europe									
Albania	6.27	6.34	6.63	4.83	3.65	3.39	2.85	1.96	1.65
Belarus	6.87	7.80	8.14	6.66	5.35	3.22	4.30	2.95	3.24
Bosnia-Herzegovina	7.33	7.83	7.72	7.05	5.51	4.03	4.16	3.29	2.55
Bulgaria	7.03	6.78	6.95	6.89	6.96	5.33	4.48	3.95	3.93
Croatia	6.80	7.21	7.43	7.20	6.16	4.64	4.83	3.95	3.74
Czech Republic	6.69	6.61	6.39	7.16	7.06	5.24	3.64	2.98	3.67
Estonia	6.58	6.78	6.95	6.50	5.78	4.43	4.78	3.54	4.26
Georgia	6.29	7.55	7.55	6.44	5.07	3.51	4.46	3.21	3.16
Hungary	6.98	5.94	6.70	7.52	6.17	5.13	4.18	3.35	4.07
Latvia	6.87	7.21	7.31	6.26	5.49	4.83	4.96	3.47	4.10
Lithuania	7.28	7.74	7.37	5.94	5.10	4.73	4.38	3.54	3.86
Macedonia	7.15	7.08	6.92	6.33	5.21	3.91	3.37	2.54	1.87
Moldova	5.95	7.22	7.59	7.09	5.11	3.41	3.24	2.30	2.29
Montenegro	6.41	6.69	7.05	6.62	5.46	3.51	3.79	2.79	2.48
Poland	6.15	6.40	7.63	7.48	6.10	3.55	3.55	3.00	3.48
Romania	8.38	5.54	6.76	6.73	5.61	4.04	4.30	3.31	3.21
Russia	6.51	7.47	8.08	6.98	5.48	2.70	4.42	2.46	2.92
Serbia	6.50	6.72	7.20	7.95	6.74	4.40	4.78	3.96	3.58
Slovakia	6.65	6.98	7.17	7.09	5.57	3.99	3.12	2.48	2.78
Slovenia	7.35	7.66	7.49	7.37	6.03	4.58	4.27	3.53	4.15
Ukraine	6.67	7.29	7.64	6.67	5.63	3.75	5.32	2.70	3.51

Source: Euromonitor International from national statistics

Table 22.28

Population Forecasts at January 1st 2011-2021

'000

	2011	2012	2013	2014	2015	2016	2017	2018	2019	2020	2021
Western Europe											
Austria	8,404	8,443	8,480	8,517	8,554	8,593	8,631	8,666	8,699	8,730	8,761
Belgium	10,951	11,041	11,132	11,222	11,310	11,396	11,480	11,562	11,640	11,716	11,789
Cyprus	1,116	1,128	1,140	1,153	1,165	1,175	1,186	1,196	1,207	1,218	1,227
Denmark	5,561	5,581	5,602	5,622	5,641	5,658	5,675	5,691	5,708	5,725	5,743
Finland	5,375	5,401	5,426	5,450	5,475	5,499	5,523	5,547	5,571	5,594	5,617
France	63,128	63,461	63,809	64,147	64,477	64,800	65,116	65,426	65,730	66,028	66,322
Germany	81,752	81,841	81,841	81,789	81,708	81,599	81,472	81,327	81,175	81,015	80,846
Gibraltar	29	29	29	29	29	29	29	29	29	29	29
Greece	11,326	11,346	11,364	11,380	11,394	11,406	11,415	11,422	11,427	11,431	11,432
Iceland	324	328	332	335	339	343	346	350	354	358	361
Ireland	4,481	4,478	4,485	4,497	4,511	4,527	4,545	4,563	4,582	4,602	4,622
Italy	60,626	60,851	61,051	61,231	61,392	61,538	61,668	61,785	61,890	61,984	62,068
Liechtenstein	36	36	37	37	37	38	38	38	38	39	39
Luxembourg	514	521	528	536	543	550	556	563	570	577	582
Malta	418	419	421	422	423	424	425	426	427	428	428
Monaco	35	35	35	35	35	35	35	35	35	35	35
Netherlands	16,656	16,730	16,803	16,873	16,935	16,994	17,051	17,109	17,167	17,225	17,282
Norway	4,920	4,986	5,055	5,125	5,196	5,267	5,336	5,405	5,472	5,538	5,603
Portugal	10,637	10,634	10,629	10,623	10,613	10,602	10,588	10,573	10,556	10,537	10,517
Spain	46,153	46,196	46,213	46,223	46,225	46,220	46,207	46,187	46,160	46,126	46,086
Sweden	9,416	9,483	9,566	9,653	9,738	9,821	9,906	9,986	10,064	10,136	10,200
Switzerland	7,870	7,953	8,032	8,102	8,167	8,229	8,291	8,354	8,412	8,468	8,521
Turkey	73,312	74,056	74,787	75,505	76,209	76,899	77,573	78,232	78,876	79,503	80,114
United Kingdom	62,499	62,991	63,488	63,984	64,472	64,951	65,417	65,878	66,334	66,786	67,232
Eastern Europe											
Albania	3,215	3,227	3,239	3,249	3,258	3,269	3,277	3,282	3,288	3,294	3,296
Belarus	9,481	9,465	9,444	9,420	9,394	9,366	9,336	9,304	9,271	9,237	9,203
Bosnia-Herzegovina	3,844	3,843	3,841	3,840	3,837	3,833	3,828	3,823	3,816	3,809	3,800
Bulgaria	7,517	7,475	7,437	7,401	7,363	7,325	7,286	7,246	7,205	7,164	7,121
Croatia	4,412	4,401	4,392	4,383	4,374	4,365	4,356	4,347	4,337	4,327	4,316
Czech Republic	10,486	10,504	10,521	10,534	10,546	10,557	10,567	10,576	10,582	10,587	10,589
Estonia	1,340	1,339	1,338	1,338	1,337	1,337	1,336	1,335	1,334	1,333	1,331
Georgia	4,393	4,398	4,403	4,409	4,414	4,418	4,422	4,425	4,428	4,429	4,430
Hungary	9,986	9,959	9,935	9,910	9,884	9,858	9,830	9,801	9,772	9,742	9,711
Latvia	2,075	2,039	2,008	1,981	1,960	1,942	1,927	1,912	1,897	1,882	1,867
Lithuania	3,245	3,198	3,161	3,130	3,102	3,076	3,053	3,031	3,012	2,994	2,978
Macedonia	2,057	2,061	2,065	2,069	2,073	2,077	2,080	2,083	2,086	2,088	2,091
Moldova	3,556	3,532	3,505	3,478	3,453	3,431	3,413	3,397	3,379	3,358	3,342
Montenegro	620	619	619	618	618	617	617	616	616	615	615
Poland	38,189	38,212	38,233	38,253	38,269	38,279	38,284	38,281	38,270	38,248	38,216
Romania	21,424	21,385	21,345	21,303	21,260	21,214	21,166	21,115	21,061	21,004	20,943
Russia	142,914	142,862	142,813	142,762	142,707	142,644	142,564	142,461	142,330	142,169	141,976
Serbia	7,275	7,240	7,202	7,163	7,122	7,082	7,041	6,999	6,956	6,913	6,870
Slovakia	5,397	5,404	5,412	5,420	5,427	5,434	5,440	5,446	5,451	5,455	5,458
Slovenia	2,050	2,055	2,061	2,067	2,072	2,077	2,081	2,085	2,088	2,091	2,093
Ukraine	45,598	45,453	45,312	45,174	45,036	44,897	44,757	44,616	44,471	44,323	44,170

Source: Euromonitor International from national statistics

Population 22

Table 22.29

Children Aged 0-14 Years Forecasts at January 1st 2011-2021

'000

	2011	2012	2013	2014	2015	2016	2017	2018	2019	2020	2021
Western Europe											
Austria	1,235	1,224	1,219	1,218	1,219	1,221	1,225	1,227	1,230	1,231	1,233
Belgium	1,857	1,876	1,896	1,919	1,943	1,965	1,989	2,014	2,038	2,059	2,076
Cyprus	195	194	193	193	193	193	194	195	196	196	197
Denmark	995	986	978	971	964	956	950	947	943	941	940
Finland	888	889	891	896	901	906	912	918	922	926	930
France	11,594	11,643	11,729	11,800	11,865	11,894	11,934	11,986	12,043	12,097	12,145
Germany	10,941	10,834	10,698	10,585	10,486	10,386	10,319	10,266	10,229	10,191	10,168
Gibraltar	5	5	5	5	5	5	5	5	5	5	5
Greece	1,624	1,628	1,634	1,645	1,655	1,660	1,664	1,665	1,665	1,665	1,662
Iceland	67	68	68	69	70	71	71	72	73	74	75
Ireland	977	992	1,007	1,023	1,038	1,053	1,067	1,080	1,092	1,103	1,113
Italy	8,513	8,531	8,540	8,537	8,525	8,494	8,463	8,428	8,382	8,323	8,266
Liechtenstein	6	6	6	6	6	6	6	6	6	6	6
Luxembourg	90	91	92	93	93	94	95	96	97	98	100
Malta	62	60	59	58	58	57	57	57	58	58	58
Monaco	5	5	5	5	5	5	5	5	5	5	5
Netherlands	2,907	2,897	2,884	2,866	2,845	2,820	2,800	2,783	2,768	2,762	2,762
Norway	922	924	931	940	950	961	975	990	1,005	1,019	1,034
Portugal	1,608	1,602	1,597	1,590	1,576	1,563	1,546	1,527	1,507	1,489	1,470
Spain	6,965	7,027	7,072	7,106	7,122	7,115	7,088	7,054	6,995	6,925	6,847
Sweden	1,565	1,584	1,613	1,645	1,678	1,710	1,743	1,771	1,796	1,819	1,839
Switzerland	1,191	1,195	1,202	1,208	1,215	1,221	1,231	1,242	1,251	1,261	1,269
Turkey	18,542	18,410	18,216	17,999	17,739	17,501	17,301	17,205	17,132	17,032	16,918
United Kingdom	10,915	11,007	11,112	11,232	11,365	11,512	11,663	11,800	11,914	12,008	12,086
Eastern Europe											
Albania	710	694	680	665	650	640	628	616	605	597	589
Belarus	1,414	1,431	1,458	1,476	1,502	1,519	1,539	1,560	1,580	1,598	1,611
Bosnia-Herzegovina	573	563	552	542	533	526	521	517	514	511	508
Bulgaria	1,035	1,044	1,060	1,074	1,079	1,085	1,088	1,090	1,091	1,087	1,081
Croatia	669	659	652	647	644	642	644	647	651	654	655
Czech Republic	1,511	1,531	1,550	1,569	1,587	1,603	1,615	1,625	1,633	1,635	1,630
Estonia	206	209	213	217	221	224	226	229	231	231	231
Georgia	733	735	740	747	754	761	767	771	774	774	772
Hungary	1,461	1,451	1,447	1,445	1,445	1,439	1,433	1,426	1,420	1,412	1,400
Latvia	285	282	280	279	278	277	277	276	274	272	269
Lithuania	488	480	477	474	473	474	478	483	487	492	496
Macedonia	359	355	353	352	352	351	351	352	353	354	356
Moldova	592	587	582	580	582	580	583	588	590	587	583
Montenegro	118	117	116	115	114	113	112	111	109	108	107
Poland	5,749	5,730	5,730	5,745	5,766	5,786	5,812	5,840	5,860	5,864	5,848
Romania	3,247	3,245	3,239	3,225	3,210	3,193	3,183	3,174	3,160	3,137	3,105
Russia	21,989	22,464	22,977	23,407	23,862	24,258	24,632	24,923	25,126	25,305	25,472
Serbia	1,099	1,091	1,087	1,085	1,084	1,082	1,075	1,065	1,053	1,042	1,037
Slovakia	825	825	827	830	834	839	846	854	860	863	865
Slovenia	291	295	300	305	310	314	319	323	328	331	334
Ukraine	6,496	6,530	6,596	6,675	6,774	6,870	6,971	7,055	7,115	7,151	7,177

Source: Euromonitor International from national statistics

　　　　　　　　　　　　　　　　　　　　　　　　　　　　　　　Table 22.30

Persons of Working Age (15-64 Years) Forecasts at January 1st 2011-2021

'000

	2011	2012	2013	2014	2015	2016	2017	2018	2019	2020	2021
Western Europe											
Austria	5,689	5,720	5,730	5,739	5,749	5,763	5,775	5,784	5,789	5,793	5,791
Belgium	7,212	7,243	7,275	7,304	7,334	7,363	7,390	7,408	7,424	7,439	7,452
Cyprus	789	798	807	815	823	828	833	838	842	847	849
Denmark	3,632	3,626	3,624	3,625	3,627	3,630	3,632	3,632	3,631	3,631	3,629
Finland	3,547	3,533	3,514	3,493	3,475	3,459	3,447	3,432	3,421	3,412	3,403
France	40,852	40,827	40,756	40,686	40,630	40,599	40,597	40,570	40,556	40,535	40,522
Germany	53,966	54,104	54,094	53,997	53,783	53,533	53,251	52,931	52,603	52,251	51,863
Gibraltar	19	19	19	19	19	19	19	19	19	19	19
Greece	7,517	7,485	7,461	7,448	7,446	7,413	7,390	7,366	7,353	7,335	7,314
Iceland	217	219	221	223	224	226	227	228	229	230	231
Ireland	2,984	2,952	2,929	2,910	2,892	2,877	2,863	2,850	2,838	2,826	2,816
Italy	39,812	39,776	39,739	39,686	39,668	39,666	39,681	39,695	39,706	39,691	39,660
Liechtenstein	25	25	26	26	26	26	26	26	27	27	27
Luxembourg	352	357	362	367	372	376	380	383	387	391	394
Malta	296	295	294	292	291	290	288	286	285	283	281
Monaco	23	23	23	23	22	22	22	22	22	22	22
Netherlands	11,154	11,117	11,091	11,082	11,077	11,079	11,079	11,072	11,066	11,051	11,029
Norway	3,256	3,294	3,332	3,371	3,411	3,450	3,487	3,519	3,550	3,579	3,606
Portugal	7,098	7,084	7,065	7,038	7,020	6,997	6,976	6,956	6,938	6,914	6,888
Spain	31,310	31,140	30,987	30,848	30,720	30,606	30,509	30,413	30,328	30,236	30,136
Sweden	6,113	6,114	6,122	6,133	6,146	6,163	6,184	6,206	6,228	6,250	6,264
Switzerland	5,350	5,387	5,421	5,447	5,468	5,489	5,507	5,523	5,538	5,548	5,556
Turkey	49,373	50,132	50,915	51,718	52,402	53,062	53,800	54,378	54,940	55,437	55,766
United Kingdom	41,178	41,297	41,355	41,446	41,555	41,664	41,775	41,896	42,031	42,182	42,339
Eastern Europe											
Albania	2,189	2,209	2,230	2,249	2,266	2,280	2,292	2,301	2,307	2,307	2,302
Belarus	6,767	6,745	6,707	6,639	6,601	6,528	6,470	6,411	6,350	6,282	6,217
Bosnia-Herzegovina	2,731	2,734	2,735	2,733	2,728	2,717	2,702	2,683	2,661	2,638	2,614
Bulgaria	5,152	5,087	5,023	4,958	4,897	4,832	4,782	4,729	4,676	4,628	4,579
Croatia	2,986	2,980	2,971	2,961	2,945	2,923	2,901	2,875	2,850	2,826	2,802
Czech Republic	7,346	7,284	7,218	7,157	7,101	7,044	6,989	6,938	6,891	6,850	6,814
Estonia	906	901	894	887	879	874	867	861	856	851	845
Georgia	3,030	3,031	3,028	3,023	3,014	3,003	2,990	2,975	2,960	2,944	2,930
Hungary	6,854	6,828	6,785	6,736	6,683	6,629	6,579	6,530	6,467	6,394	6,331
Latvia	1,429	1,403	1,377	1,352	1,330	1,314	1,298	1,283	1,270	1,255	1,240
Lithuania	2,221	2,189	2,161	2,134	2,107	2,079	2,050	2,022	1,997	1,974	1,949
Macedonia	1,458	1,464	1,465	1,463	1,461	1,460	1,458	1,452	1,447	1,441	1,434
Moldova	2,564	2,544	2,520	2,491	2,459	2,428	2,395	2,360	2,327	2,296	2,269
Montenegro	424	423	422	421	420	419	417	416	414	413	411
Poland	27,253	27,170	27,035	26,861	26,668	26,454	26,215	25,963	25,709	25,462	25,212
Romania	14,992	14,938	14,891	14,831	14,730	14,631	14,534	14,427	14,328	14,217	14,100
Russia	103,062	102,574	101,958	101,260	100,226	99,201	98,212	97,348	96,750	96,135	95,414
Serbia	4,960	4,937	4,900	4,853	4,801	4,743	4,701	4,647	4,599	4,548	4,501
Slovakia	3,904	3,901	3,889	3,872	3,855	3,831	3,800	3,769	3,739	3,710	3,681
Slovenia	1,420	1,416	1,410	1,403	1,394	1,384	1,374	1,362	1,350	1,339	1,327
Ukraine	32,137	32,002	31,822	31,544	31,154	30,771	30,400	30,094	29,850	29,594	29,319

Source: Euromonitor International from national statistics

22

Population

Population Statistics

Table 22.31

Persons Aged 65 Years and Over Forecasts at January 1st 2011-2021

'000

	2011	2012	2013	2014	2015	2016	2017	2018	2019	2020	2021
Western Europe											
Austria	1,480	1,499	1,531	1,560	1,586	1,609	1,630	1,655	1,679	1,706	1,737
Belgium	1,883	1,923	1,961	1,998	2,034	2,069	2,102	2,140	2,178	2,218	2,261
Cyprus	132	136	140	145	150	154	159	164	169	175	180
Denmark	934	968	1,000	1,027	1,050	1,072	1,092	1,113	1,134	1,153	1,173
Finland	941	980	1,021	1,061	1,099	1,134	1,165	1,197	1,227	1,256	1,285
France	10,682	10,990	11,324	11,660	11,983	12,306	12,585	12,870	13,131	13,396	13,654
Germany	16,844	16,903	17,049	17,207	17,438	17,680	17,901	18,129	18,343	18,573	18,816
Gibraltar	5	5	5	5	5	5	5	5	5	5	5
Greece	2,185	2,233	2,269	2,287	2,293	2,333	2,361	2,391	2,409	2,431	2,456
Iceland	40	41	42	44	45	47	48	50	51	53	55
Ireland	520	533	548	564	580	597	615	633	652	672	692
Italy	12,302	12,543	12,772	13,007	13,199	13,378	13,524	13,663	13,803	13,969	14,142
Liechtenstein	5	5	5	6	6	6	6	6	6	7	7
Luxembourg	72	73	75	76	78	79	81	83	85	87	89
Malta	61	64	67	71	74	77	79	82	84	87	89
Monaco	8	8	8	8	8	8	8	8	8	8	8
Netherlands	2,595	2,716	2,828	2,925	3,013	3,095	3,172	3,254	3,333	3,412	3,490
Norway	742	768	792	814	835	856	875	896	918	940	963
Portugal	1,931	1,948	1,967	1,995	2,018	2,042	2,066	2,091	2,111	2,134	2,159
Spain	7,878	8,030	8,154	8,269	8,383	8,499	8,610	8,720	8,837	8,964	9,103
Sweden	1,737	1,785	1,830	1,874	1,914	1,949	1,979	2,009	2,040	2,068	2,097
Switzerland	1,330	1,370	1,408	1,447	1,484	1,520	1,553	1,589	1,623	1,659	1,696
Turkey	5,397	5,515	5,656	5,788	6,068	6,335	6,472	6,650	6,804	7,034	7,430
United Kingdom	10,406	10,686	11,021	11,307	11,552	11,774	11,980	12,182	12,389	12,596	12,807
Eastern Europe											
Albania	317	323	329	336	343	350	357	365	376	389	405
Belarus	1,299	1,289	1,279	1,305	1,291	1,319	1,326	1,333	1,341	1,358	1,375
Bosnia-Herzegovina	540	546	554	564	576	590	605	623	641	659	678
Bulgaria	1,329	1,344	1,355	1,369	1,387	1,408	1,417	1,427	1,438	1,448	1,461
Croatia	757	761	769	775	785	800	811	824	836	846	859
Czech Republic	1,629	1,689	1,753	1,809	1,858	1,910	1,962	2,013	2,059	2,102	2,144
Estonia	228	229	231	234	237	240	242	245	248	251	255
Georgia	630	632	635	639	645	654	665	679	694	711	729
Hungary	1,671	1,680	1,703	1,729	1,756	1,790	1,818	1,845	1,885	1,936	1,980
Latvia	360	354	351	350	351	351	352	353	353	354	357
Lithuania	536	528	523	521	522	523	525	526	527	528	532
Macedonia	241	243	248	254	260	266	271	279	286	294	301
Moldova	400	401	403	407	412	423	436	449	462	474	489
Montenegro	78	79	81	82	84	86	88	90	92	94	97
Poland	5,188	5,312	5,468	5,648	5,834	6,039	6,257	6,479	6,701	6,922	7,157
Romania	3,184	3,202	3,215	3,246	3,320	3,391	3,449	3,514	3,573	3,649	3,738
Russia	17,863	17,824	17,878	18,094	18,620	19,186	19,720	20,190	20,455	20,729	21,090
Serbia	1,217	1,211	1,215	1,225	1,237	1,256	1,264	1,287	1,304	1,323	1,333
Slovakia	668	679	697	717	738	764	793	823	852	881	912
Slovenia	339	345	352	360	368	379	388	399	410	421	432
Ukraine	6,965	6,922	6,894	6,955	7,108	7,256	7,386	7,467	7,506	7,578	7,674

Source: Euromonitor International from national statistics

CHAPTER TWENTY-THREE

Retailing

Retailing Statistics

Table 23.1

Retail Sales 2006-2011
US$ billion

	2006	2007	2008	2009	2010	2011
Western Europe						
Austria	68.1	75.6	82.2	78.2	74.9	78.6
Belgium	80.9	93.2	102.6	98.7	96.4	102.1
Cyprus	3.4	3.5	3.7	3.5	3.5	3.5
Denmark	43.4	50.1	53.8	50.3	48.1	49.9
Finland	38.7	44.9	49.8	47.3	46.2	49.3
France	456.6	511.0	557.0	528.8	513.8	544.0
Germany	469.7	522.4	574.0	549.2	530.3	553.1
Gibraltar	0.1	0.1	0.1	0.1	0.1	0.1
Greece	65.9	75.8	81.7	74.9	63.1	55.8
Iceland	1.9	2.0	2.1	2.2	2.3	2.4
Ireland	38.8	44.8	47.6	44.4	40.1	40.3
Italy	355.1	398.5	435.7	411.0	392.5	408.5
Liechtenstein	0.3	0.3	0.3	0.3	0.3	0.3
Luxembourg	3.6	3.7	3.8	3.8	3.9	4.0
Malta	1.3	1.3	1.3	1.3	1.3	1.4
Monaco	0.3	0.3	0.3	0.3	0.3	0.3
Netherlands	101.8	114.6	127.2	121.7	117.3	124.5
Norway	47.3	54.1	58.2	54.4	58.0	64.2
Portugal	47.6	53.5	59.8	57.5	54.7	56.1
Spain	266.6	300.2	320.9	290.5	270.5	275.5
Sweden	64.2	73.7	78.7	69.4	75.9	87.2
Switzerland	73.9	79.6	90.5	92.4	98.0	109.0
Turkey	128.5	155.3	160.2	136.7	148.9	153.5
United Kingdom	548.3	614.6	572.0	493.0	501.7	543.4
Eastern Europe						
Albania	0.6	0.7	0.8	0.8	0.8	0.8
Belarus	7.6	9.5	12.8	11.9	13.6	16.6
Bosnia-Herzegovina	3.5	4.1	4.8	4.4	4.2	4.5
Bulgaria	8.7	10.1	11.4	10.9	10.8	11.5
Croatia	13.3	14.6	16.2	13.8	12.8	13.5
Czech Republic	28.3	33.7	41.2	36.5	36.2	39.8
Estonia	4.1	5.4	5.8	4.7	4.7	5.2
Georgia	4.1	4.5	5.1	4.3	4.1	4.1
Hungary	29.6	35.3	38.6	32.8	31.0	30.8
Latvia	5.4	7.2	8.1	5.9	5.3	5.7
Lithuania	6.4	8.2	9.4	7.2	6.6	7.2
Macedonia	1.6	2.0	2.3	2.1	2.0	2.2
Moldova	0.5	0.6	0.7	0.7	0.7	0.7
Montenegro	0.6	0.6	0.6	0.6	0.6	0.6
Poland	79.0	93.4	112.5	90.5	95.5	99.1
Romania	21.7	29.3	34.0	29.3	27.9	29.5
Russia	255.3	324.3	390.6	311.3	363.9	430.9
Serbia	11.4	13.4	14.4	11.7	10.3	11.8
Slovakia	12.6	15.5	17.9	15.6	15.0	15.9
Slovenia	6.4	7.8	9.3	9.2	9.1	9.8
Ukraine	45.9	55.5	66.3	45.4	46.9	51.4

Source: Euromonitor International from national statistics

European Marketing Data and Statistics 2013 – © Euromonitor International Ltd 2012

Table 23.2

Store-Based Retailer Sales by Grocery/Non-Grocery Split 2011

US$ billion

	Grocery Retailers	Non-Grocery Retailers	Total
Western Europe			
Austria	26.7	47.6	74.3
Belgium	49.4	49.1	98.6
Cyprus	1.4	2.0	3.4
Denmark	27.3	19.3	46.5
Finland	21.8	23.2	44.9
France	276.4	233.6	509.9
Germany	244.0	265.3	509.2
Gibraltar	0.0	0.1	0.1
Greece	29.0	26.0	55.0
Iceland	0.8	1.5	2.3
Ireland	19.8	19.5	39.2
Italy	166.3	233.0	399.3
Liechtenstein	0.1	0.2	0.3
Luxembourg	2.0	1.8	3.8
Malta	0.5	0.8	1.3
Monaco	0.1	0.2	0.3
Netherlands	49.0	69.1	118.1
Norway	30.8	31.2	61.9
Portugal	27.3	27.3	54.6
Spain	128.6	134.2	262.8
Sweden	40.9	41.9	82.8
Switzerland	53.3	51.0	104.3
Turkey	78.4	69.3	147.7
United Kingdom	237.8	249.8	487.5
Eastern Europe			
Albania	0.4	0.4	0.8
Belarus	9.4	6.9	16.3
Bosnia-Herzegovina	2.6	1.8	4.4
Bulgaria	5.5	5.9	11.4
Croatia	9.3	4.0	13.3
Czech Republic	17.6	19.4	37.0
Estonia	2.6	2.5	5.1
Georgia	3.1	1.0	4.1
Hungary	16.4	13.3	29.7
Latvia	3.3	2.3	5.6
Lithuania	4.6	2.4	7.0
Macedonia	1.5	0.6	2.1
Moldova	0.3	0.4	0.7
Montenegro	0.3	0.3	0.6
Poland	53.3	40.8	94.1
Romania	18.8	9.9	28.8
Russia	227.5	186.2	413.7
Serbia	7.1	4.5	11.6
Slovakia	8.3	6.8	15.1
Slovenia	5.9	3.6	9.5
Ukraine	25.2	24.3	49.5

Source: Euromonitor International from national statistics

23

Retailing

Retailing Statistics · **Table 23.3**

Store-Based Retailer Outlets by Grocery/Non-Grocery Split 2011
Number of outlets

	Grocery Retailers	Non-Grocery Retailers	Total
Western Europe			
Austria	10,829	26,515	37,344
Belgium	24,421	47,812	72,233
Cyprus	2,182	4,454	6,635
Denmark	9,353	14,840	24,193
Finland	5,842	18,988	24,830
France	93,968	204,229	298,197
Germany	107,192	193,875	301,067
Gibraltar	28	59	87
Greece	70,913	68,738	139,651
Iceland	491	1,668	2,158
Ireland	7,756	11,181	18,937
Italy	279,303	646,732	926,035
Liechtenstein	66	152	218
Luxembourg	1,037	1,765	2,801
Malta	1,064	1,940	3,004
Monaco	56	108	163
Netherlands	33,082	73,694	106,776
Norway	8,557	25,086	33,643
Portugal	37,453	80,451	117,904
Spain	152,878	375,445	528,323
Sweden	12,772	34,267	47,039
Switzerland	17,180	30,146	47,326
Turkey	352,089	269,064	621,153
United Kingdom	94,715	192,343	287,058
Eastern Europe			
Albania	3,077	2,678	5,754
Belarus	26,091	21,129	47,220
Bosnia-Herzegovina	10,079	6,640	16,719
Bulgaria	35,184	45,608	80,792
Croatia	10,537	15,360	25,897
Czech Republic	24,410	60,555	84,965
Estonia	1,738	2,735	4,473
Georgia	6,746	2,738	9,484
Hungary	41,007	94,313	135,320
Latvia	5,790	6,342	12,132
Lithuania	6,008	7,263	13,271
Macedonia	9,870	9,709	19,579
Moldova	2,584	2,258	4,842
Montenegro	2,183	1,867	4,050
Poland	145,972	157,129	303,101
Romania	66,692	52,996	119,688
Russia	306,704	484,483	791,187
Serbia	32,505	18,395	50,900
Slovakia	15,391	21,704	37,095
Slovenia	2,759	3,077	5,836
Ukraine	88,166	103,787	191,953

Source: Euromonitor International from national statistics

        Table 23.4

Grocery Retailer Sales by Type 2011
% of total

	Hypermarkets	Supermarkets	Discounters	Convenience Stores	Forecourt Retailers	Independent Small Grocers	Food/Drink Tobacco Specialists	Other Grocery Retailers	Total
Western Europe									
Austria	10.45	43.43	27.42	2.96	4.13	1.09	9.32	1.19	100.00
Belgium	7.21	40.16	10.83	8.67	1.08	15.22	14.38	2.46	100.00
Cyprus	6.59	27.14	13.55		1.35	17.74	22.64	10.98	100.00
Denmark	21.62	30.28	26.74	7.88	5.40	1.95	5.84	0.28	100.00
Finland	30.83	29.13	4.03	24.29	2.47	0.65	8.30	0.31	100.00
France	42.07	33.25	8.35	2.82	0.94	3.21	8.32	1.02	100.00
Germany	18.98	27.56	34.77	0.32	4.90	5.63	6.59	1.25	100.00
Gibraltar		54.90			4.16	14.06	8.72	18.16	100.00
Greece	3.64	39.85	4.85	0.89	0.37	8.05	16.93	25.41	100.00
Iceland		58.90		8.94	6.78	4.46	18.75	2.17	100.00
Ireland	3.97	37.04	5.46	33.38	4.06	3.69	11.97	0.42	100.00
Italy	17.92	34.80	8.62	10.86	0.13	11.52	15.77	0.38	100.00
Liechtenstein		75.32				8.09	16.59		100.00
Luxembourg	11.05	41.99	7.18	8.36	2.49	15.98	10.14	2.82	100.00
Malta		58.91	5.22	16.98	4.01	5.41	9.34	0.11	100.00
Monaco		57.22			1.44	9.78	31.43	0.14	100.00
Netherlands	3.43	64.99	11.96	2.22	4.06	2.74	6.83	3.77	100.00
Norway	8.68	31.22	44.21	2.43	2.78	0.22	9.82	0.64	100.00
Portugal	18.70	48.22	10.77	1.98	1.01	5.12	11.21	3.00	100.00
Spain	14.89	48.91	7.92	1.34	1.22	1.89	21.57	2.26	100.00
Sweden	20.92	43.31	4.08	10.30	3.37	3.24	14.00	0.80	100.00
Switzerland	12.05	49.95	10.75	3.27	4.89	2.22	16.73	0.14	100.00
Turkey	5.60	27.38	12.00		1.23	39.77	13.58	0.43	100.00
United Kingdom	45.12	21.95	3.21	14.26	2.85	4.49	6.81	1.31	100.00
Eastern Europe									
Albania		27.54			9.49	15.69	15.25	32.02	100.00
Belarus	4.76	12.55	1.77		1.47	35.66	5.86	37.93	100.00
Bosnia-Herzegovina	12.96	25.14	0.22	8.75	2.15	30.79	16.27	3.73	100.00
Bulgaria	15.87	24.78	3.55	5.98	2.30	28.84	15.28	3.40	100.00
Croatia	24.26	27.19	4.71	22.00	5.17	6.06	3.93	6.68	100.00
Czech Republic	40.44	15.07	15.81	9.45	1.71	7.14	8.64	1.75	100.00
Estonia	21.96	27.09	11.90	24.03	4.01	6.89	3.03	1.08	100.00
Georgia	0.99	14.15		1.66	1.37	49.90	5.52	26.39	100.00
Hungary	30.52	9.31	10.78	30.72	1.86	7.55	8.91	0.35	100.00
Latvia	14.92	23.69	6.97	41.26	1.90	8.35	2.76	0.16	100.00
Lithuania	23.32	48.90	4.58	10.92	1.50	7.32	1.58	1.89	100.00
Macedonia	0.92	24.29	3.92	0.21	1.63	40.35	14.55	14.13	100.00
Moldova		30.43				17.34	16.85	35.38	100.00
Montenegro		31.10			0.97	42.04	21.87	4.02	100.00
Poland	18.93	15.74	17.29	12.63	1.95	24.00	5.33	4.13	100.00
Romania	30.79	10.54	5.51	0.08	0.99	12.20	15.43	24.46	100.00
Russia	10.63	36.79		5.82	0.24	29.13	2.59	14.79	100.00
Serbia	15.89	14.43	1.31	8.15	1.82	46.56	7.57	4.28	100.00
Slovakia	26.09	26.35	3.07	18.69	1.67	9.72	11.59	2.81	100.00
Slovenia	26.47	35.96	9.12	14.39	9.43	1.32	1.39	1.92	100.00
Ukraine	11.30	38.00		2.84	0.92	22.18	2.49	22.26	100.00

Source: Euromonitor International from national statistics

Retailing Statistics

Table 23.5

Non-Grocery Retailer Sales by Type 2011

% of total

	Department Stores	Variety Stores	Mass Merchandisers	Health and Beauty Specialist Retailers	Apparel Specialist Retailers
Western Europe					
Austria		0.67		15.34	14.90
Belgium	2.40	1.37		20.30	21.83
Cyprus	13.27	5.27		7.90	19.91
Denmark	2.95	2.21	0.39	17.45	24.19
Finland	8.10	6.63	1.16	15.98	10.09
France	2.45	2.28		26.92	15.66
Germany	3.33	1.57		32.10	15.56
Gibraltar	7.95	6.60		17.83	20.63
Greece	4.12	0.48		22.55	20.63
Iceland		5.77		11.44	12.83
Ireland	25.16	4.90		14.68	18.83
Italy	0.68	1.33		22.48	23.02
Liechtenstein	11.97	0.81		17.76	19.09
Luxembourg	1.76	2.96		17.20	21.67
Malta	8.71	7.29		11.57	22.84
Monaco	4.38	3.42		23.78	17.15
Netherlands	4.95	4.33		19.25	15.05
Norway	0.31	2.96		11.82	20.19
Portugal	2.10	5.88		20.35	15.74
Spain	9.59	1.82		19.39	19.14
Sweden	2.69	3.02	1.60	16.56	18.44
Switzerland	9.94	1.38		16.06	20.08
Turkey	2.47	0.02		11.25	31.73
United Kingdom	9.99	6.67		10.57	26.92
Eastern Europe					
Albania	1.59			22.10	18.85
Belarus	6.09			15.70	20.59
Bosnia-Herzegovina	13.76			36.53	17.70
Bulgaria				17.37	28.64
Croatia	2.77			26.27	15.86
Czech Republic	2.82	12.11		21.65	9.58
Estonia	4.06			13.37	11.02
Georgia				16.00	28.93
Hungary	0.60	7.34		31.24	10.41
Latvia	3.04	0.19		25.07	20.33
Lithuania		1.84		33.40	16.99
Macedonia				19.75	20.10
Moldova	1.90			26.44	6.15
Montenegro				15.06	17.67
Poland	0.86	2.24		23.94	16.00
Romania	1.68			23.86	7.35
Russia	0.63	0.11		11.40	8.93
Serbia				42.97	19.05
Slovakia	3.96	5.40		25.63	19.32
Slovenia	1.59	0.06		32.34	15.22
Ukraine		0.80		15.21	20.38

Source: Euromonitor International from national statistics

Non-Grocery Retailer Sales by Type 2011 *(continued)*

% of total

	Home and Garden Specialist Retailers	Electronics and Appliance Specialist Retailers	Leisure and Personal Goods Specialist Retailers	Other Non-Grocery Retailers	Total
Western Europe					
Austria	38.78	10.89	13.53	5.89	100.00
Belgium	20.77	13.51	15.34	4.48	100.00
Cyprus	26.50	8.92	12.98	5.25	100.00
Denmark	25.17	10.74	15.03	1.87	100.00
Finland	32.49	8.02	9.82	7.71	100.00
France	22.54	10.01	17.69	2.46	100.00
Germany	23.49	10.65	12.88	0.43	100.00
Gibraltar	15.73	9.93	16.50	4.83	100.00
Greece	25.42	8.26	13.48	5.08	100.00
Iceland	34.75	11.51	22.24	1.46	100.00
Ireland	15.82	5.88	12.30	2.43	100.00
Italy	22.93	5.59	12.95	11.02	100.00
Liechtenstein	9.33	9.41	14.18	17.45	100.00
Luxembourg	24.52	7.30	19.59	4.99	100.00
Malta	17.43	11.01	17.90	3.24	100.00
Monaco	24.56	11.51	12.07	3.13	100.00
Netherlands	27.68	8.93	15.26	4.55	100.00
Norway	34.15	11.32	18.13	1.11	100.00
Portugal	21.86	9.02	19.51	5.53	100.00
Spain	16.88	6.66	23.52	3.00	100.00
Sweden	27.19	12.24	13.50	4.75	100.00
Switzerland	12.96	8.72	13.74	17.12	100.00
Turkey	16.21	23.70	14.52	0.09	100.00
United Kingdom	16.23	9.82	16.14	3.66	100.00
Eastern Europe					
Albania	20.26	7.74	18.43	11.03	100.00
Belarus	19.68	5.56	9.03	23.34	100.00
Bosnia-Herzegovina	17.80	9.30	4.43	0.49	100.00
Bulgaria	21.21	13.76	15.46	3.56	100.00
Croatia	27.22	9.65	17.44	0.79	100.00
Czech Republic	23.73	9.27	11.47	9.37	100.00
Estonia	41.50	7.14	20.31	2.61	100.00
Georgia	4.95	34.33	6.03	9.76	100.00
Hungary	13.27	7.51	19.36	10.26	100.00
Latvia	29.13	7.28	9.52	5.44	100.00
Lithuania	22.21	9.15	11.19	5.22	100.00
Macedonia	33.79	14.18	10.65	1.53	100.00
Moldova	24.23	9.25	18.83	13.20	100.00
Montenegro	28.08	21.90	12.78	4.50	100.00
Poland	20.49	13.80	17.50	5.17	100.00
Romania	27.72	14.87	12.18	12.34	100.00
Russia	19.15	12.53	10.20	37.04	100.00
Serbia	12.93	10.87	10.53	3.66	100.00
Slovakia	18.15	7.20	15.96	4.38	100.00
Slovenia	33.61	3.58	12.55	1.06	100.00
Ukraine	16.02	10.24	7.02	30.32	100.00

Source: Euromonitor International from national statistics

23

Retailing

Retailing Statistics

Table 23.6

Non-Store Retailer Sales by Type 2011

US$ billion

	Vending	Homeshopping	Internet Retailing	Direct Selling	Total
Western Europe					
Austria	0.54	1.00	2.51	0.23	4.28
Belgium	0.35	0.30	2.61	0.31	3.57
Cyprus	0.00	0.00	0.08	0.01	0.09
Denmark	0.09	0.26	2.94	0.09	3.38
Finland	0.08	0.18	3.87	0.20	4.33
France	0.90	4.91	25.11	3.12	34.04
Germany	2.59	13.84	23.99	3.43	43.86
Gibraltar	0.00	0.00	0.00		0.00
Greece	0.02	0.09	0.46	0.20	0.77
Iceland	0.00	0.01	0.07	0.00	0.08
Ireland	0.14	0.18	0.68	0.08	1.08
Italy	0.53	1.60	4.26	2.83	9.23
Liechtenstein	0.00	0.00	0.00		0.01
Luxembourg	0.00	0.01	0.18	0.01	0.20
Malta	0.00	0.00	0.06	0.00	0.07
Monaco	0.00	0.00	0.01		0.01
Netherlands	0.56	0.78	4.89	0.15	6.37
Norway	0.06	0.61	1.38	0.20	2.25
Portugal	0.39	0.30	0.55	0.28	1.52
Spain	9.01	0.80	2.09	0.84	12.75
Sweden	0.15	0.47	3.59	0.20	4.40
Switzerland	0.62	1.43	2.29	0.34	4.68
Turkey	0.00		1.27	4.59	5.86
United Kingdom	0.73	8.27	45.01	1.82	55.83
Eastern Europe					
Albania	0.00	0.00	0.00	0.02	0.02
Belarus	0.00	0.02	0.12	0.20	0.34
Bosnia-Herzegovina	0.00	0.01	0.00	0.04	0.05
Bulgaria	0.01	0.00	0.06	0.08	0.15
Croatia	0.03	0.02	0.12	0.08	0.25
Czech Republic	0.10	0.22	2.07	0.37	2.76
Estonia	0.01	0.02	0.04	0.02	0.09
Georgia	0.01	0.00	0.02	0.03	0.07
Hungary	0.05	0.10	0.62	0.26	1.03
Latvia	0.00	0.03	0.05	0.03	0.12
Lithuania	0.01	0.01	0.18	0.04	0.24
Macedonia	0.00	0.01	0.00	0.02	0.03
Moldova	0.00	0.00	0.00	0.02	0.02
Montenegro	0.00	0.00	0.00	0.01	0.01
Poland	0.10	0.15	3.91	0.83	5.00
Romania	0.01	0.03	0.37	0.36	0.76
Russia	0.49	3.75	9.11	3.87	17.22
Serbia	0.01	0.02	0.04	0.11	0.18
Slovakia	0.04	0.08	0.54	0.15	0.81
Slovenia	0.02	0.06	0.17	0.03	0.29
Ukraine	0.02	0.13	0.80	0.90	1.86

Source: Euromonitor International from national statistics

Table 23.7

Non-Store Retailer Sales by Type (% Analysis) 2011

% of total

	Vending	Homeshopping	Internet Retailing	Direct Selling	Non-Store Retailing
Western Europe					
Austria	12.6	23.4	58.6	5.4	100.0
Belgium	9.8	8.3	73.1	8.8	100.0
Cyprus	1.2	0.1	86.3	12.4	100.0
Denmark	2.7	7.8	86.8	2.7	100.0
Finland	1.8	4.1	89.4	4.7	100.0
France	2.6	14.4	73.8	9.2	100.0
Germany	5.9	31.6	54.7	7.8	100.0
Gibraltar	7.3	22.2	70.5		100.0
Greece	2.8	11.5	60.0	25.8	100.0
Iceland	0.7	11.5	86.4	1.4	100.0
Ireland	13.0	16.3	63.0	7.6	100.0
Italy	5.8	17.4	46.2	30.6	100.0
Liechtenstein	3.6	20.1	76.3		100.0
Luxembourg	1.1	4.8	89.6	4.5	100.0
Malta	2.1	6.7	86.2	5.0	100.0
Monaco	2.8	16.0	81.2		100.0
Netherlands	8.8	12.2	76.7	2.3	100.0
Norway	2.9	27.0	61.2	8.9	100.0
Portugal	25.5	20.0	36.0	18.5	100.0
Spain	70.7	6.3	16.4	6.6	100.0
Sweden	3.3	10.7	81.5	4.5	100.0
Switzerland	13.3	30.5	49.0	7.2	100.0
Turkey	0.0		21.7	78.3	100.0
United Kingdom	1.3	14.8	80.6	3.3	100.0
Eastern Europe					
Albania	0.1	2.5	2.5	94.9	100.0
Belarus	1.1	6.1	35.9	56.8	100.0
Bosnia-Herzegovina	2.2	26.2	4.3	67.2	100.0
Bulgaria	6.4	1.7	37.7	54.2	100.0
Croatia	13.3	8.2	46.7	31.8	100.0
Czech Republic	3.7	8.1	75.0	13.2	100.0
Estonia	8.9	25.8	45.0	20.3	100.0
Georgia	10.9	2.7	35.6	50.8	100.0
Hungary	4.8	10.0	60.3	24.9	100.0
Latvia	2.7	27.1	41.4	28.8	100.0
Lithuania	5.0	3.6	73.6	17.8	100.0
Macedonia	0.7	23.0	6.7	69.6	100.0
Moldova	0.1	2.5	1.2	96.2	100.0
Montenegro	13.5	2.0	14.2	70.2	100.0
Poland	2.1	3.1	78.3	16.6	100.0
Romania	0.7	3.4	48.3	47.6	100.0
Russia	2.9	21.8	52.9	22.5	100.0
Serbia	7.2	10.8	22.8	59.2	100.0
Slovakia	4.9	9.8	67.0	18.3	100.0
Slovenia	8.4	20.6	59.3	11.8	100.0
Ukraine	1.3	7.2	43.1	48.4	100.0

Source: Euromonitor International from national statistics

CHAPTER TWENTY-FOUR

Travel and Tourism

Travel and Tourism Statistics   **Table 24.1**

Average Tourist Nights in Accommodation Establishments 1990, 1995, 2000, 2006-2011

Nights

	1990	1995	2000	2006	2007	2008	2009	2010	2011
Western Europe									
Austria	4.90	4.80	4.00	3.46	3.41	3.40	3.38	3.36	3.35
Belgium									
Cyprus	12.80	11.02	6.70	6.32	6.19	6.27	5.72	5.59	5.45
Denmark									
Finland		1.84	1.90	1.82	1.82	1.81	1.80	1.80	1.79
France			1.88	1.82	1.84	1.84	1.81	1.81	1.80
Germany	2.20	2.39	2.32	2.19	2.18	2.17	2.17	2.17	2.16
Gibraltar									
Greece				4.15	4.08	4.10	4.05	4.03	4.02
Iceland			1.86	1.80	1.80	1.80	1.80	1.80	1.80
Ireland									
Italy	3.53	3.55	3.50	3.27	3.26	3.26	3.26	3.26	3.26
Liechtenstein			2.12	2.10	2.20	2.20	2.20	2.22	2.23
Luxembourg		2.36	2.10	1.90	1.90	2.00	1.90	1.90	1.90
Malta			8.30	8.40	8.12	7.75	7.53	7.30	7.08
Monaco	2.96	2.84	2.87	2.92	2.88	3.00	3.05	3.09	3.14
Netherlands	2.39	1.93	1.90	1.80	1.78	1.76	1.76	1.75	1.74
Norway	1.73	1.61	1.67	1.62	1.63	1.65	1.64	1.64	1.64
Portugal	4.60	4.09	3.60	3.00	3.00	2.90	2.80	2.75	2.68
Spain	5.57	4.26	3.83	3.26	3.22	3.24	3.25	3.26	3.27
Sweden									
Switzerland	3.50	3.01	2.50	2.40	2.33	2.33	2.29	2.26	2.24
Turkey	3.43	4.00	4.20	2.90	2.94	3.12	3.13	3.19	3.26
United Kingdom									
Eastern Europe									
Albania		3.16	2.44	3.50	3.20	2.30	2.18	1.96	1.76
Belarus				3.00	3.04	2.99	2.91	2.89	2.86
Bosnia-Herzegovina			2.30						
Bulgaria		3.50	3.90	4.07	3.80	3.60	3.50	3.37	3.28
Croatia		5.29	5.49	4.33	4.17	4.07	4.00	3.90	3.83
Czech Republic	2.40	3.10	3.30	2.71	2.71	2.75	2.75	2.76	2.77
Estonia		1.81	1.53	2.01	2.00	1.91	1.87	1.84	1.80
Georgia				8.00	6.00	4.00	2.67	1.56	
Hungary	3.70	3.18	2.86	2.63	2.58	2.50	2.50	2.47	2.45
Latvia		2.85	2.90	2.23	2.11	2.15	2.19	2.22	2.24
Lithuania		2.15	2.22	2.10	1.97	1.87	1.93	1.89	1.87
Macedonia	3.20	3.60	3.90	3.80	3.80	3.70	3.60	3.56	3.50
Moldova				2.90	2.70	2.90	2.90	2.90	2.95
Montenegro									
Poland	1.37	1.43	2.00	1.93	1.95	1.93	1.89	1.88	1.86
Romania	2.96	3.40	3.20	3.18	2.94	2.89	2.82	2.72	2.67
Russia				5.30	6.71	7.17	7.80	8.47	8.93
Serbia				2.70	2.63	2.67	2.60	2.57	2.56
Slovakia	3.20	3.40	3.10	2.80	2.70	2.60	3.10	3.18	3.31
Slovenia		3.73	3.31	2.97	2.96	2.86	2.87	2.84	2.81
Ukraine			2.70						

Source: Euromonitor International from national statistics

Table 24.2

Average Tourist Nights in the Country 1990, 1995, 2000, 2006-2011

Nights

	1990	1995	2000	2006	2007	2008	2009	2010	2011
Western Europe									
Austria			4.60	4.30	4.26	4.23	4.20	4.18	4.17
Belgium				2.29	2.31	2.28	2.27	2.27	2.26
Cyprus	10.28	7.99	7.52	9.60	9.20	9.20	8.89	8.73	8.63
Denmark				5.01	5.08	5.06	5.14	5.17	5.19
Finland			2.06	2.21	2.16	2.16	2.16	2.15	2.14
France	6.90	8.17	7.48	6.59	6.63	6.64	6.66	6.67	6.67
Germany				2.20	2.20	2.30	2.30	2.32	2.35
Gibraltar	3.00								
Greece				5.56	5.37	5.40	5.32	5.27	5.24
Iceland			1.80	1.80	1.80	1.70	1.70	1.68	1.65
Ireland	11.00	8.42	7.40	7.60	7.30	8.10	8.10	8.21	8.41
Italy				3.81	3.81	3.87	3.88	3.90	3.91
Liechtenstein	1.91	2.10	2.10	2.10	2.20	2.20	2.30	2.34	2.38
Luxembourg		3.00	2.80	2.70	2.60	2.60	2.40	2.33	2.27
Malta	9.26	9.80	8.40	9.50	8.90	8.50	8.50	8.23	8.06
Monaco									
Netherlands			2.70	2.50	2.54	2.50	2.52	2.52	2.52
Norway									
Portugal	7.40	7.00	6.70	3.85	4.20	4.00	3.89	3.90	3.82
Spain	4.83	5.20	5.50	5.20	5.11	5.12	4.99	4.94	4.89
Sweden				2.33	2.14	2.31	2.40	2.42	2.49
Switzerland				2.50	2.48	2.50	2.43	2.41	2.39
Turkey	8.33	9.00	4.19	3.92	3.82	4.17	4.17	4.24	4.35
United Kingdom	10.90	9.40	8.08	8.40	7.70	7.70	7.70	7.51	7.46
Eastern Europe									
Albania			2.67	2.20	2.60	2.30	2.60	2.72	2.75
Belarus									
Bosnia-Herzegovina					2.30	2.20	2.20	2.57	2.61
Bulgaria	6.00	6.60	8.35	5.82	5.39	5.24	5.06	4.90	4.79
Croatia				5.43	5.33	5.38	5.41	5.41	5.41
Czech Republic	3.32	3.13	3.50	3.12	3.09	3.01	3.33	3.39	3.48
Estonia		1.90	1.90	2.12	2.11	2.05	1.99	1.96	1.93
Georgia			7.10						
Hungary	6.58	6.39	3.51	3.04	2.95	2.85	2.86	2.82	2.79
Latvia			2.60	2.29	2.29	2.24	2.90	3.04	3.20
Lithuania		3.50	3.20	2.52	2.41	2.26	2.34	2.29	2.25
Macedonia				2.20	2.30	2.30	2.30	2.32	2.33
Moldova				3.40	2.90	2.80	2.50	2.26	2.09
Montenegro					6.55	6.76	6.41	8.12	8.54
Poland		4.70	4.80	3.40	2.90	4.00	4.20	4.41	4.82
Romania			2.48	2.30	2.30	2.30	2.09	2.03	1.96
Russia				5.20	6.10	7.00	7.63	8.28	8.86
Serbia				2.16	2.12	2.16	2.28	2.31	2.36
Slovakia			3.90	3.20	3.10	3.00	2.90	2.82	2.75
Slovenia	3.10	3.12	3.12	2.78	2.78	2.73	2.71	2.69	2.67
Ukraine			5.30						

Source: Euromonitor International from national statistics

24

Travel and Tourism

Travel and Tourism Statistics   **Table 24.3**

Domestic Tourist Nights 1990, 1995, 2000, 2006-2011

'000 nights

	1990	1995	2000	2006	2007	2008	2009	2010	2011
Western Europe									
Austria	15,152	16,302	18,031	20,277	21,285	21,903	22,273	23,029	25,296
Belgium	2,707	3,054	4,045	4,737	5,220	5,422	5,604	6,169	6,964
Cyprus	166	346	597	1,114	1,169	1,159	1,320	1,331	1,380
Denmark	5,205	3,908	4,592	5,840	6,445	6,279	5,708	6,064	5,939
Finland	8,209	8,464	9,786	10,676	11,182	11,339	10,930	11,440	12,674
France	89,353	90,349	108,774	127,869	131,117	130,555	127,904	130,390	138,324
Germany	125,601	145,147	163,429	165,355	170,234	173,028	172,756	179,920	181,701
Gibraltar									
Greece	11,346	11,908	14,628	14,249	16,675	16,840	18,367	19,104	19,590
Iceland	225	246	291	387	437	429	386	404	402
Ireland		6,698	6,786	7,978	8,791	8,794	8,452	7,352	7,675
Italy	125,053	123,467	136,392	140,397	141,311	141,187	139,790	140,024	139,595
Liechtenstein	1	1	3	3	3	3	4	4	4
Luxembourg	109	89	67	77	78	78	89	84	94
Malta				310	331	335	351	351	386
Monaco									
Netherlands	6,396	8,799	14,027	15,783	17,831	17,657	17,052	17,533	17,722
Norway	8,485	9,862	11,398	12,859	13,458	13,328	13,227	13,595	15,000
Portugal	7,103	7,580	9,693	12,350	12,968	13,024	13,243	13,783	15,248
Spain	57,154	58,281	83,382	115,088	116,597	113,083	109,757	113,236	113,014
Sweden	13,033	14,771	16,586	18,606	19,574	20,042	19,871	20,975	21,439
Switzerland	13,587	12,316	14,013	15,229	15,473	15,855	15,451	15,792	17,990
Turkey	6,878	9,624	16,351	21,476	22,223	20,809	22,340	23,920	21,806
United Kingdom	77,915	88,346	139,000	102,010	105,231	103,020	106,116	90,210	89,272
Eastern Europe									
Albania		123	228	323	375	360	370	385	388
Belarus				3,649	3,739	3,624	3,275	3,572	3,019
Bosnia-Herzegovina		69	561	543	598	625	539	545	597
Bulgaria	14,578	3,735	3,036	4,342	4,867	5,370	4,676	4,548	4,937
Croatia		3,125	2,933	2,886	2,951	2,946	2,522	2,333	2,178
Czech Republic	7,752	6,952	12,655	8,854	9,206	9,686	9,328	9,478	9,562
Estonia		325	459	989	1,175	1,120	944	1,025	1,013
Georgia			2,115	5,581	5,303	5,160	5,678	7,283	7,723
Hungary		3,972	5,479	7,284	7,662	7,794	7,201	7,435	7,578
Latvia		600	669	855	979	941	600	674	625
Lithuania		331	303	934	1,082	1,057	755	853	938
Macedonia	738	464	443	267	283	277	267	261	278
Moldova			119	282	234	225	195	213	237
Montenegro		1,829	1,476	1,200	331	348	326	343	390
Poland		4,038	9,353	13,910	15,898	17,300	17,036	19,112	21,281
Romania	33,935	18,128	13,862	14,929	16,259	16,580	13,932	12,733	13,094
Russia				42,630	44,334	44,218	45,719	46,827	48,795
Serbia			6,968	3,120	3,187	3,230	2,648	2,465	2,674
Slovakia	3,990	2,180	2,843	3,142	3,264	3,684	3,427	3,592	3,587
Slovenia	1,279	2,066	1,860	1,746	1,839	2,175	2,234	2,138	2,257
Ukraine			7,986	9,691	10,427	10,628	9,155	9,588	10,399

Source: Euromonitor International from national statistics

European Marketing Data and Statistics 2013 – © Euromonitor International Ltd 2012

Table 24.4

International Tourist Nights 1990, 1995, 2000, 2006-2011

'000 nights

	1990	1995	2000	2006	2007	2008	2009	2010	2011
Western Europe									
Austria	61,894	56,198	53,617	57,114	57,882	60,462	57,798	58,315	62,581
Belgium	6,874	7,900	10,184	10,633	10,976	11,120	10,333	10,854	11,905
Cyprus	10,149	14,181	16,790	13,227	13,129	13,151	11,488	12,268	11,986
Denmark	5,429	4,146	4,608	4,807	4,635	4,552	4,258	4,874	4,953
Finland	2,468	2,926	3,562	4,339	4,635	4,768	4,198	4,297	4,602
France	55,322	54,339	71,768	69,551	73,152	71,725	63,837	65,516	67,067
Germany	29,765	27,184	34,641	42,821	44,442	45,218	43,472	48,382	49,341
Gibraltar									
Greece	35,012	37,474	46,212	42,459	47,410	47,234	45,926	46,453	46,457
Iceland	420	598	895	1,341	1,480	1,517	1,554	1,621	1,659
Ireland	8,277	11,348	17,564	18,834	19,737	19,285	15,393	12,774	12,802
Italy	66,012	84,566	97,221	107,859	113,017	110,492	106,829	114,153	114,531
Liechtenstein	149	127	131	115	126	131	118	111	107
Luxembourg	1,085	1,051	1,196	1,284	1,360	1,297	1,193	1,095	1,186
Malta	6,425	7,632	7,015	6,978	7,585	7,416	6,390	7,124	7,765
Monaco		626	861	916	944	944	778	818	927
Netherlands	8,102	9,581	15,695	15,976	16,328	14,962	14,429	16,175	16,390
Norway	3,537	4,985	4,967	4,896	5,052	4,871	4,404	4,782	5,199
Portugal	16,710	20,357	24,102	25,216	26,769	26,204	23,214	23,608	25,670
Spain	71,741	101,000	143,762	151,940	155,093	155,347	141,228	153,911	154,164
Sweden	3,193	3,694	4,679	5,604	5,842	5,830	6,087	6,363	6,539
Switzerland	21,041	18,386	19,914	19,619	20,892	21,478	20,138	20,416	22,926
Turkey	13,271	18,438	20,377	46,588	56,491	56,873	59,874	66,540	61,598
United Kingdom	64,416	55,451	53,131	64,951	64,253	61,633	59,608	48,554	46,023
Eastern Europe									
Albania		89	98	137	173	131	170	182	185
Belarus				688	791	1,001	1,042	1,180	1,030
Bosnia-Herzegovina			254	574	672	697	646	681	773
Bulgaria	11,519	5,299	5,104	11,776	11,868	11,641	9,378	10,455	11,133
Croatia		4,575	15,057	17,807	17,988	17,605	16,085	17,011	16,955
Czech Republic	5,377	8,386	12,919	17,035	17,838	17,741	16,013	16,881	16,568
Estonia		608	1,253	2,772	2,668	2,727	2,555	3,003	3,114
Georgia			2,730	3,997	3,447	3,045	3,029	3,503	3,522
Hungary		6,894	8,062	8,524	8,635	8,489	7,773	8,183	8,274
Latvia		662	691	1,745	1,780	1,913	1,588	1,787	1,736
Lithuania		418	579	1,451	1,509	1,544	1,323	1,510	1,730
Macedonia	474	243	439	392	457	475	469	473	514
Moldova		99	85	202	194	191	135	146	157
Montenegro		344	366	1,453	3,062	3,234	2,388	2,341	2,549
Poland		3,161	4,945	7,911	8,409	7,939	7,478	8,029	8,704
Romania	4,085	2,326	2,085	3,169	3,497	3,251	2,582	2,685	2,743
Russia				10,637	10,616	10,228	10,114	9,930	9,915
Serbia			376	949	1,240	1,195	1,184	1,169	1,308
Slovakia	1,459	2,340	2,761	3,911	3,969	3,978	2,908	3,043	2,949
Slovenia	3,889	2,059	2,758	3,401	3,707	4,051	3,684	3,715	3,944
Ukraine			948	1,549	1,635	1,646	1,394	1,435	1,532

Source: Euromonitor International from national statistics

24

Travel and Tourism

Travel and Tourism Statistics | **Table 24.5**

Expenditure by Tourists 1985, 1990, 1995, 2000, 2006-2011

US$ million

	1985	1990	1995	2000	2006	2007	2008	2009	2010	2011
Western Europe										
Austria	2,723	7,723	11,657	8,463	9,626	10,561	11,432	10,817	10,770	10,956
Belgium	2,050	5,471	9,215	9,429	15,574	17,506	19,822	17,923	16,745	16,537
Cyprus	78	111	293	413	967	1,479	1,571	1,275	1,222	1,252
Denmark	1,410	3,676	4,280	4,669	7,428	8,791	9,678	9,260	8,876	9,364
Finland	777	2,740	2,319	1,852	3,424	3,983	4,501	4,373	4,248	4,329
France	4,557	12,424	16,328	17,906	32,693	38,261	41,570	38,575	36,935	36,762
Germany			52,194	52,824	74,123	83,156	91,598	81,044	77,695	77,922
Gibraltar										
Greece	368	1,090	1,322	4,558	2,997	3,423	3,930	3,381	2,945	2,727
Iceland	94	278	282	471	1,076	1,326	1,103	533	537	569
Ireland	429	1,159	2,030	2,600	6,862	8,656	10,413	8,773	7,519	6,441
Italy	1,880	14,045	12,420	15,685	23,152	27,329	30,927	27,864	26,716	26,232
Liechtenstein										
Luxembourg				1,318	3,138	3,476	3,837	3,650	3,511	3,474
Malta	50	134	200	200	320	376	431	440	441	469
Monaco										
Netherlands	3,416	7,376	11,455	12,191	17,087	19,110	21,825	20,757	21,152	20,971
Norway	1,722	3,679	4,221	4,558	11,586	14,043	14,228	12,366	10,091	9,141
Portugal	235	867	2,141	2,228	3,340	3,937	4,328	3,776	3,729	3,945
Spain	1,010	4,254	4,461	5,572	16,697	19,724	20,363	16,911	16,859	17,015
Sweden	1,967	6,134	5,621	8,048	11,151	13,496	14,618	11,856	12,959	13,821
Switzerland	2,399	5,817	7,346	6,335	9,252	10,116	10,923	10,628	11,076	11,579
Turkey	324	520	912	1,713	2,743	3,260	3,506	4,147	4,581	5,044
United Kingdom	6,369	19,063	24,268	38,262	63,319	71,519	68,792	50,559	54,139	57,847
Eastern Europe										
Albania			5	272	965	1,268	1,555	1,585	1,526	1,588
Belarus			87	243	586	606	668	588	601	622
Bosnia-Herzegovina				78	170	203	304	236	213	200
Bulgaria	74	257	195	538	1,478	1,880	2,311	1,755	1,459	1,424
Croatia			421	568	737	985	1,113	1,013	994	1,025
Czech Republic			1,633	1,276	2,765	3,648	4,585	4,077	3,940	4,410
Estonia			91	204	586	670	808	606	649	697
Georgia				110	167	176	203	181	165	174
Hungary	208	477	1,070	1,651	2,126	2,949	4,037	3,638	3,729	3,817
Latvia			24	247	704	927	1,142	799	735	713
Lithuania			108	253	909	1,144	1,497	1,131	1,075	1,066
Macedonia			27	34	71	102	136	100	100	106
Moldova			56	73	190	233	288	243	203	217
Montenegro						37	43	49	53	55
Poland	184	423	5,500	3,313	7,224	7,753	9,903	7,327	8,294	8,944
Romania		103	697	425	1,310	1,543	2,176	1,473	1,199	1,074
Russia			11,599	8,848	18,112	21,217	23,778	20,763	22,424	24,781
Serbia					322	1,194	1,449	1,076	982	1,051
Slovakia			330	296	1,060	1,533	2,165	2,098	1,916	1,941
Slovenia			524	511	974	1,144	1,395	1,355	1,245	1,242
Ukraine				576	2,834	3,569	4,023	3,330	3,375	3,964

Source: Euromonitor International from national statistics

Table 24.6

Receipts from Tourism 1985, 1990, 1995, 2000, 2006-2011

US$ million

	1985	1990	1995	2000	2006	2007	2008	2009	2010	2011
Western Europe										
Austria	5,084	13,410	14,593	9,998	16,510	18,559	21,630	19,176	18,798	18,901
Belgium	1,663	3,718	5,719	6,592	10,311	11,017	11,801	9,967	9,459	9,347
Cyprus	380	1,258	1,783	1,941	2,381	2,686	2,770	2,188	2,052	2,019
Denmark	1,326	3,322	3,672	3,671	5,587	5,976	6,242	5,679	5,445	5,742
Finland	501	1,170	1,676	1,406	2,380	2,837	3,220	2,814	2,733	2,773
France	7,942	20,185	27,527	30,981	46,512	54,209	57,230	40,160	48,436	48,640
Germany			18,028	18,611	32,888	36,101	40,021	34,781	33,951	34,548
Gibraltar	15	112								
Greece	1,428	2,587	4,136	9,219	14,402	15,550	17,416	14,681	13,001	12,948
Iceland	41	139	167	227	478	601	624	555	591	619
Ireland	531	1,447	2,688	3,387	5,369	6,074	6,356	4,894	3,728	3,768
Italy	8,758	20,016	27,723	27,493	38,257	42,660	46,192	40,311	40,419	41,078
Liechtenstein	20									
Luxembourg				1,686	3,636	4,032	4,491	4,180	4,283	4,510
Malta	149	496	660	610	767	913	959	827	847	825
Monaco	300									
Netherlands	1,661	3,636	5,762	7,197	11,382	13,339	13,346	12,408	12,644	12,536
Norway	755	1,570	2,386	2,050	3,613	4,222	4,807	4,082	4,372	4,698
Portugal	1,137	3,555	4,339	5,243	8,416	10,175	10,980	9,707	9,302	9,306
Spain	8,151	18,593	25,388	31,454	51,297	57,734	61,978	53,337	51,861	51,122
Sweden	1,190	2,916	3,462	4,064	8,170	10,642	11,026	10,275	11,039	12,019
Switzerland	3,145	6,789	9,365	7,576	10,808	12,183	14,458	13,816	14,492	14,973
Turkey	1,482	3,308	4,957	7,636	16,853	18,487	21,951	21,250	22,771	25,240
United Kingdom	7,120	14,003	18,554	21,769	34,796	38,698	36,424	30,498	34,664	38,778
Eastern Europe										
Albania			7	398	1,012	1,378	1,714	1,827	1,584	1,821
Belarus			23	93	286	324	363	369	403	325
Bosnia-Herzegovina			7	233	607	729	826	681	660	633
Bulgaria	343	320	473	1,074	2,612	3,713	4,306	3,776	3,531	3,521
Croatia			1,351	2,758	7,990	9,233	11,280	9,000	8,536	9,260
Czech Republic	307	470	2,875	2,973	5,541	6,388	7,204	6,477	6,439	7,503
Estonia			353	505	1,024	1,036	1,189	1,090	1,167	1,379
Georgia				97	313	384	447	470	477	504
Hungary	512	1,000	1,723	3,733	4,254	4,739	6,033	5,712	5,943	6,218
Latvia			20	131	480	671	803	723	646	696
Lithuania			124	391	1,038	1,153	1,343	1,092	1,219	1,455
Macedonia		45	19	38	129	186	228	218	213	227
Moldova			57	39	115	167	212	168	169	172
Montenegro						629	755	659	687	776
Poland	118	358	6,600	5,677	7,239	10,599	11,768	9,011	9,338	10,122
Romania	182	106	590	359	1,308	1,610	1,991	1,228	1,078	1,028
Russia	163	410	4,312	3,430	7,628	9,447	11,795	9,297	10,062	10,663
Serbia					342	866	944	866	788	885
Slovakia			620	433	1,521	2,026	2,589	2,341	2,169	2,388
Slovenia			1,082	961	1,797	2,283	2,837	2,518	2,409	2,396
Ukraine				736	3,485	4,597	5,768	3,576	3,539	4,063

Source: Euromonitor International from national statistics

24

Travel and Tourism

Travel and Tourism Statistics   **Table 24.7**

Rooms in Tourist Accommodation 1990, 1995, 2000, 2006-2011
'000

	1990	1995	2000	2006	2007	2008	2009	2010	2011
Western Europe									
Austria	317.8	309.7	286.8	282.0	285.6	286.6	288.9	290.3	291.5
Belgium		59.7	61.9	67.8	67.7	67.9	68.7	69.0	69.4
Cyprus	24.5	35.0	43.4	44.4	43.8	42.9	42.0	41.8	41.2
Denmark	35.6	38.3	32.0	36.0	37.1	37.6	39.1	41.0	42.0
Finland	46.5	54.0	54.9	54.9	54.7	54.8	55.1	55.3	55.4
France	547.0	596.7	589.2	612.4	614.5	612.1	612.5	624.0	626.5
Germany		819.0	877.1	897.0	899.1	915.6	926.6	939.9	950.8
Gibraltar									
Greece	232.8	283.4	313.0	364.2	368.0	375.1	383.0	368.8	367.0
Iceland	3.3	4.9	6.0	8.0	8.5	9.1	9.0	9.4	10.0
Ireland	22.8	36.8	60.4	63.4	67.6	72.9	74.5	73.3	75.1
Italy	938.1	944.1	966.1	1,034.7	1,058.9	1,079.5	1,088.1	1,095.3	1,105.0
Liechtenstein		0.6	0.6	0.6	0.6	0.6	0.6	0.6	0.6
Luxembourg	7.9	8.2	7.7	7.4	7.6	7.6	7.8	8.5	8.7
Malta	34.2				17.5	18.3	18.4	18.0	18.1
Monaco			2.2	2.6	2.8	2.6	2.6	2.8	2.9
Netherlands	60.7	71.3	82.0	94.5	99.0	98.2	100.5	103.2	104.3
Norway	54.0	60.0	65.2	69.5	71.0	72.4	75.4	78.4	80.4
Portugal	79.4	90.0	97.7	117.6	118.0	121.0	120.7	124.5	126.3
Spain	603.0	564.6	677.1	810.6	821.1	838.5	863.1	884.6	901.6
Sweden	82.0	100.0	96.1	101.7	103.8	106.6	108.2	110.4	112.2
Switzerland	146.9	143.5	140.8	142.5	141.6	141.7	142.6	142.8	143.1
Turkey	82.1	133.2	155.4	241.3	251.5	266.9	286.1	281.4	289.3
United Kingdom		440.0	463.0	616.8	616.0	616.0	648.2	651.0	660.3
Eastern Europe									
Albania		3.0	3.0	4.8	6.9	8.7	8.5	9.0	10.1
Belarus			2.0	13.3	13.7	13.9	14.6	14.8	15.9
Bosnia-Herzegovina		1.1	4.4	9.0	10.8	11.1	11.8	12.5	13.4
Bulgaria		57.0		95.6	103.8	108.0	111.9	111.2	113.2
Croatia		85.4	81.3	77.3	77.5	77.2	73.8	72.6	71.0
Czech Republic	63.1	53.7	96.4	101.6	106.9	111.8	114.5	113.4	119.7
Estonia		5.2	7.6	12.8	13.9	14.6	14.9	14.7	14.9
Georgia			8.7	10.0	8.3	8.6	9.4	9.8	10.6
Hungary	34.0	47.8	57.9	66.9	65.6	65.8	67.3	69.1	70.1
Latvia		5.4	6.4	9.7	10.0	11.6	12.4	13.0	13.8
Lithuania		5.3	5.9	10.8	11.0	11.1	12.0	12.1	12.4
Macedonia	6.0	6.0	6.6	7.0	7.2	5.0	5.4	5.9	5.6
Moldova		2.6	3.0	2.5	2.3	2.4	2.5	2.5	2.6
Montenegro	16.0	16.0	15.8	17.9	18.0	18.1	18.8	18.9	19.8
Poland	43.4	48.2	60.9	88.4	93.9	103.7	109.5	119.2	131.5
Romania	87.1	95.5	95.4	111.8	112.2	116.9	121.7	126.2	129.9
Russia		214.1	183.4	208.3	219.4	247.9	254.2	271.9	294.0
Serbia				22.6	24.0	25.1	25.4	25.5	26.3
Slovakia	14.5	23.4	28.4	35.9	41.6	42.5	43.6	35.8	35.8
Slovenia		16.2	16.3	16.4	17.3	21.7	22.0	21.7	23.5
Ukraine			44.8	40.2	41.0	42.2	42.8	44.9	46.3

Source: Euromonitor International from national statistics

    Table 24.8

Bed-Places in Tourist Accommodation 1990, 1995, 2000, 2006-2011

'000

	1990	1995	2000	2006	2007	2008	2009	2010	2011
Western Europe									
Austria	587.8	583.8	580.7	572.5	573.7	579.8	587.9	589.3	593.4
Belgium		154.7	158.6	172.9	172.0	170.9	170.9	170.3	169.7
Cyprus	51.8	73.1	84.5	89.5	87.8	85.7	84.3	83.9	82.8
Denmark	88.5	99.0	62.9	70.8	73.4	73.5	77.4	81.5	83.7
Finland	97.4	113.0	117.3	119.0	118.9	119.2	120.2	121.1	121.7
France	1,082.1	1,193.3	1,178.3	1,224.8	1,229.1	1,224.2	1,225.0	1,248.0	1,253.1
Germany		1,490.9	1,649.2	1,690.9	1,703.3	1,737.9	1,813.0	1,721.8	1,726.8
Gibraltar									
Greece	438.4	535.8	594.0	693.3	700.9	715.9	732.3	705.7	703.9
Iceland	6.3	8.8	12.5	16.8	17.9	19.3	18.9	19.9	21.2
Ireland	45.2	79.8	140.2	148.8	157.4	168.7	163.6	151.7	150.4
Italy	1,703.5	1,738.0	1,854.1	2,087.0	2,142.8	2,201.8	2,227.8	2,253.3	2,282.8
Liechtenstein	1.2	1.2	1.2	1.3	1.3	1.2	1.1	1.1	1.1
Luxembourg			14.7	14.4	14.6	14.4	14.7	16.2	16.6
Malta	37.9	37.3	40.6	39.4	38.1	38.9	39.1	39.1	39.4
Monaco				5.3	4.2	5.9	5.7	6.2	6.4
Netherlands	111.3	142.5	173.0	192.1	200.3	198.6	203.9	211.8	214.8
Norway	112.7	131.2	140.6	151.3	154.3	157.3	169.2	175.5	181.1
Portugal	179.3	204.1	223.0	264.0	264.7	274.0	273.8	279.5	283.4
Spain	1,102.3	1,074.0	1,315.7	1,615.3	1,642.4	1,682.6	1,733.4	1,784.7	1,822.7
Sweden	125.9	173.1	188.3	201.3	207.4	218.2	221.8	224.4	229.0
Switzerland	269.8	265.0	259.7	271.6	270.1	270.5	274.0	275.2	276.5
Turkey	165.0	274.1	332.3	507.2	530.8	563.3	601.0	597.9	615.7
United Kingdom	993.5	879.7	1,111.0	1,255.7	1,250.5	1,238.7	1,410.8	1,452.2	1,506.0
Eastern Europe									
Albania		4.7	4.8	9.2	14.7	17.9	17.7	19.2	21.6
Belarus		1.0	14.4	24.1	24.6	24.4	25.7	25.5	27.4
Bosnia-Herzegovina		1.9	9.1	20.0	22.4	23.0	24.5	26.0	27.9
Bulgaria	114.3	114.2	120.2	211.6	231.3	239.7	249.2	245.4	249.2
Croatia		205.2	199.5	165.9	166.0	166.0	152.3	151.7	154.8
Czech Republic		131.2	236.5	236.1	248.0	257.8	260.7	255.9	268.0
Estonia		10.6	16.3	26.1	28.6	29.8	30.8	30.3	30.8
Georgia			17.2	20.5	16.7	17.6	18.7	18.5	19.4
Hungary	85.3	119.1	143.6	158.8	154.1	154.5	157.5	161.4	163.3
Latvia		14.0	11.9	19.7	20.7	23.5	25.4	27.4	29.2
Lithuania		10.5	11.1	21.5	21.9	22.0	23.8	24.3	25.0
Macedonia	15.1	15.0	16.1	16.8	17.1	10.9	11.9	13.0	12.0
Moldova		5.3	5.6	4.5	4.3	4.4	4.7	4.8	5.0
Montenegro	34.3	35.1	32.2	42.3	43.1	43.2	43.8	45.4	45.4
Poland	90.4	93.3	120.3	178.1	190.4	210.5	221.6	241.0	266.1
Romania	168.0	205.7	199.3	228.1	228.1	237.9	248.4	258.2	266.3
Russia		426.1	346.1	431.0	447.1	500.0	518.2	551.4	593.2
Serbia				49.1	52.5	55.1	55.7	56.3	57.9
Slovakia	33.6	53.9	73.0	91.0	105.7	108.8	109.6	74.6	70.5
Slovenia		33.9	33.5	34.4	36.2	48.3	48.6	43.9	47.0
Ukraine			102.9	72.5	73.8	75.7	77.9	80.1	84.9

Source: Euromonitor International from national statistics

Travel and Tourism Statistics   **Table 24.9**

Hotel Bed Occupancy Rates 1990, 1995, 2000, 2006-2011

% of beds occupied

	1990	1995	2000	2006	2007	2008	2009	2010	2011
Western Europe									
Austria	32.1	33.6	35.2	37.6	39.2	39.7	37.3	37.3	37.1
Belgium		31.3							
Cyprus	62.3	58.6	65.1	59.9	61.8	63.5	56.1	55.3	53.8
Denmark	34.7	35.5	37.4	43.0	44.0	42.0	38.0	36.9	35.3
Finland	48.6	45.0	47.8	49.9	51.6	51.9	47.6	47.1	46.1
France	52.4	49.5	60.3	60.4	61.9	61.4	58.1	57.5	56.6
Germany		33.9	35.0	35.9	36.7	36.5	35.7	35.7	35.4
Gibraltar	40.8								
Greece		56.6	65.0	59.8	57.0	56.7	51.1	49.2	47.4
Iceland	41.0	44.8	46.0	47.0	46.7	47.4	46.0	45.8	45.6
Ireland			65.0	64.0	64.0	58.0	55.0	53.0	50.6
Italy	41.5	40.0	42.7	40.8	41.8	40.2	38.8	38.4	37.6
Liechtenstein	33.4	28.4	30.9	25.6	27.9	30.9	30.0	31.0	31.7
Luxembourg		19.4	26.2	29.9	31.6	28.5	25.7	24.8	23.2
Malta	56.4	55.5	47.0	51.2	59.9	57.7	50.6	50.4	47.9
Monaco	55.7	49.5	71.5	58.8	63.6	61.1	62.3	62.9	63.7
Netherlands	38.5	35.3	48.5	45.3	46.7	45.0	42.3	41.5	40.1
Norway	35.4	36.7	37.5	38.9	39.5	37.8	34.8	33.7	32.2
Portugal	29.9	38.0	42.2	48.3	50.3	47.3	42.2	40.5	37.9
Spain	52.3	60.7	58.9	56.4	56.0	53.5	49.4	47.6	45.3
Sweden	31.0	32.0	35.0	36.1	37.2	36.0	35.0	34.7	34.0
Switzerland	44.0	38.5	42.3	41.7	43.6	44.5	42.6	43.1	43.2
Turkey	48.2	47.0	36.8	47.3	51.1	51.5	48.9	48.5	48.0
United Kingdom	57.0	44.0	43.0	47.0	48.0	44.0	43.0	41.9	40.3
Eastern Europe									
Albania		32.4	20.0	63.0	63.0	61.0	63.9	64.2	64.5
Belarus				49.3	50.4	51.7	46.1	45.3	44.2
Bosnia-Herzegovina			15.0						
Bulgaria		36.5	28.3	35.8	33.2	32.1	26.3	24.2	22.2
Croatia	16.6	11.1	24.8	34.8	35.2	34.2	34.0	33.8	33.3
Czech Republic	46.0	28.8	46.0	35.8	35.8	35.7	32.8	32.2	31.3
Estonia		35.0	48.0	47.0	44.0	42.8	37.6	35.5	33.6
Georgia			34.0						
Hungary	55.4	45.4	46.7	42.4	45.0	43.8	39.1	38.4	36.9
Latvia			32.0	35.6	36.5	33.2	22.3	19.3	15.5
Lithuania		23.0	28.4	42.1	46.3	44.9	34.0	32.2	29.1
Macedonia	10.9	10.6	15.0	10.8	11.8	18.9	16.9	18.3	19.7
Moldova		10.5	19.8	30.9	28.3	28.6	20.6	17.9	15.1
Montenegro					6.1	19.3	24.5	31.0	37.7
Poland	39.5	42.7	39.6	42.2	46.1	45.1	40.6	40.2	38.6
Romania		52.1	35.2	33.6	36.0	35.9	28.4	27.0	24.6
Russia		38.0	37.0	35.0	36.0	35.0	35.0	34.8	34.8
Serbia				22.7	23.1	21.9	18.9	17.9	16.5
Slovakia	48.7	31.9	29.2	35.7	33.7	31.9	22.4	18.9	14.9
Slovenia		33.4	39.4	47.6	47.4	43.9	39.8	37.7	35.1
Ukraine			24.0						

Source: Euromonitor International from national statistics

Table 24.10

International Tourist Arrivals 1990, 1995, 2000, 2006-2011

'000

	1990	1995	2000	2006	2007	2008	2009	2010	2011
Western Europe									
Austria		17,173	17,982	20,269	20,773	21,935	21,355	21,941	22,553
Belgium		5,560	6,457	6,995	7,045	7,165	6,815	7,179	7,417
Cyprus		2,100	2,686	2,401	2,416	2,404	2,141	2,173	2,434
Denmark		3,417	3,535	4,742	4,770	4,503	4,316	4,406	4,684
Finland			2,714	3,375	3,519	3,583	3,423	3,531	3,592
France		60,033	77,190	77,916	80,853	79,218	76,824	80,268	82,650
Germany		14,847	18,983	23,569	24,421	24,884	24,220	26,862	28,088
Gibraltar									
Greece		10,130	13,095	16,039	16,165	15,939	14,915	15,008	17,061
Iceland		474	634	971	1,058	1,106	1,235	1,170	1,305
Ireland		4,821	6,646	8,001	8,332	8,026	7,189	6,311	6,118
Italy		31,052	41,181	41,058	43,654	42,734	43,239	45,487	46,275
Liechtenstein		59	62	55	58	59	52	49	51
Luxembourg	694	768	852	908	917	879	849	804	797
Malta		1,116	1,216	1,124	1,244	1,291	1,183	1,332	1,498
Monaco		233	300	313	328	324	265	280	305
Netherlands		6,574	10,003	10,739	11,008	10,104	9,921	10,883	11,373
Norway		2,880	3,104	4,070	4,377	4,347	4,288	4,710	4,802
Portugal		9,511	12,097	11,282	12,321	12,520	12,175	12,471	12,805
Spain		38,803	47,898	58,004	58,666	57,192	52,231	52,440	54,296
Sweden		1,255	1,492	4,729	5,224	4,555	4,678	4,791	4,953
Switzerland		6,946	7,821	7,863	8,440	8,608	8,294	8,512	7,986
Turkey		7,083	9,586	18,916	22,248	24,994	25,506	25,867	27,587
United Kingdom		21,675	23,221	30,654	30,870	30,142	28,199	28,112	28,548
Eastern Europe									
Albania		843	551	1,032	1,062	1,337	1,792	2,034	2,181
Belarus		161	60	90	105	92	94	104	114
Bosnia-Herzegovina		37	171	256	306	322	311	366	378
Bulgaria		3,466	2,785	5,158	5,151	5,780	5,739	6,047	6,247
Croatia		1,324	5,831	8,659	9,307	9,415	9,335	9,111	9,711
Czech Republic			4,666	6,435	6,680	6,649	6,032	6,158	6,473
Estonia		530	1,220	1,940	1,900	1,970	1,900	2,048	2,130
Georgia		85	387	983	1,052	1,290	1,500	1,602	1,677
Hungary			11,207	9,259	8,638	8,814	9,058	9,818	10,135
Latvia			509	1,535	1,653	1,684	1,323	1,551	1,733
Lithuania		662	1,083	2,180	1,486	1,611	1,341	1,508	1,807
Macedonia		147	224	202	230	255	259	257	266
Moldova			19	13	13	7	7	7	7
Montenegro		68	69	378	984	1,031	1,044	1,128	1,223
Poland		19,215	17,400	15,670	14,975	12,960	11,890	12,319	12,750
Romania		2,963	3,274	4,059	5,193	5,960	5,095	4,913	4,937
Russia		9,250	19,072	20,168	20,527	21,566	19,420	20,269	22,390
Serbia			469	696	646	645	655	674	
Slovakia		903	1,053	1,612	1,685	1,766	1,298	1,318	1,379
Slovenia		732	1,090	1,617	1,751	1,958	1,824	1,844	1,940
Ukraine			6,431	18,936	23,122	25,449	20,798	19,675	20,969

Source: Euromonitor International from national statistics

24

Travel and Tourism

Travel and Tourism Statistics   **Table 24.11**

Tourist Arrivals by Method 2011

'000

	Air	Rail	Land	Sea
Western Europe				
Austria	5,502	2,497	14,170	120
Belgium	1,599	2,031	3,755	40
Cyprus	2,344			90
Denmark	2,951	862	1,895	269
Finland	1,886	263	637	987
France	34,271	12,287	27,819	4,593
Germany	11,756	1,660	14,625	61
Gibraltar	65		6	5
Greece	11,088	129	4,611	1,232
Iceland	1,336			17
Ireland	4,767	81	149	654
Italy	21,969	2,731	17,529	1,883
Liechtenstein			69	
Luxembourg	312	87	397	
Malta	1,476			22
Monaco	46	66	189	18
Netherlands	4,901	1,338	4,895	239
Norway	2,162	129	1,811	932
Portugal	8,591	117	4,609	57
Spain	44,438	258	11,373	768
Sweden	5,921	754	1,845	1,252
Switzerland	5,439	971	6,367	
Turkey	21,939	104	8,419	2,784
United Kingdom	22,044	2,757	245	3,212
Eastern Europe				
Albania	454	131	1,525	561
Belarus	221	1,506	3,083	
Bosnia-Herzegovina	65	19	294	
Bulgaria	2,622	99	3,463	62
Croatia	1,223	34	8,368	85
Czech Republic	8,043	509	4,306	
Estonia	161	75	607	1,393
Georgia	384	158	1,809	32
Hungary	6,140	2,337	1,761	20
Latvia	268	75	1,185	30
Lithuania	636	94	1,026	60
Macedonia	86	18	167	
Moldova	224	145	592	
Montenegro	279	56	798	94
Poland	4,529	1,316	7,090	261
Romania	1,440	209	5,924	45
Russia	5,397	6,128	9,842	1,017
Serbia	206	43	442	
Slovakia	434	172	2,782	13
Slovenia	395	189	1,325	30
Ukraine	728	8,425	3,713	231

Source: Euromonitor International from national statistics

Table 24.12

Tourist Arrivals by Region 2011

'000

	Africa	Americas	East Asia/Pacific	Europe	Middle East	South Asia
Western Europe						
Austria	41	643	669	21,042	106	52
Belgium	66	418	267	6,563	24	80
Cyprus	8	27	17	2,317	59	6
Denmark		151	99	4,434		
Finland	7	156	328	3,066	10	26
France	2,002	5,941	3,662	70,119	926	
Germany	188	2,927	2,087	22,570	316	
Gibraltar						
Greece	30	868	228	15,871	63	2
Iceland	2	103	41	1,158		
Ireland	37	782	200	5,100		
Italy	262	3,582	1,393	40,559	234	246
Liechtenstein	1	2	1	47		
Luxembourg		28		769		
Malta		18		1,464	16	
Monaco	2	32	12	255	5	
Netherlands	95	1,144	768	9,367		
Norway		143	28	4,631		
Portugal		707	45	12,053		
Spain		2,823	251	51,222		
Sweden		263	251	4,439		
Switzerland	76	775	853	6,036	112	133
Turkey	319	602	615	23,068	1,375	1,607
United Kingdom	597	4,001	2,079	20,880	623	368
Eastern Europe						
Albania		80	40	2,059	1	1
Belarus		1	1	112		
Bosnia-Herzegovina		9	5	363		
Bulgaria	2	88	46	6,062	23	26
Croatia	13	196	303	9,199		
Czech Republic	22	427	526	5,497		
Estonia	2	36	32	2,061		
Georgia	1	21	12	1,625	3	15
Hungary	26	721	281	9,107		
Latvia	7	84	49	1,579	3	11
Lithuania	2	47	45	1,713		
Macedonia		9	4	252		
Moldova				7		
Montenegro		8	2	1,213		
Poland	22	361	230	12,097	17	22
Romania	7	104	55	4,741	17	12
Russia	40	534	1,589	20,075	43	109
Serbia		16	9	649		
Slovakia	2	31	58	1,286	1	1
Slovenia	3	57	100	1,780		
Ukraine	10	165	44	20,700	28	20

Source: Euromonitor International from national statistics

24

Travel and Tourism